D1281066

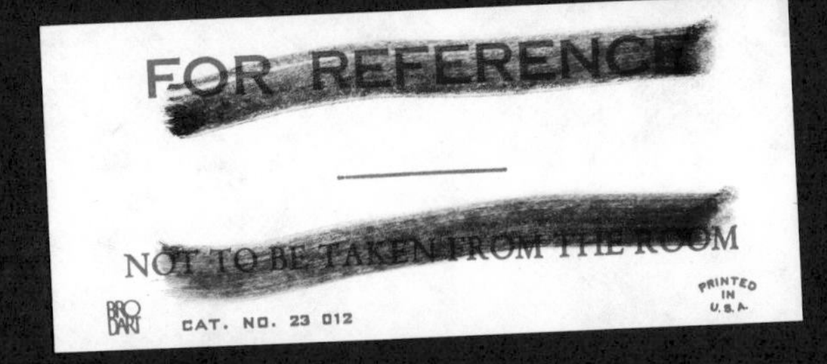
FOR REFERENCE
NOT TO BE TAKEN FROM THE ROOM
BRODART
CAT. NO. 23 012
PRINTED IN U.S.A.

University of Lowell
O'Leary Library

Author Newsletters and Journals

WITHDRAWN
UML LIBRARIES

WITHDRAWN
UML LIBRARIES

AMERICAN LITERATURE, ENGLISH LITERATURE, AND WORLD LITERATURES IN ENGLISH: AN INFORMATION GUIDE SERIES

Series Editor Theodore Grieder, Curator, Division of Special Collections, Fales Library, New York University, New York, New York

Associate Editor: Duane DeVries, Associate Professor, Polytechnic Institute of New York, Brooklyn

Other books on world literatures in this series:

BLACK AFRICAN LITERATURE IN ENGLISH—*Edited by Bernth Lindfors**

ASIAN LITERATURE IN ENGLISH—*Edited by George Anderson**

AUSTRALIAN LITERATURE TO 1900—*Edited by Barry Andrews and W.H. Wilde**

MODERN AUSTRALIAN POETRY, 1920-1970—*Edited by Herbert C. Jaffa*

MODERN AUSTRALIAN PROSE—*Edited by A. Grove Day**

ENGLISH-CANADIAN LITERATURE TO 1900—*Edited by R.G. Moyles*

MODERN ENGLISH-CANADIAN POETRY—*Edited by Peter Stevens*

MODERN ENGLISH-CANADIAN PROSE—*Edited by Helen Hoy**

INDIAN LITERATURE IN ENGLISH, 1827-1977—*Edited by Amritjit Singh and Rajiva Verma**

IRISH LITERATURE, 1800-1875—*Edited by Brian McKenna*

IRISH LITERATURE, 1876-1950—*Edited by Brian McKenna**

NEW ZEALAND LITERATURE TO 1977—*Edited by J.E.P. Thomson**

SCOTTISH LITERATURE IN ENGLISH—*Edited by William Aitken**

WEST INDIAN LITERATURE IN ENGLISH—*Edited by Priscilla Tyler**

*in preparation

The above series is part of the
GALE INFORMATION GUIDE LIBRARY

The Library consists of a number of separate series of guides covering major areas in the social sciences, humanities, and current affairs.

General Editor: Paul Wasserman, Professor and former Dean, School of Library and Information Services, University of Maryland

Managing Editor: Denise Allard Adzigian, Gale Research Company

Author Newsletters and Journals

AN INTERNATIONAL ANNOTATED BIBLIOGRAPHY OF SERIAL PUBLICATIONS CONCERNED WITH THE LIFE AND WORKS OF INDIVIDUAL AUTHORS

Volume 19 in the American Literature, English Literature, and World Literatures in English Information Guide Series

Margaret C. Patterson

Book Review Editor
LITERARY RESEARCH NEWSLETTER

Gale Research Company
Book Tower, Detroit, Michigan 48226

Library of Congress Cataloging in Publication Data

Patterson, Margaret C
Author newsletters and journals.

(American literature, English literature, and world literatures in English ; v. 19) (Gale information guide library)
Includes index.
1. Authors—Periodicals—Bibliography. I. Title.
Z6513.P37 [PN4836] 016.809 79-63742
ISBN 0-8103-1432-0

Copyright © 1979 by
Margaret C. Patterson

No part of this book may be reproduced in any form without permission in writing from the publisher, except by a reviewer who wishes to quote brief passages or entries in connection with a review written for inclusion in a magazine or newspaper. Manufactured in the United States of America.

VITA

Margaret C. Patterson is the author of the LITERARY RESEARCH GUIDE (Gale Research, 1976), which was selected by both CHOICE and the LIBRARY JOURNAL as one of the outstanding reference books of the year. The GUIDE is currently being revised for publication in a paperback second edition by the Modern Language Association of America. Professor Patterson has been a bibliographer for the MLA INTERNATIONAL BIBLIOGRAPHY since 1972, and the book review editor of the LITERARY RESEARCH NEWSLETTER since 1976. She taught for several years in the English Department at the University of Florida, and in 1978 was a research editor on the WELLESLEY INDEX TO VICTORIAN PERIODICALS at Wellesley College, her alma mater.

CONTENTS

PREFACE

THE SCOPE

This international annotated Guide includes publishing and bibliographical information on 1,129 titles which fulfill both of the following qualifications:

1. These publications are interested in collecting and distributing criticism, bibliographies, biographical information, textual studies, reviews, and related scholarship on the life and works of one author--such as Whitman, Chaucer, Claudel, Joyce, Hesse, Strindberg, or Dostoevsky. A total of 435 authors from 28 different countries have inspired these 1,129 titles.

2. These publications are serials--that is, they are continuing projects published either regularly or irregularly, and they have no scheduled termination date, although many do cease publication after a few years, or even months, for financial or other reasons.

They are, therefore, like the DICKENSIAN which, since 1905, has produced 386 issues with remarkable regularity; like STUDIES ON VOLTAIRE AND THE EIGHTEENTH CENTURY, which has no scheduled month of publication but which between 1955 and 1978 managed to produce 175 volumes; or like the MARY WOLLSTONECRAFT NEWSLETTER, which two years after its creation in 1972 changed its scope and title to WOMEN AND LITERATURE and, with the change, went beyond the limits established for this Guide. These publications may be monthlies, quarterlies, annuals, or they may emerge only when enough material has accumulated to produce a respectable volume, but they all are "serials," no matter how long they survive or how frequently they appear.

Occasionally a title sounds as if it should be a continuing publication, but it is not. This is true particularly of the "Cahiers" in French literature. The CAHIERS DE L'AMITIÉ CHARLES PÉGUY, for example, is given a full annotation in this book because it represents a series of critical studies that have been published annually since 1947, whereas the series entitled Cahier Victor Hugo (a series, and therefore not italicized or capitalized) is concerned solely with publishing works by Hugo, not criticism about him and is, therefore, not included here. In one or two cases (see, for example, the series entitled Cahiers Simone Weil), critical editions of an author's work have been included because

(1) their voluminous notes and commentary make a unique contribution to scholarship, and (2) little or no other criticism of any great import is available. The most popular type of "Cahiers" contains both primary and secondary material, such as CAHIERS DES AMIS DE HAN RYNER, which includes critical essays, bibliographies, and news for members as well as previously unpublished material. All such "Cahiers" are listed and described in this Guide.

In a few instances, the decision to include or omit a title has been difficult. La Revue des Lettres Modernes and Archives des Lettres Modernes, for instance (see Albert Camus, entries 1 and 2, for a full description), contain several excellent subseries which almost every year publish critical works on the more important French authors. There are special Archives subseries on Gérard de Nerval, Claudel, Hugo, Apollinaire, Bernanos, Montesquieu, Gide, Camus, and Malraux, and special La Revue subseries on Bernanos, Apollinaire, Claudel, Barbey d'Aurevilly, Camus, Gide, Cocteau, Malraux, Jacob, Rimbaud, Suarès, Giono, Mauriac, Céline, Valéry, and Verne. All of these are cited and described in this book.

Both Archives and La Revue have also published, however, critical works on a great many other authors--and whether these random volumes will develop into a series in the future is as yet an undetermined question. The one volume on John Bunyan which was published by Archives in 1958 might develop into a series, it is true; but for the purpose of this project, no authors covered by Archives or La Revue are included in this Guide unless two or more titles have been published to indicate the beginnings of a genuine series. One important exception to this is that if the author has other publications devoted exclusively to the study of his life and work, then it seemed wise to add information about the Archives or La Revue title because the chance that it might be the first of a series is greatly improved. Thus, Goethe, with twenty-three other titles focusing on his work, has in addition a citation for the Archives series, even though only one title has been published so far.

If the subject limitations for this Guide has been a little difficult to establish, the limits of time and place have not--there are none. The twenty-eight countries represented in this Guide extend from Switzerland to Brazil, Sweden to Japan, India to Belgium, as well as to Argentina, Austria, Canada, Cuba, Denmark, England (which includes Scotland, Ireland, and Wales), France, Germany, Greece, Hungary, Italy, Martinique, the Netherlands, Norway, Poland, Portugal, Russia, Spain, the United States, and Venezuela. Appendix 1 contains a further breakdown of these countries by native authors and number of publications produced in their honor.

The time span covered by this Guide extends from the Greek and Roman Empires, represented by Aristotle, Cicero, and Vergil, through the Middle Ages, Renaissance, Enlightenment, and nineteenth century to the twentieth, during which no fewer than 207 different authors from around the world, from Sherwood Anderson to Stefan Zweig, have so far had journals and other publications created to study their life and works. Appendix 2 shows how the growing interest in such a method of research has resulted in the specialized study of 435 writers, philosophers, and statesmen spanning 2,500 years of literary history.

The standard primary and secondary bibliographies of these famous men and women have long neglected the author newsletter and journal as a reliable source of scholarship. Because they rarely cite more than the most venerable titles (and even then their facts are extremely brief and all too often inaccurate), they thus leave to relative obscurity hundreds of other titles that might be less ambitious in budget and circulation but not less worthy in research possibilities. This Guide, with its comprehensive accumulation of all information on all author newsletters and journals, will, therefore, enlarge most existing bibliographies and perhaps stimulate the creation of many more. And with this, the project attains its desired goal--that of making the authors and their works more accessible to scholars.

THE BY-PRODUCTS

Research projects should have moments of pleasure as well as intellectual triumph. And this one did. The most enjoyable and most illuminating moments came, of course, during the examination of the periodicals themselves. To discover what the experienced scholar-editor deemed important about his literary celebrity; to note the rise and fall of many titles which somehow lacked the inspiration, dedication, or--alas, and more likely--the application of time and money to survive; to admire the feeble starts and then steady growth of others that were endowed with a firm and knowledgeable editorial hand; to linger over news notes written decades ago in another cultural world; to scan the brilliant arguments of philosopher-editors who had decided to give over a large portion of their own lives to study the life and works of other, earlier philosophers--these were the by-products that brought pleasure, as well as value, to this project.

The first task of locating titles and leads to titles from hundreds of different reference books and sources in various languages, with a steadily increasing amount of contradictory information was, as usual, the difficult and at times discouraging part of the research procedure; but the final months spent working with the content of the periodicals and with the thoughts of literary scholars and dedicated editors were solidly rewarding. About 1,000 of the 1,129 titles in this Guide were examined and evaluated personally by the editor, and matters bibliographical were often abandoned, with some regularity and no little delight, for more important matters of the soul--the wit and wisdom of learned men.

In one of the best of these publications, the JOHNSONIAN NEWS LETTER (which, incidentally, claims to have been the first of the genre "newsletters"), the editors justifiably applaud their own small (twelve-page) but healthy (thirty-nine-year-old) contribution to scholarship. They mention several other publications that by age and circulation figures have proved their unique value--for instance, the SHAKESPEARE NEWSLETTER, which was founded in 1951 and is still edited by Louis Marder who, almost single-handedly, sends it out six times a year to its 2,800 subscribers. Then, the JOHNSONIAN editors comment, "More and more, the need for sharing information among active scholars has become evident" (December 1975). And, indeed, that need is why this Guide exists.

In another periodical, an editor refers wistfully to the good old days when we could go to the annual Modern Language Association convention anticipating three full days of animated discussion-- and, yes, argument--about our favorite author or title with the most dedicated scholars in the world. Now, with administrators pressuring faculty to teach a little of everything and publish besides, we dutifully schedule our time at MLA with a variety of seminars and centuries, only occasionally taking the time to exchange and develop ideas through leisurely, informal conversations.

Where can we now find that concentration, that distillation, of scholarship--critical, biographical, bibliographical, historical, textual--that we must have so that we can aspire to lecture brilliantly and write provocatively in our specialized field? Within the pages, of course, of the quarterly newsletter, scholarly journal, or thick, well-edited annual that represents hundreds of hours of research, writing, and editing, hundreds of hours devoted to the author and century that we have selected as our own life's interest. These publications that limit their scope to one author are--along with the current proliferation of specialized primary and secondary bibliographies and reviews of research--the scholar's method of coping with today's ever-increasing amount of knowledge and ever-diminishing number of quiet hours for research. They offer us a practical way to keep abreast of developments in our field--and a pleasant way, as well.

This pleasure is felt by the editors of and contributors to these journals as well as by their readers. Do we not share and understand the pride of the editor of the OWL OF MINERVA when, in answer to our query about special features of his Hegel quarterly that might interest future readers, he replies, "The OWL is the finest such publication in the world." And do we not experience a rare moment of understanding when we ask an English editor, "Any special issues?" and receive the very gentle answer, "One tries to make every issue special."

And many editors do. Some of these publications are works of art as well as of literature (see the MILTON QUARTERLY and BLAKE: AN ILLUSTRATED QUARTERLY). Others are splendid examples of particularly helpful bibliography (see, for example, the JAMES JOYCE QUARTERLY). Others have prevailed over oppression, wars, and purges (AURORA: JAHRBUCH DER EICHENDORFF-GESELLSCHAFT, first published in 1929 in Poland). Some are, not surprisingly, aged warriors (DANTE STUDIES and ANALECTA BOLLANDIA have been published continuously since 1882). Others are memorable for their originality in format and approach (PAIDEUMA--Ezra Pound). Others seem, for mystifying reasons, to have sprung full-grown to satisfy what was apparently a long-unrecognized need. ERASMUS IN ENGLISH, founded in 1970, already has a circulation of 3,050 in 52 countries, and the CHESTERTON REVIEW, even younger, is well-armed for the future with 1,263 subscribers.

Even the most ardent admirers of Samuel L. Clemens will probably be surprised to learn that the MARK TWAIN JOURNAL has a circulation of 10,000. Thoreau would be surprised, perhaps elated, at the news that, since the beginning of World War II, his supporters have produced no fewer than 146 issues of the THOREAU SOCIETY BULLETIN for some 1,200 subscribers. The WILLA CATHER PIONEER MEMORIAL NEWSLETTER has a circulation of 6,000; the THOMAS HARDY YEAR BOOK, 3,500; the SHAKESPEARE QUARTERLY, FITZGERALD/HEMINGWAY ANNUAL, and THROUGH CASA GUIDI WINDOWS (Browning) have 3,000 subscribers each; the BYRON JOURNAL, 2,000; and (there is hope for the world) even VERGILIUS has 1,700 subscribers.

The survey of international interest in Appendix 1 shows that literary genius spans the centuries, crosses national borders, and speaks above the clamor of social and political issues. Dante serial publications appear in Argentina, Canada, and Russia; Goethe in Australia and England; Whitman and Yeats in Japan; Shakespeare in Armenia and Austria; Doyle in Denmark and Sweden. The BURNS CHRONICLE, established in 1892, reports that there are 329 Robert Burns clubs scattered throughout the world--all very active indeed. In these days when international communication seems to be having its problems, it is encouraging to discover that the THOMAS HARDY YEAR BOOK has subscribers in 57 countries and the JOHN LOCKE NEWSLETTER in 40 countries, that scholars from 40 different nations around the world contribute articles and news to MOREANA, and that 30 percent of those who subscribe to the JAMES JOYCE QUARTERLY live in foreign lands. Such facts help us to understand what Whitman meant when he said, "I ask not good fortune; I _am_ good fortune."

THE APPRAISAL

The examination of these author serial publications, volume by volume, issue by issue, has produced the following observations and suggestions:

1. The most successful editors are good publicity agents. They maintain contact with serials and humanities librarians in large or specialized libraries, with departments of English in universities and colleges in America and overseas, with established literary scholars, respected periodicals and their editors, literary agents, and publishing houses that specialize in scholarly publications. They attend important conferences and seminars, read all new publications in their field, and they write, write, write.

2. The most successful periodicals have good business managers who insist on reasonable production costs and reasonable subscription rates, but economy is not a factor in their publication's format and content. These periodicals are readable, attractive, convenient, lucid, imaginative, provocative, stimulating--but most of all, they are memorable, in appearance and in scholarship. They are, furthermore, printed on schedule and delivered without mishap.

3. The most respected editors solicit and require scholarly research of the highest quality. An unblemished reputation for accuracy and insight seems to attract contributors and subscribers who in their turn tend to produce scholarship of accuracy and insight.

4. The best editors recognize the fact that most readers turn first to the section in the periodical containing current news items about seminars, conferences, new publications, work in progress, and activities of members. By making their periodical the primary source for such information, these editors enlist a reliable core of interested subscribers. Currency is always a major feature in the best author newsletters and journals--currency in book reviews, articles, bibliographies, and, last but not least, in indexes.

The one serious criticism that must be made of almost all the publications that were examined concerns this last item--indexing. When the periodicals themselves were compared with the questionnaires returned to us by their editors, we discovered with dismay that too many editors either do not know where their publications are indexed or abstracted, or do not think it important to supply their readers with this information. They do not, in other words, inform their readers where to go to locate--in the most professional, efficient manner--the scholarship so carefully solicited and presented within their highly specialized publications.

Some editors give their readers no indexes at all in the individual issues (such omissions are noted in this Guide with the annotation, "No index"). Many, but not enough, editors do provide an annual index. A very few conscientious editors see to it that cumulated indexes are available at three- or five-year intervals. But almost no editor includes on his inside front cover, along with his other important publishing and manuscript information, any mention of the professional indexing and abstracting publications which analyze his journal's contributions year after year and provide scholars with a key to its contents.

Readers should know, for instance, that the easiest way to locate articles in that excellent quarterly review MENCKENIANA, published since Spring 1962, is by consulting the title, author, and/or subject indexes of ABSTRACTS OF ENGLISH STUDIES, AMERICAN LITERATURE, AMERICAN HUMANITIES INDEX, ANNUAL BIBLIOGRAPHY OF ENGLISH LANGUAGE AND LITERATURE, MISSISSIPPI QUARTERLY, MLA INTERNATIONAL BIBLIOGRAPHY, or TWENTIETH CENTURY LITERATURE. And they should know that access to material in the interdisciplinary TEILHARD REVIEW, which is almost unequaled today for its purity of ideas and clarity of prose, is easiest through either the PHILOSOPHER'S INDEX, FRENCH XX BIBLIOGRAPHY: CRITICAL AND BIOGRAPHICAL REFERENCES FOR THE STUDY OF FRENCH LITERATURE SINCE 1885, or CATHOLIC PERIODICAL AND LITERATURE INDEX.

We can make the plea, then, that the editors of every publication listed within these pages take careful note of the indexing and abstracting information provided for them at the end of the annotations and that they print this information in the next issue of their own publications, preferably on the inside front cover near the copyright information. They might also wish to insert in their editorial page or news-and-notes section a reminder to their readers that the easy way to locate any one specific article or subject in their journal is to use those indexing services responsible for examining and listing its contents. We might also ask that these editors send copies of their publications to all indexing and abstracting services that might be interested in analyzing their contents.

ABSTRACTS OF ENGLISH STUDIES cannot abstract articles if AES editors do not know a publication exists. Very few of us have the time to read every issue of even our most admired newsletters and journals--we need indexes.

A few editors might note that the publication entitled PMLA (PUBLICATIONS OF THE MODERN LANGUAGE ASSOCIATION) is not an indexing service. It is a literary periodical which contains only scholarly articles and news for MLA members. The title which should be cited as an indexer of newsletter and journal publications is the MLA INTERNATIONAL BIBLIOGRAPHY, which is far removed, in both budget and staff, from PMLA.

And this might be the place to mention that editors who compile bibliographies of works by and about these famous authors hinder efficient research procedure when they fail to include an accurate list of all periodicals consulted during the process of compilation. Librarians and experienced researchers use these lists, and if they do not find the desired periodical title included there, they cast the bibliography aside without looking further. MISSISSIPPI QUARTERLY, for instance, could improve its excellent annual bibliography by providing a complete list of its sources to show it analyzes the contents of POE STUDIES, the FLANNERY O'CONNOR BULLETIN, and several other publications that focus on a single author.

THE FUTURE

Newsletters and journals that devote their pages to the life and works of one individual author are, almost invariably, nonprofit organizations that were created solely because their editors were convinced of the worth of their subject. With very few exceptions, they depend on subscription money for their existence, and their subscribers are necessarily limited to a relatively small number of intellectuals. But many of these publications make unique and substantial contributions to scholarship. They deserve the support of institutions and individuals alike--what better cause is there than a project which seeks to "learn and propagate the best that is known and thought in the world."

GUIDELINES FOR THE READER

1. Authors are listed alphabetically under their given names, not their pseudonyms. Cross references from pseudonyms to given names are provided. In Appendixes 1, 2, and 4, pseudonyms are placed in brackets after the given name for easy identification.

2. Periodicals are listed alphabetically, letter-by-letter, under each author. Names and titles are spelled as they appear in the originating periodicals or reference sources.

3. Queries were sent to hundreds of periodicals currently being published throughout the world, if addresses were available. If queries were not answered, this fact is noted in the annotation because librarians and scholars will want to know that the only available address may be incorrect or that the title may no longer be in existence and cannot be traced.

4. All available bibliographical information has been included on all available titles, new or old. Defunct periodicals are fully described and evaluated as an aid for acquisitions librarians, researchers considering interlibrary loan channels, and scholars interested in the historical aspects of their subject. When very little information other than the title itself is available, even that is cited in the hope that it will stimulate further investigation. In some cases, information will appear to be incomplete, as in a few periodicals where facts were found on the "new" series and not on the assumed "old" series, or in the numerous cases where no evidence could be found of the publisher's name and only the city could be cited. In all cases, readers can be certain that all information located in the periodicals themselves and in the numerous related reference books has been accumulated here for their convenience. See Appendix 7 for a list of sources and their abbreviations.

5. Explanation of entry items:

    Author's name, pseudonym in brackets, and birth and death dates (when available).

Guidelines for the Reader

Author's nationality and areas of interest. Not everyone, for example, knows Césaire's country of origin, and most are surprised to learn that Wilhelm Busch was a poet as well as an illustrator.

Title. The title chosen for the main entry is the title which appears on the title page of the most recent issue of the publication; spelling and hyphenation of the original are retained. With every title change, the new title is given a separate entry because changes of editors, addresses, and format usually occur at the same time. When the title change is accompanied by an expansion in coverage that takes the periodical outside the scope of this Guide (as when the MARY WOLLSTONECRAFT NEWSLETTER became WOMEN AND LITERATURE) no entry and no information is provided for the new title. Cross references to previous or succeeding titles of the main entry are indicated, and readers should consult those entries for complete information on the periodical when it functioned under those names. The title of a series (such as Cahiers André Gide) is in upper and lower case letters in order to help scholars distinguish the series from the individual volumes within the series which are in full caps (such as LE CENTENAIRE, published in 1972 as a part of the series Cahiers André Gide).

Abbreviation of title. Enclosed within parentheses after the titles are their abbreviations as they appear in the MODERN LANGUAGE ASSOCIATION INTERNATIONAL BIBLIOGRAPHY, Klapp, and other indexing and abstracting publications.

Editor's name and address. In general, the name of the *present* editor of journals still in existence is cited in the annotation, and the *last* editor of journals no longer being published. Other officers are listed when the publication indicated such a need, and in several instances earlier noteworthy editors are cited. Occasionally, no information on the editor could be found.

Sponsor's name and address. In a few cases, editor-sponsor-publisher is one person.

Publisher's name and address. In several older publications, only the name of the city, and not of the publisher, is indicated on the title page.

Date of first publication. The date is followed by a dash and a space if the periodical is still being published: 1923-- . If the date of the first issue could not be located, the first available number and date is cited. Note that if the periodical ever appeared under another title, that title has its own entry and all information pertinent to that title, including dates, is enumerated in that entry.

Frequency of publication. The reader will thus have some idea of the regularity and reliability of the publication.

Price. The most recent price of current periodicals and the range of prices in periodicals no longer being published are provided (when available) as an aid to both the history-oriented researcher and to the acquisitions librarian who needs to order back copies. Frequently a periodical will cite different subscription fees for students, individuals, and institutions in its own country and a flat fee for overseas subscriptions--for example, "Kr 16-30; $7." Native subscription rates are printed first; foreign rates, second.

Pages. The approximate number of pages is provided in brackets so that readers and acquisition librarians can estimate the substance of the individual publications.

Circulation figures are provided when editors responded to this question in our query.

Latest issue examined. The most recent issue examined for this Guide is cited so that the reader will have some idea of the accuracy and currency of the facts in the entry. Readers should remember that in some cases years elapse between publications of a series, especially in foreign titles. When the most recent available issue is several years old, as in the case of CAHIERS GASTON BATY, that fact is noted as follows: "Vol. 9 not yet published (1979)."

Annotation. The description and evaluation of each publication progresses generally from articles, bibliographies, and book reviews to news, notes, and indexing information. Omission of indexes in scholarly publications is noted.

Language of the periodical is indicated only if it is other than English, even when it is published in a non-English-speaking country. The notation reads "In English or French" when the contents are printed in one or the other language; it reads "In English and French" when a translation is provided.

Availability of reprints, used copies, microform, and their prices are noted for the convenience of acquisition librarians and specialists--all are of course subject to change. Note that Kraus Reprints supplies reprints of out-of-print titles and that Kraus Periodicals specializes in second-hand material.

Indexing information. When annual and cumulated indexes are provided by the periodical, that fact is noted; when important scholarly publications fail to provide an annual index, that, too, is noted. When the contents of the periodicals are analyzed by indexing and abstracting services, the titles of those services are listed at the end of the annotation ("Indexed by . . . ") so that readers will know the best sources to use when trying to locate articles in back or current issues. This last feature was researched with special care for this Guide; for instance, we found that CONRADIANA was analyzed by nine different indexing sources, whereas other library reference books responsible for such information cite only one indexing source. See Appendix 4 for a list of the indexing publications and the periodicals they analyze. See Appendix 7 for a list of the sources consulted and their abbreviations.

Alternate titles. Frequently the various indexing and abstracting publications refer to a periodical by inaccurate or informal versions of its copyrighted title. For this Guide, the source for the form of the main entry is always the title page of the periodical itself, when it is available, with other versions being listed at the end of the annotation. All variants are listed in the Title Index with a reference to the main entry.

Alternate information. Contradictory or unsubstantiated information that could be neither verified not refuted by available issues of the periodical, reference books, or queries to the editors is included here in the hope that exposure will resolve the problem.

6. Addenda. The Addenda (p. 357), like the main author-periodical section, is arranged alphabetically by author. It contains information on thirty-six additional titles and fifteen additional authors that was located after the remainder of the book had been prepared for the binder. Readers will have to consult both sections for complete coverage.

7. Appendixes. The main section of author-periodical entries is followed by seven appendixes: four analyze the results of the research by country, century, sponsoring institution, and indexing and abstracting services; three list information on publishers, foreign terms, and sources consulted. Additions and corrections will be received with gratitude.

ACKNOWLEDGMENTS

Special thanks for special contributions are extended to

Editors all over the world, some of whom, like Mme. Romain Rolland, wrote long letters explaining the history and scope of their publications. They include Charles Wirz (curator of the Voltaire Institute and Museum in Geneva), E.M. John (Tennyson Society, Lincoln, England), Pierre Michel (Amis de Montaigne, Paris), P. Bernanos (COURRIER GEORGES BERNANOS, Paris), Ian Campbell (Carlyle Society, Edinburgh), Eberhard Galley (Heinrich-Heine-Institut, Düsseldorf), Claude Martin (Centre d'Études gidiennes, Bron, France), Abbé Germain Marc'hadour (MOREANA, Angers, France), Maurice Amour (Société Chateaubriand, Paris), and many, many more.

Numerous colleagues who sent notes on newly created periodicals and other inaccessible information: William White (Oakland University), Richard A. Altick (Ohio State University), Richard Tobias (VICTORIAN STUDIES, University of Pittsburgh), Vincent Tollers (LITERARY RESEARCH NEWSLETTER, State University of New York at Brockport), Mary Ann O'Donnell (Manhattan College), Richard Centing (UNDER THE SIGN OF PISCES, Ohio State University Library), Louis Marder (SHAKESPEARE NEWSLETTER, University of Illinois), J. Theodore Johnson, Jr. (PROUST RESEARCH ASSOCIATION NEWSLETTER, University of Kansas), David L. Greene (BAUM BUGLE, Piedmont College), Kenneth Blackwell (Bertrand Russell Archives, McMaster University), Janice M. Benario (VERGILIUS, Georgia State University), Gregory Guzman (VINCENT OF BEAUVAIS NEWSLETTER, Bradley University), Mary Lewis Chapman (LITERARY SKETCHES, Williamsburg, Va.), Jack W. Herring (Armstrong Browning Library, Baylor University), Robert W. Morrison (Burns Society of the City of New York), Edmund A. Bojarski (CONRADIANA, McMurry College), Julian Wolff (BAKER STREET JOURNAL, New York), James C. Cowan (D.H. LAWRENCE REVIEW, University of Arkansas), Bob Mowery (ARTHUR MACHEN JOURNAL, Wittenberg University), Marjorie M. Johnson (University of Northern Colorado Library), Betty Adler (MENCKENIANA, Enoch Pratt Free Library, Baltimore), Walter Harding (THOREAU SOCIETY BULLETIN, State University College at Geneseo, New York), and many more.

Robert A. Colby (Queens College), who examined the index and made several important suggestions and additions.

Acknowledgments

Ronald de Waal (Colorado State University Library), who generously shared his current list of Sherlockian journals and newsletters.

Ernst Schürer (Department of German, Pennsylvania State University) and Raymond Gay-Crosier (Department of Romance Language and Literature, University of Florida), both of whom suggested sources, supplied names and titles, read the early manuscript, and made valuable comments on style and form.

Reference and serial librarians at the University of Massachusetts in Boston, the University of Florida, Wellesley College, the Boston Public Library, and the Widener Library at Harvard. They gave generously of their time, effort, and imagination.

Editors of the BULLETIN OF BIBLIOGRAPHY, who granted permission to reprint certain information which originally appeared in the December 1973 issue of their publication.

And most of all, I wish to express my sincere gratitude to Theodore Grieder (New York University), Duane DeVries (Polytechnic Institute of New York), and Denise Allard Adzigian, Gale Research Co. Their advice on every phase of the work has been invaluable.

M.C.P.

AUTHORS AND THEIR PERIODICALS

ALAIN

See Chartier, Émile-Auguste.

ALAIN-FOURNIER

See Fournier, Henri-Alban.

ALGER, HORATIO (1832-99)

American author of boys' books

1. Horatio Alger Society. MEMBERSHIP ROSTER. Sponsor and publisher: Horatio Alger Society, 4907 Allison Drive, Lansing, Mich. 48910. 1970-- .

2. NEWSBOY. Editor: Jack Bales. Sponsor and publisher: Horatio Alger Society, 4907 Allison Drive, Lansing, Mich. 48910. July 1962-- . Monthly. $10. [16 p.] Circulation: 300.

   Brief critical articles on the life, works, and times of Horatio Alger; news notes--"Random Reports from Algerland"; information on Alger book sales and membership activities such as the publication of Ralph Gardner's BIBLIOGRAPHY OF THE WORKS OF HORATIO ALGER (Wayside Press, 1971; 165 p.); occasional special issues; occasional bibliographies and book reviews; reports of work in progress; illustrations. Annual index is planned. Index for July 1962-June 1972 (vols. 1-10, no. 10).

AMPÈRE, ANDRÉ-MARIE (1775-1836)

French physicist, historian

1. BULLETIN DE LA SOCIÉTÉ DES AMIS D'ANDRÉ-MARIE AMPÈRE. Sponsor: Société des Amis d'André-Marie Ampère, 170, avenue Jean-Jaurès,

Lyon, France. 1931-(?).

Brief articles; news. In French.

Alternate address: Musée Ampère, Poleymieux (Rhone), France.

ANDERSEN, HANS CHRISTIAN (1805-75)

Danish author of fairy tales, poet, novelist, dramatist

1. ANDERSENIANA. Editors: Niels Oxenvad and H. Topsøe-Jensen, Universitetsbiblioteket, Copenhagen, Denmark. Sponsor and publisher: H.C. Andersens Hus, Odense Bys Museer, 5000 Odense, Denmark. 1933-46 (vols. 1-13); new series, 1947-69 (vols. 1-6); third series, 1970 (vol. 1, no. 1)-- . Annual. Kr 20-33.75. [100-130 p.] Circulation: 1,000. Last issue examined: vol. 3, no. 3, 1976.

   Long scholarly essays comparing Andersen's folktales with those of other countries and examining his sources from and influences on other literatures; studies of his life, environment, travels; occasional special surveys, such as "H.C. Andersen i Polen . . . 1844-1960"; "H.C. Andersen-litteraturen"--annual survey of research, with reviews of the most important international publications; abstracts; international contributors; news notes; numerous illustrations and facsimiles. Cumulative index for each volume by title, name, and subject. In Danish.

   Indexed by MLA INTERNATIONAL BIBLIOGRAPHY.

ANDERSON, SHERWOOD (1876-1941)

American novelist

1. Sherwood Anderson. Subseries of La Revue des Lettres Modernes. 1963-- . Irregular. Equivalent numbers are provided below for the parent series (La Revue des Lettres Modernes) and the individual author series on Anderson.

Anderson subseries	La Revue series	Date
No. 1	Nos. 78-80	1963

   In French. See Camus, Albert, entry 1, for a full description of La Revue des Lettres Modernes.

   Indexed by BULLETIN CRITIQUE, Klapp, and MLA INTERNATIONAL BIBLIOGRAPHY.

2. SHERWOOD ANDERSON SOCIETY NEWSLETTER. See WINESBURG EAGLE (entry 3, below).

3. WINESBURG EAGLE (WE). Editor: Welford D. Taylor. Sponsor and publisher: Sherwood Anderson Society, P.O. Box 51, University of Richmond, Richmond, Va. 23173. November 1975-- . 2/yr. (November, April). Free with membership ($5). [8 p.] Last issue examined: vol. 3, 1977.

Official publication of the Sherwood Anderson Society, which was formed to help further Anderson scholarship and to increase interest in the man and his work. Biographical, critical, and bibliographical articles; news and notes of interest to Anderson scholars; report of progress on Ray Lewis White's comprehensive Anderson bibliography and the annual supplement in the EAGLE; interviews; notes on textual problems; memoirs; reviews; news of publications by members; drawings. The title is frequently cited incorrectly as the SHERWOOD ANDERSON SOCIETY NEWSLETTER.

Indexed by MLA INTERNATIONAL BIBLIOGRAPHY.

ANNUNZIO, GABRIELE D' (1863-1938)

Italian poet, novelist, dramatist, soldier

1. QUADERNI DANNUNZIANI (QD). Director: Emilio Mariano. Sponsor and publisher: Il Vittoriale degli Italiani, Gardone Riviera, Brescia, Italy. 1941-43 (nos. 1-5); new series, 1955-- . Irregular. L.4.500-24.000. [85-400 p.] Last issues examined: nos. 42-43, 1976.

Long biographical and critical studies; brief notes on D'Annunzio's works, his influence, and his interaction with his associates; previously unpublished letters, works, and other documents; occasional comprehensive bibliographies covering several years of D'Annunzio scholarship; inventories of D'Annunzio manuscripts and other holdings in the Fondazione "Il Vittoriale degli Italiani"; facsimiles. In Italian.

Indexed by BIBLIOGRAPHIE DE LA LITTÉRATURE FRANÇAISE, FRENCH VII, and MLA INTERNATIONAL BIBLIOGRAPHY.

APOLLINAIRE, GUILLAUME

See Kostrowitzky, Wilhelm.

AQUINAS, SAINT THOMAS (1225?-74)

Italian scholar, philosopher

1. AQUINAS: RIVISTA INTERNAZIONALE DI FILOSOFIA. Editor: Aniceto Molinaro. Sponsor and publisher: Department of Philosophy, Pontificia Università Lateranense, Piazza San Giovanni in Laterano, 4, 00184 Rome, Italy. 1958-- . 3/yr. L.6.000; L.8.000 (foreign); $12. [175 p.] Last issue examined: no. 20, 1977.

Not confined to St. Thomas Aquinas--long scholarly articles extend to other philosophers such as Peirce, Kant, and Heidegger. Comprehensive international bibliographies on research in philosophy in general; long review articles as well as briefer reviews, mainly of Italian publications. In Italian.

Indexed by BIBLIOGRAPHIE DE LA LITTÉRATURE FRANÇAISE, MLA INTERNATIONAL BIBLIOGRAPHY, and PHILOSOPHER'S INDEX.

2. AQUINAS LECTURE. Sponsor: Aristotelian Society of Marquette University, Milwaukee, Wis. 53233. Publisher: Marquette University Press. 1938-- . Annual. $4-5. [40-160p.] Last issue examined: 1977.

   Each lecture focuses on a specific subject related in some way to the philosophy of St. Thomas Aquinas. The 1977 lecture, for example, is entitled THE PROBLEM OF EVIL. Contains bibliographies.

3. AQUINAS PAPER. Sponsor: Aquinas Society of London: Publisher: Aquin Press, Gloucestershire, England. 1950-71 (nos. 1-40). Irregular. Free with membership (20 shillings); $5 (U.S.). [10-30 p.]

   Coverage extends beyond Aquinas to Boethius, existentialism, and other philosophical subjects, but the Society existed to "stimulate interest in the teachings of St. Thomas and their relevance to present day problems." Contains reprints of lectures delivered to the Aquinas Society, each one on a different subject, such as THE HISTORICAL CONTEXT OF THE PHILOSOPHICAL WORKS OF ST. THOMAS AQUINAS (1958).

   Alternate title:

   Aquinas Society of London. AQUINAS PAPER

4. THOMAS IM GESPRÄCH. Publisher: Heidelberg, Germany (BRD). 1958-(?). Irregular. Last issue examined: no. 5, 1961.

   In German.

ARISTOTLE (384-322 B.C.)

Greek philosopher

1. Studia aristotelica. Sponsor: University of Padua (Padova), Centro per la storia della tradizione aristotelica, Facoltà di lettera e filosofía, Padua, Italy. Publisher: Editrice Antenore, Padua. 1958-- . Irregular (a series). [160-600 p.] Last issue examined: vol. 5, 1970.

   Each volume is devoted to a specific subject, such as LOGIC AND METAPHYSICS IN ARISTOTLE (vol. 5, 1970). Contains specialized bibliographies, such as that of Aristotle's works (vol. 1, 1958); title and subject indexes. In English, French, Italian, or Latin. Vol. 6 not yet published (1978).

ARNOLD, MATTHEW (1822-88)

English critic, poet

1. ARNOLDIAN. Supersedes ARNOLD NEWSLETTER (see entry 2). Editor: Richard R. Wohlschlaeger, Department of English, U.S. Naval Academy, Annapolis, Md. 21402. Sponsor and publisher: U.S. Naval Academy. Fall 1975 (vol. 3, no. 1)-- . 3/yr. Vols. 1 and 2, $3; thereafter, free (subscription list limited to 400). [15 p.] Circulation: 250. Last issue examined: vol. 5, 1978.

   Brief scholarly articles and notes dealing with the life and literature of Arnold, his family, and his circle; bibliographical, biographical, prosodic, and interpretive subjects; occasional long review essays of recent Arnoldian scholarship and on any subject relevant to the study of Victorian literature; "Notes of Interest"--comments on new publications, work in progress, library holdings; report of the MLA seminar, with abstracts of the papers; previously unpublished letters; annual bibliography of Arnold scholarship; queries; abstracts of dissertations; facsimiles.

2. ARNOLD NEWSLETTER. Superseded by ARNOLDIAN (see entry 1). Editor: Nadean Bishop, Department of English, Eastern Michigan University, Ypsilanti, Mich. 48197. Sponsor: Department of English, Eastern Michigan University, vols. 1-2, no. 1; vol. 2, nos. 2-4, U.S. Naval Academy. Spring 1973-Spring 1975 (vols. 1-2, no. 4). Vol. 1 contains three issues; vol. 2, four issues. $2.50. [15 p.]

   Established to "stimulate scholarship in the Arnold circle." Ongoing census of biographical materials and manuscripts in libraries; surveys of research possibilities and of scholarship in foreign countries; brief interpretive articles; annual bibliography of Arnold scholarship; book reviews; news of MLA seminars.

Indexed by ABSTRACTS OF ENGLISH STUDIES and ANNUAL BIBLIOGRAPHY OF ENGLISH LANGUAGE AND LITERATURE.

AROUET, FRANÇOIS MARIE [VOLTAIRE] (1694-1778)

French satirist, poet, dramatist

1. Archives des Lettres Modernes. 1960-- . Irregular. Series numbers for the issues on Voltaire are provided below.

Voltaire subseries	Archives series	Date
Unnumbered	No. 30	1960
Unnumbered	No. 32	1960
Unnumbered	No. 37	1961
Unnumbered	No. 146	1973

   In French. See Camus, Albert, entry 2, for a full description of Archives des Lettres Modernes.

Indexed by BULLETIN CRITIQUE, Klapp, and MLA INTERNATIONAL BIBLIOGRAPHY.

2. BULLETIN DE L'INSTITUT VOLTAIRE EN BELGIQUE. Sponsor: Institut Voltaire en Belgique, 64, rue des Deux-Églises, 4 Brussels, Belgium. 1961-- .

In French.

3. STUDIES ON VOLTAIRE AND THE EIGHTEENTH CENTURY (SVEC). Editor: Haydn Mason. Sponsor: The Voltaire Foundation, Thorpe Mandeville House, Banbury, Oxfordshire, England. Publisher: The Voltaire Foundation, Taylor Institution, Oxford, England. 1955-- . Irregular (15-20 vols./yr.). Price varies. [200-300 p.] Last issue examined: vol. 175, 1978.

Long scholarly studies of Voltaire's works, ideas, friendships, and influence; occasional reports on the progress of and corrections to the definitive edition; occasional bibliographies; international contributors; illustrations; no index. Formerly referred to as PUBLICATIONS DE L'INSTITUT ET MUSÉE VOLTAIRE, Geneva, Switzerland. In English or French.

Indexed by BIBLIOGRAPHIE DE LA LITTÉRATURE FRANÇAISE, BIBLIOGRAPHY OF FRENCH SEVENTEENTH CENTURY STUDIES, ENGLISH LANGUAGE NOTES, Klapp, MLA INTERNATIONAL BIBLIOGRAPHY, PHILOLOGICAL QUARTERLY, and REVUE D'HISTOIRE LITTÉRAIRE.

Alternate title:

TRAVAUX SUR VOLTAIRE ET LE DIX-HUITIÈME SIÈCLE

AUDOUX, MARGUÈRITE (1863-1937)

French author

See Philippe, Charles-Louis, entry 1.

AUGUSTINE, SAINT (354-430)

Early Christian church father, philosopher

1. ANALECTA AUGUSTINIANA. Sponsor and publisher: Institutum Historicum Ord. S. Augustini, via del Sant'Uffizio, 25, 00193 Rome, Italy. 1905-- . Annual. L.12.000-16.000. [300-450 p.] Last issue examined: vol. 39, 1976.

Long scholarly studies of the influence of Saint Augustine down through the ages; occasional surveys of research; name index. In Latin, Spanish, Italian, German, or English.

2. L'ANNÉE THÉOLOGIQUE AUGUSTINIENNE. Supersedes SENS CHÉTIEN; superseded by REVUE DES ÉTUDES AUGUSTINIENNES (see entry 9). Sponsor and publisher: Société augustinienne, Paris. 1940-54 (nos. 1-14). Annual.

   In French.

   Alternate title, 1940-51, no. 3:
   L'ANNÉE THÉOLOGIQUE

3. AUGUSTINIANA: REVUE POUR L'ÉTUDE DE SAINT AUGUSTIN ET DE L'ORDRE DES AUGUSTINS. Editors: Augustinian Fathers. Sponsor and publisher: Institut Historique Augustinien, Pakenstraat 109, B-3030, Héverlée-Louvain, Belgium. April 1951-- . Quarterly. 450 BF (Belgium); 650 BF (foreign). [200-340 p.] Last issue examined: vol. 27, 1977.

   Scholarly studies on philosophical questions that focus on St. Augustine and the order; occasional special issues, such as BIBLIOGRAPHIE HISTORIQUE DE L'ORDRE DE SAINT AUGUSTIN, 1945-75 (1976); textual studies toward a critical edition; occasional comprehensive bibliographies covering several years of Augustinian scholarship; long scholarly book reviews; list of books received; annual index. Index to vols. 1-25 in vol. 26 (1976). In French, English, German, Italian, or Latin.

   Indexed by L'ANNÉE PHILOLOGIQUE and MLA INTERNATIONAL BIBLIOGRAPHY.

4. AUGUSTINIAN STUDIES. Editor: Robert P. Russell, O.S.A. Sponsor and publisher: Augustinian Institute, Villanova University, Villanova, Pa. 19085. 1970-- . Annual. $10. [210-50 p.] Last issue examined: vol. 7, 1976.

   Annual publication of the Augustinian Institute, devoted to scholarly, international studies on the life, teachings, and influence of Augustine through the ages, such as "Jean Calvin et Saint Augustin" (in vol. 3) and "Two Notes on Augustine, Charlemagne, and Romance" (in vol.5); review articles of recent important publications. In English, German, Italian, Latin, Spanish, or French.

   Indexed by L'ANNÉE PHILOLOGIQUE, CATHOLIC PERIODICAL AND LITERATURE INDEX, and PHILOSOPHER'S INDEX.

5. AUGUSTINIANUM: PERIODICUM QUADRIMESTRE INSTITUTI PATRISTICI "AUGUSTINIANUM." Editor: Vittorino Grossi. Sponsor: Institutum Patristicum "Augustinianum," via del San Uffizio, 25, I-00193 Rome. April 1961-- . 3/yr. L.13.000. [190-235 p.] Last issue examined: vol. 17, 1977.

Long scholarly studies on philosophical questions--not confined to St. Augustine; numerous brief reviews of international publications. In Italian or German.

Indexed by L'ANNÉE PHILOLOGIQUE and MLA INTERNATIONAL BIBLIOGRAPHY.

Alternate subtitle:

PERIODICUM QUADRIMESTRE COLLEGII INTERNATIONALIS AUGUSTINIANA (Rome)

6. AUGUSTINUS: REVISTA TRIMESTRAL PUBLICADA POR LOS PADRES AUGUSTINOS RECOLETOS. Director: Victorino Capanaga. Secretary: José Oroz, Agustinos Recoletos, 2, Salamanca, Spain. 1956-- . Quarterly (occasionally published in 1-2 issues/yr.). 700 pesetas; $10 (U.S.). [100-110 p.] Last issue examined: vol. 23, 1978.

Inspired by St. Augustine's life and works, but not devoted to him exclusively. Long scholarly studies on Augustinian philosophy as it appears throughout history; "Boletin Agustiniano"--a survey and evaluation of recent research; exceptionally well-annotated, comprehensive, international bibliography of recent scholarship; numerous brief reviews of important international publications; bibliographical references; list of books received; no index. In Spanish.

Indexed by L'ANNÉE PHILOLOGIQUE, MLA INTERNATIONAL BIBLIOGRAPHY, and PHILOSOPHER'S INDEX.

7. ESTUDIO AGUSTINIANO. Director: Constantino Mielgo. Sponsor and publisher: Estudio Teológico Agustiniano, Paseo de Filipinos, 7, Valladolid, Spain. 1966-- . 3/yr. 250-400 pesetas; $7 (U.S.). [150-90 p.] Last issue examined: vol. 11, no. 2, May-August 1976.

Long scholarly studies on every phase of Augustinian philosophy--not confined to St. Augustine except in the way his life and teaching have permeated our culture; numerous brief reviews of important international publications arranged according to subject; indexed by subject. In Spanish.

Alternate titles:

ARCHIVO TEOLÓGICO AGUSTINIANO

ARCHIVO AGUSTINIANO

8. RECHERCHES AUGUSTINIENNES (RechA). Supplement of REVUE DES ÉTUDES AUGUSTINIENNES (see entry 9). Sponsor and publisher: Études Augustiniennes, 8, rue François-Ier, 75008 Paris. 1958-- . Irregular. 80-170 Fr. [180-500 p.] Last issue examined: vol. 11, 1976.

Collections of scholarly essays on special subjects that, for reasons of space and scope, could not be included in the REVUE, such as "Augustin et Camus" (in vol. 6) or "Les Voyages de Saint Augustin" (in vol. 1); bibliographies. In French, Italian, or English.

Indexed by FRENCH XX and MLA INTERNATIONAL BIBLIOGRAPHY.

9. REVUE DES ÉTUDES AUGUSTINIENNES (REA). Supersedes L'ANNÉE THÉOLOGIQUE AUGUSTINIENNE (see entry 2). Editor: Jacques Fontaine and others. Sponsor: Études Augustiniennes, 8, rue François-Ier, 75008 Paris. Published with the approval of the Centre National de la Recherche Scientifique. 1955-- . Quarterly (published in two issues/yr.). 120 Fr; 124 Fr or $29 (foreign). [200-240 p.] Last issue examined: vol. 23, 1977.

Only occasional mention of St. Augustine, but the content is based on his teaching and influence--coverage extends to all early philosophers and their works. Learned essays; bibliographies; numerous book reviews; illustrations; index. Includes "Bulletin Augustinien," a comprehensive annotated, international bibliography of scholarship arranged by genre and subject. In French, English, German, or Latin. Supplement: RECHERCHES AUGUSTINIENNES (see entry 8).

Indexed by L'ANNÉE PHILOLOGIQUE, BIBLIOGRAPHIE DE LA LITTÉRATURE FRANÇAISE, MLA INTERNATIONAL BIBLIOGRAPHY, and PHILOSOPHER'S INDEX.

10. Saint Augustine Lectures. Sponsor and publisher: Augustinian Institute, Villanova University Press, Villanova, Pa. 19085. 1960-- . Irregular. [$2-4.] Last issue examined: no. 13, 1974.

Contemporary studies, such as "Augustine on Immortality" (no. 8, 1969), by outstanding scholars. In English or French.

AUSTEN, JANE (1775-1817)

English novelist

1. Jane Austen Society. REPORT. Sponsor: Jane Austen Society. Secretary: Sir Hugh Smiley, Ivalls, Bentworth, Alton, Hampshire, England. 1940(?)-- . Annual. £5 (life membership). [10-25 p.]

Reprints of addresses delivered to the Society's annual meetings, generally on Jane Austen's friendships, family, possessions, works, travels, and homes; information on the purchase and contents of her home in Chawton, near Winchester; news of Society activities, including the annual meeting; lists of members; financial report; numerous photographs. Facsimile reprints for 1949-65 are available from William Dawson (£2.50).

BACON, FRANCIS (1561-1626)

English philosopher, essayist

1. AMERICAN BACONIANA. Sponsor and publisher: Bacon Society of America, National Arts Club, 15 Gramercy Park, New York, N.Y. President: Willard Parker. February 1923-January 1931 (vols. 1-2, no. 7). Irregular. $1. [60-160 p.]

   Concerned with Bacon's genius, his life and methods of work, his associates and his times, especially in relation to the plays generally attributed to Shakespeare, to the alleged ciphers in Bacon's manuscripts, and to handwriting; book reviews; report of society meetings around the world; occasional bibliographies and news of acquisitions; numerous illustrations, portraits, and facsimiles.

2. BACONIANA (Chicago). May-October 1892 (vol. 1, nos. 1-2).

3. BACONIANA: THE JOURNAL OF THE FRANCIS BACON SOCIETY. Supersedes Bacon Society, London. JOURNAL (see entry 5). Sponsor and publisher: Francis Bacon Society, 50a, Old Brompton Road, London S.W.7 (former name, 1885-1948: Bacon Society). May-October 1892 (vol. 1); new series, August 1893-October 1902 (vols. 1-10, nos. 1-40); third series, January 1903-- . Irregular (2-4/yr.). Free with membership (£2.10; $5); £1 per issue. [60-100 p.]. Last issue examined: vol. 59, 1976.

   Official journal of the Francis Bacon Society--seeks to encourage the study of Bacon's life, works, and influence. Articles, notes, and editorials exploring and expounding the theory the Francis Bacon was the author of the works generally credited to Shakespeare; studies of Bacon's style and philosophy; correspondence from readers; book reviews; news of the Society; illustrations and photographs. Index for 1886-1907 in the April 1907 issue, pp. 129-36. Reprints available from Kraus Reprint (1892-1964, $1,000); and from Walter J. Johnson (1892-1970, $1,000).

   Alternate title:

   JOURNAL OF THE BACON SOCIETY

   Alternate subtitle, 1903-17:

   A QUARTERLY MAGAZINE

4. BACONIANA LETTER. Sponsor and publisher: Francis Bacon Society, London. March 1951--(?) .

5. Bacon Society, London. JOURNAL. Superseded by BACONIA (see entry 3). Sponsor: Bacon Society, 5, Grosvenor Square, London, W.1. Publisher: George Redway, York Street, Covent Garden, London, June 1886-January 1891 (vols. 1-2, no. 11). Irregular (about 3/yr.). [60-80 p.]

   Organ of the Bacon Society--"To study the works of Francis Bacon, as Philosopher, Lawyer, Statesman, and Poet, also his character, genius, and life, his influence on his own and succeeding times, and the tendencies and results of his writing. . . . To investigate Bacon's supposed authorship of certain works unacknowledged by him, including the Shakespearian dramas and poems." Contains proceedings of the Society; reprints of lectures on the Shakespeare-Bacon controversy; essays on textual, linguistic, and historical questions; name and subject index. Reprints available from Kraus Reprint and Walter J. Johnson.

   Alternate title:

   JOURNAL OF THE BACON SOCIETY

BAILLON, ANDRÉ (1875-1932)

Belgian novelist, man of letters

1. CAHIERS ANDRÉ BAILLON. Publisher: E. Malfrère, France. March 1935-(?). 10 Fr. [125 p.]

   Collections of critical essays; reprints of some of Baillon's works. In French.

BALZAC, HONORÉ (1799-1850)

French novelist

1. L'ANNÉE BALZACIENNE (AB; ABalzac). Supersedes ÉTUDES BALZACIENNES (see entry 10). Editor: Pierre-Georges Castex. Associate editor: Madeleine Fargeaud, 87, rue de Courcelles, 75017 Paris. Sponsor: Groupe d'Etudes balzaciennes, Musée Balzac, 47, rue Raynouard, 75016 Paris. Publisher: Garnier Frères, Paris. Manuscripts: Michel Lichtlé, Les Parcs de la Nove, Bt 5, 13, rue de la Nove, 93170 Bagnolet, France. 1960-- . Annual (Spring). Free with membership (100 Fr; 110 Fr, foreign); $20. [375-425 p.] Last issue examined: 1978.

   Long documented studies of the life and works of Balzac and his associates; new biographical material; source studies on the influence of his travels and friendships; in every issue, "Bibliographie balzacienne," which includes bibliographies, biographies, surveys, books, articles, book reviews; "Revue Bibliophilique"--report of new editions of Balzac's work; numerous long book reviews and review articles; previously unpublished letters and other documents; critical notes; news of international events and publications, both completed and in progress; report of meetings, visitors, and displays at Balzac's house; report of activities of the Société des Amis d'Honoré de Balzac; list of articles appearing in previous volumes of L'ANNÉE BALZACIENNE; international contributors; index. In French.

Indexed by BIBLIOGRAPHIE DE LA LITTÉRATURE FRANÇAISE, Klapp, MLA INTERNATIONAL BIBLIOGRAPHY, and REVUE D'HISTOIRE LITTÉRAIRE.

2. BALZAC, JOURNAL POLITIQUE, LITTÉRAIRE ET ARTISTIQUE. PARAISSANT LE PREMIER DE CHAQUE MOIS. Publisher: Oziou. Bureaux, 235, faubourg Saint-Honoré; 5, rue de Savoie. September-December 1884 (nos. 1-4); January 1885 (no. 1); new series, November 1900-September 1901 (nos. 1-4). [8 p.]

   In French.

3. BALZAC A SACHÉ. Editor: Paul Métadier, Chateau de Saché, 37190 Saché (Indre-et-Loire), France. Sponsor and publisher: Société Honoré de Balzac de Touraine, Tours, France. 1951-- . Irregular. 300 Fr. [30-60 p.]. Last issue examined: no. 14, 1975.

   Brief critical and biographical articles; report of Society activities, expositions, television programs, films; previously unpublished material; report on the Museum's acquisitions and number of visitors; maps; reproductions and photographs; occasional facsimiles. In French.

   Indexed by BIBLIOGRAPHIE DE LA LITTÉRATURE FRANÇAISE.

   Alternate title:

   Association des Amis de Saché. BALZAC A SACHÉ

4. BALZAC BULLETIN. Sponsor: Balzac Society of Brooklyn, New York. 1939-(?).

   Alternate information in REVUE D'HISTOIRE LITTÉRAIRE: 1941-61 (nos. 1-34).

5. BALZACIANA. Publisher: a la cité des Livres, 27, rue Saint-Sulpice, Paris. 1925-(?). Irregular. [22 p.]

   Short examinations of specific aspects of Balzac's work. In French.

6. BALZACIEN. Sponsor: Société nationale des Amis de Balzac, Paris.

January-June 1912 (nos. 1-4); May 1913; new series, May-June 1918 (nos. 1-2).

In French.

Alternate subtitles:

1912-13: BULLETIN LITTÉRAIRE DE LA SOCIÉTÉ NATIONALE DES AMIS DE BALZAC

1918: BULLETIN MENSUEL DES TRAVAUX ET DE LA PROPAGANDE DE LA MAISON DE BALZAC

7. Balzac Society of America. PUBLICATIONS. 1946(?)-(?).

8. BULLETIN DE LA SOCIÉTÉ DES AMIS D'HONORÉ DE BALZAC. Sponsor and publisher: Société des Amis de Balzac, Paris. 1952-56 (nos. 1-22).

9. COURRIER BALZACIEN. Superseded by ÉTUDES BALZACIENNES (see entry 10). Editor: Jean A. Ducourneau, 17, rue d'Astorg, 75008 Paris. Sponsor: Société des Amis de Balzac, 3, rue Edmond Gondinet, 75013 Paris. December 1948-December 1950 (nos. 1-10). Monthly (irregular). [20-30 p.]

Essays on the life and works of Balzac; book reviews; previously unpublished works; bibliographies--primary and secondary, including book reviews; "L'Année Balzac"--news of Society activities and of international events; "Calendrier balzacien" --chronological report of events in Balzac's life; report of works in progress; facsimiles. Index to nos. 1-10 in no. 10. In French.

Indexed by BIBLIOGRAPHIE DE LA LITTÉRATURE FRANÇAISE and BULLETIN CRITIQUE.

10. ÉTUDES BALZACIENNES (EB). Supersedes LE COURRIER BALZACIEN (see entry 9); superseded by L'ANNÉE BALZACIENNE (see entry 1). Editor: Jean A. Ducourneau, 3, rue de Grenelle, 75006 Paris. Publisher: Paris. New series, March/June 1951-March 1960 (vols. 1-10; suspended January 1953-November 1958). [30-80 p.]

Long historical, biographical, textual, and literary studies; brief interpretive articles; previously unpublished works; bibliographies of new editions, critical works, and Balzac manuscripts in collections; bibliographical notes on early editions and reissues; book reviews; calendar of Balzac's life; news of films, Balzac's home, Society activities; photographs and facsimiles. Index to vols. 1-10 (1951-60) in vol. 10. In French.

Indexed by BULLETIN CRITIQUE, Klapp, and MLA INTERNATIONAL BIBLIOGRAPHY.

11. Études balzaciennes. Publisher: G. Courville, Paris. No. 2 (1938)-(?). Irregular (a series).

    Not to be confused with the periodical described in the preceding entry. Each volume is concerned with a specific subject. In French.

BARBEY D'AUREVILLY, JULES AMÉDÉE (1808-89)

French poet, novelist

1. Barbey d'Aurevilly. Subseries of La Revue des Lettres Modernes. Editor: Jacques Petit. 1966-- . Annual. Equivalent numbers are provided below for the parent series (La Revue des Lettres Modernes) and the individual author series on Barbey d'Aurevilly.

Barbey d'Aurevilly	La Revue Series	Date
No. 1	Nos. 137-40	1966
No. 2	Nos. 162-65	1967
No. 3	Nos. 189-92	1968
No. 4	Nos. 199-202	1969
No. 5	Nos. 234-37	1970
No. 6	Nos. 260-63	1971
No. 7	Nos. 285-89	1972
No. 8	Nos. 351-54	1973
No. 9	Nos. 403-08	1974
No. 10	Nos. 491-97	1977

In French. See Camus, Albert, entry 1, for a full description of La Revue des Lettres Modernes.

Indexed by BULLETIN CRITIQUE, Klapp, and MLA INTERNATIONAL BIBLIOGRAPHY.

2. Bibliothèque Barbey d'Aurevilly. Publisher: Minard, Paris. 1974-- .

    Each volume focuses on a specific subject--a regrouping of criticism originally published in Lettres Modernes. In French.

3. CAHIER AUREVILLIENS. Sponsor: Société Barbey d'Aurevilly, Paris. Publisher: Paris. June 1935-December 1939 (vols. 1-5, nos. 1-10). 2/yr.(?)

    Biographical, bibliographical, and interpretive articles on Barbey d'Aurevilly; previously unpublished works; "Bibliographie aurevillienne" in every issue: news of Society events; list of members; occasional illustrations and facsimiles. In French. Reprints available from Slatkine Reprints (1935-39, 220 Fr).

Alternate title:

BULLETIN DE LA SOCIÉTÉ BARBEY D'AUREVILLY

BARBIERI, CESARE (1877?-1956)

Italian-born American sponsor of the arts, engineer

1. CESARE BARBIERI COURIER (CBC). Editor: Michael R. Campo. Sponsor: Cesare Barbieri Center of Italian Studies, Trinity College, Hartford, Conn. 06106. November 1958-Fall 1967 (ceased publication in pamphlet form with vol. 9, no. 2); 1968 (vol. 10, enlarged form)-- . Annual. $1; free to friends of the Barbieri Center. [25-30 p.] Last issue examined: 1977.

   Only brief references to the life and works of Barbieri--designed to provide information on Italian culture and the affairs of the Cesare Barbieri Center, which was established by a Barbieri endowment. Contains short articles and notes on Italian archaeology, music, art, theatre, sports, dance, and history; surveys of scholarship; studies of comparative literature; book reviews; occasional poems; news on symposia and exhibits; illustrations.

Indexed by FRENCH VII and MLA INTERNATIONAL BIBLIOGRAPHY.

BARLACH, ERNST (1870-1938)

German poet, dramatist, sculptor, graphic artist

1. Ernst Barlach-Gesellschaft. DEN MITGLIEDERN UND FREUNDEN ZUR JAHRESWENDE. Editor: Hans Harmsen. Sponsor and publisher: Ernst Barlach-Gesellschaft, Hamburg, Germany (BRD). 1961(?)-- . Annual(?). [70-85 p.]

   Studies of Barlach's life, drama, letters, symbolism, philosophy, and newly discovered fragments; brief biographical and critical articles on Barlach's life and works; brief book reviews; includes "Berichte" and "Jahresberichte"--news of the Gesellschaft activities; news of work in progress; facsimiles with explanatory notes. Absorbed the Gesellschaft's JAHRESGABE (see entry 2) with the 1971/72 issue. In German.

Indexed by Köttelwesch.

Alternate titles:

ZUR JAHRESWENDE, DEN MITGLIEDERN ALS GRUSS

DEN MITGLIEDERN UND FREUNDEN ZUR JAHRESWENDE UND ALS JAHRESGABE

2. Ernst Barlach-Gesellschaft. JAHRESGABE. Sponsor and publisher: Ernst Barlach-Gesellschaft, Ratzeburg, Germany (BRD). 1947-70(?). 2/yr.(?) [15 p.]

Brief notes on Barlach's life, works, and influence on his contemporaries; previously unpublished letters and other documents. In German or English.

Alternate title:

Ernst Barlach-Gesellschaft. MITGLIEDERGABE

3. JAHRBUCH DER BARLACH-GESELLSCHAFT (JBG). Sponsor: Ernst Barlach-Gesellschaft. 195(?)-(?). Annual.

Brief articles; news of Gesellschaft activities. In German.

Indexed by MLA INTERNATIONAL BIBLIOGRAPHY.

BARRAULT, JEAN-LOUIS (1910-)

French actor, producer

See Renaud, Madeleine.

BATY, GASTON (1885-1952)

French drama producer

1. CAHIERS GASTON BATY. Editor: André-Charles Gervais, 172, rue de l'Université, 75007 Paris. Sponsor: Association des Amis de Gaston Baty, Direction des Arts et des Lettres, 53, rue Saint-Dominique, 75007 Paris. Publisher: Garnier-Arnoul, Paris. 1963-- . Annual. 7-16 Fr. [50-90 p.] Last issue examined: vol. 8, 1971.

Collections of long (5-30 p.) studies on Baty's technique and influence, his themes, relationship to the classics, and contributions to the renewal of the French theatre; reminiscences; previously unpublished fragments; abstracts of dissertations; news of interest to Baty admirers; no index. In French. Vol. 9 not yet published (1979).

Indexed by BIBLIOGRAPHIE DE LA LITTÉRATURE FRANÇAISE, FRENCH VII, and FRENCH XX.

BAUDELAIRE, CHARLES (1821-67)

French poet

1. Archives des Lettres Modernes. 1959-- . Irregular. [30-72 p.]. Series numbers for the issues on Baudelaire are provided below.

Baudelaire subseries	Archives series	Date
Unnumbered	No. 18	1958
Unnumbered	Nos. 19-20	1959
	Nos. 19-20, 2nd ed.	1969
Unnumbered	No. 23	1959
	No. 23, 2nd ed.	1968

In French. See Camus, Albert, entry 2, for a full description of Archives des Lettres Modernes.

Indexed by BULLETIN CRITIQUE, Klapp, and MLA INTERNATIONAL BIBLIOGRAPHY.

2. BULLETIN BAUDELAIRIEN. Editors: Claude Pichois, William T. Bandy, R.P. Poggenburg, Box 1830, Station B, Vanderbilt University, Nashville, Tenn. 37235. Sponsor: Center for Baudelaire Studies, Vanderbilt University. Paris office: J. Corti, 11, rue de Médicis, Paris. August 1965-- . 2/yr. (April, August), plus bibliographical supplement. $3; $4, air mail. [20-30 p.] Circulation: 450. Last issue examined: vol. 13, 1978.

Editors are interested in scholarship on Baudelaire and his circle, either biographical, textual, exegetical, or bibliographical. The Center for Baudelaire Studies is not a museum but a research library focusing on the life, works, and influence of Baudelaire throughout the world. It collects first editions, reprints, periodicals which published Baudelaire's works, and thousands of items containing criticism of his work.

Brief (5-6 p.) critical articles (strict space limitation); annual bibliography in August of books, articles, Ph.D. and M.A. theses, and scholarship from all parts of the world, edited by René Rancoeur, Centre W.T. Bandy d'études baudelairiennes, Vanderbilt University; news notes; work in progress; international contributors; occasional illustrations; index for 1965-70 (vols. 1-5). A cumulative index is planned for every five years. In French, with occasional material in English.

Indexed by BIBLIOGRAPHIE DE LA LITTÉRATURE FRANÇAISE, FRENCH VI, FRENCH XX, Klapp, MLA INTERNATIONAL BIBLIOGRAPHY, and REVUE D'HISTOIRE LITTÉRAIRE.

3. Centre d'études baudelairiennes. PUBLICATIONS. Sponsor: Center for

Baudelaire Studies, Vanderbilt University, Nashville, Tenn. 37235. 1972-- . Irregular. $2. Last issue examined: no. 2, 1976.

4. CRAMÉRIEN: BULLETIN D'INFORMATION DES AMIS DE SAMUEL CRAMER. Editor: Mme. M. Rosec-Le Roy, 31, rue St-Antoine, 75004 Paris. Sponsor: Amis de Samuel Cramer (Cramer-Club). August 1969-- . Irregular. 13 Fr. [4-10 p.] Last issue examined: vol. 3, no. 6, 1975.

   Dedicated to research on the life and works of Baudelaire, his family and friends, as well as on writers and artists with the Baudelaire spirit--for example, Gérard de Nerval, Huysmans, Proust, and Asselineau. Brief articles with information on Baudelaire's life and contemporaries; notes on criticism of his works, new periodicals and other publications, meetings, activities of Baudelaire scholars, translations. In French, with occasional contributions in English. Vol. 4 not yet published (1978).

   Indexed by BIBLIOGRAPHIE DE LA LITTÉRATURE FRANÇAISE.

5. Études baudelairiennes. Editors: William T. Bandy, Claude Pichois, James S. Patty, Robert Kopp, and others. Publisher: Éditions de la Baconnière, Neuchâtel, Switzerland. 1969-- . Irregular (a series). 30-80 Fr. [200-300 p.] Last issue examined: vol. 8, 1977.

   Long critical studies of themes, influences, research problems; emphasis on literary history; comprehensive bibliographies; surveys of research; previously unpublished works; book reviews; long descriptions of expositions, congresses, films, festivals; occasional special issues, such as MÉLANGES OFFERTS AU PROFESSOR W.T. BANDY (vol. 3); illustrations; no indexes. In French.

   Indexed by BULLETIN CRITIQUE, Klapp, and REVUE D'HISTOIRE LITTÉRAIRE.

BAUM, L. FRANK (1856-1919)

American author of children's books

1. BAUM BUGLE: A JOURNAL OF OZ (BaumB). Editor: Jerry V. Tobias, 1213 Kansas Street, Norman, Okla. 73069. Bibliographer: Peter E. Hanff. Review editor: David L. Greene. Sponsor: International Wizard of Oz Club, 220 North 11th Street, Escanaba, Mich. 49829 (corporate address: Box 95, Kinderhook, Ill. 62345). June 1957-- . 3/yr. (Spring, Autumn, Winter). $3.50. [30 p.] Circulation: 1,600.

   Interested in material related to Baum and the illustrators and authors of the Oz books. Biographical, bibliographical, scholarly, and popular articles; annotated bibliographies; "Oz Behind the Footlights"; "Oz in the News"; "Footnotes to Oz" (etymology of Oz words and names); occasional primary material; occasional special issues; book reviews; news notes; illustrations--generally reproductions of early Baum-Oz material. Cumulative index is in progress. The Oz Club also publishes a directory of members, THE OZ TRADING POST (a quarterly medium of exchange for collectors), and OZIANA (an annual of original stories and poems, $1 per issue).

Indexed by AMERICAN LITERATURE and MLA INTERNATIONAL BIBLIOGRAPHY.

BENNETT, ARNOLD (1867-1931)

English novelist, dramatist

1. ARNOLD BENNETT NEWSLETTER (ABN). Editor and publisher: Anita Miller, 334 Hawthorn, Glencoe, Ill. 60022. January 1975-- . 2/yr. Free; back issues, $1. [10-25 p.] Last issue examined: vol. 2, 1977.

   Information of all kinds on current work on Bennett, the Edwardian novel in general, H.G. Wells, Frank Swinnerton, Pauline Smith, and others in the Bennett circle. Short critical articles; book reviews and excerpts from reviews; notes on new editions, paperbacks, television programs; queries.

Indexed by MLA INTERNATIONAL BIBLIOGRAPHY.

BERGMAN, HJALMAR (1883-1931)

Swedish dramatist, novelist, short-story writer

1. HJALMAR BERGMAN SAMFUNDET ÅRSBOK (HBSÅ). Editor: Gunnar Qvarnström. Sponsor: Hjalmar Bergman Society. 1959-- . Annual. [100-240 p.] Last issue examined: 1976.

   Monographs or collections of long scholarly articles on Bergman's expressionism, symbolism, life, relationship with other authors, and works; studies of his place in literary history and critical approaches to his writings; previously unpublished works; bibliographies of international Bergman scholarship, including books, articles, films, recordings, microform; notes on performances and annual meetings; financial report; list of members; photographs and sketches. In Swedish.

Indexed by MLA INTERNATIONAL BIBLIOGRAPHY.

BERGSON, HENRI LOUIS (1859-1941)

French philosopher

1. ÉTUDES BERGSONIENNES (Étbergson). Editor: André Robinet. Sponsor: Association des Amis d'Henri Bergson. Publisher: Albin Michel (early volumes); Presses Universitaires de France (later volumes). 1948-- . Irregular. 25-30 Fr. [125-200 p.] Last issue examined: vol. 11, 1976.

   Long critical essays on Bergson's philosophy and his relationship with his predecessors, contemporaries, and such followers as Leibniz, Kant, and Einstein; "Bibliographie bergsonienne," edited by Angèle Kremer-Marietti--works by and about Bergson, listed and discussed or surveyed and evaluated, arranged by year and critic's name; notes on ideas, interpretations, conversations; occasional book reviews; news of Association meetings, lectures, and the Bergson Chair at the University of Nice; no index. In French.

   Indexed by FRENCH VII, FRENCH XX, and Klapp.

BERNANOS, GEORGES (1888-1948)

French novelist

1. Archives Bernanos. Subseries of Archives des Lettres Modernes. 1966-- . Irregular. Equivalent numbers are provided below for both the parent series (Archives des Lettres Modernes) and the individual author series on Bernanos.

Bernanos subseries	Archives series	Date
No. 1	No. 70	1966
No. 2	No. 105	1969
No. 3 (2 vols.)	No. 136	1972-73
No. 4	No. 143	1973
No. 5	No. 150	1974
No. 6	No. 154	1974

   In French. See Camus, Albert, entry 2, for a full description of Archives des Lettres Modernes.

   Indexed by BULLETIN CRITIQUE, FRENCH VII, FRENCH XX, Klapp, and MLA INTERNATIONAL BIBLIOGRAPHY.

2. Bibliothèque Bernanos. Publisher: Minard, Paris. 1959-- . Irregular. 30-34 Fr. [200-250 p.] Last issue examined: no. 8, 1972.

   Each volume focuses on a specific subject--a regrouping of criticism originally published in Lettres Modernes. In French.

3. BULLETIN DE LA SOCIÉTÉ DES AMIS DE GEORGES BERNANOS. Supersedes Société des Amis de Georges Bernanos. BULLETIN (see entry 6); superseded by COURRIER GEORGES BERNANOS (see entry 4). Editor: Daniel Pezeril. Sponsor: Société des Amis de Georges Bernanos, 252, rue Saint-Jacques, 75005 Paris. Publisher: Paillart, Abbeville, France. New series, May 1961-69 (nos. 41-60). Quarterly. 12 Fr. [15 p.]

   Devoted to spreading the thoughts of Bernanos, to making available previously unpublished material, and to publishing critical studies, interviews, surveys, and biographical and bibliographical research. Index for December 1949-66 (nos. 1-58) in no. 60 (1969). In French.

   Indexed by FRENCH VII.

   Alternate titles:

   BULLETIN DE L'ASSOCIATION DES AMIS DE GEORGES BERNANOS

   Société des Amis de Georges Bernanos. BULLETIN

4. COURRIER GEORGES BERNANOS. Supersedes BULLETIN DE LA SOCIÉTÉ DES AMIS DE GEORGES BERNANOS (see entry 3). Editor: Jean-Loup Bernanos, 211, boulevard Raspail, 75014 Paris. December 1969-- . 3-4/yr. 30 Fr; 38 Fr (foreign). [15 p.] Last issue examined: no. 17, December 1974.

   Concerned mainly with reprinting inaccessible or previously unpublished writings or extracts of writings by Bernanos and with reprinting criticism from other publications. Brief critical and biographical notes; numerous extracts concerning Bernanos from critical articles in other periodicals; previously unpublished works, with evaluations and notes; occasional bibliographies of works by and about Bernanos--new editions, criticism, dissertations, television programs, chapters in books, and articles in periodicals; occasional book reviews; interviews; calendar of Bernanos-related activities and interests--colloquia, conferences, readings, publications; letters to the editor. In French. No. 18 not yet published (1978).

   Indexed by BIBLIOGRAPHIE DE LA LITTÉRATURE FRANÇAISE, FRENCH XX, and Klapp.

5. Études bernanosiennes. Subseries of La Revue des Lettres Modernes. Editor: Michel Estève. 1960-- . Annual. Equivalent numbers are provided below for the parent series (La Revue des Lettres Modernes) and the individual author series on Bernanos.

Bernanos subseries	La Revue Series	Date
No. 1	Nos. 56-57	1960
No. 2	Nos. 67-68	1961-62
Nos. 3/4	Nos. 81-84	1963
No. 5	Nos. 108-10	1964
No. 6	Nos. 127-29	1965
No. 7	Nos. 141-45	1966
No. 8	Nos. 153-56	1967
No. 9	Nos. 175-79	1968
No. 10	Nos. 203-08	1969
No. 11	Nos. 228-33	1970
No. 12	Nos. 254-59	1971
No. 13	Nos. 290-97	1972
No. 14	Nos. 340-45	1973
No. 15	Nos. 409-12	1974
No. 16	Nos. 504-09	1977

In French. See Camus, Albert, entry 1, for a full description of La Revue des Lettres Modernes.

Indexed by BULLETIN CRITIQUE, FRENCH VII, FRENCH XX, Klapp, and MLA INTERNATIONAL BIBLIOGRAPHY.

6. Société des Amis de Georges Bernanos. BULLETIN (new series). Supersedes BULLETIN PERIODIQUE; superseded by BULLETIN DE LA SOCIÉTÉ DES AMIS DE GEORGES BERNANOS (see entry 3). Editor: Michel Estève, 33, rue Carvès, Montrouge (Seine), France. Treasurer: Camille Sautet, 51, rue de la Chapelle, 75018 Paris. Sponsor and publisher: Société des Amis de Georges Bernanos, Paris. December 1949-September 1960 (nos. 1-40). Quarterly. 250 Fr (10 NF). [16-32 p.]

Brief critical articles on the life and works of Bernanos; previously unpublished material; reminiscences; excerpts from reviews of plays; bibliographies of primary and secondary works, including articles about Bernanos in newspapers and journals; news of Society activities. Back issues available at Minard, Paris, and at Librairie La Hune, 170, boulevard St-Germain, Paris. In French.

The BULLETIN PÉRIODIQUE (also titled PERIODICUM MUNDANEUM) was sponsored by the Union of International Associations, Brussels, Belgium, and included material about, but was not devoted primarily to, Bernanos. Editor and publisher: Camille Sautet, 15, rue Francois-Bonvin, 75015 Paris. 1927(?)-April 1947.

Indexed by FRENCH VII.

BERNARDINO DA SIENA, SAINT (1380-1444)

Italian Franciscan monk

1. BULLETTINO DI STUDI BERNARDINIANI. Publisher: Siena, Italy. 1935-44/50 (vols. 1-10).

   Index for vols. 1-10. In Italian. Reprints available from Walter Johnson ($45).

BERRYMAN, JOHN (1914-72)

American poet, short-story writer

1. JOHN BERRYMAN STUDIES: A SCHOLARLY AND CRITICAL JOURNAL (JBerS). Editors and publishers: Ernest C. Stefanik, Jr., and Cis Stefanik, 805 West First Avenue, Derry, Pa. 15627. Sponsor: The Rook Society. January 1975-77. Quarterly (January, April, July, October). $5; $9 (institutions). [30-50 p.] Last issue examined: vol. 3, 1977.

   Devoted to scholarship on the writings of John Berryman and other middle-generation American poets. Research-based biographical and critical articles; textual studies; bibliographies of critical books and articles and of reprints and new editions of Berryman's works; book reviews; contemporary poems. Temporarily suspended publication (1978).

Indexed by ABSTRACTS OF ENGLISH STUDIES and MLA INTERNATIONAL BIBLIOGRAPHY.

BEYLE, MARIE HENRI [STENDHAL] (1783-1842)

French novelist, critic

1. Collection stendhalienne. Editor: V. del Litto ("Beauregard"), 3, rue Maurice-Gignoux (Montée Rabot), 3800 Grenoble, France. Publisher: Éditions du Grand Chêne, Lausanne, Switzerland. 1958-- . Irregular (a series). 15-60 Fr. Last issue examined: vol. 19, 1975.

   Long critical studies on Stendhal, including four book-length comprehensive bibliographies of current scholarship (vols. 1, 5, 9, 17). Each volume is devoted to a specific subject, such as STENDHAL LECTEUR DE MME. DE STAËL (vol. 16). In French.

2. DIVAN: REVUE DE LITTÉRATURE ET D'ART. Editor: H. Martineau. Publisher: Éditions du Divan, Paris. 1909-58 (vols. 1-50, nos. 1-307); suspended September 1914-September 1915, November 1915-January 1916. Quarterly.

Numerous articles on Stendhal's life and works--not devoted to him, but a good source for well-researched material. In French. Reprints available from Walter J. Johnson (1909-58, $1,040); second-hand sets from Kraus Periodicals (1909-58, $670).

Indexed by Klapp and MLA INTERNATIONAL BIBLIOGRAPHY.

3. ÉTUDES STENDHALIENNES. Editor: François Michel. Publisher: Mercure de France, Paris; Le Divan, Paris. 1931-- . Irregular. 10-60 Fr. [55-400 p.]

Some new biographical and interpretive studies, but mainly reprints of critical works originally published in other sources such as DIVAN and LE MONDE; book reviews; index. In French.

4. Société des Amis du Musée de Stendhal. BULLETIN. Sponsor: Société des Amis du Musée de Stendhal. Publisher: 5, rue Hauquelin, Grenoble (Isère), France.

In French.

5. STENDHAL CLUB: REVUE TRIMESTRIELLE (SC; StCl). Editor: V. del Litto ("Beauregard"), 3, rue Maurice-Gignoux (Montée Rabot), 38000 Grenoble, France. Publisher: Éditions du Grand Chêne, Lausanne, Switzerland. Dépot: Librairie Nicaise, 145, boulevard St-Germain, 75006 Paris. October 1958-July 1975 (nos. 1-68); new series, October 1975 (no. 69)-- . Quarterly (October, January, April, July). 105 Fr; 135 Fr (foreign). [80-120 p.] Last issue examined: vol. 21, no. 81, 1978.

Long biographical and interpretive studies; "Bibliographie stendhalienne"--international bibliography in October containing information on new editions, translations, previously unpublished works, autographs, television programs, books and articles; critical notes on problem areas; short book reviews; previously unpublished documents; news notes of lectures, events, necrology, and scholarship recently completed throughout the world; queries and answers; reader's forum; occasional special numbers, such as STENDHAL AUX ÉTATS-UNIS (no. 78, January 1978); illustrations; annual index by author, subject, and title. In French. Scattered issues available in reprint from Walter J. Johnson ($5 per issue).

Indexed by BIBLIOGRAPHIE DE LA LITTÉRATURE FRANÇAISE, BULLETIN CRITIQUE, ENGLISH LANGUAGE NOTES, FRENCH VI, FRENCH XX, Klapp, MLA INTERNATIONAL BIBLIOGRAPHY, and REVUE D'HISTOIRE LITTÉRAIRE.

6. Stendhal-Club, Grenoble. Editions du Stendhal-Club. Publisher: Paris. 1922-35 (nos. 1-35).

    Stendhal's works, but occasionally accompanied by helpful criticism. In French. Reprints available from Slatkine Reprints (1922-35, 160 Fr per title). Distributor in Paris: H. Champion.

BLACKMORE, RICHARD DODDRIDGE (1825-1900)

English novelist

1. BLACKMORE STUDIES. Sponsor: Blackmore Society, 24 Linhope Street, Clarence Gate, London N.W.1. 1969-(?). 1-2/yr. $2.50 (individuals); $5 (institutions). Circulation: 600.

    Literary, topographical, bibliographical material relating to Blackmore's life and works; bibliographies; book reviews; illustrations. Supplied only to members of the Blackmore Society. No reply to query.

BLAKE, WILLIAM (1757-1827)

English poet, engraver, painter

1. BLAKE: AN ILLUSTRATED QUARTERLY. Supersedes BLAKE NEWSLETTER (see entry 2). Editors: Morris Eaves, Department of English, University of New Mexico, Albuquerque, N. Mex. 87131; and Morton D. Paley, Department of English, University of California, Berkeley, Calif. 94720. Associate editor for Great Britain: Frances A. Carey, Assistant Curator, Department of Prints and Drawings, British Museum, London. Sponsor and publisher: Department of English, University of New Mexico. Summer 1977 (vol. 11)-- . Quarterly (Summer, Fall, Winter, Spring). $12 (individuals); $10 (surface mail); $15 (overseas, air mail). [60-70 p.] Last issue examined: BLAKE 43, vol. 12, 1978.

    Long articles on Blake's work, with particular attention given to his art; notes on interpretations, dating problems, and textual problems and corrections; discussions; comprehensive annual checklist of Blake scholarship; special checklists such as those of "Blake among the Slavs" and "Dissertations on Blake: 1963-1975"; special bibliographical issues; book reviews; news of recent publications, book and art sales, festivals and conferences; numerous illustrations and facsimiles; quality format; annual index.

Indexed by AMERICAN HUMANITIES INDEX, ANNUAL BIBLIOGRAPHY OF ENGLISH LANGUAGE AND LITERATURE, ENGLISH LANGUAGE NOTES, and MLA INTERNATIONAL BIBLIOGRAPHY.

OVER 150 YEARS PASS, DURING WHICH THE PICTURE OF THE "ANCIENT BRITONS" IS LOST....
ARTHUR HAS JUST RETURNED FROM SCHOOL, AFTER LEARNING ABOUT BLAKE.
HELLO ARTHUR
LATER THAT DAY
I WONDER IF OUR ANCESTORS STOWED THOSE THREE NUDE MEN INTO OUR ATTIC?
WHO?
THEY ARE THE "ANCIENT BRITONS", THREE NUDE MEN, THE MOST BEAUTIFUL, MOST STRONG AND MOST UGLY, OVERTHROWING AN ARMY OF ARMED ROMANS.
THE STRONG MAN REPRESENTS THE HUMAN SUBLIME, THE BEAUTIFUL MAN THE HUMAN PATHETIC, THE UGLY IS HUMAN REASON
IT WAS NOT GREEK IN CHARACTER AND WAS 10 FOOT by 14
BUT WHY DONT YOU JUST LOOK AT MODERN NUDE PAINTINGS, LIKE OTHER HEALTHY YOUNG LADS?
BECAUSE MODERN MAN IS LIKE A CORPSE
WE CAN SEARCH THROUGH THE JUNK IN THE ATTIC
WHAT BLISS! WHAT JOY! THIS MUST GO TO THE NATION
OUTSIDE THE TATE GALLERY
HURRAH! HERE COME BLAKE'S LONG-LOST BRITONS
150th BLAKE ANNIVERSARY
IN THE GALLERY.......
I GUESSED IT HAD BEEN STOWED AWAY SOMEWHERE, EVER SINCE 1810, AND FORGOTTEN....
BBC
YOU MODERN BRITONS COULD MAKE THIS VISION TRUE. SEARCH YOUR ATTICS AND CELLARS.
YOU COULD DO THE NATION, BLAKE, AND YOURSELF A FAVOUR: FIND THE PICTURE
Drawn by MARTIN READ
Inspired by Ruthven Todd
Phrased from "Blake Records" edited by
Chosen by Michael Davis G.E. Bentley Jnr.

2. BLAKE NEWSLETTER: AN ILLUSTRATED QUARTERLY (BlakeN; BNL). Superseded by BLAKE: AN ILLUSTRATED QUARTERLY (see entry 1). Editors: Morris Eaves, Department of English, University of New Mexico, Albuquerque, N. Mex. 87131; Morton D. Paley, Department of English, Boston University, Boston, Mass. 02215. Sponsor: Department of English, University of New Mexico. June 15, 1967-77 (vols. 1-10). Quarterly. $4 (individuals); $5 (institutions); $8 (foreign air mail). [20-40 p.] Circulation: 600.

Brief articles on every aspect of Blake scholarship--biographical, textual, historical, interpretive, and art criticism; brief discussions of controversial areas in Blake's work; news notes on lectures, exhibitions, library holdings, videotapes, and television programs; annual checklist in the fall issue of recent Blake scholarship, plus an average of two special bibliographical issues per year with such material as "A Checklist of Blake Slides," or a checklist of material useful for Blake classes (Summer 1976) which includes visual aids, out-of-print books, works in progress; long book reviews; report of work in progress; report of MLA Blake seminar and other conferences; numerous excellent reproductions of Blake art; special issues, like nos. 29-30, "Blake among the Victorians," and no. 31, Blake's paintings for the FAERIE QUEENE; annual index in the Spring issue of articles and books reviewed, arranged by author and title, and of illustrations, arranged by title (publication of this index is occasionally delayed, as it was in 1975); striking format with bold art work.

Indexed by AMERICAN HUMANITIES INDEX, ANNUAL BIBLIOGRAPHY OF ENGLISH LANGUAGE AND LITERATURE, ENGLISH LANGUAGE NOTES, MLA ABSTRACTS, MLA INTERNATIONAL BIBLIOGRAPHY, PHILOLOGICAL QUARTERLY, and YEAR'S WORK IN ENGLISH STUDIES.

3. BLAKE STUDIES (BlakeS; BS). Editors and publishers: Kay Parkhurst Easson and Roger R. Easson, American Blake Foundation, Department of English, Memphis State University, Memphis, Tenn. 38152. Associate editor: Robert N. Essick. Fall 1968-- . 2/yr. (Winter, Spring). $7.50 (U.S., Canada); $8.50 (foreign). [90-110 p.] Circulation: 660. Last issue examined: vol. 8, 1978.

Editorial policy stresses preference for interdisciplinary studies of art and literary criticism as applied to Blake's work. Long articles by American scholars on Blake as author and artist--occasional contributions by English critics; long scholarly book reviews in each issue; brief evaluative annotations on publications related to Blake, as on a Fuseli biography or a Mellon collection of English drawings; abstracts of dissertations; bibliographical references; letters to the editor; book exchange; occasional news of seminars, expositions, and library or art museum holdings; numerous reproductions of Blake's art; index. Available on microform from University Microfilms International.

Indexed by ABSTRACTS OF ENGLISH STUDIES, AMERICAN HUMANITIES INDEX, ANNUAL BIBLIOGRAPHY OF ENGLISH LANGUAGE AND LITERATURE, ENGLISH LANGUAGE NOTES, MLA INTERNATIONAL BIBLIOGRAPHY, PHILOLOGICAL QUARTERLY, and YEAR'S WORK IN ENGLISH STUDIES.

BLOCH, JEAN-RICHARD (1884-1947)

French essayist, novelist, dramatist, journalist

1. EUROPE: REVUE LITTÉRAIRE MENSUELLE. Editor: Pierre Gamarra, 21, rue de Richelieu, 75001 Paris. February 1923-- . Monthly. 75 Fr; 143 Fr (foreign). Last issue examined: no. 576, 1977.

   Contains a regular report from Les Amis de Jean-Richard Bloch. In French.

   Indexed by BIBLIOGRAPHIE DE LA LITTÉRATURE FRANÇAISE, FRENCH VII, FRENCH XX, and Klapp.

BLONDEL, MAURICE (1861-1949)

French neo-Catholic philosopher

1. BULLETIN DES AMIS DE MAURICE BLONDEL. Supersedes COURRIER DES AMIS DE MAURICE BLONDEL (see entry 2). 1952 (no. 3)--(?).

2. COURRIER DES AMIS DE MAURICE BLONDEL. Superseded by BULLETIN DES AMIS DE MAURICE BLONDEL (see entry 1). Publisher: Aix-en-Provence, France. 1950-51 (nos. 1-2).

3. ÉTUDES BLONDÉLIENNES. Sponsor and publisher: Presses Universitaires de France, Paris. 1951-54 (nos. 1-3). Annual. [120-79 p.]

   Critical essays on Blondel's works, philosophy, and friendships; notes toward a revised edition of his works; dialogues on his ideas; previously unpublished material. In French.

   Indexed by BULLETIN CRITIQUE and FRENCH VII.

BLOY, LÉON (1846-1917)

French apocalyptic Catholic writer

1. Archives des Lettres Modernes. 1969-- . Irregular. Series numbers for the issues on Bloy are provided below.

Bloy subseries	Archives series	Date
Unnumbered	No. 23	1968
Unnumbered	No. 99	1969

In French. See Camus, Albert, entry 2, for a full description of Archives des Lettres Modernes.

Indexed by BULLETIN CRITIQUE, FRENCH XX, Klapp, and MLA INTERNATIONAL BIBLIOGRAPHY.

2. BLOYANA. Editor: Léonce Trépanier. Publisher: 6764, rue Chambord, Montréal, Canada. June 1962-(?). Irregular. $2. Last issue examined: no. 7, 1968.

   Brief articles on Bloy's philosophy and technique; reminiscences; previously unpublished works. In French.

   Indexed by FRENCH VII and FRENCH XX.

3. CAHIERS LÉON-BLOY. Publisher: La Rochelle, France. 1924-39 (nos. 1-15); 1952 (no. 16).

   In French. Reprints available from Slatkine Reprints (1924-52, 450 Fr).

BLUM, LÉON (1872-1950)

French essayist, critic, politician

1. BULLETIN DE LA SOCIÉTÉ DES AMIS DE LÉON BLUM. Supersedes BULLETIN DES AMIS DE LÉON BLUM (see entry 2); superseded by CAHIERS LÉON BLUM (see entry 3). Sponsor and publisher: Société des Amis de Léon Blum, 18, rue Duret, 75016 Paris. Treasurer: Cécile Constant, 15, rue Gazan, 75014 Paris. December 1966-73 (nos. 14-17). Irregular. 3-20 Fr. [30-50 p.]

   Report of Society activities--participation in the International Socialist Conference, exhibitions; report on the progress of the publication of Blum's works, now complete in nine volumes (Albin Michel, Paris); reprints of lectures; no index. In French.

2. BULLETIN DES AMIS DE LÉON BLUM. Superseded by BULLETIN DE LA SOCIÉTÉ DES AMIS DE LÉON BLUM (see entry 1). Sponsor and publisher: Société des Amis de Léon Blum, 18, rue Duret, 75016 Paris. June 1952-February 1966 (nos. 1-13). Irregular. 1.50 Fr. [8-15 p.]

   Biographical and critical notes; report on the progress of the publication of Blum's works; financial statement; no index. In French.

   Alternate title:

   Société des Amis de Léon Blum. BULLETIN

3. CAHIERS LÉON BLUM. Supersedes BULLETIN DE LA SOCIÉTÉ DES AMIS

DE LÉON BLUM (see entry 1). Editor: Dominique Hamon, 9, rue des Tournelles, 94230 CACHAN, France. Sponsor and publisher: Société des Amis de Léon Blum, 9, rue des Tournelles, 94230 CACHAN. Treasurer: Mme. Catherine Malamoud, 7, rue de la Cité universitaire, 75014 Paris. May 1977-- . 2/yr. 20 Fr. [45-50 p.] Last issue examined: nos. 2-3, 1978.

Designed to foster interest in Blum and his times. Studies of his ideas and tactics; previously unpublished material; reminiscences. In French.

BLUNCK, HANS FRIEDRICH (1888-1961)

German poet, novelist, dramatist, folklorist

1. HANS FRIEDRICH BLUNCK-JAHRBUCH. Sponsor Hans Friedrich Blunck-Gesellschaft, Hamburg-Altona, Germany (BRD). Publisher: Plön, Heide in Holstein, Germany (BRD). 1963-- . Irregular. [240 p.] Last issue examined: Jahrbuch 2, 1968.

   An occasional publication of the Gesellschaft that includes long studies on Blunck's life and works--his youth, religion, friendship with Thomas Mann and other contemporaries, philosophy, and influence on other authors and literatures; previously unpublished material; surveys of Blunck scholarship; list of critical works; international editorial board; facsimiles. In German. The Gesellschaft also publishes other individual works of criticism on Blunck.

   Indexed by Köttelwesch.

   Alternate titles:

   JAHRBUCH DER GESELLSCHAFT ZUR FÖRDERUNG DES WERKES VON HANS FRIEDRICH BLUNCK

   Gesellschaft zur Förderung des Werkes von Hans Friedrich Blunck. JAHRBUCH

BOCCACCIO, GIOVANNI (1313-75)

Italian poet, prose writer

1. BOCCACCIO. Sponsor: American Boccaccio Association, Sea Cliff, New York. 1974-- .

2. PUBLICATIONS. Ente Nazionale Giovanni Boccaccio. President: Carlo Pelligrini. Sponsor: Ente Nazionale Giovanni Boccaccio, Florence, Italy. Publisher: Leo S. Olschki, Florence. 1971-- . Irregular. L.6.000-8.000. [300-600 p.] Last issue examined: no. 2, 1974.

Collections of long scholarly studies on a specific subject, such as IL BOCCACCIO NELLA CULTURA FRANCESE; bibliographical references; name index. In Italian. No. 3 not yet published (1978).

3. STUDI SUL BOCCACCIO (SBoc). Editor: Giorgio Padoan. Director: Vittore Branca. Sponsor: Ente Nazionale Giovanni Boccaccio, Florence, Italy. Publisher: G.C. Sansoni Editore, Florence. 1963-- . Irregular. L.11.000-17.500. [400 p.] Last issue examined: vol. 9, 1975-76.

   Long studies of Boccaccio's life, works, chronology of works, letters, technique, language, influence on other authors, and contributions to literature; examinations of translations and editions through the centuries; comprehensive bibliographies of scholarship in his own country in the English language, and in other countries and languages; long review articles of books and articles in periodicals; brief news notes on international congresses and celebrations; bibliographical references. In Italian or English. Second-hand copies available from Kraus Periodicals (1963-69, $110).

   Indexed by MLA INTERNATIONAL BIBLIOGRAPHY.

BODIN, JEAN (1530-96)

French lawyer, political philosopher

1. Société Jean Bodin. RECUEIL. Sponsor: Société Jean Bodin pour l'histoire comparative des institutions, avenue Jeanne 44, 1050 Brussèls, Belgium. Secretary general: J. Gilissen, 155, avenue des Statuaires, 1180 Brussels, Belgium. Publisher: Éditions de la Librairie Encyclopedique, Brussels. 1936-- . Irregular. [280-750 p.] Last issue examined: vol. 39, 1976.

   Founded to encourage the scientific study of the history of institutions--not focused on Jean Bodin, but inspired by his teachings. Each volume is concerned with a specific subject. In French.

   Alternate titles:

   Institut Solvay. Institut de sociologie. REVUE

   REVUE DE L'INSTITUT DE SOCIOLOGIE SOLVAY

BOEHME, JACOB (1575-1624)

German philosopher, theologian

1. JACOB BOEHME SOCIETY QUARTERLY. Editor: C.A. Muses. Sponsor

and publisher: Jacob Boehme Society, P.O. Box 296, Woodside, N.Y. 11377; and 50-38 40th Street, Long Island City, N.Y. Autumn 1952-Winter 1956 (vols. 1-4, no. 2). Quarterly. $3-5. [32 p.]

"Devoted to the thought of Jacob Boehme--Philosophus Centralis--and dedicated to his spirit of impartial truth to modern applications of that truth." Brief informal interpretations of his ideas and his relationship to Paracelsus, Bacon, Edward Taylor, and others; book reviews; facsimiles and reproductions. Alternate spelling: Jakob Böhme.

BOLÍVAR, SIMÓN (1783-1830)

Venezuelan statesman, revolutionary leader

1. BOLETÍN DE LA SOCIEDAD BOLIVARIANA DE PANAMÁ. 1931--(?). Irregular. Sponsor and publisher: Sociedad Bolivariana de Panamá, Apartado de Correos 829, Panamá. [100-120 p.] Last issue examined: no. 55, 1957.

   Articles on the life and contributions of Bolívar and on the historical development of the country; numerous illustrations and photographs; no index. In Spanish.

   Alternate title:

   Sociedad Bolivariana de Panamá. BOLETÍN

2. REVISTA BOLIVARIANA. Supersedes REVISTA DE LA SOCIEDAD BOLIVIANA (see entry 4). Editor: Roberto Velandia, 1975-- . Sponsor: Sociedad Bolivariana de Colombia, Casa Bolivariana, Calle 19 A No. 4-40 Este, Bogotá, D.E., Colombia. December 1926-January 1931 (nos. 1-24; new series, March 1935-June 1966 (nos. 1-83); 1976 (no. 84)-- . Irregular. $3. [110-20 p.] Last issue examined: no. 86, 1976.

   Organ of the Sociedad Bolivariana de Colombia. Numerous brief articles on Bolívar, San Martín, and other heroes of South American history; criticism of his government, reforms, and effect on other countries; reprints of important historical documents; analysis of historical events; bibliography of Bolívar scholarship; illustrations. In Spanish.

   Indexed by AMERICA: HISTORY AND LIFE.

3. REVISTA DE LA SOCIEDAD BOLIVARIANA DE VENEZUELA. Editor: Luis Villalba-Villalba and J.A. Escalona-Escalona. Sponsor and publisher: Sociedad Bolivariana de Venezuela, Apartado 874, San Jacinto à Traposos, Caracas, Venezuela. July 1939-October 1969 (nos. 1-100); second series, April 1974 (no. 101)-- . Quarterly (irregular). [90-130 p.] Last issue examined: vol. 32, no. 108, 1975.

   Organ of the Sociedad Bolivariana de Venezuela. Essays discussing the ideas and activities of Bolívar and his followers; homages and commemorations; long review articles; notes on the activities of the Sociedad, the international congresses, and events and publications of interest to Bolívar scholars; illustrations, plates, portraits, maps; index. Index for vols. 1-15, nos. 1-49 (1939-55). In Spanish. Vol. 33 not yet published (1978).

Alternate title:

Sociedad Bolivariana de Venezuela. REVISTA

4. REVISTA DE LA SOCIEDAD BOLIVIANA. Superseded by REVISTA BOLIVARIANA (see entry 2). December 1926-April 1928 (vol. 1, nos. 1-12). Irregular.

BOLLAND, JEAN DE (1596-1665)

Flemish Jesuit hagiologist, editor

1. ANALECTA BOLLANDIA: REVUE CRITIQUE D'HAGIOGRAPHIE. Editors: Maurice Coens, Baudouin de Gaiffier, François Halkin, Paul Devos, Joseph van der Straeten-Bollandistes. Sponsor and publisher: Société des Bollandistes, 24, boulevard Saint-Michel, B-1040 Brussels, Belgium. 1882-- . Quarterly (published in two issues per year). 900 Fr; $26. [250-500 p.] Circulation: 1,250. Last issue examined: vol. 95, 1977.

The Society is named after Bolland, and its members are Belgian Jesuits engaged in several publications, including a critical history of the Saints, using original documents. The ANALECTA, therefore, is not concerned with Bolland except in the perpetuation of the way of life and the philosophy which he himself espoused. Long scholarly studies of biographies, manuscripts, editorial problems; brief notes on textual problems, little-known manuscripts, acquisitions; long scholarly book reviews of international publications; list of books received. Cumulated indexes to vols. 1-40, 41-60, 61-80, arranged by critic, subject, and reviews. Text in English, German, French, Latin, or other Western languages. Second-hand copies available from Kraus Periodicals (1882-1969, $1,179).

Indexed by Köttelwesch and MLA INTERNATIONAL BIBLIOGRAPHY.

BONAPARTE, NAPOLEON (1769-1821)

French emperor, soldier

1. SOUVENIR NAPOLÉONIEN. President: Guy Godlewski. Secretary General: Comte Walewski. Subscriptions: 82, rue de Monceau, 75008 Paris. 1937-- . 6/yr. 40 Fr; 60 Fr (foreign). [30-35 p.] Last issue examined: vol. 41, no. 302, January 1978.

Brief articles on Napoleon's life and influence--his relationship to Madame de Staël, Benjamin Constant, Goethe, Chateaubriand, the French Academy, and the theatre; brief biographical notes; brief book reviews; reports of activities of the various branches of the Souvenir Napoléonien in the French provinces; news of group expeditions, forgotten monuments, tours, meetings, awards, exhibitions, and members' activities; occasional bibliographies of periodicals containing articles concerning Napoleon; numerous illustrations. In French.

BOSCO, HENRI (1888-1976)

French novelist

1. BULLETIN DU CENTRE HENRI BOSCO. Publisher: Centre d'études sur l'oeuvres d'Henri Bosco, U.E.R. Lettres et Sciences humaines, 2, rue Tréfilerie, 42 St-Étienne, France. June 1971-- .

   In French.

2. CAHIERS DE L'AMITIÉ HENRI BOSCO. Editor: Jean Onimus. Sponsor and publisher: Fonds de documentation Henri Bosco, Université de Nice, Bibliothèque de l'Université, Section-Lettres, 100, boulevard Edouard-Herriot, 06200 Nice, France. November 1972-- . 3/yr. 20-30 Fr. [15-40 p.] Circulation: 150. Last issue examined: no. 14, 1977.

   Long studies on Bosco's technique, such as the images in his novels or his surrealism; brief articles on his ideas, his life, and his contributions to French literature; occasional bibliographies of works by and about Bosco; previously unpublished works, such as extracts from his journals and letters to and from his friends; report of organization activities and of research accomplished in the Fonds de documentation Henri Bosco; financial report. In French.

   Indexed by BIBLIOGRAPHIE DE LA LITTÉRATURE FRANÇAISE, FRENCH XX, Klapp, and REVUE D'HISTOIRE LITTÉRAIRE.

   Alternate title for issue no. 1:

   BULLETIN HENRI BOSCO

BOSSUET, JACQUES-BÉNIGNE (1627-1704)

French humanist, theologian

1. BULLETIN DES AMIS DE BOSSUET. Sponsor: Société des Amis de Bossuet, 12, rue Notre-Dame, 77100 Meaux (Seine-et-Marne), France. 1931-35; 1973(?)-- . Irregular.

Long critical articles on, for example, the women in Bossuet's works; news and notes; bibliographies. In French.

Indexed by BIBLIOGRAPHIE DE LA LITTÉRATURE FRANÇAISE.

Alternate title:

AMIS DE BOSSUET

2. REVUE BOSSUET. Editor: M. Levesque. Sponsor: Comité pour le monument de Bossuet, Paris. 1900-1904 (vols. 1-5); new series, 1905-11 (supplements 1-8). Quarterly.

Previously unpublished works and documents, including Bossuet's will, an inventory of his possessions, and a record of his activities; bibliographies; research notes and problems; book reviews; illustrations; portraits; facsimiles; index. In French. Reprints available from Slatkine Reprints (1968).

BOURDALOUE, LOUIS (1632-1704)

French Jesuit priest, teacher

1. REVUE BOURDALOUE. Publisher: Lille, France. 1902-04. Previously unpublished letters, sermons, and other works, with notes and explanations; bibliographies. In French.

BOUTELLEAU, JACQUES [JACQUES CHARDONNE] (1884-1968)

French novelist

1. CAHIERS JACQUES CHARDONNE. Sponsor: Amis de Jacques Chardonne. Publisher: Association des Amis de Jacques Chardonne, 28, rue A.-Briand, 95530 La Frette-sur-Seine, France. 1971-- . Irregular.

Brief articles on Chardonne's works and ideas; proposals for a new edition; bibliographies of works by Chardonne. In French.

Indexed by BIBLIOGRAPHIE DE LA LITTÉRATURE FRANÇAISE.

BOYLESVE, RENÉ

See Tardiveau, René M.A.

BRAND, MAX

See Faust, Frederick.

BRASILLACH, ROBERT (1910-45)

French novelist, critic

1. Amis de Robert Brasillach. BULLETIN. Sponsor and publisher: Association des Amis de Robert Brasillach, Case Saint-François 1214, 1002 Lausanne, Switzerland. 1950-- . Quarterly. Free with membership (30 Swiss Fr; 40 French Fr; 400 Belgian Fr). [8-16 p.] Last issue examined: nos. 69-72, 1975-76.

   Brief notes on members' activities, society lectures, radio programs, conferences, memorials, dinners, and the Robert Brasillach Prize; interviews; announcements of new editions and new criticism. In French.

   Alternate title:

   BULLETIN DE L'ASSOCIATION DES AMIS DE ROBERT BRASILLACH

2. CAHIERS DES AMIS DE ROBERT BRASILLACH (CahBrasillach). Editors: Pierre Favre and Jean-Claude Fontanet. Sponsor: Association des Amis de Robert Brasillach, Case postale 2755, 1002 Lausanne, Switzerland. Publisher: Éditions des Sept-Couleurs, Paris. 1950-- . Irregular. Free with membership (30 Swiss Fr; 40 French Fr; 400 Belgian Fr). [100-300 p.] Last issue examined: no. 22, 1977.

   Studies of the life, family, works, and social background of Brasillach, his relationship with other writers and countries, classical and contemporary, and the resulting influences; previously unpublished works; brief notes on his characters, literary criticism, development, friendships, new editions, reception in other countries; occasional collections of critical essays on a specific title; occasional poems or quotations from the Brasillach canon; reprints of criticism from other sources; occasional list of members; occasional facsimiles and illustrations. Index for nos. 1-16. In French. Second-hand copies available from Kraus Periodicals (1951-70, $50).

   Indexed by BIBLIOGRAPHIE DE LA LITTÉRATURE FRANÇAISE, FRENCH VII, FRENCH XX, and Klapp.

   Alternate titles:

   Amis de Robert Brasillach. CAHIERS

   Association des Amis de Robert Brasillach. CAHIERS

BRECHT, BERTOLT (1898-1956)

German dramatist, poet, novelist, critic

1. BRECHT HEUTE--BRECHT TODAY: JAHRBUCH DER INTERNATIONALEN

BRECHT-GESELLSCHAFT (BrechtH). Superseded by BRECHT-JAHRBUCH (see entry 2). Editors: John Guegi, Reinhold Grimm, Jost Hermand, Walter Hinck, Eric Bentley, Ulrich Weisstein, John Spalek, Gisela Bahr. Sponsor: International Brecht Society. Publisher: Athenäum Verlag, Frankfurt/am/Main, Germany (BRD). 1971-73 (nos. 1-3). Annual. Free with membership ($10; $18, senior; $7, students). [200-280 p.]

The International Brecht Society, "through its publications and regular international symposia . . . encourages the free and open discussion of any and all views on the relationship of the arts to the contemporary world." Collections of long scholarly essays on aspects of Brecht's works, their influence, and related subjects, such as "Bertolt Brecht and George Bernard Shaw" or "Brecht's Soviet Connection: Tretiakov" (no. 3, 1973); numerous reviews of relevant international scholarship; bibliographical references; international contributors; no index. In German, English, or French. Members of the Society receive BRECHT HEUTE and COMMUNICATIONS (see entry 3), a newsletter containing news of interest to Brecht scholars and a Brecht bibliography.

Indexed by Köttelwesch and MLA INTERNATIONAL BIBLIOGRAPHY.

Alternate title:

Internationale Brecht-Gesellschaft. JAHRBUCH

2. BRECHT-JAHRBUCH (BrechtJ). Supersedes BRECHT HEUTE (see entry 1). Editors: John Guegi, Department of Comparative Literature, University of Maryland, College Park, Md. 20742; Reinhold Grimm and Jost Hermand, Department of German, University of Wisconsin, Madison, Wis. 53706. Sponsor: Internationale Brecht-Gesellschaft. Publisher: Suhrkamp, Frankfurt/am/Main, Germany (BRD). 1974-- . Annual. Free with membership ($10; $18, senior; $7, students). [180-200 p.] Last issue examined: 1977.

Collections of critical essays by international scholars on the life, travels, friendships, works, ideas, themes, and influence of Brecht, and "on the relationship of the arts to the contemporary world"; comments on performances in various countries of the world; long reviews of important books and dissertations; previously unpublished letters; bibliographical references; international contributors; no index. The Gesellschaft sponsors publications, conducts regular international symposia, and welcomes new members from any field and any country. In English, French, or German.

Indexed by Köttelwesch and MLA INTERNATIONAL BIBLIOGRAPHY.

3. COMMUNICATIONS. Sponsor: International Brecht Society.

News of interest to Brecht scholars; continuing Brecht bibliography. See BRECHT HEUTE, entry 1.

BREMOND, HENRI (1865-1933)

French literary critic, historian

1. Études bremondiennes. Publisher: Éditions Montaigne, Aubier, Paris. 1967-- . Irregular. 18-42 Fr. [300 p.] Last issue examined: no. 4, 1975.

   Reprints of Bremond's work with copious notes and explanations; previously unpublished letters and other material, such as correspondence with Blondel; bibliographical references; illustrations and facsimiles; name index. In French.

BRONTË

Charlotte (1816-55)
Emily (1818-48) English authors
Anne (1820-49)
Branwell (1817-48)

1. BRONTË SOCIETY: TRANSACTIONS (BST). Editor: Charles H. Lemon. Sponsor: Brontë Society. Subscriptions: Brontë Parsonage Museum, Haworth, Keighley, West Yorkshire BD22 8DR, England. Representative in the U.S.: Diane McGuire, Moorland, Long Pasture Road, Little Compton, R.I. 02837. 1895-- . Annual (Fall). Free with membership (£2; $6). [80-100 p.] Circulation: 2,000. Last issue examined: pt. 88, vol. 17, no. 3, 1978.

   Numerous source, historical, and biographical studies; information concerning the social and cultural background of the authors; studies of the Brontë family, friends, and acquaintances; occasional bibliographies, such as "The Brontes in the American Periodical Press of Their Day" and, annually since 1969, "A Brontë Reading List" of critical books and articles; previously unpublished letters and other documents; brief book reviews; annual report of the Society with, in the early issues, a list of members; notes on Society activities--excursions, lectures, museum and parsonage acquisitions, awards for research; list of Brontë Society publications; illustrations; facsimiles; portraits; maps. Analytical index by subject and author for 1895-1967 (vols. 1-15).

   Vols. 1-9 (parts 1-49, 1895-1939) available at the Brontë Parsonage Museum. Parts 50-82 (1940-72) also available from William Dawson (£80). Parts 19-40 include the 15th-36th annual reports of the Society, for 1908-30. (Preceding reports, for 1894-1907, were issued separately.) Parts 41 (1930) to the present include the report of the honorary corresponding secretary.

Indexed by ABSTRACTS OF ENGLISH STUDIES, ANNUAL BIBLIOGRAPHY OF ENGLISH LANGUAGE AND LITERATURE, BRITISH HUMANITIES INDEX, MLA INTERNATIONAL BIBLIOGRAPHY, VICTORIAN STUDIES, and YEAR'S WORK IN ENGLISH STUDIES.

Alternate titles:

BRONTË SOCIETY PUBLICATIONS

TRANSACTIONS AND OTHER PUBLICATIONS OF THE BRONTË SOCIETY

BROWNING

Robert (1812-89)
Elizabeth Barrett (1806-61) English poets

1. BAYLOR BROWNING INTERESTS. Editor: Jack W. Herring, Director, Armstrong Browning Library, Baylor University, Box 6336, Waco, Tex. 76706. Sponsor: Armstrong Browning Library. December 1927-- . Irregular (as material and budget permit). $1-3.50. [40 p.] Last issue examined: no. 24, 1975.

   Each publication is concerned with one specific aspect of Browning scholarship. Critical, biographical, bibliographical, or textual studies; reprints of Browning letters and accounts; previously unpublished works; new editions with introductory notes; catalogs of library holdings, national and international; catalogs of exhibitions; bibliographies of foreign Browningiana; photographs; portraits; facsimiles such as the Old Yellow Book manuscripts; occasional indexes. No. 25 not yet published (1978).

   Alternate titles:

   Baylor Browning Interests Series

   BAYLOR BULLETIN

   Baylor University Browning Interests

2. Boston Browning Society. YEAR-BOOK. Sponsor: Boston Browning Society. 1887-- . Annual (occasional omissions).

   Report of activities; bylaws; list of members.

3. BROWNING INSTITUTE STUDIES (BIS). Editor: William S. Peterson, Department of English, University of Maryland, College Park, Md. 20742. Sponsor and publisher: Browning Institute, Box 2983, Grand Central

Station, New York, N.Y. 10017. President: Peter N. Heydon. June 1973-- . Annual. $20; free with membership ($15; student, $3); additional copies, $12. [225-40 p.] Circulation: 1,000. Last issue examined: vol. 7, 1979.

Official journal of the Browning Institute. Long biographical, textual, and critical studies of Robert and Elizabeth Barrett Browning and their circle, and, since 1979, scholarship on all aspects of Victorian literary and cultural history; annual annotated bibliography of works by and about the Brownings; reprints of library holdings; in each issue one long review-essay examining several new Browning-related books; film reviews, as of PIPPA PASSES; previously unpublished letters; annual report of the Institute with list of members and bylaws; illustrations and facsimiles; index.

Indexed by AMERICAN HUMANITIES INDEX, ANNUAL BIBLIOGRAPHY OF ENGLISH LANGUAGE AND LITERATURE, MLA INTERNATIONAL BIBLIOGRAPHY, and VICTORIAN STUDIES.

4. BROWNING MAGAZINE. Sponsor: Robert Browning Guild, England. 1922-23 (nos. 1-3).

5. BROWNING NEWSLETTER (BN). Superseded by STUDIES IN BROWNING AND HIS CIRCLE (see entry 11). Editor: Warner Barnes, Armstrong Browning Library, Baylor University, Box 6336, Waco, Tex. 76706. Sponsor: Armstrong Browning Library. October 1968-Fall 1972 (nos. 1-9). 2/yr. (Spring, Fall). $3; $2 per copy. [70-80 p.] Circulation: 300.

Concentrates on research with a checklist of recent publications in every issue and an annual review of the year's scholarship on Elizabeth and Robert Browning. Contains brief source studies; notes on characters, allusions, style, literary tradition, biographical background; long book reviews; report on work in progress, including dissertations; previously unpublished letters and poems; news and descriptions of library acquisitions throughout the world, library catalogs, exhibitions, and international symposia; queries; photographs and facsimiles. No long critical articles or explications. Cumulative index for 1968-72 (nos. 1-9).

Indexed by ABSTRACTS OF ENGLISH STUDIES, ANNUAL BIBLIOGRAPHY OF ENGLISH LANGUAGE AND LITERATURE, INDEX TO BOOK REVIEWS IN THE HUMANITIES, and MLA INTERNATIONAL BIBLIOGRAPHY.

6. Browning Society, London. ANNUAL REPORT. Sponsor: Browning Society, London. 1882-91 (nos. 1-10).

Issued in the Society's PAPERS, vols. 1-3 (see entry 8).

Alternate title:

REPORT OF THE BROWNING SOCIETY'S COMMITTEE

7. Browning Society, London. MONTHLY ABSTRACT OF PROCEEDINGS. Sponsor: Browning Society, London. Meetings 1-80 (October 1881-90).

 Issued in the Society's PAPERS, vols. 1-3 (see entry 8). Only occasional issues are in print.

8. Browning Society, London. PAPERS. Founder and editor: Frederick J. Furnivall. Sponsor: Browning Society, London. Publisher: Trübner, London. 1881-91 (vols. 1-3, pts. 1-13, nos. 1-67, excepting pt. 6, which was never published).

 About sixty-eight papers read at meetings of the London Browning Society by such noted scholars as W.M. Rossetti and J.A. Symonds; bibliographies of works by and about Browning; reports of Society events and plans. Reprints available from Kraus Reprint and Walter J. Johnson ($100).

 The Browning Society was reestablished in 1970 (see BROWNING SOCIETY NOTES, entry 9). See also William S. Peterson, INTERROGATING THE ORACLE: A HISTORY OF THE LONDON BROWNING SOCIETY (Athens: Ohio University Press, 1969).

9. BROWNING SOCIETY NOTES (BS NOTES). Editor: John Woolford, Fitzwilliam College, Cambridge University, Cambridge, England. Treasurer: R.E. Bolton, Browning Society of London, 9, Lakenheath, Southgate, London N14 4RJ. Sponsor: Browning Society of London. June 1970-- . 3/yr. U.K.: £2.50 (individuals) and £3 (institutions); foreign £7.50 (individuals) and £9 (institutions); back issues, £2.50 or $7.50. [30-45 p.] Circulation: 200. Last issue examined: vol. 8, 1978.

 Long (6-12 p.) critical articles concentrating on single poems or groups of poems, such as the love lyrics, which have tended to be critically neglected; articles on material newly acquired or never previously published; reprints of conferences and lectures; brief reports of research in progress in England; news of Browning sites; reviews of dramatic productions and broadcasts connected with the Brownings; reviews of recently published books and articles; news of interest to Browning scholars; occasional special issues, including one on the works of Elizabeth Barrett Browning; occasional illustrations. Cumulated index to vols. 1-7 (1970-77) in vol. 7, no. 3.

 Indexed by ANNUAL BIBLIOGRAPHY OF ENGLISH LANGUAGE AND LITERATURE, BROWNING INSTITUTE STUDIES, MLA INTERNATIONAL BIBLIOGRAPHY, STUDIES IN BROWNING AND HIS CIRCLE, VICTORIAN POETRY, and VICTORIAN STUDIES.

10. BULLETIN OF THE NEW YORK BROWNING SOCIETY. Editors: Current presidents and program chairmen. Sponsor: New York Browning Society. 1907-65. 4-8/yr. Free to members. [4-20 p.] Circulation: 100.

 Reports on the programs and lectures at the New York Browning Society meetings.

11. STUDIES IN BROWNING AND HIS CIRCLE: A JOURNAL OF CRITICISM, HISTORY, BIBLIOGRAPHY (SBHC). Supersedes BROWNING NEWSLETTER (see entry 5). Editor: Jack W. Herring, Director, Armstrong Browning Library, Baylor University, Box 6336, Waco, Tex. 76706. Sponsor: Armstrong Browning Library. Spring 1973-- . 2/yr. (December, June), 1973-75; quarterly since 1976. $5. [100-150 p.] Circulation: 400. Last issue examined: vol. 6, 1978.

    Long (15-25 p.) critical and biographical articles on Elizabeth and Robert Browning, their family and friends, and the Victorian period; bibliographies, including a checklist of recently published books, articles, reviews, and dissertations; checklists of library acquisitions throughout the world; review of the year's research; report of work in progress, including dissertations; previously unpublished letters and photographs; long book reviews; brief notes and queries; comments on exhibitions, library catalogs, lectures, performances, and seminars; illustrations; facsimiles; no index. The Armstrong Browning Library has the largest collection of Browning work and memorabilia in the world and is interested in all current trends of Browning scholarship--critical, biographical, and editorial.

    Indexed by ABSTRACTS OF ENGLISH STUDIES, AMERICAN HUMANITIES INDEX, ANNUAL BIBLIOGRAPHY OF ENGLISH LANGUAGE AND LITERATURE, INDEX TO BOOK REVIEWS IN THE HUMANITIES, MLA INTERNATIONAL BIBLIOGRAPHY, VICTORIAN STUDIES, and YEAR'S WORK IN ENGLISH STUDIES.

12. THROUGH CASA GUIDI WINDOWS: THE BULLETIN OF THE BROWNING INSTITUTE. Editor: Publications Committee of the Browning Institute, 9 Maplewood Court, Greenbelt, Md. 20770. Sponsor: Browning Institute, Box 2983, Grand Central Station, New York, N.Y. 10017. March 1975-- . 1-2/yr. Free to British and American libraries, to Friends of Casa Guidi, and to members of the Browning Institute (dues, $15). [6-8 p.] Circulation: 3,000. Last issue examined: no. 2, 1976.

    News about activities of the Browning Institute--annual meeting, election of officers, and members' activities in Florence, Italy; report on the progress of the restoration of Casa Guidi, the Brownings' home at 8 Piazza S. Felice, Palazzo Guidi, Rome, Italy; description of the Browning Institute publications and of films relating to the Brownings; "Browning Society Notes" --news of activities of Browning societies all over the world-- Boston (90th year), San Diego, London, and others; illustrations; no index.

BUDÉ, GUILLAUME (1468-1540)

French humanist, author

1. Association Guillaume Budé. ACTES DE CONGRES. Sponsor and publisher:

Association Guillaume Budé. 1932-- . Irregular (10th Congress, Toulouse, 1978). [10-15 p.] Free to members.

Report of the International Congress of Linguists. Published as a supplement to LETTRES D'HUMANITÉ, issue no. 4 of the Association's BULLETIN (see entry 2). In French.

2. BULLETIN DE L'ASSOCIATION GUILLAUME BUDÉ: REVUE DE CULTURE GÉNÉRALE (BAGB; BGB; BABudé). Sponsor: Association Guillaume Budé. President: Fernand Robert. Publisher: Société d'édition les Belles Lettres. October 1923-(?); publication suspended, April 1940-July 1946; new series, July 1946-December 1950 (nos. 1-12); third series, March 1951-December 1953; fourth series, March 1954-- . Quarterly (three bulletins; fourth issue is the supplement, LETTRES D'HUMANITÉ). 45-55 Fr. [130-60 p.] Last issue examined: 1978.

Interested in classical humanism, linguistics, philology, literature--occasional references to Budé. Long essays on Homer, the place of Latin in contemporary curriculums, and other international classical subjects; bibliographic surveys; occasional book reviews; library acquisitions; report of the meeting of the Association's General Assembly, the activities of the various branches of the Association, and other colloquia and symposia; list of members attending and subjects under discussion; lists of publications of Librairie Guillaume Budé, Les Belles Lettres, and other series; report of work in progress; annual index by author and subject. Index for October 1923-April 1940 (nos. 1-67). In French. Second-hand copies available from Kraus Periodicals (1923-67, some missing issues, $558, including BULLETIN DES JEUNES, entry 3); reprints available from Walter J. Johnson (1923-66, $495). Beginning in 1950, the bulletin includes LETTRES D'HUMANITÉ, which were previously published separately, 1942-49 (vols. 1-8); index, 1946-55.

Indexed by L'ANNÉE PHILOLOGIQUE, BIBLIOGRAPHIE DE LA LITTÉRATURE FRANÇAISE, BIBLIOGRAPHY OF FRENCH SEVENTEENTH CENTURY STUDIES, BULLETIN CRITIQUE, ENGLISH LANGUAGE NOTES, FRENCH XX, Klapp, Köttelwesch, MLA INTERNATIONAL BIBLIOGRAPHY, and REVUE D'HISTOIRE LITTÉRAIRE.

Alternate title:

Association Guillaume Budé, Paris. BULLETIN

3. BULLETIN DES JEUNES DE L'ASSOCIATION GUILLAUME BUDÉ (Humanisme contemporain). Editor: Jean Malye, 95, boulevard Raspail, 75006 Paris. April 1960-- . 3/yr.

News of meetings, excursions. In French. Second-hand copies available from Kraus Periodicals (1960-62, nos. 2-7).

Indexed by BIBLIOGRAPHIE DE LA LITTÉRATURE FRANÇAISE.

BULWER-LYTTON, EDWARD GEORGE (1803-73)

English novelist, dramatist

1. BULWER-LYTTON CHRONICLE. Editors: H.C. Brown, Eric F.J. Ford. Sponsor: Bulwer-Lytton Circle, High Orchard, 125 Markyate Road, Dagenham, Essex RM8 2LB, England. 1973-- . Irregular. £2.

   Encourages interest in the social novel. Critical articles; bibliographies; work in progress; book reviews; news notes; occasional illustrations; index in progress.

   Indexed by ABSTRACTS OF ENGLISH STUDIES.

BURCKHARDT, JACOB (1818-97)

Swiss historian of art and culture

1. JACOB BURCKHARDT STUDIEN. Publisher: Van Gorcum, Assen, Netherlands. 1970-- . 35 Fl.

   Articles; bibliographies. In German. Alternate spelling: Jakob Burchkhardt.

BURKE, EDMUND (1729-97)

Irish-born English statesman, author

1. BURKE NEWSLETTER. Superseded by STUDIES IN BURKE AND HIS TIME (see entry 2). Editor: Peter J. Stanlis. Publisher: University of Detroit Press, 4001 West McNichols, Detroit, Mich. 48221. Summer 1959-Spring 1967 (vols. 1-8, nos. 1-29). Quarterly (Summer 1959-Summer 1964); 3/yr. (Fall 1964-Spring 1967).

   Long articles and book reviews by international contributors; reports of work in progress; news of symposia, lectures. Index to vols. 1-5 (Summer 1959-Summer 1964) and vols. 6-13 (Fall 1964-1972; see STUDIES IN BURKE AND HIS TIME, entry 2).

   First seven numbers were first published in MODERN AGE (Summer 1959-Winter 1960/61). All back issues available--8 vols., with indexes, $21.

2. STUDIES IN BURKE AND HIS TIME: A JOURNAL DEVOTED TO BRITISH, AMERICAN, AND CONTINENTAL CULTURE, 1750-1800 (SBHT; SIB). Supersedes BURKE NEWSLETTER (see entry 1); superseded by EIGHTEENTH CENTURY: A JOURNAL OF THEORY AND INTERPRETATION. Editors: Jeffrey R. Smitten and Joel C. Weinsheimer, Texas Technological University, Box 4530, Lubbock, Tex. 79409. Managing editor: Steven R. Phillips. Sponsor: Texas Technological University. Fall 1967 (vol. 9,

no. 1, also called no. 30)-1978 (vol. 19). 3/yr. (Fall, Winter, Spring). $8 (individuals); $10 (institutions). [100 p.] Circulation: 800.

Interested in any aspect of the life and thoughts of Edmund Burke and in all aspects of the period 1750-1800, including its lingering influence and all ideas that support or oppose its philosophies. Long (10-15 p.) critical articles; numerous long book reviews in every issue; occasional bibliographies of scholarship on Burke; international contributors; occasional illustrations and facsimiles; cumulated index every five years. Index by subject and author for 1964-72 (vols. 6-13), $1. All back issues available, $2.50.

Indexed by ABSTRACTS OF ENGLISH STUDIES, AMERICA: HISTORY AND LIFE, AMERICAN HUMANITIES INDEX, ANNUAL BIBLIOGRAPHY OF ENGLISH LANGUAGE AND LITERATURE, ENGLISH LANGUAGE NOTES, Klapp, MLA ABSTRACTS, MLA INTERNATIONAL BIBLIOGRAPHY, PHILOLOGICAL QUARTERLY, and YEAR'S WORK IN ENGLISH STUDIES.

BURNS, ROBERT (1759-96)

Scottish poet

1. BURNS CHRONICLE. Editor: 1955-75, James Veitch, Newbigging, Tweedsmuir, Biggar, Lanarkshire, Scotland; since 1975, Arthur Daw. Sponsor and publisher: Burns Federation, Kilmarnock, Scotland. 1892-1925 (nos. 1-34); second series, 1926-50 (nos. 1-25); 1951; third series, 1952-75 (vols. 1-24); fourth series, 1976-- . Annual. £1.50-2.25. [200 p.] Circulation: 3,000. Last issue examined: vol. 3, 1978.

Long scholarly studies on Burns, Scott, Currie, and other contemporaries--editorial policy is to encourage more numerous, shorter articles; translations of foreign criticism; occasional book reviews; reports of international events; occasional poems in the Burns style; photographs; facsimiles; illustrations; advertisements. Includes the constitution, minutes of the annual conference, news and addresses of the 329 international Burns Clubs, and, since 1965, the JUNIOR BURNS CHRONICLE, with news of Burns Clubs for young people.

Indexed by AMERICAN HUMANITIES INDEX and ANNUAL BIBLIOGRAPHY OF ENGLISH LANGUAGE AND LITERATURE.

Alternate titles:

BURNS FEDERATION, 1892-1925

BURNS CHRONICLE AND CLUB DIRECTORY, 1926-50

SCOTS CHRONICLE, 1951

BURNS CHRONICLE or ANNUAL BURNS CHRONICLE AND CLUB DIRECTORY, 1952--

2. Burns Federation. QUARTERLY BULLETIN. 1930-37 (nos. 1-29).

3. Burns Society of the City of New York. OCCASIONAL PAPERS. Secretary: Robert W. Morrison, 1869 Cider Mill Road, Union, N.J. 07083. Sponsor: Burns Society, 281 Park Avenue South, New York, N.Y. 10010. 1871-(?).

BURROUGHS, EDGAR RICE (1875-1950)

American author of adventure stories

1. BARSODMIAN. Editor: Paul C. Allen, 84 Charlton Road, Rochester, N.Y. 14617. 1952-- . 2-3/yr. (no. 15, 1969). $.60 per copy.

   Brief articles and notes; informal book reviews; bibliographies; illustrations.

2. BURROUGHS BIBLIOPHILE. Editor: Vernell W. Coriell, 6657 Locust Street, Kansas City, Mo. 64131. 1964-(?). Irregular. $5.

   Reprints of rare books, limited editions, and collectors' items, with notes and introductions.

3. BURROUGHS BULLETIN. Editor: Vernell W. Coriell, 6657 Locust Street, Kansas City, Mo. 64131. Sponsor: House of Greystoke for the Burroughs Bibliophiles. June 1947-- . Monthly. Free with membership ($15, includes other publications). [25 p.] Circulation: 2,800.

   Interested in Burroughs--the man, his works, and the art forms that have used the characters in his novels. Brief articles; reprints of inaccessible material; annual bibliography; reviews; special issues; illustrations; no index.

4. ERBANIA. Editor: D. Peter Ogden, 8001 Fernview Lane, Tampa, Fla. 33615. April 1956-- . Irregular (3 issues in 1976). $3/four issues. [16 p.] Circulation: 500. Last issue examined: no. 40, 1976.

   Essays and reviews of Burroughs' work as it appears in books, films, and radio; bibliographies; news of interest to Burroughs enthusiasts; illustrations.

5. ERB-DOM AND THE FANTASY COLLECTOR. Editor: C.E. Cazedessus, Jr., Route 2, Box 119, Clinton, La. 70722. May 1960-- . 5/yr. $9. [35 p.] Circulation: 1,000.

   Interested in all aspects of Burroughs' work plus art and science fiction films; infrequent book reviews; colored illustrations.

6. ERBIVORE. Editor: Philip J.C. Currie, 8198 avenue de l'Épee, Montreal

P.2, H3N 2Q1, Quebec, Canada. 1967-- . Irregular (no. 5, 1972). $2 for 4 nos.

Articles; news; book reviews. No reply to query.

7. GRIDLEY WAVE. Editor: Vernell W. Coriell, 6657 Locust Street, Kansas City, Mo. 64131. Sponsor: Burroughs Bibliophiles. 1959-- . Monthly. Free with membership ($15, includes other publications). [3 p.]

News and notes; bibliographies; report of work in progress; book, art, and film reviews; illustrations. Sent to members of the Burroughs Bibliophiles as a newsletter along with the BURROUGHS BULLETIN (see entry 3).

8. JASOOMIAN. Editor: Don Frailey, 2481 Eucalyptus Way, San Bruno, Calif. 94066. (?)-- . 2/month. $9.

No reply to query.

BUSCH, WILHELM (1832-1908)

German humorous illustrator, poet

1. JAHRBUCH DER WILHELM-BUSCH-GESELLSCHAFT (JbBusch). Supersedes Wilhelm-Busch-Gesellschaft. MITTEILUNGEN (see entry 2); superseded by WILHELM-BUSCH-JAHRBUCH (see entry 3). Editor: Friedrich Bohne. Sponsor and publisher: Wilhelm-Busch-Gesellschaft, Georgengarten 1, 3 Hannover, Germany (BRD). 1949-64 (nos. 15-30). Annual (irregular). [70-135 p.]

Numerous essays examining Busch's life and technique, both literary and artistic; studies of his influence on other artists; articles on his two most famous characters, Max and Maurice, and on their long-suffering Teacher Temple; numerous excellent reproductions of Busch's art; brief notes on new editions and Gesellschaft and museum activities; chronicle of events; index. Some reference sources continue to use the title JAHRBUCH DER WILHELM-BUSCH-GESELLSCHAFT in the 1970's even though the name was changed in 1964. In German.

Indexed by Köttelwesch.

2. Wilhelm-Busch-Gesellschaft. MITTEILUNGEN. Superseded by JAHRBUCH DER WILHELM-BUSCH-GESELLSCHAFT (see entry 1). Sponsor: Wilhelm-Busch-Gesellschaft, Rustplatz 15, Hannover, Germany (BRD). May 1932-February 1943 (nos. 1-14). Annual. [20-120 p.]

Long articles on Busch's realism, his relationship to Hogarth, his technique and contributions, and details of his life; occasional bibliographies of critical works; previously unpublished letters; book reviews; report of the Gesellschaft--activities, finances, gifts, and list of members; report of holdings and acquisitions at the Wilhelm-Busch-Museum; numerous sketches, reproductions, and facsimiles that illustrate Busch's genius and humor. Nos. 5-14 (June 1936-February 1943) include VERÖFFENTLICHUNGEN AUS DEM WILHELM-BUSCH-ARCHIV (published separately, 1931-32, nos. 1-3). In German.

Indexed by Köttelwesch.

Alternate title:

MITTEILUNGEN DER WILHEM-BUSCH-GESELLSCHAFT

3. WILHELM-BUSCH-JAHRBUCH: MITTEILUNGEN DER WILHELM-BUSCH-GESELLSCHAFT. Supersedes JAHRBUCH DER WILHELM-BUSCH-GESELLSCHAFT (see entry 1). Editors: Friedrich Bohne and Ingrid Haberland. Sponsor and publisher: Wilhelm-Busch-Gesellschaft, Georgengarten 1, 3 Hannover, Germany (BRD). 1964 (no. 31)-- . Annual. Free with membership (DM18; $18). [70-95 p.] Last issue examined: MITTEILUNGEN no. 43, 1977.

Essays on Busch's religious and social philosophy, on the themes in his work, and on his life, artistic ability, and influence on other art and literature; textual studies; accomplishments of the Gesellschaft--conferences, library acquisitions, membership report, meetings, necrology; Wilhelm-Busch-Museum report--number of researchers and country of their origin; numerous portraits, sketches, facsimiles, and photographs to illustrate Bushch's talent, wit, and imagination. Some reference sources continue to use the title JAHRBUCH DER WILHELM-BUSCH-GESELLSCHAFT (see entry 1). In German.

Indexed by Köttelwesch.

BUTLER, SAMUEL (1835-1902)

English novelist, satirist, scholar

1. SAMUEL BUTLER NEWSLETTER. Editors: James A. Donovan, Jr., 4100 Cathedral Avenue, Apt. 711, Washington, D.C. 20016; and R. Balfour Daniels, 20 North Wynden Drive, Houston, Tex. 77056. Sponsor: Samuel Butler Society. Winter 1978-- . $5. [15 p.]

Interested in stimulating further study and scholarship on Butler and his theories on evolution, psychology, religion, arts, sciences, machines, technology, satire, music, and autobiography. Critical articles; bibliographies; abstracts; news and notes.

BUZZATI, DINO (1906-)

Italian journalist, editor, novelist

1. CAHIERS DINO BUZZATI. Sponsor: Association des Amis de Dino Buzzati.

Sponsor: Association des Amis de Dino Buzzati, 6, place Saint-Sulpice, 75279 Paris. Publisher: Éditions Robert Laffont, Paris. 1977-- . Annual. 45 Fr. [250 p.] Last number examined: no. 2, 1978.

BYRON, GEORGE GORDON, LORD (1788-1824)

English poet

1. Byron Foundation Lecture. Sponsor and publisher: University of Nottingham, England. 1912-- . Annual. [20-35 p.]

   Each issue is devoted to a specific subject, such as critical studies of Byron's poetry, prose, ideas, and influence, but other subjects and authors are also covered; occasional bibliographies.

   Alternate title:

   Byron Memorial Lecture

2. BYRON JOURNAL. Editors: Robert Escarpit, Leslie A. Marchand, Andrew Rutherford et al. Sponsor: Byron House in association with the Byron Society, 6, Gertrude Street, London SW10 0JN. Publisher: Byron Society and BYRON SOCIETY JOURNAL. 1973-- . Annual. Free with membership (£4); £1.50 per issue. [80-100 p.] Circulation: 2,000. Last issue examined: vol. 6, 1978.

   Editorial, biographical, and critical articles; short book reviews; news notes; reprints of lectures; previously unpublished letters, such as those from Augusta Leigh; illustrations; facsimiles; advertisements. Includes report of the International Byron Society, which has branches in 21 countries, including Austria, Canada, France, Germany, Ceylon, Cyprus, Greece, Italy, Japan, Netherlands, Poland, Portugal, Rumania, Switzerland, and the United States (American Committee, John Clubbe, Department of English, University of Kentucky, Lexington, Ky. 40506).

   Indexed by MLA INTERNATIONAL BIBLIOGRAPHY.

3. BYRON MONOGRAPHS. Sponsor: University of Texas, Austin, Tex. 78712. 1948-(?).

4. Byron Society. JOURNAL. Editor: Francis Lewis Randolph. Sponsor: Byron Society, 318 St. James' Place, Philadelphia, Pa. 19106. Publisher: Falcon Press, Philadelphia, Pa. 1972-73 (nos. 1-2).

   Studies of previously unpublished letters; reprints of letters; facsimiles. No longer published because of the death of the editor, but plans are in progress to combine the Byron Society of Philadelphia with the Byron Society in London.

Alternate title:

JOURNAL OF THE BYRON SOCIETY

CABELL, JAMES BRANCH (1879-1958)

American novelist, essayist

1. CABELLIAN: A JOURNAL OF THE SECOND AMERICAN RENAISSANCE. Editor: Julius Rothman, 75 Noble Street, Lynbrook, N.Y. 11563. Sponsor: Cabell Society. November 1968-Spring 1972 (vols. 1-4, no. 2). One issue, 1968; 2/yr., 1969-72. $7. [50-70 p.] Circulation: 300.

   Brief but scholarly biographical, critical, and bibliographical articles on Cabell's life, works, sources, relationship with his contemporaries, and influences; occasional bibliographies of criticism, library holdings, and book sales; surveys of research, past and present; numerous book reviews in every issue; occasional poems; report of the Cabell Society; notes on members' activities, lectures, and awards; photographs; index to each volume. Early issues are devoted solely to Cabell, but later issues include articles on other writers of the twentieth-century American literary renaissance. Reprints available from Kraus Reprint ($34, three vols.) and Walter J. Johnson ($38, vols. 1-2, 1968-70); microfilm available from University Microfilms International.

   Indexed by ABSTRACTS OF ENGLISH STUDIES, AMERICAN LITERATURE, MISSISSIPPI QUARTERLY, and MLA INTERNATIONAL BIBLIOGRAPHY.

2. KALKI. Editors: Paul Spencer, 665 Lotus Avenue, Oradell, N.J. 07649, and William L. Godshalk, Department of English, University of Cincinnati, Cincinnati, Ohio 45221. Sponsor: James Branch Cabell Society, 172 Balsam Road, Wayne, N.J. 07470. 1965-- . Quarterly. $5 (individuals); $10 (institutions). [30-45 p.] Circulation: 400. Last issue examined: no. 27, 1977.

   Brief critical articles on sources, influences, new biographical facts, structure, style, and every aspect of Cabell's life and work; occasional long interpretive studies; frequent bibliographies of "Cabell in Print" and Cabell criticism; "Jurgen's Pawnshop"--books for sale, exchange, and wanted; "The View from Mespec Moor"--informal notes and comments from readers; "From the Third Window"--editor's column, with information about new editions, reviews, activities; long book reviews; queries; illustrations; annual title, author, and subject index published separately. Available on microfilm.

   Indexed by AMERICAN HUMANITIES INDEX, ANNUAL BIBLIOGRAPHY OF ENGLISH LANGUAGE AND LITERATURE, MLA INTERNATIONAL BIBLIOGRAPHY.

Alternate subtitles:

THE CABELLIAN QUARTERLY

STUDIES IN JAMES BRANCH CABELL (appears on front cover of vols. 1-4, no. 1, and on verso since vol. 4, no. 2)

CALVIN, JOHN (1509-64)

French-born Swiss theologian, reformer

1. CAHIERS CALVINISTES. Sponsor: Société Calviniste de Belgique, 66, rue J.-Wilson, Brussels, Belgium. January 1961-- . Irregular.

   In French. No reply to query.

   Alternate title:

   Société Calviniste de Belgique. CAHIER

   Alternate information: Sponsor: 275, avenue Charles-Quint, Brussels, Belgium (query returned--addressee unknown). 1957-- .

CAMUS, ALBERT (1913-60)

French novelist, essayist, dramatist

1. Albert Camus. Subseries of La Revue des Lettres Modernes, described below. Editor: Brian T. Fitch. 1968-- . Annual (irregular). Equivalent numbers are provided below for the parent series (La Revue des Lettres Modernes) and the individual author series on Camus.

Camus subseries	La Revue series	Date
Unnumbered	Nos. 64-66	1961
Unnumbered	Nos. 90-93	1963
No. 1	Nos. 170-74	1968
No. 2	Nos. 212-16	1969
No. 3	Nos. 238-44	1970
No. 4	Nos. 264-70	1971
No. 5	Nos. 315-22	1972
No. 6	Nos. 360-65	1973
No. 7	Nos. 419-24	1975
No. 8	Nos. 479-83	1976

La Revue des Lettres Modernes: histoire des idées et des littératures (RLM). Publisher: Minard, Paris. 1954-- . Irregular. 8-50 Fr. [150-300 p.] Last issue examined: no. 546, 1979.

An ambitious publishing program which is made up of several different series founded at different times, each one under the supervision of a different editor and each one concerned with the publication of scholarship on one specific author.

For instance, the series on Georges Bernanos, which was formed in 1960, produced its sixteenth volume in 1977. Other authors covered by these special series:

Apollinaire	Jacob
Barbey d'Aurevilly	Malraux
Camus	Mauriac
Céline	Rimbaud
Claudel	Suarès
Cocteau	Valéry
Gide	Verne
Giono	

The major portion of each volume is usually historical, biographical, or interpretive criticism, either in the form of one long study or as a collection of critical essays by international contributors exploring one aspect of the chosen author's life or works, such as the theatre of Camus (no. 7 in his series). Each volume may also include bibliographies of published or unpublished works by the author; previously unpublished material with explanatory notes; biographical contributions in the form of reminiscences or newly discovered documents; surveys of translations or editorial problems; textual studies; several book reviews; research or interpretive notes; long explications; news of events, work in progress, and seminars of interest to the author's admirers; illustrations. In addition, almost every volume contains a bibliography of current scholarship on the chosen author, edited by Peter C. Hoy. In French.

Indexed by BULLETIN CRITIQUE, FRENCH VII, FRENCH XX, Klapp, MLA ABSTRACTS, MLA INTERNATIONAL BIBLIOGRAPHY, and REVUE D'HISTOIRE LITTÉRAIRE.

2. Archives Albert Camus. Subseries of Archives des Lettres Modernes, described below. 1960-- . Irregular. Equivalent numbers are provided below for the parent series (Archives des Lettres Modernes) and the individual author series on Camus.

Camus subseries	Archives series	Date
No. 1	No. 34	1960
No. 1, 2nd ed.	No. 34, 2nd ed.	1968
No. 2	No. 122	1971
No. 3	No. 156	1975

Archives des Lettres Modernes: études de critique et d'histoire littéraire (ALM). Publisher: Minard, Paris. 1957-- . Approximately 1/month. 5-40 Fr. [30-130 p.] Last issue examined: vol. 179, 1978.

Small pamphlets containing critical studies of a single aspect of an author's life or work, such as CAMUS ET HUGO (no. 156, 1975). Subjects range from a study of the author's place in literary history to book reviews on a single subject or title, bibliographical surveys, presentation of generally inaccessible material, or analyses of texts. Most volumes include bibliographical references. Individual author subseries begin publication on the date indicated in the author's entry. Equivalent numbers are usually provided for both the parent series (Archives des Lettres Modernes) and the individual author series (in this case, Archives Albert Camus); however, the latter occasionally were not assigned author series numbers when they were first published. In French.

Indexed by BULLETIN CRITIQUE, FRENCH VII, FRENCH XX, Klapp, MLA INTERNATIONAL BIBLIOGRAPHY, and REVUE D'HISTOIRE LITTÉRAIRE.

3. Bibliothèque Albert Camus. Publisher: Minard, Paris. 1961-- . Irregular. 25-35 Fr. Last issue examined: no. 6, 1973.

Each volume focuses on a specific subject--a regrouping of criticism originally published in Lettres Modernes. In French.

4. Cahiers Albert Camus. Editors: Jean-Claude Brisville, Roger Grenier, Roger Quilliot, and Paul Viallaneix. Publisher: Gallimard, Paris. 1971-- . Irregular (a series). 25-35 Fr. [250-300 p.] Last issue examined: vol. 3, 1978.

Concerned primarily with the presentation and publication of unpublished or inaccessible material, but the long introductions and numerous notes make these volumes valuable to critics, and the editors welcome studies that will throw a new light on Camus' contributions. Includes critical studies of Camus' works, bibliographies, and analyses of the writings of Camus' youth. In French. One translation of this series has been published by Knopf under the title Albert Camus Cahier (New York, 1972).

Indexed by FRENCH XX.

CARLETON, WILLIAM (1794-1869)

Irish novelist

1. CARLETON NEWSLETTER (CarlN). Superseded by EIRE 19: A JOURNAL OF 19TH CENTURY IRISH LIFE. Editors: Eileen Sullivan Ibarra, Logic Department, University of Florida, Gainesville, Fla. 32611; and Daniel J. Casey, English Department, State University of New York, Oneonta, N.Y. 13820. Sponsor: University College, University of Florida. July 1970-April 1975 (vols. 1-5, no. 2). 3/yr. $2. [8 p.] Circulation: 200.

Brief critical and biographical articles; bibliographies of library holdings; book reviews; news and notes; report of work in progress.

Indexed by ANNUAL BIBLIOGRAPHY OF ENGLISH LANGUAGE AND LITERATURE.

CARLYLE, THOMAS (1795-1881)

Scottish-born English author

1. Carlyle House Memorial Trust, London. GENERAL MEETING. Sponsor: Carlyle House, 24, Cheyne Row, Chelsea, London. 1896-March 1929 (nos. 1-34). Annual.

   The Carlyle House is presently administered by the National Trust.

2. Carlyle Society. OCCASIONAL PAPERS. Vice-president of the Carlyle Society: Ian Campbell, English Department, University of Edinburgh, David Hume Tower, George Square, Edinburgh EH8 9JX, Scotland. Sponsor: Thomas Green bequest to the Carlyle Society, Edinburgh, Scotland. 1965-- . Irregular. Price varies (free to £1). [18 p.] Circulation: 100. Last issue examined: vol. 6, 1974.

   Subjects range from CARLYLE AND MILL (1965) and CARLYLE AND GOETHE (1972) to CARLYLE AND THE MODERN WORLD (1971). Publications are generally revised versions of lectures delivered to the Carlyle Society.

3. Carlyle Society. THOMAS GREEN LECTURES. Vice-president of the Carlyle Society: Ian Campbell, English Department, University of Edinburgh, David Hume Tower, George Square, Edinburgh EH8 9JX, Scotland. Sponsor: Thomas Green bequest to the Carlyle Society. 1959-- . Irregular. Free. [18 p.] Circulation: 100. Last issue examined: no. 5, 1974.

   Reprints of lectures delivered to the Carlyle Society on Carlyle, Burns, and their times, such as GERMAN ROMANCE AND GERMAN ROMANTICISM: A CASE FOR CARLYLEAN AMBIVALENCE.

CARROLL, LEWIS

See Dodgson, Charles Lutwidge.

CARVALHO, JOAQUIM DE (1892-1959)

Portuguese medieval and Renaissance scholar

1. MISCELÂNEA DE ESTUDOS A JOAQUIM DE CARVALHO (MEJC). Sponsor: Biblioteca-Museu Joaquim de Carvalho, Figueira da Foz, Portugal. Publisher: Publicações Europa-América, Lisbon, Portugal. 1959-(?).

2/yr. (irregular). [100-110 p.] Last issue examined: no. 9, 1963.

Articles on Carvalho, his life, and the relationship of his philosophy with that of Spinoza, Descartes, and others. In Portuguese. No. 10 not yet published (1978).

Indexed by MLA INTERNATIONAL BIBLIOGRAPHY.

CASANOVA DE SEINGALT, JACQUES (1725-98)

Italian adventurer, author of French stories

1. CASANOVA GLEANINGS: REVUE INTERNATIONALE D'ÉTUDES CASANOVIENNES ET DIX-HUITIÈMISTES. Founding editor: J. Rives Childs, Château des Baumettes, 06000 Nice, France, or Richmond, Va. Current editor: Francis-L. Mars, 17, rue Georges-Ville, 06300 Nice. Sponsor and publisher: Istituto Francesedi Studi Storici, Venice. 1958-73 (vols. 1-18); new series, 1974 (vol. 19, no. 1)-- . Annual. $5; 22 Fr. [30-60 p.] Last issue examined: vol. 20, 1977.

   Critical articles on Casanovian themes and allusions; significance of the illustrations of his works; studies of Casanova's writings, including memoirs and letters; previously unpublished works; annual supplement to Casanoviana--eighteenth supplement in vol. 19 (1976), edited by J. Rives Childs; book reviews; facsimiles and photographs. In English or French. Alternate spelling: Giacomo Casanova de Seingalt.

Indexed by BIBLIOGRAPHIE DE LA LITTÉRATURE FRANÇAISE and Klapp.

CATHER, WILLA (1876-1947)

American novelist

1. WILLA CATHER PIONEER MEMORIAL. Superseded by WILLA CATHER PIONEER MEMORIAL AND EDUCATIONAL FOUNDATION (see entry 2). Summer 1957-Spring 1965 (vols. 1-9, no. 1).

2. WILLA CATHER PIONEER MEMORIAL AND EDUCATIONAL FOUNDATION. Supersedes WILLA CATHER PIONEER MEMORIAL (see entry 1); superseded by WILLA CATHER PIONEER MEMORIAL NEWSLETTER (see entry 3). Fall 1965-Fall 1975 (vol. 9, no. 2-vol. 19, no. 3).

3. WILLA CATHER PIONEER MEMORIAL NEWSLETTER. Supersedes WILLA CATHER PIONEER MEMORIAL AND EDUCATIONAL FOUNDATION (see entry 2). Editor: Miriam Mountford. Literary issue editor: Bernice Slote, 201 Andrews Hall, University of Nebraska, Lincoln, Nebr. 68508. Sponsor: Willa Cather Pioneer Memorial, Red Cloud, Nebr. 68970.

Spring 1976 (vol. 20, no. 1)-- . 2-4/yr. $5. [4-6 p.] Circulation: 6,000. Last issue examined: vol. 21, 1978.

News of meetings of the national Cather Circles; report of the annual Cather conference in Red Cloud; report of museum acquisitions, relevant publications, donations, tours, television specials, grants, MLA seminars, restoration of Cather buildings, ceremonies (including the dedication of a bronze plaque at 5 Bank Street, Greenwich Village, where Cather lived for fourteen years and wrote many novels including MY ANTONIA); no index. Twice a year, since 1972, special literary issues have featured reprints of generally inaccessible material, previously unpublished works, early reviews, interviews, primary and secondary bibliographical information, explications, and short critical articles.

Indexed by AMERICAN HUMANITIES INDEX.

CATHLIN, LÉON (1882-?)

French novelist

1. CAHIERS LÉON CATHLIN. Editor: Berthe Bricage. Publisher: 12, rue Olivier-Noyer; 18, rue de Ronde, Lons-le-Saunier, France. October 1957-September 1960. Quarterly. [15-20 p.]

In French.

CÉLINE, LOUIS-FERDINAND

See Destouches, Louis-Ferdinand.

CERVANTES SAAVEDRA, MIGUEL DE (1547-1616)

Spanish novelist, poet, dramatist

1. ANALES CERVANTINOS (ACer). Director: Francisco Sanchez-Castañer. Publisher: Consejo Superior de Investigaciones Científicas, Instituto Miguel de Cervantes de Filología Hispanica, Duque de Medinaceli 4, Madrid-14, Spain. 1951-- . Irregular. 450 pesetas. [250-300 p.] Last issue examined: vol. 15, 1976.

Long scholarly articles on Cervantes, his works, his times, and the extent of his influence on such authors as Dickens; several reviews of international publications in every volume; "Bibliografía Cervantina," a long, critically annotated bibliography of international scholarship appearing in books and articles related to Cervantes--the most comprehensive source in the field, divided into general studies, biographies, new editions, genres, and individual titles; "Cronica Cervantina"--brief news notes on international cultural and political events relating to Cervantes, new publications, benefits, ceremonies, production of plays and television or radio programs, anniversaries, dedications, conferences; facsimiles, maps, and portraits; index. In Spanish, with occasional essays in English or French. Second-hand copies available from Kraus Periodicals (1951-61/62, $195); reprints from Walter J. Johnson (1951-73, $350).

Indexed by MANUAL DE BIBLIOGRAFÍA DE LA LITERATURA ESPAÑOLA and MLA INTERNATIONAL BIBLIOGRAPHY.

CÉSAIRE, AIMÉ (1913-)

Martinique poet, political leader

1. CAHIERS CÉSAIRIENS. Editors: Lilyan Kesteloot, c/o Ministre de Culture, IFAN, B.P. 206, Dakar, Sénégal, or Centre d'Études Francophones, Université Paris-Nord, avenue J.-B. Clément, 93430 Villetaneuse, France; and Thomas A. Hale, French Department, Pennsylvania State University, University Park, Pa. 16802. Publisher: Pennsylvania State University. Spring 1974-- . Annual. $6/four issues. [40 p.] Last issue examined: vol. 4, 1977.

   Bulletin concerning research on Aimé Césaire in international universities. Interpretive essays; textual studies of the changes Césaire made in his own work; bibliographies of theses, critical works, histories, and translations; long reviews of translations, biographies, critical works, new editions; abstracts of dissertations; news of seminars, dissertations, colloquia, programs; international contributors. In French or English.

Indexed by FRENCH XX and MLA INTERNATIONAL BIBLIOGRAPHY.

CHANEY, WILLIAM H. (1821-1903)

American author

1. CHANEY CHRONICLE: LONDON NORTHWEST. Editor and publisher: David H. Schlottmann, 929 South Bay Road, Olympia, Wash. 98506. 1972-- . 1-2/yr. $.50 per copy. [10 p.] Circulation: 30.

   A companion publication to WHAT'S NEW ABOUT LONDON, JACK? (see Jack London, who is generally believed to be Chaney's son). News and notes; book reviews; occasional bibliographies; reprints of articles written by Chaney on spiritualism and astrology.

CHARDONNE, JACQUES

See Boutelleau, Jacques.

CHARTIER, ÉMILE AUGUSTE [ALAIN] (1868-1951)

French philosopher, teacher, essayist

1. Association des Amis d'Alain. ANNUAIRE. Publisher: Le Vésinet (Seine et Oise), France.

   Distributed to subscribers to the Association's BULLETIN (see entry 2). In French.

2. Association des Amis d'Alain. BULLETIN. Editor: Jean Miquel, 7, rue Dante, 75005 Paris. Sponsor: Amis d'Alain, Secrétariat, 4, rue Valette, 75005 Paris. Treasurer: Michel Algrain, 4, rue Molière, 75001 Paris. December 1954-- . 2/yr. 30 Fr; 10 Fr (students). [100 p.] Last issue examined: no. 45, 1978.

   Brief articles on Alain's teaching and philosophy, his friendships and his writings; occasional bibliographies; previously unpublished works; notes on association events and members' activities, international expositions, seminars on Alain and his associates, interviews with his acquaintances. In French.

   Indexed by BIBLIOGRAPHIE DE LA LITTÉRATURE FRANÇAISE, FRENCH VII, and FRENCH XX.

   Alternate titles:

   ASSOCIATION DES AMIS D'ALAIN BULLETIN

   Association des Amis d'Alain. BULLETIN D'INFORMATIONS

3. CAHIERS ALAIN. Sponsor: Association des Amis d'Alain, 75, avenue Émile-Thiébaut, Le Vésinet (Seine et Oise), France. 1962-63 (nos. 1-2).

   Contents later issued in the Association's BULLETIN (see entry 2). In French.

CHATEAUBRIAND, FRANÇOIS-RENÉ, VICOMTE DE (1768-1848)

French author

1. CAHIERS CHATEAUBRIAND. Publisher: Société Chateaubriand, Paris. 1947-(?). Irregular. Last issue examined: vol. 3, 1951.

2. Société Chateaubriand. BULLETIN (BSChat). Formerly GRAND BULLETIN (see entry 3) and PETIT BULLETIN (see entry 4). Sponsor: Société Chateaubriand, La Vallée-aux-Loups, 87, rue Chateaubriand, Châtenay-Malabry, Hauts-de-Seine, France. Secrétariat Général de la Société Chateaubriand: Maurice Amour, 122, boulevard de Courcelles, 75017 Paris. Libraire Chrétien de la Société Chateaubriand: 178, Faubourg St-Honoré, 75008 Paris. Publisher: Éditions A.-G. Nizet. New series,

1955-- . Annual. 50 Fr; 60 Fr (foreign). [100-120 p.] Last issue examined: no. 20, 1977.

Biographical, bibliographical, and interpretive articles; critical notes; detailed critical bibliographies of works by and about Chateaubriand; previously unpublished works and letters; book reviews; descriptive annotations of Chateaubriand manuscripts and new editions; report of work in progress and future publications; news of the annual assembly and reports of international society activities; list of members, including officers in foreign countries; numerous portraits, illustrations, and facsimiles. Index for 1930-59 (30 Fr); index for 1960-69 (30 Fr). In French.

Indexed by BIBLIOGRAPHIE DE LA LITTÉRATURE FRANÇAISE, BULLETIN CRITIQUE, ENGLISH LANGUAGE NOTES, FRENCH XX, Klapp, MLA INTERNATIONAL BIBLIOGRAPHY, and REVUE D'HISTOIRE LITTÉRAIRE.

Alternate title:

BULLETIN DE LA SOCIÉTÉ CHATEAUBRIAND

3. Société Chateaubriand. GRAND BULLETIN. Superseded by PETIT BULLETIN (see entry 4) and BULLETIN (see entry 2). Sponsor: Société Chateaubriand (see previous entry). Old series: 1930-37 (nos. 1-6). Irregular (approximately 1/yr.). 60 Fr. [60-160 p.]

Report on Society activities, new editions, critical works; previously unpublished or inaccessible works; book reviews; photographs and facsimiles. In French.

Indexed by MLA INTERNATIONAL BIBLIOGRAPHY.

4. Société Chateaubriand. PETIT BULLETIN. Supersedes GRAND BULLETIN (see entry 3); superseded by BULLETIN (see entry 2). Sponsor: Société Chateaubriand (see entry 2). 1948-54 (nos. 1-6). Annual. 10 Fr.

Brief notes of Society news. In French.

CHATRIAN, ALEXANDRE [ERCKMANN-CHATRIAN] (1826-90)

French regional novelist

See Erckmann, Émile.

CHAUCER, GEOFFREY (1345-1400)

English poet

1. CHAUCER RESEARCH REPORT. Editor: Thomas A. Kirby. Sponsor: Committee on Chaucer Research and Bibliography, MLA. Annual feature

of the CHAUCER REVIEW (see entry 2). [30 p.] Last issue examined: no. 37, Chaucer Research, 1976.

Includes information on work in progress: projects approved and being encouraged; completed projects--books, articles, desiderata, and dissertations; and recent publications. Offprints available from CHAUCER REVIEW, 215 Wagner Building, Pennsylvania State University, University Park, Pa. 16802 ($.50).

2. CHAUCER REVIEW: A JOURNAL OF MEDIEVAL STUDIES AND LITERARY CRITICISM (ChauR). Editors: Robert W. Frank, Jr., 117 Burrowes Building, Pennsylvania State University, University Park, Pa. 16802; and Bruce A. Rosenberg, Department of English, Brown University, Providence, R.I. 02912. Sponsor: Issued with the cooperation of the Chaucer Group of the Modern Language Association. Publisher: Pennsylvania State University Press. July 1966-- . Quarterly (Summer, Fall, Winter, Spring). Individuals: $12, $34/three yrs.; overseas: $16, $46/three yrs. Institutions: $20, $57/three yrs.; overseas: $21, $60/three yrs. [70-100 p.] Circulation: 1,356. Last issue examined: vol. 13, 1979.

Long, documented articles on Chaucer's language, characters, style, irony, use of conventions, life, and contributions to medieval literature; annual bibliography of Chaucer scholarship; occasional bibliographies on individual works; report of work in progress in the summer issue (see CHAUCER RESEARCH REPORT, previous entry); book reviews; abstracts of featured articles are placed in the front of each issue; occasional news items; report of the Chaucer Library Committee to the MLA Chaucer Division at the annual convention; advertisements; annual index.

Indexed by ABSTRACTS OF ENGLISH STUDIES, ANNUAL BIBLIOGRAPHY OF ENGLISH LANGUAGE AND LITERATURE, HUMANITIES INDEX, MLA ABSTRACTS, MLA INTERNATIONAL BIBLIOGRAPHY, and YEAR'S WORK IN ENGLISH STUDIES.

3. Chaucer Society, London. PUBLICATIONS. Publisher: For the Chaucer Society by Paul, Trench, Trübner, London. First series, 1868-1912 (vols. 1-99); second series, 1869-1925 (vols. 1-56). Irregular. Price varies.

Each volume concerns a specific subject. Critical studies of the life, works, and language of Chaucer; source studies; diagrams of genealogy of manuscripts; parallel-text editions; facsimiles; illustrations; bibliographies; rhyme, subject, and name indexes. Scattered volumes have been published by the Early English Text Society, and some volumes were also issued by the Philological Society. Reprints available from Kraus Reprint and Johnson Reprint (first series, 1868-1912, $1,100); and from Walter J. Johnson (first series, 1868-1912, $1,540).

the chaucer review

A JOURNAL OF MEDIEVAL STUDIES AND LITERARY CRITICISM

Published with the cooperation of the Chaucer group
of the Modern Language Association
by The Pennsylvania State University Press

Vol. 10, No. 3 Winter, 1976

4. Chaucer Society, London. REPORTS. Editor: Frederick J. Furnivall, 3, St. George's Square, Primrose Hill, London N.W. March 1869-September 1881 (nos. 1-10). Annual. Two guineas. [4-8 p.]

   Report on editing problems and progress of new Chaucer editions; financial statement; list of members; list of publications of the Society.

CHESTERTON, GILBERT KEITH (1874-1936)

English essayist, novelist, journalist, poet

1. CHESTERTON REVIEW: THE JOURNAL OF THE CHESTERTON SOCIETY. Editor: Ian Boyd, Department of English, St. Thomas More College, University of Saskatchewan, 1437 College Drive, Saskatoon, Saskatchewan S7N 0W6, Canada. Sponsor: The Chesterton Society. Fall/Winter 1974-- . 2/yr. $5 (Canadians); $6 (non-Canadians); $7 (institutions); $8 (non-Canadian institutions); £2 (Great Britain). [50-150 p.] Circulation: 1,263, including 376 outside North America. Last issue examined: vol. 4, 1978.

   Concerned with "the promotion of a critical interest in all aspects of the life and works of G.K. Chesterton." Critical and biographical studies on sources, influences, comparisons, style; review articles; previously unpublished works; reprints of inaccessible early works; surveys of Chesterton's popularity and influence in foreign lands; extensive news and comments concerning national and international Chesterton Society meetings and financial status, seminars in North American and foreign countries, work in progress, new publications; reminiscences; brief notes; letters to the editor; bibliographies; poems; international contributors; annual index. The Chesterton Society has branch secretaries in England, Australia, Canada, France, Japan, Poland, and the United States.

   Indexed by AMERICA: HISTORY AND LIFE and HISTORICAL ABSTRACTS.

   Alternate subtitle, Fall-Winter, 1974:

   NEWSLETTER OF THE G.K. CHESTERTON SOCIETY

CHOPIN, KATE O'FLAHERTY (1851-1904)

American short-story writer, novelist

1. KATE CHOPIN NEWSLETTER. Editor: Emily Toth, Department of English, University of North Dakota, Grand Forks, N. Dak. 58201. Spring 1975-77 (vols. 1-2). 3/yr. (Winter, Spring, Fall). $5 (individuals); $3 (students); $10 (institutions).

   "Interested in articles on both well-known and forgotten writers, on books and journals and diaries, and in theoretical articles defining the powers and limits of regionalism." First three issues were concerned solely with Kate Chopin; since then, coverage has been extended to all women regionalists whose work "shows a strong sense of place," such as Mary E. Wilkins Freeman, Ruth McEnery Stuart, Sarah Orne Jewett, Grace King, Doris Lessing, Eudora Welty, and Joan Didion. Brief critical articles; book reviews; notes.

Indexed by AMERICAN HUMANITIES INDEX and MLA INTERNATIONAL BIBLIOGRAPHY.

CHOQUETTE, ROBERT (1905-)

American-born Canadian poet, novelist, dramatist

1. CAHIERS DU CERCLE ROBERT CHOQUETTE. Editors: Le Père André Melancon, Jean-Marie Moreau, and Roland Laferrière. Sponsor and publisher: Collège de Saint-Laurent (Collège d'enseignement général et professionnel), 625 boulevard Ste-Croix, Saint Laurent, Quebec H4L 3X7, Canada. 1956-64 (nos. 1-9). Irregular. [40-65 p.]

   Dedicated to Choquette, a graduate of the Collège de Saint-Laurent. Composed mainly of poems in Choquette's honor, with a few essays and stories; brief introductions.

CICERO, MARCUS TULLIUS (106-43 B.C.)

Roman orator, statesman, philosopher

1. CICERONIANA: RIVISTA DI STUDI CICERONIANI. Editor: Virgilio Paladini, Piazza dei Cavalieri di Malta 2, Rome, Italy. Sponsor: Centro di studi ciceroniani, Rome, Italy. 1959-(?). Irregular. L.4.000. [200 p.] Last issue examined: nos. 3-6, 1961-64.

   Long documented essays on textual problems, sources, translations; notes on editions, interpretations, Cicero's life and travels, his reception and influence; book reviews and review articles; occasional facsimiles and diagrams. In Italian, Latin, German, or English.

2. COLLANA DI STUDI CICERONIANI. Editor: Ettore Paratore. Publisher: Centro de studi Ciceroniani, Rome, Italy. 1961-(?). Irregular. [150 p.] Last issue examined: vol. 2, 1962.

   Collections of biographical, historical, theological, and thematic studies of Cicero and his work. In English or Italian.

CLAUDEL, PAUL (1868-1955)

French dramatist, poet

1. Archives Paul Claudel. Subseries of Archives des Lettres Modernes. 1958-- . Irregular. Equivalent numbers are provided below for both the parent series (Archives des Lettres Modernes) and the individual author series on Claudel.

Claudel subseries	Archives series	Date
No. 1	No. 8	1958
No. 2	No. 53	1964
No. 3	No. 58	1965
No. 4	No. 63	1965
No. 5	No. 69	1966
No. 6	No. 77	1967
No. 7	No. 87	1968
No. 8	No. 100	1969
No. 8, 2nd ed.	No. 100, 2nd ed.	1971
No. 9	No. 120	1971
No. 10	No. 148	1973
No. 11	No. 152	1974

In French. See Camus, Albert, entry 2, for a full description of Archives des Lettres Modernes.

Indexed by BULLETIN CRITIQUE, FRENCH VII, FRENCH XX, Klapp, and MLA INTERNATIONAL BIBLIOGRAPHY.

Alternate title:

Archives claudéliennes

2. Bibliothèque Paul Claudel. Publisher: Minard, Paris. 1958-- . Irregular (a series). Last issue examined: no. 6, 1976.

Each volume focuses on a specific subject--a regrouping of critical works originally published in Lettres Modernes. In French.

3. BULLETIN DE LA SOCIÉTÉ PAUL CLAUDEL. Editor: Charles Galpérine, 11, boulevard Lannes, 75016 Paris. Sponsor· Société Paul Claudel, 13, rue du Pont-Louis-Philippe, 75004 Paris. Publisher: Dumas, St-Étienne, France. 1958-- . Quarterly. 40 Fr; 45 Fr (foreign). [25-70 p.] Circulation: 1,000. Last issue examined: no. 69, 1978.

Commentaries on works; historical and biographical essays; discussions of new translations; bibliographies of recent international Claudel scholarship, including theses; long book, television, and play reviews; abstracts; report of archive acquisitions; report of Society meetings and colloquia; previously unpublished letters; "Calendrier"--news of international theatre productions, conferences, reunions, and other Society activities; letters to the editor; numerous illustrations, photographs, and facsimiles. Available on microfilms. Checklist of nos. 1-36, edited by Renée Nantet and Jacqueline Veinstein (1970). In French.

Indexed by BIBLIOGRAPHIE DE LA LITTÉRATURE FRANÇAISE, FRENCH VII, FRENCH XX, Klapp, and REVUE D'HISTOIRE LITTÉRAIRE.

4. BULLETIN DE LA SOCIÉTÉ PAUL CLAUDEL DU JAPON. 1968-- . Annual. [50 p.]

Brief articles on Claudel scholarship in Japan; long scholarly studies of the works; news of events; interviews. In Japanese.

Indexed by BIBLIOGRAPHIE DE LA LITTÉRATURE FRANÇAISE.

5. Cahier Canadien Claudel (CCanC). Editor: Eugene Roberto. Sponsor and Publisher: University of Ottawa Press, for Paul Claudel Society of Canada, 65 Hastey Avenue, Ottawa, Ontario K1N 6N5. 1963-- . Irregular (a series). $3-6. [150-350 p.] Last issue examined: vol. 8, 1975.

The Paul Claudel Society of Canada seeks to encourage communication among all those who are interested in Claudel's work, to encourage research, and to publish original studies. Each volume is either a long study of a single work, such as L'ENDORMIE (1963), or a collection of studies by various authors, with bibliographical references, of Claudel's friendships, basic themes, influence, or style, such as CLAUDEL ET L'AMERIQUE (I, 1964; II, 1969). Occasional bibliographies; occasional book reviews; information on the Society in Canada and a list of its members; facsimiles, photographs, and illustrations; indexes in some volumes. In French, with occasional English contributions. Vol. 9 not yet published (1978).

Indexed by FRENCH VII, FRENCH XX, Klapp, and MLA INTERNATIONAL BIBLIOGRAPHY.

6. Cahiers Paul Claudel. Editorial secretary: Charles Galpérine, 11, boulevard Lannes, 75016 Paris. Sponsor: published with the approval of the Société Paul Claudel, 13, rue du Pont-Louis-Philippe, 75004 Paris. Publisher: Gallimard, Paris. 1959-- . Irregular (a series). 30-40 Fr. [300-400 p.] Last issue examined: vol. 10, 1974.

Each volume is concerned with a different subject; as, for example, CLAUDEL DIPLOMATE (1962). Occasionally these include critical editions of Claudel's letters, journals, plays, prose, or poetry, with fully half the book devoted to copious notes, relevant news items, introductions discussing new biographical, textual, or interpretive material, and indexes. Contains "Claudeliana" (an occasional feature with information on new editions, translations, dramatic productions, and international Society events); previously unpublished works; short book reviews; occasional bibliographies, primary or secondary, on specific subjects such as criticism in foreign countries; illustrations and portraits; occasional indexes. In French. Vol. 11 not yet published (1978).

Indexed by BULLETIN CRITIQUE, FRENCH VII, FRENCH XX, Klapp, and REVUE D'HISTOIRE LITTÉRAIRE.

7. CLAUDEL NEWSLETTER. Superseded by CLAUDEL STUDIES (see entry 8). Editor: Harold A. Waters, Department of Languages, University of Rhode Island, Kingston, R.I. 02881. Sponsors: University of Rhode Island, Cultural Services of the French Embassy, and Paul Claudel Society. April 1968-February 1972 (nos. 1-9). 2-3 yr. Free to Claudelians and libraries. Circulation: 500.

 Brief articles; book reviews; notes and queries; Society events. In English or French.

 Indexed by BIBLIOGRAPHIE DE LA LITTÉRATURE FRANÇAISE and FRENCH XX.

 Alternate title:

 CLAUDEL'S NEWSLETTER

8. CLAUDEL STUDIES (ClaudelS). Supersedes CLAUDEL NEWSLETTER (see entry 7). Editor and publisher: Moses M. Nagy, Department of French, University of Dallas, Irving, Tex. 75061. Sponsors: University of Dallas and Cultural Services of the French Embassy. November 1972-- . 2/yr. $5 (U.S.); $5.50 (foreign); $3 per issue; $6 (subscription and membership in the Paul Claudel Society). [90-100 p.] Circulation: 500. Last issue examined: vol. 5, 1978.

 Long (10 p.) critical articles on themes, style, influences, translations, travels, friendships; previously unpublished works; news notes concerning Society activities in all parts of the world--meetings, dramatic productions, readings; reports of work in progress; book reviews; list of members; no index. In English or French.

 Indexed by BIBLIOGRAPHIE DE LA LITTÉRATURE FRANÇAISE, FRENCH XX, Klapp, MLA ABSTRACTS, MLA INTERNATIONAL BIBLIOGRAPHY, and MODERN DRAMA (Toronto).

9. Paul Claudel. Subseries of La Revue des Lettres Modernes. Editor: Jacques Petit. 1959-- . Irregular. Equivalent numbers are provided below for both the parent series (La Revue des Lettres Modernes) and the individual author series on Claudel.

Three New Poems by Floyd Dell

MARK TWAIN JOURNAL

Huckleberry Finn.

I first read this delightful book in my fourteenth year on board an old ship in a great river. I must have read it all through once at least in each succeeding year, always with much delight in the people, the unfolding tale & the unfailing river. I can have read no book more frequently nor with more glad content. As for the writer, I can but quote an old song:-
"I wish in Heaven his soul may dwell"

John Masefield.

Some Recollections of John Masefield

Thomas Caldecot Chubb

Claudel subseries	La Revue series	Date
Unnumbered	Nos. 44-45	1959
No. 1	Nos. 101-03	1964
No. 2	Nos. 114-16	1965
No. 3	Nos. 134-36	1966
No. 4	Nos. 150-52	1967
No. 5	Nos. 180-82	1968
No. 6	Nos. 209-11	1969
No. 7	Nos. 245-48	1970
No. 8	Nos. 271-75	1971
No. 9	Nos. 310-14	1972
No. 10	Nos. 366-69	1973
No. 11	Nos. 391-97	1974
No. 12	Nos. 510-15	1977

In French. See Camus, Albert, entry 1, for a full description of La Revue des Lettres Modernes.

Indexed by BULLETIN CRITIQUE, FRENCH VII, FRENCH XX, Klapp, and MLA INTERNATIONAL BIBLIOGRAPHY.

10. Société Claudel en Belgique. BULLETIN RÉGIONAL. Sponsor: Amis de Paul Claudel en Belgique. Secrétariat: 1, rue de Crehen, Hannut, Belgium. 1960-- . Irregular. Last issue examined: no. 18, 1973.

Brief articles on the relationship of Claudel with Belgian authors and literature; reprints of material of interest to Belgian scholars; occasional special issues, such as PAUL CLAUDEL ET LÉOPOLD LEVAUX, with critical notes and reprints of letters. In French.

Indexed by BIBLIOGRAPHIE DE LA LITTÉRATURE FRANÇAISE, FRENCH VII, and FRENCH XX.

Alternate title:

AMIS DE PAUL CLAUDEL EN BELGIQUE

CLEMENS, SAMUEL L. [MARK TWAIN] (1835-1910)

American humorist, author

1. Mark Twain Association of America, Chicago. REPORT OF THE ANNUAL MEETING. 1942-(?). [2 p.]

See also TWAINIAN (entry 7).

2. MARK TWAIN JOURNAL (MTJ). Supersedes MARK TWAIN QUARTERLY (see entry 6). Editor: Cyril Clemens, Kirkwood, Mo. 63122. Sponsor: 1954-55, Mark Twain Journal Associates; since Summer 1955, Mark Twain Memorial Association. Summer 1954 (vol. 9, no. 4)-- . 2/yr. (Summer, Winter). $3; $5/two yrs.; $7/three yrs. [20-30 p.] Circulation: 10,000. Last issue examined: vol. 19, 1979.

Brief articles on Twain's themes, characters, style, friendships, worldwide reputation, wit, and wisdom; numerous reprints from his works; numerous reminiscences from people who had known Twain or whose family and friends had met him--always with details of Twain's witty conversations; contributors such as H.G. Wells, Shaw, T.S. Eliot, Sandburg, Frost, O'Neill; previously unpublished documents; occasional book reviews; occasional poems; facsimiles of Twain's letters or notes; sketches, photographs, or facsimiles on every cover; portraits and reproductions. Cumulative index for 1936-65. Reprints of first twelve volumes (1936-65) available from Kraus Reprint ($92). Available in microform from University Microfilms International.

Indexed by ABSTRACTS OF ENGLISH STUDIES, AMERICAN HUMANITIES INDEX, AMERICAN LITERATURE, AMERICAN LITERATURE ABSTRACTS, ANNUAL BIBLIOGRAPHY OF ENGLISH LANGUAGE AND LITERATURE, Leary, MISSISSIPPI QUARTERLY, MLA ABSTRACTS, MLA INTERNATIONAL BIBLIOGRAPHY, TWENTIETH CENTURY LITERATURE, and VICTORIAN STUDIES.

3. Mark Twain Library and Memorial Commission, Hartford. NEWSLETTER. 1955-64.

4. Mark Twain Memorial Association. Publisher: Webster Groves, Mo. 63119.

Biographical series. 1934-- .

Each volume is concerned with a specific subject, such as MARK TWAIN AND HARRY S. TRUMAN.

Alternate title: Historical Series or Studies

Fiction Series. 1937-- .

Poetry Series. 1939.

Studies. No. 5 (1932-(?).

5. MARK TWAIN MEMORIAL NEWSLETTER. Sponsor: Mark Twain Memorial, 351 Farmington Avenue, Hartford, Conn. 06105. March 1955-- . 3-4/yr. Free with membership ($7.50, individual; $15, group). [8 p.]

Club news--meetings, lectures, acquisitions, plans; report on activities at the Mark Twain home, Nook Farm.

6. MARK TWAIN QUARTERLY. Superseded by MARK TWAIN JOURNAL (see entry 2). Editor: Cyril Clemens. Sponsor and publisher: International Mark Twain Society, Mark Twain Hotel, St. Louis, Mo.; Webster

Groves, Mo. 63119. Fall 1936-Winter 1953 (vols. 1-9, no. 3). Quarterly (Spring, Summer, Fall, Winter). $.30-$1 per issue. [20-25 p.]

Brief articles--reminiscences, memorials, surveys of influence in foreign lands; book reviews; "Here and There"--news on awards, worthwhile books; occasional special issues in honor of illustrious members of the Society, such as A.E. Housman and G.K. Chesterton, shortly after their deaths; facsimiles; cumulative index at the end of each annual volume.

7. TWAINIAN: (DISCOVERING MARK TWAIN). Editor: George H. Brownell, 1939-50; Secretary, Chester L. Davis, 1950-- . Sponsor: 1939-41, Mark Twain Society of Chicago; 1942-45, Mark Twain Association of America; since January 1947, Mark Twain Research Foundation, Perry, Mo. 63462. January 1939-June 1941 (vols. 1-3, no. 1); new series, January 1942 (vol. 1, no. 1)-- . Irregular until Summer 1944; Fall 1944-Fall 1945, monthly; bimonthly since January 1946. By annual membership only in U.S. and Canada ($5). [2-8 p.] Circulation: 400. Last issue examined: vol. 37, 1978.

Concerned with the wisdom of Mark Twain as taught by his life and writing. Reprints of material related to Twain; reminiscences; annual reprints of entries in ABSTRACTS OF ENGLISH STUDIES, usually in the January-February issue; occasional book reviews on scholarly, not subjective, works; news notes; no index.

Indexed by ABSTRACTS OF ENGLISH STUDIES, AMERICA: HISTORY AND LIFE, AMERICAN HUMANITIES INDEX, AMERICAN LITERATURE, ANNUAL BIBLIOGRAPHY OF ENGLISH LANGUAGE AND LITERATURE, and MLA INTERNATIONAL BIBLIOGRAPHY.

Subtitle, May/June 1969-January/February 1973:

MARK TWAIN--YESTERDAY AND TODAY

COCTEAU, JEAN (1889-1963)

French poet, dramatist

1. Cahiers Jean Cocteau. Sponsor: Société des Amis de Jean Cocteau. Secrétariat: 6, rue Bonaparte, Paris. Publisher: Gallimard, Paris. 1969-- . Irregular (a series). 30 Fr; 15 Fr (students). [120-40 p.] Last issue examined: vol. 7, 1978.

Long critical studies of Cocteau's life, works, and influence, such as JEAN COCTEAU ET SON THÉÂTRE (1975); reprints of his works; short reminiscences; previously unpublished material--poems and letters to and from Cocteau; primary and secondary bibliographies; information on films, radio and television programs, exhibitions, dramatic productions, international expositions, and lectures; report of the Society's activities; illustrations. In French.

Cahiers Jean Cocteau 5

nrf

Cahiers Jean Cocteau

5

JEAN COCTEAU ET SON THÉÂTRE

Gallimard

Indexed by BIBLIOGRAPHIE DE LA LITTÉRATURE FRANÇAISE, BULLETIN CRITIQUE, FRENCH XX, Klapp, and MLA INTERNATIONAL BIBLIOGRAPHY.

2. Jean Cocteau. Subseries of La Revue des Lettres Modernes. Equivalent numbers are provided below for both the parent series (La Revue des Lettres Modernes) and the individual author series on Cocteau. Editors: Jean-Jacques Kihm (deceased); P. Chanel. 1972-- . Irregular.

Cocteau subseries	La Revue series	Date
No. 1	Nos. 298-303	1972

In French. See Camus, Albert, entry 1, for a full description of La Revue des Lettres Modernes.

Indexed by BULLETIN CRITIQUE, FRENCH XX, Klapp, and MLA INTERNATIONAL BIBLIOGRAPHY.

COLETTE

See Jouvenal, Sidonie-Gabrielle de.

COLLIER, JOHN (1901-)

English-born American short-story writer

1. PRESENTING MOONSHINE. Editors: Charles E. Yenter and Morley Fox, 1015 South Steele Street, Tacoma, Wash. 98405. July 1969-- . Monthly, then irregular. Free. [24 p.] Circulation: 100.

Devoted to the study of bibliography, with emphasis on Collier. News and notes of interest to local book collectors--for example, a list of the Serif Series (checklists and bibliographies of works by or about prominent authors); bibliographies by and about Collier; occasional descriptive bibliographical entries for individual Collier works; illustrations.

Indexed by ANNUAL BIBLIOGRAPHY OF ENGLISH LANGUAGE AND LITERATURE.

CONRAD, JOSEPH [JOSEPH CONRAD THEODORE KORZENIOWSKI] (1857-1924)

Polish-born English novelist

1. CONRADIANA: A JOURNAL OF JOSEPH CONRAD. Editors: David L. Higdon and Donald W. Rude, Department of English, Texas Technological University, Box 4530, Lubbock, Tex. 79409. Sponsor: Dean of the Graduate School and Director of Academic Publications, in cooperation with the International Center for Arid and Semi-Arid Land Studies.

CONRADIANA
CONRADIANA
VOLUME IX: 1
Conradiana Volume IX, Number 1: 1977
Texas Tech University/Lubbock, Texas

Publisher: Texas Technological University. September 1968-- . 3/yr. (Spring, Summer, Autumn). $7.50 (U.S.); $8.50 (foreign). [60-100 p.] Circulation: 950. Last issue examined: vol. 10, 1978.

Long (15-25 p.) critical articles on Conrad and his works--the plot, characters, style, sources, and themes in the novels; textual, biographical, and bibliographical studies; annual bibliography of Conrad scholarship, including dissertations, in the fall issue; since November 1975, report of research in progress as well as of research forthcoming and recently completed; abstracts; news of international symposia, musical programs, memorials, activities of Conrad societies all over the world; queries from international sources; long book reviews of international publications; international editorial board; list of forthcoming essays; occasional illustrations; annual index in no. 3 of every volume. Vols. 1-2 available in microfilm from University Microfilms International; vols. 1-5 in reprint from Walter J. Johnson ($60).

Indexed by ABSTRACTS OF ENGLISH STUDIES, AMERICAN HUMANITIES INDEX, ANNUAL BIBLIOGRAPHY OF ENGLISH LANGUAGE AND LITERATURE, INDEX TO BOOK REVIEWS IN THE HUMANITIES, MLA ABSTRACTS, MLA INTERNATIONAL BIBLIOGRAPHY, TWENTIETH CENTURY LITERATURE, and VICTORIAN STUDIES.

2. L'EPOQUE CONRADIENNE: BULLETIN ANNUEL DE LA SOCIÉTÉ CONRADIENNE FRANÇAISE. Editor: F. Lombard, Maître de Conférences a l'Université de Limoges, 13, rue de Genève, 87100 Limoges, France. 1975-- . Annual.

   Critical articles on Conrad's work and his relationship to other writers; translations of critical works from other countries. In English.

3. ITALIAN JOSEPH CONRAD SOCIETY NEWSLETTER. Editor: Mario Curreli, University of Pisa, Italy. No. 3, 1975-- .

   Notes on Conrad's life and works; bibliographies of critical works (mostly by Italian authors) and of theses; news on activities of Conrad societies. In Italian.

4. Joseph Conrad Society. PAMPHLET SERIES. Sponsor: Joseph Conrad Society, United Kingdom. Treasurer: Margaret Rishworth, Olinda, Beacon Hill Road, Hindhead, Surrey, England. Autumn 1975-- . Irregular. £1-1.25. [16-24 p.] Last issue examined: no. 4, 1976.

   Each pamphlet covers a different subject, such as TOUR OF JOSEPH CONRAD'S HOMES IN KENT (by Conrad's son, Borys); personal memoirs; reprints of out-of-print material; photographs.

5. JOSEPH CONRAD TODAY: THE NEWSLETTER OF THE JOSEPH CONRAD SOCIETY OF AMERICA. President and editor: Adam Gillon, English

Department, State University of New York, New Paltz, N.Y. 12561. Vice-president and treasurer: Peter D. O'Connor, State University College of New York, Oswego, N.Y. 13126. Sponsor: Joseph Conrad Society of America, New Paltz, N.Y. 12561. October 1975-- . Quarterly(October, January, April, July). Free with membership (U.S., $4; Canada and foreign, $4.50); U.S. institutions: $5.50, $9/two yrs., $13.50/three yrs.; Canada and foreign institutions: $6, $10/two yrs., $14/three yrs. [8 p.] Last issue examined: vol. 3, 1978.

Brief articles on Conrad's literary relationship with other writers, especially (in 1976 issues) with American writers such as Thoreau, Pynchon, and Faulkner; news of MLA seminars and of international societies and conferences; occasional book reviews; notes and queries.

6. JOURNAL OF THE JOSEPH CONRAD SOCIETY (U.K.). Editor: John Crompton, School of Education, University of Newcastle upon Tyne, England. Sponsor: Joseph Conrad Society (U.K.). 1974-- . $3.50.

Brief critical articles on Conrad's plots, style, characters.

Alternate title:

JOSEPH CONRAD SOCIETY NEWSLETTER (U.K.).

CONSTANT DE REBECQUE, HENRI BENJAMIN (1767-1830)

French author, politician

1. CAHIERS BENJAMIN CONSTANT (CBC). Editor: René Le Grand Roy, 2, Chemin des Crêts-de-Champel, 1206 Geneva, Switzerland. Sponsor: Association des Amis de Benjamin Constant, Librairie Bonnard, 3, rue Langallerie, Lausanne, Switzerland. 1955-August 1969(?). Irregular (no. 2, 1957; no. 3, 1961; no. 4, 1967).

Collections of essays on Constant's life, family, and friendships with various illustrious contemporaries, including Mme. de Staël (q.v.); previously unpublished documents; studies of his political ideas, textual problems, writings; bibliographies; book reviews. In French.

Indexed by Klapp.

Alternate title:

CAHIERS CONSTANT

CORNEILLE, PIERRE (1606-84)

French dramatist

1. CAHIERS PIERRE CORNEILLE. Sponsor: Société Pierre Corneille, 77, rue Thiers, Rouen, France. March 1964 (nos. 1-2)-(?). [35-40 p.]

Brief articles on Corneille's family and friends. In French.

Indexed by Klapp.

COURIER, PAUL-LOUIS (1772-1825)

French scholar, author

1. CAHIERS PAUL-LOUIS COURIER. Editor: Gabriel Spillebout, 3, place du Chardonnet, 37000 Tours, France. Sponsor and publisher: Société des Amis de Paul-Louis Courier, 37270 Mairie de Véretz (Indre-et-Loire), France. November 1968-- . Irregular (2-3/yr.). 20 Fr; 30 Fr (foreign); 10 Fr (students). [25-45 p.] Last issue examined: no. 18, 1977.

   Brief articles on Courier's relationship with his contemporaries, his contributions to literature, his writing style, reactions by later critics in periodicals; previously unpublished letters and other documents; catalogs of his portraits; bibliographies; notes on newly discovered editions, special expositions, Society and membership activities, meetings of the General Assembly. In French.

   Indexed by BIBLIOGRAPHIE DE LA LITTÉRATURE FRANÇAISE.

2. Société des Amis de Paul-Louis Courier. PUBLICATIONS, Series A. Sponsor: Société des Amis de Paul-Louis Courier, 17, rue Claude-Debussy, Tours, France. Publisher: 37270 Mairie de Véretz (Indre-et-Loire), France. 1974-- . Irregular. [100 p.]

   Vol. 1 contains brief papers prepared for the 1972 symposium at the Sorbonne on the history of French literature--studies of Courier's childhood, his inspiration from Voltaire, his attitude toward the Revolution and the classics, his interest in the pamphlet genre. In French.

   Indexed by REVUE D'HISTOIRE LITTÉRAIRE.

   Alternate title:

   PUBLICATIONS DE LA SOCIÉTÉ DES AMIS DE PAUL-LOUIS COURIER

COUTÉ, GASTON (1880-1911)

French poet

1. AMIS DE GASTON COUTÉ. Sponsor: Musée G. Couté, Hôtel de Ville, Meung-sur-Loire (Loiret), France. 1947-(?). Irregular. Last issue examined: no. 3, 1955.

   In French.

COWARD, NOEL (1899-1977)

English actor, composer, dramatist

1. NOEL COWARD NEWSLETTER. Editor: Archie K. Loss, Division of Arts and Humanities, Behrend College, Pennsylvania State University, Station Road, Erie, Pa. 16510.

   Planned but not yet published (1978).

CRAMER, SAMUEL (1842-1913)

Dutch theologian

1. CRAMÉRIEN: BULLETIN D'INFORMATION DES AMIS DE SAMUEL CRAMER.

   Devoted to research on the life and times, work and contributions of Baudelaire (see Baudelaire, entry 4).

CRANE, HART (1899-1932)

American poet

1. HART CRANE NEWSLETTER. Editors and publishers: Warren Herendeen, Department of English, Mercy College, Dobbs Ferry, N.Y. 10522; and Donald G. Parker, Manhattan Community College, City University of New York. February 1977-- . 2/yr. $5; $9/two yrs. [45-50 p.] Circulation: 250. Last issue examined: vol. 1, no. 2, 1977.

   Brief critical essays and textual studies; bibliographies; book reviews; illustrations; no index.

CRANE, STEPHEN (1871-1900)

American novelist, poet, short-story writer

1. STEPHEN CRANE NEWSLETTER (SCraneN). Editor: Joseph Katz, Department of English, University of South Carolina, Columbia, S.C. 29208. October 1966-Fall 1970 (vols. 1-5, no. 1). 4/yr. $2 (individual); $3 (U.S. libraries). [12 p.] Circulation: 400.

   Brief articles, chiefly on textual problems but also on subjects such as the meager sales and royalties of RED BADGE OF COURAGE at the first part of the century, on problem areas in the novels, and on Crane's own life, including his brief disappearance in Havana; quarterly checklist of Crane scholarship; occasional special annotated checklists, such as that for Crane criticism during his lifetime; announcements of new editions, translations; numerous previously unpublished Crane letters, dispatches to his newspaper, and other material; book, film, and play reviews; work in progress; reprints of early advertisements of Crane's works; queries; facsimiles.

Indexed by ABSTRACTS OF ENGLISH STUDIES, AMERICAN HUMANITIES INDEX, AMERICAN LITERATURE, ANNUAL BIBLIOGRAPHY OF ENGLISH LANGUAGE AND LITERATURE, Leary, and MLA INTERNATIONAL BIBLIOGRAPHY.

CROCE, BENEDETTO (1866-1952)

Italian philosopher

1. RIVISTA DI STUDI CROCIANI (RSC). Editor: Alfredo Parente. Sponsor and publisher: Società napoletana di storia patria, Piazza Municipio, Maschio Angioiono, 80133 Naples, Italy. January-March 1964-- . Quarterly. L.10.000; L.13.000 (foreign). [120-50 p.] Last issue examined: vol. 14, 1977.

   Long scholarly studies of Croce's beliefs and arguments, including his interaction with contemporaries and his philosophical differences from or similarities to the thought of such authors as Goethe, Marx, Einstein, Beltrani; analyses of previously unpublished documents; long review articles, generally of Italian publications; "Miscellanea"--brief comments and queries by readers; cumulative author index in the fourth issue of each annual volume. In Italian, French, or English.

   Indexed by BIBLIOGRAPHIE DE LA LITTÉRATURE FRANÇAISE, FRENCH VII, FRENCH XX, MLA INTERNATIONAL BIBLIOGRAPHY, and PHILOSOPHER'S INDEX.

CURWOOD, JAMES OLIVER (1878-1927)

American author of adventure stories

1. CURWOOD COLLECTOR. Editor and publisher: Ivan A. Conger, 1825 Osaukie Road, Owosso, Mich. 48867. January 1972-- . Irregular (1-3/yr). $3 (U.S. and Canada); $3.50 (elsewhere). [8-16 p.] Circulation: 200.

   Short stories by Curwood; articles about films based on his works; occasional critical and biographical articles; reproductions of old newspaper clippings, letters, advertisements; occasional bibliographies of Curwood's works, new editions, movies; letters to the editor; illustrations. Back issues available for vols. 1-2 (4 issues each), $2.

CUSANUS, NICOLAUS [NIKOLAUS VON CUES/KUES] (1401-64)

German theologian, statesman, philosopher, humanist

1. Cusanus-Gesellschaft. BUCHREIHE. Editors: Josef Koch and Rudolf Haubst. Sponsor: Cusanus-Gesellschaft. Publisher: Verlag Aschendorff, Münster, Germany (BRD). 1964-- . Irregular. DM10-25. Last issue examined: no. 6, 1975.

   Monographs concerned with such subjects as NIKOLAUS VON KUES: SKIZZE EINER BIOGRAPHIE (1964). In German.

2. Cusanus-Gesellschaft. KLEINE SCHRIFTEN. Sponsor: Cusanus-Gesellschaft. Publisher: Paulinus-Verlag, Trier, Germany (BRD). 1963-- . Irregular. DM2-8; $1.50. [20-100 p.] Last issue examined: no. 10, 1977.

   Each volume is on a different subject, such as DAS GLOBUS-SPIEL DES NIKOLAUS VON KUES (1965). Bibliographies; numerous illustrations and photographs. In German.

   Alternate title:

   KLEINE SCHRIFTEN DER CUSANUS-GESELLSCHAFT

3. MITTEILUNGEN UND FORSCHUNGSBEITRÄGE DER CUSANUS-GESELLSCHAFT (MFCG). Editor: Rudolf Haubst. Sponsor: Vereinigung zur Förderung der Cusanus-Forschung, Cusanus-Institut, Johannes Gutenberg-Universität, Mainz, Germany (BRD). Publisher: Matthias-Grünewald-Verlag, Mainz. 1961-- . Annual. DM30-46. [125-300 p.] Last issue examined: vol. 12, 1977.

   Long scholarly studies of specific titles, their interpretation, themes, and structure; critical, textual, and biographical essays; numerous analyses of problems with the manuscripts; occasional comprehensive, international bibliographies covering several years of Cusanus scholarship, such as "Cusanus-Bibliographie, 1920-61" (vol. 1) and a supplement for the years 1967-73 (vol. 10); long scholarly reviews of international articles and monographs; facsimiles and maps; indexes for names and locations. In German.

   Indexed by Köttelwesch and MLA INTERNATIONAL BIBLIOGRAPHY.

DANIÉLOU, CARDINAL JEAN (1905-74)

French Jesuit philosopher, educator, author

1. BULLETIN DES AMIS DU CARDINAL DANIÉLOU. Editor: Annick Lalle-

mand. Sponsor and publisher: Société des Amis du Cardinal Daniélou, 24, boulevard Victor Hugo, 92200 Neuilly-sur-Seine, France. September 1975-- . Annual. 30 Fr. [50-100 p.] Last issue examined: 1976.

Previously unpublished material, including letters and spiritual notes; reminiscences; bibliographies of Daniélou's works; news of editions, translations, activities of the organization. In French.

DANNAY, FREDERIC [ELLERY QUEEN] (1905-)

American coauthor, with Manfred B. Lee, of the Ellery Queen mysteries

1. ELLERY QUEEN REVIEW. Supersedes QUEEN CANON BIBLIOPHILES (see entry 2). Editor: The Reverend Robert E. Washer, 82 East 8th Street, Oneida Castle, N.Y. 13421. 1971-(?). $3.50/four issues.

   Query returned--addressee unknown.

2. QUEEN CANON BIBLIOPHILES. Superseded by ELLERY QUEEN REVIEW (see entry 1). Editor: The Reverend Robert E. Washer, 82 East 8th Street, Oneida Castle, N.Y. 13421. 1965(?)-1970(?).

   Query returned--addressee unknown.

DANTE ALIGHIERI (1265-1321)

Italian poet

1. L'ALIGHIERI: RASSEGNO BIBLIOGRAFICA DANTESCA. Supersedes GIORNALE DANTESCO (see entry 19). Sponsor: Casa di Dante, Rome, Italy. Administrator: Silvio Zennaro, Piazza S. Sonnino 5, Rome. Publisher: Rassegna Bibliografica Dantesca, Rome. 1960-- . 2/yr. (published in one volume). L.5.000; L.8.000 (foreign). [70-100 p.] Last issue examined: vol. 17, 1976.

   Long scholarly articles on specific aspects of Dante's life and works, such as his relationship to Petrarch and Boccaccio; long scholarly reviews of books and articles; annual bibliography of Dante scholarship in Italy; brief critical annotations for selected books and articles; notices; explicative notes, such as on Francesca; annual index. In Italian, with occasional contributions in English and other languages.

   Indexed by MLA INTERNATIONAL BIBLIOGRAPHY.

   Former titles:

   L'ALIGHIERI: RIVISTA DI COSE DANTESCHE (April 1889-February 1893)

GIORNALE DANTESCO (1893-December 1915)

NUOVO GIORNALE DANTESCO (January 1917-September 1921)

GIORNALE DANTESCO (1921-43?)

2. L'ALIGHIERI: RIVISTA DI COSE DANTESCHE. Superseded by GIORNALE DANTESCO (see entry 19). Editors: Francesco Pasqualigo (1889-93) and Cristoforo Pasqualigo (1893). Publisher: Leo S. Olschki, Verona (1890) and Venice (1891-93), Italy. April 1889-February 1893 (vols. 1-4). Monthly. L.15. [30-70 p.]

Interpretative, biographical, and linguistic studies; bibliographies; notes on new publications; report on Dante Society activities; book reviews; queries; letters. Index for 1889-1910 and 1911-27. In Italian.

3. American Dante Society. YEAR BOOK. Sponsor: American Dante Society, New York. 1890/91-(?). [80 p.]

Reprints of lectures on Dante's life and works; report of Society activities; list of members.

Alternate title:

YEAR BOOK OF THE AMERICAN DANTE SOCIETY

4. ANNALI DELL'ISTITUTO DI STUDI DANTESCHI (AISD). Sponsor: Universita Cattolica del Sacro Cuore, Milan, Italy. Publisher: Società Editrice Vita e Pensiero, Milan. 1967-- . Annual. [400-500 p.]

Subseries of the university's publications in science, philology, and literature--collections of essays concerned with Dante and his works. In Italian.

Indexed by MLA INTERNATIONAL BIBLIOGRAPHY.

Alternate title:

Istituto di Studi Danteschi. ANNALI

5. ANNUAL REPORT OF THE DANTE SOCIETY, WITH ACCOMPANYING PAPERS. Superseded by DANTE STUDIES (see entry 16). Sponsor: Dante Society, Cambridge, Mass. Publisher: John Wilson and Son, University Press, Cambridge, Mass. May 1882-1965 (vols. 1-83). Annual, 1882-1919; intervals of 2-3 yrs., 1920-36; discontinued, 1937-50; annual, 1951-65. [30-100 p.]

Biographical and critical studies; reprints of lectures; annual Dante bibliography of new editions, critical books and articles, with citations of reviews; report on establishment of and acquisitions by the Dante Library at Harvard; news of Society activities; lists of members.

6. BIBLIOTECHINA DI STUDI DANTESCHI. Editor: Aldo Vallone. Publisher: Angelo Signorelli, Rome, Italy. 1971-- .

 In Italian.

7. BULLETIN DE LA SOCIÉTÉ D'ÉTUDES DANTESQUE DU CENTRE UNIVERSITAIRE MÉDITERRANÉEN (BSED). Sponsor and publisher: Société Études Dantesque du Centre Universitaire Méditerranéen, 65, Promenade-des-Anglais, 06034 Nice, France. 1950-- . Irregular. 20-25 Fr. [80-100 p.] Last issue examined: vol. 21, 1973-74.

 Long biographical and critical studies, such as those of Dante in exile and his reliance on astrology and allegory; detailed examinations of his use of language, with numerous quotations. In French.

 Indexed by MLA INTERNATIONAL BIBLIOGRAPHY.

 Alternate title:

 Société d'Études Dantesques. BULLETIN.

8. BULLETTINO DELLA SOCIETÀ DANTESCA ITALIANA. Superseded by STUDI DANTESCHI (see entry 24). Editor: Michele Barbi. Sponsor: Società dantesca italiana, Florence, Italy. Publisher: Salvadore Landi, Florence. First series, March 1890-99 (nos. 1-15); new series, 1893-1921 (vols. 1-28). Irregular, 1890-93; monthly, 1893/94-1905; quarterly, 1906-21. [240-400 p.]

 Long scholarly essays; annual annotated bibliography of Dante criticism; notes on new publications; news of Society events; list of members; facsimiles. Index for 1893-1903 (vols. 1-10). In Italian.

 Subtitle, 1893-21:

 RASSEGNA CRITICA DEGLI STUDI DANTESCHI

 Alternate title:

 Società dantesca italiana. BULLETTINO

9. CUADERNOS DE LA DANTE. Sponsor: Asociación Dante Alighieri, Buenos Aires, Argentina. 1946-- .

10. DANTE. June 1925-June 1928.

11. Dante Society (Cambridge, Mass.).

 See DANTE STUDIES (entry 16).

12. Dante Society (Cambridge, Mass.). PRIZE ESSAYS. 1887-1942. Irregular.

13. Dante Society (London). ANNUAL REPORT. 1904-11. Irregular.

14. Dante Society (London). DANTE SOCIETY LECTURES. Sponsor: Dante Society, 38, Conduit Street, W., London. Publisher: Athenaeum Press, London. 1904-09 (nos. 1-3). [240-45 p.]

    Reprints of lectures delivered at Dante Society meetings--informal, undocumented. In English or Italian.

15. Dante Society (Toronto). OCCASIONAL PAPERS. Sponsor: Dante Society of Toronto. Publisher: University of Toronto Press, Toronto, Canada. 1966-- .

16. DANTE STUDIES, WITH THE ANNUAL REPORT OF THE DANTE SOCIETY (DSARDS). Supersedes ANNUAL REPORT OF THE DANTE SOCIETY (see entry 5). Editor: Anthony L. Pellegrini, Department of Romance Languages, Harpur College, State University of New York at Binghamton, N.Y. 13901. Sponsor: 1882-1966, Dante Society, Cambridge, Mass.; since 1966, Dante Society of America, Boylston Hall, Harvard University, Cambridge, Mass. 02138, in cooperation with the State University of New York at Binghamton and the SUNY Press. Publisher: Baker and Taylor, Somerville, N.J. 1966 (vol.84)-- . Annual (December). Free with membership ($12; family $15). [130-230 p.] Circulation: 600. Last issue examined: vol. 95, 1977.

    Reports of 1881-1965 include "accompanying papers"--critical texts, lists of new additions to library collections (especially Harvard's), translations, interpretive essays, first efforts at a concordance. Since 1953 Anthony L. Pellegrini has been editor of one of the periodical's outstanding features, the annual annotated "American Dante Bibliography," covering all Dante translations, studies, and reviews of the preceding year "that are in any sense American." Since 1966, each volume has contained several long critical essays of "philological, theoretical, interpretive, and comparative interest"; occasional book reviews; annual report, with news of events, announcement of the Dante Prize, and lists of officers and members; portraits and illustrations. Index for 1882-1967 in vol. 86 (1968). In English, with occasional material in Italian.

    Vols. 13-38 (1894-1921) were published for the Society by Ginn, Boston. SUMMARY OF THE FIRST FIFTEEN ANNUAL REPORTS OF THE DANTE SOCIETY was published in Cambridge, Mass. in 1955 (26 p.). Single copies of the current issues are available from the State University of New York Press. Reprints are available from Kraus Reprint (1882-1966, $230).

XCIII

DANTE STUDIES

1975

DANTE STUDIES
with the Annual Report of the Dante Society

XCIII

1975

Indexed by MLA INTERNATIONAL BIBLIOGRAPHY.

Alternate titles from 1881 to 1965:

ANNUAL REPORT OF THE DANTE SOCIETY, WITH ACCOMPANYING PAPERS

REPORT OF THE DANTE SOCIETY

17. DANTOVSKIE CHTENIA. Editor: Igor Belza. Sponsor: Akademiia nauka USSR; Casa Editrice Nauka, Moscow. 1968-- . Irregular. [200-280 p.] Last issue examined: no. 3, 1973.

Collections of character, stylistic, interpretive, and biographical studies by different scholars; occasional illustrations; no index. In Russian.

Title in Italian:

LETTURE DANTESCHE

18. DEUTSCHE DANTE-JAHRBUCH (DDJ). Supersedes JAHRBUCH DER DEUTSCHEN DANTE-GESELLSCHAFT (see entry 20). Editor: Marcella Roddewig, Metzkauserstrasse 21, 4 Düsseldorf-Gerresheim, Germany (BRD). Sponsor: Deutsche Dante-Gesellschaft, Köln and Munich, Germany (BRD). Publisher: Hermann Böhlaus Nachfolger, Köln. 1920-25 (vols. 5-9); new series, 1928 (vol. 10, or new series, vol. 1)-- . Annual. DM35-50. [200-240 p.] Last issue examined: vols. 51-52, 1976-77.

Scholarly studies of Dante's influence on authors and literatures of other countries; criticisms of various translations and editions; interpretive essays, especially on the religious and philosophical aspects of Dante's works; occasional bibliographies covering several years of Dante scholarship; long book reviews; occasional illustrations; index of proper names. In German. Second-hand copies available from Kraus Periodicals (1920-67, $450); reprints from Walter J. Johnson (1920-54, $395).

Indexed by Klapp, Köttelwesch, and MLA INTERNATIONAL BIBLIOGRAPHY.

Alternate title:

JAHRESGABE DER DEUTSCHEN DANTE-GESELLSCHAFT

19. GIORNALE DANTESCO. Supersedes L'ALIGHIERI: RIVISTA DI COSE DANTESCHE (see entry 2); superseded by L'ALIGHIERI: RASSEGNO BIBLIOGRAFICA DANTESCA (see entry 1). Editors: Guiseppe L. Passerini, 1894-1915; Luigi Pietrobono, 1921-43. Publisher: Leo S. Olschki, Venice. 1893-December 1915 (vols. 1-23); suspended publication, 1916-20 (replaced by NUOVO GIORNALE DANTESCO (see entry 23); 1921-27 (vols. 24-30); suspended publication, 1928-29; new series, 1930-

43 (vols. 31-43, or n.s. vols. 1-13). Monthly, 1894-1904; bimonthly, 1905-15; quarterly, 1921-27; annual, 1930-43. [50-100 p.]

Long studies of Dante's life, works, background, characters; annotated bibliography of Dante scholarship; book reviews; report of Society activities; annual analytical index. Index for 1889-1910 and 1911-27. In Italian.

20. JAHRBUCH DER DEUTSCHEN DANTE-GESELLSCHAFT. Superseded by DEUTSCHE DANTE-JAHRBUCH (see entry 18). Editors: Karl Witte, vols. 1-3; J.A. Scartazzini, vol. 4. Sponsor: Deutsche Dante-Gesellschaft. Publisher: F.A. Brockhaus, Leipzig, Germany (DDR). 1867-77 (vols. 1-4); suspended 1878-1919. [400-680 p.]

Long scholarly studies of Dante's life and works; textual studies and emendations; international bibliographies of Dante scholarship; report of the Dante Gesellschaft; list of members; portraits, maps, and facsimiles; no index. In German, with occasional contributions in English.

Alternate title:

Deutsche Dante-Gesellschaft. JAHRBUCH

21. MITTEILUNGSBLATT DER DEUTSCHEN DANTE-GESELLSCHAFT. Sponsor: Deutsche Dante-Gesellschaft. Publisher: Bonn and Köln, Germany (BRD). 1970(?)-- . Annual.

In German.

Indexed by Köttelwesch.

Alternate title:

Deutsche Dante-Gesellschaft. MITTEILUNGSBLATT

22. NUOVE LETTURE DANTESCHE. Sponsor: Casa di Dante, in Roma, Palazzetto degli Anguillara, Piazza Sonnino, 5, Rome, Italy. Publisher: Felice le Monnier, Florence, Italy. 1966-- . Annual. L.8.000-10.000. [300-400 p.] Last issue examined: vol. 7, 1974.

Each volume contains a collection of critical studies by Italian scholars on a specific title in Dante's canon; no index. In Italian. Vol. 8 not yet published (1978).

23. NUOVO GIORNALE DANTESCO. Supersedes and superseded by GIORNALE DANTESCO (see entry 19). Editor: Guiseppe L. Passerini. Publisher: La Direzione, Florence, Italy. January 1917-September 1921 (vols. 1-5). 3/yr.(1917-20); quarterly, 1921.

Numerous long scholarly essays on Dante's works, characters, influence; annotated "Bibliografia dantesca"; news of Society events, members' activities, international research, lectures, and conferences. Index for 1889-1910 and 1911-27. In Italian.

24. STUDI DANTESCHI (SD). Supersedes BULLETTINO DELLA SOCIETÀ DANTESCA ITALIANA (see entry 8). Editors: Founded by Michele Barbi, 1920-43; since 1971, Gianfranco Contini and Francesco Mazzoni. Sponsor: Società dantesca italiana. Publisher: G.C. Sansoni, Florence, Italy. Subscriptions: LICOSA, via Lamarmore 45, 50121 Florence. Distributor in England: Interbrook Ltd., 12 Fitzroy Street, London W.1. 1920-43 (vols. 1-27); publication suspended, 1944-48; 1949 (vol. 28)-- . Irregular. L.11.00; £7.50; $17. [200-370 p.] Last issue examined: vol. 50, 1973.

    Long critical articles on Dante's life and works; brief notes on specific problems; comprehensive international bibliographies covering several years of Dante scholarship--the best in the field, arranged by year, general subject, title of Dante's work, with annotations for both books and articles in periodicals; book reviews; news of Society activities; illustrations. Index for vols. 1-20 in vol. 20. In Italian, with occasional material in English, French, or German. Second-hand copies available from Kraus Periodicals (1920-69, $918); reprints from Walter J. Johnson (vols. 1-46, $885). Vol. 51 not yet published (1978).

    Indexed by MLA INTERNATIONAL BIBLIOGRAPHY.

DANTIN, LOUIS

See Seers, Eugène.

DE GAULLE, CHARLES (1890-1970)

French statesman, soldier

1. ESPOIR: REVUE DE L'INSTITUT CHARLES DE GAULLE. Sponsor: Institut Charles de Gaulle. September 1972-- . Quarterly. Last issue examined: no. 17, 1976.

    Previously unpublished material, including de Gaulle's letters to Claudel; critical articles on contemporaries, including Malraux.

    Indexed by FRENCH XX.

2. ÉTUDES GAULLIENNES. Editor: Jean-Paul Cointet, 4, square Émile-Zola, 75015 Paris. Director: Charles Dédeyan. Sponsor and publisher: Cercles Universitaires d'Études et de Recherches Gaulliennes. President: Jean-Paul Bled, 26, rue de la Canardière, 67100 Strasbourg-Meinau, France. January 1973-- . Quarterly. 60 Fr; 50 Fr (members); 70 Fr

(foreign). [85-200 p.] Last issue examined: vol. 5, 1977.

Designed to analyze the spirit, sources, and themes of General de Gaulle and to study the different aspects of this work. Long studies of de Gaulle's influence on French and international affairs and ideas both during and after his lifetime; reminiscences; biographical articles, such as those on his travels and speeches; book reviews; reports of the various branches of the Cercles Universitaires; reports of the annual international colloquia. In French.

DEGÉE, OLIVIER [JEAN TOUSSEUL] (1890-1944)

Belgian author

1. CAHIERS JEAN TOUSSEUL. Editor: Jean Paul Bonnami, 6, boulevard du Château, Ath, Belgium. Sponsor: Association des Amis de Jean Tousseul. October 1946-- . Quarterly. $4. Circulation: 1,500.

   Interested in the French influence on Belgian literature, especially that of Jean Tousseul. Brief critical articles; bibliographies; book reviews; illustrations. In French. Second-hand copies available from Kraus Periodicals (1946-56, $25).

Indexed by BIBLIOGRAPHIE DE LA LITTÉRATURE FRANÇAISE and Klapp.

DELISLE, LÉOPOLD (1826-1910)

French medievalist, head of the Bibliothèque nationale

1. CAHIERS LÉOPOLD DELISLE: REVUE TRIMESTRIELLE DE LA SOCIÉTÉ PARISIENNE D'HISTOIRE ET D'ARCHÉOLOGIE NORMANDES (Cah.L. Delisle). Editor: Michel Nortier, 26, rue de Sucy, 94450 Limeil-Brévannes, France. Sponsor: Société Parisienne d'Histoire et d'Archéologie Normandes (S.P.H.A.N.), 14 bis, rue Charles-VII, 94130 Nogent-sur-Marne, France. Publisher: Jouve, with the approval of Centre National de la Recherche Scientifique. 1947-- . Irregular. 25-30 Fr. [35-80 p.] Last issue examined: vol. 26, 1977.

   Inspired by the scholarship and contributions of Delisle, but only incidentally concerned with his personal works. Each volume is devoted to a specific subject, such as ENQUÊTE SUR LE FOLKLORE DE LA FORÊT ET DE L'ARBRE EN NORMANDE (1975). Bibliographies; illustrations. In French.

Indexed by Klapp.

DESCARTES, RENÉ (1596-1650)

French mathematician, philosopher

1. CAHIERS DU CERCLE DESCARTES. 1936-39.

   Occasional articles on Descartes. In French.

DESTOUCHES, LOUIS-FERDINAND [LOUIS-FERDINAND CÉLINE] (1894-1961)

French novelist, dramatist

1. Archives Céline. Subseries of Archives des Lettres Modernes. 1971-- . Irregular. 12 Fr. [95 p.] Equivalent numbers are provided below for both the parent series (Archives des Lettres Modernes) and the individual series on Céline.

Céline subseries	Archives series	Date
No. 1	No. 129	1971
No. 2	No. 164	1976

   In French. See Camus, Albert, entry 2, for a full description of Archives des Lettres Modernes.

   Indexed by BULLETIN CRITIQUE, FRENCH XX, Klapp, and MLA INTERNATIONAL BIBLIOGRAPHY.

2. L.-F. Céline. Subseries of La Revue des Lettres Modernes. Editor: Jean-Pierre Dauphin. 1974-- . Irregular. Equivalent numbers are provided below for both the parent series (La Revue des Lettres Modernes) and the individual author series on Céline.

Céline subseries	La Revue series	Date
No. 1	Nos. 398-402	1974
No. 2	Nos. 462-67	1976

   In French. See Camus, Albert, entry 1, for a full description of La Revue des Lettres Modernes.

   Indexed by BULLETIN CRITIQUE, FRENCH XX, Klapp, and MLA INTERNATIONAL BIBLIOGRAPHY.

DEUBEL, LÉON (1879-1913)

French author

1. Société des Amis de Léon Deubel. BULLETIN. Editor: Eugène Chatot, 16, rue Jules-Dumien, 75020 Paris. Publisher: Subervie, Rodez, France. 1927-(?). Irregular. Last issue examined: vols. 35-36, 1961.

   Articles on Deubel's friendships and influence; letters. In French.

Indexed by BIBLIOGRAPHIE DE LA LITTÉRATURE FRANÇAISE, FRENCH VII, and Klapp.

Alternate title:

BULLETIN DE LA SOCIÉTÉ DES AMIS DE LÉON DEUBEL

DEWEY, JOHN (1859-1952)

American philosopher, teacher

1. DEWEY NEWSLETTER. Editor: Jo Ann Boydston, Center for Dewey Studies, 803 South Oakland, Southern Illinois University, Carbondale, Ill. 62901. Sponsor: Center for Dewey Studies, Southern Illinois University. January 1967-- . Quarterly, 1967-70; 2/yr., since 1971. Free. [4-6 p.] Circulation: 800. Last issue examined: vol. 12, 1978.

   Interested in cooperative research on Dewey material--brief progress reports on the publication of new editions, anthologies, awards to work in progress; accounts of discoveries of new Dewey manuscripts, location of quotations, new biographical tidbits; brief bibliographies of current scholarship; notes on gifts and other library acquisitions; deletions and additions to the Dewey canon; contributions to a checklist of Dewey criticism; assessment of publications, such as the selection of Dewey's poems as approved by MLA's Center for Editions of American Authors; book reviews; translations of criticism from foreign publications; news of completed dissertations; report on the John Dewey Research Fund; looseleaf format; no index.

2. STUDIES IN EDUCATIONAL THEORY. Sponsor: John Dewey Society. 1963-- . Irregular. $6. Last issue examined: vol. 7, 1970.

DICKENS, CHARLES (1812-70)

English novelist

1. CDRC REPORT: A NEWS LETTER. Superseded by DICKENS STUDIES (see entry 3). Sponsor and publisher: Charles Dickens Reference Center, Lesley College, Cambridge, Mass. 02138. September 1963-64(?). Irregular. [12 p.]

   CDRC (pronounced Cedric): Charles Dickens Reference Center, "a library research institute dedicated to the encouragement and advancement of the studies of the novelist's life and works." Brief articles and notes; quotations.

2. DICKENSIAN. Editor: Andrew Sanders, 48, Doughty Street, London WC1N 2LF, or Birkbeck College, Malet Street, London WC1E 7HX. Sponsor and publisher: Dickens Fellowship, The Dickens House, 48,

Doughty Street, London WC1N 2LF. January 1905-- . 3/yr. (January, May, September). Free with membership (£2); nonmembers: U.K., £3, and overseas, £3.50; institutions: U.K., £4, and overseas, £4.50. [60-200 p.] Circulation: 2,250. Last issue examined: vol. 74, no. 386, 1978.

Official organ of the Dickens Fellowship. Emphasizes biography and history but encourages critical articles on every aspect of Dickens' life and work; tries to give wide coverage to activities of the Fellowship, which has branches in Australia, Canada, Ceylon, the Netherlands, Japan, New Zealand, South Africa, South America, and the United States. Annual survey (since 1968) in the September issue of all work on Dickens in scholarly journals during the previous year; numerous brief book reviews in every issue; reports of the annual conference, lectures given at Society functions by such noted scholars as Chesterton, Orwell, and Priestley, events of the Dickens Festival, and chronology of coming events; news of members' activities all over the world, television programs, tours, films, performances; information on British theses completed; letters to the editor; obituaries; list of international branches of the Dickens Fellowship; illustrations, plates, and portraits; reproductions of "Phiz" and Cruikshank. Annual index by author, subject, and title is included in the January issue for the preceding year. Index for 1905-34 (vols. 1-30) and 1935-60 (vols. 31-56). Reprints available from Kraus Reprint (1905-68, $1,097; 1969-72, $64) and from Walter J. Johnson (1905-72 with index, $1,160). Microfiche available from Harvester Press (1905-74, £195). Frank T. Dunn has prepared A CUMULATIVE ANALYTICAL INDEX TO "THE DICKENSIAN," 1905-74 (Hassocks, Sussex: Harvester Press, 1976).

Indexed by ABSTRACTS OF ENGLISH STUDIES, ANNUAL BIBLIOGRAPHY OF ENGLISH LANGUAGE AND LITERATURE, BRITISH HUMANITIES INDEX, INDEX TO BOOK REVIEWS IN THE HUMANITIES, MLA INTERNATIONAL BIBLIOGRAPHY, and VICTORIAN STUDIES.

Alternate subtitles:

MAGAZINE FOR DICKENS LOVERS AND MONTHLY RECORD OF DICKENS FELLOWSHIP

MAGAZINE FOR DICKENS LOVERS

QUARTERLY MAGAZINE FOR DICKENS LOVERS

3. DICKENS STUDIES: A JOURNAL OF MODERN RESEARCH AND CRITICISM (DS; DiS). Supersedes CDRC REPORT (see entry 1); superseded by DICKENS STUDIES ANNUAL (see entry 4). Editors: Laurence P. Senelick, 65 Sparks Street, Cambridge, Mass. 02116; Noel C. Peyrouton. Sponsor: Emerson College, 148 Beacon Street, Boston, Mass. 02116. January 1965-May 1969 (vols. 1-5). 3/yr. (January, May, September), 1965-67; 2/yr. (March, October), 1967-69. $3.50. [50-100 p.]

Long articles on Dickens' life and background, his novels, literary technique, contributions to periodicals, and influence on other literatures; book reviews; facsimiles.

Indexed by ANNUAL BIBLIOGRAPHY OF ENGLISH LANGUAGE AND LITERATURE, MLA INTERNATIONAL BIBLIOGRAPHY, and YEAR'S WORK IN ENGLISH STUDIES.

4. DICKENS STUDIES ANNUAL (DSA). Supersedes DICKENS STUDIES (see entry 3). Editor: Robert B. Partlow, Jr., Department of English, Southern Illinois University, Carbondale, Ill. 62901. Sponsor: Southern Illinois University Press, P.O. Box 3697, Carbondale, Ill. 62901. Publisher: Southern Illinois University Press, and Feffer and Simons, London and Amsterdam. November 1970-- . Annual (November). $15, hardbound. [200-300 p.] Circulation: 1,800. Last issue examined: vol. 7, 1978.

Interested in every aspect of Dickens' life, times, and work. Long (20 p.) critical essays on the characters, themes, plot, and style in the novels, including Dickens' social comments and humor; scholarly prefaces describe and evaluate the essays contained in the volume, survey their position in contemporary scholarship, refer to past studies, and make suggestions for future research possibilities; occasional illustrations and portraits; subject, title, and author index in each volume.

Indexed by ABSTRACTS OF ENGLISH STUDIES, AMERICAN HUMANITIES INDEX, ANNUAL BIBLIOGRAPHY OF ENGLISH LANGUAGE AND LITERATURE, MLA INTERNATIONAL BIBLIOGRAPHY, VICTORIAN STUDIES, and YEAR'S WORK IN ENGLISH STUDIES.

5. DICKENS STUDIES NEWSLETTER (DSN). Editor: Duane DeVries, Department of Humanities, Polytechnic Institute of New York, 333 Jay Street, Brooklyn, N.Y. 11201. Review editor: Jerome Meckier, Department of English, University of Kentucky, Lexington, Ky. 40506. Sponsor: 1970-71, DICKENS STUDIES ANNUAL (see entry 4); since 1971, Dickens Society. Publisher: Office of Academic Publication, University of Louisville, Building M55D, 500 South Preston Street, P.O. Box 35260, Louisville, Ky. 40232. March 1970-- . Quarterly (March, June, September, December). Free with membership ($7); $1.75 per issue. [32 p.] Circulation: 500. Last issue examined: vol. 9, 1978.

Brief critical or biographical articles; checklist of works by and about Dickens in every quarterly issue--includes new editions, critical books and articles, reviews, films, tapes, plays, readings, objective testing devices; special bibliographies; numerous long book reviews; news and notes of meetings, projects, symposia, awards, member and Society activities; announcements of forthcoming publications and special events; occasional reports of work in progress; report from the MLA meeting of the Dickens Society; letters to the editor; occasional illustrations; annual index in the December issue. Vol. 1 issued in three numbers.

DICKENS STUDIES NEWSLETTER

Vol. VII, No. 2
June 1976

Indexed by ABSTRACTS OF ENGLISH STUDIES, AMERICAN HUMANITIES INDEX, ANNUAL BIBLIOGRAPHY OF ENGLISH LANGUAGE AND LITERATURE, ENGLISH LANGUAGE NOTES, MLA INTERNATIONAL BIBLIOGRAPHY, VICTORIAN STUDIES, and YEAR'S WORK IN ENGLISH STUDIES.

DICKINSON, EMILY (1830-86)

American poet

1. AUCTION OF THE MIND: A JOURNAL OF EMILY DICKINSON STUDIES.

   Announced but never published.

2. EMILY DICKINSON BOOKS (ED BOOKS). Sponsors: Mary Gaumond, Frederick L. Morey, and Stacy Tuthill. Publisher: ED BOOKS, 4508 38th Street, Brentwood, Md. 20722. 1975-- . Irregular. Price varies.

   Short studies of Emily Dickinson's poetry.

3. EMILY DICKINSON BULLETIN (EDB). Editor: Frederick L. Morey, 4508 38th Street, Brentwood, Md. 20722. Publisher: Higginson Press, 4508 38th Street, Brentwood, Md. 20722. January 1968-78. 2/yr. (June, December). Individuals: $5/first yr., $14/three-yr. renewals; institutions: $10/first yr., $30/three-yr. renewals. [25-50 p.] Circulation: 100. Superseded by DICKINSON STUDIES (see Addenda).

   Critical, biographical, and bibliographical articles, frequently by the editor, on Dickinson's poetry and times; numerous explications; annual bibliography in December; occasional issues focus on special aspects, such as Dickinson in Brazil or Japan; reviews; notes; announcements of MLA seminars and new publications, including the annotated Dickinson bibliography planned for publication in 1980; annual index. Index for January 1968-December 1974 (nos. 1-26) arranged by author, subject, and periodical title. Membership in the Emily Dickinson Society includes subscriptions to the EMILY DICKINSON BULLETIN and the HIGGINSON JOURNAL OF POETRY (see Higginson, Thomas, entry 1.).

Indexed by AMERICAN HUMANITIES INDEX, ANNUAL BIBLIOGRAPHY OF ENGLISH LANGUAGE AND LITERATURE.

DIDEROT, DENIS (1713-84)

French philosopher, author

1. Archives des Lettres Modernes. 1966-- . Irregular. Series numbers for the issues on Diderot provided below.

Diderot subseries	Archives series	Date
Unnumbered	No. 68	1966
Unnumbered	No. 79	1967
Unnumbered	No. 177	1977

In French. See Camus, Albert, entry 2, for a full description of Archives des Lettres Modernes.

Indexed by BULLETIN CRITIQUE, Klapp, and MLA INTERNATIONAL BIBLIOGRAPHY.

2. Diderot Studies (DidS). Editors: Otis E. Fellows, Columbia University, New York, N.Y. 10023; and Diana Guiragossian, Indiana University, Bloomington, Ind. 47401. Sponsors and publishers: 1949-52, Syracuse University Press, Syracuse, N.Y. 13210; since 1953, Librairie Droz, Geneva. 1949-- . Irregular (a series). $13-22. [150-450 p.] Last issue examined: vol. 18, 1975.

Collections of long (10-20 p.) essays representing "various critical approaches and diverse points of view" on Diderot's life and works--textual problems, poetic experiences, translations, politics, analyses and views about specific titles; numerous long book reviews and review articles on eighteenth-century authors and ideas; international contributors; no index. In French or English.

Indexed by Klapp and MLA INTERNATIONAL BIBLIOGRAPHY.

DIEUDONNÉ, LUCIEN [LUCIEN JEAN] (1870-1908)

French novelist, poet

See Philippe, Charles-Louis, entry 1.

DISRAELI, BENJAMIN, 1ST EARL OF BEACONSFIELD (1804-81)

English statesman, writer

1. DISRAELI NEWSLETTER (DN). Editor: J.P. Matthews. Sponsor and publisher; Disraeli Project, Queen's University, Kingston, Canada K7L 3N6. April 1976-- . 2/yr. (April, October). Free. [25-40 p.] Circulation: 1,000. Last issue examined: vol. 1, no. 2, October 1976.

Created for the purpose of gathering and disseminating information about Disraeli in behalf of the forthcoming edition of his letters. The editors intend to include "discoveries, research methods, desiderata, and questions which we and you may wish to ask on specific problems." Short, unpretentious, and sometimes witty articles on Disraeli, Victorian politics, and Victorian literature and society; book reviews.

Indexed by MLA INTERNATIONAL BIBLIOGRAPHY and VICTORIAN STUDIES.

DODGSON, CHARLES LUTWIDGE [LEWIS CARROLL] (1832-98)

English author, mathematician

1. BANDERSNATCH: THE LEWIS CARROLL SOCIETY NEWSLETTER. Editor: Brian Sibley, 55, Heath Cottages, Chislehurst Common, Chislehurst, Kent, England. Sponsor: Lewis Carroll Society, 69, Ashby Road, Woodville, Burton-on-Trent, Staffordshire, England. 1973-- . Irregular. Free with membership (£4 or $9, individuals; £5 or $11, institutions). Last issue examined: no. 16, 1976.

   "A light-hearted newsletter [that] keeps members informed with details of Society activities, and news of books, plays, films, and Carrollian ephemera."

2. CARROLL STUDIES. Sponsor: Lewis Carroll Society of North America, New York. Secretary: 617 Rockford Drive, Silver Spring, Md. 20902. 1975-- . Free with membership ($10). [16 p.] Last issue examined: vol. 2, 1977.

   "An occasional chapbook series." Interested in material concerned with the life, work, time, and influence of Lewis Carroll. No. 1 (1975) is a briefly annotated, international bibliography of Carroll scholarship published during 1974--new editions, reference works, biographies, and criticism in books and periodicals (supplements are scheduled). Index by title, author, and subject.

3. JABBERWOCKY: THE JOURNAL OF THE LEWIS CARROLL SOCIETY (England). Editor: Selwyn H. Goodacre. Sponsor: Lewis Carroll Society, 69, Ashby Road, Woodville, Burton-on-Trent, Staffordshire, England. Secretary: Edward Wakeling, 36, Bradgers Hill Road, Luton, Bedfordshire, England. October 1969-- . Quarterly. Free with membership (£4 or $9, individuals; £5 or $11, institutions; £2 or $6, students). [28-36 p.] Circulation: 350. Last issue examined: vol. 6, 1977.

   Informal articles on Carroll's life and work, especially as the material pertains to his stories about Alice; descriptions and evaluations of all new editions of Carroll's works and of all scholarship relating to him, such as studies of his illustrators and biographies of his friends; occasional bibliographies or bibliographic essays; book, play, and film reviews; occasional special issues devoted to one subject; previously unpublished material; reprints of inaccessible material; news of translations, work in progress, annual symposia of the Society (activity reports are in the Society newsletter, BANDERSNATCH, see entry 1); letters to the editor with textual corrections, suggested explications, and collectors' news; occasional illustrations and facsimiles. Index is planned.

Indexed by VICTORIAN STUDIES.

Alternate subtitle, October 1969-Summer 1972:

THE LEWIS CARROLL SOCIETY MAGAZINE

DOSTOEVSKY, FEODOR (1821-81)

Russian novelist

1. Dostoevsky Research Association. Editors: Nadine Popluiko-Natov, Department of Slavic Languages and Literatures, George Washington University, Washington, D.C. 20006; and N.V. Pervushin, Department of Russian, McGill University, Montreal 2, Canada. 1971-- .

   Report on international meetings and exchange of information; newsletter planned.

2. International Dostoevsky Society. BULLETIN (IDS Bulletin). Editors: Rudoff Neuhäuser, University of Klagenfurt, A-9010 Klagenfurt, Austria; and Martin Rice, Department of Germanic and Slavic Languages, University of Tennessee, Knoxville, Tenn. 37916. Sponsor: University of Tennessee. February 1972-- . Annual. $2.25 (individuals); $4.25 (institutions); $1.25 (students). [95-100 p.] Circulation: 100. Last issue examined: vol. 6, 1976.

   Resumés of research papers delivered at the symposia; extensive bibliographies, including the most complete current international bibliographical information on Dostoevsky to be found anywhere, in both Slavic and non-Slavic languages; book reviews and long review articles; news of the North American Dostoevsky Society annual meeting and of the Dostoevsky symposia which are held every three or four years; news of conferences, lectures, members' publications, theatre productions, fellowships, work in progress; international contributors and international editorial board. The editor encourages short notes and observations concerning the life and work of Dostoevsky and solicits queries relating to current research projects. In English, Russian, or French.

   Alternate titles:

   BULLETIN OF THE INTERNATIONAL DOSTOEVSKY SOCIETY

   Title in French: SOCIÉTÉ INTERNATIONALE DES ÉTUDES DOSTOIEVSKIENNES

   Title in Russian: MEZHDUNARODNAIA ASSOTSIATSIIA DOSTOEVSKOVEDOV

DOUCET, JACQUES (1853-1929)

French poet, artist

1. CAHIERS JACQUES DOUCET. Publisher: Paris. 1934-(?).

   In French.

DOYLE, SIR ARTHUR CONAN (1859-1930)

English novelist

1. ADVENTURESSES OF SHERLOCK HOLMES NEWSLETTER (ASH). Editor: Kate Karlson, 151 West 16th Street, Apt. 3E, New York, N.Y. 10011. Managing editor: Pat Moran, 12 West 19th Street, New York, N.Y. April 1975-- . Quarterly (January, April, July, October). $3. [5 p.] Circulation: 80. Last issue examined: vol. 2, no. 3, October 1976.

   "The only feminist Sherlockian publication." Articles on Sherlockian thoughts; book or movie reviews; poetry; letters to the editor; news items of interest to women Sherlockians. To be retitled SERPENTINE MUSE.

2. ARNSWORTH CASTLE BUSINESS INDEX. Sponsor: Arnsworth Castle, Scion Society of the Baker Street Irregulars, Pittsburgh, Pa. June 1960-February 1964 (nos. 1-16). Irregular.

   Bibliographical series by Robert H. Schutz.

3. BAKER STREET CAB LANTERN. Editor: Ted Bergman, Storkvagen 10, 181 35 Lidingo, Sweden. Sponsor: Solitary Cyclists of Sweden, Stockholm. 1963-- . Annual. Last issue examined: no. 11, 1973.

   Articles; book reviews; bibliographies; illustrations. Text in Swedish and English. No reply to query.

4. BAKER STREET CHRISTMAS STOCKING: BEING A MISCELLANY OF HOLMESIAN TRIVIA CONTRIVED TO CONVEY IRREGULAR GREETINGS AT CHRISTMAS. Editor and sponsor: [James] Bliss Austin, 114 Buckingham Road, Pittsburgh, Pa. 15215. Publisher: Hydraulic Press, 114 Buckingham Road, Pittsburgh, Pa. 15215. 1953-56, 1958-60, 1962-- . Annual. Free (limited to 50 copies). [4-13 p.]

   A Christmas annual. Brief articles on textual, biographical, and bibliographical problems, allusions, character analyses; previously unpublished works, such as a series of cartoons based on a Sherlock Holmes story; facsimiles and illustrations. Recent back issues available.

5. BAKER STREET COLLECTING. Editors: G.L. Puhl and Ray Funk. February 1968-September 1969. Irregular.

Articles; illustrations.

6. BAKER STREET GASOGENE: A SHERLOCKIAN QUARTERLY. Editor: Peter A. Ruber. 1961-62 (vol. 1, nos. 1-4). Quarterly.

   Articles; illustrations.

7. BAKER STREET JOURNAL: A QUARTERLY OF SHERLOCKIANA (BSJ). Editor: Julian Wolff, 33 Riverside Drive, New York, N.Y. 10023. Publisher: Fordham University Press, Box L, Bronx, N.Y. 10458. Sponsor: Baker Street Irregulars, New York. January 1946-49; suspended publication, 1950; new series, 1951-- . Quarterly. $10. Circulation: 1,100. Last issue examined: vol. 28, 1978.

   Articles; bibliography in every issue; reviews; news and notes; illustrations; Christmas annual; annual subject index. BAKER STREET JOURNAL 1946-69: A CUMULATED INDEX TO THE BAKER STREET JOURNAL, available from Julian Wolff ($5). SUBJECT INDEX TO BAKER STREET JOURNAL, VOLUMES 20-24, 1970 to 1974, comp. Donald A. Redmond, 178 Barrie Street, Kingston, Ontario, Canada K7L 3K1 ($3; 28 p.). Reprints available from Walter J. Johnson (1946-49, 1951-69, $565).

   Indexed by ABSTRACTS OF ENGLISH STUDIES, AMERICAN HUMANITIES INDEX, ANNUAL BIBLIOGRAPHY OF ENGLISH LANGUAGE AND LITERATURE, MLA INTERNATIONAL BIBLIOGRAPHY, and VICTORIAN STUDIES.

   Alternate subtitle:

   AN IRREGULAR QUARTERLY OF SHERLOCKIANA

8. BAKER STREET MISCELLANEA. Editors: William D. Goodrich, 182 Forest Avenue, Winnetka, Ill. 60093; John Nieminski and Donald K. Pollock, Jr. Sponsor: Advisory Committee on Popular Culture, Northeastern Illinois University, Chicago, Ill. 60625. Publisher: Sciolist Press, Box 2579, Chicago, Ill. 60690. April 1975-- . Quarterly. $4; $6 (overseas); $1.50 per issue. [30 p.] Circulation: 200. Last issue examined: no. 7, 1976.

   Articles investigating Holmes's biography and commenting on plots, characters, influences; occasional specialized articles, such as a reference guide to Doyle's allusions to geographical locations, military units, and other subjects (no. 7, 1976); reprints of lectures and papers; reprints of parodies; book reviews; poems; puzzles; news of paperback and other editions, television programs, films, plays, conventions, annual dinners; sketches; no index.

9. BAKER STREET PAGES. Editors: Chris Redmond, 178 Barrie Street,

Kingston, Ontario, Canada K7L 3K1; and Glenn Holland and Andrew Page, 3130 Irwin Avenue, Bronx, N.Y. 10463. Sponsor: Baker Street Pageboys. July 1965-July 1970 (nos. 1-54); new series, June 1971-July 1972. Monthly. Circulation: 100. $.40 per copy.

Occasional Christmas annuals, as in 1966.

10. BULLETIN. Editor: James R. Stefanie. Sponsor: Unknowns of Buffalo, N.Y. July 1963-July 1964. Monthly.

Articles; illustrations.

11. CANADIAN HOLMES. Editor: Ira Blatt, 120 Bedford Road, Toronto, Ontario, Canada M5R 2K2. Sponsor: Bootmakers of Toronto, 221B Central Library, College and St. George Streets, Toronto M5T 1R3. Fall 1973-- . Irregular, 1973-76; quarterly since 1977. Free. [10 p.] Circulation: 150.

Editorial policy "goes on the theory that Holmes and Watson were or are reál persons, and that Arthur Conan Doyle was Watson's literary agent. It is mainly intended to amuse rather than inform, and will interest those who are involved with Sherlock Holmes as collectors or connoisseurs." Critical essays; brief notes and news; parodies; illustrations.

12. COMMONPLACE BOOK. Editor: W.T. Rabe. Sponsor: Old Soldiers of Baker Street, 2271 Pinecrest Avenue, Ferndale, Mich. 48220. Summer 1964-June 1969 (vols. 1-5, no. 19). Irregular.

Reprints of articles and reviews; illustrations.

13. CORMORANTS' RING. Editor: Dean W. Dickensheet. Sponsor: Trained Cormorants of Los Angeles County, Calif. September 1958-September 1960. Irregular.

Articles; illustrations.

14. DEVON COUNTRY CHRONICLE: SERVING THE PARISHES OF GRIMPEN, THORSLEY AND HIGH BARROW. Editor: Robert W. Hahn, 509 South Ahrens Avenue, Lombard, Ill. 60148. Sponsor: Hugo's Companions, B.S.I. December 1964-- . Irregular (5-6/yr.). $3. Circulation: 200. Last issue examined: vol. 12, no. 5, 1976.

Concerned not only with Sherlock Holmes but also with the age of Victoria and the mystery-detective-suspense field in general. Critical essays; short short stories; poems; bibliographies; book reviews; news and notes; illustrations; cartoons; index.

15. ENCYCLICAL LETTER. Editors: Russell McLauchlin and W.T. Rabe, Detroit, Mich. Sponsor: Amateur Mendicant Society. April 1953-(?).

16. FEATHERS FROM THE NEST. Editor: Vic Hale, 11911 N.E. Halsey, Portland, Oreg. 97220. Sponsor: The Noble and Most Singular Order of the Blue Carbuncle, 7033 N.E. Flanders, Portland, Oreg. 97213. October 1971-- . Irregular (4-6/yr.). $2; $4, new members. Circulation: 50. Last issue examined: vol. 7, no. 1, March 1977.

    Brief articles; reviews; bibliographies; illustrations.

17. GAMEBAG. Sponsor: Gamekeepers of Northern Minnesota, Buhl, Minn. 55713. 1965-69. Circulation: limited to 50.

    A Christmas annual. Articles; illustrations.

18. GARROTER. Editors: P. Stephen Clarkson and Rose M. Vogel. 1041 Camelot Gardens Drive, St. Louis, Mo. 63125. Sponsor: The Cavendish Squares, St. Louis. March 1972-- . 2/yr. $.60.

    Critical articles; book reviews; illustrations by Sue Murphy. No reply to query.

19. GENERAL COMMUNICATION. Editor and publisher: The Reverend Benton Wood, 4400 Gulf Drive, Holmes Beach, Fla. 33510. Sponsor: Baker Street Irregulars. June 1972-- . 6/yr. Free. [2 p.] Circulation: 60.

    Brief notes on references in the media to Sherlock Holmes and the canon.

20. GROWLER. Editors: R. Cogan Clyne and George J. McCormack. Sponsor: Diogenes Club of Brooklyn, N.Y. 1950; November 1958.

21. HOLMESIAN OBSERVER. Superseded by HOLMESIAN OBSERVER--1975 ANNUAL (see entry 22). Editor: Andrew Page, 3130 Irwin Avenue, Bronx, N.Y. 10463. Sponsor: Three Garridebs Scion of the Baker Street Irregulars. March 1971-June 1974 (vols. 1-4, no. 2). Irregular. [20 p.] $1 per issue.

    Critical articles; news notes; occasional book reviews; special annual volumes. Back issues available from the editor.

22. HOLMESIAN OBSERVER--1975 ANNUAL. Supersedes HOLMESIAN OBSERVER (see entry 21). Editor: Andrew Page, 3130 Irwin Avenue, Bronx, N.Y. 10463. 1975-- . Annual. $2. [45 p.]

    Critical articles on the Sherlock Holmes canon.

23. HOLMESWORK. Editor: Robert M. Broderick, 49 Woodale Road, Philadelphia, Pa. 19118. Sponsor: The Master's Class, Gwynedd Valley, Pa. April 1974-- .

    Articles; illustrations.

24. HURLSTONE PAPERS: A QUARTERLY OF HOLMESIANA. Editors: William J. Walsh and P. Stephen Clarkson, 6 Ernst Drive, Suffern, N.Y. 10901. Sponsor: The Musgrave Ritualists Beta, Suffern, N.Y. Summer 1971-(?).

    No reply to query.

25. INVESTIGATIONS: AN IRREGULAR JOURNAL OF ATLANTA-AREA SHERLOCKIANA. Editor: Mrs. E.M. Hughes, Atlanta, Ga. Sponsor: Confederates of Wisteria Lodge. January 1971-(?).

    Articles; illustrations.

26. IRREGULAR REPORT. Editor: Poul Arenfalk. Sponsor: Literary League, The King of Scandinavia's Own Sherlockians, Copenhagen, Denmark. April 1960-November 1965. Irregular.

    Articles; news.

27. JOURNAL OF THE AMATEUR MENDICANT SOCIETY OF MADISON, WISCONSIN. Editor: Perri Corrick, 1308 Spring Street, Apartment 211, Madison, Wis. 53715. Publisher: Perriwinkle Press. Spring 1972-(?).

    Articles; illustrations by William Jensen. No reply to query.

28. KANSAS CITY DAILY JOURNAL. Editor and publisher: Jon L. Lellenberg, 4501 West 90th Street, Shawnee Mission, Kans. 66207. Sponsor: The Great Alkali Plainsmen of Greater Kansas City, Scion Society of The Baker Street Irregulars. February 1976-- . 5-6/yr. $1. [2-6 p.] Circulation: 50. Last issue examined: no. 5, November 1976.

    Notes on new publications about Sherlock Holmes and about Holmes productions on stage, television, radio, and film, with an occasional book or film review; news about other Sherlockian events that Plainsmen might wish to attend; occasional challenge questions about controversial or unresolved scholarly problems in the canon; an occasional puzzle or quiz; local news of Sherlockian interest to the Plainsmen; occasional commentary about the history of the Plainsmen, founded in 1963; summaries of meetings; occasional illustrations.

29. LAB NOTES: A QUARTERLY OF SHERLOCKIANA. Editors: William McCullam and Donald E. Novorsky, Fairmount Road, Newbury, Ohio 44065. Sponsor: The Creeping Men of Cleveland. April 1973-(?). $5 (members); $2 (nonmembers).

    Articles; illustrations. No reply to query.

30. LENS. Editor: Robert M. Broderick, 49 Woodale Road, Philadelphia, Pa. 19118. Sponsor: The Master's Class. July 1975-- .

31. MEDICAL BULLETIN. Editor: Mary Holmes. Subscriptions: W.P. Blake,

2410 Eighth Avenue, Greeley, Colo. 80631. Sponsor: Dr. Watson's Neglected Patients, Littleton, Colo. 80120. January 1975-(?). $3.

No reply to query.

32. MONTGOMERY'S CHRISTMAS ANNUAL. 1950-55. Annual.

Articles; illustrations. Privately printed in Philadelphia, Pa.

33. NORTHUMBERLAND DISPATCH. Editor: Jackie Geyer, 312 Princeton Avenue, Pittsburgh, Pa. 15229. Sponsor: The Pittsburgh Scion of the Baker Street Irregulars, Fifth Northumberland Fusiliers, Pittsburgh, Pa. Publisher: Q.J. Bailey, 9329 Doral Drive, Pittsburgh, Pa. 15237. August 1974-- . Monthly. $3.60. [6-8 p.] Circulation: 40. Last issue examined: April 1977.

Brief informal articles on crimes and famous criminals; brief notes on Holmes's allusions, names, locations; book, film, theatre, and television reviews; recent acquisitions of interest to members; excerpts from current Sherlockian books; parodies; pastiches; quizzes, games, and puzzles; detailed reports of the monthly meetings, members' activities, Sherlockian dinners; correspondence; original illustrations.

34. NOTES BY THE SUB-LIBRARIAN. January 1959-68. 3/yr., January 1959-February 1950; annual, 1961-68. Circulation: limited to 75.

A Christmas annual. Privately printed in Indianapolis.

35. NOTES FROM A NOTORIOUS CARD CLUB. Supersedes NOTORIOUS CANARY-TRAINERS MANUAL (see entry 36). Editor: Susan Flaherty, N62 W15127 Tepee Court, Menomonee Falls, Wis. 53051. Sponsor: The Notorious Canary-Trainers of Madison and The Bagatelle Card Club of Milwaukee. 1976-(?).

Articles; illustrations. No reply to query.

36. NOTORIOUS CANARY-TRAINERS MANUAL. Superseded by NOTES FROM A NOTORIOUS CARD CLUB (see entry 35). Editor: Susan Flaherty, N62 W15127 Tepee Court, Menomonee Falls, Wis. 53051. Winter-Fall 1975 (nos. 1-4).

Articles; illustrations.

37. PONDERINGS BY THE POLITICIAN. 1951-56.

A Christmas annual. Privately printed in Los Angeles, Calif.

38. PONTINE DOSSIER. Editor: Luther Norris, 3844 Watseka Avenue, Culver City, Calif. 90230. Sponsor: Praed Street Irregulars, Culver City, Calif. February 1967-- . Quarterly, 1967-69; annual since 1970. $5. Last issue examined: vol. 2, no. 1, 1973.

Articles on the Pontine and Sherlockian tales; illustrations. No reply to query.

39. REPORT CARD. Editor: Glen J. Shea, 5 Pine Hill Road, Jewett City, Conn. 06351. Sponsor: Board School Beacons, Scion Society of the Baker Street Irregulars, Owings Mills, Md., and Jewett City, Conn. June 1971-- . 2/yr. Free to members. [2 p.] Circulation: 50. Last issue examined: no. 15, February 1975.

    News notes on book sales, moving pictures, annual meetings of the Baker Street Irregulars, TV programs, parodies; information on forthcoming publications and Sherlockian activities. Applications for membership: P. Stephen Clarkson, 3612 Briarstone Road, Randallstown, Md. 21133.

40. REPORT OF THE ANDERSON MURDERERS OF NORTH CAROLINA. Editor and publisher: J. David Kiser, P.O. Box 84, Skyland, N.C. 28776. Sponsor: Anderson Murderers of North Carolina, Sherlock Holmes Society of North Carolina. June 1976-- . Quarterly. Free (members); $1 (nonmembers). [1 p.] Circulation: 50. Last issue examined: no. 5, May 1977.

    Summaries of meetings; news of forthcoming gatherings and publications of interest to Sherlockians.

41. SCANDAL SHEET. Editor: Robert A.W. Lowndes, 717 Willow Avenue, Hoboken, N.J. 07030. Subscriptions: Norman S. Nolan, 68 Crest Road, Middletown, N.J. 07748. Sponsor: Scandalous Bohemians of New Jersey. January 1971-(?). Irregular. $2 per issue. Last issue examined: vol. 2, no. 1, April 1972.

    Articles; occasional bibliographies; book reviews. No reply to query.

42. SHADES OF SHERLOCK. Editor: Bruce Kennedy, 200 Diplomat Drive, Apartment 7D, Mount Kisco, N.Y. 10549. Sponsor: Three Students Plus, Chappaqua, N.Y. October 1966-(?). 6/yr. in 1966-67; 2/yr. since 1968. $.40 ($.25 per issue). Circulation: 100.

    Articles; book reviews in every issue; bibliography in the last issue of every other year; two special annuals published in 1966 and 1967; illustrations.

43. SHERLOCK HOLMES ÅRBOK. Editor: A.D. Henriksen. Publisher: Martins Forlag, Copenhagen, Denmark. 1965-67. Annual. [100 p.]

    Critical essays; illustrations. In Danish.

44. SHERLOCK HOLMES JOURNAL. Editor: Nicholas R. Utechin. Honorary editor: Marquis of Donegall, Holmes Society, The Studio, 39 Clabon Mews, London, S.W.1, England. Subscriptions: W.R. Michell, 5 Manor

Close, Warlingham, Surrey CR3 9SF, England. Sponsor: Sherlock Holmes Society of London. May 1952-- . 2/yr. $12. [35-40 p.] Last issue examined: vol. 13, 1976.

Brief articles on literary and geographical allusions in the works; analyses of problems in the plots, contradictions in descriptions, and personalities of the characters; book reviews; numerous informal editorial notes on current theatrical productions, new publications, activities of members, tours to places mentioned in the stories; reports of annual dinners and celebrations of Holmes's birthday; notes from book collectors; list of members; illustrations; cumulated index every second year. A selected subject index is in progress.

45. SHERLOCKIANA: MEDDELELSER FRA SHERLOCK HOLMES KLUBBEN I DANMARK. Editor: Henry Lauritzen, Vesterbro 60, 9000 Aalborg, Denmark. Publisher: Sherlock Holmes Klubben i Danmark (The Danish Baker Street Irregulars). Spring 1956-- . 4/yr. $3. [10 p.] Circulation: 150. Last issues examined: nos. 2-3, 1976.

Brief articles; numerous brief book reviews in every issue on Holmesian and other mystery publications; occasional bibliographies; notes and news of interest to members; occasional short mystery stories; list of new members; numerous illustrations; no index. In Danish or English.

46. SHERLOCKIAN MEDDLER. Editor: John Farrell, 1367 West 6th Street, San Pedro, Calif. 90732. Sponsor: Non-Canonical Calabashes, The Sherlock Holmes Society of Los Angeles. 1973-(?).

Articles; illustrations. No reply to query.

47. SIDELIGHTS ON HOLMES. Editor: John Sikorski. Sponsor: Priory Scholars of Fenwick High School. 1966-69 (vols. 1-3, no. 1?). Quarterly.

48. STUDIES IN SCARLET. Editors: Steven Thomashefsky and Robert Enright, 104 Brightwood Avenue, Pearl River, N.J. 10965. June 1965-66.

No reply to query.

49. THREE PIPE PROBLEMS. Editor: Bradley Kjell, 1732 Sexton Drive, Rockford, Ill. 61108. Sponsor: Baker Street Irrationals. September 1970-(?). Last issue examined: nos. 1-2, 1970.

News and notes. No reply to query.

50. UNDERGROUND JOTTINGS: THE NEWSLETTER OF THE BAKER STREET UNDERGROUND. Editor: Andrew Jay Peck, 306 Highland Road, Ithaca,

N.Y. 14850. November 1971-72 (vol. 1, nos. 1-4).

Query returned--forwarding address unknown.

51. VERMISSA HERALD: A JOURNAL OF SHERLOCKIAN AFFAIRS. Editors: William A. Berner and Herbert A. Eaton, 4712 17th Street, San Francisco, Calif. 94117. Sponsor: The Scowrers and Molly Maguires of San Francisco. Old series, Spring 1962-Fall 1963 (3 issues); new series, January 1967-- . 3/yr. $2 (U.S.); $2.75 (overseas). Circulation: 200. Last issue examined: vol. 6, 1972.

Articles; occasional bibliographies; occasional book reviews; illustrations. No reply to query.

52. VICTORIAN JOURNAL. Editor: Tom Mengert. Sponsor: Victorian Gentlemen, Tacoma, Wash. 1970-December 1971 (vol. 1, nos. 1-4). Quarterly.

DREISER, THEODORE (1871-1945)

American novelist

1. DREISER NEWSLETTER (DreiN). Editors: Robert P. Saalbach and Richard W. Dowell. Managing editor: Frederic E. Rusch. Sponsor: English Department, Indiana State University, Terre Haute, Ind. 47809. Spring 1970-- . 2/yr. (Spring, Fall). $2.50 (four issues); $3.50 (overseas). [24 p.] Circulation: 300. Last issue examined: vol. 8, 1977.

"Dedicated to stimulating, coordinating, and reporting Dreiser scholarship"--interested particularly in bibliographical materials. Brief notes on Dreiser's life and works, his literary style and reception here and abroad; occasional long critical articles; annotated checklist in every Fall issue of the previous year's scholarship; news and notes about lectures, MLA seminars, new editions and other publications, and, in 1976, plans for a Dreiser Studies Association; occasional reports of work in progress; book reviews; special features, such as a series of articles by foreign scholars on Dreiser's reputation abroad, and airmail interviews with outstanding Dreiser scholars; occasional illustrations; cumulated index at three-year intervals.

Indexed by ABSTRACTS OF ENGLISH STUDIES, AMERICAN HUMANITIES INDEX, ANNUAL BIBLIOGRAPHY OF ENGLISH LANGUAGE AND LITERATURE, and MISSISSIPPI QUARTERLY.

DROSTE-HÜLSHOFF, ANNETTE VON (1797-1848)

German poet

1. JAHRBUCH DER DROSTE-GESELLSCHAFT: WESTFÄLISCHE BLÄTTER FÜR

THE
DREISER
NEWSLETTER
CENTENARY YEAR
SPRING 1971

DICHTUNG UND GEISTESGESCHICHTE (JbDroste). Editor: vols. 3-4, Clemens Heselhaus. Sponsor: Droste-Gesellschaft. Publisher: Verlag Regensberg, Münster, Germany (BRD). 1947-- . Irregular (vol. 2, 1948-50; vol. 3, 1954-59; vol. 4, 1962; vol. 5, 1972). [160-260 p.]

Studies of friendships, early publications, textual problems, ideas, and literary technique; occasional bibliographies covering several years of Droste scholarship; reviews of books and articles; reports of progress of the collected works; reprints of early reviews. In German. The JAHRBUCH is a publication of SCHRIFTEN DER DROSTE-GESELLSCHAFT (see entry 3).

Indexed by Köttelwesch.

Alternate title:

Droste-Gesellschaft. JAHRBUCH

2. KLEINE BEITRÄGE ZUR DROSTE-FORSCHUNG (KBDF). Editor: Winfried Woesler. Publisher: A. Laumannsche Verlagsbuchhandlung, Dülmen, Westphalia, Germany (BRD). 1971-- . Irregular (no. 2, 1972-73; no. 3, 1974-75). DM15. [140-60 p.] Last issue examined: no. 4, 1976-77.

Long scholarly studies of individual titles, library holdings, friendships, correspondence, background, influence, travels, literary style; previously unpublished letters; review articles. In German.

Indexed by Köttelwesch and MLA INTERNATIONAL BIBLIOGRAPHY.

3. SCHRIFTEN DER DROSTE-GESELLSCHAFT (SDG). Sponsor: Droste-Gesellschaft, 44 Münster, Germany (BRD). 1929-- . Irregular. DM30. Last issue examined: vol. 18, 1972.

Each volume is concerned with a specific aspect of scholarship --biography, bibliography, interpretation, or research. One of its publications is the JAHRBUCH DER DROSTE-GESELLSCHAFT (see entry 1). Nos. 1-6 (1929-41) include the VERÖFFENTLICHUNGEN DER ANNETTE VON DROSTE-GESELLSCHAFT. In German. Vol. 19 not yet published (1978).

Indexed by MLA INTERNATIONAL BIBLIOGRAPHY.

Alternate titles:

Annette von Droste-Gesellschaft

Droste-Gesellschaft. SCHRIFTEN

DU BELLAY, JOACHIM (1522-60)

French poet

1. AMIS DU PETIT LYRÉ. Sponsor: Association et Musée Joachim Du Bellay, Le Grand Logis, Maine-et-Loire, Liré, France. 1960-(?).

   Brief articles. In French.

DU BOS, CHARLES (1882-1939)

French literary critic, essayist

1. CAHIERS CHARLES DU BOS. Sponsor and publisher: Société des Amis de Charles du Bos, 76 bis, rue de Saints-Pères, 75007 Paris. Published with the approval of the Caisse Nationale des Lettres. President: Jean Mouton. December 1956-- . Annual. 25-50 Fr. [45-80 p.] Last issue examined: vol. 21, 1977.

   Devoted to preserving the memory of du Bos, to acquainting the public with his works, and to encouraging the publication of his works. Collections of long scholarly studies of du Bos's life, works, style, and philosophy; examination of his influence in other countries and on other authors, such as Curtius and Gide; bibliographies of du Bos scholarship; descriptions of newly acquired documents; previously unpublished letters, like those to Berenson, Marcel, Maritain; news notes on completed scholarship, awards. In French.

   Indexed by BIBLIOGRAPHIE DE LA LITTÉRATURE FRANÇAISE, FRENCH VII, FRENCH XX, Klapp, and REVUE D'HISTOIRE LITTÉRAIRE.

2. Charles du Bos. Subseries of La Revue des Lettres Modernes. 1960-- . Irregular. Series numbers for the issues on du Bos are provided below.

du Bos subseries	La Revue series	Date
Unnumbered	Nos. 54-55	1960

   In French. See Camus, Albert, entry 1, for a full description of La Revue des Lettres Modernes.

   Indexed by BULLETIN CRITIQUE, FRENCH VII, FRENCH XX, Klapp, and MLA INTERNATIONAL BIBLIOGRAPHY.

DUDEVANT, MME., LUCILE-AURORE DUPIN [GEORGE SAND] (1804-76)

French novelist

1. Archives des Lettres Modernes. 1962-- . Irregular. Series numbers for the issues on Sand are provided below:

Sand subseries	Archives series	Date
Unnumbered	No. 44	1962

In French. See Camus, Albert, entry 2, for a full description of Archives des Lettres Modernes.

Indexed by BULLETIN CRITIQUE, Klapp, and MLA INTERNATIONAL BIBLIOGRAPHY.

2. Association "Les Amis de George Sand." BULLETIN DE LIAISON. No. 1, 1977-- . [20-25 p.]

   Brief critical and biographical articles.

   Indexed by REVUE D'HISTOIRE LITTÉRAIRE.

3. BERRY DE GEORGE SAND. Sponsor: Fondation Sand. Publisher: G. Smeets-Sand, Gargilesse (Indre), France. No. 2, March 1964-(?).

   An information bulletin of the Fondation Sand. In French.

4. NEWSLETTER. Sponsor and publisher: Friends of George Sand, University Center for Cultural and Inter-Cultural Studies, Hofstra University, Hempstead, N.Y. 11550. 1978-- . 3/yr. $5 (individuals); $8 (institutions); $3 (students).

   Designed "to coordinate research and scholarship, to serve as a clearinghouse for information, to establish scholarly exchanges, meetings, and seminars, and to give George Sand her rightful place as a writer." Contains articles concerning Sand's life, work, her circle, and her influence.

DULLIN, CHARLES (1885-1949)

French actor, director, comédie improvisée

1. Association Charles Dullin. BULLETIN. Editor: de Linières. Sponsor: Association Charles Dullin, 14, rue des Volontaires, 75015 Paris. December 1959-60(?).

   Brief critical articles. In French.

   Indexed by FRENCH VII.

   Alternate title:

   ASSOCIATION CHARLES DULLIN BULLETIN

   Alternate address in LIBRAIRIE FRANÇAISE: 33, rue St-Dominique.

DUMAS, ALEXANDRE, PÈRE (1802-70)

French dramatist

1. Association des Amis d'Alexandre Dumas. BULLETIN. Sponsor: Amis d'Alexandre Dumas. Secrétariat Général: Mme. C. Neave, 1 bis, rue Champflour, 78160 Marly-le-Roi, France. 1971(?)-- . Irregular. [40-50 p.] Last issue examined: no. 5, 1976.

   Brief notes on the life, family, and works of Alexandre Dumas, père; examinations of the plot, themes, technique, and characters in his writings; reprints of letters to such famous authors as Hugo; news of the Association's activities. In French.

   Indexed by BIBLIOGRAPHIE DE LA LITTÉRATURE FRANÇAISE and REVUE D'HISTOIRE LITTÉRAIRE.

   Alternate title:

   BULLETIN DE L'ASSOCIATION DES AMIS D'ALEXANDRE DUMAS

2. DUMASIAN: THE MAGAZINE OF THE DUMAS ASSOCIATION. Editor: Alfred Evans, 59 Bolling Hall Road, Bradford 4, Yorkshire, England. Sponsor: Dumas Association, Keighley, England. Spring 1956-August 1960 (nos. 1-11). Quarterly.

   Query returned--addressee unknown.

   Indexed by FRENCH VI.

DURRELL, LAWRENCE (1912-)

English novelist, poet

1. DEUS LOCI: THE LAWRENCE DURRELL NEWSLETTER. Editor: James A. Brigham, Department of English, Okanagen College, 1000 K.L.O. Road, Kelowna, British Columbia V1Y 4X8, Canada; and Ian C. MacNiven, State University of New York, Maritime College, Bronx, N.Y. 10465. September 1977-- . Quarterly. $3.50.

   A focus for scholarship on Durrell. Contains critical articles; bibliographies of new or uncollected Durrelliana; notes and queries section; reviews; lists of works in progress; correspondence.

EDWARDS, LEO

See Lee, Edward Edson.

EICHENDORFF, BARON JOSEPH FREIHERR VON (1788-1857)

German lyric poet, novelist, critic

1. AURORA: EICHENDORFF-ALMANACH, JAHRESGABE DER EICHENDORFF-STIFTUNG e. V. EICHENDORFFBUND. Supersedes AURORA: EIN ROMANTISCHER ALMANACH (see entry 2); superseded by AURORA: JAHRBUCH DER EICHENDORFF-GESELLSCHAFT (see entry 3). Editors: Karl Freiherr von Eichendorff, Adolf Dyroff, Karl Schodrok (1936-69), and others. Sponsor: Eichendorff-Gesellschaft. Publisher: Verlag Eichendorff-Stiftung, Würzburg, Germany (BRD). 1953-69 (vols. 13-29). Annual. [100-125 p.]

   Long articles on Eichendorff's style, political ideas, friendships; annual bibliographies of new editions and criticism; previously unpublished works; book reviews; facsimiles, reproductions, portraits, and photographs. In German.

   Indexed by ENGLISH LANGUAGE NOTES and MLA INTERNATIONAL BIBLIOGRAPHY.

2. AURORA: EIN ROMANTISCHER ALMANACH. Superseded by AURORA: EICHENDORFF-ALMANACH (see entry 1). Editor: Karl Schodrok. Sponsor: Eichendorff-Gesellschaft. Publisher: Verlag "Der Oberschlesier," Oppeln (Opole), Poland. 1929-43 (vols. 1-12); suspended 1944-52. Annual. [100-150 p.]

   Long essays on Eichendorff's use of myth, the structure of his plots, and the characters in his novels; reports from the Deutsche Eichendorffmuseum and from the various branches of the Eichendorff-Gesellschaft; facsimiles, illustrations, and photographs; index. In German.

   Alternate title:

   JAHRESGABE DER DEUTSCHEN EICHENDORFF-STIFTUNG

3. AURORA: JAHRBUCH DER EICHENDORFF-GESELLSCHAFT. Supersedes AURORA: EICHENDORFF-ALMANACH (see entry 1). Editor: Franz Heiduk, Würzburg, Germany (BRD). Sponsor: Eichendorff-Gesellschaft, Schönleinstrasse 3, 8700 Würzburg 2, Postfach 988, Germany (BRD). 1970-71 (vols. 30-31)-- . Annual. DM20-30. [130-200 p.] Last issue examined: vol. 37, 1977.

   Long critical essays on Eichendorff, his contemporaries, their ideas and influences, textual and editorial problems; numerous long book reviews; mainly of German publications; annual bibliography of Eichendorff scholarship edited by Hans M. Meyer since 1953; news notes of Gesellschaft activities, important publications, performances; illustrations and facsimiles; numerous portraits; summary of contents in English; annual index. Index for 1929-70/71 (vols. 1-30/31) in vols. 30-31, edited by Heinz Linduschka and Franz Heiduk. In German, with occasional material in English.

Indexed by ENGLISH LANGUAGE NOTES, Köttelwesch, and MLA INTERNATIONAL BIBLIOGRAPHY.

4. EICHENDORFF-KALENDER (EK). Publisher: Regensburg, Germany (BRD). 1910-30 (vols. 1-19).

   Cumulative index for 1910-30, edited by Heinz Linduschka and Franz Heiduk, in AURORA: JAHRBUCH DER EICHENDORFF-GESELLSCHAFT (vol. 34, 1974).

ELIOT, GEORGE

See Evans, Mary Ann.

ELIOT, THOMAS STEARNS (1888-1965)

American-born English poet, critic, dramatist

1. T.S. Eliot Memorial Lectures. Sponsor: Yale University, New Haven, Conn. 06520. Publisher: Yale University Press, New Haven, Conn., and Oxford University Press, New York. 1970-- . Irregular. [150 p.]

   Concerned with the history and criticism of literature and ideas--not confined solely to Eliot and his works.

2. T.S. ELIOT NEWSLETTER. Superseded by T.S. ELIOT REVIEW (see entry 3). Spring-Fall 1974 (vol. 1, nos. 1-2).

   For a full description of the contents, see the following entry.

3. T.S. ELIOT REVIEW: AN INTERNATIONAL JOURNAL OF ELIOT SCHOLARSHIP (TSER). Supersedes T.S. ELIOT NEWSLETTER (see entry 2); superseded by YEATS-ELIOT REVIEW: A JOURNAL OF CRITICISM AND SCHOLARSHIP (see Yeats, W.B., entry 3). Editors: Shyamal Bagchee, Department of English, University of Alberta, Edmonton, Alberta, Canada T6G 2J9; and Desmond E.S. Maxwell. Spring 1975 (vol. 2, no. 1)-Fall 1977 (vol. 4, nos. 1-2). 2/yr. Two-yr. subscriptions only: individuals--$5 (Canada), $5.50 (U.S.); institutions--$6 (Canada), $7 (U.S.). [20 p.]

   Interested in scholarship on Eliot and related figures like Wyndham Lewis, Ezra Pound, and W.B. Yeats. Short, research-based articles and notes on all aspects of Eliot studies; bibliographical essays; annotated "Bibliographical Update"; brief notes explicating specific lines and references; long book reviews and review articles; news notes; queries and answers; work in progress; abstracts; reports of completed work, including dissertations, and recent publications; special issues, such as a supplementary bibliography of Eliot criticism, 1916-65.

Indexed by ABSTRACTS OF ENGLISH STUDIES, AMERICAN HUMANITIES INDEX, AMERICAN LITERATURE, JOURNAL OF MODERN LITERATURE, MLA ABSTRACTS, MLA INTERNATIONAL BIBLIOGRAPHY, and TWENTIETH CENTURY LITERATURE.

ÉLUARD, PAUL

See Grindel, Eugène.

EMERSON, RALPH WALDO (1803-82)

American philosopher, author

1. EMERSON NEWSLETTER. Editor: Jane Emerson James, 432 North Winnebago Drive, Greenwood, Mo. 64034. December 1970-(?). Quarterly.

   Notes about the Emerson family; illustrations. No longer in print.

2. EMERSON SOCIETY QUARTERLY: A JOURNAL OF THE AMERICAN RENAISSANCE. Superseded by ESQ: A JOURNAL OF THE AMERICAN RENAISSANCE (see entry 3). Editor: Kenneth W. Cameron. Sponsor and publisher: Emerson Society, Box 1080, Hartford, Conn. 1955-68 (nos. 1-53).

   Issues for nos. 1-65 have no volume number but constitute vols. 1-17. Subject and author index for 1955-65 (nos. 1-41); index for books reviewed. For a full description of the contents, see the following entry.

   Indexed by ABSTRACTS OF ENGLISH STUDIES, AMERICAN LITERATURE, ANNUAL BIBLIOGRAPHY OF ENGLISH LANGUAGE AND LITERATURE, Leary, MLA INTERNATIONAL BIBLIOGRAPHY, and VICTORIAN STUDIES.

3. ESQ: A JOURNAL OF THE AMERICAN RENAISSANCE. Supersedes EMERSON SOCIETY QUARTERLY (see entry 2). Editors: Robert C. McLean, Department of English, Washington State University, Pullman, Wash. 99164; and G.R. Thompson, Department of English, Purdue University, Lafayette, Ind. 47907. Publisher: Washington State University Press, Pullman, Wash. 99164. 1969 (no. 54)-- . Quarterly. $10; $6 (students). [60-100 p.] Circulation: 1,000. Last issue examined: vol. 25, 1979.

   Devoted to the study of nineteenth-century American literature with emphasis on Romanticism and reciprocal relationships with European literature--no longer interested solely in Emerson, Poe, Thoreau, Melville, and their times, but general Romanticism, American Transcendentalism, and the relationship of nineteenth-century American philosophy and history to the arts. In spite of this wide coverage, the editors emphasize that they will "focus on that Romantic Transcendental tradition emanating out of New England . . . of which Emerson is a principal figure." Long (20 p.) critical, source, and influence studies; biographical and bibliographical scholarship on all figures of the century; occasional monographic supplements; occasional long review articles on new publications, such as "Melville and His Biographers" (3rd quarter, 1976); occasional bibliographies--author, subject, or title; illustrations; portraits; facsimiles. Cumulated index planned for every ten years. Some numbers issued in parts.

Indexed by ABSTRACTS OF ENGLISH STUDIES, AMERICAN HUMANITIES INDEX, AMERICAN LITERATURE, AMERICAN LITERATURE ABSTRACTS, ANNUAL BIBLIOGRAPHY OF ENGLISH LANGUAGE AND LITERATURE, ENGLISH LANGUAGE NOTES, Leary, MLA ABSTRACTS, MLA INTERNATIONAL BIBLIOGRAPHY, PHILOLOGICAL QUARTERLY, and YEAR'S WORK IN ENGLISH STUDIES.

ERASMUS, DESIDERIUS (1466-1536)

Dutch philosopher, scholar

1. ERASMUS IN ENGLISH (ErasmusE). Chairman, Collected Works of Erasmus: R.M. Schoeffel. Sponsor: Canada Council. Publisher: University of Toronto Press, Toronto, Canada. 1970-- . Irregular. Free. Circulation: 3,050 in 52 countries. [12-36 p.] Last issue examined: no. 9, 1978.

The editors' stated purpose is "to provide information about the progress of the Collected Works of Erasmus (CWE) and about Erasmus studies in general, and to serve as a clearinghouse for information and a forum for articles, notes, reviews . . . related to Erasmian studies." Includes progress report on the collected works; information concerning financial support; brief critical articles, with bibliographical references, interpreting the works and ideas of Erasmus and his contemporaries; biographical and bibliographical essays; notes on textual problems; book reviews and review articles; selected bibliography of recent international publications of interest to Erasmian scholars; occasional bibliographies of library holdings and special studies, such as "Erasme en Roumanie: Une bibliographie" (no. 6, 1973); queries; news notes; illustrations, numerous facsimiles, reproductions, and portraits. Author and title index for 1970-73 (nos. 1-6). For additional information on Erasmus, see More, Saint Thomas, entry 1.

Title on first page:

A NEWSLETTER PUBLISHED BY UNIVERSITY OF TORONTO PRESS.

Indexed by MLA INTERNATIONAL BIBLIOGRAPHY.

2. ERASMUS STUDIES: A SERIES OF STUDIES CONCERNED WITH ERASMUS AND RELATED SUBJECTS. Sponsor: Humanities Research Council of Canada (Canada Council and Andrew W. Mellon Foundation). Publisher: University of Toronto Press, Toronto, Canada. 1973-- . Irregular. $15. [200 p.] Last issue examined: no. 2, 1977.

   Learned monographs on single aspects of Erasmus' work and influence, such as UNDER PRETEXT OF PRAISE: SATIRIC MODE IN ERASMUS' FICTION (1973); bibliographies of primary and secondary sources; subject, name, and title index.

ERCKMANN, ÉMILE [ERCKMANN-CHATRIAN] (1822-99)

French regional novelist

1. BULLETIN DE LA SOCIÉTÉ ERCKMANN-CHATRIAN. Publisher: Nancy, France. 1914-32 (nos. 1-18).

   Critical studies and information on Erckmann and Chatrian. In French.

ERCKMANN-CHATRIAN

See Erckmann, Émile.

ERNST, PAUL C.F. (1866-1933)

German critic, dramatist, short-story writer

1. MITTEILUNGEN DER PAUL-ERNST-GESELLSCHAFT. Editors: Heinrich Steinmeyer, Hauptstrasse 58, Postfach 279, 4690 Herne 2, Germany (BRD); and Karl Vogel, Barkhovenallee 26, 4300 Essen-Heidhausen, Germany (BRD). Sponsor and publisher in 1936-40: Paul-Ernst-Gesellschaft, Hubertusstrasse 4, Munich; in 1968, Düsseldorf, Germany (BRD). September 1936-March 1940 (nos. 5-7); 1968(?)-- . Annual. [15-25 p.] Last issue examined: 1977.

   Report to members and friends of new publications, celebrations in Ernst's honor, performances of his works, his family's activities, location and movements of his manuscripts, photographs, and library; account of Gesellschaft conferences, activities, membership, financial statement; brief bibliographies of criticism in periodicals and newspapers; excerpts from Ernst's manuscripts--poems and articles; brief book reviews; lists of new publications. In German.

Alternate title:

Paul-Ernst-Gesellschaft. MITTEILUNGEN

2. Paul-Ernst-Gesellschaft. JAHRBUCH. Sponsor: Paul-Ernst-Gesellschaft. Publisher: Julius Beltz, Langensalza, Germany (DDR). 1936-39 (nos. 1-4). Annual. [250-320 p.]

   Each volume is concerned with a specific subject, for example, PAUL ERNST UND DAS DRAMA (1939). In German.

   Alternate title:

   JAHRBUCH DER PAUL-ERNST-GESELLSCHAFT

3. Paul-Ernst-Gesellschaft. JAHRESGABE. Sponsor: Paul-Ernst-Gesellschaft, Düsseldorf, Germany (BRD). 1971/72-- . Annual. [60-260 p.] Last issue examined: vol. 4, 1976-77.

   Long studies of one specific subject, such as Ernst's drama--its reception and technique; previously unpublished letters and other documents; reprints and criticism of early works. In German.

   Indexed by Köttelwesch.

4. WILLE ZUR FORM: BLÄTTER DER PAUL-ERNST-GESELLSCHAFT. Editor: Karl August Kutzbach, Schumannstrasse 39, 53 Bonn 1, Germany (BRD). Sponsor and publisher: Paul-Ernst-Gesellschaft, Ackerstrasse 12, 468 Wanne-Eickel, Germany (BRD). January 1957-Fall 1965 (nos. 1-11); new series, 1970 (no. 1)-- . Irregular. [40-60 p.]

   New editions or reprints of selected works by Ernst, accompanied by numerous critical, interpretive, and biographical essays; occasional brief book reviews; notes. Index for 1957-65 (nos. 1-11), edited by Karl August Kutzbach. In German. Future publications are uncertain.

   Indexed by Köttelwesch.

ERWIN VON STEINBACH (1244-1318)

German architect

1. SCHRIFTEN DER ERWIN VON STEINBACH-STIFTUNG. Editor: Christian Hallier. Sponsor and publisher: Erwin von Steinbach-Stiftung, Bockenheimer Landstrasse 138, Frankfurt/am/Main, Germany (BRD). 1968-- . Irregular. DM12-20. [150 p.] Last issue examined: vol. 5, 1976.

   Monographs on the history and culture of Germany, not solely on Erwin von Steinbach but inspired by him; bibliographies; index. In German.

   Alternate title:

   Erwin von Steinbach-Stiftung. SCHRIFTEN

2. STUDIEN DER ERWIN VON STEINBACH-STIFTUNG. Editor: Christian Hallier. Sponsor and publisher: Erwin von Steinbach-Stiftung, Bockenheimer Landstrasse 136, Frankfurt/am/Main, Germany (BRD). 1965-- . Irregular. $7. [150-250 p.] Last issue examined: vol. 4, 1975.

   Long scholarly studies, a few on specific aspects of Steinbach's life but most on writers and philosophers who are related in some way to his craft and structures; critical essays, such as those on his relationship to Goethe and Romanticism; news of organization activities and the Erwin von Steinbach Prize; photographs. In German.

   Indexed by Köttelwesch.

   Alternate title:

   Erwin von Steinbach-Stiftung. STUDIEN

ESDAILE, ARUNDELL (1880-1956)

English librarian, bibliographer, author

1. Arundell Esdaile Memorial Lecture. Sponsor: English Association, London, and Library Association, Chaucer House, Malet Place, London W.C.1. 1960-(?). Irregular. Last issue examined: no. 3, 1964.

   Concerned not only with Esdaile's numerous accomplishments in bibliography and library science but also with the organization of famous libraries and the problems of other bibliographers.

EVANS, MARY ANN [GEORGE ELIOT] (1819-80)

English novelist

1. GEORGE ELIOT FELLOWSHIP REVIEW (GEFR). Editor and publisher: Kathleen M. Adams, 71, Stepping Stones Road, Coventry CV5 8JT, England. Treasurer: Mrs. E. Lenton, 150, Attleborough Road, Nuneaton CV11 4JW, England. Sponsor: George Eliot Fellowship. June 1970-- . Annual. £1 (individuals); £1.50 (married couples); £10 (life membership). [20-30 p.] Circulation: 300. Last issue examined: no. 6, 1975.

   Critical essays; reviews, news of Fellowship activities; announcements of ceremonies, lectures, literary outings, readings, and the annual dinner. The Fellowship also publishes an annual review of activities.

   Indexed by MLA INTERNATIONAL BIBLIOGRAPHY.

FARIGOULE, LOUIS H.J. [JULES ROMAINS] (1885-1972)

French poet, dramatist, novelist

1. CAHIERS DES HOMMES DE BONNE VOLONTÉ. Publisher: Flammarion, Paris. April 1948-March 1950 (nos. 1-4).

   In French.

2. Société des Amis de Jules Romains. BULLETIN. Sponsor: Société des Amis de Jules Romains, 50, rue Corvisart, 75013 Paris. President: André François-Poncet. Publisher: U.E.R. de l'Université de Saint-Étienne, B.P. 127, 42023 St.-Étienne Cedex, France. October 1974-- . Irregular. Last issue examined: vol. 4, no. 11, 1978.

   Brief notes on Romains as poet and professor, his influence, and his reception in the United States; bibliographies of criticism; facsimiles of manuscripts; previously unpublished works; news of Society activities. In French.

   Indexed by BIBLIOGRAPHIE DE LA LITTÉRATURE FRANÇAISE.

   Alternate title:

   BULLETIN DES AMIS DE JULES ROMAINS

FAULKNER, WILLIAM (1897-1962)

American novelist, short-story writer

1. FAULKNER CONCORDANCE NEWSLETTER. Incorporated in the NEWSLETTER OF THE SOCIETY FOR THE STUDY OF SOUTHERN LITERATURE. Editor: Robert H. Moore, Department of English, University of Maryland, College Park, Md. 20742. Sponsor: Faulkner Concordance Project, Library, United States Military Academy, West Point, N.Y. 10996. Project officials: chairman, Jack L. Capps, USMA; textual editor: James B. Meriweather, University of South Carolina; executive secretary: Robert H. Moore, University of Maryland. December 1972-November 1976 (nos. 1-5). Irregular. [8 p.]

   Report on assimilation of unpublished manuscripts and typescripts; report on work in progress--editorial decisions, financial assistance, conferences; bibliography of publications concerning the concordance; list of libraries where the NEWSLETTER and the completed concordances are available.

   Indexed by MISSISSIPPI QUARTERLY.

2. FAULKNER STUDIES. Superseded by CRITIQUE: STUDIES IN MODERN FICTION. Founding editors (several others for later issues): James R. Baker, John R. Marvin, and Tom E. Francis. Spring 1952-Winter 1954 (vols. 1-3, no. 4, eleven issues). Quarterly. $2. [20-30 p.]

   Brief critical articles and notes on Faulkner's symbolism, characters, structure; reprints of early Faulkner material; selective, annotated bibliographies; book reviews; news of interest to Faulkner scholars; index to each volume. Reprints available from Kraus Reprint ($14) and from Walter J. Johnson ($17).

3. FAULKNER STUDIES (Miami). Editor: Barnett Guttenberg, Box 248, University of Miami, Coral Gables, Fla. 33124. December 1978-- . Annual. $20. [300 p.]

   A forum for Faulkner scholarship and a guide to Faulkner research. Includes long critical essays; reviews; bibliographies; information on work in progress; illustrations; index.

4. William Faulkner. Subseries of La Revue des Lettres Modernes. 1957-- . Irregular. Series numbers for the issues on Faulkner are provided below.

Faulkner subseries	La Revue series	Date
Unnumbered	Nos. 27-29	1957
Unnumbered	Nos. 40-42	1959

   In French. See Camus, Albert, entry 1, for a full description of La Revue des Lettres Modernes.

Indexed by MLA INTERNATIONAL BIBLIOGRAPHY.

FAUST, FREDERICK [MAX BRAND] (1892-1944)

American author

1. FAUST COLLECTOR. Editor and publisher (with permission of the Faust family heirs): William J. Clark, 11744 1/2 Gateway Boulevard, Los Angeles, Calif. 90064. February 1969-February 1971 (nos. 1-9; publication suspended). 4/yr. $2.

FÉNELON, FRANÇOIS (1651-1715)

French prelate, writer

1. REVUE FÉNELON. 1910-12. Quarterly.

   Occasional articles on Fénelon. In French.

FITZGERALD, F. SCOTT (1896-1940)

American novelist, short-story writer

1. FITZGERALD/HEMINGWAY ANNUAL (FHA). Supersedes FITZGERALD NEWSLETTER (see entry 2). Editors: Matthew J. Bruccoli and Richard L. Layman, Department of English, University of South Carolina, Columbia, S.C. 29208; and Margaret M. Duggan, Montclair State College, Upper Montclair, N.J. 07043. Sponsor and publisher: Gale Research, Detroit, Mich. 1969-- . Annual. $17-24. [150-500 p.] Circulation: 3,000. Last issue examined: 1978.

   The first several volumes contain long (20 p.) critical, biographical, and interpretive essays; brief notes and comments on editions, interpretations, textual problems, acquaintances of the authors; annual checklists of Hemingway and Fitzgerald scholarship; specialized bibliographies, such as those of Fitzgerald reprints and translations; information on work in progress; brief news notes; long book reviews; previously unpublished works, such as Fitzgerald short stories and letters and Hemingway reviews; reports from the annual conference proceedings; interviews; photographs, illustrations, and facsimiles. About one-third of each volume is devoted to Fitzgerald, one-third to Hemingway, and the remainder to reviews, bibliographical material, and announcements. Back copies available from Microcard Editions. The 1978 volume concentrates on previously unpublished work by and about Fitzgerald and Hemingway, with some critical studies, current book reviews, and up-to-date bibliographical material on the authors and the 1920's.

   Indexed by AMERICAN HUMANITIES INDEX, AMERICAN LITERATURE, ANNUAL BIBLIOGRAPHY OF ENGLISH LANGUAGE AND LITERATURE, MLA ABSTRACTS, MLA INTERNATIONAL BIBLIOGRAPHY, and TWENTIETH CENTURY LITERATURE.

2. FITZGERALD NEWSLETTER (FitzN; FN). Superseded by FITZGERALD/HEMINGWAY ANNUAL (see entry 1). Editor and sponsor: Matthew J. Bruccoli, Department of English, University of South Carolina, Columbia, S.C. 29208. Spring 1958-Winter 1968 (nos. 1-40, plus special issue, Winter 1963). Quarterly. $2. [3-25 p.] Circulation: 500.

   Brief notes on plot or character problems in Fitzgerald's works; news on the availability and price of first editions and other inaccessible material; checklist of criticism in every issue; previously unpublished material; news of television programs, recordings, films, plays, library acquisitions; suggestions for research projects; notes on work in progress and forthcoming publications. Five-year index for Spring 1963-Winter 1968 (nos. 21-40). Issue nos. 1-29 were published without covers. "A corrected and revised version of the original newsletter" was published in 1969 in one bound volume by NCR/Microcard Editions.

Indexed by AMERICAN LITERATURE, AMERICAN LITERATURE ABSTRACTS, ANNUAL BIBLIOGRAPHY OF ENGLISH LANGUAGE AND LITERATURE, Leary, and MLA INTERNATIONAL BIBLIOGRAPHY.

FLAUBERT, GUSTAVE (1821-80)

French novelist

1. AMIS DE FLAUBERT (AFl). Supersedes Amis de Flaubert. BULLETIN (see entry 2). Editor: André Dubuc, 701, rue de Robert-Pinchon, 76230 Boisguillaume-lès-Rouen (Seine-Maritime), France. Sponsor: Association des Amis de Flaubert, 1, rue de Lourdines, 76100 Rouen, France. Publisher: Pavillon de Croisset, 76830 par Dieppedalle (Seine-Maritime), Rouen, France. 1962-- . 2/yr. Free with membership (38 Fr; 44 Fr, foreign). [50 p.] Last issue examined: no. 51, 1977.

   Brief notes and explications of problem areas in Flaubert's works; textual studies; biographical and interpretive articles; source and dating notes; each May, a bibliography of the previous year's Flaubert scholarship; previously unpublished documents; reprints of early criticism; brief comments on new publications; occasional illustrations. In French.

   Indexed by BIBLIOGRAPHIE DE LA LITTÉRATURE FRANÇAISE, FRENCH VI, FRENCH XX, Klapp, MLA INTERNATIONAL BIBLIOGRAPHY, and REVUE D'HISTOIRE LITTÉRAIRE.

   Alternate title:

   BULLETIN DE LA SOCIÉTÉ DES AMIS DE FLAUBERT

2. Amis de Flaubert. BULLETIN. Superseded by AMIS DE FLAUBERT (see entry 1). Editor: André Dubuc, 11, rue de Robert-Pinchon, 76230 Boisguillaume-lès-Rouen (Seine-Maritime), France. Sponsor: Amis de Flaubert, Pavillon de Croisset, à Canteleu (Seine-Maritime), Rouen, France. 1951-62 (nos. 1-20). 2/yr. [50-60 p.]

   Articles on Flaubert and his friends; previously unpublished letters, poems, and other material; bibliographies of Flaubert scholarship; notes on activities of the Society; list of members. In French.

3. Archives des Lettres Modernes. 1964-- . Irregular. Series numbers for the issues on Flaubert are provided below.

Flaubert subseries	Archives series	Date
Unnumbered	No. 56	1964
Unnumbered	No. 110	1970
Unnumbered	No. 145	1973

   In French. See Camus, Albert, entry 2, for a full description of Archives des Lettres Modernes.

Indexed by BULLETIN CRITIQUE, FRENCH VI, Klapp, and MLA INTERNATIONAL BIBLIOGRAPHY.

FLEG, EDMOND (1874-1963)

French poet, dramatist, novelist

1. Société des Amis d'Edmond Fleg. BULLETIN. Sponsor: Société des Amis d'Edmond Fleg. Secrétariat: L. Algazi, 123, boulevard Montmorency, 75016 Paris. 1967-- . Irregular. [50 p.] Last issue examined: no. 2, 1969.

   Critical and biographical articles; previously unpublished works; reprints of letters. In French.

   Indexed by BIBLIOGRAPHIE DE LA LITTÉRATURE FRANÇAISE.

   Alternate title:

   BULLETIN DE LA SOCIÉTÉ DES AMIS D'EDMOND FLEG

FONTANE, THEODOR (1819-98)

German novelist, critic

1. FONTANE-BLÄTTER (FB; F'-Bll). Editor: Joachim Schobess, Leiter des Fontane-Archivs. Sponsor: Theodor-Fontane-Archive der Deutschen Staatsbibliothek, Dortustrasse 30/34, 15 Potsdam, Germany (DDR), with the cooperation of Kreis der Freunde Theodor Fontane. Subscription address: Deutscher Buchexport, Leninstrasse 16, 701 Leipzig, Germany (DDR), or Brandenburgische Landes- und Hochschulbibliothek, Dortustrasse 30/34, 15 Potsdam, Germany (DDR). 1965-- . Irregular (vol. 1, nos. 1-8, 1965-69; vol. 2, nos. 1-8, 1969-73). DM2.50. [25-80 p.] Last issue examined: vol. 4, no. 1, 1977.

   Long studies of Fontane's influence on contemporary authors and ideas; source, biographical, and critical studies; reports on library and archive holdings and acquisitions, both primary and secondary; report of progress on research in the Fontane Archiv; news of currently interesting publications; numerous previously unpublished letters, works, and other pertinent documents; long book reviews; news notes; occasional illustrations and photographs; index. Index for vol. 2 in vol. 2, no. 8. A supplement (SONDERHEFT) has been issued irregularly since 1968 (vol. 4, 1976). In German.

   Indexed by Köttelwesch and MLA INTERNATIONAL BIBLIOGRAPHY.

FORESTER, CECIL SCOTT (1899-1966)

English novelist

1. C.S. FORESTER NEWSLETTER (?). Editor: John A. Hogan, 6, Fremantle Road, High Wycombe, Buckinghamshire, England. Sponsor: C.S. Forester Society.

   Announced, but not yet published (1978).

FORSTER, JOHN (1812-76)

English journalist, historian, critic, biographer, editor

1. JOHN FORSTER NEWSLETTER. Editor: Alec W.C. Brice, Department of English, University of Saskatchewan, Saskatoon, Canada S7N 0W0. March 1978-- . Annual. [25 p.]

   Devoted to the objective assessment of Forster's achievement as a man of letters and his influence on authors like Browning, Tennyson, Landor, Bulwer-Lytton, Gaskell, Ainsworth, and Wilkie Collins. Long and short articles centering on Forster, his circle, and his works, including his biographies of Dickens, Landor, and Goldsmith.

FOUCAULD, CHARLES, VICOMTE DE (1858-1916)

French soldier, Saharan explorer, ascetic

1. Association Charles de Foucauld. BULLETIN. Sponsor: Association Charles de Foucauld, 5, rue Monsieur, 75007 Paris. 1924(?)-(?). Irregular. Last issues examined: nos. 27-31, March-December 1931.

   Alternate title:

   BULLETIN DE L'ASSOCIATION CHARLES DE FOUCAULD

2. CAHIERS CHARLES DE FOUCAULD. Publisher: Éditions Arthaud, Seine, France. October 1946-56 (vols. 1-44). Quarterly. [150-80 p.]

   Collections of critical essays on Foucauld's spirituality, life, works, friends, influence, and importance to France; previously unpublished documents; bibliographies; occasional special issues, such as those about Maréchal Lyautey or the ethnogeography of the Sahara. In French.

   Indexed by BULLETIN CRITIQUE.

Alternate information in BRITISH UNION-CATALOGUE OF PERIODICALS: 1946-57.

FOURNIER, HENRI-ALBAN [ALAIN-FOURNIER] (1886-1914)

French novelist

1. Amis de Jacques Rivière et d'Alain Fournier. BULLETIN.

   See entry 1 for Rivière, Jacques.

2. Archives des Lettres Modernes. 1961-- . Irregular. The series number for the issue on Alain-Fournier is provided below.

Alain-Fournier	Archives series	Date
Unnumbered	No. 51	1963

   In French. See Camus, Albert, entry 2, for a full description of Archives des Lettres Modernes.

   Indexed by BULLETIN CRITIQUE, FRENCH VII, FRENCH XX, Klapp, and MLA INTERNATIONAL BIBLIOGRAPHY.

3. DOSSIERS DE LA SOCIÉTÉ DES AMIS DE JACQUES RIVIÈRE ET ALAIN-FOURNIER.

   See entry 2 for Rivière, Jacques.

FRANCE, ANATOLE

See Thibault, Jacques Anatole François.

FREDERIC, HAROLD (1856-98)

American novelist, journalist

1. FREDERIC HERALD. Editor: Thomas F. O'Donnell, State University at Brockport, Brockport, N.Y. 14420. Sponsor: Utica College, Utica, N.Y. 13502. September 1967-January 1970 (nos. 1-9). 3/yr. Free. Circulation: 300.

   Short notes on the canon, textual problems, technique; brief book reviews; previously unpublished letters and other materials; news items; occasional bibliographies of theses and primary and secondary works; illustrations.

   Indexed by MLA INTERNATIONAL BIBLIOGRAPHY.

FREUD, SIGMUND (1856-1939)

Austrian founder of psychoanalysis

1. ÉTUDES FREUDIENNES. Director: Conrad Stein. Publisher: Éditions Denoël, Paris. November 1969-- . Irregular. 20 Fr. [240-70 p.] Last issues examined: nos. 11-12, 1976.

   Coverage extends to such authors as Joyce and Claudel, and to every aspect of psychoanalysis. Collections of biographical and analytical essays as well as letters and poems that expound on the Freudian philosophy; no index. In French.

   Indexed by BIBLIOGRAPHIE DE LA LITTÉRATURE FRANÇAISE and Klapp.

2. SIGMUND FREUD HOUSE BULLETIN. Editors: H. Leupold-Löwenthal and E. Lingens. Sponsor: Sigmund Freud Society, Berggasse 19, A-1090 Vienna, Austria. Publisher: Sigmund-Freud-Gesellschaft. 1975-- . Irregular. Free with membership ($7). [35-40 p.] Last issue examined: vol. 1, no. 2, 1977.

   Aims to give members of the Society information about the beginnings of psychoanalysis. Reprints and abstracts of lectures concerned with Freud and his ideas; articles on Freud's library and on collections of his works; report of Society activities, international congresses, and conferences; occasional photographs. In English and German.

FREYTAG, GUSTAV (1816-95)

German novelist, dramatist

1. GUSTAV-FREYTAG-BLÄTTER (GFB). Editor: Rupprecht Leppla. Sponsor: Deutsche Gustav-Freytag-Gesellschaft, Rheinstrasse 55-57, 62 Wiesbaden, Germany (BRD). May 1954-- . Annual (irregular). DM10; DM15 (institutions); DM22.50 (foreign institutions). [50-140 p.] Circulation: 500. Last issues examined: vol. 20, nos. 36-37, 1976.

   Long articles on Freytag's philosophy, works, contributions to the theatre, correspondence; reprints of Freytag newspaper articles and other publications; previously unpublished letters, with explanatory notes; translations of early criticism; occasional bibliographies; book reviews; report of members' activities; illustrations. In German.

   Indexed by Köttelwesch and MLA INTERNATIONAL BIBLIOGRAPHY.

   Alternate subtitles:

   MITTEILUNGEN DER DEUTSCHEN GUSTAV-FREYTAG-GESELLSCHAFT

   ORGAN DER DEUTSCHEN GUSTAV-FREYTAG-GESELLSCHAFT

FRÖDING, GUSTAF (1860-1911)

Swedish poet

1. Gustaf-Fröding-sällskapet. SKRIFTSERIE. Sponsor: Gustaf-Fröding-sällskapet. Publisher: NWT:s Förlag, Karlstad, Sweden. 1969-- . Annual. Skr 25-35. [30-170 p.] Last issue examined: vol. 9, 1977.

   Critical and biographical essays explaining Fröding's technique and influence, with numerous quotations from his works; numerous poems by Fröding and poems in his honor written in his style; bibliographies of primary and secondary works; list of members; photographs and facsimiles. In Swedish.

FUSTEL DE COULANGES, NUMA-DENIS (1830-89)

French historian

1. CAHIERS DU CERCLE FUSTEL DE COULANGES. Publisher: Paris. 1928-(?); new series, March 1955-December 1959 (nos. 2-6).

   A few brief critical articles on the writer; news. In French.

   Alternate title:

   Cercle Fustel de Coulanges. CAHIERS

GANDHI, MOHANDAS KARAMCHAND (1869-1948)

Hindu nationalist, spiritual leader

1. GANDHIAN THOUGHT. Sponsor: R. Achuthan, New Delhi, India. 1969-- .

2. GANDHI MARG: A QUARTERLY JOURNAL OF GANDHIAN THOUGHT (GM) (English edition). Supersedes the Nidhi's QUARTERLY BULLETIN. Editors: G. Ramachandran and T.K. Mahadevan. Sponsor: Gandhi Peace Foundation, 221-23 Deen Dayal Upadhyaya Marg, New Delhi 110-001, India. Publisher: T.K. Mahadevan. January 1957-April 1977. Quarterly. $7. [60-80 p.]

   Collections of articles on Gandhi's life, martyrdom, philosophy, and influence in the world, the relationship between his and other beliefs, the contemplation of present and future problems and of Gandhi's influence in their solution; occasional articles relating Gandhi's philosophy to the themes and style of contemporary literature; personal reminiscences. Available from University Microfilms International.

   Indexed by AMERICA: HISTORY AND LIFE, FRENCH VII, FRENCH XX, and MLA INTERNATIONAL BIBLIOGRAPHY.

Alternate title:

JOURNAL OF THE GANDHI PEACE FOUNDATION

3. Gandhi Memorial Lecture. Sponsor: School of Oriental and African Studies, University of London, England. Distributor: Luzac and Company, 46, Great Russell Street, London W.C.1. 1969-- . Irregular (a series).

4. Gandhi Memorial Lectures (Nairobi). Publisher: For University College, Nairobi, East Africa, by Oxford University Press, New York, and Ely House, London, England. 1969-- . Irregular (a series). [100 p.]

   Founded by a grant from the Gandhi Memorial Academy Society and concerned with intellectual, political, and cultural subjects as well as with Gandhi.

5. GANDHI SERIES. Sponsor: Bharatiya Vidya Bhavan, Bombay, India. 1960-- .

GARCÍA LORCA, FEDERICO (1898-1936)

Spanish poet, dramatist

1. GARCÍA LORCA REVIEW. Editor: Grace Alvarez-Altman, State University College of New York, Department of Foreign Language and Literature, Brockport, N.Y. 14420. Fall 1973-- . 2/yr. (published in one vol.). $3; back issues £4. [130-40 p.] Last issue examined: vol. 5, 1977.

   Long critical studies of the works--their themes, structure, characters, tragic elements; bibliographical surveys, such as "Lorca in Portuguese," "Lorca and the Theater of the Absurd," and "A Catalogue of Lorca's Drawings" (vol. 4, nos. 1-2); occasional book reviews; programs of the MLA seminars; facsimiles and occasional photographs, like that of Lorca in Vermont. In Spanish or English.

   Indexed by MLA INTERNATIONAL BIBLIOGRAPHY.

GARIBALDI, GUISEPPE (1807-82)

Italian patriot

1. STUDI GARIBALDINI. Sponsor: Istituto "Civitas garibaldini." Publisher: Bergamo, Italy. 1960-- .

   Issued as a supplement to BERGOMUN, new series. In Italian.

GEORGE, HENRY (1839-97)

American economist, reformer

1. HENRY GEORGE NEWS. Supersedes THE FREEMAN. Editor: Lancaster M. Greene. Sponsor: Henry George School of Social Science, 50 East 69th Street, New York, N.Y. 10021. September 1943-- . 6/yr. $2; $5/three yrs. [4-16 p.] Circulation: 3,000. Last issue examined: vol. 42, 1978.

   Not confined to the life and works of Henry George, but the contents emanate from his philosophy and teachings. Brief articles on economic issues as they affect the individual--campus unrest, property rights, urban environment, tax reform, real estate; "Brief Cases"--comments on past and present problems; notes on prices, meetings, conferences.

   Alternate subtitle:

   NEWS AND VIEWS ON ECONOMICS

GÉRARD DE NERVAL

See Labrunie, Gérard.

GHIL, RAIMOND (?-1948)

French poet

1. Amis de Raimond Ghil. PREMIER RECEUIL COLLECTIF. Editor: Michel Esserent. Sponsor: Amis de Raimond Ghil, Lamalous-les-Bains, France. Publisher: Éditions de la Revue du Languedoc, France. 1952-(?). [100 p.]

   Critical studies; illustrations. In French.

GIDE, ANDRÉ (1869-1951)

French writer, editor

1. André Gide. Subseries of La Revue des Lettres Modernes. Editor: Claude E. Martin, 3, rue Alexis-Carrel, 69110 Ste-Foy-lès-Lyon, France. 1970-- . Irregular. Equivalent numbers are provided below for both the parent series (La Revue des Lettres Modernes) and the individual author series on Gide.

Gide subseries	La Revue series	Date
No. 1	Nos. 223-27	1970
No. 2	Nos. 280-84	1971
No. 3	Nos. 331-35	1972
No. 4	Nos. 374-79	1973

Gide subseries	La Revue series	Date
No. 5	Nos. 439-44	1975
No. 6	Unnumbered	1977

Each volume concerns a different subject. In French. See Camus, Albert, entry 1, for a full description of La Revue des Lettres Modernes.

Indexed by BULLETIN CRITIQUE, FRENCH XX, Klapp, and MLA INTERNATIONAL BIBLIOGRAPHY.

2. Archives André Gide. Subseries of Archives des Lettres Modernes. 1964-- . Irregular. Equivalent numbers are given below for both the parent series (Archives des Lettres Modernes) and the individual author series on Gide.

Gide subseries	Archives series	Date
No. 1	No. 54	1964
No. 2	No. 117	1970
No. 3	No. 134	1972
No. 4	Unnumbered	1977

In French. See Camus, Albert, entry 2, for a full description of Archives des Lettres Modernes.

Indexed by BULLETIN CRITIQUE, FRENCH VII, FRENCH XX, Klapp, and MLA INTERNATIONAL BIBLIOGRAPHY.

3. Bibliothèque André Gide. Publisher: Minard, Paris. 1967-- . Irregular. 30-70 Fr. [100-450 p.] Last issue examined: no. 5, 1977.

Each volume focuses on a specific subject--a regrouping of criticism originally published as Lettres Modernes. In French.

4. BULLETIN DES AMIS D'ANDRÉ GIDE (BAAG). Editor: Claude E. Martin, 3, rue Alexis-Carrel, 69110 Ste-Foy-lès-Lyon, France. Sponsor and publisher: Bibliothèque André Gide, Le Centre d'études gidiennes, Université de Lyon II, 69500 Bron, France. July 1968-- . Quarterly. 35 Fr; 40 Fr (foreign); included in membership of the Association des Amis d'André Gide, Unité d'Études françaises, Université de Lyon II (50 Fr; 35 Fr, students). [60-85 p.] Circulation: 700. Last issue examined: no. 40, 1978.

Brief articles on Gide's life, works, and background; reprints of early book reviews and criticism; reminiscences; previously unpublished letters to and from Gide; descriptions and comments on new editions of Gide's letters, translations, articles in periodicals, dissertations, work in progress; bibliographies, such as that of translations, library holdings, or Gide criticism; "Varia"--news and notes on publications, letters, manuscripts, meetings, activities of the Association, its members, publications, and budget; lists of new members; photographs; index. Available in vol. 1 (nos. 1-17, 1968-72) and vol. 2 (nos. 18-24, 1973-74). In English or French.

Indexed by BIBLIOGRAPHIE DE LA LITTÉRATURE FRANÇAISE, FRENCH XX, Klapp, and REVUE D'HISTOIRE LITTÉRAIRE.

Alternate titles:

Association des Amis d'André Gide. BULLETIN D'INFORMATIONS

BULLETIN D'INFORMATIONS DE L'ASSOCIATION DES AMIS D'ANDRÉ GIDE

BULLETIN DE L'ASSOCIATION DES AMIS D'ANDRÉ GIDE

5. Cahiers André Gide (CAG). Editor: Claude E. Martin, 3, rue Alexis-Carrel, 69110 Ste-Foy-lès-Lyon, France. Sponsor: Issued in cooperation with the Association des Amis d'André Gide. Secrétariat: Unité d'Études françaises, Université de Lyon II, chemin de l'Hippodrome, 69500 Bron, France. Siège social: 17, rue de l'Université, 75008 Paris. Publisher: Gallimard, Paris. 1969-- . Annual (a series). 40-90 Fr. [300-700 p.] Last issue examined: vol. 8, 1978.

Each volume is devoted to a special subject and has a distinctive title, such as LES CAHIERS DE LA PETITE DAME (1976). Mainly reprints of letters and journals, accompanied by numerous notes and helpful critical material; primary and secondary bibliographies--comprehensive and international; bibliographical references; contributions by such well-known authors as Malraux; information on activities of the Association des Amis d'André Gide with list of members; occasional illustrations and portraits; indexes in some volumes. In French.

Indexed by BIBLIOGRAPHIE DE LA LITTÉRATURE FRANÇAISE, FRENCH XX, and Klapp.

6. PRÉTEXTE: CAHIER ANDRÉ GIDE. Editors: Jean-Jacques Thierry and Jean-Louis Ornequint, 116, rue Gatti-de-Gamond, Brussels, Belgium. Sponsor: Wladimir de Goghnieff, 7, villa de la Martinique, Boulogne-sur-Seine, France. Publisher: Librairie Gallimard, 15, boulevard Raspail, 75015 Paris. February 1952-(?). Quarterly. [100-120 p.] Last issue examined: no. 3, 1953.

Each volume is on a different subject--for example, RILKE, GIDE, ET VALÉRY. Brief biographical, bibliographical, psychological, and thematic articles and notes, mainly on Gide but occasionally on other authors as well; bibliography. In French.

Alternate title:

Collection Études gidiennes, Les Éditions de la Revue PRÉTEXTE

GIONO, JEAN (1895-1970)

French novelist

1. Association des Amis de Jean Giono. BULLETIN. Sponsor: Association des Amis de Jean Giono, CCP 53.6657 Marseilles, France. President: Henri Fluchère, Emeritus Dean, Faculté des Lettres, Aix-en-Provence, "Tras Castel," 04220 Sainte-Tulle, France. Secretary: Louis Michel, Les Chauvinets, 04100 Manosque, France. Spring 1973-- . Irregular. [65-135 p.] Last issue examined: no. 6, 1976.

   Interested in relevant information and documents on Giono, critical studies of the works; international contributors. In French.

   Indexed by BIBLIOGRAPHIE DE LA LITTÉRATURE FRANÇAISE, FRENCH XX, and Klapp.

   Alternate title:

   BULLETIN. Association des Amis de Jean Giono.

2. Jean Giono. Subseries of La Revue des Lettres Modernes. Editor: Alan J. Clayton, Department of Romance Languages, Tufts University, Medford, Mass. 02155. 1974-- . Irregular. Equivalent numbers are provided below for both the parent series (La Revue des Lettres Modernes) and the individual author series on Giono.

Giono subseries	La Revue series	Date
No. 1	Nos. 385-90	1974
No. 2	Nos. 468-73	1976

   In French. See Camus, Albert, entry 1, for a full description of La Revue des Lettres Modernes.

   Indexed by BULLETIN CRITIQUE, FRENCH XX, Klapp, and MLA INTERNATIONAL BIBLIOGRAPHY.

GIRAUDOUX, JEAN (1882-1944)

French author

1. Archives des Lettres Modernes. 1961-- . Irregular. Series numbers for the issues on Giraudoux are given below.

Giraudoux subseries	Archives series	Date
Unnumbered	No. 35	1961
Unnumbered	No. 56	1964
Unnumbered	No. 108	1969
Unnumbered	No. 125	1971

In French. See Camus, Albert, entry 2, for a full description of Archives des Lettres Modernes.

Indexed by BULLETIN CRITIQUE, FRENCH VII, FRENCH XX, Klapp, and MLA INTERNATIONAL BIBLIOGRAPHY.

2. CAHIERS JEAN GIRAUDOUX (CJG). Sponsor: Société des Amis de Jean Giraudoux, Pavillon du Festival, rue Louis-Jouvet, 87 Bellac, France. Publisher: Éditions Bernard Grasset, Paris. 1972-- . Irregular. 10-15 Fr. [100-150 p.] Last issue examined: no. 7, 1978.

   Designed to facilitate the study of Giraudoux's work. Includes brief critical and biographical articles examining his contribution to the theatre, the sources for his ideas and style, his influence; previously unpublished letters to friends and family, with numerous notes and explanations; occasional bibliographies of Giraudoux scholarship; occasional photographs. In French.

Indexed by BIBLIOGRAPHIE DE LA LITTÉRATURE FRANÇAISE, BULLETIN CRITIQUE, FRENCH XX, Klapp, MLA INTERNATIONAL BIBLIOGRAPHY, and REVUE D'HISTOIRE LITTÉRAIRE.

GISSING, GEORGE (1857-1903)

English novelist, critic, essayist

1. GISSING NEWSLETTER. Editor: Pierre Coustillas (University of Lille), 10 rue Gay-Lussac, 59110-La Madeleine, France. Sponsor: C.C. Kohler, 12, Horsham Road, Dorking, Surrey RH4 2JL, England. January 1965-- . Quarterly. £1.50 (individuals); £3 (libraries). [10-25 p.] Circulation: 200. Last issue examined: vol. 14, 1978.

   Brief, informal information for Gissing enthusiasts; occasional studies of plots, characters, or themes in the novels; bibliography in every issue of recently published books and articles, with citations for their reviews; reprints of lectures, such as on Gissing's sociological themes; informal news notes, like that on Gissing's grave in France; announcements of new editions and future scholarly publications; reminiscences by acquaintances of Gissing's family; notes on allusions and quotations in Gissing's works; book reviews; letters to the editor; no index.

GLASGOW, ELLEN (1874-1945)

American novelist

1. ELLEN GLASGOW NEWSLETTER. Editor: Edgar E. MacDonald. Sponsor: Ellen Glasgow Society, Box 565, Ashland, Va. 23005. October 1974-- . 2/yr. $1. [20 p.] Circulation: 225. Last issue examined: no. 9, 1978.

   Interested in encouraging Glasgow studies by disseminating news of Glasgow scholarship and publications. Articles on her life, acquaintances, and contemporaries; news and notes concerning library acquisitions, films, business of the Society, MLA seminars; reprints of letters to and from her friends; occasional comments on recently published criticism and bibliographies; reviews; report of work in progress; illustrations, reproductions, and facsimiles.

   Indexed by MISSISSIPPI QUARTERLY and MLA INTERNATIONAL BIBLIOGRAPHY.

GOBINEAU, JOSEPH-ARTHUR, COMTE DE (1816-82)

French diplomat, writer, Orientalist

1. Archives des Lettres Modernes. 1967-- . Irregular. The series number for the issue on Gobineau is provided below.

Gobineau subseries	Archives series	Date
Unnumbered	No. 75	1967

   In French. See Camus, Albert, entry 2, for a full description of Archives des Lettres Modernes.

   Indexed by BULLETIN CRITIQUE, Klapp, and MLA INTERNATIONAL BIBLIOGRAPHY.

2. ÉTUDES GOBINIENNES. Editor: Jean Gaulmier, 74, rue Desnouettes, 75015 Paris. Publisher: Librairie Klincksieck, Paris. Directors: A.B. Duff and Jean Gaulmier. November 1966-- . Annual. 40-60 Fr. [200-300 p.] Last issue examined: vol. 8, 1974-75.

   Scholarly essays on Gobineau's life, literary style, and influence in foreign countries; previously unpublished or inaccessible documents, letters, and family papers, accompanied by explanatory notes; annual "Bibliographie Gobineau"; news of conferences, work in progress, new editions; brief book reviews; occasional special issues, such as the one in honor of the centenary of "Les Pléïades" (1974-75); portraits, photographs, illustrations, and facsimiles. In French. Vol. 9 not yet published (1978).

Indexed by BIBLIOGRAPHIE DE LA LITTÉRATURE FRANÇAISE, BULLETIN CRITIQUE, and Klapp.

GODWIN, MARY WOLLSTONECRAFT

See Wollstonecraft, Mary.

GÖRRES, JOSEPH VON (1776-1848)

German journalist, man of letters

1. HISTORISCHES JAHRBUCH DER GÖRRES-GESELLSCHAFT (HJb). Sponsor: Görres-Gesellschaft, Freiburg/Köln/Munich, Germany (BRD). 1880-- . Annual. Last issue examined: vol. 95, 1975.

   Occasional long scholarly articles on Görres' beliefs and on his contributions to history. Index for vols. 1-34. In German. Second-hand copies available from Kraus Periodicals (1951-67, $180).

   Indexed by Köttelwesch.

2. LITERATURWISSENSCHAFTLICHES JAHRBUCH (LJGG; LwJb). Sponsor: Görres-Gesellschaft, Berlin, Germany (BRD). Publisher: Duncker und Humblot, Berlin. 1926-39 (nos. 1-9); publication suspended, 1939-60; new series, 1960-- . Annual. Last issue examined: no. 14, 1973.

   Inspired by Görres, but devoted to literature in general. In German.

   Indexed by ENGLISH LANGUAGE NOTES, FRENCH VII, and MLA INTERNATIONAL BIBLIOGRAPHY.

   Alternate title:

   LITERATURWISSENSCHAFTLICHES JAHRBUCH DER GÖRRES-GESELLSCHAFT.

3. PHILOSOPHISCHES JAHRBUCH DER GÖRRES-GESELLSCHAFT (PhJb; PJGG). Sponsor: Görres-Gesellschaft, Freiburg/Munich, Germany (BRD). 1888-1942; suspended publication, 1943-45; 1946-51; suspended publication, 1952; 1953-- . Annual.

   Inspired by Görres' life and works, but devoted to philosophy in general. In German. Index for 1888-1907 (vols. 1-20). Second-hand copies available from Kraus Periodicals (1888-1950, $1,226).

   Indexed by Köttelwesch and MLA INTERNATIONAL BIBLIOGRAPHY.

GOETHE, JOHANN WOLFGANG VON (1749-1832)

German poet, novelist, dramatist

1. Archives des Lettres Modernes. 1969-- . Irregular. The series number for the issue on Goethe is provided below.

Goethe subseries	Archives series	Date
Unnumbered	No. 107	1969

In German. See Camus, Albert, entry 2, for a full description of Archives des Lettres Modernes.

Indexed by BULLETIN CRITIQUE, FRENCH XX, Klapp, and MLA INTERNATIONAL BIBLIOGRAPHY.

2. AUSTRALIAN GOETHE SOCIETY PROCEEDINGS (AGoethe). Sponsor and publisher: Australian Goethe Society, Victorian Branch, Melbourne, Australia. 1949-(?). Irregular. [70-90 p.] Last issue examined: vol. 6, 1956-59.

Lectures on the works of Goethe and related subjects; book reviews; summary of Society activities--its several branches, Goethe Prizes. In German or English.

Indexed by Köttelwesch.

Alternate title:

PROCEEDINGS OF THE AUSTRALIAN GOETHE SOCIETY

3. CHRONIK DES WIENER GOETHE-VEREINS (Chronik; CWGV). Superseded by JAHRBUCH DES WIENER GOETHE-VEREINS (see entry 23). Sponsor and publisher: Verlag des Wiener Goethe-Vereins, Vienna, Austria. October 1886-1959 (vols. 1-63). Annual. [60-160 p.]

Reprints of lectures; news of membership activities throughout the year--performances, museum and library events, meetings; later issues contain critical, biographical, bibliographical, and textual studies; facsimiles. Index for vols. 1-20. In German.

Indexed by Köttelwesch and MLA INTERNATIONAL BIBLIOGRAPHY.

Alternate title:

CHRONIK WIENER GOETHEVEREIN

4. ENGLISH GOETHE SOCIETY: PUBLICATIONS (PEGS). Editors since 1972: Frank M. Fowler, Department of German, Queen Mary College, Mile End Road, London E.1; Brian A. Rowley and Ann C. Weaver. Sponsor: English Goethe Society. Publisher: University College,

London W.C.1, England. 1886-1912 (nos. 1-14); new series, 1923-39 (nos. 1-14); suspended publication, 1940-45; 1946-71; new series, 1973-- . Annual. £4; £2 (students). [100-170 p.] Last issue examined: no. 47, 1978.

Founded originally to promote the study of Goethe's work and thought, but later extended to include other fields of German literature. Long scholarly essays on Goethe's influence, ideas, literary style, specific titles and characters; reprints of papers read at conferences; brief surveys of research; chronicle of Society events--rules, finances, prizes, list of members. Vols. 1-41 (1924-71) are available from Dawson's (£115). INDEX TO PUBLICATIONS, 1886-1970, available from the Treasurer, Department of German, University College, London W.C.1 (£1). In English or German.

Indexed by ENGLISH LANGUAGE NOTES, FRENCH VII, Köttelwesch, and MLA INTERNATIONAL BIBLIOGRAPHY.

Alternate title:

PUBLICATIONS OF THE ENGLISH GOETHE SOCIETY

5. GOETHE: NEUE FOLGE DES JAHRBUCHS DER GOETHE-GESELLSCHAFT (Weimar; JbGG). Editors: Hans Wahl, 1947-49; Andreas B. Wachsmuth, 1949-71. Publisher: Hermann Böhlaus Nachfolger, Weimar, Germany (DDR). 1947-71 (vols. 10-33). Annual.

For complete information, see entry 15: GOETHE-JAHRBUCH (Weimar).

Alternate title:

GOETHE

6. GOETHE: VIERMONATSSCHRIFT DER GOETHE-GESELLSCHAFT: NEUE FOLGE DES JAHRBUCHS. Editor: Hans Wahl. Publisher: Verlag der Goethe-Gesellschaft, Weimar, Germany (DDR). 1938-44 (vols. 3-9). Quarterly.

For complete information, see entry 15: GOETHE-JAHRBUCH (Weimar).

Alternate title:

GOETHE

7. GOETHE: VIERTELJAHRESSCHRIFT DER GOETHE-GESELLSCHAFT: NEUE FOLGE DES JAHRBUCHS. Editor: Hans Wahl. Publisher: Verlag der Goethe-Gesellschaft, Weimar, Germany (DDR). 1936-37 (vols. 1-2). Quarterly.

For complete information, see entry 15: GOETHE-JAHRBUCH (Weimar).

Alternate title:

GOETHE

8. GOETHE ALMANACH. Publisher: Bellaria-Verlag, Vienna. 1948-(?). [400 p.]

Partly critical essays and partly excerpts from Goethe's works; reprints of letters to and from Beethoven, Stifter, Carlyle; poems; portraits; no index. In German.

9. GOETHE-ALMANACH AUF DAS JAHR (Goethe-Al). Editors: Helmut Holtzhauer and Hans Henning. Publisher: Aufbau-Verlag, Berlin. 1967-71(?). [360-400 p.]

Long biographical and critical studies on Goethe, his themes, and his relationship with such authors as Schiller and Herder; numerous excerpts from his works; previously unpublished letters and other documents; descriptions of library holdings; "Tatigkeitsbericht"--news of all Goethe organizations in the German Democratic Republic; facsimiles and illustrations. In German.

Indexed by Köttelwesch and MLA INTERNATIONAL BIBLIOGRAPHY.

10. GOETHEANA. Publisher: Buenos Aires, Argentina. December 1947-April 1948 (nos. 1-3).

11. Goethe-Gesellschaft (Weimar). JAHRESBERICHT. 1886-- .

Nos. 1-28 appeared in vols. 7-34 (1886-1913) of GOETHE-JAHRBUCH (Weimar; see entry 15). From 1913 to 1935, information in nos. 29-50 on Gesellschaft conferences, programs, members and officers, finances, library, and international branches was included in the JAHRBUCH DER GOETHE-GESELLSCHAFT (entry 21); from 1936 to 1939, in GOETHE (see entries 6-7). In German.

12. Goethe-Gesellschaft (Weimar). SCHRIFTEN. Editors: different editors for almost every volume. Sponsor: Goethe-Gesellschaft, Weimar, Germany (DDR). Publisher: Verlag der Goethe-Gesellschaft, 1885-1941; since 1949, Hermann Böhlaus Nachfolger, Weimar, Germany (DDR). 1885-1941 (vols. 1-52); new series, 1949 (vol. 1/vol. 53)-- . Irregular. DM15-25. [130-750 p.] Last issue examined: vol. 60, 1974.

Almost exclusively critical editions of Goethe documents, but there are occasional monographs concerning Goethe's life, correspondence, works, influence, and contemporaries; facsimiles and illustrations. Includes REGISTER DER GOETHE-JAHRBÜCHER, 1880-1968 (no. 59). In German. Second-hand copies available from Kraus Periodicals (1885-1958), $495); reprints from Walter J. Johnson (1885-1962, $565). Vol. 61 not yet published (1978).

Alternate title:

SCHRIFTEN DER GOETHE-GESELLSCHAFT (Weimar)

13. GOETHE JAHRBUCH: ANUARIO GOETHE. Editor: Hans Von Foerster, Casilla de Correo 938, Buenos Aires, Argentina. Publisher: Goethe-Buchhandlung, Buenos Aires. 1949-(?). Annual. [120-225 p.] Last issue examined: no. 18, 1966.

Not devoted to Goethe, but the first few issues do include informal biographical and critical articles about him; later issues contain information only on German cities, German and South American scholars, and occasional short stories. In German or Spanish.

Alternate titles:

ANUARIO DI GOETHE

GOETHE-JAHRBUCH FÜR SÜDAMERIKA

GOETHEANA PERIODICO LITERARIO

14. GOETHE-JAHRBUCH (Tokyo; GJbTokyo). Sponsor: Goethe-Gesellschaft in Japan. 1932-(?); new series, 1959-- . Annual. [200-225 p.] Last issue examined: vol. 19, 1977.

Long critical articles on Goethe's works; interdisciplinary studies; news notes. In Japanese, with summaries in German.

Indexed by ENGLISH LANGUAGE NOTES and Köttelwesch.

15. GOETHE-JAHRBUCH (Weimar; GJb). Editor: since 1975, Karl-Heinz Hahn. Sponsor: Goethe-Gesellschaft, Burgplatz 4, Weimar 53, Germany (DDR). Publisher: Hermann Böhlaus Nachfolger, Weimar. 1972 (vol. 89)-- . Annual. Free with membership (DM25); $15. [280-380 p.] Last issue examined: vol. 94, 1977.

Long scholarly articles by international contributors on Goethe's life and works, his interest in art and artists, his relationship with past and contemporary authors; since 1952, a comprehensive annual, analytical, international bibliography, "Goethe-Bibliographie," edited by Hans Henning; numerous long book reviews; information on works in progress; news from German and other European Gesellschaften; facsimiles and illustrations; author index. In German. Second-hand copies available from Kraus Periodicals (1880-1961, $594); reprints from Walter

J. Johnson (1880-1963, $895).

Cumulative index, REGISTER DER GOETHE-JAHRBÜCHER 1880-1968, edited by Konrad Kratzsch (Weimar: Hermann Böhlaus, 1970; 177 p.) This is no. 59 of the Goethe-Gesellschaft (Weimar). SCHRIFTEN (see entry 12).

The 1972 volume is numbered 89 in continuation of the combined numbering of its predecessors:

GOETHE-JAHRBUCH, 1880-1913 (vols. 1-34). Vols. 7-34 include JAHRESBERICHT, nos. 1-28. Annual.

JAHRBUCH DER GOETHE-GESELLSCHAFT (Weimar), 1914-35 (vols. 1-21) (see entry 21). Annual.

GOETHE: VIERTELJAHRESSCHRIFT DER GOETHE-GESELLSCHAFT, 1936-37 (vols. 1-2) (see entry 7). Quarterly.

GOETHE: VIERMONATSSCHRIFT DER GOETHE-GESELLSCHAFT, 1938-44 (vols. 3-9) (see entry 6). Quarterly.

Suspended publication, 1945-46.

GOETHE: NEUE FOLGE DES JAHRBUCHS DER GOETHE-GESELLSCHAFT, 1947-71 (vols. 10-33) (see entry 5). Annual.

Indexed by Klapp, Köttelwesch, MLA INTERNATIONAL BIBLIOGRAPHY, and PHILOLOGICAL QUARTERLY.

16. GOETHE-KALENDER AUF DAS JAHR (GK). Editor: Otto Julius Bierbaum and others. Sponsor: Frankfurter Goethe-museum, Frankfurt/am/Main, Germany (BRD). Publisher: Dieterich, Leipzig, Germany (DDR). 1906-14; suspended 1915-16; 1917-(?). Annual. [120-280 p.]

Informal articles on Goethe's family and contemporaries; surveys of his influence and reception; reprints of his stories, with accompanying critical comments; previously unpublished letters; numerous quotations and poems or excerpts from poems; photographs, portraits, and facsimiles; numerous advertisements; no index. In German. Second-hand copies available from Kraus Periodicals (1906-40, $110).

Alternate title:

GOETHE KALENDER

17. GOETHE- UND SCHILLERSTUDIEN. Publisher: Munich, Germany (BRD). 1905-(?).

18. Goethezeit. Editors: Bernhard Gajek, Gerhard Kaiser, Hans-Joachim Mähl, Karl Pestalozzi, and Erich Trunz. Publisher: Athenäum Verlag, Frankfurt/am/Main, Germany (BRD). 1969-77. Irregular (a series; vols. 2-3, 1971; vol. 4, 1974; vols. 5-6, 1972). $8-21. [200-600 p.] Last issue examined: vol. 7, 1977.

Each volume is concerned with one specific aspect of the life or works of Goethe or other philosophers such as Brentano or Kierkegaard. Some volumes are written by a single author; others are collections of essays by well-known scholars. Bibliographies in every volume; indexes in some volumes; occasional illustrations. In German.

The comprehensive, analytical bibliography on the life and times of Goethe which appears in the annual publication BIBLIOGRAPHIE DER DEUTSCHEN SPRACH- UND LITERATURWISSENSCHAFT, by Köttelwesch, is also entitled "Goethezeit."

Indexed by MLA INTERNATIONAL BIBLIOGRAPHY.

19. Goethe-Zeit und Goethe-Kreis. SCHRIFTENREIHE. Editors: Friedrich List and Hans Kaesser. Publisher: Verlag für Angewandte Wissenschaften, Baden-Baden, Germany (BRD). 1954-(?). Irregular. [30-80 p.] Last issues examined: nos. 1-2, 1954.

Monographs examining the background and contemporaries of Goethe; illustrations. In German. Two more volumes were announced but have not been located.

20. JAHRBUCH DER GOETHE-GESELLSCHAFT (Japan). Editor: Shusuke Okamoto. Sponsor: Goethe-Gesellschaft, Kansai-Gebiet, Osaka, Japan. 1955-59 (vols. 1-5). Annual.

Articles; news. In Japanese, with summaries in German.

21. JAHRBUCH DER GOETHE-GESELLSCHAFT (Weimar; JbGG; JGG). Editors: Hans G. Gräf, 1914-22; Max Hecker, 1923-35. 1914-35 (vols. 1-21). Annual. 200-300 p.

Name and subject index in each volume. Cumulative name and subject index 1914-34 (vols. 1-20), in vol. 21 (1936). International list of members, supplement to vol. 12, 1926. Includes JAHRESBERICHT, 1913/14-1934/35 (nos. 29-50), see entry 11. See entry 15, GOETHE-JAHRBUCH (Weimar), for complete information. In German.

Indexed by MLA INTERNATIONAL BIBLIOGRAPHY.

Alternate title:

Goethe-Gesellschaft (Weimar). JAHRBUCH

22. JAHRBUCH DES FREIEN DEUTSCHEN HOCHSTIFTS. Editor: Detlev Lüders. Publisher: Max Niemayer Verlag, Tübingen, Germany (BRD). 1902-40; suspended publication, 1941-61; new series, 1962-- . Annual. $25-35. [500-600 p.] Last issue examined: 1977.

Organ of the Goethe-Museum des Freien Deutschen Hochstifts in Frankfurt/am/Main, Germany (BRD). Interested in all aspects of German literature, especially Goethe, his contemporaries, and their interaction with past and present cultures; notes, articles, and illustrations of the Museum collection; news of activities--exhibitions, lectures, list of members; international contributors. Preceded by its BERICHTE, 1861-1901. In German.

Indexed by ENGLISH LANGUAGE NOTES, Köttelwesch, and MLA INTERNATIONAL BIBLIOGRAPHY.

Alternate title:

Freies Deutsches Hochstift. JAHRBUCH

23. JAHRBUCH DES WIENER GOETHE-VEREINS: NEUE FOLGE DER CHRONIK (JWGV). Supersedes CHRONIK DES WIENER GOETHE-VEREINS (see entry 3). Editor: Robert Mühlher. Publisher: Verlag des Wiener Goethe-Vereins, Reitschulgasse 2, A-1010, Vienna 1, Austria. New series, 1960 (vol. 64)-- . Annual. As 50; As 150 (foreign). [150-60 p.] Last issue examined: vol. 80, 1976.

At first only a register of society lectures and activities, but later the central Austrian publication for Goethe scholarship of all kinds--critical, bibliographical, textual, biographical. Extends coverage to contemporaries, such as Watteau, and to other authors, such as Rilke; reprints of lectures delivered to the Wiener Goethe-Verein; numerous bibliographical references; numerous book reviews; news of activities--calendar of lectures, financial report, list of officers; occasional contributions from the United States; illustrations. In German. Reprints available from Kraus Reprint (1886-1937, $200; 1936-66); and from Walter J. Johnson (1886-1937, $200). Alternate spelling: JAHRBUCH DES WIENER GOETHEVEREINS.

Indexed by ENGLISH LANGUAGE NOTES, Köttelwesch, and MLA INTERNATIONAL BIBLIOGRAPHY.

Alternate title:

Wiener Goethe-Verein. JAHRBUCH

24. MIT GOETHE DURCH DAS JAHR: EIN KALENDER FÜR DAS JAHR. . . . Editor: Effi Biedrzynski et al. Publisher: Artemis Verlag, Zurich. 1954-- . Annual. DM5. [100-120 p.] Last issue examined: 1977.

Quotations, biographical data, and excerpts from letters and other works arranged by date; numerous illustrations; facsimiles. In German.

GOLDONI, CARLO (1707-93)

Italian dramatist, poet

1. STUDI GOLDONIANI (SGoldoniani). Sponsor: Casa di Goldoni, S. Toma 2794, 30125 Venice, Italy. 1968-- . Irregular. L.3.000-4.600. [170 p.] Last issue examined: vol. 4, 1976.

   Subseries of the publications of the Casa di Goldoni. Long scholarly essays on Goldoni compositions, translations, poems; surveys of his influence in other countries; previously unpublished sonnets and other works; occasional comprehensive bibliographies covering several years of Goldoni scholarship. In Italian. Vol. 5 not yet published (1978).

   Indexed by MLA INTERNATIONAL BIBLIOGRAPHY.

   Alternate subtitle:

   PUBBLICAZIONI DELLA CASA DI GOLDONI

GOURMONT, RÉMY DE (1858-1915)

French novelist, poet, dramatist

1. IMPRIMERIE GOURMONTIENNE. Publisher: Paris, France. 1920-23 (nos. 1-10). Quarterly.

   In French.

   Alternate information in UNION LIST OF SERIALS: Discontinued in 1925(?).

GRAVES, ROBERT (1895-)

English poet, novelist, critic

1. FOCUS ON ROBERT GRAVES. Editor: Ellsworth Mason, Head, Special Collections, University of Colorado Libraries, Boulder, Colo. 80302. Sponsor: University of Colorado Libraries. January 1972-- . Irregular (nos. 2-3, December 1973; nos. 4, June 1974; no. 5, June 1976). Free to Graves scholars, collectors, and interested libraries. [16 p.]

   Compiles biographical, bibliographical, and book-collecting information about Robert Graves; articles about Graves and his relationships to other writers; occasional bibliographies and book reviews; news and notes.

   Indexed by ANNUAL BIBLIOGRAPHY OF ENGLISH LANGUAGE AND LITERATURE and MLA INTERNATIONAL BIBLIOGRAPHY.

GREENAWAY, KATE (1846-1901)

English artist, illustrator

1. UNDER THE WINDOW. Sponsor: Kate Greenaway Society, James L. Lowe, Director, 3709 Gradyville Road, Newton Square, Pa. 19073. March 1971-(temporarily suspended). Quarterly. $2. Circulation: 350.

   Official publication of the Kate Greenaway Society. Brief articles; directory of members; advertisements. Letter from editor says this has been temporarily suspended.

GREGORY VII, SAINT (c. 1020-85)

Italian pope

1. STUDI GREGORIANI PER LA STORIA DELLA "LIBERTAS ECCLESIAE." Editor: Giovanni Battista Borino, 1947-66; since 1970, Alfonso M. Stickler. Publisher: Pontificio Ateneo Salesiano, Rome, Italy. 1947-60 (vols. 1-7); new series, 1961(?)-- . Irregular. L.14.500-20.000. Last issue examined: vol. 10, 1975.

   Not confined solely to Pope Gregory VII, his life and works, but concerned with the total concept and influence of the Middle Ages--the social, political, cultural, religious, and intellectual reforms of his times; long scholarly essays by international contributors; illustrations and graphs. Index to vols. 1-6 in vol. 8. In Italian, French, German, or English. Second-hand copies available from Kraus Periodicals (1947-60, $110). Vol. 11 not yet published (1978).

   Alternate title, 1947-60 (vols. 1-7):

   STUDI GREGORIANI PER LA STORIA DE GREGORIO VII E DELLA RIFORMA GREGORIANA

GREY, ZANE (1872-1939)

American novelist

1. ZANE GREY COLLECTOR. Editor: Reverend G.M. Farley, 1613 Virginia Avenue, Hagerstown, Md. 21740. April 1968-75 (vols. 1-7, nos. 1-29). Quarterly. $2. [14 p.] Circulation: 200.

   Brief notes and news; reprints of inaccessible material; bibliography in special supplementary printing; information on rare works; occasional book reviews; illustrations; looseleaf format. Back issues available.

GRILLPARZER, FRANZ (1791-1872)

Austrian dramatist, poet, novelist

1. GRILLPARZER-FORUM FORCHTENSTEIN: VORTRÄGE, FORSCHUNGEN, BERICHTE (GFF). Editors: Johann Hüttner and Otto G. Schindler, Institut für Theaterwissenschaft, Universität Wien, Hofburg, Batthyanystiege, A-1010 Vienna. Sponsor: Grillparzer-Forum Forchtenstein, Eisenstadt, Austria. Publisher: Hermann Böhlaus Nachfolger, Graz/Vienna/Köln; and Rötzer-Verlag, Eisenstadt, Austria. 1965-- . Annual. [100-200 p.] Last issue examined: 1977.

   Reprints of lectures at the annual Grillparzer forum on the author's life and works, his technique and philosophy, his themes, theory, satire, and criticism; annual international bibliography of Grillparzer scholarship--new editions, critical books and articles; current surveys of Grillparzer research; list of officers; calendar of activities--"Tätigkeitsbericht"; international contributors; illustrations. In German.

   Indexed by Köttelwesch and MLA INTERNATIONAL BIBLIOGRAPHY.

2. JAHRBUCH DER GRILLPARZER-GESELLSCHAFT (JGG; GrJb; JGrG). Editor: since 1966, Johann Gunert. Sponsor: Grillparzer-Gesellschaft, Vienna. Publisher: third series, Bergland Verlag, Vienna. 1890-1915 (vols. 1-25); 1920, 1924, 1926, 1930-34 (vols. 26-33); new series, 1941-44; third series, 1953-- . Irregular. $8-22. [150-435 p.] Last issue examined: vol. 12, 1976.

   Long critical essays on Grillparzer and his contemporaries--their artistic theories, mutual influence, language, themes, and style; reprints of letters, journals, and other previously unpublished material; surveys of research; occasional special bibliographies, as in series 3, vol. 1, "Grillparzer-Bibliographie, 1937-52"; occasional book reviews, some brief, some long and scholarly; information concerning activities of the Gesellschaft and its international branches; long biographical sketches of contributing authors; international contributors; portraits, illustrations, facsimiles; index to the third series in the back of each annual volume. The Grillparzer-Gesellschaft also occasionally publishes individual volumes of criticism and research. In German. Second-hand copies available from Kraus Periodicals (1890-1905, $120); reprints from Walter J. Johnson (1890-1915, 1930, $295).

   Indexed by Köttelwesch and MLA INTERNATIONAL BIBLIOGRAPHY.

   Alternate title:

   Grillparzer-Gesellschaft. JAHRBUCH

GRIMM

Jacob (1785-1863)
Wilhelm (1786-1859) German philologists

1. BRÜDER GRIMM GEDENKEN. Editor: Ludwig Denecke (vol. 2). Publisher: N.G. Elwert Verlag, Marburg an der Lahn, Germany (BRD). 1963-- . Irregular. DM46. [300 p.] Last issue examined: vol. 2, 1975.

   Long studies of the Grimm brothers' philological accomplishments; research in the folktales of all the European countries; articles on early editions of the folktales and on illustrators and translations; brief notes on friendships, language; illustrations. In German.

2. Brüder Grimm Gesellschaft. JAHRESGABE. Editor: Else Hünert-Hofmann. Publisher: Kassel, Germany (BRD). 1970/72-- .

GRINDEL, EUGÈNE [PAUL ÉLUARD] (1895-1952)

French poet

1. CAHIERS PAUL ÉLUARD. Editor: Michel Launay, 81, avenue de la Lanterne, 06 Nice, France. Sponsor and publisher: Centre de la Civilisation Française et Européenne du Vingtième Siècle, Université de Nice, 117, rue de France, 06 Nice. May 1972-- . 3/yr. (irregular). 30 Fr. [50-70 p.] Last issue examined: no. 4, November 1973.

   Short articles on Éluard's theology, language, writings, pseudonym; reprints of previously published criticism; previously unpublished documents, such as extracts from letters; contributions to a bibliography and a concordance of Éluard's works. In French. Vol. 5 not yet published (1978).

   Indexed by BIBLIOGRAPHIE DE LA LITTÉRATURE FRANÇAISE.

GROTH, KLAUS (1819-99)

German poet

1. JAHRESGABE DER KLAUS-GROTH-GESELLSCHAFT (KGGJ). Editors: Bernhard Weihmann and Magdalena Weihmann. Sponsor: Klaus-Groth-Gesellschaft. Publisher: Westholsteinische Verlagsanstalt Boyens, Heide in Holstein, Germany (BRD). 1959-- . Annual. DM7-14. [100-200 p.] Last issue examined: vol. 19, 1975-76.

   Collections of long scholarly essays on the life, works, and influence of Klaus Groth; studies of his associates, correspondence, the literature he influenced, problems in specific titles; reports from the Groth Museum and Gesellschaft; survey of library holdings; interviews; list of new members; illustrations and photographs. In German.

Indexed by Köttelwesch and MLA INTERNATIONAL BIBLIOGRAPHY.

Alternate title:

Klaus-Groth-Gesellschaft. JAHRESGABE

GUÉRIN

Eugénie de (1805-48)
Maurice de (1810-39) French authors, brother and sister

1. L'AMITIÉ GUÉRINIENNE (AGuérin; AmG). Editors: F. Barthe and P. Damien Bertrand, 26, avenue Bouloc-Torcatis, 81400 Carmaux, France. Sponsor: Amis de Guérin, 3, rue Justin-Alibert, Albi, France. January 1964-- . Quarterly. $1.95. [35 p.] Last issue examined: no. 50, 1976.

   Brief studies of individual titles; biographical information; evaluations of Guérin contributions, friendships, technique; previously unpublished documents; reprints of letters from family, friends, and others; reminiscences. In French.

   Indexed by BIBLIOGRAPHIE DE LA LITTÉRATURE FRANÇAISE, ENGLISH LANGUAGE NOTES, Klapp, and REVUE D'HISTOIRE LITTÉRAIRE.

   Alternate information in RÉPERTOIRE DE LA PRESSE and in REVUE D'HISTOIRE LITTÉRAIRE: 1933-- . Address: 12, rue Matabiau, Toulouse, France.

   Alternate information in LISTE DES SOCIÉTÉS SAVANTES: Amis des Guérin, chez l'Abbé Decahors, Lauzerte (Tarn-et-Garonne), France.

2. Archives des Lettres Modernes. 1965-- . Irregular. The series number for the issue on Guérin is provided below.

Guérin subseries	Archives series	Date
Unnumbered	No. 60	1965

   In French. See Camus, Albert, entry 2, for a full description of Archives des Lettres Modernes.

   Indexed by BULLETIN CRITIQUE, Klapp, and MLA INTERNATIONAL BIBLIOGRAPHY.

GUILLAUMIN, ÉMILE (1873-1951)

French regional novelist

See Philippe, Charles-Louis, entry 1.

GUTENBERG, JOHANNES (c. 1400- c. 1468)

German printer

1. GUTENBERG-JAHRBUCH (GJ). Editors: Aloys Ruppel, 1926-69; Hans Widmann, 1970-76. Sponsor and publisher: Gutenberg-Gesellschaft, Mainz, Germany (BRD). Secretary: E. Born, Liebfrauenplatz 5, Mainz, Germany (BRD). 1926-- . Annual. [400-540 p.] Last issue examined: 1977.

   Scholarly studies and reports on the history of printing and book binding all over the world from the times of Johannes Gutenberg to the present; emphasis on the early history, with occasional references to Gutenberg; bibliography of Gesellschaft publications and reports; international contributors; numerous excellent facsimiles and colored reproductions of early illustrations and art work. Cumulative index: REGISTER ZUM GUTENBERG-JAHRBUCH 1926-60 (1962; 198 p.). In German, English, or Italian. Reprints available from Kraus Reprint (1926-44/49, vols. 1-19/24, $403); and from Walter J. Johnson (1926-72, vols. 1-47, with index, $1,695). Second-hand copies from Kraus Periodicals (1926-68, vols. 1-43 plus index, $1,188).

   Indexed by BIBLIOGRAPHIE DE LA LITTÉRATURE FRANÇAISE, Klapp, Köttelwesch, and MLA INTERNATIONAL BIBLIOGRAPHY.

   Other publications of the Gutenberg-Gesellschaft:

   JAHRESBERICHT, 1901-26; included in Jahrbuch, 1926-- .

   KLEINE DRUCKE, 1926-- . Irregular. Last issue examined: no. 102, 1977.

   SONDERVERÖFFENTLICHUNGEN, 1922-40.

   TÄTIGKEITSBERICHT, 1918-26 (alternate title for JAHRESBERICHT).

   VERÖFFENTLICHUNGEN, 1902-(?). Irregular. Last issue examined: vol. 23, 1934.

2. SCHRIFTEN DES GUTENBERG-MUSEUMS. Editor and publisher: Rolf Bernhart, Darmstadt, Germany (BRD). 1967-- . Irregular. $5. [35 p.] Last issue examined: vol. 5, 1973.

   Concerned with early printing practices and illustrations, not solely with Gutenberg. In German. Vol. 6 not yet published (1978).

3. SCHWEIZERISCHES GUTENBERGMUSEUM: ZEITSCHRIFT FÜR BUCHDRUCKGESCHICHTE, GRAPHIK- UND ZEITUNGSKUNDE. Editor: Max Mittler. Sponsor and publisher: Schweizerisches Gutenbergmuseum, Musée Gutenberg suisse, Bern, Switzerland. 1925 (no. 11)-- . Quarterly. S Fr 15; S Fr 17 (foreign); $4.50. [40-90 p.] Last issue examined: vol. 58, 1972.

    Concerned with the art of book publishing, binding, and printing, not solely with Gutenberg. Scholarly articles; brief book reviews; numerous illustrations, facsimiles, and photographs; international in coverage and interest. In German.

    Previous titles:

    GUTENBERGSTUBE, 1914-18 (nos. 1-4)

    GUTENBERGMUSEUM, 1919-24 (nos. 5-10)

    Alternate subtitle:

    REVUE D'HISTOIRE DE L'IMPRIMERIE, DES ARTS GRAPHIQUES, ET DE LA PRESSE

HÄBERLIN, PAUL (1878-1960)

Swiss educator, philosopher

1. GESCHÄFTSSTELLE DER PAUL-HÄBERLIN-GESELLSCHAFT. Sponsor: Paul Häberlin-Gesellschaft, 5022 Rombach, Switzerland. 1948-(?). Irregular. DM1-7. Last issue examined: vol. 7, 1964.

    Each volume concerns a different subject--studies either by Häberlin or about his ideas and work. In German.

2. Paul Häberlin-Gesellschaft. SCHRIFTEN. Sponsor: Paul Häberlin-Gesellschaft. Publisher: Schweizer Spiegel Verlag, Zurich. 1965-- . Irregular. S Fr 10. [20-200 p.] Last issue examined: vol. 4, 1974.

    Monographs on the philosophy of education, especially as it relates to Häberlin's ideas and activities; glossary; bibliographies; index. In German. Vol. 5 not yet published (1978).

    Alternate title:

    SCHRIFTENREIHE DER PAUL HÄBERLIN-GESELLSCHAFT

HANSJAKOB, HEINRICH (1837-1916)

German theologian

1. HANSJAKOB-JAHRBUCH. Sponsor: Heinrich-Hansjakob-Gesellschaft, Burgunderstrasse 11, 7800 Freiburg im Breisgau, Germany (BRD). President: Max Müller. Publishers: in 1958, Rombach, Freiburg im Breisgau, Germany (BRD); in 1969, Badenia Verlag, Karlsruhe, Germany (BRD). 1957-- . Irregular (no. 2, 1958; no. 3, 1969; no. 4, 1972; no. 5, 1975). [130-50 p.]

   Collections of long scholarly articles on Hansjakob's life and works, his family, political ideas, friendships; previously unpublished letters; occasional surveys of completed scholarship; bibliographical references; occasional photographs and facsimiles; no index. The JAHRBUCH is one of the publications of the VERÖFFENTLICHUNGEN described in the following entry. In German.

   Indexed by Köttelwesch.

2. Heinrich-Hansjakob-Gesellschaft. VERÖFFENTLICHUNGEN. Sponsor and publisher: Heinrich-Hansjakob-Gesellschaft, Burgunderstrasse 11, 7800 Freiburg im Breisgau, Germany (BRD). President: Max Müller. 1957(?)-- . Irregular. Last issue examined: no. 10, 1975.

   Each volume is on a specific subject, such as WEBER, MAX: HEINRICH HANSJAKOB, AUS SEINEM LEBEN UND SEINEM WERKEN (1970, 2 vols.); photographs; no index. The HANSJAKOB-JAHRBUCH (see entry 1) is included in this series, vol. 5 of the JAHRBUCH being no. 10 of the series. In German.

HARDY, THOMAS (1840-1928)

English novelist, poet

1. Monographs on the Life, Times, and Works of Thomas Hardy. Editor: James Stevens Cox, "Birling," Mount Durand, St. Peter Port, Guernsey, C.I. via Britain. Publisher: Toucan Press, Mount Durand, St. Peter Port, Guernsey, C.I. via Britain. 1968-- . Irregular (a series). [10-30 p.] Last issue examined: no. 72, 1971.

   Each issue focuses on a specific subject, such as ROUND DORSET WITH HARDY (1969) or THOMAS HARDY AT MAX GATE (1969). Long biographical or critical studies, or brief notes on the life, works, and times of Hardy and such contemporaries as Barnes and Powys; reminiscences by personal acquaintances of the Hardy family; reprints of letters; notes on Hardy's allusions, his illustrators, friendships, peculiarities, favorite dog, conversations, influence; numerous photographs and illustrations.

2. THOMAS HARDY SOCIETY REVIEW. Editor: F.B. Pinion, 65, Ranmoor Crescent, Sheffield S10 3GW, England. Sponsor: Thomas Hardy Society. Secretary: The Reverend John Yates, The Vicarage, Haselbury, Plucknett, Crewkerne, Somerset TA18 7PB, England. American representative: Harold Orel, Department of English, University of Kansas, Lawrence, Kans. 66045. 1975-- . Annual. Free with membership (£1.50); 30p or $.80 per issue. [30-40 p.] Last issue examined: vol. 1, no. 3, 1977.

   Aims to publish "informed critical views and inquiry concerning Thomas Hardy's works and life." Short critical articles and notes; new biographical information on Hardy, his marriage, friends; brief reviews of new editions and criticism; report of the Annual Summer School lectures and the Annual Walk.

3. THOMAS HARDY YEAR BOOK (THY). Editors: James S. and G. Stevens Cox, "Birling," Mount Durand, St. Peter Port, Guernsey, C.I. via Britain. September 1970-- . Annual (Autumn). £1.40 [80-125 p.] Circulation: 3,500. Last issue examined: vol. 6, 1977.

   "Devoted to publishing essays and articles about the life and times of Thomas Hardy; about the writer's environment, both physical and cultural; and about Dorset writers, especially those of the nineteenth century." Long scholarly studies of themes, characters, style, allusions in Hardy's works; numerous brief notes on his illustrators, descriptions (as of bell ringing or rural crafts), homes, use of names, travels; queries; occasional reports on scholarship concerning the Powys family, who were friends of Hardy; bibliographies of forthcoming books, slides and books for sale; reports of work in progress; brief book reviews; numerous photographs, illustrations, and facsimiles. Until 1975, distributed by Richard Abel; since 1976, by Blackwell and Mott, 49, Broad Street, Oxford OX1 3BP, England. Subscriptions went to fifty-seven different countries in 1971.

   Indexed by BRITISH HUMANITIES INDEX, MLA INTERNATIONAL BIBLIOGRAPHY, and YEAR'S WORK IN ENGLISH STUDIES.

HARTMANN, SADAKICHI (1867-1944)

American author, art historian

1. SADAKICHI HARTMANN NEWSLETTER. Editor and business correspondence: Richard Tuerk, Department of Literature and Languages, East Texas State University, East Texas Station, Commerce, Tex. 75428. Manuscripts: George Knox, Department of English, University of California, Riverside, Calif. 92502. Publisher: Department of Literature and Languages, East Texas State University. Fall 1969-Spring 1975 (vols. 1-5, no. 3). 3/yr. (Fall, Winter, Spring). $2.50. [12 p.] Circulation: 250.

Interested in scholarship on any phase of the life, career, writing, and influence of Sadakichi Hartmann. Brief critical and biographical articles; frequent bibliographies; previously unpublished works; occasional book reviews; letters to the editor; illustrations.

HAUPTMANN, GERHART (1862-1946)

German poet, dramatist, novelist

1. GERHART-HAUPTMANN-JAHRBUCH (G.H.-Jb). Editor: Felix A. Voigt. Publishers: 1936-37, Maruschke und Berendt-Verlag, Breslau, Germany (now Poland); 1948, Verlag Deutsche Volksbücherei, Goslar, Germany (BRD). 1936-48; new series, 1948-(?). Irregular. [160-270 p.]

   Long studies on Hauptmann's life and works--his travels, reception, influence, and dramatic and poetic technique; reminiscences by friends and colleagues; reprints of poems and fragments of his other works; occasional bibliographies of primary and secondary works; occasional surveys of scholarship; poems in his honor; illustrations, sketches, and portraits. Vols. 1-2 contain VERÖFFENTLICHUNGEN AUS DEM GERHART-HAUPTMANN-ARCHIV. In German.

   Indexed by Köttelwesch.

2. GERHART-HAUPTMANN-SCHRIFTEN. Publisher: Goslar, Germany (BRD). 1947-(?).

   No verification of scope.

3. GERHART-HAUPTMANN-STUDIEN. 1936-(?).

   Essays on Hauptmann's early life and work--no verification that this is a serial. In German.

   Alternate title:

   HAUPTMANN-STUDIEN

HAWTHORNE, NATHANIEL (1804-64)

American novelist, short-story writer

1. NATHANIEL HAWTHORNE JOURNAL (NHJ). Editor: C.E. Frazer Clark, Jr., 1700 Lone Pine Road, Bloomfield Hills, Mich. 48013. Publisher: Microcard Editions. June 1971-- . Annual (November). $19, hardbound. [300 p.] Circulation: 500. Last issue examined: 1975.

Devoted to scholarship concerning work by and about Hawthorne, especially fresh interpretations and new bibliographical studies. Long, documented critical, textual, and biographical studies; brief explicative notes; previously unpublished or neglected works by Hawthorne and his acquaintances; reproductions and facsimiles from Clark's extensive collection; bibliographies, such as "Hawthorne in Portuguese" and the annual "Recent Hawthorne Scholarship"; long book reviews; brief comments on other new publications; numerous photographs and illustrations; no index.

Indexed by AMERICAN HUMANITIES INDEX, AMERICAN LITERATURE, ANNUAL BIBLIOGRAPHY OF ENGLISH LANGUAGE AND LITERATURE, and MLA INTERNATIONAL BIBLIOGRAPHY.

2. NATHANIEL HAWTHORNE SOCIETY NEWSLETTER. Editor: A. Monke, Hawthorne-Longfellow Library, Bowdoin College, Brunswick, Maine 04011. Sponsor: Nathaniel Hawthorne Society. Spring 1975-- . 2/yr. $4.

HEBBEL, FRIEDRICH (1813-63)

German dramatist, poet, novelist, critic

1. HEBBEL-FORSCHUNGEN. Editors: 1907-19, R.M. Werner and W. Bloch-Wunschmann; 1923-33, Richard M. Wagner. Publisher: Behr's Verlag, Berlin, Germany (DDR). 1907-33 (nos. 1-23). [200-250 p.]

   Each volume concerns a specific subject, such as HEBBEL UND KLEIST (no. 21); bibliographical references; name and subject indexes in some volumes.

2. Hebbelgemeinde. JAHRESGABE. Publisher: Heide in Holstein, Germany (BRD). 1932-(?). Irregular.

3. HEBBEL-JAHRBUCH (HJb). Editors: Detlef Cölln, 1939-59; since 1975, Ludwig Koopmann, Heinz Stolte, and Hilmar Grundmann. Sponsor: Hebbel-Gesellschaft, Wesselburen, Germany (BRD). Publisher: Westholsteinische Verlagsanstalt Boyens, Heide in Holstein, Germany (BRD). 1939-43; suspended publication, 1944-48; 1949-- . Annual. DM15-20. [120-200 p.] Last issue examined: 1977.

   Collections of long scholarly essays on the life, works, and influence of Hebbel--the theory and structure of his drama, his use of myth and history, themes of justice and responsibility, and peculiarities of language; occasional Hebbel bibliographies, including library holdings; newly discovered documents; reminiscences; reports from the Hebbel-Gesellschaft;

activities of the Hebbel-Bibliothek and the Hebbel-Museum; photographs and illustrations. In German.

Indexed by Köttelwesch and MLA INTERNATIONAL BIBLIOGRAPHY.

4. HEBBEL-KALENDAR: EIN JAHRBUCH. Editors: R.M. Werner and Walther Bloch, Berlin. 1905-(?).

HEGEL, GEORG (1770-1831)

German philosopher

1. HEGEL-ARCHIV. Publisher: Leipzig, Germany (DDR). 1912-16 (nos. 1-3).

2. HEGEL-JAHRBUCH. Editor and president: Wilhelm Raimund Beyer, Internationale Hegel-Gesellschaft, Richard-Strele-Strasse 16, A 5020 Salzburg, Austria. Sponsor: Hegel-Gesellschaft, Munich, Germany (BRD). Publisher: 1961-73, Verlag Anton Hain, Meisenheim am Glan, Germany (BRD); since 1974, Pahl-Rugenstein Verlag, Koln, Germany (BRD). 1961-- . Annual. DM50-85. [300-500 p.] Last issue examined: 1975.

Papers prepared for the International Hegel conferences--collections of long scholarly essays, with bibliographical references, concerning every aspect of Hegel's life and works, his terminology, influence, and interpretation; some studies of related theories, such as those of Marx, Rousseau, Lenin and their interaction to the present; brief report of accomplishments at the Hegel Congress--discussion topics, attendance, future plans; international contributors; no index. In German, with occasional contributions in English or French.

Indexed by PHILOSOPHER'S INDEX.

3. HEGEL-STUDIEN. Editors: Friedhelm Nicolin and Otto Pöggeler, Hegel-Archiv der Ruhr-Universität, Overbergstrasse 17, 4630 Bochum, Postfach 2148, Germany (BRD). Sponsor: Hegel-Kommission der Rheinisch-Westfälischen Akademie der Wissenschaften. Publisher: Bouvier Verlag, Bonn, Germany (BRD). 1961-- . Irregular. DM40-80. [350-450 p.] Last issue examined: vol. 13, 1978.

Collections of essays on Hegel's life, friendships, works, interaction with other authors and literatures; annual annotated, international bibliography of Hegel scholarship--books, articles, and reviews; numerous long review-articles that usually are valuable essays in themselves; numerous brief reviews; occasional contributors from outside Germany; no index. In German, English, or French.

Indexed by Köttelwesch.

4. HEGEL-STUDIEN/BEIHEFT. Editors: Friedhelm Nicolin and Otto Pöggeler. Sponsor: Hegel-Archiv, Erste Fährgasse 7, Bonn, Germany (BRD); Association hégelienne internationale. Publisher: Bouvier Verlag, Bonn, Germany (BRD). 1964-- . Irregular. DM40-90. [220-350 p.] Last issue examined: no. 18, 1978.

   Each volume concentrates on a specific subject, either in the form of one long, extended study (frequently, dissertations) or as a collection of essays by international scholars; indexes and bibliographies in some volumes. In French or German. Supplements HEGEL-STUDIEN (entry 3, above).

5. OWL OF MINERVA: QUARTERLY JOURNAL OF THE HEGEL SOCIETY OF AMERICA. Editor: Lawrence S. Stepelevich. Sponsor: Hegel Society of America, 3369 University Station, Charlottesville, Va. 22903. Publisher: Philosophy Department, Villanova University, Villanova, Pa. 19085. Treasurer: Donald Verene, Hegel Society of America, Department of Philosophy, 246 Sparks Building, Pennsylvania State University, University Park, Pa. 16802. Summer 1969-- . Quarterly (September, December, March, June). $5. [8 p.] Circulation: 600. Last issue examined: vol. 9, 1978.

   Occasional long articles on such timely subjects as "Recent French Hegel Scholarship"; a valuable source for long book reviews on important international publications; numerous brief notes on other new critical works, reprints, editions, and forthcoming books; occasional bibliographies; report of work in progress; notes on activities of the Hegel Society of America (meeting every second year), the International Hegel Association (colloquium every second year), international congress (every sixth year), and other events and meetings relating to the study of Hegel; no index. In English.

   Indexed by PHILOSOPHER'S INDEX.

6. RECHERCHES HEGELIENNES: BULLETIN D'INFORMATION DU CENTRE DE RECHERCHE ET DE DOCUMENTATION SUR HEGEL ET MARX. Editor: Jacky Mercier. Sponsor and publisher: Université de Poitiers, 8, rue René Descartes, 86022 Poitiers, France. May 1970-- . Irregular. [20-40 p.] Last issue examined: no. 6, 1972.

   Bibliographies of works by and about Marx and Hegel, including reviews and dissertations; book reviews; report of congresses, seminars; news of activities at the Centre; name and subject index. Available on microfiche. In French.

HEIDEGGER, MARTIN (1889-1976)

German philosopher

1. Heideggeriana. Publisher: Marzorati, Milan, Italy. 1967-(?). Irregular (a series). [320 p.]

Critical editions with numerous notes and appendixes that might be helpful to scholars, such as GELASSENHEIT DI MARTIN HEIDEGGER (1967). In Italian.

HEINE, HEINRICH (1797-1856)

German poet, satirist, journalist

1. GUTE TAMBOUR: LITERARISCH-KULTURELLE BLÄTTER UM HEINRICH HEINE UND SEINE GEISTESGENÖSSEN. Publisher: Winterstrasse 9-11, 2 Hamburg-Altona, Germany (BRD). December 1961-(?). Irregular.

2. HEINE-JAHRBUCH (HeineJ). Editor: Eberhard Galley, Director of City Library, Am Brambusch 10, 4 Düsseldorf, Germany (BRD). Sponsors: originally, City of Düsseldorf, Bilkerstrasse 14, 4 Düsseldorf; later, Heinrich-Heine-Institut, Grabbeplatz 7, and Heinrich-Heine-Gesellschaft, Humboldtstrasse 2, Geschäftstelle Neuss, Dusseldorf. Publisher: Hoffmann und Campe Verlag, Hamburg, Germany (BRD). 1962-- . Annual. DM18; DM20 (foreign). [130–240 p.] Last issue examined: vol. 16, 1977.

   Long critical, textual, and biographical articles; studies of Heine's relationship with other authors and of his place in literary history; "Heine-Literatur"--annual, comprehensive, international bibliography of Heine scholarship, with supplements; indexes of library holdings; numerous long book reviews, mainly of German publications (since 1974); calendar of Gesellschaft activities--lectures, exhibitions, performances; numerous illustrations and facsimiles; index in each volume. HEINE-INDEX in progress. In German, with occasional contributions in English. Second-hand copies available from Kraus Periodicals (1962-69, $35).

   Indexed by ENGLISH LANGUAGE NOTES, Köttelwesch, and MLA INTERNATIONAL BIBLIOGRAPHY.

3. HEINE STUDIEN. Publisher: Hoffmann und Campe Verlag, Hamburg, Germany (BRD). 1971(?)-- .

   Essays; bibliographies; facsimiles; report of Internationaler Heine-Kongress (1972). In German.

4. Heinrich Heine-Gesellschaft. MITTEILUNGEN. Sponsor and publisher: Heinrich Heine-Gesellschaft, Drakestrasse 1a, Düsseldorf. 1966-- . 2/yr.

5. Heinrich Heine-Gesellschaft. SCHRIFTEN. Sponsor and publisher: Heinrich Heine-Gesellschaft, Postrasse 24, Düsseldorf. 1964-- . Irregular (a series). DM3; $1. [20-50 p.] Last issue examined: vol. 5, 1972.

Long studies on one aspect of Heine interest, such as HEINRICH HEINE IM WIDERSTREIT DER MEINUNGEN, 1825-1965, or ÜBER DIE IRONIE BEI HEINRICH HEINE (no. 1). In German. Vol. 6 not yet published (1978).

Alternate title:

SCHRIFTEN DER HEINRICH HEINE-GESELLSCHAFT

HEMINGWAY, ERNEST (1899-1961)

American novelist, short-story writer

1. Ernest Hemingway. Subseries of La Revue des Lettres Modernes. 1957-- . Irregular. Series numbers for the issues on Hemingway are provided below.

Hemingway subseries	La Revue series	Date
Unnumbered	Nos. 31-34	1957

In French. See Camus, Albert, entry 1, for a full description of La Revue des Lettres Modernes.

Indexed by FRENCH VII, Klapp, and MLA INTERNATIONAL BIBLIOGRAPHY.

2. FITZGERALD/HEMINGWAY ANNUAL. See Fitzgerald, F. Scott, entry 1.

3. HEMINGWAY NOTES. Editors: Taylor Alderman, Department of English, Youngstown State University, Youngstown, Ohio 44503; and Kenneth Rosen, Department of English, Dickinson College, Carlisle, Pa. 17013. Sponsor: Dickinson College. Spring 1971-Spring 1974 (vols. 1-4, no. 1). 2/yr. (Spring, Fall). $3; $5/two yrs. [25-35 p.] Circulation: 250.

Biographical, bibliographical, textual, and critical articles; international bibliography of current Hemingway books, articles, dissertations, and new editions; "Briefs"--news of unpublished material, auctions, conferences; queries; occasional book and film reviews. Available from University Microfilms International.

Indexed by ABSTRACTS OF ENGLISH STUDIES and AMERICAN HUMANITIES INDEX.

HERBERT, GEORGE (1593-1633)

English poet

1. GEORGE HERBERT JOURNAL. Editor: Sidney Gottlieb, Department of English, Sacred Heart University, P.O. Box 6460, Bridgeport, Conn. 06606. Sponsor: Sacred Heart University. Fall 1977-- . 2/yr. (Spring, Fall). $7; $10 (foreign). [60-80 p.]

    Long critical articles; brief notes on conferences, meetings, and major work in progress; critical exchanges; queries and answers; annual bibliography of work relevant to Herbert; book reviews; annual index.

Indexed by ABSTRACTS OF ENGLISH STUDIES and SEVENTEENTH-CENTURY NEWS.

HERZL, THEODOR (1860-1904)

Hungarian-born Austrian Jewish writer, founder of Zionism

1. THEODOR HERZL JAHRBUCH. Editor and sponsor: Tulo Nussenblatt. Publisher: Heinrich Glanz Verlag, Vienna. 1937--(?). [335 p.]

    Long biographical and critical essays on Herzl's contributions to Zionism; bibliographical references; previously unpublished letters to family and friends, including Martin Buber; facsimiles. In German.

HESSE, HERMANN (1877-1962)

German novelist, poet

1. HERMANN-HESSE-LITERATUR. Editor: Martin Pfeifer, Mittelbuchen, Hanau, Germany (BRD). 1966-(?). Annual.

    Includes bibliography of Hesse scholarship. In German.

2. HERMANN HESSE NEWSLETTER. Editor: Marjorie Strickland, Apt. 2B, 517 East 77th Street, New York, N.Y. 10021. Sponsor: Hermann Hesse Society. 1975-- . Free with membership ($15); $10 (students).

    Organized for the free exchange of ideas, scholarship, and creative works on the themes explored by Hesse. News notes concerning lectures, discussions, public readings, and the creation of a Hesse reference library.

HIGGINSON, THOMAS WENTWORTH (1823-1911)

American Unitarian clergyman, editor, soldier, writer

1. HIGGINSON JOURNAL OF POETRY. Editor: Frederick L. Morey, 4508 38th Street, Brentwood, Md. 20722. Publisher: Higginson Press Enterprises. 1971-- . 2/yr. Available only to members of the ED Society (see Dickinson, Emily). [50 p.] Circulation: 200.

   Interested in Colonel T.W. Higginson and his relationship with Emily Dickinson, other women poets, and current social and cultural issues of his time. Critical articles and notes concerning Emily Dickinson and her poetry; book reviews; occasional special issues such as "Jung and Literature" (1978); illustrations.

   Indexed by ANNUAL BIBLIOGRAPHY OF ENGLISH LANGUAGE AND LITERATURE.

HÖLDERLIN, FRIEDRICH (1770-1843)

German poet

1. Hölderlin-Archiv. VERÖFFENTLICHUNGEN. Sponsor: Hölderlin-Archiv, Landesbibliothek, Stuttgart, Germany (BRD). 1953-- . Irregular. Last issue examined: vol. 3, 1961.

   In German.

2. HÖLDERLIN-JAHRBUCH (HöJb). Supersedes IDUNA: JAHRBUCH DER HÖLDERLIN-GESELLSCHAFT (see entry 4). Editors: Bernhard Böschenstein, 34, rue de Saint Jean, Geneva, Switzerland; Alfred Kelletat. Sponsor: Friedrich Hölderlin-Gesellschaft. Publisher: J.C.B. Mohr, Tübingen, Germany (BRD). 1947-- . Irregular. DM48; $8-20. [130-370 p.] Last issue examined: vol. 19, 1975-77.

   Long biographical and interpretive essays on such subjects as Hölderlin's relationship with the French Revolution or with other poets and authors, past and contemporary; reprints of previously unpublished letters and other documents; occasional comprehensive bibliographies such as the "Hölderlin-Bibliographie 1971-73" in vol. 19; reports of the annual meeting of the Hölderlin-Gesellschaft, the Hölderlin colloquia, and the Hölderlin-Archiv; occasional illustrations; index. In German, with some English material. Second-hand copies available from Kraus Periodicals (1947-67/68, $215, includes IDUNA, see entry 4); reprints from Walter J. Johnson (1944-1973/74, $380).

Indexed by ENGLISH LANGUAGE NOTES, Köttelwesch, and MLA INTERNATIONAL BIBLIOGRAPHY.

3. HÖLDERLIN-STUDIEN. 1967-(?).

4. IDUNA: JAHRBUCH DER HÖLDERLIN-GESELLSCHAFT. Superseded by HÖLDERLIN-JAHRBUCH (see entry 2). Sponsor: Hölderlin-Gesellschaft, 1944-46.

After dissolution of the Hölderlin-Gesellschaft in March 1946, IDUNA was superseded by the HÖLDERLIN-JAHRBUCH (see entry 2), which was published by the Friedrich Hölderlin-Gesellschaft, founded October 1946. In German. Secondhand copies available from Kraus Periodicals (see HÖLDERLIN-JAHRBUCH).

5. SCHRIFTEN DER HÖLDERLIN-GESELLSCHAFT. Sponsor and publisher: Friedrich Hölderlin-Gesellschaft, Tübingen, Germany (BRD). 1949-- . Irregular. [400 p.] Last issue examined: vol. 9, 1975.

Each volume is concerned with a specific subject, such as HÖLDERLIN: BEITRÄGE ZU SEINEM VERSTÄNDNIS IN UNSER JAHRHUNDERT (1961). In German.

Alternate title:

Hölderlin-Gesellschaft. SCHRIFTEN

HOFFMANN, AUGUST HEINRICH [HOFFMANN VON FALLERSLEBEN] (1798-1874)

German poet, philologist, librarian, literary historian

1. Hoffmann von Fallersleben-Gesellschaft. JAHRESGABE. Sponsor and publisher: Hoffmann von Fallersleben-Gesellschaft, Fallersleben, Germany (BRD). 1957(?)-- . Irregular. [100-120 p.] Last issue examined: 1964.

Studies of Hoffmann's life and works; detailed chronology and examination of his family and background, with interpretations relating his life to his poetry; report of progress on new editions; notes on buildings named in his honor and on other ceremonies; special issues devoted to other authors and their work; illustrations, facsimiles, and photographs. In German.

Alternate title:

JAHRESGABE DER HOFFMANN VON FALLERSLEBEN-GESELLSCHAFT

2. MITTEILUNGS-BLÄTTER DER HOFFMANN VON FALLERSLEBEN-GESELLSCHAFT. Editor: Theodor Kröger, Kirchstrasse 4, 3183 Wolfsburg-

Fallersleben, Germany (BRD). Sponsor: Hoffmann von Fallersleben-Gesellschaft. 1953(?)-- . Annual. [8-16 p.] Last issue examined: no. 50, 1973.

Brief articles on events in Hoffmann's life, on his friends, family, travels; report of activities of the Gesellschaft, its members, and the Museum; occasional brief book reviews; illustrations and photographs. In German.

HOFFMANN, ERNST T.A. (1776-1822)

German composer, author of humorous tales

1. MITTEILUNGEN DER E.T.A. HOFFMANN-GESELLSCHAFT (MHG). Sponsor: E.T.A. Hoffmann-Gesellschaft, Gönnerstrasse 2/II, 8600 Bamberg, Germany (BRD). 1938-- . Irregular. Free with membership (DM20); nonmembers (DM30 per issue). [70-80 p.] Circulation: 850. Last issue examined: vol. 23, 1977.

   Long articles on the themes, problems, style, and relationship of Hoffmann's musical compositions and literary works, his life in Bamberg and his influences; occasional bibliographies covering several years of Hoffmann scholarship and musical performances; numerous brief book reviews of important international publications, including dissertations; list of new members; international contributors; occasional photographs; no index. In German. Second-hand copies available from Kraus Periodicals (1938-68, $65); reprints from Walter J. Johnson (1938-74, $220).

   Indexed by ENGLISH LANGUAGE NOTES, Köttelwesch, and MLA INTERNATIONAL BIBLIOGRAPHY.

   Alternate title:

   E.T.A. Hoffmann-Gesellschaft. MITTEILUNGEN

HOFFMANN VON FALLERSLEBEN

See Hoffmann, August Heinrich.

HOFMANNSTHAL, HUGO VON (1874-1929)

Austrian dramatist, poet, essayist

1. HESPERUS: EIN JAHRBUCH VON HUGO VON HOFMANNSTHAL. Publisher: Leipzig, Germany (DDR). 1909-(?).

2. HOFMANNSTHAL-BLÄTTER: VERÖFFENTLICHUNGEN DER HUGO VON HOFMANNSTHAL-GESELLSCHAFT, FRANKFURT-AM-MAIN (HBl).

Editor: Norbert Altenhofer, Postfach 90 05 11, D-6000 Frankfurt/am/Main, Germany (BRD). Sponsor: Hugo von Hofmannsthal-Gesellschaft, Postfach 90 05 11, D-6000 Frankfurt/am/Main, Germany (BRD). Publisher: Lothar Stiehm Verlag, Heidelberg, Germany (BRD). Autumn 1968-- . Irregular. DM60; $12. [85-140 p.] Last issue examined: no. 16, 1976.

Articles on Hofmannsthal's life, travels, works, and relationship with other authors; "Hofmannsthal-Bibliographie" (edited by Hans-Albrecht Koch)--extensive international bibliography, primary and secondary, including dissertations, with supplements for previous years; bibliographies of library holdings in Germany and in other countries; occasional reviews of research accomplishments and possibilities; previously unpublished letters and other documents, with explanatory notes; book reviews; report of publications and past and future activities of the Hofmannsthal-Gesellschaft; news and notes on symposia, library holdings; list of new members; facsimiles. In German.

Indexed by Köttelwesch and MLA INTERNATIONAL BIBLIOGRAPHY.

3. HOFMANNSTHAL-FORSCHUNGEN. Director: Wolfram Mauser, Deutsches Seminar der Universität, Werthmannplatz, D-78 Freiberg im Breisgau, Germany (BRD). Sponsor: Hugo von Hofmannsthal-Gesellschaft, with the cooperation of Arbeitsstelle Basel der kritischen Hofmannsthal-Ausgabe, Petersplatz 14, CH 4051 Basel, Switzerland. 1971-- . Irregular. DM14-22. [100-240 p.] Last issue examined: vol. 5, 1977.

Long studies of Hofmannsthal's life and works, including such surveys as "Hofmannsthals Dramatisches Werk in Russland" (1971); reprints of scholarly papers and debates prepared for conferences; report of activities of the Gesellschaft; comprehensive bibliographies or surveys of scholarship; bibliographical references; international contributors; no index. In German.

HOHENHEIM, THEOPHRASTUS BOMBASTUS VON [PARACELSUS] (1493-1541)

Swiss-born German alchemist, physician

1. SALZBURGER BEITRÄGE ZUR PARACELSUSFORSCHUNG. Editor: Sepp Domandl, general secretary of the Gesellschaft. Sponsor: Internationale Paracelsus-Gesellschaft, Rathaus, I. Stock, Salzburg, Austria. Publisher: Notring-Verlag, Vienna. 1960-- . Irregular. AS 12-190. [30-200 p.] Last issue examined: vol. 15, 1977.

Studies of Paracelsus' life and work, sometimes as brief essays with bibliographical references, and sometimes as long monographs, such as PARACELSUS STUDIEN (1970); occasional bibliographies, such as "Auswahl-Bibliographie der neueren Paracelsus-Literature"; reproductions, maps, and facsimiles. In German.

HOPKINS, GERARD MANLEY (1844-89)

English poet, priest

1. ANNUAL HOPKINS LECTURE. Sponsor and publisher: Hopkins Society, Roselands, 162 Turkey Street, Enfield, Middlesex EN1 4NW, England. 1970-76 (nos. 1-7). Annual. Free with membership ($6); back issues, $1.50. [20 p.]

   Reprints of lectures on one facet of Hopkins' life and works, such as HOPKINS AND LITERARY CRITICISM (1974).

2. ANNUAL HOPKINS SERMON. Sponsor and publisher: Hopkins Society, Roselands, 162 Turkey Street, Enfield, Middlesex EN1 4NW, England. 1969-75 (nos. 1-7). Annual. Free with membership ($6); $.50 per issue. [5 p.]

   Sermons delivered on the anniversary of Hopkins' birth--related to his life, beliefs, and works.

3. HOPKINS QUARTERLY: A JOURNAL DEVOTED TO CRITICAL AND SCHOLARLY INQUIRY INTO THE LIFE AND WORKS OF GERARD MANLEY HOPKINS (HQ). Editors: Richard F. Giles and John R. Hopkins, Department of English, University of Guelph, Guelph, Ontario, Canada N1G 2W1. April 1974-- . Quarterly (April, July, October, January). $6 (U.S. and Canada); $7.50 (elsewhere); $2.50 per issue. [40-50 p.] Circulation: 200. Last issue examined: vol. 5, 1979.

   Long (15 p.) critical, appreciative, and explicative articles on Hopkins' imagery, themes, language, dramatic monologues, verse structure, literary associates, and every phase of his life, works, and thoughts; news notes on seminars, exhibitions, and progress of the International Hopkins Association; queries and forum; references to work in progress; occasional book reviews; annual index in January; beginning in April 1979, an annual comprehensive, current, and critical bibliography with contributors from around the world. Cumulative author, subject, and title index to vols. 1-2 (April 1974-January 1976).

   Indexed by ABSTRACTS OF ENGLISH STUDIES, MLA INTERNATIONAL BIBLIOGRAPHY, and VICTORIAN STUDIES.

4. HOPKINS RESEARCH BULLETIN. Sponsor and publisher: Hopkins Society, Roselands, 162 Turkey Street, Enfield, Middlesex EN1 4NW, England. Spring 1970-76 (nos. 1-7). Annual. Free with membership ($6); back issues, $1.50. [25-40 p.]

   Short articles on such newly discovered material as personal correspondence or books owned by Hopkins and his family; annual bibliography of Hopkins scholarship; checklists of recent criticism; brief notes on work in progress; previously unpublished material; interviews; items of interest--auctions, awards, seminars, and excursions; facsimiles and illustrations; selective index.

The Hopkins Society also published the ANNUAL HOPKINS LECTURES (see entry 1) and ANNUAL HOPKINS SERMON (see entry 2). Membership in the Society included a subscription to both of these as well as to the BULLETIN: $6 (individual); $12 (libraries); $30 (patron); $300 (benefactor).

Indexed by ANNUAL BIBLIOGRAPHY OF ENGLISH LANGUAGE AND LITERATURE and VICTORIAN STUDIES.

HOUSMAN, ALFRED EDWARD (1859-1936)

English poet, Latin scholar

1. HOUSMAN SOCIETY JOURNAL (HSJ). Editors: Graham and Jennifer Speake, 74 Duns Tew, Oxford, England. Sponsor: Housman Society, London. Publisher: Turner and Devereux, 254 Temple Chambers, Temple Avenue, London E.C.4. 1974-- . Annual. £1 (members); £2.50 (non-members). [60 p.]

   Interested in publishing "critical researches related to the poetry, prose, and classical scholarship of A.E. Housman and the works of his brother Laurence and sister Clemence and for the review of books concerned with same." Long essays on Housman's poetic and prose style, life at college, classical background; source and textual studies; critiques of poems; short notes on problems of content or allusions; survey of scholarship; personal recollections; book reviews; brief notes on forthcoming books, acquisitions, library holdings; occasional sketches.

Indexed by ANNUAL BIBLIOGRAPHY OF ENGLISH LANGUAGE AND LITERATURE, MLA INTERNATIONAL BIBLIOGRAPHY, and VICTORIAN STUDIES.

HOWARD, ROBERT E. (1906-36)

American author

1. AMRA. Editors: "The Amraëditorial Horde," Box 8243, Philadelphia, Pa. 19101. 1956-- . Irregular (2 in 1974). $6/ten issues. Circulation: 1,245.

   Interested in the "sword and sorcery" tales of Robert E. Howard.

2. HOWARD COLLECTOR. Editor: Glenn Lord, P.O. Box 775, Pasadena, Tex. 77501. Summer 1961-1973 (publication suspended). 2/yr. $1.20. Circulation: 350.

   Informal notes on Howard's life and works; news items; occasional book reviews.

HOWELLS, WILLIAM DEAN (1837-1920)

American critic, novelist, poet

1. HOWELLS SENTINEL. Editors: nos. 1-6, Rudolf and Clara Kirk; no. 7, David J. Burrows, Department of English, Douglass College, Rutgers University, New Brunswick, N.J. 08901. March 1951-May 1964 (nos. 1-7). Irregular. Free. [10 p.]

   Brief articles and notes concerning Howells' life and works; bibliography edited by George Arms and William M. Gibson; report of meetings of the Howells group (associated with MLA).

HUGO, VICTOR MARIE, COMTE (1802-85)

French poet, novelist, dramatist

1. Archives hugoliennes. Subseries of Archives des Lettres Modernes. 1961-- . Irregular. Equivalent numbers are provided below for both the parent series (Archives des Lettres Modernes) and the individual author series on Hugo.

Hugo subseries	Archives series	Date
No. 1	No. 38	1961
No. 2	No. 41	1962
No. 3	No. 43	1962
No. 4	No. 44	1962
No. 5	No. 67	1966
Unnumbered	No. 78	1967
No. 6	No. 94	1968
No. 7	No. 96	1968

   In French. See Camus, Albert, entry 2, for a full description of Archives des Lettres Modernes. See also Archives Albert Camus, no. 3 (Archives des Lettres Modernes, no. 156).

   Indexed by BULLETIN CRITIQUE, FRENCH VI, Klapp, and MLA INTERNATIONAL BIBLIOGRAPHY.

2. BULLETIN DE LA FONDATION VICTOR HUGO. Supersedes FONDATION VICTOR HUGO (see entry 4). Publisher: Paris. 1928-32 (nos. 2-6).

3. BULLETIN DE LA SOCIÉTÉ VICTOR HUGO. Publisher: Paris. 1906-16 (nos. 1-22).

4. FONDATION VICTOR HUGO. Superseded by BULLETIN DE LA FONDATION VICTOR HUGO (see entry 2). Publisher: Paris. 1927 (no. 1). Quarterly.

   Alternate information in UNION LIST OF SERIALS: FONDATION VICTOR HUGO, Paris Bibliothèque. 1934-- .

HUME, DAVID (1711-76)

Scottish philosopher, historian

1. HUME STUDIES. Editor: John W. Davis, Department of Philosophy, Talbot College, University of Western Ontario, London, Ontario N6A 3K7, Canada. Sponsor: Faculty of Arts, University of Western Ontario. 1975-- . 2/yr. (April, November). $3.50 (individuals); $5.50 (institutions). [30-50 p.] Last issue examined: vol. 4, 1978.

   Devoted to historical and systematic research on David Hume. Long documented essays on Hume's work; brief comments on his contemporaries, his influence, letters, manuscripts, and life; Hume bibliographies; notes and news on workshops of the Canadian Society for Eighteenth Century Studies and other research projects; notes on symposia, projected works; book reviews; announcements of books received. In English, French, German, or Italian. Back issues available from Micromedia Limited, Box 34, Station S, Toronto, Ontario M5M 4L6, Canada.

   Indexed by AMERICA: HISTORY AND LIFE and PHILOSOPHER'S INDEX.

HUYSMANS, JORIS-KARL (1848-1907)

French novelist, art critic

1. BULLETIN DE LA SOCIÉTÉ J.-K. HUYSMANS (BSH). Editor: Paul-Courant (formerly Pierre Lambert), 15, boulevard de Port-Royal, 75013 Paris. Sponsor: Société J.-K. Huysmans, 22, rue Guynemer, 75006 Paris. Publisher: Éditions du Divan, Paris. March 1928-- . Irregular. [20 Fr.] Last issue examined: vol. 15, no. 67, 1977.

   Articles on Huysmans' relationships with other writers and his contribution to French literature; notes on newly discovered documents; previously unpublished letters and works; brief "Notes et Echos" with information on Huysmans' realism, friendships, ideas on astrology and painting, allusions, contemporary radio programs, and old reviews; bibliographies of critical books, articles, and book reviews; report of Society activities and other news of interest to members; list of members. In French. Second-hand copies available from Kraus Periodicals (1928-58, $120); reprints from Slatkine Reprints (1928-47, 210 Fr; 10 Fr per issue, since 1948).

Indexed by BIBLIOGRAPHIE DE LA LITTÉRATURE FRANÇAISE, BULLETIN CRITIQUE, FRENCH VII, FRENCH XX, Klapp, and REVUE D'HISTOIRE LITTÉRAIRE.

Alternate titles:

CAHIERS J.-K. HUYSMANS

Société J.-K. Huysmans. BULLETIN

ISBEN, HENRIK (1828-1906)

Norwegian poet, dramatist

1. IBSENÅRBOK (IÅ). Editors: Daniel Haakonsen, Else Høst, Einar Østvedt, John Northam. Sponsor: Universitetsforlaget, Box 1071, Blindern, Oslo 3, Norway. Publisher: Norges Almenvitenskapelige Forskningsråd. 1952-- . Annual. S kr 40-110. [180-240 p.] Last issue examined: 1977.

   Comparisons of Ibsen's technique with that of dramatists in other countries and generations; studies of his influence on style and concept from his own times to contemporary drama; close analyses of specific titles; surveys of Ibsen performances throughout the world; proceedings of the International Ibsen Seminar; bibliographies of international Ibsen scholarship--books, articles, dissertations; bibliographical references. Distributed by Humanities Press, 303 Park Avenue, New York, N.Y. 10010. In English or Norwegian.

Indexed by Köttelwesch and MLA INTERNATIONAL BIBLIOGRAPHY.

Alternate titles:

IBSEN ÅRBOK

IBSENFORBUNDET: ÅRBOK

IBSEN YEARBOOK

JACOB, MAX [MORVEN LE GAËLIQUE] (1876-1944)

French Cubist poet

1. CAHIERS MAX JACOB. Sponsor and publisher: Amis de Max Jacob, 120, boulevard Raspail, 75006 Paris. March 1951-57 (nos. 1-7). Annual. 50 Fr. [60 p.]

   Critical commentary and reprints of Jacob's works.

2. Max Jacob. Subseries of La Revue des Lettres Modernes. Editor: Jean de Palacio. 1973-- . Irregular. Equivalent numbers are provided below for both the parent series (La Revue des Lettres Modernes) and the individual author series on Jacob.

Jacob subseries	La Revue series	Date
No. 1	Nos. 336-39	1973
No. 2	Nos. 474-78	1976

In French. See Camus, Albert, entry 1, for a full description of La Revue des Lettres Modernes.

Indexed by BULLETIN CRITIQUE, FRENCH XX, Klapp, and MLA INTERNATIONAL BIBLIOGRAPHY.

JAURÈS, JEAN (1859-1914)

French Socialist leader, author

1. BULLETIN DE LA SOCIÉTÉ D'ÉTUDES JAURÉSIENNES. Sponsor: Société d'Études jaurésiennes, 131, rue de l'Abbé-Groult, 75015 Paris. Secrétariat: Jean-Pierre Rioux, 25, rue Damrémont, 75018 Paris. June 1960-- . Quarterly. 38 Fr; 15 Fr (student). [15-30 p.] Last issue examined: no. 68, 1978.

    Brief articles and notes on Jaurès' relationship with other writers, his environment, philosophy, literary technique, social criticism, lectures, travels, journals, public reception, political and cultural ideas; extracts from his letters and early publications; brief bibliographies; report of the annual meeting of the Society; facsimiles. In French.

    Indexed by BIBLIOGRAPHIE DE LA LITTÉRATURE FRANÇAISE, FRENCH VII, and FRENCH XX.

    Alternate title:

    Société d'Études jaurésiennes. BULLETIN

JEAN, LUCIEN

French novelist, poet

See Lucien Jean (pseudonym for Lucien Dieudonné 1870-1908), under Philippe, Charles-Louis, entry 1.

JEAN PAUL

See Richter, Jean Paul Friedrich.

JEFFERS, ROBINSON (1887-1962)

American poet

1. ROBINSON JEFFERS NEWSLETTER (RJN). Editor: Robert J. Brophy,

Department of English, California State College at Long Beach, 6101 East 7th, Long Beach, Calif. 90801. Sponsor: Robinson Jeffers Committee, Occidental College Library, 1600 Campus Road, Los Angeles, Calif. 90041. November 1962-- . Quarterly. $4. [2-25 p.] Circulation: 200. Last issue examined: no. 49, 1977.

Brief explications; comments on style and content; brief biographical and influence studies; occasional bibliographies of recent criticism, library holdings, and books in print of interest to Jeffers scholars--both primary and secondary works; personal reminiscences; occasional surveys of scholarship; comments on newly discovered material; abstracts; previously unpublished material; news notes on translations, meetings, library acquisitions, theatre productions, recent publications, stamps, medals, music, and art relating to Jeffers; "Collectors' Corner," with information from rare book dealers; frequent book reviews; facsimiles. Subject, author, and title index for 1962-70 (nos. 1-25). Back copies available from Tyrus G. Harmsen, College Librarian, Occidental College Library (1962-1975, $25).

Indexed by MLA INTERNATIONAL BIBLIOGRAPHY.

JOHNSON, SAMUEL (1709-84)

English essayist, moralist, scholar

1. JOHNSONIAN NEWS LETTER (JNL). Editor: John H. Middendorf, Department of English and Comparative Literature, 610 Philosophy Hall, Columbia University, New York, N.Y. 10027. December 1940-- . Quarterly (March, June, September, December). $4 (U.S. and Canada); $4.50 (foreign); back issues $1. [12 p.] Circulation: 1,200. Last issue examined: vol. 38, 1978.

   Interested in Johnson, Boswell, Richardson, Fielding, Defoe, their contemporaries, and the life and literature of 1660-1800. Originally sponsored by Group VIII of MLA and published six times a year--the first of the "newsletter" genre which has now become so popular.

   Almost all recent issues have been comprised mainly of discerning but informal comments on new books and bibliographies (with occasional elaboration of the contents); regular sections entitled "Some Recent Articles" and "Some New Books"; a few brief critical notes; news items from all over the world; and information on work in progress, work recently completed, library holdings, members' activities, and "Conferences, Conferences." Cumulative index every five years, the most recent for 1971-75 (Summer 1976). Reprints available from Walter J. Johnson (1940-70, vols. 1-30, $90); second-hand copies from Kraus Periodicals (1940-65, vols. 1-25, $70).

JOHNSONIAN NEWS LETTER

James L. Clifford–John H. Middendorf, Co-editors

610 Philosophy Hall, Columbia University, New York, N.Y. 10027

A Subject Index to the

JOHNSONIAN NEWS LETTER

Volumes XXXI – XXXV (March 1971 – December 1975)

Compiled by
Barbara Jetton
and
Cynthia Swain

(This index does not include titles of twentieth-century books and names of scholars, personal gossip, or accounts of MLA affairs, etc.)

Indexed by ANNUAL BIBLIOGRAPHY OF ENGLISH LANGUAGE AND LITERATURE and ENGLISH LANGUAGE NOTES.

2. Johnson Society. [Addresses and/or Transactions.]

See entry 3, Johnson Society. TRANSACTIONS.

3. Johnson Society. TRANSACTIONS. Editor: G.W. Nicholls, Johnson Birthplace Museum, Breadmarket Street, Lichfield WS13 6LG, Staffordshire, England. Sponsor: Johnson Society of Lichfield. President: Frederick A. Pottle. 1911-- . Annual. $5. [70-100 p.] Circulation: 600. Last issue examined: 1977.

The Johnson Society of Lichfield was founded in 1911, but all early addresses and transactions were published as individual news items in local periodicals and newspapers such as the LICHFIELD MERCURY and, therefore, had no all-encompassing title. They were not published separately, it appears, until 1938. After World War II the brief publications were usually titled ADDRESSES because they were composed only of lectures given at the Annual Johnson Society Supper in Lichfield. Since 1948, when they were finally titled "Johnson Society. TRANSACTIONS," they have included an occasional article of biographical or critical interest; the president's address delivered at annual birthday celebrations in Lichfield on Johnson's life, character, and work; occasional brief book, play, and radio reviews; notes on pilgrimages, library acquisitions; activities of the Lichfield and international Johnson clubs; the Johnson Society officer and membership lists; no index.

Volumes for 1910-53 partly reset and wholly reprinted in four volumes ($20 per volume; William Dawson). Subsequent years in reprint or in the original edition if still available are $5 per number from Dawson.

Indexed by ABSTRACTS OF ENGLISH STUDIES.

Alternate title:

TRANSACTIONS OF THE JOHNSON SOCIETY

4. NEW RAMBLER: JOURNAL OF THE JOHNSON SOCIETY OF LONDON (NRam). Editor: James H. Leicester, Broadmead, Eynsford Road, Farningham, Kent DA4 0BQ, England. Sponsor: Johnson Society of London, Broadmead, Eynsford Road, Farningham, Kent DA4 0BQ, England. Secretary: Mrs. A.G. Dowdeswell, 92, St. Paul's Road, Canonbury, London N12OP. July 1941-- . 2/yr. through 1972; annual since 1973. £1.30; $3.50. [40-65 p.] Circulation: 300. Last issue examined: Serial C, no. 18, 1977.

Devoted to Dr. Johnson and the life and ideas of the eighteenth century. Reprints of lectures read to the Johnson Society and other related meetings; brief, documented articles on Johnson's life, works, and influence; occasional brief play and book reviews; announcements of new publications and Society events; international contributors; occasional illustrations; no index.

Indexed by ABSTRACTS OF ENGLISH STUDIES, ANNUAL BIBLIOGRAPHY OF ENGLISH LANGUAGE AND LITERATURE, and MLA INTERNATIONAL BIBLIOGRAPHY.

Early subtitle:

MEMBERS' EVERCIRCULATOR

5. Samuel Johnson Society of the Northwest. TRANSACTIONS (TSJSNW). Sponsor: University of Washington, Seattle, Wash. 98105. No. 4, 1971.

Indexed by MLA INTERNATIONAL BIBLIOGRAPHY.

Alternate title:

TRANSACTIONS OF THE SAMUEL JOHNSON SOCIETY OF THE NORTHWEST

JOUVENAL, SIDONIE-GABRIELLE DE [COLETTE] (1873-1954)

French novelist

1. BULLETIN DE LA SOCIÉTÉ DES AMIS DE COLETTE. Sponsor: Société des Amis de Colette, Mairie de 89520, St-Sauveur-en-Puisaye, France; or, 9, rue de Beaujolais, 75001 Paris. President: Armand Lanoux. 1966(?)-(?). 2/yr.(?) Last issue examined: no. 10, 1970.

Brief articles on Colette's life, background, and works. In French.

Indexed by BIBLIOGRAPHIE DE LA LITTÉRATURE FRANÇAISE.

JOYCE, JAMES (1882-1941)

Irish novelist, poet, short-story writer

1. James Joyce. Subseries of La Revue des Lettres Modernes. 1959-- . Irregular. Series numbers for the issues on Joyce are provided below.

Joyce subseries	La Revue series	Date
Unnumbered	Nos. 46-48	1959
Unnumbered	Nos. 49-51	1959
Unnumbered	Nos. 117-22	1965

In French. See Camus, Albert, entry 1, for a full description of La Revue des Lettres Modernes.

Indexed by FRENCH VII, Klapp, and MLA INTERNATIONAL BIBLIOGRAPHY.

2. JAMES JOYCE MISCELLANY. Editor: Marvin Magalaner, Graduate Center, City University of New York, N.Y. 10036. Sponsor: James Joyce Society, 41 West 47th Street, New York, N.Y. 10036. Publisher: series 1, James Joyce Society; series 2-3, Southern Illinois University Press, Carbondale, Ill. 62901. 1957-62 (series 1-3). Irregular. [80-300 p.]

Collections of long critical essays on the life, works, and influence of Joyce--tributes, surveys, biographical contributions, autobiographical aspects of the works, linguistic studies; bibliographical references; no index.

Indexed by ESSAY AND GENERAL LITERATURE INDEX and MLA INTERNATIONAL BIBLIOGRAPHY.

3. JAMES JOYCE QUARTERLY (JJQ). Editor: Thomas F. Staley. Managing editor: Charlotte C. Stewart. Sponsor: University of Tulsa, 600 South College, Tulsa, Okla. 74104. Fall 1963-- . Quarterly. $7 (U.S., individuals) and $8 (U.S., institutions); $8 (foreign individuals) and $9 (foreign institutions). [60-140 p.] Circulation: 1,300 (30 percent foreign). Last issue examined: vol. 15, 1978.

Long (10-15 p.) critical articles on Joyce's life and works and his relationship with other authors and the Irish Renaissance; brief explicative notes on problem phrases or specific areas of the works; news notes on past and future conferences, the International James Joyce Symposium publications, and Joycean interests; "Current JJ Checklist" in every issue; occasional reports of work in progress; long book reviews in every issue; letters to the editor; illustrations and facsimiles. One or more special issues a year, such as the FINNEGANS WAKE issues in 1965 and 1972 and the ULYSSES issue in 1972. Five- and ten-year cumulative indexes until vol. 11--thereafter at the end of each annual volume (vols. 1-5, 1963-68, in vol. 5; vols. 1-10, 1963-72, in vol. 10), arranged by authors of the articles, notes, reviews, letters to the editor, and poems. Available in microfilm and microfiche from University Microfilms. Second-hand copies available from Kraus Periodicals (1963-68, vols. 1-5 and index, $80). Back issues available at present from Swets and Zeitlinger.

In 1975, editors began serial publication of a list of recurrent motifs in ULYSSES (comp. William M. Schutte).

Indexed by ABSTRACTS OF ENGLISH STUDIES, AMERICAN HUMANITIES INDEX, ANNUAL BIBLIOGRAPHY OF ENGLISH LANGUAGE AND LITERATURE, BIBLIOGRAPHIE DE LA LITTÉRATURE FRANÇAISE, FRENCH XX,

JAMES JOYCE QUARTERLY

Vol. 14, No. 1

Fall 1976

James Joyce Quarterly

INDEX TO BOOK REVIEWS IN THE HUMANITIES, Klapp, MLA INTERNATIONAL BIBLIOGRAPHY, TWENTIETH CENTURY LITERATURE, and YEAR'S WORK IN ENGLISH STUDIES.

4. JAMES JOYCE REVIEW (JJR). Editor: Edmund L. Epstein, Southern Illinois University, Carbondale, Ill. 62901. February 1957-February 1959 (vols. 1-3, no. 2). Quarterly. $4. Circulation: 300.

Short articles on Joyce's works, characters, language; bibliographies of critical articles, books, chapters in books; brief notes on library acquisitions, dating problems, allusions, recordings, musical settings, pamphlets; book reviews.

Indexed by MLA INTERNATIONAL BIBLIOGRAPHY and TWENTIETH CENTURY LITERATURE.

5. James Joyce Society, New York. PROCEEDINGS. 1948-- .

6. James Joyce Symposium. PAPERS. Various publishers. 1967-- . Every two yrs.

Reprints of lectures delivered at the International Symposia; bibliographies. In various languages.

7. JAMES JOYCE YEARBOOK. Editor: Maria Jolas. Publisher: Transition Workshop, Transition Press, Paris, France. 1949 (ceased publication). [195 p.]

A collection of informal essays on Joyce's life and works, with reminiscences, interviews, personal interpretations; photographs and facsimiles.

8. JOYCENOTES. Editor and Sponsor: Mrs. L. Inger, Haslemere Road, London N.8. June 1969-(?).

9. A WAKE NEWSLITTER [sic]: STUDIES OF JAMES JOYCE'S FINNEGANS WAKE (WN). Editors: Clive Hart, Department of Literature, University of Essex, Wivenhoe Park, Colchester, Essex CO4 3SQ, England; and Fritz Senn, Weiningerstrasse 55, 8103 Unterengstringen, Switzerland. Sponsor and publisher: Department of Literature, University of Essex. March 1962-December 1963 (nos. 1-18); new series, February 1964 (vol. 1, no.1)-- . Irregular through 1963; 6/yr., since 1964. £2.50; $6. [15-25 p.] Circulation: 650. Last issue examined: vol. 15, 1978.

Interested mainly in scholarship on FINNEGANS WAKE, but occasionally includes notes on Joyce's other works. Short critical articles and explications; queries; news of recent editions and work in progress; reviews of books only if they focus directly on FINNEGANS WAKE; occasional special issues, as on the Greek in the novel (June 1975). Cumulated index for 1962-71 (nos. 1-18; new series, vols. 1-8).

Indexed by ABSTRACTS OF ENGLISH STUDIES and MLA INTERNATIONAL BIBLIOGRAPHY.

KANT, IMMANUEL (1724-1804)

German philosopher

1. KANTSTUDIEN: ERGÄNZUNGSHEFTE. Editor: Ingeborg Heidemann. Sponsor: Kantgesellschaft Landesgruppe Reinland-Westfalen. Publisher: Bouvier Verlag, Bonn, Germany (BRD). 1906-30 (nos. 1-65); new series, 1937 (nos. 1-2); 1952 (no. 66)-- . Irregular. DM70-75. [100-300 p.] Last issue examined: no. 109, 1976.

   Each volume deals with a specific subject--for example, GOETHES ÄSTHETIK (1957) or FORCE, COSMOS, MONADS, AND OTHER THEMES OF KANT'S EARLY THOUGHT (1973); bibliographies of works consulted. In German, with occasional volumes in English. Second-hand copies available from Kraus Periodicals.

2. KANT-STUDIEN: PHILOSOPHISCHE ZEITSCHRIFT DER KANT-GESELLSCHAFT (KSt). Editors: Gerhard Funke, Am Gonsenheimer, Spiess 6 1X, 6500 Mainz, Germany (BRD); and Joachim Kopper, Hochgesandstrasse 1, 6500 Mainz, Germany (BRD). Sponsor: Kant-Gesellschaft, Hamburg, Germany (BRD). Publisher: Walter de Gruyter, Berlin. 1897-June 1936 (vols. 1-41, nos. 3-4); suspended 1937-41; 1942-43 (vol. 42, nos. 1-3); new series, 1944 (vol. 44); suspended 1945-52; 1953 (vol. 45)-- . Annual through 1957; quarterly since 1958 (irregular). DM75-90; $39-64. [125-50 p.] Last issue examined: vol. 69, 1978.

   Long essays on Kant, his contemporaries, and his influence on later generations; bibliographies, some of which focus on a specific area, such as "Italian articles, 1971-72" and some of which are surveys, such as the one on research in Russia from 1917 to 1971; numerous reviews and review articles of international publications; abstracts of articles in international periodicals; previously unpublished letters and other documents; research notes; information on activities of the Kant-Gesellschaft, the Leibniz colloquia, congresses; international reviewers, critics, and editors; list of members; illustrations, portraits, facsimiles, diagrams; no annual index. Index for 1897-1969 (vol. 1-60). Organ of the Kant-Gesellschaft since 1904. In German, English, or French. Second-hand copies available from Kraus Periodicals (vols. 1-62, $1584); reprints from Walter J. Johnson (1897-1971, $2,295). Alternate spelling: KANTSTUDIEN.

Indexed by L'ANNÉE PHILOLOGIQUE, BIBLIOGRAPHIE DE LA LITTÉRA-

TURE FRANÇAISE, ENGLISH LANGUAGE NOTES, FRENCH VII, INDEX TO BOOK REVIEWS IN THE HUMANITIES, Köttelwesch, MLA INTERNATIONAL BIBLIOGRAPHY, PHILOLOGICAL QUARTERLY, PHILOSOPHER'S INDEX, and VICTORIAN STUDIES.

3. PHILOSOPHISCHE MONATSHEFTE DER KANT-STUDIEN. Sponsor: Kant-Gesellschaft, Berlin. 1925-26 (vols. 1-2).

Two supplements. Second-hand copies available from Kraus Periodicals ($30).

KEATS, JOHN (1795-1821)

English poet

1. KEATS-SHELLEY JOURNAL (KSJ). Editor: Rae Ann Nager, Houghton Library, Harvard University, Cambridge, Mass. 02138. Book review editor: Betty T. Bennett, Office of the Graduate School, State University of New York, Stony Brook, N.Y. 11794. Publisher and sponsor: Keats-Shelley Association of America, Carl H. Pforzheimer Library, Room 815, 41 East 42nd Street, New York, N.Y. 10017. January 1952-- . Annual. Free with membership ($12.50). Circulation: 1,000. Last issue examined: vol. 27, 1978.

Interested in not only Keats and Shelley but also Byron, Hunt, Hazlitt, and their circles. Long (10-20 p.) scholarly studies, mainly interpretations of individual works or analyses of style; brief notes on sources, images, influences, allusions, and problem areas in the authors' works; comprehensive annotated annual bibliography, published separately--the best single source for scholarship in books, articles, and dissertations; numerous book reviews or review articles in every issue, such as "Recent Biographies of Mary Wollstonecraft" (1976); news of the annual meeting of members and directors of the Keats-Shelley Association and of the Byron Society; news of poetry contests, conferences, activities at Keats's house; facsimiles. Publication of the annual bibliography was delayed in the early 1970's but became current in 1976 with an issue that covered 1974-76 (vols. 23-25). The first twelve annual bibliographies (1950-62) are available in a one-volume edition with a single cumulated index, and a second volume covers the years 1962-74 (Lincoln: University of Nebraska, 1964, 1978). Reprints available from Kraus Reprint (1952-70, $177.50; 1969-70, $20); and from Walter J. Johnson (1952-67, $115).

Indexed by ABSTRACTS OF ENGLISH STUDIES, ANNUAL BIBLIOGRAPHY OF ENGLISH LANGUAGE AND LITERATURE, ENGLISH LANGUAGE NOTES, HUMANITIES INDEX, MLA ABSTRACTS, MLA INTERNATIONAL BIBLIOGRAPHY, VICTORIAN STUDIES, and YEAR'S WORK IN ENGLISH STUDIES.

Alternate subtitles:

A PERIODICAL DEVOTED TO KEATS, SHELLEY, BYRON, HUNT AND THEIR CIRCLES

KEATS, SHELLEY, BYRON, HUNT, AND THEIR CIRCLES

2. KEATS-SHELLEY MEMORIAL BULLETIN, ROME (KSMB). Supersedes Keats-Shelley Memorial, Rome. BULLETIN (see entry 3). Editor: Dorothy Hewlett, Keats-Shelley Memorial Association, Longfield Cottage, Longfield Drive, Sheen Common, London S.W.14. Sponsor: Keats-Shelley Memorial Association, 12 Runnymede, Courtlands, Sheen Road, Richmond, Surrey, England. 1950 (no. 3)-- . Annual. £2.50. [30-50 p.] Circulation: 800-1,000. Last issue examined: no. 28, 1977.

Brief critical and biographical articles; bibliographies of the collection; previously unpublished material; occasional book reviews; news and notes about tours, lectures, members' activities, recent publications, book and manuscript sales, exhibitions, recordings, work in progress; portraits, plates, illustrations, and facsimiles. BIBLIOGRAPHICAL INDEX TO THE KEATS-SHELLEY MEMORIAL BULLETIN, I-XX, 1910-1969, comp. S. Darrel Sheraw, available from the editor or from William Dawson ($1.25). Issues for 1910-72 (vols. 1-23), with the bibliographical index to vols. 1-20, may be obtained from Dawson. Reprints for 1910-71 (vols. 1-22) may be obtained from Walter J. Johnson ($65).

The Keats-Shelley Memorial Association maintains the Memorial House, 26, Piazza di Spagna, Rome, Italy, where Keats died in 1821. In 1910 and 1913, the BULLETIN was sponsored by the Memorial House.

Indexed by ANNUAL BIBLIOGRAPHY OF ENGLISH LANGUAGE AND LITERATURE, ENGLISH LANGUAGE NOTES, MLA INTERNATIONAL BIBLIOGRAPHY, and YEAR'S WORK IN ENGLISH STUDIES.

3. Keats-Shelley Memorial, Rome. BULLETIN (KSMRB). Superseded by KEATS-SHELLEY MEMORIAL BULLETIN (see entry 2). Editors: Sir Rennell Rodd and H. Nelson Gay. Publisher: Macmillan, London. 1910; 1913 (nos. 1-2); publication suspended, 1913-50.

Brief essays on Keats's life, family, works, and friendships with other authors; previously unpublished works; history of the institution; reprints of lectures; list of Memorial House holdings; commemorative poems; list of donors; illustrations and portraits. Reprints available from Walter J. Johnson and from Gregg Associates, Brussels.

Alternate titles:

BULLETIN OF THE KEATS-SHELLEY MEMORIAL, ROME

BULLETIN. Keats-Shelley Memorial, Rome

BULLETIN AND REVIEW OF THE KEATS-SHELLEY MEMORIAL, ROME

KELLER, GOTTFRIED (1819-90)

Swiss poet, novelist

1. Gottfried Keller-Gesellschaft. JAHRESBERICHT. Sponsor and publisher: Gottfried Keller-Gesellschaft, Zurich, Switzerland. Secretary: Egon Wilhelm, Postfach 474, 8610 Uster 1, Switzerland. 1932-- . Annual. $15-20. [20-35 p.] Last issue examined: vol. 45, 1976.

   Long essays on one specific subject, such as Keller's realism and love of nature; news of the Gesellschaft--annual report, financial status, membership lists and activities; bibliographical references; list of publications. In German.

   Indexed by Köttelwesch.

KIERKEGAARD, SØREN (1813-55)

Danish philosopher

1. KIERKEGAARDIANA. Editor: Niels Thulstrup. Sponsor: Søren Kierkegaard Selskabet (Kierkegaard Society), Hanevangen 7, 2730 Herlev, DK Denmark. Publisher: Ejnar Munksgaard, Copenhagen, vols. 1-8; vol. 9, Rosenkilde og Bagger, Copenhagen; vol. 10, C.A. Reitzels Beghandel, Nørregade 20, Copenhagen. 1955-- . Every other yr. D Kr 80-120. [100-400 p.] Last issue examined: vol. 10, 1974.

   Collections of long scholarly studies on Kierkegaard's philosophy, religion, relationship with other writers like Luther or Heine, and contemporary reception; numerous long book reviews of international publications; occasional bibliographies, such as that of dissertations (vol. 9); notes on international Society activities, festschriften, lectures; photographs. In Danish, English, or German.

2. KIERKEGAARD SELSKABETS POPULAERE SKRIFTER. Sponsor: Søren Kierkegaard Selskabet (Kierkegaard Society), Hauser Plads 12[1], 1127 Copenhagen, Denmark. Publisher: Ejnar Munksgaard, Copenhagen. 1951-- . Irregular. Kr 10-25. [150-330 p.] Last issue examined: vol. 15, 1970.

   Each volume concerns a different subject, such as KIERKEGAARD STUDIES IN SCANDINAVIA (vol. 1); bibliographies; indexes. In Danish, with occasional contributions in English.

   Alternate title:

   Søren Kierkegaard selskabet. POPULAERE SKRIFTER

3. MEDDELELSER FRA SØREN KIERKEGAARD SELSKABET. Sponsor: Søren Kierkegaard Society, Copenhagen, Denmark. 1949–March 1955 (vols. 1-5, no. 2). Quarterly. Kr 15; $2.50; Kr 75 (institutions).

   Numerous reviews and review articles; notes on Society activities, important publications, and lectures; occasionally, a critical survey of all Kierkegaardian literature. Cumulative index for vols. 1-5 in vol. 5, no. 2. In Danish or German.

   Alternate title:

   REPORTS FROM THE SØREN KIERKEGAARD SOCIETY.
   QUARTERLY REVIEW

4. PUBLICATIONS OF THE KIERKEGAARD SOCIETY, COPENHAGEN. Sponsor: Kierkegaard Society. Publisher: Munksgaard, Copenhagen, vols. 1-2; Rosenkilde, Copenhagen, vols. 3-4. 1951-- . Irregular (vol. 2, 1962; vol. 3, 1969; vol. 4, 1971). Kr 20-40. [130-330 p.]

   Monographs on Kierkegaard's ideas, such as KIERKEGAARDS VERSTÄNDNIS DER EXISTENZ (1969); bibliographies; no index. In Danish, with long summaries in English or German. Vol. 5 not yet published (1978).

KIPLING, RUDYARD (1865-1936)

English novelist, poet, short-story writer

1. KIPLING JOURNAL (KJ). Editor: Roger Lancelyn Green, Poulton Hall, Poulton-Lancelyn, Wirral, Cheshire L63 9LN, England. Sponsor: Kipling Society, 18, Northumberland Avenue, London WC2N 5BJ. March 1927-- . Quarterly. Free with membership (£4; U.S., $10; overseas, £5); libraries (£8; U.S., $20; overseas, £10). [20 p.] Circulation: 1,000. Last issue examined: vol. 45, 1978.

   Organ of the Kipling Society. Brief biographical or interpretive articles; notes on sources, influences, allusions; occasional bibliographies; occasional book reviews; abstracts; news of meetings, recent Kipling-related publications, work in progress; queries; letters to the editor; lists of officers and new members; no annual index. Indexes to vols. 1-24, 25-28, 29-32, 33-36. Reprints of selected volumes available from Walter J. Johnson.

   Indexed by ABSTRACTS OF ENGLISH STUDIES, ANNUAL BIBLIOGRAPHY OF ENGLISH LANGUAGE AND LITERATURE, BRITISH HUMANITIES INDEX, MLA INTERNATIONAL BIBLIOGRAPHY, TWENTIETH CENTURY LITERATURE, and VICTORIAN STUDIES.

2. KIPLING NOTE BOOK: ILLUSTRATIONS, ANECDOTES, BIBLIOGRAPHICAL AND BIOGRAPHICAL FACTS ANENT THIS FOREMOST WRITER OF

FICTION. Editor: Milburg F. Mansfield. Publisher: Milburg F. Mansfield and A. Wessels, 22 East 16th Street, New York, N.Y. February 1899-January 1900 (nos. 1-12). Monthly. $1.50.

Informal biographical notes; unofficial information on Kipling's early works; comments on foreign reviews; contributions toward a bibliography of Kipling's works; reprints of inaccessible material; illustrations.

Alternate title:

KIPLINGIANA: BIOGRAPHICAL AND BIBLIOGRAPHICAL NOTES ANENT RUDYARD KIPLING

3. Kipling Society. REPORT AND ACCOUNTS. 1939-(?).

KIRCHER, ATHANASIUS (1602-80)

German Jesuit, scholar

1. STUDIA KIRCHERIANA. Editors: Olaf Hein and Helmut Kastl. Sponsor: Internationale Athanasius Kircher Forschungs Gesellschaft. Publisher: Edizioni del mondo, Wiesbaden Germany (BRD). 1974-- . DM280. [200 p.]

Extensive studies of Kircher's work, life, and influence, including Kircher's themes as they are treated by other scholars; bibliography; name index. Each monograph covers a different subject; vol. 1, for instance, is the first biography of Kircher ever written. In German, English, French, Italian, or other Western languages. Vol. 2 not yet published (1978).

Alternate title:

SCHRIFTENREIHE DER INTERNATIONALEN ATHANASIUS KIRCHER FORSCHUNGSGESELLSCHAFT, Wiesbaden-Rom

KLEIST, HEINRICH VON (1777-1811)

German poet, dramatist, novelist

1. Archives des Lettres Modernes. 1961-- . Irregular. The series number for the issue on Kleist is provided below.

Kleist subseries	Archives series	Date
Unnumbered	No. 35	1961

In French. See Camus, Albert, entry 2, for a full description of Archives des Lettres Modernes.

Indexed by BULLETIN CRITIQUE, Klapp, and MLA INTERNATIONAL BIBLIOGRAPHY.

2. JAHRBUCH DER KLEIST-GESELLSCHAFT (KlJb; JKG).

See entry 4: SCHRIFTEN DER KLEIST-GESELLSCHAFT.

Indexed by MLA INTERNATIONAL BIBLIOGRAPHY.

3. JAHRESGABE DER HEINRICH-VON-KLEIST-GESELLSCHAFT. Editor: Walter Müller-Seidel. Sponsor: Heinrich-von-Kleist-Gesellschaft. Publisher: Erich Schmidt, Berlin. 1962-- . Irregular. DM20-65. [75-300 p.] Last issue examined: 1973-74.

Studies and interpretations of Kleist's life and works--comparisons with earlier and later authors and titles; numerous essays on the "Marionettentheater"; reprints of lectures; surveys of his influence on modern literature; bibliographies; report of Gesellschaft activities. In German.

Indexed by Köttelwesch.

Alternate title:

Heinrich von Kleist-Gesellschaft. JAHRESGABE

4. SCHRIFTEN DER KLEIST-GESELLSCHAFT. Sponsor: Kleist-Gesellschaft. Publisher: Weidmannsche Buchhandlung, Berlin. 1921-39 (vols. 1-19). Annual. [150-400 p.]

Biographical and interpretive essays; reprints of Kleist's notes; occasional lists of performances of his plays; bibliography of Kleist scholarship, 1914-21, in vol. 1 (1921); annual bibliographies in vols. 2-4 (1922-24); bibliography for 1925-30 in vols. 11-12 (1929-30) and for 1931-37 in vol. 17 (1937), with occasional annotations; illustrations, portraits, and facsimiles. Vols. 1-4, 7-14, and 17 include the JAHRBUCH of the Gesellschaft, with a report of activities, performances of plays, statistics. In German. Reprints available from John Benjamins; and from Walter J. Johnson (1922-39, $135).

According to some sources, this title is continued by the SCHRIFTEN sponsored and published by the Kleist-Gesellschaft, Frankfurt-an-der-Oder.

KNOX, JOHN (1505-72)

Scottish reformer, writer, statesman

1. Foyer John Knox Lecture. Sponsor: John Knox House Association, Geneva, Switzerland. 1955-- . Irregular. Last issue examined: no. 11, 1970.

Reprints of lectures. In English, French, German, or Spanish.

Alternate title:

John Knox House Lecture

KOLBENHEYER, EDWIN GUIDO (1878-1962)

German poet, philosopher

1. BAUHÜTTEN-BRIEF: ZEITSCHRIFT FÜR DIE FREUNDE DER DICHTUNG UND DES GEDANKENWERKES VON E.G. KOLBENHEYERS. Editor: Walter Oesterhelt, Burkardstrasse 11, 721 Rottweil a. N. Germany (BRD). Sponsor: Kolbenheyer-Gesellschaft. Publisher: L.C. Wittich, Darmstadt, Germany (BRD). 1955-71 (temporarily suspended). Annual. Free with membership (DM2). [30-35 p.] Last issue examined: no. 35, 1971.

    Official organ of the Kolbenheyer-Gesellschaft. Long scholarly studies of Kolbenheyer's philosophy as it is expressed in his published works, notes, and journals; reprints of lectures delivered at the Kolbenheyer-Gesellschaft meetings; reprints of important excerpts from the works; occasional poems by Kolbenheyer; occasional photographs; no index. In German.

KORZENIOWSKI, JOSEPH CONRAD THEODORE

See Conrad, Joseph.

KOSTROWITZKY, WILHELM [GUILLAUME APOLLINAIRE] (1880-1918)

French poet

1. Archives Guillaume Apollinaire. Subseries of Archives des Lettres Modernes. 1969-- . Irregular. Equivalent numbers are provided below for both the parent series (Archives des Lettres Modernes) and the individual series on Apollinaire.

Apollinaire subseries	Archives series	Date
No. 1	No. 101	1969
No. 2	No. 103	1969
No. 3	No. 112	1970
No. 4	No. 118	1970
No. 5	No. 126	1971
No. 6	No. 138	1972

In French. See Camus, Albert, entry 2, for a full description of Archives des Lettres Modernes.

Indexed by BULLETIN CRITIQUE, FRENCH VII, FRENCH XX, Klapp, and MLA INTERNATIONAL BIBLIOGRAPHY.

2. Bibliothèque Guillaume Apollinaire. Sponsor: Amis de Guillaume Apollinaire, A.S.B.L., Stavelot, Belgium. Publisher: Minard, Paris. 1956-- . Irregular (a series). 20-45 Fr. [150-300 p.] Last issue examined: no. 9, 1976.

   Critical studies, critical editions, and lectures delivered at conferences on Apollinaire's works. Published originally in the series Lettres Modernes. In French.

   Indexed by FRENCH XX.

3. FLÂNEUR DES DEUX RIVES: BULLETIN D'ÉTUDES APOLLINARIENNES. Editor: Pierre-Marcel Adéma, 18, rue des Écoles, 75005 Paris. Secretary: Michel Décaudin. March 1954-June 1955 (nos. 1-6). Quarterly. [26 p.]

   A bulletin of Apollinaire studies. Brief critical essays; previously unpublished or inaccessible material; bibliographies of new editions and critical works, including articles in periodicals; interviews and reminiscences; news of recent and forthcoming publications, conferences, expositions, books received, prizes; poems. In French.

   Alternate title:

   CAHIERS APOLLINAIRE

4. Guillaume Apollinaire. Subseries of La Revue des Lettres Modernes. Editor: Michel Décaudin. Spring 1962-- . Annual (irregular). 8-14 Fr. Equivalent numbers are provided below for both the parent series (La Revue des Lettres Modernes) and the individual series on Apollinaire.

Apollinaire subseries	La Revue series	Date
No. 1	Nos. 69-70	1962
No. 2	Nos. 85-89	1963
No. 3	Nos. 104-07	1964
No. 4	Nos. 123-26	1965
No. 5	Nos. 146-49	1966
No. 6	Nos. 166-69	1967
No. 7	Nos. 183-88	1968
No. 8	Nos. 217-22	1969
No. 9	Nos. 249-53	1970
No. 10	Nos. 276-79	1971
No. 11	Nos. 327-30	1972
No. 12	Nos. 380-84	1973
No. 13	Nos. 450-55	1976
No. 14	Nos. 530-36	1978

   Each volume concerns a different subject, such as APOLLINAIRE ET LES SURRÉALISTES. In French. See Camus, Albert, entry 1, for a full description of La Revue des Lettres Modernes.

Indexed by BULLETIN CRITIQUE, FRENCH VII, FRENCH XX, Klapp, and MLA INTERNATIONAL BIBLIOGRAPHY.

Alternate title:

Serie Guillaume Apollinaire

5. QUE VLO-VE?: BULLETIN DE L'ASSOCIATION INTERNATIONALE DES AMIS DE GUILLAUME APOLLINAIRE. Editor: Victor Martin-Schmets, 66, rue de la Pépinière, B-5000 Namur, Belgium. Treasurer for France: Michel Décaudin, 24, rue des Bernardins, 75005 Paris. Treasurer for Belgium and other countries: Les Amis de Guillaume Apollinaire, c/o Armand Huysmans, B-4970 Stavelot, Belgium. Sponsor: Association internationale des Amis de Guillaume Apollinaire. January 1973 (no. 1)-- . 2/yr. 22 Fr (33 Fr includes ACTES des colloques de Stavelot). [16 p.] Last issue examined: no. 10, 1976.

Brief biographical and critical articles; resumés of activities of the Association and the Stavelot Museum--lectures, seminars, awards; report of acquisitions; portraits and facsimiles. In French.

Indexed by BIBLIOGRAPHIE DE LA LITTÉRATURE FRANÇAISE, FRENCH XX, Klapp, and REVUE D'HISTOIRE LITTÉRAIRE.

Alternate title:

BULLETIN DE L'ASSOCIATION INTERNATIONALE DES AMIS DE GUILLAUME APOLLINAIRE

KRISHNAMURTI, JIDDU (1895-)

Indian religious leader

1. WAYSIDE QUARTERLY BULLETIN. Editors: Joan Atwater and Mary Radcliffe, P.O. Box 333, St. Helena, Calif. 94574. Publisher: Wayside Press. 1970(?)-- . Quarterly. $2. [60 p.] Circulation: 350.

Interested in the work of Jiddu Krishnamurti--poetry, brief articles, letters; concerned with the problems of daily living.

LABRUNIE, GÉRARD [GÉRARD DE NERVAL] (1808-55)

French poet

1. Archives nervaliennes. Subseries of Archives des Lettres Modernes. 1957-- . Irregular. Equivalent numbers are provided below for both the parent series (Archives des Lettres Modernes) and the individual author series on Nerval.

Nerval subseries	Archives series	Date
No. 1	No. 1	1957
No. 2	No. 3	1957
No. 3	No. 48	1963
No. 4	No. 49	1963
No. 5	No. 59	1965
No. 6	No. 92	1968
No. 7	No. 93	1968
No. 8	No. 104	1969
No. 9	No. 127	1971
No. 10	No. 130	1971
No. 11	No. 131	1971

In French. See Camus, Albert, entry 2, for a full description of Archives des Lettres Modernes.

Indexed by BULLETIN CRITIQUE, Klapp, and MLA INTERNATIONAL BIBLIOGRAPHY.

2. Gérard de Nerval. Subseries of La Revue des Lettres Modernes, 1960/61-- . Irregular. Series numbers as provided below for the issues on Nerval.

Nerval subseries	La Revue series	Date
Unnumbered	Nos. 58/59	1960/61

In French. See Camus, Albert, entry 1, for a full description of La Revue des Lettres Modernes.

Indexed by BULLETIN CRITIQUE, FRENCH VI, Klapp, and MLA INTERNATIONAL BIBLIOGRAPHY.

3. Nouvelle bibliothèque nervalienne. Publisher: Minard, Paris. 1959-- . Irregular (a series). 20-50 Fr. [300-500 p.]. Last issue examined: Critical works, no. 5, 1972.

A new multivolume edition of Gérard de Nerval's published and previously unpublished works, letters, and other documents--accompanied by biographical, critical, source, textual, and influence studies; bibliographical references and bibliographies; illustrations, plates, and facsimiles. The series also includes separate book-length critical works, such as THÉMATIQUE DE NERVAL. In French.

Indexed by FRENCH VI.

LACORDAIRE, JEAN-BAPTISTE-HENRI (1802-61)

French Dominican, ecclesiastic

1. CAHIERS LACORDAIRE. Sponsor: Association Saint-Vincent-Ferrier,

Dijon, France. 1960-63(?) (nos. 1-18). Quarterly.

Contains a few essays about Lacordaire and his work. In French.

LA FONTAINE, JEAN DE (1621-95)

French author of fables, ballads, comedies

1. Amis de La Fontaine. BULLETIN. 1922-40.

   Occasional articles on the works of La Fontaine. In French.

2. Archives des Lettres Modernes. 1959-- . Irregular. The series number for the issue on La Fontaine is provided below.

La Fontaine subseries	Archives series	Date
Unnumbered	No. 27	1959

   In French. See Camus, Albert, entry 2, for a full description of Archives des Lettres Modernes.

Indexed by BULLETIN CRITIQUE, Klapp, and MLA INTERNATIONAL BIBLIOGRAPHY.

LAGERLÖF, SELMA (1858-1940)

Swedish novelist, poet

1. LAGERLÖFSTUDIER. Editors: Bengt Ek, Inge Jonsson, Ying Toijer-Nilsson. Sponsor: Selma Lagerlöfsällskapet. 1958-- . Irregular (no. 4, 1971). [200-300 p.] Last issue examined: no. 5, 1976.

   Long scholarly studies of the novels and other works, including memoirs; articles on contemporaries and mutual influences; reminiscences by relatives and acquaintances; previously unpublished or inaccessible works; brief news of international assemblies and important publications; portraits and facsimiles; no index. In Swedish.

LAMB, CHARLES (1775-1834)

English essayist, critic

1. Ç.L.S. BULLETIN. Supersedes Charles Lamb Society. MONTHLY BULLETIN (see entry 5); superseded by CHARLES LAMB BULLETIN (see entry 2). Editors: September 1948-January 1972, H.G. Smith, Blakesmoor, 61, Salisbury Avenue, St. Albans, England; April-October 1972, Basil Savage, 46, Brookfield, Highgate West Hill, London N6 6AT. Sponsor:

Charles Lamb Society. President: Ian Jack. Secretary: A.D.G. Cheyne, Charles Lamb's House, 64, Duncan Terrace, London N1 8AG. May 1941-October 1972 (nos. 51-216). Bimonthly, May-(?)1941; quarterly, 1941-72 (January, April, July, October). £1.50; $3.50; $4.50 (libraries). [4-8 p.]

Organ of the Charles Lamb Society, with reports from numerous international branches. Brief notes and articles on Lamb, his sister Mary, and his contemporaries; news of social events and excursions, competitions, members' activities, recent scholarship; book reviews; occasional bibliographies. Back issues available from Florence S. Reeves, 33, Alma Street, London NW5 3DH.

Alternate title:

Charles Lamb Society. JOURNAL

2. CHARLES LAMB BULLETIN: THE JOURNAL OF THE CHARLES LAMB SOCIETY (ChLB). Supersedes C.L.S. BULLETIN (see entry 1). Editor: Basil Savage, 46, Brookfield, Highgate West Hill, London N6 6AT; and Mary R. Wedd, 14 Valley Drive, Sevenoaks, Kent TN13 2EG, England. Sponsor: Charles Lamb Society, London. President: Ian Jack. Secretary: A.D.G. Cheyne, Charles Lamb's House, 64, Duncan Terrace, London N1 8AG. New series, January 1973-- . Quarterly (January, April, July, October). London: £2.50 (doubles, £3); provincial members £1.50 (doubles, £2); overseas, $5 (individuals), $7.50 (institutions). [20-50 p.] Circulation: 500. Last issue examined: no. 24, 1978.

Editorial policy is "to study the life, works, and times of Charles Lamb and his circle, to stimulate the Elian spirit of friendliness and humor, and to form a collection of Eliana." Long (10 p.) scholarly, biographical, and interpretive studies, not only on Lamb but also on Clare, Coleridge, and others; reprints of lectures delivered to the Society; long book reviews; notes on new publications, seminars, exhibitions, Society activities; list of new members; annual report and financial statement; facsimiles and illustrations.

Indexed by ENGLISH LANGUAGE NOTES and MLA INTERNATIONAL BIBLIOGRAPHY.

3. Charles Lamb Society. ANNUAL REPORT AND FINANCIAL STATEMENT. Sponsor and publisher: Charles Lamb Society, Charles Lamb's House, 64, Duncan Terrace, London N1 8AG. President: Ian Jack. 1935-- . Annual. [3-12 p.] Last issue examined: 40th, 1974.

Report of monthly lectures, excursions, acquisitions, commemorations, and expenditures; list of current members.

4. Charles Lamb Society. BULLETIN.

 Supplement, 1936-41.

5. Charles Lamb Society. MONTHLY BULLETIN. Superseded by C.L.S. BULLETIN (see entry 1). Sponsor: Charles Lamb Society, London. May 1935-April 1941 (nos. 1-50). Monthly.

6. ELIAN NOTEBOOK. Sponsor: Charles Lamb Society, London. 1950-(?).

 Each volume is concerned with a specific subject. No reply to query.

 Alternate title:

 ELIAN BOOKLETS

LARBAUD, VALÉRY (1881-1957)

French poet, critic, translator, author of fiction

1. CAHIERS DES AMIS DE VALÉRY LARBAUD. Sponsor: Amis de Valéry Larbaud, Mlle. Kuntz, Bibliothèque Municipale, Centre Culturel Valéry Larbaud (Fonds Larbaud), 15, rue du Maréchal-Foch, 03200 Vichy (Allier), France. 1967-- . Irregular. 10-35 Fr. [45-70 p.] Last issue examined: no. 15, 1977.

 Articles on Larbaud's life, works, and influence in France and other countries; information on the Larbaud Prize, expositions, the annual cocktail party; reminiscences; previously unpublished documents, such as letters from Philippe and Dujardin; bibliographies of library holdings and acquisitions; facsimiles and photographs. In French.

 Indexed by BIBLIOGRAPHIE DE LA LITTÉRATURE FRANÇAISE, BULLETIN CRITIQUE, FRENCH XX, Klapp, and REVUE D'HISTOIRE LITTÉRAIRE.

 Alternate titles:

 Amis de Valéry Larbaud. CAHIERS

 Association internationale des Amis de Valéry Larbaud. CAHIERS DES AMIS DE VALÉRY LARBAUD, Vichy

LA VARENDE, JEAN MALLARD, VICOMTE DE (1887-1959)

French novelist

1. AMIS DE LA VARENDE. Editor: 63, rue Renequin, 75017 Paris. Spon-

sor: Amis de La Varende, 36, rue du Bac, 75007 Paris. Publisher: Firmin-Didot, 56, rue Jacob, 75006 Paris. January 1963-- . Irregular. Last issue examined: no. 10, June 1973.

Brief articles analyzing La Varende's works and life. In French.

Indexed by BIBLIOGRAPHIE DE LA LITTÉRATURE FRANÇAISE, FRENCH VII, and Klapp.

Alternate title:

BULLETIN DES AMIS DE LA VARENDE

LAWRENCE, DAVID HERBERT (1885-1930)

English novelist, poet, short-story writer

1. D.H. LAWRENCE NEWS AND NOTES. Editor and publisher: Dexter Martin, Department of English, South Dakota University, Brookings, S. Dak. 57006. October 1959-Fall 1962 (vols. 1-2, no. 3). 3-4/yr. $1. [8-16 p.]

   Editorial intent is "to spread interest in Lawrence without idealizing him." Brief critical and biographical articles; informal notes on censorship, new editions of Lawrence's works, new criticism, films, work in progress; announcements of exhibitions, library acquisitions; bibliographies of English and American hardbound and paperbound editions.

   Indexed by ABSTRACTS OF ENGLISH STUDIES.

2. D.H. LAWRENCE NEWSLETTER. Editor: Keith Cushman, Department of English, University of North Carolina at Greensboro, Greensboro, N.C. 27412. Sponsor: D.H. Lawrence Society. Membership chairman: David Farmer, Box 7219, Humanities Research Center, University of Texas, Austin, Tex. 78712. 1977-- . Irregular. Last issue examined: no. 2, Fall 1977.

   Founded to "serve as a means of communication among the Society's members." Published initially in the D.H. LAWRENCE REVIEW (see entry 3).

3. D.H. LAWRENCE REVIEW (DHLR). Editor: James C. Cowan, Box 2474, University of Arkansas, Fayetteville, Ark. 72701. Sponsor: University of Arkansas. Spring 1968-- . 3/yr. (Spring, Summer, Fall). $7 (individuals); $8 (institutions); $8 (foreign); $2.50 per issue. [120-70 p.] Circulation: 600. Last issue examined: vol. 11, 1978.

   A forum for criticism, scholarship, reviews, and bibliographies of Lawrence and his circle. Long (25 p.) scholarly articles on Lawrence's life, loves, friendships, works, influence, and style; English language bibliography of Lawrence scholarship in the Spring issue; foreign language bibliographies published irregularly; reminiscences; previously unpublished material; several review articles in every issue; film and play reviews; "Laurentiana"--news of D.H. Lawrence Society activities, MLA seminars, library acquisitions, dissertations and research completed, work in progress; brief survey of recent publications on Lawrence; letters from readers; illustrations, photographs, and facsimiles; annual index. Occasional special issues on specific areas of Lawrence's work or on his associates, such as the Dorothy Brett letters, with extensive notes (Spring 1976). Available in microform from University Microfilms International.

Indexed by ABSTRACTS OF ENGLISH STUDIES, AMERICAN HUMANITIES INDEX, ANNUAL BIBLIOGRAPHY OF ENGLISH LANGUAGE AND LITERATURE, MLA INTERNATIONAL BIBLIOGRAPHY, TWENTIETH CENTURY LITERATURE, and YEAR'S WORK IN ENGLISH STUDIES.

4. D.H. Lawrence Studies. Editor: Sadanobu Kai, Ritsumeikan University, Kyoto, Japan. Sponsor: D.H. Lawrence Society of Japan. 1973-- . Annual (a series). Last issue examined: vol. 3, 1975.

Collections of essays, each volume on a different subject, such as SONS AND LOVERS; bibliographies of critical works. In Japanese, with summaries in English.

5. JOURNAL OF THE D.H. LAWRENCE SOCIETY. Editor: John S. Poynter. Sponsor and publisher: D.H. Lawrence Society, 8a, Victoria Street, Eastwood, Nottinghamshire, England. 1976-- . Irregular. £.70. [20-25 p.] Last issue examined: vol. 1, no. 3, 1978.

Brief articles on Lawrence's stories--their sources, style, and characters; previously unpublished or inaccessible material, such as letters and poems; reminiscences by friends of the Lawrences; news of interest to Lawrence scholars, such as a report of the death of the man who was assumed by some to have been Frieda Lawrence's lover and the source of the plot for LADY CHATTERLEY'S LOVER; letters to the editor; bibliographical references; photographs. The Society sponsors lectures, organizes walks and exhibitions, notifies members of performances, and preserves Lawrence homes and memorabilia in Eastwood.

6. NETHERMERE NEWS. Sponsor: D.H. Lawrence Association, Nottingham, England. January 1973-- .

LAWRENCE, T.E. (1885-1935)

English author, soldier, adventurer

1. T.E. LAWRENCE STUDIES. Editor: J.M. Wilson. Sponsor and publisher: T.E. Lawrence Studies, Apt. 5, 75, West Hill, London SW15 2UL. Spring 1976-- . Vol. 1: 2/yr. (Spring, Autumn); annual beginning with vol. 2. $14.50. [80-85 p.]

   "Aims to provide material for an impartial assessment of T.E. Lawrence's career." Articles on his relationship with such notables as Churchill, Buchan, Shaw, Sassoon, Hardy; reminiscences; in every issue, a descriptive bibliography (catalogue raisonné), with annotations, of works by and about Lawrence; surveys of collections; authoritative reviews of books and articles that stress accuracy and correction; annotated list of works received and forthcoming; register of current research; book exchange; news of book auctions, television programs, and press coverage; sketches and photographs.

LAZARE, BERNARD (1865-1903)

French essayist

1. CAHIERS BERNARD LAZARE. Editor: A. Scherr. Sponsor: Cercle Bernard Lazare, in collaboration with NEW OUTLOOK (Tel Aviv) and ISRAËL HORIZONS (New York). Publisher: CAHIERS BERNARD LAZARE, 17, rue de la Victoire, 75009 Paris. 1957-- . 3-4/yr. 20 Fr; with membership in the Cercle Bernard Lazare, 40 Fr. [16 p.] Last issues examined: nos. 63-64, 1977.

   Originally inspired by the life and work of Bernard Lazare, but now devoted to articles on current political and cultural issues; brief book reviews; announcements of meetings, new publications, necrology, memorials. In French.

LEACOCK, STEPHEN (1869-1944)

Canadian humorist, political scientist

1. NEWSPACKET. Sponsor: Stephen Leacock Associates, P.O. Box 854, Orillia, Ontario, Canada. Spring 1970-- . Quarterly.

   No reply to query.

LEE, EDWARD EDSON [LEO EDWARDS] (1884-1944)

American author of boys' books

1. TUTTER BUGLE. Editor: Robert L. Johnson. Sponsor: Leo Edwards' Juvenile Jupiter Detectives, John L. Tornquist, 4645 Vincent Avenue, South Minneapolis, Minn. 55410. 1973-- . 2/month. $3. [8 p.] Circulation: 85.

   Query returned--addressee unknown.

LEE, MANFRED B. [ELLERY QUEEN] (1905-71)

Co-author, with Frederic Dannay, of the Ellery Queen mysteries

See Dannay, Frederic.

LEIBNIZ, GOTTFRIED WILHELM (1646-1716)

German philosopher, mathematician, logician

1. STUDIA LEIBNITIANA: SONDERHEFT. Editors: Kurt Müller and Wilhelm Totok, Geschaftsstelle der Gottfried-Wilhelm-Leibniz-Gesellschaft, Niedersächsische Landesbibliothek, 3 Hannover, Am Archiv 1, Germany (BRD); Heinrich Schepers, Leibniz-Forschungsstelle der Westfälischen Wilhelms-Universität, 44 Münster, Rothenburg 32, Germany (BRD). Publisher: Franz Steiner Verlag, Wiesbaden, Germany (BRD). 1969-- . Irregular. DM15-55; $8-16. [70-300 p.] Last issue examined: vol. 10, 1978.

   Long studies on such specific subjects as LEIBNIZ ON HUMAN FREEDOM (vol. 2, 1970). In German.

2. STUDIA LEIBNITIANA: ZEITSCHRIFT FÜR GESCHICHTE DER PHILOSOPHIE UND DER WISSENSCHAFTEN. Editors: Kurt Müller and Wilhelm Totok, Geschaftsstelle der Gottfried-Wilhelm-Leibniz-Gesellschaft, Niedersächsische Landesbibliothek, Waterloostrasse 8, 3000 Hannover 1, Germany (BRD); Heinrich Schepers, Leibniz-Forschungsstelle der Westfälischen Wilhelms-Universität, 44 Münster, Rothenburg 32, Westfalia, Germany (BRD). Sponsor: Gottfried-Wilhelm-Leibniz-Gesellschaft. Publisher: Franz Steiner Verlag, Wiesbaden, Germany (BRD). 1969-- . Quarterly, 1969-72; since 1973, 2/yr. DM40-85; $12-41. [150-70 p.] Last issue examined: vol. 10, 1978.

   Since 1974, brief abstracts precede each of the scholarly essays on Leibniz's principles and philosophy, language, unpublished manuscripts, sources, and influence; bibliographical references; important comprehensive Leibniz bibliography, analytical and international, with information on new editions, critical books, critical articles in periodicals, reviews, completed dissertations; numerous long reviews and review articles on important international publications; notes on conferences, work in progress, translations, new publications; abstracts of complete works; international contributors. Since 1968, occasional supplements have been published that concentrate on a specific subject, such as the reports of the international Leibniz congresses, or DIE MATHEMATISCHEN STUDIEN VON G.W. LEIBNIZ ZUR KOMBINATORIK (no. 16, 1976; DM110). In English, German, or French. Alternate spelling: Leibnitz, Lubeniecz.

Indexed by BIBLIOGRAPHIE DE LA LITTÉRATURE FRANÇAISE, PHILOLOGICAL QUARTERLY, and PHILOSOPHER'S INDEX.

Alternate subtitles:

VIERTELJAHRSCHRIFT FÜR PHILOSOPHIE UND GESCHICHTE DER WISSENSCHAFTEN

ZEITSCHRIFT FÜR GESCHICHTE DER PHILOSOPHIE UND DER WISSENSCHAFTEN VOM 16. BIS 18 JAHRHUNDERT

LENAU, NIKOLAUS

See Strehlenau, Nikolaus Niembsch von.

LENIN, NIKOLAI (1870-1924)

Russian Communist leader

1. LENINSKII SBORNIK. Publisher: Izd-vo Politicheskoi Literatury, Moscow. 1924-- . Irregular (vols. 1-27, 1924-34; vols. 28-32, 1936-38; vol. 33, 1940; vols. 34-35, 1942-45; vols. 36, 1959; vol. 37, 1970; vol. 38, 1975). [400-550 p.]

   Concerned mainly with the publication of previously unpublished letters and other documents, but also includes notes on the life and contributions of Lenin to history; reports of the Lenin symposia; portraits and facsimiles; detailed index. Index for vols. 1-20 (1924-32). In Russian. Reprints available from Walter J. Johnson (1924-59, $695).

LESSING, DORIS (1919-)

English novelist, dramatist, short-story writer

1. DORIS LESSING NEWSLETTER. Editor: Dee Seligman, 35 Prospect Street, Sherborn, Mass. 01770. 1977-- . 2/yr. $4. [10-15 p.]

   A newsletter designed to keep people in touch with current research on Lessing, with some material on related authors. Editorial policy encourages brief articles that will help further constructive research, and solicits notes and queries to which readers can respond. Occasional bibliographies and book reviews; news of conferences, new publications by and about Lessing, and activities of Lessing scholars.

LESSING, GOTTHOLD EPHRAIM (1729-81)

German dramatist, critic, poet

1. LESSING YEARBOOK (LY). Editors: Jerry Glenn and Gottfried Merkel, University of Cincinnati, Cincinnati, Ohio 45221; Karl S. Guthke, Harvard University, Cambridge, Mass. 02138, and others. Sponsor: American Lessing Society. Secretary: Edward P. Harris, Department of Germanic Languages and Literatures, University of Cincinnati. Publisher: Max Hueber Verlag, Ismaning, Germany (BRD). Distributed by Rand McNally, Foreign Languages Department, P.O. Box 76000, Chicago, Ill. 60680. 1969-- . Annual. Free with membership (DM35; $14). [250-300 p.] Last issue examined: vol. 10, 1978.

   "Founded for the purpose of encouraging and furthering the scholarly study of Lessing and his times . . . to reemphasize Lessing's humanism and his continuing importance throughout the world." Scholarly essays on his philosophy and literary technique; essays on such contemporary poets as Hagedorn, Hölty, and Goethe; studies in the cultural, religious, and political background; numerous book reviews, usually of German publications, reviewed by American scholars; news of the American Lessing Society. In English or German.

   Indexed by ENGLISH LANGUAGE NOTES, Köttelwesch, MLA INTERNATIONAL BIBLIOGRAPHY, and PHILOLOGICAL QUARTERLY.

LEWIS, CLIVE STAPLES (1898-1963)

English novelist, critic, essayist

1. BULLETIN OF THE NEW YORK C.S. LEWIS SOCIETY (CSLBull). Editor: Eugene McGovern, 32 Park Drive, Ossining, N.Y. 10562. Sponsor: New York C.S. Lewis Society. Correspondence: Mrs. John Kirkpatrick, 466 Orange Street, New Haven, Conn. 06511. December 1969-- . Monthly. Free with membership ($7). [10-15 p.] Circulation: 350. Last issue examined: vol. 9, no. 4, February 1978.

   Brief critical notes on language, content, sources, influence, friendships, religion, myth; occasional bibliographies; book reviews; news notes on Dorothy Sayers, Charles Williams, and Lewis activities in the media of interest to the general reader; annual index. See also Tolkien, J.R.R., entries 2, 8, 9, 11, 12.

   Indexed by MLA INTERNATIONAL BIBLIOGRAPHY.

Alternate titles:

C.S.L. BULLETIN

CSL: BULLETIN

2. CHRONICLE OF THE PORTLAND C.S. LEWIS SOCIETY. Editor: Carole Sperou, 1224 S.E. 41st Street, Portland, Oreg. 97214. Sponsor: Portland C.S. Lewis Society. 1972-- . Quarterly. $5. [10-15 p.] Last issue examined: January-March 1978.

Brief, informal biographical and critical notes; news of members' activities.

Alternate title:

CHRONICLE. Portland C.S. Lewis Society

3. LAMPPOST. Editor: George Musacchio, California Baptist College, Riverside, Calif. 92504. Sponsor: Southern California C.S. Lewis Society. 1976-- . $6. [8-10 p.]

Brief, informal notes concerning Lewis' life and works; news of members' activities.

LEWIS, SINCLAIR (1885-1951)

American novelist

1. SINCLAIR LEWIS NEWSLETTER (SLN). Editor: James Lundquist, Department of English, St. Cloud State College, St. Cloud, Minn. 56301. Sponsor: Department of English, St. Cloud State College. April 1969-76 (temporarily suspended). $1. [10-25 p.] Circulation: 500. Last issues examined: vols. 7-8, 1975-76.

Numerous brief biographical and critical articles and notes on Lewis, his contemporaries and followers; interviews and reminiscences; reprints of letters; occasional notes on library holdings, radio programs, new publications; book reviews; occasional photographs.

Indexed by ABSTRACTS OF ENGLISH STUDIES and ANNUAL BIBLIOGRAPHY OF ENGLISH LANGUAGE AND LITERATURE.

LEWIS, WYNDHAM (1884-1957)

English author, critic, artist

1. LEWISLETTER. Editor: Tom Kinninmont, Publishing Research Project, National Library, Edinburgh, Scotland. Sponsor: W.L. Society. Secretary: Frank Kirkpatrick, 148 Bellahouston Drive, Glasgow G52, Scotland. December 1974-- . 2/yr. Last issue examined: no. 7, October 1977.

Brief informal critical and biographical articles covering Lewis' literary and artistic talents; occasional brief surveys of recent critical works, biographies, and new editions; occasional checklists of primary and secondary works (no. 5, October 1976); reprints of inaccessible works and previously unpublished material, such as his correspondence with Thomas Sturge Moore; news of Lewis happenings--location of collections, availability of reproductions, exhibitions, new publications of Lewis scholarship, symposia, radio programs, films.

LINDSAY, VACHEL (1879-1931)

American poet

1. VACHEL LINDSAY ASSOCIATION. Editor and sponsor: Elizabeth E. Graham, 502 South State Street, Springfield, Ill. 62704. November 1946-- . Irregular.

   Occasional copies of lectures, brochures, reprints. Sponsor displays her collection of Lindsayana June-August and upon request.

LOCKE, JOHN (1632-1704)

English philosopher

1. John Locke Lectures. Publisher: Oxford, England. 1955-(?).

2. LOCKE NEWSLETTER. Editor: Roland Hall, Department of Philosophy, University of York, Heslington, York YO1 5DD, England. November 1970-- . Annual. Free (early issues, £2 or $5.50). [100 p.] Circulation: 600. Last issue examined: vol. 7, 1976.

   Long documented articles on Locke's epistemology, political theory, ethics, editions; supplements to the Locke bibliography; notes on accuracy of editions; queries and replies; "Recent Reviews"--list of periodicals where reviews of Locke scholarship can be found; book reviews in vol. 2 and succeeding issues; list of recent publications, forthcoming articles, and books in Locke's library; report of work in progress; news of conferences; international audience--forty different countries. Index (vols. 1-5) in vol. 6 (1975).

   Indexed by PHILOSOPHER'S INDEX.

LONDON, JACK (1876-1916)

American novelist

1. JACK LONDON NEWSLETTER. Editor and publisher: Hensley C.

Woodbridge, Department of Foreign Languages and Literatures, Faner Hall, Southern Illinois University, Carbondale, Ill. 62901. July-December 1967-- . 2/yr. in 1967-68; 3/yr., since 1969. $5. [20-60 p.] Circulation: 300. Last issue examined: vol. 10, 1977.

Brief critical articles on London's novels, short stories, and poems, his stormy life, and his humor; critical material on Jesse Stuart, his life and works, and a regular Stuart bibliography, both primary and secondary; occasional supplements to the 1973 edition of JACK LONDON: A BIBLIOGRAPHY (Kraus Reprint); occasional specialized bibliographies, including one of the numerous memorial publications at the time of London's death; notes on translations, book sales, library collections; news of events and recent publications; film reviews; works by and about both London and Stuart reviewed regularly; previously unpublished material; queries; international contributors; no index. Microfilm available from University Microfilms International.

Indexed by ABSTRACTS OF ENGLISH STUDIES, AMERICAN HUMANITIES INDEX, AMERICAN LITERATURE ABSTRACTS, ANNUAL BIBLIOGRAPHY OF ENGLISH LANGUAGE AND LITERATURE, and MLA INTERNATIONAL BIBLIOGRAPHY.

2. LONDON COLLECTOR. Editor: Richard Weiderman, 1420 Pontiac Road, S.E., Grand Rapids, Mich. 49506. June 1970-- . Approximately l/yr. $1/four issues. [2 p.] Circulation: 200.

Each issue is on a different subject. Collections of short critical articles on London's life, his works, and his contemporaries; occasional bibliographies; occasional reports of work in progress; book reviews; news notes; occasional illustrations; no index.

3. WHAT'S NEW ABOUT LONDON, JACK? Editor: David H. Schlottmann, 929 South Bay Road, Olympia, Wash. 98506. July 1971-- . Irregular, as news accumulates. $3.50/twelve issues. [5-10 p.] Circulation: 100.

Comments on critical books and articles; occasional bibliographies; reprints of rare items; news and notes; information on new editions and second-hand books. See also William H. Chaney.

LOTI, PIERRE

See Viaud, Julien.

LUDWIG, OTTO (1813-65)

German author of realistic stories

1. OTTO LUDWIG-JAHRBUCH. Supersedes OTTO LUDWIG-KALENDER

(entry 2). Sponsor: Otto Ludwig-verein, Weimar, Germany (DDR). 1938-(?).

2. OTTO LUDWIG-KALENDER. Superseded by OTTO LUDWIG-JAHRBUCH (see entry 1). 1929-37 (nos. 1-9).

LUTHER, MARTIN (1483-1546)

German religious reformer

1. LUTHER: ZEITSCHRIFT DER LUTHER-GESELLSCHAFT. Editors: Walther von Loewenich, Bernhard Lohse, and Erwin Mülhaupt. Sponsor: Luther-Gesellschaft, Grindelallee 7, 2 Hamburg 13, Germany (BRD). Publisher: Vandenhoeck und Ruprecht, Göttingen, Germany (BRD). 1919-41 (nos. 1-23); 1953 (no. 1)-- . 3/yr. DM6.50. [40-50 p.] Last issue examined: 1974.

   Long studies on Luther's theology, his influence on his contemporaries and on our times, his critics, and the Reformation; occasional book reviews on important German publications; international editorial board; no index. In German. Reprints available from Walter J. Johnson (1919-71, $335).

   Alternate titles:

   LUTHER

   LUTHER: MITTEILUNGEN DER LUTHERGESELLSCHAFT (1953-61)

   LUTHER: VIERTELJAHRESSCHRIFT (vols. 9-20, no. 1, 1927-38)

2. Luther-Akademie. STUDIEN. Publisher: Gütersloher Verlagshaus Gerd Mohn, Gütersloh, Germany (BRD). 1931-49 (?) (nos. 1-17); new series, 1953-59 (?) (nos. 1-7).

3. LUTHER-JAHRBUCH (LJb). Sponsor: Luthergesellschaft. Publisher: Verlag Friedrich Wittig, Hamburg, Germany (BRD). 1919-- . Annual (irregular). [150-200 p.] Last issue examined: vol. 44, 1977.

   Organ for the publication of international Luther research. Long scholarly articles on Luther's life and works and the effect of his ideas on other countries and literatures; occasional comprehensive analytical bibliographies of Luther scholarship covering several years; textual studies; name index. Vol. 24 (1957) contains a Luther bibliography for 1940-53. In German. Reprints available from Walter J. Johnson (1919-71, $380) and from John Benjamins.

   Indexed by Köttelwesch and MLA INTERNATIONAL BIBLIOGRAPHY.

Alternate titles:

JAHRBUCH DER LUTHER-GESELLSCHAFT

LUTHERJAHRBUCH

4. LUTHER-KALENDER. Publisher: Leipzig, Germany (DDR). 1909, 1911.

5. MARTIN LUTHER. Sponsor: Österreichischer Freundeskreis der Luther-Gesellschaft; Evangelischer Bund; Martin Luther-Bund. Publisher: Oberkirchenrat Jakob Wolfer, Vienna, Austria. 1972-- . 2/yr. Circulation: 1,000.

6. Martin Luther Lectures. Editor: Gerhard L. Belgum. Sponsor: Luther College, Decorah, Iowa 52101. Publisher: Luther College Press. 1957-61 (vols. 1-5). Annual. [150-200 p.]

   Each volume contains reprints of lectures delivered annually at Luther College, such as LUTHER IN THE TWENTIETH CENTURY (1961). No index.

7. SCHRIFTENREIHE DER LUTHER-GESELLSCHAFT. Sponsor: Luther-Gesellschaft. Publisher: Gütersloher Verlagshaus Gerd Mohn, Gütersloh, Germany (BRD). 1933-40 (nos. 7-14). [80 p.]

   Each volume contains essays on a specific subject; bibliographies; illustrations. In German.

   Alternate title:

   Luthergesellschaft. SCHRIFTENREIHE

LYDGATE, JOHN (1370?-1451?)

English poet, priest

1. LYDGATE NEWSLETTER. Editors: C. David Benson and Jay Schleusener, 417 Hamilton Hall, Columbia University, New York, N.Y. 10027. Sponsor: Lydgate Society of America. January 1972-(?). Quarterly. $2. [15 p.]

   Brief informal articles and notes on the late medieval period and its literary scholars, especially Lydgate; reviews on medieval literature, history, and theology; news notes.

   Indexed by ANNUAL BIBLIOGRAPHY OF ENGLISH LANGUAGE AND LITERATURE.

LYTTON, EDWARD GEORGE, BULWER-

See Bulwer-Lytton, Edward.

MACDONALD, JOHN D. (1916-)

American author

1. JDM BIBLIOPHILE. Editors: Len and June Moffatt, P.O. Box 4456, Downey, Calif. 90241. March 1965-- . 2/yr. $.50 per issue (or submission of an article, review, or news item). [28 p.] Circulation: 300.

   Brief critical and biographical articles; frequent bibliographies and book reviews; letters from members; news and announcements; book exchange.

MACHADO DE ASSIS (ASSIZ), JOAQUIM (1839-1908)

Brazilian writer, poet

1. BOLETIM DA SOCIEDADE DOS AMIGOS DE MACHADO DE ASSIS. Editor: Plínio Doyle. Sponsor: Sociedade dos Amigos de Machado de Assis, Sede-Rua São José, 38, Livrario São José, Rio de Janeiro, Brazil. September 1958-September 1961 (nos. 1-7). 2/yr. (irregular). [30-50 p.]

   Numerous critical studies of the works; biographical studies on friendships and influence; bibliographies of "Machadiana"--new editions, translations, criticism in foreign periodicals; previously unpublished documents; facsimiles, with explanatory notes; portraits. In Portuguese.

   Alternate title:

   REVISTA

MACHEN, ARTHUR (1863-1947)

Welsh novelist, essayist, journalist

1. AMS OCCASIONAL (ARTHUR MACHEN SOCIETY OCCASIONAL). Editor: Bob Mowery, Thomas Library, Wittenberg University, Springfield, Ohio 45501. Sponsor: Arthur Machen Society. Secretary: Adrian Goldstone, 35 Lee Street, Mill Valley, Calif. 94941. 1965(?)-(?). Irregular. [20-25 p.] Circulation: 200.

   Long critical articles; occasional comparisons with similar authors, such as Lovecroft; book reviews; news notes. No reply to query.

2. ARTHUR MACHEN JOURNAL: A QUARTERLY PUBLICATION OF THE ARTHUR MACHEN SOCIETY. Sponsor: Arthur Machen Society. Publisher: Candlelight Press, New York. Summer 1963-(?). Irregular. [30 p.]

Reminiscences by friends and family, with quotations from letters; drawings and facsimiles.

MAETERLINCK, MAURICE (1862-1949)

Belgian dramatist, critic, poet

1. Fondation Maurice Maeterlinck. ANNALES (AFM; AFMM). Editor: Robert Van Nuffel, 123 avenue des Statuaires, 1180 Uccle-Brussels, Belgium. Sponsor: Fondation Maurice Maeterlinck, Ghent, Belgium. 1956-- . Annual. BF550. [50-150 p.] Last issue examined: vol. 22, 1976.

   Long biographical or critical essays examining Maeterlinck's reception and influence in other countries, themes in his works, specific titles, friends, and critics; previously unpublished documents; inventory of his library; report of the international conference; activities of members; awards; news of past and forthcoming meetings. In French.

   Indexed by BIBLIOGRAPHIE DE LA LITTÉRATURE FRANÇAISE, FRENCH VII, FRENCH XX, Klapp, MLA INTERNATIONAL BIBLIOGRAPHY, and REVUE D'HISTOIRE LITTÉRAIRE.

   Alternate titles:

   ANNALES DE LA FONDATION M. MAETERLINCK

   ANNALES FONDS MAETERLINCK

MAISTRE, JOSEPH MARIA, COMTE DE (1753-1821)

French writer, diplomat

1. REVUE DES ÉTUDES MAISTRIENNES. Sponsor: L'Institut de formation et de recherches en littérature, Université de Louvain. Publisher: Société d'édition les Belles Lettres. 1975-- . Annual. 30-50 Fr. [150-200 p.] Last issue examined: vol. 4, 1978.

   Founded to spread knowledge of the works of Joseph de Maistre. Contains critical editions, biographical studies, bibliographies. In French.

MALLARMÉ, STÉPHANE (1842-98)

French symbolist poet

1. DOCUMENTS STÉPHANE MALLARMÉ. Editor: Carl-Paul Barbier. Publisher: Librairie Nizet, Paris. 1968-- . Irregular. [400-500 p.] Last issue examined: no. 6, 1977.

Critical and historical studies of Mallarmé's works; previously unpublished material, including letters and other inaccessible papers; translations; chronology of life and works; genealogical charts of the family; explanatory notes and introductions; no index. In French.

MALRAUX, ANDRÉ (1901-76)

French novelist, critic

1. André Malraux. Subseries of La Revue des Lettres Modernes. Editor: Walter G. Langlois. 1972-- . Irregular. Equivalent numbers are provided below for both the parent series (La Revue des Lettres Modernes) and the individual author series on Malraux.

Malraux subseries	La Revue series	Date
No. 1	Nos. 304-09	1972
No. 2	Nos. 355-59	1973
No. 3	Nos. 425-31	1975

In French. See Camus, Albert, entry 1, for a full description of La Revue des Lettres Modernes.

Indexed by BULLETIN CRITIQUE, FRENCH XX, Klapp, and MLA INTERNATIONAL BIBLIOGRAPHY.

Alternate title:

Série André Malraux

2. Archives André Malraux. Subseries of Archives des Lettres Modernes. 1964-- . Irregular. Equivalent numbers are provided below for both the parent series (Archives des Lettres Modernes) and the individual author series on Malraux.

Malraux subseries	Archives series	Date
No. 1	No. 52	1964
No. 2	No. 98	1969
No. 3	No. 121	1971
No. 4	No. 157	1975

In French. See Camus, Albert, entry 2, for a full description of Archives des Lettres Modernes.

Indexed by BULLETIN CRITIQUE, FRENCH VII, FRENCH XX, Klapp, and MLA INTERNATIONAL BIBLIOGRAPHY.

3. Bibliothèque André Malraux. Publisher: Minard, Paris. 1964-- . Irregular. Last issue examined: no. 6, 1976.

Each volume focuses on a specific subject--a regrouping of criticism originally published in Lettres Modernes. In French.

4. MÉLANGES MALRAUX MISCELLANY (MMM). Editor: Walter G. Langlois, Box 3231 University Station, University of Wyoming, Laramie, Wyo. 83071. Sponsor: Malraux Society. Spring 1969-- . 2/yr. (Spring, Autumn). $6/two yrs. (4 issues). [30-60 p.] Circulation: 350. Last issues examined: vols. 9-10, 1977-78.

   Official organ of the Malraux Society. Long (15 p.) critical, historical, bibliographical, and biographical studies relating to Malraux; occasional bibliographies, such as "Malraux et le cinema" (1972, 1976) and his obituaries and other commemorative items after his death; report of work in progress; long book reviews in every issue; news of the Society's annual meeting and the MLA seminars; occasional illustrations, facsimiles, and reprints. Index for vols. 1-3 included in vol. 3, no. 2; index for vols. 4-6 in vol. 7, no. 1 (Spring 1975). In English or French.

   Indexed by BIBLIOGRAPHIE DE LA LITTÉRATURE FRANÇAISE, FRENCH XX, MLA ABSTRACTS, and MLA INTERNATIONAL BIBLIOGRAPHY.

   Alternate title:

   MALRAUX MISCELLANY

MANN, HEINRICH (1871-1950)

German novelist, dramatist, critic, essayist

1. Arbeitskreis Heinrich Mann. MITTEILUNGSBLATT. Editors: Siegfried Sudhof and Walter Biedermann. Sponsor: Amt für Kultur, Senat der Hansestadt Lübeck, Germany (BRD). 1972-- . Irregular. [60-70 p.] Last issue examined: vol. 10, 1977.

   Critical articles on Mann's novels, themes, ideas, and activities; notes on his interaction with associates in his own and other countries; biographical studies of Mann's work in exile, his friendships, his family, and their activities; surveys of his reception in other countries; reprints of letters to his family and friends; numerous Heinrich Mann bibliographies--primary and secondary; indexes of library holdings; long book reviews; news of seminars and symposia all over the world and of the annual Heinrich Mann Conference in Germany; news of exhibitions, necrology, sales and prices, new editions, newly discovered manuscripts; international contributors. In German or English.

   Indexed by Köttelwesch.

MANN, THOMAS (1875-1955)

German novelist, essayist, critic

1. BLÄTTER DER THOMAS-MANN-GESELLSCHAFT (BTMG). Sponsor: Thomas-Mann-Gesellschaft, Rämistrasse 5, Postfach, 8024 Zurich, Switzerland. President: Max Rynchner, 1958-65; Robert Faesi, 1965-72(?); since 1974, Erwin Jaeckle and others. Publisher: Europa Verlag, Zurich. 1958-- . Annual (irregular). 7.50 S Fr; 5 Fr (students). [50-100 p.] Last issue examined: no. 15, 1975.

   Close studies of the contents of the Archiv holdings; with bibliographies and comments; most issues concentrate on a specific area of Mann's life or works, such as the letters written in exile which are located in the Thomas-Mann Archivs, Zurich; previously unpublished letters from such figures as Stefan Zweig, with analyses and notes; list of members; financial report. In German.

   Indexed by Köttelwesch and MLA INTERNATIONAL BIBLIOGRAPHY.

   Alternate titles:

   THOMAS MANN BLÄTTER

   Thomas-Mann-Gesellschaft. BLÄTTER

2. Thomas Mann-Studien (ThMS). Editor: Hans Wysling, Director of the Thomas-Mann Archiv. Sponsor: Thomas-Mann-Archiv der Eidgenössischen Technischen Hochschule, Zurich, Switzerland. Publisher: Francke Verlag, Bern, Switzerland; Munich, Germany (BRD). 1967-- . Irregular (a series; vol. 2, 1972; vol. 3, 1974). DM45-48; S Fr 50. [240-350 p.]

   Scholarly studies on the life and contributions of Thomas Mann, such as STUDIEN ZU MYTHUS UND PSYCHOLOGIE BEI THOMAS MANN (1972); reprints of letters, essays, lectures, and other works with numerous notes, factual data, and explanations; bibliographies; portraits and facsimiles; name, title, and subject indexes. In German.

   Indexed by MLA INTERNATIONAL BIBLIOGRAPHY.

MARKHAM, EDWIN (1852-1940)

American poet

1. MARKHAM REVIEW (MarkhamR). Editor: Joseph W. Slade, Horrmann Library, Wagner College, Staten Island, N.Y. 10301. Sponsor: Wagner College. February 1968-- . 3/yr. from 1968 to 1975; quarterly, since 1976 (Fall, Winter, Spring, Summer). Free to 1975; $4, since 1975. [4-20 p.] Circulation: 2,000. Last issue examined: vol. 7, 1978.

An outgrowth of the Edwin Markham Archives at Wagner College, which announced in 1975 that it would henceforth be concentrating on minor American literary, political, and social figures of the period 1865-1940. Brief articles on American literary figures and aspects of the American literary scene, with occasional research on Markham as well as on Henry James, Wolfe, Chopin, Henry Adams, O'Neill, and Crane; interested in interdisciplinary coverage, "especially of minor figures and neglected trends"; brief critical notes; news about sales, library acquisitions, and the new James Branch Cabell Library at Virginia Commonwealth University in Richmond; occasional bibliographies and book reviews; occasional reports of work in progress; frequent photographs, illustrations, or facsimiles. Available in microform from University Microfilms International.

Indexed by ABSTRACTS OF ENGLISH STUDIES, AMERICAN HUMANITIES INDEX, ANNUAL BIBLIOGRAPHY OF ENGLISH LANGUAGE AND LITERATURE, MLA ABSTRACTS, MLA INTERNATIONAL BIBLIOGRAPHY, and YEAR'S WORK IN ENGLISH STUDIES.

MARTÍ, JOSÉ (1853-95)

Cuban poet, essayist

1. ANUARIO MARTIANO. Director: Salvador Morales. Sponsor: Consejo Nacional de Cultura, Departamento Colección Cubana. Publisher: Sala Martí, Biblioteca Nacional José Martí, Plaza de la Revolución, Havana. 1969-- . Annual. [350-450 p.] Last issue examined: vol. 7, 1977.

   Long documented articles on the life and work of José Martí, his influence, and his reception in other countries; extensive "Bibliografía martiana" of the previous year's studies; previously unpublished letters and other documents; several long book reviews; reminiscences; news notes of the José Martí Foundation and events in international Martí societies; evaluations of recent Martiano publications; index. In Spanish.

2. ARCHIVO JOSÉ MARTÍ (AJM). Sponsor: July-December 1940, Consejo corporativo de educación, sanidad, y beneficencia; December 1940-52, Ministerio de educación, Havana, Cuba. July 1940-52 (nos. 1-22). Irregular.

   Biographical and interpretive studies; occasional bibliographies of Martí scholarship; notes and commentaries on Martí's life and works; portraits. News of the comprehensive bibliography of Martí scholarship: ARCHIVO JOSÉ MARTÍ: REPERTORIO CRÍTICO: MEDIO SIGLO DE ESTUDIOS MARTIANOS, by Carlos Ripoll (New York: E. Torres, 1971; 276 p.). In Spanish.

Indexed by MLA INTERNATIONAL BIBLIOGRAPHY.

3. REVISTA MARTINIANA: PUBLICACIÓN MENSUAL CONSAGRADO AL ESTUDIO DE LA VIDA Y LA OBRA DE JOSÉ MARTÍ. Publisher: Havana, Cuba. October 1921-September 1927 (vols. 1-6). Monthly.

   Dedicated to the study of the life and works of José Martí.

MASSIGNON, LOUIS (1883-1962)

French scholar

1. MÉLANGES LOUIS MASSIGNON. Sponsor: Institut français de Damas. 1956-57 (nos. 1-3).

MAUPASSANT, GUY DE (1850-93)

French novelist, short-story writer

1. BEL AMI. Sponsor: Association des Amis de Guy de Maupassant, 60, rue Vaneau, 75007 Paris. 1951-61 (nos. 1-8). Irregular.

   Brief articles on Maupassant as journalist, on his writing style, and on the structure and themes of his stories; previously unpublished works. In French.

   Indexed by Klapp.

   Alternate title:

   BULLETIN DE LA SOCIÉTÉ DES AMIS DE GUY DE MAUPASSANT

MAURIAC, FRANÇOIS (1885-1970)

French novelist, essayist, dramatist

1. Archives François Mauriac. Subseries of Archives des Lettres Modernes. 1969-- . Irregular. Equivalent numbers are provided below for both the parent series (Archives des Lettres Modernes) and the individual author series on Mauriac.

Mauriac subseries	Archives series	Date
Unnumbered	No. 106	1969
No. 1	No. 140	1972

   In French. See Camus, Albert, entry 2, for a full description of Archives des Lettres Modernes.

   Indexed by BULLETIN CRITIQUE, FRENCH XX, Klapp, and MLA INTERNATIONAL BIBLIOGRAPHY.

2. CAHIERS FRANÇOIS MAURIAC: BULLETIN DE L'ASSOCIATION DES AMIS DE FRANÇOIS MAURIAC. Sponsor: Association des Amis de François Mauriac. Bibliothèque municipale, 3, rue Mably, 33000 Bordeaux-Cedex, France, or 173, boulevard St-Germain, 75006 Paris. Publisher: B. Grasset, Paris. Spring 1974-- . Annual. 30-118 Fr; $6. [300-350 p.] Last issue examined: vol. 5, 1977.

   Collections of critical studies on Mauriac's themes and ideas (like the problem of evil in his works), his friendships and patriotism, his critics; previously unpublished works. In French.

   Indexed by BIBLIOGRAPHIE DE LA LITTÉRATURE FRANÇAISE, FRENCH XX, Klapp, and REVUE D'HISTOIRE LITTÉRAIRE.

   Alternate title:

   BULLETIN DE L'ASSOCIATION DES AMIS DE FRANÇOIS MAURIAC

3. François Mauriac. Subseries of La Revue des Lettres Modernes. Editor: Jacques Monférier. 1974-- . Irregular. Equivalent numbers are provided below for both the parent series (La Revue des Lettres Modernes) and the individual author series on Mauriac.

Mauriac subseries	La Revue series	Date
Unnumbered	Nos. 403-07	1974
No. 1	Nos. 432-38	1975

   In French. See Camus, Albert, entry 1, for a full description of La Revue des Lettres Modernes.

   Indexed by BULLETIN CRITIQUE, FRENCH XX, Klapp, and MLA INTERNATIONAL BIBLIOGRAPHY.

MAURRAS, CHARLES (1868-1952)

French poet, essayist, journalist

1. Archives des Lettres Modernes.

   See entry 1 under Bernanos, Georges. Archives Bernanos, no. 6 (Archives des Lettres Modernes, no. 154), is concerned partly with Maurras.

2. CAHIERS CHARLES MAURRAS. Founding editors: Georges and Marguerite Calzant. Manager: Guy Kloeckner, 13, rue Saint-Florentin, 75008 Paris. April 1960-- . Quarterly. 85 Fr; 90 Fr (foreign). [40-90 p.] Last issue examined: no. 64, 1977.

   Brief critical and biographical essays on Maurras' political ideas and problems, the intensity of his convictions, his travels, journals, poems, conflicts and contributions, his ideas on the church, nationalism, and democracy; reminiscences; quotations or excerpts from his works; occasional photographs and facsimiles. Analytical index for 1960-66 (nos. 1-20), 1967-74 (nos. 21-52), and 1975-77 (nos. 53-64), arranged by title of Maurras' work, subject matter, critic's name, author of quotation or letter, and subject of photograph or facsimile. In French. Reprints available from Walter J. Johnson (1960-68, $95).

Indexed by BIBLIOGRAPHIE DE LA LITTÉRATURE FRANÇAISE, FRENCH VII, FRENCH XX, Klapp, and REVUE D'HISTOIRE LITTÉRAIRE.

3. ÉTUDES MAURRASSIENNES. Sponsor: Centre Charles Maurras, B.P. 76, 13607 Aix-en-Provence, France. American correspondent: Raymond Denegri, Centre Charles Maurras, 40 Octavia Street, San Rafael, Calif. 94901. 1972-- . Annual. [200-250 p.] Last issue examined: vol. 3, 1974.

Each volume is concerned with a specific subject, such as papers prepared for the third Maurras colloquium in 1972. Brief essays on Maurras' friendships with such figures as Bernanos and Renan; studies of the autobiographical features in his writings, his ideas on history and politics, his philosophy and themes, and the influence of Renan, Taine, and the literatures of other countries and authors; surveys of Maurras scholarship; no index. In French. Vol. 4 not yet published (1978).

Indexed by BIBLIOGRAPHIE DE LA LITTÉRATURE FRANÇAISE and REVUE D'HISTOIRE LITTÉRAIRE.

MAY, KARL (1842-1912)

German author of adventure novels

1. BEITRÄGE ZUR KARL-MAY-FORSCHUNG. Editor: Heinz Stolte. Sponsor and publisher: Karl-May-Verlag, Bamberg, Germany (BRD). 1966-- . Irregular. DM7-17. [200-250 p.] Last issue examined: vol. 3, 1972.

Each volume concentrates on a specified area of May's life and work--for example, KARL MAY UND EMMA POLLMER: DIE GESCHICHTE EINER EHE (1972). Critical and biographical essays; previously unpublished letters and other documents; chronologies; occasional bibliographies; photographs and facsimiles; index. In German. Vol. 4 not yet published (1978).

2. JAHRBUCH DER KARL-MAY-GESELLSCHAFT (JKMG). Editors: Claus Roxin, Heinz Stolte, and Hans Wollschäger. Sponsor: Karl-May-Gesellschaft, Swebenbrunnen 8c, 2000 Hamburg 72, Germany (BRD). Publisher: Hansa-Verlag, Hamburg. 1970-- . Annual. DM20-32. [250-90 p.] Last issue examined: vol. 7, 1977.

Long biographical analyses of key periods of May's life; long critical studies of specific aspects of his works; textual studies; occasional review articles of important recent publications; report of Gesellschaft activities; occasional sketches and facsimiles. In German.

Indexed by Köttelwesch and MLA INTERNATIONAL BIBLIOGRAPHY.

Alternate titles:

KARL-MAY-JAHRBUCH

Karl-May-Gesellschaft. JAHRBUCH

3. MITTEILUNGEN DER KARL-MAY-GESELLSCHAFT. Sponsor and publisher: Karl-May-Gesellschaft, Swebenbrunnen 8c, 2000 Hamburg 72, Germany (BRD). Director: Hansotto Hatzig, Nadlerstrasse 40, 6800 Mannheim 51, Germany (BRD). September 1969-- . Quarterly (September, December, March, June). DM2. [25-40 p.] Last issue examined: no. 32, 1977.

Brief articles on May's life, literary style, and influence; discussion of the canon and of library holdings; notes on new editions, seminars, celebrations, films, books and other publications; facsimiles and illustrations; no index. In German.

Alternate subtitle:

VIERTELJAHRESSCHRIFT

MAYNARD, FRANÇOIS DE (1582/83-1646)

French poet

1. Association des Amis de Maynard. BULLETIN. Sponsor: Association des Amis de Maynard, "La Petite Rivière," Epirè, 49170 St. Georges-sur-Loire, France. December 1971-- . Annual. 25 Fr; 60 Fr (benefactors). [30-55 p.] Last issue examined: no. 7, 1977.

Critical and biographical articles examining Maynard's cultural background, friends, influences, and style; previously unpublished works; first installment of a comprehensive "Bibliographie Maynardienne"--primary and secondary works; report of Association activities, including annual meetings, reunions, members' publications; questions and answers; facsimiles. No index. Index for 1971-74 (nos. 1-4) in no. 5 (1975). In French. Alternate spelling: Mainard.

Indexed by BIBLIOGRAPHIE DE LA LITTÉRATURE FRANÇAISE.

Alternate titles:

Association des Amis de Maynard. CAHIER

BULLETIN. Association des "Amis de Maynard"

MAZZINI, GUISEPPE (1805-72)

Italian patriot, lawyer

1. BOLLETTINO DEL DOMUS MAZZINIANA (BDM). Editor: Ezio Tongiorgi. Sponsor and publisher: Domus Mazziniana, via Mazzini, 71, Pisa, Italy. 1955-- . 2/yr. L.6.000. [180-300 p.] Last issue examined: vol. 23, 1977.

   Long scholarly studies of Mazzini's ideas and influence on both his contemporaries and succeeding generations; previously unpublished material; occasional special bibliographies, such as "Mazzini, 1872-1972" (nos. 1-2, 1974); annotated bibliographies in every issue of books, articles, and reviews. In Italian, with occasional contributions in English.

   Indexed by MLA INTERNATIONAL BIBLIOGRAPHY.

MELVILLE, HERMAN (1819-91)

American novelist, poet, short-story writer

1. EXTRACTS (AN OCCASIONAL NEWSLETTER OF THE MELVILLE SOCIETY). Founding editor: Hennig Cohen, Department of English, University of Pennsylvania, Philadelphia, Pa. 19174; since 1976, no. 25, Donald Yannella, Department of English, Glassboro State College, Glassboro, N.J. 08028. June 1969-- . Quarterly. $5. [20 p.] Circulation: 500. Last issue examined: no. 33, 1978.

   Brief notes of interest to Melville students on style, sources, and editions; descriptions--not scholarly reviews--of new and forthcoming books; occasional bibliographies of dissertations or other related scholarship; reports of research in progress; report of the annual spring meeting of the Melville Society, with summaries of lectures and news of activities; illustrations, facsimiles, and reproductions.

   Indexed by ABSTRACTS OF ENGLISH STUDIES, AMERICAN LITERATURE, Leary, and MLA INTERNATIONAL BIBLIOGRAPHY.

   Alternate title:

   MELVILLE SOCIETY EXTRACTS

2. MELVILLE ANNUAL. Subseries of Kent Studies in English. Sponsor: Kent State University Press, Kent, Ohio 44242. 1965-68 (vols. 1-2). Irregular. [150-200 p.]

   Papers presented at the annual Melville-Hawthorne symposia in 1965 (BARTLEBY THE SCRIVENER) and 1966 (MELVILLE AND HAWTHORNE IN THE BERKSHIRES).

3. Melville Society. SPECIAL PUBLICATIONS. Sponsor: Melville Society of America. Editor: Donald Yannella, Department of English, Glassboro State College, Glassboro, N.J. 08028. 1973-- . Irregular. [100 p.] Last issue examined: no. 3, 1976.

   Publications on special subjects, such as a DIRECTORY OF MELVILLE DISSERTATIONS (1973).

4. MELVILLE SOCIETY NEWSLETTER. Editor: Tyrus Hillway, University of Northern Colorado, Greeley, Colo. 80631. Sponsor: Melville Society of America. February 1945-December 1960 (vols. 1-15). Quarterly (occasionally 5/yr.). Free with membership.

   Brief critical or biographical articles; bibliographies of critical works; news notes.

Indexed by Leary.

MENCKEN, HENRY LOUIS (1880-1956)

American editor, author

1. MENCKENIANA: A QUARTERLY REVIEW. Founding editor: Betty Adler. Current editor: Frederick N. Rasmussen. Sponsor and publisher: Enoch Pratt Free Library, 400 Cathedral Street, Baltimore, Md. 21201. Spring 1962-- . Quarterly (Spring, Summer, Fall, Winter). Free with membership ($5; student, $3). [16 p.] Circulation: 600. Last issue examined: vol. 67, 1978.

   Long articles on Mencken's life, philosophy, and works; annotated bibliographic checklist and editorial comments on current books in each issue; news relating to Mencken--new editions of his works, his discerning comments on other publications, reports on preservation of his home, posthumous awards, activities at the Mencken Room in the Enoch Pratt Free Library, Mencken Day, formation of the Mencken Society (1975); numerous H.L. Mencken quotations; occasional previously unpublished documents, such as a letter to Mencken from James Joyce; reprints of correspondence, such as a letter from Joseph Conrad to Mencken revealing a sincere respect for Mencken's work and a sincere humility about his own; no index. Address of the Mencken Society: Box 1524, University of Maryland, College Park, Md. 20742. Available on microform from University Microfilms International.

Indexed by ABSTRACTS OF ENGLISH STUDIES, AMERICAN HUMANITIES INDEX, AMERICAN LITERATURE, ANNUAL BIBLIOGRAPHY OF ENGLISH LANGUAGE AND LITERATURE, MISSISSIPPI QUARTERLY, MLA INTERNATIONAL BIBLIOGRAPHY, and TWENTIETH CENTURY LITERATURE.

MENÉNDEZ (Y) PELAYO, MARCELINO (1856-1912)

Spanish critic, historian

1. Amigos de Menéndez y Pelayo. ALMANAQUE. Sponsor: Amigos de Menéndez y Pelayo, Madrid, Spain. 1932-(?). Annual.

   Articles on the author's intellectual ideas and universality; laws and purpose of the organization. In Spanish.

   Subtitle:

   AGRUPACIÓN DE AMIGOS DE MENÉNDEZ Y PELAYO: PUBLICACIONES

2. BOLETÍN DE LA BIBLIOTECA MENÉNDEZ PELAYO (BBMP). Sponsor: Sociedad Menéndez Pelayo. Director: Ignacio Aguilera y Santiago. Publisher: Biblioteca de Menéndez Pelayo, Rubio 6, Santander, Spain. 1919-38; 1945-- . Quarterly (published in one volume). Pesetas 500 (Spain); 720 (foreign). [400-440 p.] Last issue examined: vol. 53, 1977.

   Long scholarly articles on Menéndez Pelayo, Jorge Manrique, and other classical Spanish authors; bibliographical, textual, thematic, interpretive studies; previously unpublished material with extensive notes; book reviews on Spanish language and literature; list of publications by several cultural organizations; bibliographical references; international contributors; list of members; no index. In Spanish. Modern spelling frequently omits the "y" in the author's name: Menéndez (y) Pelayo.

   Indexed by AMERICA: HISTORY AND LIFE, BIBLIOGRAPHIE DE LA LITTÉRATURE FRANÇAISE, ENGLISH LANGUAGE NOTES, and MLA INTERNATIONAL BIBLIOGRAPHY.

   Alternate title:

   REVISTA BIMESTRAL DE LA SOCIEDAD MENÉNDEZ Y PELAYO

MERCIER, LOUIS (1740-1814)

French dramatist

1. AMIS DE LOUIS MERCIER. Publisher: Souchon, Roanne, France. May

1952-53 (nos. 1-4).

In French.

MICKIEWICZ, ADAM (1798-1855)

Polish poet, professor

1. MICKIEWICZ-BLÄTTER. Editor: Herman Buddensieg. Sponsor: Im Auftrage des Mickiewicz-Gremiums der deutschen bundesrepublik. Publisher: Heidelberg, Germany (BRD). 1956-(?). Annual. [100 p.] Last issue examined: vol. 13, 1968.

    Biographical and critical articles, such as that on his relationship with Schiller. Ten-year index in vol. 11, no. 31 (1966). In German.

    Indexed by Köttelwesch.

MILL, JOHN STUART (1806-73)

English philosopher, economist

1. MILL NEWS LETTER. Editors: John M. Robson and Michael Laine, Department of English, Victoria College, University of Toronto, Toronto M5S 1K7, Canada. Sponsor and publisher: University of Toronto Press in association with Victoria College. Fall 1965-- . 2/yr. Free. [20-25 p.] Circulation: 510. Last issue examined: vol. 13, 1978.

    Brief critical articles on such subjects as Mill's conservation theory, his opinion of the death penalty (favorable), his meeting with Wordsworth, his father's plan for his education, and his relationship to Shelley, Carlyle, and other nineteenth-century authors; announcements of new projects, progress of the collected works, conferences; checklist in every issue of new Mill-related books and articles in periodicals; report of work in progress; queries; long book reviews; abstracts of dissertations; previously unpublished material; "Milliana"--excerpts from personal talks or contacts with J.S. Mill. Vol. 3, no. 2 (Spring 1968), was never published.

    Indexed by ABSTRACTS OF ENGLISH STUDIES, AMERICAN HUMANITIES INDEX, ANNUAL BIBLIOGRAPHY OF ENGLISH LANGUAGE AND LITERATURE, PHILOSOPHER'S INDEX, and VICTORIAN STUDIES.

MILLER, HENRY (1891-)

American novelist, esayist

1. HENRY MILLER LITERARY SOCIETY NEWSLETTER. Editor: Edward P.

Schwartz, 1521 Hennepin Avenue, Minneapolis, Minn. 55403. Sponsor: Henry Miller Literary Society. 1958-October 1963. Irregular. [4 p.] Circulation: 700.

Editor's stated purpose: to call the public's attention to the issue of censorship, its legality, and the rights of authors and booksellers. Articles on the censorship of Miller's work and the ensuing court proceedings; in each issue a bibliography of "New Miller Items"; reprints of letters from Miller and others; chronicle of Miller's activities; announcements of television programs, recordings, publications by members of the Society, and works in progress; occasional "Capsule Reviews." The Society disbanded when Miller's works were freed from censorship.

2. INTERNATIONAL HENRY MILLER LETTER. Publisher: Henk VanGelre, Van Oldenbarneveltstraat 21, Nijmegen, Netherlands. June 1961–(?). $1. Irregular. Last issue examined: no. 2, December 1961.

Alternate address: Fransestraat 5, Nijmegen, the Netherlands.

MILOSZ, OSCAR VENCESLAS (OR VLADISLAS) DE LUBICZ (1877-1939)

Lithuanian-born French poet, dramatist, diplomat

1. Amis de Milosz. CAHIERS DE L'ASSOCIATION. Sponsor: Amis de Milosz, 6, rue José-María-de-Heredia, 75007 Paris. Publisher: Éditions André Silvaire, Paris. 1967-- . Irregular. 10-20 Fr. [50-60 p.] Last issue examined: vol. 12, 1976.

Interested in scholarship pertaining to the life and works of Milosz and in the acquisition of material by and about him. Essays on events in his life, his writings, and his translations of Goethe; previously unpublished letters and other documents; report of radio and television programs, expositions, work in progress, performances, completed editions, articles in newspapers and periodicals, reviews, and criticism; news of the activities of the Association--meetings, excursions, financial report, list of members; occasional photographs and sketches. In French.

Indexed by BIBLIOGRAPHIE DE LA LITTÉRATURE FRANÇAISE, FRENCH XX, and Klapp.

Alternate titles:

CAHIERS DES AMIS DE MILOSZ

CAHIERS DE L'ASSOCIATION "LES AMIS DE MILOSZ"

2. CAHIERS CONSACRÉS À OSCAR VENCESLAS DE LUBICZ MILOSZ. Edi-

tors: Natalie Clifford Barney and Jean de Boschère, La Châtre, France. October 1939-July 1941 (nos. 1-4).

Articles; news. In French.

MILTON, JOHN (1608-74)

English poet, scholar

1. MILTON AND THE ROMANTICS. Editor: Luther L. Scales, Jr., Department of English, Journalism, and Philosophy, Box 8023, Georgia Southern College, Statesboro, Ga. 30458. November 1975-- . Annual. $1.50/yr.; $2/two yrs. [10-30 p.] Last issue examined: vol. 2, 1976.

    Essays and notes on relationships among Milton and the Romantics; list of "Books Received" comparing the two eras; poems by Blake and Keats on Milton.

    Indexed by AMERICAN HUMANITIES INDEX and ENGLISH LANGUAGE NOTES.

2. MILTON NEWSLETTER. Superseded by MILTON QUARTERLY (see entry 3). Editor: Roy C. Flannagan, Box 337, Ellis Hall, Ohio University, Athens, Ohio 45701. Sponsor: Department of English, Ohio University, and Milton Society of America. 1967-69 (vols. 1-3, no. 4). Quarterly. $2; $2.50 (foreign); $5/three yrs. [15-20 p.]

    Short, documented biographical and critical articles; book reviews; editorial comments on books of interest; notes on recordings, work in progress, activities of members; abstracts of critical articles; annual index in the last issue of each year. Available on microfilm from University Microfilms International ($4.25 per volume).

3. MILTON QUARTERLY (Milton Q). Supersedes MILTON NEWSLETTER (see entry 2). Editor: Roy C. Flannagan, Box 337, Ellis Hall, Ohio University, Athens, Ohio 45701. Sponsor: Department of English, Ohio University, and Milton Society of America. March 1970 (vol. 4, no. 1)-- . Quarterly (March, May, October, December). $8/yr. and $20/three yrs. (individual); $10/yr. and $25/three yrs. (libraries). [25-40 p.] Circulation: 1,000. Last issue examined: vol. 12, 1978.

    Short feature articles on Milton's images, illustrations, language, analogues, characterizations, symbolism, rhyme; occasional articles on related fields in the seventeenth century; occasional bibliographies; annual reviews of Milton studies; abstracts of important articles and lectures; long book reviews in every issue and occasional reviews of tapes or records; brief editorial comments on "Books of Interest"; report on work in progress and dissertations recently completed; personal notes; news on seminars, conferences, lectures, book prices, and awards; progress reports

MILTON
QUARTERLY

on studies by Miltonians and other seventeenth-century scholars; occasional colored reproductions on the cover; illustrations; annual index which includes articles, reviews, "Books of Interest," abstracts, dissertations, and miscellaneous news notes. Available on microfilm from University Microfilms International ($4.25 per volume).

Indexed by ABSTRACTS OF ENGLISH STUDIES, AMERICAN HUMANITIES INDEX, ANNUAL BIBLIOGRAPHY OF ENGLISH LANGUAGE AND LITERATURE, MLA ABSTRACTS, MLA INTERNATIONAL BIBLIOGRAPHY, and YEAR'S WORK IN ENGLISH STUDIES.

4. MILTON SOCIETY OF AMERICA: PROCEEDINGS. Editor: John Shawcross, 20 Vernon Terrace, Bloomfield, N.J. 07003. Sponsor: Milton Society of America. December 1948-- . Annual. Free with membership ($2). Circulation: 375.

Annual report of work in progress by members of the Society.

5. MILTON STUDIES (Milton S). Manuscripts and editorial comments: James D. Simmonds, Department of English, University of Pittsburgh, Pittsburgh, Pa. 15260. Sponsor: Milton Society of America. Secretary of the Milton Society: Albert C. Labriola, Duquesne University, Pittsburgh, Pa. 15219. Publisher: University of Pittsburgh Press, Pittsburgh, Pa. 15260. Overseas orders: Feffer and Simons. 1969-- . Annual. $8-15. [200-300 p.] Circulation: 1,500. Last issue examined: vol. 11, 1978.

A forum for Milton scholarship and criticism; interpretation of his poetry and prose as well as of "his contemporaries, the traditions which affected his thought and art, contemporary political and religious movements, his influence on other writers, or the history of critical response to his work"; historical, political, biographical, literary, intellectual, religious approaches; studies of style, allusions, symbolism, source, and themes; international contributors; occasional illustrations; no reviews and no index.

Indexed by ABSTRACTS OF ENGLISH STUDIES, AMERICAN HUMANITIES INDEX, ANNUAL BIBLIOGRAPHY OF ENGLISH LANGUAGE AND LITERATURE, MLA ABSTRACTS, MLA INTERNATIONAL BIBLIOGRAPHY, and YEAR'S WORK IN ENGLISH STUDIES.

MOLIÈRE

See Poquelin, Jean-Baptiste.

MONTAIGNE, MICHEL (1533-92)

French essayist, moralist

1. Archives des Lettres Modernes. 1966-- . Irregular. The series number for the issue on Montaigne is provided below.

Montaigne subseries	Archives series	Date
Unnumbered	No. 71	1966

In French. See Camus, Albert, entry 2, for a full description of Archives des Lettres Modernes.

Indexed by BULLETIN CRITIQUE, Klapp, and MLA INTERNATIONAL BIBLIOGRAPHY.

2. BULLETIN. Société des Amis de Montaigne. Superseded by BULLETIN DES AMIS DE MONTAIGNE (see entry 4). Sponsor: Société des Amis de Montaigne, 40, rue des Écoles, Paris. Publisher: A. Durel, Libraire de la Société des Amis de Montaigne, Paris. 1913-14; suspended 1915-20; 1921; suspended 1922-36. 10 Fr. [50-100 p.]

Historical and critical studies of Montaigne's works; new translations; news of banquets, excursions; report of conferences; list of members; facsimiles. In French.

Alternate title:

BULLETIN DE LA SOCIÉTÉ DES AMIS DE MONTAIGNE

3. BULLETIN DE LA SOCIÉTÉ DES AMIS DE MONTAIGNE (BSAM; BAM). Supersedes BULLETIN DES AMIS DE MONTAIGNE (see entry 4). Editors: 1949-68, Georges Guichard; since 1969, Pierre Michel, 6, villa Chanez, 75016 Paris. Sponsor and publisher: Société des Amis de Montaigne, with the approval of the Direction générale des Arts et des Lettres. U.S. subscription address: Donald M. Frame, 512 Philosophy Hall, Columbia University, New York, N.Y. 10027. Second series, 1949-56 (nos. 15-19); third series, January 1957-December 1964 (nos. 1-32); fourth series, January 1965-December 1971 (nos. 1-27); fifth series, January 1972 (no. 1)-- . 2-3/yr. 40 Fr; 50 Fr (foreign). [60-100 p.] Circulation: 70 universities in the United States; 30 in France. Last issues examined: nos. 25-26, 1978.

Dedicated to the study of Montaigne, his works and times. Numerous long scholarly essays on his influence, language, the fable and essay forms, his travels and humor; brief notes on problem areas in his works; bibliographical surveys of scholarship in progress and completed, including that in other countries; book reviews; international editorial board and contributors; list of new members; news of conferences and Society activities. Analytical index to the third series, 1957-64 (nos. 1-32), in no. 32, 1964, and to the fourth series, 1965-71 (nos. 1-27), in nos. 3-4, 1972, fifth series. In French.

Reprints available from Slatkine Reprints (1913-64, 530 Fr).

Indexed by BIBLIOGRAPHIE DE LA LITTÉRATURE FRANÇAISE, FRENCH VI, FRENCH XX, Klapp, MLA INTERNATIONAL BIBLIOGRAPHY, and REVUE D'HISTOIRE LITTÉRAIRE.

Alternate title:

Amis de Montaigne, Paris. BULLETIN

4. BULLETIN DES AMIS DE MONTAIGNE. Supersedes BULLETIN (see entry 2); superseded by BULLETIN DE LA SOCIÉTÉ DES AMIS DE MONTAIGNE (see entry 3). Editors: 1937-40, Auguste Salles; 1940-49, Georges Guichard. Sponsor and publisher: Société des Amis de Montaigne, published with the approval of the Direction générale des Arts et des Lettres. Second series, June 1937-January 1949 (nos. 1-14). 2-3/yr. 10 Fr. [50-70 p.]

Brief biographical, bibliographical, textual, and critical articles and notes; previously unpublished works and other documents by Montaigne and his contemporaries; primary and secondary bibliographies of books and articles; book reviews; news of Society activities; list of members; illustrations; portraits. In French.

MONTESQUIEU, CHARLES LOUIS, BARON (1689-1755)

French lawyer, philosopher

1. Archives Montesquieu. Subseries of Archives des Lettres Modernes. 1965-- . Irregular. Equivalent numbers are provided below for both the parent series and the individual author series on Montesquieu.

Montesquieu subseries	Archives series	Date
No. 1	No. 61	1965
No. 2	No. 116	1970
No. 3 (2 vols.)	No. 132	1971
No. 4	No. 139	1972
No. 5	No. 151	1974
No. 6	No. 158	1975
No. 7	No. 166	1976

In French. See Camus, Albert, entry 2, for a full description of Archives des Lettres Modernes.

Indexed by BULLETIN CRITIQUE, Klapp, and MLA INTERNATIONAL BIBLIOGRAPHY.

Alternate title:

Série Montesquieu

MOORE, MARIANNE (1887-   )

American poet

1. MARIANNE MOORE NEWSLETTER. Editor: Patricia C. Willis. Sponsor: Philip H. and A.S.W. Rosenbach Foundation, 2010 DeLancey Place, Philadelphia, Pa. 19103. Spring 1977-- . 2/yr. (Spring, Fall). $4 (U.S.); $4.50 (other countries). [20 p.]

   Descriptions of furnishings, personal possessions, and manuscripts in the Marianne Moore Collection; brief articles, notes, and queries; forum for the exchange of ideas; announcements of projects planned and descriptions of those completed; biographical data, such as the note on Moore's editorship of THE DIAL; facsimiles of materials from the collection, including manuscripts of previously unpublished works, drafts and revisions, letters, sketches, and source items; photographs and illustrations.

   Indexed by AMERICAN HUMANITIES INDEX.

MORE, SAINT THOMAS (1478-1535)

English humanist, statesman

1. MOREANA: BULLETIN THOMAS MORE. Editor: Abbé Germain Marc'hadour, B.P. 858, 49005 Angers CEDEX, France. Sponsor: Amici Thomae Mori, 29, rue Volney, B.P. 808, 49005 Angers Cedex, France. President: E.E. Reynolds; international secretary: Abbé Germain Marc'hadour. Life membership in Amici Thomae Mori: $500. Subscriptions: U.S., Brother Michael Grace, S.J., 6525 North Sheridan Road, Chicago, Ill. 60626; and British Isles, Francis Murray, 12 Hammet Street, Taunton, Somerset TA1 1RL, England. September 1963-- . Quarterly. $18 (individuals); $30 (institutions). [100-120 p.] Circulation: 1,000. Last issue examined: no. 57, 1978.

   Official organ of the Amici Thomae Mori. Provides an international forum for research, documentation, and friendly discussion about the world of Thomas More, especially his relationship with Erasmus, Henry VIII, and the Reformation. Long critical articles on all of More's works, his friends and foes, the theologians, printers, biographers, statesmen, poets, and scholars of the period; survey of his influence in other countries; bibliographies; translations; news notes on conferences, symposia, films, plays, unveiling of plaques and statues; report of work in progress, book reviews; quotations from More's works; contributors from about forty countries; numerous illustrations, facsimiles, and reprints. Index for each annual volume in the following Spring issue. Special issues: two Festschriften (1967 and 1971), THOMAS MORE AND THE U.S.A. (1976), and the CENTENNIAL ISSUE (1977) for the fifth centennial of More's birth. Cumulative index for 1963-

73 (vols. 1-10) in no. 40 (February 1974, 136 p.), $10 or 45 Fr. Back numbers: $6 per issue, $20 per volume, $15 per special issue. In French or English.

Indexed by ABSTRACTS OF ENGLISH STUDIES, AMERICA: HISTORY AND LIFE, ANNUAL BIBLIOGRAPHY OF ENGLISH LANGUAGE AND LITERATURE, BIBLIOGRAPHIE DE LA LITTÉRATURE FRANÇAISE, ÉTUDES ANGLAISES (PARIS), MANUAL DE BIBLIOGRAFÍA DE LA LITTERATURA ESPAÑOLA, MLA ABSTRACTS, MLA INTERNATIONAL BIBLIOGRAPHY, NEO-LATIN NEWS, REVUE D'HISTOIRE LITTÉRAIRE, and YEAR'S WORK IN ENGLISH STUDIES.

2. Thomas More Lectures. Publisher: Yale University Press, 92A Yale Station, New Haven, Conn. 06520. 1970-- . Irregular. Price varies.

3. Thomas More Society of London. OCCASIONAL PUBLICATIONS. Sponsor: Thomas More Society of London: Publisher: Blackwell and Mott. First series, 1948; second series, 1949-(?). [100-200 p.]

   Papers read to the Society on philosophy and ethics--not confined solely to Thomas More's life and works.

MORRIS, WILLIAM (1834-96)

English artist, poet

1. JOURNAL OF THE WILLIAM MORRIS SOCIETY (England). Editor: R.C.H. Briggs, 25, Lawn Crescent, Kew, Surrey, England. Sponsor: William Morris Society, Kelmscott House, 26, Upper Mall, Hammersmith, London W.6. Winter 1961-- . Irregular (four issues per volume; no issues for 1972 and 1973). Free with membership (England: £3.50, individuals; £5, corporate members; £50, life members); includes the JOURNAL, ANNUAL REPORT (see entry 3), news bulletins, and NEWS FROM ANYWHERE (see entry 2). [30-35 p.] Circulation: 900. Last issue examined: vol. 3, no. 3, 1977.

   Brief articles on Morris, his contemporaries, his admirers, his interest in the graphic arts and in the Icelandic sagas, his part in the Kelmscott Press and its influence; occasional selective bibliographies on Morris and his circle; occasional book reviews; illustrations.

Indexed by ANNUAL BIBLIOGRAPHY OF ENGLISH LANGUAGE AND LITERATURE and VICTORIAN STUDIES.

Alternate title:

   William Morris Society. JOURNAL

2. NEWS FROM ANYWHERE. Editors: Barbara and Joseph Dunlap, 420 Riverside Drive, No. 12G, New York, N.Y. 10025. Sponsor: William Morris Society, Kelmscott House, 26, Upper Mall, Hammersmith, London W.6. October 1958 (a brief letter containing "sundry items of information"); March 1959-- . Annual. Free with membership (see JOURNAL, entry 1). [30-70 p.] Circulation: 225. Last issue examined: no. 15, 1974.

   Articles on Morris' works, friendships, talent with textiles, stained glass, and printing; extensive scholarly notes on auctions, current prices of Morris books, library holdings, and private collections, lectures, excursions, members' activities; bibliographies of books by and about Morris; report of the first academic conference in the United States (1973); notes on members of Morris' family; occasional editorial comments on new books; reprints of selections from Morris' works; reproductions; illustrations. No. 16 not yet published (1978).

3. William Morris Society and Kelmscott Fellowship. ANNUAL REPORT (formerly William Morris Society. ANNUAL REPORT). Sponsor: 1955-67, William Morris Society; since 1967, William Morris Society and Kelmscott Fellowship (amalgamated in 1966). Publisher: Kelmscott House, 26, Upper Mall, London W.6. 1955-- . Annual (Spring). Free with membership (see JOURNAL, entry 1). [15-30 p.] Last issue examined: no. 22, 1977-78.

   News from international branches; numerous reports on work in progress, tours, conferences, bibliographies, lectures, exhibitions, publications, memorials, establishment of the William Morris Centre at Kelmscott Manor, and other events concerned with Morris affairs; notices of books received that pertain not only to Morris but also to fine printing and binding; notes from North America; "Matters of Interest to the Society"--news on printing houses and special editions; comments on new books.

MORVEN LE GAËLIQUE

See Jacob, Max.

MOUNIER, EMMANUEL (1905-50)

French personalist philosopher

1. BULLETIN DES AMIS D'EMMANUEL MOUNIER. Sponsor: Amis d'Emmanuel Mounier, 19, rue Jacob, 75006 Paris. Publisher: Grévin, Lagny, Paris. February 1952-- . 2/yr.

   In French.

Alternate address in LIBRAIRIE FRANÇAISE: Centre Esprit, 19, rue d'Antony, Châtenay-Malabry (Seine), France.

MURATORI, LUDOVICO ANTONIO (1672-1750)

Italian antiquary, historian, librarian

1. ARCHIVIO MURATORIANO: STUDI E RICERCHE (AM). Publisher: Città di Castello. 1904-22 (nos. 1-22); 1957(?)-64(?).

   In Italian.

   Indexed by MLA INTERNATIONAL BIBLIOGRAPHY.

MUSIL, ROBERT (1880-1942)

Austrian novelist

1. MUSIL-FORUM. Editors: Jürgen C. Thöming, D 2848 Vechta, Dorotheenstrasse 10, Vienna, Austria; Karl H. Danner, Wolfgang Freese, Murray G. Hall, Ulrich Karthaus, Renate Schröder-Werle. Sponsor: Internationale Robert-Musil-Gesellschaft, D 6600 Saarbrücken 11, Universität, Bau 35, Vienna. Publisher: Universitäts-Druckerei der Universität des Saarlandes. 1975-- . 2/yr. DM25; DM10 (students). [100-150 p.] Last issue examined: vol. 4, 1978.

   Numerous biographical and interpretive articles; reprints of letters; interviews with other important authors, such as Brecht; textual studies; surveys of research; long book reviews; news on research projects, seminars, meetings; report of activities of the Gesellschaft; facsimiles; index. The MUSIL-FORUM began publication of a WISSENSCHAFTLICHES BEIHEFT in 1976. In German.

2. Musil-Studien (MusilS). Editors: Karl Dinklage and Karl Corino. Sponsor: Robert-Musil-Archiv, Klagenfurt, Austria. Publisher: Wilhelm Fink Verlag, Munich, Germany (BRD). 1971-- . Irregular (a series). DM20-60. [200-500 p.] Last issue examined: vol. 6, 1976.

   Each volume concentrates on a special area--for example, DAS BILD DES DICHTERS BEI ROBERT MUSIL (1976). Collections of long scholarly essays on Musil's life and works; bibliographies of works consulted; bibliographical references; occasional facsimiles and portraits; index. In German.

   Indexed by MLA INTERNATIONAL BIBLIOGRAPHY.

3. Robert Musil Gesellschaft. PUBLICATIONS. Publisher: Vienna, Austria. 1934-38.

MUSSET, ALFRED DE (1810-57)

French poet, novelist, dramatist

1. Archives des Lettres Modernes. 1962-- . Irregular. The series number for the issue on Musset is provided below.

Musset subseries	Archives series	Date
Unnumbered	No. 46	1962
Unnumbered	No. 173	1977

In French. See Camus, Albert, entry 2, for a full description of Archives des Lettres Modernes.

Indexed by BULLETIN CRITIQUE, Klapp, and MLA INTERNATIONAL BIBLIOGRAPHY.

2. CAHIERS ALFRED DE MUSSET. Sponsor: Société Alfred de Musset. Publisher: L. Giraud-Badin. January 1934 (nos. 1-2). [40 p.]

Scholarship on Musset and his times; illustrations; facsimiles. In French. Reprints available from Slatkine Reprints (1934, 30 Fr).

Alternate title:

BULLETIN DE LA SOCIÉTÉ ALFRED DE MUSSET

3. MUSSETTISTE. Sponsor: Société littéraire des Mussettistes, Paris. 1907-24 (nos. 1-17).

In French.

NADEL, HENRI

See Vendel, Henri.

NAPOLEON

See Bonaparte, Napoleon.

NER, HENRI [HAN RYNER] (1861-1938)

French philosopher, critic, novelist, dramatist

1. CAHIERS DES AMIS DE HAN RYNER. Editor: Louis Simon, 3, allée du Château, 93320 Les Pavillon-sous-Bois (Seine-Saint-Denis), France. Sponsor: Société des Amis de Han Ryner. 1939-45; new series, 1946-- . Quarterly. 5 Fr per issue; $3-7. [15-32 p.] Last issue examined: nos. 127-28, 1977-78.

The Society aims to maintain communication among the followers of Han Ryner's works and ideas, to spread his ideas through publications and conferences, to publish previously unpublished works, to reedit others, and to encourage the performance of his dramatic works. Short articles on sources, technique, influence, and friendships, especially with Romain Rolland; news of reunions, newly published works; reminiscences of friends and relatives; notes on the location of primary and secondary works, including references to Ryner in other publications; previously unpublished letters and notes; reprints of Ryner's articles in newspapers and other inaccessible publications; report on the activities and publications of members. There is an annual index in the last issue of each year. In French.

Indexed by BIBLIOGRAPHIE DE LA LITTÉRATURE FRANÇAISE, BULLETIN CRITIQUE, FRENCH VII, FRENCH XX, and Klapp.

NEWMAN, CARDINAL JOHN HENRY (1801-90)

English theologian

1. NEWMAN STUDIEN. Editors: Heinrich Fries and Werner Becker. Sponsor: Internationale Cardinal Newman Kuratorium, Nürnberg, Germany (BRD). Publisher: Glock und Lutz, Nürnberg, Germany (BRD). 1948-- . Irregular. DM45. [250-350 p.] Last issue examined: vol. 9, 1974.

   Long documented studies of Newman's life, work, contributions, and influence on today's issues; "Newman-Bibliographie"--comprehensive annual bibliography by Johannes Artz of new editions in all languages, and of critical books, monographs, and articles from all over the world; no index. In German, French, or English. Includes VERÖFFENTLICHUNGEN DES CARDINAL NEWMAN KURATORIUMS.

NIETZSCHE, FRIEDRICH (1844-1900)

German philosopher, classical scholar, poet

1. ARIADNE: JAHRBUCH DER NIETZSCHE-GESELLSCHAFT. Editors: Ernst Bertram and others. Sponsor and publisher: Nietzsche-Gesellschaft, Munich, Germany (BRD). 1925-(?). [150 p.]

   A collection of essays on Nietzsche by such famous scholars as Thomas Mann, André Gide, Rimbaud, and Hugo von Hofmannsthal; no index. In German.

2. BULLETIN DE LA SOCIÉTÉ FRANÇAISE D'ÉTUDES NIETZSCHÉENNES. Sponsor and publisher: Société française d'études nietzschéennes, Paris. June 1946-52(?); new series, November 1961-(?). Irregular. [10-30 p.] Last issue examined: no. 2, March 1963.

Brief notes on the ideas and influence of Nietzsche; book reviews; list of members and their financial contributions. In French.

Alternate title:

Société française d'études nietzschéennes. BULLETIN

3. ENGADINE. Editor: Pierre Lance, 27, rue Lacépède, 75005 Paris. Sponsor: Nietzsche Society, Paris. Autumn 1969-- . Quarterly (suspended in 1977, with plans to resume publication in Autumn 1978). 16 Fr. [30-35 p.] Last issue examined: no. 32, Summer 1977.

   Organ of the Nietzsche Society. Interpretations of Nietzsche's ideas and influence; brief critical articles; containing translations of Nietzsche's works; bibliographies; queries and answers; letters to the editor; announcements of new books, television programs. In French.

4. ÉTUDES NIETZSCHÉENNES. Editor: Armand Quinot. Sponsor and publisher: Société française d'études Nietzschéennes, 1, Traverse Sylvacanne, Aix-en-Provence, France. March 1948-September 1949 (nos. 1-7). Irregular. [70-80 p.]

   Brief informal essays on the life and works of Nietzsche and his relationship with such figures as Wagner and Gobineau; previously unpublished letters; brief book reviews; no index. In French.

5. Friedrich Nietzsche. Subseries of La Revue des Lettres Modernes. 1960-- . Irregular. Series numbers for the issues on Nietzsche are provided below.

Nietzsche subseries	La Revue series	Date
Unnumbered	Nos. 54-55	1960
Unnumbered	Nos. 76-77	1962-63

   In French. See Camus, Albert, entry 1, for a full description of La Revue des Lettres Modernes.

   Indexed by FRENCH VII, Klapp, and MLA INTERNATIONAL BIBLIOGRAPHY.

6. Gesellschaft der Freunde des Nietzsche-Archivs. JAHRESGABE. Publisher: Leipzig, Germany (DDR). 1926-42. Annual.

   Reprints available from Walter J. Johnson (1926-42, $120).

7. Monographien und Texte zur Nietzsche-Forschung. Publisher: Walter de Gruyter, Berlin. 1972-- . Irregular (a series). DM80-100; $30-40. [300-500 p.] Last issue examined: vol. 4, 1977.

8. Nietzsche Gesellschaft, Munich. JAHRESBERICHT. 1924-(?).

List of members; financial report.

9. NIETZSCHE-STUDIEN: INTERNATIONALES JAHRBUCH FÜR DIE NIETZSCHE-FORSCHUNG (NietzscheS). Editors: Mazzino Montinari, via d'Annunzio 237, 1-50135 Florence; Wolfgang Müller-Lauter, Adolf-Martens-Strasse 11, D 1 Berlin 45; and Heinz Wenzel, Harnackstrasse 16, D 1 Berlin 33. Publisher: Walter de Gruyter, Berlin. 1972-- . Annual. DM30-130. [400-470 p.] Last issue examined: vol. 7, 1978.

Long studies of Nietzsche's philosophy and ethics, his reception and influence; comparisons of his beliefs with those of such philosophers in other countries and eras as Hegel, Heidegger, and Dostoevsky; critical studies of his poetry, writing style, structure, language; occasionally, an international Nietzsche bibliography to supplement the original edition of 1960; long review articles--occasionally of older controversial titles; analytical index of references to Nietzsche's works and to other philosophers and authors; international contributors; facsimiles. In English or German.

Indexed by Köttelwesch and MLA INTERNATIONAL BIBLIOGRAPHY.

NIKOLAUS VON CUES/KUES

See Cusanus, Nicolaus.

NIN, ANAÏS (1903-77)

American novelist

1. Amis de Anaïs Nin. BULLETIN. Publisher: Paris, France.

2. UNDER THE SIGN OF PISCES: ANAÏS NIN AND HER CIRCLE. Editor: Richard R. Centing, Ohio State University Libraries, 1858 Neil Avenue Mall, Columbus, Ohio 43210. Sponsor: Ohio State University Libraries. Publisher: Publications Committee, Ohio State University Libraries. Winter 1970-- . Quarterly. $5; $2 per issue. [18 p.] Circulation: 500. Last issue examined: vol. 9, 1978.

Brief critical, bibliographical, and textual articles on Anaïs Nin and her circle--Henry Miller, Lawrence Durrell, Otto Rank; brief checklists of critical material in books and periodicals; reprints of personal correspondence; original articles by Nin; memoirs by her friends; abstracts of articles and lectures; book reviews; "New Nin Publications," a continuing feature with news of prices, availability, and out-of-print publications; comments on Anaïs Nin appearances, lectures, tours, interviews, films; occasional special issues, such as that on Lawrence

Durrell in Spring 1975; photographs of Nin and her associates. All volumes available: $3.50 per volume.

Indexed by AMERICAN HUMANITIES INDEX and TWENTIETH CENTURY LITERATURE.

NOCK, ALBERT JAY (1873-1945)

American editor, educator, author

1. NOCKIAN SOCIETY. Editor: Edmund A. Opitz, 30 South Broadway, Irvington, N.Y. 10533. February 1963-- . Irregular. Circulation: 350.

   News and notes of interest to Society members--relevant publications, books for sale, citation of reviews of works by Nock; occasional book reviews. No officers, no meetings, no dues, but gifts welcome.

NOËL, MARIE

See Rouget, Marie Mélanie.

NOUVEAU, GERMAIN (1851/52-1920)

French poet

1. CAHIERS GERMAIN NOUVEAU. Editor: Louis Forestier. Sponsor: Société des Amis de Germain Nouveau. Publisher: Minard, Paris. Director: M.A. Ruff. 1971-- . Irregular. [150 p.]

   Long studies on Nouveau's style, works, and relationship with other writers, such as Verlaine; brief notes on his travels and background; problems with translations; previously unpublished letters, poems, and other documents. In French.

   Indexed by BIBLIOGRAPHIE DE LA LITTÉRATURE FRANÇAISE.

   Alternate title:

   GERMAIN NOUVEAU

O'CASEY, SEAN (1884-1964)

Irish dramatist

1. SEAN O'CASEY REVIEW: AN INTERNATIONAL JOURNAL OF O'CASEY STUDIES. Editor and publisher: Robert G. Lowery, P.O. Box 333, Holbrook, N.Y. 11741. Fall 1974-- . 2/yr. $4 (individuals); $5 (institu-

tions); foreign: $5 (individuals) and $6 (institutions); back issues, $3. [40-150 p.] Last issue examined: vol. 5, 1978.

Brief biographical, bibliographical, historical, and critical articles; annual bibliography of O'Casey criticism in the fall issue of each year; report of work in progress and work completed, including dissertations; book reviews; numerous play reviews; reminiscences; notes of interest to O'Casey scholars, such as information on future publications and stage productions; reprints of letters; occasional special issues, including one for the fiftieth anniversary of THE PLOUGH AND THE STARS (Spring 1976); facsimiles and illustrations.

Indexed by ABSTRACTS OF ENGLISH STUDIES, MODERN DRAMA (Toronto), MLA ABSTRACTS, and MLA INTERNATIONAL BIBLIOGRAPHY.

O'CONNOR, FLANNERY (1925-64)

American novelist

1. FLANNERY O'CONNOR BULLETIN. Editor: Rosa Lee Walston. Associate editors: Mary B. Tate and Sarah Gordon. Sponsor and publisher: Georgia College, P.O. Box 608, Milledgeville, Ga. 31061. Autumn 1972-- . Annual. $2.50; $3 (foreign). [65-95 p.] Last issue examined: vol. 6, 1977.

   Long critical, biographical, source, and explicatory studies of O'Connor's work; brief comments, suggestions, and questions.

   Indexed by ABSTRACTS OF ENGLISH STUDIES, AMERICAN HUMANITIES INDEX, ANNUAL BIBLIOGRAPHY OF ENGLISH LANGUAGE AND LITERATURE, and MISSISSIPPI QUARTERLY.

O'HARA, JOHN (1905-)

American novelist

1. JOHN O'HARA JOURNAL. Editor: Vincent D. Balitas, 1401 Mahantongo Street, Pottsville, Pa. 17901. Sponsor: Schuylkill County Council for the Arts, 15th and Mahantongo Street, Pottsville, Pa. 17901. December 1978-- . 2/yr. $6 (individuals); $8 (institutions); $3 per issue. [50-60 p.] Circulation: 100.

   Critical articles on O'Hara's works and on life in Schuylkill County, Pennsylvania, from 1890 to 1920. News notes and bibliographies will be published as the need arises.

OLSON, CHARLES J. (1910-70)

American poet, essayist

1. OLSON: THE JOURNAL OF THE CHARLES OLSON ARCHIVES. Editor: George F. Butterick, Archives Curator, Special Collections Department, University of Connecticut Library, Storrs, Conn. 06268. Sponsor: Wilbur Cross Library, University of Connecticut. Spring 1974-- . 2/yr. $10 (institutions; $12.50 overseas); $7 (individuals; $10 overseas). [80-115 p. Last issue examined: no. 8, 1977.

   Interested in making material of the Olson Archives available to scholars and in coordinating "additional primary materials from widespread sources . . . letters, memoirs, and anecdotes, photographs, readings of Olson's work by fellow poets, notes and queries, book reviews, and, above all, original scholarship on any aspect of Olson's work and career." Poems by Olson accompanied by editorial comments on the manuscripts; occasional bibliographies, such as that of Olson's reading, research in progress, manuscript holdings in other libraries, acquisitions, and updated and revised lists of Olson scholarship; reprints of symposia and class notes; interviews; notes, addenda, corrigenda; photographs; facsimiles.

   Indexed by AMERICAN HUMANITIES INDEX and MLA INTERNATIONAL BIBLIOGRAPHY.

O'NEILL, EUGENE (1888-1953)

American dramatist

1. EUGENE O'NEILL NEWSLETTER. Editor: Frederick C. Wilkins, Department of English, Suffolk University, Boston, Mass. 02114. Sponsor and publisher: Suffolk University. May 1977-- . 3/yr. (January, May, September). $3 (individuals); $5 (libraries); $1.50 per issue. [15-25 p.] Circulation: 100. Last issue examined: vol. 2, 1979.

   Short critical, textual, biographical, interpretational, and theatrical articles; notes by actors and directors on performing O'Neill; news of recent and forthcoming publications relevant to O'Neill studies; news of recent and forthcoming stage productions; book and play reviews; letters to the editor, with responses and rebuttals; abstracts of books and articles; information on studies and dissertations in progress; inquiries; notes on seminars, conferences, and MLA events; occasional illustrations; annual index. A preview issue (unnumbered) was published in January 1977.

PAINE, THOMAS (1737-1809)

English pamphleteer, political radical

1. T.P.S. BULLETIN. Editor and secretary: R.W. Morrell. Sponsor: Thomas Paine Society, 43, Eugene Gardens, Nottingham NG2 3LF, England. President: Michael Foot. 1964-- . Annual. Free with membership ($3); $2.40 per issue. [50 p.] Circulation: 670. Last issue examined: vol. 6, 1977.

    Scholarly papers on Thomas Paine, his works and influence, his contemporaries, background, and related material, the history of science in so far as it relates to matters in which Paine had an interest, and recent matters "in that they bring out the present influence and value of Paine's philosophical, political, economic, and religious ideas"; bibliographies; book reviews; illustrations.

    Indexed by ABSTRACTS OF ENGLISH STUDIES.

    Alternate title:

    BULLETIN OF THE THOMAS PAINE SOCIETY

    THOMAS PAINE SOCIETY BULLETIN

2. T.P.S. NEWSLETTER. Editor and secretary: R.W. Morrell. Sponsor: Thomas Paine Society, 43, Eugene Gardens, Nottingham NG2 3LF, England. President: Michael Foot. 1963-- . 2/yr. Free with membership ($3).

    Notes and news about Society events, members' activities, research in progress, details about books of interest, exhibitions; no book reviews.

PARACELSUS

See Hohenheim, Theophrastus Bombastus von.

PARETO, VILFREDO (1848-1923)

Italian-born Swiss economist, sociologist

1. CAHIERS VILFREDO PARETO: REVUE EUROPÉENNE D'HISTOIRE DES SCIENCES SOCIALES. Editor: Giovanni Busino, 3, chemin du Petit-Bel-Air, 1225 Chêne-Bourg, Switzerland. Sponsor and publisher: Librarie Droz, Geneva. 1963-- . Irregular. 35-125 Fr; $12. [220-60 p.] Last issue examined: vol. 15, no. 41, 1977.

    Dedicated to the study of the life and works of Pareto, but coverage extends to social, cultural, and philosophical areas. Essays on his relationship with the university in Lausanne, his significant contributions, his interaction with European authors, literature, and governments, and the changes he helped to foster in the intellectual life of the nineteenth and twentieth centuries; reprints of rare editions; previously unpublished lectures, papers, and other documents by Pareto; textual studies toward a critical edition; discussions and interviews. In French or English.

Indexed by FRENCH XX.

PEAKE, MERVYN (1911-68)

English author, poet, painter

1. MERVYN PEAKE REVIEW. Supersedes MERVYN PEAKE SOCIETY NEWSLETTER (see entry 2). Editor: G. Peter Winnington, Les 3 Chasseurs, 1411 Orzens, Vaud, Switzerland. Sponsor and publisher: Mervyn Peake Society, Secretary, 17 Hawk's Mill Street, Needham Market, Ipswich, Suffolk, England. Autumn 1976 (no. 3)-- . 2/yr. (Spring, Autumn). Free with membership (S Fr 15; £3; libraries and institutions, S Fr 20 or £4). [40 p.]

   "Aims to provide the understanding of Mervyn Peake's work through the establishment of a responsible corpus of critical opinion." Studies of the setting and atmosphere of Peake's novels; articles on the publishing history of his works; notes on exhibitions of Peake's art, on book sales, and on recent publications concerning Peake and his work; notes on activities of the members, including visits to Peake's house in London; news of conferences, seminars, excursions, and work in progress; reproductions of Peake's illustrations.

2. MERVYN PEAKE SOCIETY NEWSLETTER. Superseded by MERVYN PEAKE REVIEW (see entry 1). Sponsor: Mervyn Peake Society, Lampeter, Wales. Autumn 1975-Spring 1976 (nos. 1-2). 2/yr. £1 or $3 per issue.

   Brief articles and notes on Peake.

   Alternate titles:

   BULLETIN. Mervyn Peake Society

   NEWSLETTER. Mervyn Peake Society

PÉGUY, CHARLES (1873-1914)

French poet, essayist

1. L'AMITIÉ CHARLES PÉGUY: FEUILLETS MENSUELS (ACPFM; ACP). Superseded by BULLETIN D'INFORMATIONS ET DE RECHERCHES (see Addenda). Editor: Auguste Martin. Sponsor: L'Amitié Charles Péguy, 4, rue Auguste-Bartholdi, 75015 Paris. August 1948-77 (nos. 1-216). Monthly. 50 Fr. [30 p.]

Long biographical and interpretive articles; accounts of Péguy's friendship with Spire, Bergson, and other contemporary authors; long evaluations of his influence and popularity today; long review articles; report of the Péguy seminar; brief notes and news items; previously unpublished letters and documents. In French.

Indexed by BIBLIOGRAPHIE DE LA LITTÉRATURE FRANÇAISE, FRENCH VII, FRENCH XX, Klapp, MLA INTERNATIONAL BIBLIOGRAPHY, and REVUE D'HISTOIRE LITTÉRAIRE.

Alternate titles:

FEUILLETS DE L'AMITIÉ CHARLES PÉGUY

FEUILLETS MENSUELS D'INFORMATIONS DE L'AMITIÉ CHARLES PÉGUY

FEUILLETS D'INFORMATIONS DE L'AMITIÉ CHARLES PÉGUY

2. CAHIERS DE L'AMITIÉ CHARLES PÉGUY (CACP). Sponsor: L'Amitié Charles Péguy, 4, rue Auguste-Bartholdi, 75015 Paris. Publisher: Minard, Paris. November 1947-- . Annual. 25-35 Fr; $5-14. [65-300 p.] Last issue examined: no. 26, 1976.

Each volume is concerned with a specific subject--for example, PÉGUY ET LE NATIONALISME FRANÇAIS (1972) or CARNET PÉGUY (1967), ed. Auguste Martin. These works may be one long study, such as an analysis of Péguy's posthumous writings, or they may be a combination of long essays and brief articles on Péguy's life, work, and influence and include summaries, extracts, or reprints of lectures, papers, books, articles, and conferences. They may also include primary and secondary bibliographies, book reviews, and accounts of events of interest to Péguy scholars--new publications, seminars, activities of international branches of the organization. In French.

Indexed by FRENCH VII, FRENCH XX, and MLA INTERNATIONAL BIBLIOGRAPHY.

Alternate title:

L'Amitié Charles Péguy. CAHIERS

3. COURRIER D'ORLÉANS. Director: Robert Burac. Sponsor and publisher: Centre Charles Péguy, 11, rue du Tabour, 45000 Orléans, France. January 1961-- . Irregular. [10-20 p.] Last issue examined: no. 52, 1977.

Long articles on Péguy's place in literary, political, and social history, with new biographical data; rereading of his works; reports on acquisitions, debates, lectures, expositions, and expeditions of interest to Péguy scholars; abstracts of theses; letters to the editor; occasional photographs and sketches. In French.

Indexed by BIBLIOGRAPHIE DE LA LITTÉRATURE FRANÇAISE.

Alternate title:

COURRIER DU CENTRE CHARLES PÉGUY D'ORLÉANS

PEIRCE, CHARLES SANDERS (1839-1914)

American philosopher, logician, scientist

1. CHARLES S. PEIRCE NEWSLETTER. Editors: Kenneth L. Ketner, Charles S. Hardwick, Christian J.W. Kloesel, and Joseph M. Ransdell. Sponsor and publisher: Institute for Studies in Pragmatism, Texas Technological University, P.O. Box 4530, Lubbock, Tex. 79409. December 1973-- . 2/yr. Free. [8 p.] Circulation: 2,000. Last issue examined: November 1977.

   Interested mainly in matters bibliographical for the purpose of informing readers "of the extensive work being done on America's most profound philosopher." Brief accounts of the International Congress on C.S. Peirce, the Charles S. Peirce Society meetings, conventions, and symposia; information on translations and new editions; queries; lists of work in progress; lists of books received; book reviews and brief notes on new international publications; illustrations.

2. TRANSACTIONS OF THE CHARLES S. PEIRCE SOCIETY: A QUARTERLY JOURNAL IN AMERICAN PHILOSOPHY. Editors: Richard S. Robin, Department of Philosophy, Mount Holyoke College, South Hadley, Mass. 01075; and Peter H. Hare, Department of Philosophy, Baldy Hall, State University of New York at Buffalo, N.Y. 14260. Sponsor: Charles S. Peirce Society, Amherst, Mass. 01002. Spring 1965-- . 3/yr. Free with membership ($12.50, individuals; $15, institutions). [70-80 p.] Last issue examined: vol. 14, 1978.

   Long, documented essays on the philosophy of Peirce, James, Russell, Dewey, and others--pragmatism, probability, the Self, ethics of belief; long scholarly book reviews of international publications concerning Peirce; supplements to the Peirce bibliography; brief news notices on meetings of the Society, national and international, on other symposia and conferences, and on the Charles S. Peirce Foundation; annual index arranged by author of the article or review.

Indexed by PHILOSOPHER'S INDEX.

Alternate title:

Charles S. Peirce Society. TRANSACTIONS

PÉREZ GALDÓS, BENITO (1843-1920)

Spanish novelist

1. ANALES GALDOSIANOS (AnG; Agald). Editor: Rodolfo Cardona, Batts Hall, Room 112, University of Texas, Austin, Tex. 78712. Sponsor and publisher: Department of Spanish and Portuguese, University of Texas. Address in Spain: Editorial Castalia, Zurbano, 39, Madrid 10. Address in the Canary Islands: Casa-Museo Pérez Galdós-Cano, 33, Las Palmas de Gran Canaría. 1966-- . Annual. $4; 250 pesetas. [150-200 p.] Circulation: 600. Last issue examined: supplement, 1978.

    Long scholarly essays on the life, work, and times of Galdós, especially in relationship to the realistic novel; occasional bibliographies of scholarship on Galdós (vols. for 1968, 1969, 1971, 1972, 1974); book reviews; news reports, such as that on the first international Galdós congress in Las Palmas, Grand Canary Islands (1973); reprints of documents related to Galdós' life and times; occasional special issues devoted to one title, such as FORTUNATA Y JACINTA (1974); index. In English and Spanish. An annual exhaustive compilation of scholarship is planned.

    Indexed by MLA INTERNATIONAL BIBLIOGRAPHY.

PERGAUD, LOUIS (1882-1915)

French author of animal stories

1. Amis de Louis Pergaud. BULLETIN. Sponsor: Amis de Louis Pergaud, 10, rue Neuve, 25700 Valentigney (Doubs), France. 1965-- . Irregular. [50 p.] Last issue examined: no. 10, 1974.

    Brief biographical and critical articles; notes on Pergaud's language and archaisms and on problem areas and episodes in his works; notes on newly discovered works; previously unpublished material; bibliographies, with supplements; news of organization activities. In French.

    Indexed by BIBLIOGRAPHIE DE LA LITTÉRATURE FRANÇAISE, FRENCH VII, FRENCH XX, Klapp, and REVUE D'HISTOIRE LITTÉRAIRE.

    Alternate title:

    AMIS DE LOUIS PERGAUD

PETRARCH, FRANCESCO PETRARCA (1304-74)

Italian poet, scholar

1. COURRIER VAUCLUSIEN. Editor: Ludovic Bernero, 9, rue Pasteur,

L'Isle-sur-Sorgue (Vaucluse), France. Sponsor: Société vauclusienne des Amis de Pétrarque. Publisher: Malé, Avignon, France. New series, 1949-- . Quarterly.

Official organ of the Society. In French.

2. DE PÉTRARQUE A DESCARTES. Sponsor and publisher: Librairie Philosophique J. Vrin, 6 place de la Sorbonne, F-75005 Paris. 1957-- . Irregular. 35-75 Fr. Last issue examined: vol. 36, 1977.

   Each volume is devoted to a specific subject. Concerned not only with Petrarch and Descartes but also with More, Erasmus, Budé, and other philosophers and humanists of this era. In French.

3. Petrarca-Haus (Köln). ITALIENISCHE STUDIEN. 1933-(?).

4. Petrarca-Institut (Köln). SCHRIFTEN UND VORTRÄGE. Publisher: Richard Scherpe Verlag, Krefeld, Germany (BRD). 1953-- . Irregular. DM6. [30-50 p.] Last issue examined: no. 18, 1965.

   Studies concerned mainly with the Italian Renaissance, including Petrarch's influence on contemporary and later writers; each issue features a different subject, such as DIDEROT UND GOLDONI; bibliographical references; no indexes. In German.

   Alternate title:

   SCHRIFTEN UND VORTRÄGE DES PETRARCA-INSTITUTS (Köln)

5. STUDI PETRARCHESCHI (SPetr). Sponsor: Accademia Petrarca di Lettere, Arti e Scienze, via dell'Orto, Arezzo, Bologna, Italy. Publisher: Libreria Editrice "Minerva," Bologna. 1948-(?). Irregular. [300-430 p.] Last issue examined: vol. 7, 1961.

   Long critical articles on the style, themes, language, characters, rhyme, and influence of Petrarch--coverage extends to related authors, both contemporary and modern; bibliographical references; report of Academy activities. In Italian.

   Indexed by MLA INTERNATIONAL BIBLIOGRAPHY.

6. STUDI SUL PETRARCA. Editors: Guiseppe Billanovich and Umberto Bosco. Sponsor: Ente nazionale Francesco Petrarca, with the collaboration of the commission for the critical edition of Petrarch's works. Publisher: Editrice Antenore, Padua, Italy. 1974-- . Irregular (a series). L.1.500-2.000. [30-50 p.] Last issue examined: no. 4, 1974.

   Each issue is on a specific aspect of Petrarch's life or works. In Italian. No. 5 not yet published (1978).

PHILIPPE, CHARLES-LOUIS (1875-1909)

French novelist, poet

1. Amis de Charles-Louis Philippe. BULLETIN. Sponsor: Amis de Charles-Louis Philippe, 5, rue Berthelot, Moulin (Allier), France. Secrétariat: 28, avenue de France, 03-Vichy, France. December 1936-- . Irregular. [90 p.] Last issue examined: no. 34, 1976.

   Concerned with the life and works of Philippe and other contemporaries such as Marguèrite Audoux, Émile Guillaumin, Lucien Jean. Brief analyses of specific aspects of Philippe's works; brief notes on episodes in his life; previously unpublished documents, such as the correspondence with Paul Claudel and André Gide; excerpts from theses; portraits. In French.

   Indexed by BIBLIOGRAPHIE DE LA LITTÉRATURE FRANÇAISE, FRENCH VII, FRENCH XX, and Klapp.

   Alternate titles:

   AMIS DE CHARLES-LOUIS PHILIPPE

   BULLETIN DES AMIS DE CHARLES-LOUIS PHILIPPE

2. Amis de Charles-Louis Philippe. CAHIERS. Sponsor: Amis de Charles-Louis Philippe, 5, rue Berthelot, Moulins (Allier), France. January 1957-(?). Irregular. [16 p.] Last issue examined: no. 15, 1967.

   News and notes on the activities of the organization and its members. In French.

   Indexed by FRENCH VII and FRENCH XX.

   Alternate title:

   Amis de Charles-Louis Philippe. CIRCULAIRE

PIRANDELLO, LUIGI (1867-1936)

Italian dramatist, novelist, short-story writer

1. PIRANDELLO STUDIES: A JOURNAL IN MODERN AND COMPARATIVE THEATRE. Editor: Philip J. Spartano. Sponsor: Brigham Young University Press, Provo, Utah. 1976-- . Annual. $6.

   Devoted to discussions of Pirandello's dramatic writings and productions of his plays, his influence on subsequent theatre, and his prose works insofar as they are related to his plays.

   Indexed by AMERICAN HUMANITIES INDEX.

2. Pubblicazioni dell'Istituto di studi pirandelliani. Sponsor: Istituto di studi pirandelliani, Rome, Italy. Publisher: Le Monnier, Florence, Italy. 1967-- . Irregular (a series). [100-150 p.] Last issue examined: no. 4, 1973.

   Each volume is concerned with a specific subject, such as L'ESSENZIALITÀ PROBLEMATICA E DIALETTICA DEL TEATRO DI PIRANDELLO (no. 4, 1973). In Italian.

PIRCKHEIMER, WILLIBALD (1470-1530)

German humanist, book collector

1. MARGINALIEN: ZEITSCHRIFT FÜR BUCHKUNST UND BIBLIOPHILIE. Editor: Lothar Lang. Sponsor: Pirckheimer-Gesellschaft, Berlin. Publisher: Aufbau-Verlag, Berlin. Subscriptions: Buchexport, Volkseigener Aussenhandelsbetrieb der Deutschen Demokratischen Republik, Leninstrasse 16, 701 Leipzig, Germany (DDR). January 1957-- . Quarterly. DM24. [75-100 p.] Last issue examined: vol. 63, 1976.

   A publication for book collectors and dealers, with only occasional references to Pirckheimer. Surveys of library holdings and special collections; bibliographies; book reviews; illustrations and facsimiles; no index. In German. Secondhand copies available from Kraus Periodicals (1957-66, $123). Alternate spelling: Wilibald Pirkheimer.

   Indexed by Köttelwesch and MLA INTERNATIONAL BIBLIOGRAPHY.

   Alternate subtitle:

   BLÄTTER DER PIRCKHEIMER-GESELLSCHAFT

PLISNIER, CHARLES (1897-1952)

Belgian novelist

1. CAHIERS DE LA FONDATION CHARLES PLISNIER. Sponsor: Fondation Charles Plisnier, 21, rue Darwin, Brussels 6, Belgium. December 1956-66(?). Irregular. [45-200 p.] Last issue examined: vol. 9, 1966.

   Aims to popularize the history and literature of the country and to publish scholarly studies of its authors' contributions to the French language and literature, especially the novel --refers only occasionally to the life and works of Charles Plisnier. Each volume concerns a different subject, such as L'ETHNIE FRANÇAISE D'EUROPE (1963). Occasional photographs. In French. Vol. 10 not yet published (1978). Alternate address: 47, rue des Palais, 1030 Brussels, Belgium.

Alternate titles:

CAHIERS DES AMIS DE CHARLES PLISNIER
Fondation Charles Plisnier. CAHIERS

2. Fondation Charles Plisnier. BULLETIN D'INFORMATION ET DE PRESSE. Sponsor: Fondation Charles Plisnier, 21, rue Darwin, Brussels 6, Belgium. April 1955--(?). Quarterly (irregular). Last issue examined: no. 15, 1959.

Contains information on activities of the Foundation and the regional committees throughout France. In French.

3. Fondation Charles Plisnier. ÉTUDES ET DOCUMENTS. Sponsor: Fondation Charles Plisnier, 21, rue Darwin, Brussels 6, Belgium. 1961-69 (nos. 1-8). Irregular. 15-45 Fr. [15-90 p.]

Studies of language and literature with only occasional reference to Charles Plisnier except for no. 4 (1962), LETTRES À MES CONCITOYENS. Occasional photographs and illustrations. In French.

POE, EDGAR ALLAN (1809-49)

American poet, critic, short-story writer

1. Edgar Allan Poe. Subseries of La Revue des Lettres Modernes. Editor: Claude Richard. 1969-- . Irregular. Series numbers for the issues on Poe are provided below.

Poe subseries	La Revue series	Date
Unnumbered	Nos. 193-98	1969

In French. See Camus, Albert, entry 1, for a full description of La Revue des Lettres Modernes.

Indexed by BULLETIN CRITIQUE, Klapp, and MLA INTERNATIONAL BIBLIOGRAPHY.

2. POE MESSENGER. Editor: W.D. Taylor. Sponsor: Poe Foundation, Edgar Allan Poe Museum, 1914-16 East Main Street, Richmond, Va. 23223. 1970-- . Approximately 1/yr. $1. [8-12 p.] Circulation: 600.

Brief critical articles and notes; bibliographies; book reviews; news notes; information on work in progress; illustrations; no index.

3. POE NEWSLETTER (PN). Superseded by POE STUDIES (see entry 5).

Editor: G.R. Thompson, Department of English, Washington State University, Pullman, Wash. 99163. Publisher: Washington State University Press. April 1968-December 1970 (vols. 1-3, no. 2). 2/yr. (Spring, Fall), with occasional supplements. $2. [24 p.]

Essays and notes on any aspect of Poe the man and the writer; bibliographical, source, influence, historical, and critical studies; general essays on Poe's contemporaries and the Gothic and Romantic philosophy; surveys of Poe scholarship; current international bibliography of criticism in books and articles, reviews, translations; "Marginalia"--notes on editions, sources, allusions, textual problems; news on symposia, new publications, papers, lectures.

Indexed by MLA INTERNATIONAL BIBLIOGRAPHY and YEAR'S WORK IN ENGLISH STUDIES.

4. Poe Society, Baltimore. ANNUAL LECTURE. Sponsor: Edgar Allan Poe Society, Baltimore, Md. 1922-- . [15 p.]

Studies of one specific aspect of Poe interests, such as THE INFLUENCE AND REPUTATION OF EDGAR ALLAN POE IN EUROPE (1962).

5. POE STUDIES (PoeS). Supersedes POE NEWSLETTER (see entry 3). Editors: G.R. Thompson, Department of English, Purdue University, Lafayette, Ind. 47907; and Alexander Hammond, Department of English, Washington State University, Pullman, Wash. 99164. Publisher: Washington State University Press. June 1971 (vol. 4, no. 1)-- . 2/yr. with occasional supplements. $3. [20-30 p.] Circulation: 700-800. Last issue examined: vol. 11, 1978.

Long articles on Poe the man and writer from any critical, historical, or scholarly approach--his predecessors, contemporaries, or followers in the dark tradition, his style or literary sources, his relationship with Romanticism and the grotesque, his influence, life, and works; annual briefly annotated bibliography from international sources; "Marginalia"--comments, notes, and queries about controversial points in his life and works--sources, textual problems, allusions, relationship to other authors such as Cooper and Baudelaire; report of work in progress; occasional checklists on individual titles; news of the Poe Studies Association and its annual meeting, the Poe Foundation in Richmond, Virginia, and the Poe Society of Virginia; announcements of lectures, forthcoming publications, completed dissertations, performances; translations of important contemporary foreign critics; extensive reviews of important Poe scholarship, including foreign publications; illustrations; no index.

Indexed by ABSTRACTS OF ENGLISH STUDIES, AMERICAN HUMANITIES INDEX, ANNUAL BIBLIOGRAPHY OF ENGLISH LANGUAGE AND LITERATURE, MISSISSIPPI QUARTERLY, MLA ABSTRACTS, MLA INTERNATIONAL BIBLIOGRAPHY, and YEAR'S WORK IN ENGLISH STUDIES.

6. POE STUDIES ASSOCIATION NEWSLETTER. Editors: Eric W. Carlson, Department of English, University of Connecticut, Storrs, Conn. 06268; John E. Reilly, Department of English, College of the Holy Cross, Worcester, Mass. 01610; and Richard P. Benton, Department of English, Trinity College, Hartford, Conn. 06106. Sponsor: Poe Studies Association. President: J. Lasley Dameron, Department of English, Memphis State University, Memphis, Tenn. 38152. May 1973-- . 2/yr. (May, November). Free to members ($3). [6 p.] Circulation: 800-900. Last issue examined: vol. 6, 1978.

    Information about the Society's annual meeting at the Modern Language Association convention and about the activities of cooperating Poe Societies in Baltimore, Richmond, and New York; news of forthcoming publications, research in progress, special conferences and lectures, and articles and studies of interest to Poe scholars; bibliographies of recent publications; report of work in progress; short book reviews.

Alternate title:

    NEWSLETTER. Poe Studies Association

POPE, ALEXANDER (1688-1744)

English poet, satirist

1. SCRIBLERIAN: A NEWSJOURNAL DEVOTED TO POPE AND SWIFT AND THEIR CIRCLE. Superseded by SCRIBLERIAN AND THE KIT-CATS (see entry 1). Editors: Peter A. Tasch, Arthur J. Weitzman, Roy S. Wolper. Sponsor and publisher: Department of English, Temple University, Philadelphia, Pa. 19122; and Northeastern University, Boston, Mass. 02115. Autumn 1968-Autumn 1971 (vols. 1-4, no. 1). 2/yr. (Autumn, Spring). $2 (individuals); $3 (libraries); $3 (overseas). [40-50 p.]

    Notes on allusions, biographical problems, specific points in the works; survey of scholarship in various countries; long book reviews of American publications; numerous brief book reviews of international publications--translations, new editions; brief summaries and comments on periodical articles; news of meetings, library holdings, papers, seminars; "Scribleriana"; international contributors; facsimiles; advertisements. Reprints available from Johnson Reprint.

Indexed by ABSTRACTS OF ENGLISH STUDIES, AMERICAN HUMANITIES INDEX, ANNUAL BIBLIOGRAPHY OF ENGLISH LANGUAGE AND LITERATURE, INDEX TO BOOK REVIEWS IN THE HUMANITIES, MLA INTERNATIONAL BIBLIOGRAPHY, and PHILOLOGICAL QUARTERLY.

Alternate subtitle, vol. 1, nos. 1-2:

A NEWSLETTER DEVOTED TO POPE, SWIFT AND THEIR CIRCLE

2. SCRIBLERIAN AND THE KIT-CATS. Supersedes SCRIBLERIAN: A NEWS-JOURNAL DEVOTED TO POPE AND SWIFT AND THEIR CIRCLE (see entry 2). Editors: Arthur J. Weitzman, Department of English, Northeastern University, Boston, Mass. 02115; Peter A. Tasch and Roy S. Wolper, Department of English, Temple University, Philadelphia, Pa. 19122. Sponsors: Northeastern University and Temple University. Spring 1972 (vol. 4, no. 2)-- . 2/yr. (Autumn, Spring). $3 (individuals, U.S. and Canada); $4 (foreign); $4 (libraries). [50-80 p.] Circulation: 1,300. Last issue examined: vol. 10, 1978.

Interested in Pope, Swift, and their circle in the late seventeenth and early eighteenth centuries--Gay, Arbuthnot, Parnell, Harley, Bolingbroke, Congreve, Addison, Steele, Vanbrugh, Marlborough. Devoted mainly to reviews, long and short, of books and articles published all over the world; "Scribleriana"--notes, queries, and ephemera from international sources with information on manuscripts, collections, auctions, new editions, members' activities, meetings of the British Society for Eighteenth-Century Studies, meetings of the MLA; letters to the editor; bibliography every fifth year; illustrations; facsimiles; advertisements; no annual index. Index for vols. 1-5 in vol. 5.

Indexed by ABSTRACTS OF ENGLISH STUDIES, AMERICAN HUMANITIES INDEX, INDEX TO BOOK REVIEWS IN THE HUMANITIES, MLA INTERNATIONAL BIBLIOGRAPHY, and PHILOLOGICAL QUARTERLY.

POQUELIN, JEAN-BAPTISTE [MOLIÈRE] (1622-73)

French comic dramatist

1. MOLIÉRISTE: REVUE MENSUELLE. Publisher: Georges Monval, Librairie Tresse and Stock, Paris. April 1879-March 1889 (vols. 1-10, nos. 1-120). Monthly.

Critical essays; source and character studies; bibliographies; play reviews; news of first performances of the plays; illustrations, plates, and portraits; indexes. In French.

POSTL, KARL ANTON [CHARLES SEALSFIELD] (1793-1864)

Swiss novelist (German-born, American citizen)

1. Charles Sealsfield-Gesellschaft. JAHRESGABE. Sponsor and publisher:

Charles Sealsfield-Gesellschaft, Stuttgart, Germany (BRD). 1964(?)-- . Annual. DM3-80. [50-350 p.] Last issue examined: 1977.

Long biographical and bibliographical studies of Sealsfield and his works, such as CHARLES SEALSFIELDS SPRACHE IM KAJÜTENBUCH (1975), and SEALSFIELD-BIBLIOGRAPHIE, 1945-65 (1966); special bibliographies, including one of Sealsfield holdings in the Albert Kresse Library in Stuttgart (1974); bibliographical notes; photographs. In German.

Alternate title:

JAHRESGABE DER CHARLES SEALSFIELD-GESELLSCHAFT, STUTTGART

POUND, EZRA (1885-1972)

American poet, editor, critic

1. PAIDEUMA: A JOURNAL DEVOTED TO EZRA POUND SCHOLARSHIP. Editors: Hugh Kenner, Eva Hesse, Donald Davie, Donald Gallup, Lewis Leary. Managing editor: Carroll F. Terrell, Department of English, 305 EM, University of Maine, Orono, Maine 04473. Sponsor: National Poetry Foundation. Publisher: University of Maine, Orono, Maine 04473. Spring 1972-- . 2/yr. in 1972; 3/yr. thereafter. $10 (individuals, U.S. and Canada) and $12 (foreign); $15 (institutions) and $17 (foreign); $3.95 per issue. [150 p.] Circulation: 1,000. Last issue examined: vol. 7, 1978.

   Divided into subject area sections as needed: The Periplum (essays); The Gallery (portraits); The Biographer; The Documentary; The Bibliographer; The Reviewer; The Explicator; The Bulletin Board; The Departments. Long articles based on scholarship, not opinion; brief notes and long studies of Pound's translations, his life, and various aspects of his works; occasional bibliographies of works by and about Pound, such as the "Annotated Checklist of Criticism on Ezra Pound, 1930-35" (Spring-Summer 1976)--total work to be completed by 1979, after which there will be annual increments; long book reviews; notes, queries, and answers about phrases, allusions, and names; letters to the editor; unpublished Pound letters and manuscripts; occasional report of work in progress; numerous notes about activities of Pound scholars; special issues; illustrations and facsimiles; index every two years. Cumulated index at end of fifth year. "Paideuma"--"the grisly roots of ideas that are in action": Ezra Pound.

   Indexed by ABSTRACTS OF ENGLISH STUDIES, AMERICAN HUMANITIES INDEX, AMERICAN LITERATURE, ANNUAL BIBLIOGRAPHY OF ENGLISH LANGUAGE AND LITERATURE, MLA INTERNATIONAL BIBLIOGRAPHY, and VICTORIAN STUDIES.

PAIDEUMA
Vol. 3 No. 1
$3.95

2. Pound Lectures in the Humanities. Sponsor: University of Idaho, Moscow, Idaho. October 1974-- . Annual. Last issue examined: vol. 4, 1978.

   Reprints of taped lectures and discussions--not always confined to Pound and his works.

3. POUND NEWSLETTER. Editor: John Edwards. January 1954-April 1956 (nos. 1-10). Quarterly. Free. [10-45 p.]

   Long critical essays; primary and secondary bibliographies; reprints of translations of Pound's poetry; "World Survey"--a collection of published opinions from international sources; information on Pound's trial for treason; annotated list of work in progress; survey of library holdings; abstracts of dissertations; letters to the editor; notes and queries. Index to nos. 1-10 in no. 10.

POWYS

Llewelyn (1884-1939), English essayist

John Cowper (1872-1963), novelist, essayist, poet

Theodore Francis (1875-1953), novelist, short-story writer

1. POWYS NEWSLETTER (PowysN). Editor: R.L. Blackmore, Hamilton, N.Y. 13346. Sponsor: Colgate University and Ford Humanities Fund. Publisher: Colgate University Press, Hamilton, N.Y. 1970-- . Irregular. Free to Powys scholars in touch with Colgate University Press; for others, $3 per issue; no prepaid subscriptions. [30-45 p.] Circulation: 300. Last issue examined: vol. 5, 1977-78.

   Reviews Powys scholarship in America and presents unpublished works primarily by John, Theodore, and Llewelyn; four other Powys children, out of a total of eleven, also wrote and published. Contains critical studies of the novels, their plots, characters, and allusions such as those to the early Christian monuments in Wales; bibliographies of American library collections, both public and private; reminiscences by members of the Powys family, and by friends and other contemporaries; reprints of letters, short stories, and other documents; report of scholarship in progress, including dissertations; news of Powys Society meetings in London (biannual), with summaries of and comments on the papers and seminars; brief news notes about MLA seminars and new and forthcoming editions and bibliographies of Powys works, especially those from the Colgate University Press; sketches.

Indexed by MLA INTERNATIONAL BIBLIOGRAPHY.

PROUDHON, PIERRE-JOSEPH (1809-65)

French Socialist, anarchist

1. CAHIERS DU CERCLE PROUDHON. 1912-13 (nos. 1-6); second series, 1914.

   Occasional articles on Proudhon's life and works. In French.

PROUST, MARCEL (1871-1922)

French novelist

1. BULLETIN DE LA SOCIÉTÉ DES AMIS DE MARCEL PROUST ET DES AMIS DE COMBRAY (BSAP; BSAMP; BMP). Editor: Henri Bonnet, 6, rue du Prieuré d'Yron, 28220 Cloyes-sur-le-Loir, France; or, 25, rue Gandon, 75013 Paris. Sponsor: Société des Amis de Marcel Proust et des Amis de Combray, Illiers-Combray, with the cooperation of the Direction Générale des Spectacles, de la Musique, et des Lettres. Administrative secretary: R. Lomp, 34, rue du Docteur-Galopin, 28120 Illiers-Combray (Eure-et-Loir), France. 1950-- . Annual. 50 Fr; 30 Fr (students). [200-300 p.] Last issue examined: no. 28, 1978.

   Long scholarly essays by international contributors on Proust's influence on the literature of other countries; studies of his ideas, friendships, and works; bibliographies of scholarship in foreign countries; previously unpublished works; numerous brief book reviews or long review-articles; interviews; news from international societies, libraries, expositions, conferences; report of the annual general assembly; letters to the editor; list of new members; portraits and facsimiles; no index. In French.

   Indexed by BIBLIOGRAPHIE DE LA LITTÉRATURE FRANÇAISE, FRENCH VI, FRENCH VII, FRENCH XX, Klapp, and REVUE D'HISTOIRE LITTÉRAIRE.

   Alternate titles:

   BULLETIN MARCEL PROUST

   Société des Amis de Marcel Proust et des Amis de Combray. BULLETIN

2. BULLETIN D'INFORMATIONS PROUSTIENNES. Sponsor: Centre d'Études Proustiennes, 45, rue d'Ulm, 75230 Paris, Cedex 05, France. Spring 1975-- . 2/yr. 35 Fr; 40 Fr (foreign). Last issue examined: no. 5, Autumn 1977.

   Articles on Proust's life, including his relationship with such contemporaries as Jacques Rivière, his association with the newspaper FIGARO, and other little-known data; notes on a broad range of Proustian interests, including library holdings; previously unpublished works; contributions toward a concordance. In French.

Indexed by BIBLIOGRAPHIE DE LA LITTÉRATURE FRANÇAISE.

3. Cahiers Marcel Proust. Publisher: Gallimard, Paris. 1927-35 (nos. 1-8); new series, 1970 (no. 1)-- . Irregular (a series). 20-30 Fr. [200-400 p.] Last issue examined: no. 8, 1976.

   A series in which each volume concerns a different subject--for example, L'ÉCRITURE DE PROUST; OU, L'ART DU VITRAIL (1971). Critical works about Proust and occasional critical editions of his works; personal responses to his ideas; reminiscences; surveys; extracts from correspondence; bibliographies; previously unpublished letters; illustrations and portraits; no index. In French. Second hand-copiês available from Kraus Periodicals (1927-35, $150).

   Indexed by BULLETIN CRITIQUE and Klapp.

4. ÉTUDES PROUSTIENNES. Subseries of Cahiers Marcel Proust, new series no. 6 (see entry 3). Editors: Jacques Bersani, Michel Raimond, and Jean-Yves Tadié. Publisher: Gallimard, Paris. 1973 (no. 1)-- . Annual. $10. [300-400 p.] Last issue examined: vol. 2, 1975.

   Collections of critical essays by Proust scholars; comprehensive bibliography, edited by René Rancoeur, listing new editions, unpublished works, critical books and articles, and bibliographies; extracts from previously unpublished material located in the Bibliothèque nationale, with notes and explanations; brief book reviews; occasional facsimiles. In French.

   Indexed by FRENCH XX and Klapp.

5. Nederlandse Verenigung van Vrienden van Marcel Proust. JAARBOEK. Sponsor: Vrienden den Marcel Proust, Andante 34, Krimpen aan den Ijssel. 1974 (?)-- . [180 p.] Last issue examined: no. 2, 1975.

   Biographical and critical articles; studies of Proust's themes and influence; bibliographies of critical works published in Holland. In Dutch, with summaries in French.

6. PROUST RESEARCH ASSOCIATION NEWSLETTER (PRAN). Editor: J. Theodore Johnson, Jr., Department of French and Italian, University of Kansas, Lawrence, Kans. 66045. Sponsor: University of Kansas, and Department of French, University of Kansas. March 1969-- . 2/yr. Free. [30-45 p.] Circulation: 300. Last issue examined: no. 18, Fall 1977.

   "Aims to provide a forum for the discussion of problems relating

Proust Research Association Newsletter

Number 16
Fall 1976

to current research on Marcel Proust"--interested not in finished articles but in "notes of an exploratory, heuristic, or methodological nature." Brief articles on Proust's style and contributions, his friendships, and his influence in foreign countries; bibliographies in every issue of new editions, critical books and articles, and book reviews; occasional book reviews; news and notes of the Association's activities, MLA seminars, lectures, programs; report of work in progress; abstracts of dissertations and papers. In English or French.

Indexed by BIBLIOGRAPHIE DE LA LITTÉRATURE FRANÇAISE, FRENCH XX, and MLA INTERNATIONAL BIBLIOGRAPHY.

Alternate title:

NEWSLETTER. Proust Research Association

QUEEN, ELLERY

See Dannay, Frederic.

RAABE, WILHELM (1831-1910)

German novelist

1. JAHRBUCH DER RAABE-GESELLSCHAFT (JRG). Editors: Josef Daum, Abt-Jerusalem-Strasse 8, 3300 Braunschweig, Germany (BRD); Hans-Jürgen Schrader and Werner Schultz. Sponsor: Raabe-Gesellschaft, Pockelstrasse 13, Universitätsbibliothek, 3300 Braunschweig. Publisher: Waisenhaus-Buchdruckerei und Verlag, Braunschweig. 1960-- . Annual. DM20-30. [170-200 p.] Last issue examined: 1977.

   Collections of long scholarly articles on Raabe's works, ideas, friendships, themes, language, humor; bibliographies of Raabe scholarship, including dissertations; previously unpublished letters; numerous reviews of books, dissertations, and new editions of Raabe's works; occasional surveys of Raabe research; bibliographical references; no index. In German.

   Indexed by ENGLISH LANGUAGE NOTES, Köttelwesch, and MLA INTERNATIONAL BIBLIOGRAPHY.

   Alternate title:

   Raabe-Gesellschaft. JAHRBUCH

2. MITTEILUNGEN DER RAABE-GESELLSCHAFT (MRG). Sponsor: Gesellschaft der Freunde Wilhelm Raabes, Geysostrasse 7, Braunschweig, Germany (BRD). Publisher: Waisenhaus-Buchdruckerei, Braunschweig. 1911-- . 3/yr. (irregularly). [40-50 p.] Last issue examined: vol. 64, 1977.

Brief articles on Raabe's life, friendships, family, humor, works, translations, ideas; bibliographies of new editions and criticism; brief notes on Gesellschaft activities throughout Germany, prizes, lectures, members, annual meetings; occasional photographs. Index every third year covering three volumes. In German.

Indexed by Köttelwesch and MLA INTERNATIONAL BIBLIOGRAPHY.

Alternate title:

Gesellschaft der Freunde Wilhelm Raabes. MITTEILUNGEN.

3. RAABE-JAHRBUCH. Editor: E.A. Roloff. Sponsor: Gesellschaft der Freunde Wilhelm Raabes, Braunschweig, Germany (BRD). Publisher: Verlag E. Appelhaus, Braunschweig. 1949-50. [160 p.]

Collections of essays on Raabe's life and works; no index. In German.

Indexed by Köttelwesch.

4. SCHRIFTEN DER RAABE-GESELLSCHAFT (SRG). Sponsor: Gesellschaft der Freunde Wilhelm Raabes, Braunschweig, Germany (BRD). Publisher: Deutsche Volksbücherei, Goslar, Germany (BRD). 1948-(?). [100 p.]

Each volume is concerned with a specific subject--for example, RAABES NOVELLENKUNST.

Indexed by MLA INTERNATIONAL BIBLIOGRAPHY.

Alternate title:

WILHELM RAABE-SCHRIFTEN

5. WILHELM RAABE-KALENDER. Editors: 1912-14, Otto and Hanns Martin Elster; 1947-48, E.A. Roloff. Sponsor: Gesellschaft der Freunde Wilhelm Raabes. Publisher: Deutsche Volksbücherei, Goslar, Germany (BRD). 1912-14; 1947-48. [150-60 p.]

Brief critical articles; numerous reprints of Raabe's works; no index. In German.

Indexed by Köttelwesch.

Alternate title:

RAABE-KALENDER

RABELAIS, FRANÇOIS (1494-1553)

French humanist, satirist

1. AMIS DE RABELAIS ET DE LA DEVINIÈRE (BAR). Supersedes BULLETIN DE L'ASSOCIATION DES AMIS DE RABELAIS ET DE LA DEVINIÈRE (see entry 2). Editor: Gabriel Spillebout, 3, place du Chardonnet, Tours, France. Sponsor: Association des Amis de Rabelais et de la Devinière, Secrétaire, 9, rue Giraudeau, 37000 Tours. 1952 (no. 2)-- . Annual. 20 Fr; 25 Fr (foreign). [20-45 p.] Last issue examined: vol. 3, no. 6, 1977.

    Brief articles and notes on Rabelais' treatment of comedy, the style and themes in GARGANTUA, his relationship with men of letters, his contemporary and modern reception, films based on his works; bibliographies on individual titles and general subjects; brief book reviews; report of Association activities; list of new members; illustrations. Cumulative index of vols. 1-2 in vol. 2, no. 10. In French.

    Indexed by BIBLIOGRAPHIE DE LA LITTÉRATURE FRANÇAISE, MLA INTERNATIONAL BIBLIOGRAPHY, and REVUE D'HISTOIRE LITTÉRAIRE.

    Alternate title:

    Association des Amis de Rabelais et de la Devinière. BULLETIN

2. BULLETIN DE L'ASSOCIATION DES AMIS DE RABELAIS ET DE LA DEVINIÈRE (BAARD). Superseded by AMIS DE RABELAIS ET DE LA DEVINIÈRE (see entry 1). Sponsor and publisher: Association des Amis de Rabelais et de la Devinière, 9, rue Girardeau, Tours, France. 1951 (no. 1). [15 p.]

    Report of meetings and discussions; list of members; includes announcement that the Association was organized to preserve Rabelais' home in Sevilly (Indre-et-Loire) and to establish a permanent museum. In French.

    Indexed by Klapp and MLA INTERNATIONAL BIBLIOGRAPHY.

3. ÉTUDES RABELAISIENNES (ER). Subseries of Travaux d'Humanisme et Renaissance. Publisher: Librairie Droz, Geneva. 1956-- . Irregular. 40-70 Fr. [100-200 p.] Last issue examined: vol. 14, 1978.

    Each volume contains either one long study on a specific subject, such as LES LANGAGES DE RABELAIS (1972), or a collection of essays by international contributors on Rabelais' life, style, textual problems, themes, structure, sources; occasional long review articles; footnotes and bibliographies; illustrations and facsimiles; index. In French, German, or English.

Indexed by BIBLIOGRAPHIE DE LA LITTÉRATURE FRANÇAISE, Klapp, MLA INTERNATIONAL BIBLIOGRAPHY, and REVUE D'HISTOIRE LITTÉRAIRE.

4. REVUE DES ÉTUDES RABELAISIENNES. Superseded by REVUE DU SEIZIÈME SIÈCLE. Sponsor: Société des études rabelaisiennes, Paris. Publisher: Honoré Champion, Paris. 1903-12 (vols. 1-10). Quarterly.

   Devoted to Rabelais and his times. Articles; notes; illustrations, portraits, maps, and facsimiles; index. In French.

RACINE, JEAN BAPTISTE (1639-99)

French dramatist

1. AMIS DE RACINE. April-December 1927.

2. BULLETIN DE LIAISON RACINIENNE. Sponsor: Academie raciniennes, Uzes, France. Publisher: La Ferté-Milon (Aisne), France. January 1951-58 (nos. 1-6).

3. CAHIERS RACINIENS (CRa). Editor: Jacques Masson-Forestier. Sponsor: Société racinienne, 45 bis, rue Madeleine Michelis, 92004 Neuilly-sur-Seine, France. 1957-- . 2/yr. $7; 30 Fr. [50-150 p.] Circulation: 1,000. Last issue examined: vols. 35-36, 1975.

   Collections of critical essays by international contributors on such subjects as newly discovered manuscripts, and themes in Racine's works; primary and secondary bibliographies in almost every issue--"Bibliographie racinienne" (ed. René Rancoeur) lists critical books and articles for individual Racine works, and "Bibliophilie racinienne" gives brief descriptions and current prices for rare editions or recent acquisitions; brief book and play reviews; queries and answers; news of awards, expositions, meetings of the Society; members' activities; occasional photographs and illustrations; facsimiles, such as those of Racine autographs. Cumulative analytical index for 1957-67 (nos. 1-20). In French. Second-hand copies available from Kraus Periodicals (1957-68, $150); reprints from Walter J. Johnson (1957-70, $325).

   Indexed by BIBLIOGRAPHIE DE LA LITTÉRATURE FRANÇAISE, BIBLIOGRAPHY OF FRENCH SEVENTEENTH CENTURY STUDIES, BULLETIN CRITIQUE, FRENCH XX, Klapp, and MLA INTERNATIONAL BIBLIOGRAPHY.

4. JEUNESSE DE RACINE. Editor: Jean Dubu, 22, rue des Primevères, Antony (Hts-de-Seine), France. Sponsor: Association "Jeunesse de Racine," 45 bis, rue Madeleine Michelis, 92004 Neuilly-sur-Seine, France. Publisher: René Soulié, La Ferté-Milon (Aisne), France. 1958-- . Annual, 1958-61; quarterly, 1962-65; annual, since 1966. $6.50.

Interpretive articles; long bibliographical studies of scholarship in France and other countries; historical surveys; book reviews. Index for 1958-67. In French.

Indexed by BIBLIOGRAPHIE DE LA LITTÉRATURE FRANÇAISE and Klapp.

RAIMUND, FERDINAND (1790-1836)

Austrian actor, dramatist

1. RAIMUND-ALMANACH. Sponsor: Raimundgesellschaft, Vienna, Austria. President: Gustav Pichler. Publisher: since 1963, Bergland Verlag, Vienna, Austria, and Wiesbaden, Germany (BRD). 1955-- . Every 4 yrs. AS30-90. [80-100 p.] Last issue examined: vol. 7, 1976.

   Long critical and biographical essays on Raimund's influence, contributions to the theatre, public reception at performances, relevance in today's world; reprints of lectures delivered at conferences; reprints of forgotten or inaccessible materials, such as plays and letters, with explanations and notes; reprints of criticism in other sources; reminiscences; memorials; chronicle of Gesellschaft activities; numerous photographs; no index. In German.

   Indexed by Köttelwesch.

RAMUZ, CHARLES-FERDINAND (1878-1947)

Swiss novelist

1. Fondation Charles-Ferdinand Ramuz. BULLETIN. Sponsor: Fondation Charles-Ferdinand Ramuz, C.P. 1184, 1002 Lausanne, Switzerland. 1961(?)-- . [40-60 p.] Last issue examined: 1975.

   Critical essays and reprints of lectures; previously unpublished correspondence between Ramuz and his contemporaries. In French. The Fondation has also published Ramuz' complete works.

   Indexed by BIBLIOGRAPHIE DE LA LITTÉRATURE FRANÇAISE, FRENCH VII, and FRENCH XX.

   Alternate title:

   FONDATION RAMUZ

RAND, AYN (1905-   )

Russian-born American novelist

1. AYN RAND LETTER. Supersedes THE OBJECTIVIST. Editor: Leonard

Peikoff. Sponsor and publisher: Ayn Rand Letter, 183 Madison Avenue, New York, N.Y. 10016. October 11, 1971-February 1976 (vols. 1-4). Monthly. [4-6 p.]

Written mainly by Ayn Rand "to discuss the application of Objectivism to modern events," with essays by other philosophers on political, ethical, and moral issues. Discussions of twentieth-century problems--enlightenment and reason as it should be applied to politics, laws, the Establishment; news of lectures, courses, and tapes on philosophical, metaphysical, and objectivist theories. Available on microform from University Microfilms International.

RANDON DE SAINT-AMAND, GABRIEL [JEHAN RICTUS] (1867-1933)

French poet

1. CAHIERS JEHAN RICTUS. Publisher: Auguste Blaizot et fils, Paris. March 1935-(?). [40 p.]

Essays; portraits; illustrations. In French.

Alternate title:

CAHIERS DE JEAN RICTUS

RANK, OTTO (1884-1939)

Austrian psychologist

1. JOURNAL OF THE OTTO RANK ASSOCIATION. Editor: Anita J. Faatz. Sponsor: Otto Rank Association, 35 West State Street, Doylestown, Bucks County, Pa. 18901. December 1966-- . 2/yr. Free with membership ($10/four issues); $2.50 per issue. [60-100 p.] Last issue examined: vol. 12, 1978.

Designed to "develop interest in [Rank's] writings . . . ; to promote further exploration of his concepts and their meaning for art, literature, psychology, psychotherapy, and the history of culture through publication, translation, discussion and research." Analyses of Rank's ideas, such as "The Genesis and Evolution of the Creative Personality; A Rankian Analysis of the Diary of Anaïs Nin" (vol. 9, no. 2); studies of his colleagues; interviews; long book reviews; excerpts from his works; bibliographies; notes and comments on recent publications by and activities of Rank followers. Index for Fall 1966-Summer 1974 (vols. 1-9, no. 1) in vol. 9. Microform available from University Microfilms International.

Indexed by AMERICAN HUMANITIES INDEX and PSYCHOLOGICAL ABSTRACTS.

Alternate title:

Otto Rank Association. JOURNAL

REINHARDT, MAX [GOLDMANN] (1873-1943)

Austrian theatrical director

1. PUBLIKATION DER MAX REINHARDT-FORSCHUNGSSTÄTTE. Sponsor: Max Reinhardt-Forschungsstätte, Salzburg, with the cooperation of the Max Reinhardt Archive, State University of New York at Binghamton, N.Y. 13901. Publisher: Otto Müller Verlag, Salzburg. 1970-- . Irregular. $7-20; DM57. [80-350 p.] Last issue examined: vol. 5, 1976.

Each volume focuses on a specific subject, such as MAX REINHARDT IN EUROPA (1973) or MAX REINHARDT UND MOLIÈRE (1972)--emphasis is placed on Reinhardt's skill, imagination, talent, and contribution to the theatre; bibliographies of international performances, reviews, and international criticism; bibliographical references; numerous photographs, illustrations, and facsimiles; indexes. In German.

Alternate titles:

Max Reinhardt-Forschungsstätte, Salzburg. PUBLIKATION

VERÖFFENTLICHUNGEN DER MAX REINHARDT-FORSCHUNGSSTÄTTE

RENAN, JOSEPH ERNEST (1823-92)

French philologist, historian

1. ANNUAIRE DE LA SOCIÉTÉ ERNEST-RENAN. Sponsor and publisher: Société Ernest-Renan, 45, rue des Écoles, 75005 Paris. 1960-- . Every three yrs. 20 Fr. [20-25 p.] Last issue examined: 1975.

Inspired by the life and works of Ernest Renan, but dedicated to the study of the history of religions and religious philosophy in general, with only occasional references to Renan; notices of meetings; lists of members. In French.

Alternate title:

Société Ernest-Renan. ANNUAIRE

2. Archives des Lettres Modernes. 1966-- . Irregular. The series number for the issue on Renan is provided below.

Renan subseries	Archives series	Date
Unnumbered	No. 66	1966

In French. See Camus, Albert, entry 2, for a full description of Archives des Lettres Modernes.

Indexed by BULLETIN CRITIQUE, Klapp, and MLA INTERNATIONAL BIBLIOGRAPHY.

3. BULLETIN DE LA SOCIÉTÉ ERNEST RENAN. Sponsor: Presses Universitaires de France, Paris. 1919-38; new series, 1952-(?).

   Alternate information in UNION LIST OF SERIALS: 1921-34.

   Alternate title:

   Société Ernest Renan. BULLETIN

4. BULLETIN DU CERCLE ERNEST-RENAN. Editor: Jean Coryne. Sponsor: Cercle Ernest-Renan, 3, rue Récamier, 75341 Paris. Founder: Prosper Alfaric. Publisher: Leroy, 61600 La Ferté-Macé, France. 1953-- . Monthly, 1953-June 1971; 6/yr., since November 1971. 40 Fr; 45 Fr (foreign). [4-6 p.] Last issue examined: vol. 25, no. 196, 1977.

   Reprints of lectures at meetings of the Cercle; reports of past and future conferences; brief comments and reviews on new publications; notes on members' activities and publications. Published as supplements of CAHIERS RENAN (see entry 5)--no. 191 is the supplement to CAHIER RENAN no. 94. In French.

   Alternate title:

   Cercle Ernest-Renan pour libres recherches d'histoire du christianisme. BULLETIN

5. CAHIERS RENAN. Sponsor: Cercle Ernest-Renan, 3, rue Récamier, 75007 Paris. 1954-- . Quarterly. Last issue examined: no. 95, 1976.

   Indexed by BULLETIN CRITIQUE.

   Alternate titles:

   CAHIERS ERNEST-RENAN

   CAHIERS DU CERCLE ERNEST-RENAN POUR LIBRES RECHERCHES D'HISTOIRE DU CHRISTIANISME

   Cercle Ernest-Renan pour libres recherches d'histoire du christianisme. CAHIERS

6. Cahiers renaniens (CahiersR). Editor: Jean Pommier (deceased). Sponsor: Société des Études renaniennes, 16, rue Chaptal, 75009 Paris. Publisher: Éditions A.-G. Nizet, Paris. 1971-73 (nos. 1-7). Irregular. 60-80 Fr. [80-240 p.]

   Each volume is concerned with a special subject, such as UN ITINÉRAIRE SPIRITUEL (no. 4, 1972). Collections of philosophical, biographical, and critical essays; reminiscences by Renan's friends; bibliographies; extensive notes and explanations accompany selections from Renan's works; portraits; no index. In French.

Indexed by BIBLIOGRAPHIE DE LA LITTÉRATURE FRANÇAISE, Klapp, MLA INTERNATIONAL BIBLIOGRAPHY, and REVUE D'HISTOIRE LITTÉRAIRE.

Alternate title:

CAHIERS ERNEST-RENAN

7. ÉTUDES RENANIENNES: BULLETIN. Editor: Corrie Siohan. Sponsor: Société des Études renaniennes, 16, rue Chaptal, 75009 Paris. Published with the approval of the Centre national des Lettres. 1970-- . Quarterly. 20 Fr; 40 Fr (foreign). [16 p.] Last issue examined: no. 33, 1977.

Brief articles on Renan's spiritualism and his influence on European spiritual history; reprints of his works and letters; studies of his ideas, technique, travels, and friendships, such as that with George Sand; reprints of lectures and papers read at Renan conferences on his life and philosophy; quotations from Renan's scientific and philosophical works; occasional book reviews; "Calendrier renanien"--chronicle of events; illustrations. In French.

Indexed by BIBLIOGRAPHIE DE LA LITTÉRATURE FRANÇAISE, Klapp, and REVUE D'HISTOIRE LITTÉRAIRE.

Alternate title, nos. 1-7:

Société des Études renaniennes. BULLETIN

RENAUD, MADELEINE (1900-   )

French actress

1. CAHIERS RENAUD-BARRAULT (CRB). Editor-in-chief: Simone Benmussa. Director: Jean-Louis Barrault. Publishers: 1965-72, Gallimard, Paris; 1972-74, Compagnie Renaud-Barrault, Théatre Récamier, 3, rue Récamier, 75007 Paris; since 1974, Gallimard, Paris. 1953-- . Quarterly. 32 Fr; $9; 36 Fr (other countries). [100-130 p.] Last issue examined: no. 96, 1977.

Inspired by the life and work of Madeleine Renaud and Jean-Louis Barrault. Concerned with theatre production and the technique of such authors as Claudel, Giraudoux, Molière, Shakespeare, and Sartre; surveys of theatre activity in other countries; numerous articles by Barrault; notes on performances and new ideas; letters; reprints of relevant material; interviews; "Opinions et Controverses"; occasional special issues, like LA

MUSIQUE EN PROJECT (1975); photographs and facsimiles. In French.

Indexed by BIBLIOGRAPHIE DE LA LITTÉRATURE FRANÇAISE, BULLETIN CRITIQUE, FRENCH VI, FRENCH VII, FRENCH XX, Klapp, Köttelwesch, and MLA INTERNATIONAL BIBLIOGRAPHY.

Alternate titles:

CAHIERS DE LA COMPAGNIE MADELEINE RENAUD--JEAN-LOUIS BARRAULT (CCRB; CMR)

Compagnie Madeleine Renaud--Jean-Louis Barrault. CAHIERS

RETTÉ, ADOLPHE (1863-1930)

French poet, symbolist

1. BULLETIN DES AMIS D'ADOLPHE RETTÉ. Sponsor: Amis d'Adolphe Retté, 3, rue des Prêtres-Saint-Séverin, 75005 Paris. October 1937-(?). Irregular. [16 p.] Last issue examined: no. 36, 1966.

   Studies of Retté's social and political ideas, and of his religious questioning. In French.

   Indexed by BIBLIOGRAPHIE DE LA LITTÉRATURE FRANÇAISE and FRENCH VII.

RICHTER, JEAN PAUL FRIEDRICH [JEAN PAUL] (1763-1825)

German humorist, poet, novelist, critic

1. HESPERUS. Supersedes JEAN PAUL BLÄTTER (see entry 3); superseded by JAHRBUCH DER JEAN-PAUL-GESELLSCHAFT (see entry 2). Founding editor: Theodor Langenmaier. Sponsor: Jean-Paul-Gesellschaft, Herderstrasse 21, Bayreuth, Germany (BRD). Secretary: Herbert Pachl. February 1951-December 1966 (nos. 1-30). 2/yr. DM10. [30-65 p.]

   Long scholarly articles on Jean Paul's life, works, ideas, influence, and relationship with other writers; book reviews; news of interest to the Gesellschaft--meetings, publications, brief biographical or critical notes; illustrations and photographs. In German.

   Indexed by Köttelwesch and MLA INTERNATIONAL BIBLIOGRAPHY.

   Alternate title:

   BLÄTTER DER JEAN-PAUL-GESELLSCHAFT

2. JAHRBUCH DER JEAN-PAUL-GESELLSCHAFT (JJPG). Supersedes HESPERUS (see entry 1). Editor: Kurt Wölfel, Deutsches Seminar der Universi-

tät Erlangen-Nürnberg, Bismarckstrasse 1, 8520 Erlangen, Germany (BRD). Sponsor: Jean-Paul-Gesellschaft, Bayreuth, Germany (BRD). Publisher: C.H. Beck'sche Verlagsbuchhandlung, Munich, Germany (BRD). 1966-- . Annual. DM29.50. [180-250 p.] Last issue examined: vol. 12, 1977.

Long studies of Jean Paul's religious, social, and political theories; biographical material; previously unpublished letters; surveys of his contemporaries, background, and influence on later writers; bibliographical references; occasional comprehensive analytical, international bibliographies of Jean Paul scholarship, such as the "Jean-Paul-Bibliographie, 1966-69" (1970); long book reviews; news of interest to members of the Gesellschaft; international contributors; facsimiles; no index. In German.

Indexed by ENGLISH LANGUAGE NOTES, Köttelwesch, and MLA INTERNATIONAL BIBLIOGRAPHY.

Alternate titles:

JEAN-PAUL-JAHRBUCH (Bayreuth)

Jean-Paul-Gesellschaft. JAHRBUCH

3. JEAN PAUL BLÄTTER. Superseded by HESPERUS (see entry 1). Sponsor: Jean-Paul-Gesellschaft, Bayreuth, Germany (BRD). March 1926-1950(?).

Brief news and notes. In German.

Alternate title:

BLÄTTER DER JEAN-PAUL-GESELLSCHAFT

4. JEAN-PAUL JAHRBUCH. Publisher: Berlin, Germany (DDR). 1925-(?).

RICTUS, JEHAN

See Randon de Saint-Amand, Gabriel.

RILEY, JAMES WHITCOMB (1849-1916)

American poet, lecturer, newspaperman

1. RILEY MEMORIAL ASSOCIATION NEWS. Sponsor: James Whitcomb Riley Memorial Association, Room 917, 124 East Market Building, Indianapolis, Ind. December 1958-(?).

Query returned--addressee unknown.

RILKE, RAINER MARIA (1875-1926)

German poet

1. BLÄTTER DER RILKE-GESELLSCHAFT (BRG). Editor: Rätus Luck, Leiter des Rilke-Archivs in der Schweizerischen Landesbibliothek, Lilienweg 18, Bern, Switzerland, and others. Sponsor and publisher: Rilke-Gesellschaft, St. Christophorus, 3906 Saas-Fee, Switzerland; and Tita van Oetinger. Secretary: Schweizerisches Rilke-Archiv, Hallwylstrasse 15, 3003 Bern, Switzerland. 1972-- . Annual. 10 S Fr. [65-80 p.] Last issue examined: vol. 4, 1976.

   Long studies of Rilke's philosophy, language, and literary technique; surveys of the status of Rilke scholarship throughout the world; explications; international bibliographies of new editions and of criticism in books and articles; reports of the Rilke Archivs in Switzerland and other countries; no index. In German.

   Indexed by Köttelwesch and MLA INTERNATIONAL BIBLIOGRAPHY.

   Alternate title:

   Rilke-Gesellschaft. BLÄTTER

2. Rainer Maria Rilke. Subseries of La Revue des Lettres Modernes. 1959-- . Irregular. The series numbers for the issue on Rilke is provided below.

Rilke subseries	La Revue series	Date
Unnumbered	No. 43	1959

   In French. See Camus, Albert, entry 1, for a full description of La Revue des Lettres Modernes.

   Indexed by FRENCH VII, Klapp, and MLA INTERNATIONAL BIBLIOGRAPHY.

RIMBAUD, ARTHUR (1854-91)

French pre-Symbolist poet

1. Archives Arthur Rimbaud. Subseries of Archives des Lettres Modernes. 1975-- . Irregular. Equivalent numbers are provided below for both the parent series (Archives des Lettres Modernes) and the individual author series on Rimbaud.

Rimbaud subseries	Archives series	Date
No. 1	No. 155	1975
No. 2	No. 160	1976

   In French. See Camus, Albert, entry 2, for a full description of Archives des Lettres Modernes.

Indexed by BULLETIN CRITIQUE, FRENCH XX, Klapp, and MLA INTERNATIONAL BIBLIOGRAPHY.

2. Arthur Rimbaud. Subseries of La Revue des Lettres Modernes. Editor: Louis Forestier. 1972-- . Irregular. Equivalent numbers are provided below for both the parent series (La Revue des Lettres Modernes) and the individual author series on Rimbaud.

Rimbaud subseries	La Revue series	Date
No. 1	Nos. 323-26	1972
No. 2	Nos. 370-73	1973
No. 3	Nos. 445-49	1976

In French. See Camus, Albert, entry 1, for a full description of La Revue des Lettres Modernes.

Indexed by BULLETIN CRITIQUE, FRENCH XX, Klapp, and MLA INTERNATIONAL BIBLIOGRAPHY.

3. BATEAU IVRE: BULLETIN DE LA SOCIÉTÉ DES AMIS DE RIMBAUD. Editors: Jean-Paul Vaillant and Pierre Petitfils. Sponsor: Société des Amis de Rimbaud, Musée Rimbaud et Bibliothèque de Charleville, Charleville, France. January 1949-66 (nos. 1-20; ceased publication?). Quarterly, then annual (new series, no. 20, 1966). 200 Fr; 240 Fr (foreign). [10 p.]

Official bulletin of the Société des Amis de Rimbaud (an earlier official publication is entitled BULLETIN DES AMIS DE RIMBAUD, see entry 5, and later official publication is ÉTUDES RIMBALDIENNES, see entry 7). Brief articles on Rimbaud's sources, friendships, childhood, critics; bibliographies of new publications--important critical works are annotated; previously unpublished letters and other works; "Echos"--notes on films, libraries, work in progress, lectures, new periodicals, and recordings. In French.

Indexed by FRENCH VII.

Alternate subtitle, 1949-61:

BULLETIN DES AMIS DE RIMBAUD

4. Bibliothèque Arthur Rimbaud. Publisher: Minard, Paris. 1968-- . Irregular. Last issue examined: no. 5, 1976.

Each volume concerns a specific subject--a regrouping of criticism originally published in Lettres Modernes. In French.

5. BULLETIN DES AMIS DE RIMBAUD. Sponsor: Amis de Rimbaud, 8, avenue d'Arches, Mézières, France; or, 5, rue Duvivier, Charleville-Mézières, France. 1931-April 1939 (nos. 1-7; ceased publication because of the beginning of World War II). Irregular. [8 p.]

Official publication of Les Amis de Rimbaud; later official publications are entitled BATEAU IVRE (see entry 3) and ÉTUDES RIMBALDIENNES (see entry 7). Brief notes, reminiscences, explications; previously unpublished works; news of the organization; facsimiles. Nos. 1-3 were issued originally as "Supplément a LA GRIVE." In French. Reprints are available from Slatkine Reprints (1931-39, 25 Fr).

Indexed by FRENCH VII.

6. Centre Culturel Arthur Rimbaud. CAHIER. Sponsor: Cooperation of Musée Rimbaud and Fonds Rimbaud, Charleville-Mézières, France. Publisher: The City of Charleville-Mézières. March 1969-- . Irregular. [35-40 p.] Last issue examined: no. 5, 1977.

Devoted to assembling and publishing all known documentation on Rimbaud, including a catalog of the library holdings and news of recent acquisitions. Brief descriptions and comments on individual books or manuscripts; calendar of activities at the Museum; reprints of lectures; comments on television programs and films; lists of new members; sketches, reproductions, and facsimiles. In French.

Indexed by Klapp.

Alternate title:

CAHIERS DU CENTRE CULTUREL ARTHUR RIMBAUD

7. ÉTUDES RIMBALDIENNES. Superseded by RIMBAUD VIVANT (see entry 9). Editor: Pierre Petitfils. Sponsor: Amis de Rimbaud, 13, rue Paul-Louis Courier, 75007 Paris. Publisher: Minard, Paris. 1969-72 (nos. 1-3). Irregular. 18-22 Fr. [100-200 p.] Last issue examined: no. 3, 1972.

Official journal of the Amis de Rimbaud, taking the place of BATEAU IVRE (see entry 3), which was the official organ of the Société des Amis de Rimbaud. Scholarly essays on the style, themes, influence, editions, and life of Rimbaud; explications; surveys of Rimbaud's reception and influence in other countries; bibliographies; previously unpublished letters, documents, and photographs; notes and impressions; short book reviews; "Échos"--news of interest to Rimbaud scholars concerning expositions, cultural events, entries in encyclopedias and histories, acquisitions by the Musée Rimbaud de Charleville, necrology; occasional facsimiles and portraits. Index for 1969-72 (nos. 1-3) in RIMBAUD VIVANT, no. 1 (see entry 9), arranged by author, subject, and title. In French. Ceased publication to make place for the series Arthur Rimbaud (entry 2) of La Revue des Lettres Modernes. In French.

Indexed by FRENCH XX, Klapp, and MLA INTERNATIONAL BIBLIOGRAPHY.

Alternate title:

Amis de Rimbaud. ÉTUDES RIMBALDIENNES

8. RIMBALDIEN. Publisher: Charleville-Mézières, France. 1945-49 (nos. 1-16).

Biographical and critical articles. In French.

Indexed by FRENCH VII.

9. RIMBAUD VIVANT: BULLETIN DES AMIS DE RIMBAUD. Supersedes ÉTUDES RIMBALDIENNES (see entry 7). Editor: Pierre Petitfils, 13, rue Paul-Louis Courier, 75007 Paris. Sponsor: Amis de Rimbaud, C.C.P., 1075-72 Paris. Published with the cooperation of the Centre National des Lettres et de la Municipalité de Charleville-Mézières, France. Secretary general: Suzanne Briet, 24, rue Gutenberg, 92110 Boulogne, France. 1973-- . Quarterly. 40 Fr; 50 Fr (foreign). [30-70 p.] Last issue examined: no. 13, 1977.

Short textual, critical, or biographical studies, with particular emphasis placed on Rimbaud's significance in today's world; previously unpublished documents; notes on new publications; glosses and notes for future editions; reviews of books and of articles in journals; occasional bibliographies of books, articles, and dissertations--international sources; Rimbaud-related extracts from articles and books; reprints of lectures to the Amis de Rimbaud; interviews and personal interpretations; "Chronique"--news of conferences, new editions, members' activities and publications, readings, necrology, and annual meetings of the organization; sketches. Index for ÉTUDES RIMBALDIENNES, 1970-72 (nos. 1-3; see entry 7) in RIMBAUD VIVANT, no. 1, arranged by author, title, and subject. In French.

Indexed by BIBLIOGRAPHIE DE LA LITTÉRATURE FRANÇAISE, FRENCH XX, Klapp, and REVUE D'HISTOIRE LITTÉRAIRE.

RIVIÈRE, JACQUES (1886-1925)

French critic, editor

1. Amis de Jacques Rivière et d'Alain-Fournier. BULLETIN. Sponsor: Association des Amis de Jacques Rivière et d'Alain-Fournier, 31, rue Arthur-Petit, 78220 Viroflay, France. 1975-- . Quarterly. Free with membership (35 Fr; 25 Fr, students). [60-150 p.] Last issue examined: no. 4, 1978.

Studies of letters, friendships, influence; descriptions of library holdings. First issue is a special number commemorating the fiftieth anniversary of Rivière's death. In French.

Indexed by FRENCH XX and Klapp.

Alternate titles:

Association des Amis de Jacques Rivière et Alain-Fournier. BULLETIN

BULLETIN DES AMIS DE JACQUES RIVIÈRE ET ALAIN-FOURNIER

2. DOSSIERS DE LA SOCIÉTÉ DES AMIS DE JACQUES RIVIÈRE ET ALAIN-FOURNIER. Editor: Alain Rivière, 31, rue Arthur Petit, 78220 Viroflay, France. Sponsor: Centre National des Lettres, 6, rue Dufrenoy, 75016 Paris. Summer 1975-- . 2/yr. [40 p.] Circulation: 500.

Brief critical articles; bibliographies; previously unpublished material; book reviews; reports of work in progress; international news notes; occasional special issues; illustrations. In French.

Indexed by REVUE D'HISTOIRE LITTÉRAIRE.

ROHMER, SAX

See Ward, Arthur S.

ROHNER, LUCIEN (1880-1916)

French poet

1. CAHIERS LUCIEN ROHNER. Editor: Mme. Lucien Rohner, 10, rue Émile-Duclaux, Paris. November 1934-July 1936. Quarterly. [24 p.]

Biographical and critical notes; portraits. In French.

ROLLAND, ROMAIN (1866-1944)

French novelist, playwright, critic, musicologist

1. BULLETIN DE L'ASSOCIATION DES AMIS DU FONDS ROMAIN ROLLAND. Editor: Jacques Saada. Sponsor: Fonds Romain Rolland, Association des Amis du Fonds Romain Rolland, Bibliothèque Sainte-Geneviève, 6, rue Vallette, 75005 Paris. Advisor: Mme. Romain Rolland, 89, boulevard Montparnasse, 75006 Paris. August 1946-- . Quarterly, then annually. Free with membership (25 Fr). [20-80 p.] Last issues examined: nos. 111-14, 1975.

Long detailed accounts of the work and influence of Romain Rolland throughout the world, country by country; report on efforts to enlarge the archives of the Fonds Romain Rolland and on plans for future editions of the Cahiers Romain Rolland (see entry 2); brief biographical and interpretive articles; studies showing influence from and to other authors and countries; previously unpublished letters and other documents; extracts from journals. In French or German.

The Fonds Romain Rolland is constituted in part by the Archives Romain Rolland and in part by the Romain Rolland à Vézelay (the future Musée-Bibliothèque Romain Rolland and Centre Jean-Christophe, which has been functioning since 1964).

Indexed by BIBLIOGRAPHIE DE LA LITTÉRATURE FRANÇAISE, FRENCH VII, FRENCH XX, and Klapp.

Alternate titles:

Académie des Universités de Paris, Fonds Romain Roland. Association des Amis du Fonds Romain Rolland. BULLETIN

Association des Amis de Romain Rolland. BULLETIN

Association des Amis du Fonds Romain Rolland. BULLETIN

BULLETIN DE L'ASSOCIATION DES AMIS DE ROMAIN ROLLAND

Fonds Romain Rolland. BULLETIN

Université de Paris, Fonds Romain Rolland. Association des Amis de Romain Rolland. BULLETIN

2. Cahiers Romain Rolland. Sponsor: Fonds Romain Rolland, Association des Amis du Fonds Romain Rolland, Bibliothèque Sainte-Geneviève, 6, rue Valette, 75005 Paris. Publisher: Albin Michel, Paris. 1948-- . Irregular (a series). [200-450 p.] Last issue examined: vol. 23, 1975.

Included here because many of the volumes contain critical introductions, appendices, and notes of interest to Rolland scholars, although the text itself is concerned mainly with the editing of previously unpublished letters, journals, and other documents. Every volume is concerned with a specific subject, such as D'UNE RIVE A L'AUTRE: HERMANN HESSE ET ROMAIN ROLLAND; comments by such noted authors and friends as Péguy, Gandhi, Tagore; illustrations; facsimiles; portraits; index. In French.

Mme. Rolland states that there is enough material for about fifty cahiers, including a special volume for Rolland's correspondence with friends in Switzerland, another for the United States, one for Tolstoi, and two for Rumania. See also Charles Péguy, entry 1, FEUILLETS DE L'AMITIÉ CHARLES PÉGUY, for numerous articles concerning the relationship of the two authors.

Indexed by FRENCH VII and FRENCH XX.

3. CAHIERS SUISSE ROMAIN ROLLAND. Editor: Pierre Hirsch. Publisher: a la Bacconiére, Neuchâtel, Switzerland. 1977-- . Irregular. 27 S Fr. [230 p.]

   Previously unpublished works, with helpful introductions, notes, and indexes of proper names mentioned in the contents. Vol. 1, BON VOISINAGE, contains the correspondence between Edmond Privat and Romain Rolland from 1915 to 1931. Future volumes will print and comment on other work relating Rolland to Switzerland.

4. ÉTUDES SUR ROMAIN ROLLAND. Publisher: Tokyo, Japan. No. 16, 1954-- . [30 p.]

   Brief essays which examine Rolland's influence on the authors and literature of his own and other countries. In French.

   Indexed by FRENCH VII.

ROLLINAT, MAURICE (1846-1903)

French poet

1. BULLETIN DE LA SOCIÉTÉ "LES AMIS DE MAURICE ROLLINAT" (BSA Rollinat). Editor: Laboureur, Chateauroux, France. Sponsor: Société "Les Amis de M. Rollinat," M.G. Lubin, 50, quai Alphonse-Le Gallo, 92100 Boulogne-sur-Seine, France. March 1956-- . Irregular. Last issue examined: no. 13, 1974.

   Brief articles on Rollinat's friendships, influence, critics; short critical notes on his technique; reminiscences; previously unpublished letters, such as those to his family and to George Sand. In French.

   Indexed by BIBLIOGRAPHIE DE LA LITTÉRATURE FRANÇAISE, FRENCH VII, FRENCH XX, Klapp, and REVUE D'HISTOIRE LITTÉRAIRE.

ROMAINS, JULES

See Farigoule, Louis H.J.

RONSARD, PIERRE DE (1524-85)

French poet, humanist

1. Association des Amis de Ronsard et du prieuré de Sainte-Côme. BULLE-

TIN. Sponsor: Association des Amis de Ronsard et du prieuré de Sainte-Côme, 8, place Foire-le-Roi, Tours (Indre-et-Loire), France.

In French.

ROOSEVELT, THEODORE (1858-1919)

Twenty-sixth president of the United States

1. THEODORE ROOSEVELT ASSOCIATION JOURNAL. Editor: John A. Gable, Box 720, Oyster Bay, N.Y. 11771. Sponsor: Theodore Roosevelt Association, Box 720, Oyster Bay, N.Y. 11771. Winter 1975-- . 2/yr. Free with membership ($5). [14-20 p.] Last issue examined: vol. 4, 1978.

   Brief articles on Roosevelt's contribution to his times and to the twentieth century, the establishment of memorials, grants, and galleries, new editions and publications, essay contests and anniversary celebrations; report of meetings of the association and its accomplishments; information on video and tape series; bibliographies; book reviews; numerous photographs.

ROUGET, MARIE MÉLANIE [MARIE NOËL] (1883-1967)

French poet, dramatist

1. CAHIERS MARIE NOËL. Sponsor: Association des Amis de Marie Noël, 19, rue Casimir-Périer, 75007 Paris. Publisher: Paris. February 1969-- . Annual. [40-45 p.] Last issue examined: no. 9, 1977.

   Articles on themes in Noël's works, her relationship with her friends, translations of her writings; reprints of letters; previously unpublished works; news of commemorative events. In French.

   Indexed by BIBLIOGRAPHIE DE LA LITTÉRATURE FRANÇAISE, FRENCH XX, and Klapp.

ROUSSEAU, JEAN-JACQUES (1712-78)

Swiss-born French philosopher, author, political theorist, composer

1. ANNALES DE LA SOCIÉTÉ JEAN-JACQUES ROUSSEAU (ASR). Editor: Jean Starobinski, président de la Société Jean-Jacques Rousseau, 12, rue de Candolle, 1200 Geneva, Switzerland. Sponsor: Société Jean-Jacques Rousseau, c/o Secretary, Charles Wirz, 26, rue Voltaire, 1201 Geneva. Publisher: A. Jullien, Geneva. 1905-- . Irregular. 15-25 Fr. [250-500 p.] Last issue examined: vol. 38, 1969-71.

Long studies on the effect of Rousseau's work on other countries and authors; essays on his ideas, themes, library collections, and individual titles; comprehensive international bibliography of books by and about Rousseau, arranged by country, with long reviews for the most important titles; "Chronique"--bibliography of articles in periodicals, arranged by subject; notes on television and radio programs, expositions, and activities of the Society; illustrations; name index. Author, subject, and illustration index for 1905-62, vols. 1-35 (Geneva: A. Jullien, 1965; 218 p.). Table of contents in the back of each volume. In French. Second-hand copies available from Kraus Periodicals (1905-66, $630); reprints from Slatkine Reprints (1905-75, 2,850 Fr). Vol. 39 not yet published (1979).

Indexed by BIBLIOGRAPHIE DE LA LITTÉRATURE FRANÇAISE, FRENCH XX, Klapp, Köttelwesch, and REVUE D'HISTOIRE LITTÉRAIRE.

Alternate title:

Société Jean-Jacques Rousseau, Geneva. ANNALES.

2. Archives des Lettres Modernes. 1962-- . Irregular. Series numbers for the issues on Rousseau are provided below.

Rousseau subseries	Archives series	Date
Unnumbered	No. 45	1962
Unnumbered	No. 81	1967

In French. See Camus, Albert, entry 2, for a full description of Archives des Lettres Modernes.

Indexed by BULLETIN CRITIQUE, Klapp, and MLA INTERNATIONAL BIBLIOGRAPHY.

3. BULLETIN D'INFORMATION: ÉTUDES ET DOCUMENTS RELATIFS A JEAN-JACQUES ROUSSEAU. Editor: François Matthey. Sponsor: Association des Amis de Jean-Jacques Rousseau, Bibliothèque de la Ville, 2000 Neuchâtel, Switzerland. 1964-- . 2/yr. (Spring, Autumn). Free with membership (10 Swiss Fr). [4-6 p.] Circulation: 300. Last issue examined: no. 20, Spring 1975.

Brief news notes on activities, events, and acquisitions by the library; reprints of newly discovered material, with descriptions and comments; bibliographies; occasional brief book reviews; list of members; occasional illustrations, portraits, or facsimiles; no index. In French.

Nos. 1-3: "Extr. de la Revue Neuchâteloise." Nos. 1-8: issued by the Association under its earlier name: Amis de la collection neuchâteloise des manuscripts de Jean-Jacques Rousseau.

Indexed by ANNALES DE LA SOCIÉTÉ JEAN-JACQUES ROUSSEAU, BIBLIOGRAPHIE DE LA LITTÉRATURE FRANÇAISE, and REVUE D'HISTOIRE LITTÉRAIRE.

Alternate title:

Association des Amis de Jean-Jacques Rousseau. BULLETIN D'INFORMATION. ÉTUDES ET DOCUMENTS

4. CAHIERS JEAN-JACQUES ROUSSEAU. 1971(?)-- . Irregular. Last issue examined: no. 2, 1972.

   Long character analyses.

RÜCKERT Friedrich (1788-1866) Heinrich (1823-75)

German father and son, statesmen, authors

1. Rückert-Gesellschaft. JAHRESGABE. Sponsor and publisher: Rückert-Gesellschaft, Schweinfurt, Germany (BRD). 1969-- . Annual (1973 volume never published). DM7.50-12. [10-80 p.] Last issue examined: 1976.

   Notes on Rückert research; news of members' activities, state celebrations, prizes; occasional special issues on specific subjects. In German.

   Alternate title:

   VERÖFFENTLICHUNGEN DES FÖRDERERKREISES DER RÜCKERT-FORSCHUNG

2. RÜCKERT-STUDIEN. Editor: Helmut Prang. Sponsor and publisher: Rückert-Gesellschaft, Schweinfurt, Germany (BRD). 1964-- . Irregular. DM25. [150-240 p.] Last issue examined: vol. 3, 1974.

   Monographs on specific subjects, such as DAS SLAWENBILD FRIEDRICH UND HEINRICH RÜCKERTS; numerous quotations from the works; bibliographies. In German. Vol. 4 not yet published (1978).

RUSSELL, BERTRAND (1872-1970)

English philosopher, social reformer

1. BERTRAND RUSSELL SOCIETY NEWSLETTER. Editor: Lee Eisler, R.D. 1, Box 409, Coopersburg, Pa. 18036. Sponsor: Bertrand Russell Society. March 1974-- . Quarterly. Free with membership ($15); $5 (students). [25 p.] Circulation: 160.

   Brief critical comments on Russell's life and work; bibliographies of primary works; news notes; occasional reports of work in progress; brief notes on new publications; occasional illustrations.

2. RUSSELL: THE JOURNAL OF THE BERTRAND RUSSELL ARCHIVES. Editor: Kenneth Blackwell, McMaster University Library, Hamilton, Ontario L8S 4L6, Canada. Sponsor and publisher: McMaster University Library Press. Spring 1971-- . Quarterly. $4 (individuals); $6 (institutions). [32 p.] Circulation: 450. Last issue examined: no. 28, 1977.

   Long (10 p.) documented essays on the works and ideas of Bertrand Russell; occasional biographical contributions, such as an article on Russell's visit to Australia; occasional bibliographies, including one of the Russell articles published in the Hearst newspapers, and others on new and forthcoming books; news and notes about the Bertrand Russell Society activities, collectors' items, visitors and researchers at the Russell Archives at McMaster University Library, availability of microfilm copies, and newly discovered Russell manuscripts; reprints of early interviews and reviews; reminiscences; previously unpublished manuscripts and letters to and from Russell; queries; reports of work in progress, including the definitive edition of Russell's works; occasional book reviews; editor's notes, such as the one about "the dreadful state of the budget" of the Archives; occasional illustrations. Index for 1971-75 (nos. 1-19) in no. 20.

   Indexed by PHILOSOPHER'S INDEX.

RYNER, HAN

See Ner, Henri.

SAINTE-BEUVE, CHARLES-AUGUSTIN (1804-69)

French poet, literary critic, man of letters

1. Archives des Lettres Modernes. 1960-- . Irregular. Series numbers for the issues on Sainte-Beuve are provided below.

Sainte-Beuve subseries	Archives series	Date
Unnumbered	No. 29	1960
Unnumbered	No. 115	1970

   In French. See Camus, Albert, entry 2, for a full description of Archives des Lettres Modernes.

   Indexed by BULLETIN CRITIQUE, Klapp, and MLA INTERNATIONAL BIBLIOGRAPHY.

SAINT-SIMON, CLAUDE-HENRI, COMTE DE (1760-1825)

French philosopher, social reformer

1. CAHIERS SAINT-SIMON. Editor: Yves Coirault. Sponsor and publisher: Librairie Klincksieck, Paris. 1973-- . 35-80 Fr. [50-320 p.] Last issue examined: no. 5, 1977.

   Scholarly essays on Saint-Simon's life and works--his relationship with Rome, problems of class, philosophy; previously unpublished works. In French.

   Indexed by BIBLIOGRAPHIE DE LA LITTÉRATURE FRANÇAISE and Klapp.

SAND, GEORGE

See Dudevant, Mme., Lucile-Aurore Dupin.

SANDOZ, MARI [SUZETTE] (1896-1966)

American biographer, historical writer

1. MARI SANDOZ HERITAGE. Publisher: Chadron, Nebr. 69337. Winter 1971-- . 2/yr.

SAN MARTÍN, JOSÉ DE (1778-1850)

Argentine general, revolutionary leader

1. SAN MARTÍN. 1961(?)-(?). 6/yr. Sponsor: Instituto Sanmartiniano de Mexico(?).

2. SAN MARTÍN: REVISTA DEL INSTITUTO NACIONAL SANMARTINIANO. Sponsor and publisher: Instituto Nacional Sanmartiniano, Plaza Grand-Bourg, Buenos Aires 25, Argentina. August 1935-55 (nos. 1-36). Quarterly. [100-170 p.]

   Long articles discussing San Martín's ideas, activities, and contribution to the history of the country--coverage extends to other leaders and heroes; brief reviews of books and articles; brief notes on ceremonies and activities in Argentina and other countries; news of the Institute; illustrations, portraits, and facsimiles. In Spanish.

SARTRE, JEAN PAUL (1905-)

French philosopher, dramatist, novelist, teacher

1. Archives des Lettres Modernes. 1968-- . Irregular. Series numbers for

the issues on Sartre are provided below.

Sartre subseries	Archives series	Date
Unnumbered	No. 89	1968
Unnumbered	No. 144	1973
Unnumbered	No. 159	1976

In French. See Camus, Albert, entry 2, for a full description of Archives des Lettres Modernes. See also Archives des Lettres Modernes, no. 134 (no. 3, Archives André Gide).

Indexed by BULLETIN CRITIQUE, FRENCH XX, Klapp, and MLA INTERNATIONAL BIBLIOGRAPHY.

SAUSSURE, FERDINAND DE (1857-1913)

Swiss linguistics professor

1. CAHIERS FERDINAND DE SAUSSURE (CFS). Sponsor: Société genevoise de linguistique, Geneva, Switzerland. Publisher: Librairie Droz, Geneva. 1941-- . Annual (irregular). 20-40 Fr. [70-200 p.] Last issue examined: vol. 31, 1977.

   Each volume concerns a different subject, such as MÉLANGES DE LINGUISTIQUE OFFERTS A HENRI FREI. The volumes are seldom concerned with Saussure; rather, they are inspired by and dedicated to him. Unpublished essays based on lecture notes and other research; bibliographical references; illustrations. In French or English.

   Indexed by Klapp, Köttelwesch, and MLA INTERNATIONAL BIBLIOGRAPHY.

   Subtitle in Köttelwesch:

   REVUE DE LINGUISTIQUE GÉNÉRALE

SCANTREL, FÉLIX-ANDRÉ-YVES [ANDRÉ SUARÈS] (1868-1948)

French poet

1. André Suarès. Subseries of La Revue des Lettres Modernes. Editor: Yves-Alain Favre. 1973-- . Irregular. Equivalent numbers are provided below for both the parent series (La Revue des Lettres Modernes) and the individual author series on Suarès.

Suares subseries	La Revue series	Date
No. 1	Nos. 346-50	1973
No. 2	Nos. 484-90	1976

In French. See Camus, Albert, entry 1, for a full description of La Revue des Lettres Modernes.

Indexed by BULLETIN CRITIQUE, FRENCH XX, Klapp, and MLA INTERNATIONAL BIBLIOGRAPHY.

2. Archives André Suarès. Subseries of Archives des Lettres Modernes. 1972-- . Irregular. Equivalent numbers are provided below for both the parent series (Archives des Lettres Modernes) and the individual author series on Suarès.

Suarès subseries	Archives series	Date
No. 14	No. 142	1972

In French. See Camus, Albert, entry 2, for a full description of Archives des Lettres Modernes.

Indexed by BULLETIN CRITIQUE, FRENCH XX, Klapp, and MLA INTERNATIONAL BIBLIOGRAPHY.

3. Bibliothèque André Suarès. Publisher: Minard, Paris. 1975-- . Irregular.

Each volume is centered on a specific subject--new editions and regrouping of criticism originally published in Lettres Modernes. In French.

SCHILLER, FRIEDRICH VON (1759-1805)

German poet, dramatist, historian

1. Deutsche Schillergesellschaft. VERÖFFENTLICHUNGEN (VDS). Supersedes VERÖFFENTLICHUNGEN DES SCHWÄBISCHEN SCHILLERVEREINS. Publisher: Ernst Klett, Stuttgart, Germany (BRD). 1905-37 (nos. 1-16); 1948 (no. 17)-- . Irregular. DM55. [300-650 p.] Last issue examined: vol. 30, 1974.

Each volume concerns a different subject--for example, SCHILLERS DON KARLOS (1974) or JEAN-PAUL-BIBLIOGRAPHIE (1963)--with coverage frequently extending beyond Schiller and his works. Bibliographies; portraits. In German. Vol. 31 not yet published (1978).

Indexed by MLA INTERNATIONAL BIBLIOGRAPHY.

Alternate title:

VERÖFFENTLICHUNGEN DER DEUTSCHEN SCHILLERGESELLSCHAFT

2. JAHRBUCH DER DEUTSCHEN SCHILLERGESELLSCHAFT (JDSG; JSG). Editors: Fritz Martini, Walter Müller-Seidel, Bernhard Zeller. Sponsor:

Deutsche Schillergesellschaft. Director: Walter Scheffler, Schiller-Nationalmuseum, 7142 Marbach am Neckar, Germany (BRD). Publisher: Alfred Kröner Verlag, Stuttgart, Germany (BRD). 1957-- . Annual. DM22-38. [400-700 p.] Last issue examined: vol. 21, 1977.

Long scholarly studies of the work and influence of Schiller and his contemporaries; analyses of previously unpublished works; textual, critical, and biographical approaches; occasional Schiller bibliographies; illustrations, portraits, and facsimiles. Since 1956, the JAHRBUCH has included "Jahresbericht der Deutschen Schillergesellschaft," also entitled "Die Deutsche Schillergesellschaft" (published separately, 1953-55), with news of events, members' activities, the Schiller-Nationalmuseum, and important publications and acquisitions. Cumulated index for 1957-76 (vols. 1-20). In German.

Indexed by ENGLISH LANGUAGE NOTES, Klapp, Köttelwesch, MLA INTERNATIONAL BIBLIOGRAPHY, and PHILOLOGICAL QUARTERLY.

Alternate titles:

Deutsche Schillergesellschaft. JAHRBUCH

JAHRBUCH DER SCHILLER-GESELLSCHAFT

SCHILLER-JAHRBUCH

3. Schwäbischer Schiller-Verein, Marbach-Stuttgart. RECHENSCHAFTS-BERICHT. Editor: Otto von Güntter. Publisher: Ernst Klett, Stuttgart, Germany (BRD). 1897-1941 (nos. 1-45). Annual. [70-90 p.]

Long scholarly studies of Schiller's youth, early writings, background, friendships, influence, philosophy; critical essays on contemporaries and other authors influenced by his ideas; previously unknown works, with analyses; descriptions of library holdings and acquisitions; surveys of research; lists of members. In German.

SCHNEIDER, REINHOLD (1903-58)

German poet, essayist

1. Reinhold-Schneider-Gesellschaft. MITTEILUNGEN. Publisher: Aumühle bei Hamburg, Germany (BRD). 1974 (nos. 10-11)-- . [90 p.]

Long critical articles exploring Schneider's beliefs and execution of those beliefs; biographical essays on critical periods of his life, his friendships, and his influences. In German.

Indexed by Köttelwesch.

Alternate title:

MITTEILUNGEN DER REINHOLD-SCHNEIDER-GESELLSCHAFT

2. SCHRIFTEN DER REINHOLD-SCHNEIDER-STIFTUNG. Sponsor: Reinhold-Schneider-Stiftung, Hamburg, Germany (BRD). Publisher: Freiburg, Germany (BRD). 1973-- . Irregular.

   In German.

   Alternate title:

   Reinhold-Schneider-Stiftung. SCHRIFTEN

SCHNITZLER, ARTHUR (1862-1931)

Austrian dramatist, novelist, physician

1. JOURNAL OF THE INTERNATIONAL ARTHUR SCHNITZLER RESEARCH ASSOCIATION (IASRA). Superseded by MODERN AUSTRIAN LITERATURE. Editor: Vincent LoCicero, Chatham College, Pittsburgh, Pa. 15232. Sponsor: International Arthur Schnitzler Research Association. President: Robert O. Weiss, State University of New York, Binghamton, N.Y. 03901. Publisher: State University of New York. November 1961-Winter 1967 (vols. 1-6, no. 4). Quarterly. Free with membership ($5); $3 (students); $1 per issue. [50-70 p.]

   Subjects range from analyses of Schnitzler's literary style and influence on other authors to examinations of all "vital aspects of Austrian culture." Studies of Schnitzler's Vienna, Grillparzer's works, Hofmannsthal's plays, autobiography, and film; reprints of lectures delivered at conferences; occasional bibliographies; book reviews; news and announcements of theatre symposia, members' publications and activities, MLA conferences; list of members. In English, German, or French.

   Title also in German:

   ZEITSCHRIFT DER INTERNATIONALEN ARTHUR SCHNITZLER FORSCHUNGSGESELLSCHAFT

   Alternate subtitle:

   NACHRICHTEN DER INTERNATIONALEN ARTHUR SCHNITZLER FORSCHUNGSGESELLSCHAFT

SCHOPENHAUER, ARTHUR (1788-1860)

German philosopher

1. JAHRBUCH DER SCHOPENHAUER-GESELLSCHAFT. Superseded by SCHOPENHAUER-JAHRBUCH (see entry 3). Editor: Arthur Hubscher. Sponsor: Schopenhauer-Gesellschaft. Publisher: Carl Winter, Universitatsverlag, Heidelberg, Germany (BRD). 1912-44 (vols. 1-31); suspended operation 1945-47. Annual. [200-450 p.]

Long articles investigating the biography, philosophy, and historical aspects of Schopenhauer; "Schopenhauer-Bibliographie" --brief, but with annotations; long book reviews; honorary poems; lists of members and financial reports; news notes of interest to the Gesellschaft; no index. In German. Second-hand copies available from Kraus Periodicals (1912-19, $96; 1920-69, $693); reprints from Walter J. Johnson (1912-72, $855).

Alternate title:

Schopenhauer-Gesellschaft. JAHRBUCH

2. Schopenhauer Gesellschaft. BERICHT. 1912-17 (nos. 1-6).

Discontinued as a separate publication.

3. SCHOPENHAUER-JAHRBUCH (SchopJb). Supersedes JAHRBUCH DER SCHOPENHAUER-GESELLSCHAFT (see entry 1). Editor: Arthur Hübscher. Sponsor: Schopenhauer-Gesellschaft, Beethovenstrasse 48, D-6000 Frankfurt/am/Main, Germany (BRD). Publisher: Verlag Waldemar Kramer, Frankfurt/am/Main. 1948 (vol. 32)-- . Annual. DM35-40. [135-75 p.] Last issue examined: vol. 59, 1978.

Long scholarly articles about Schopenhauer's influence in his own times and ours; annual annotated bibliography of Schopenhauer scholarship; previously unpublished material; notes about activities and acquisitions of the Schopenhauer Archivs; occasional surveys of scholarship, including one on "Schopenhauer i Polen" (vol. 57, 1976); brief notes from the editor and readers on important publications and events, and on problem areas in Schopenhauer's life and works; international contributors; facsimiles. In German.

Indexed by BIBLIOGRAPHIE DE LA LITTÉRATURE FRANÇAISE, Köttelwesch, PHILOSOPHER'S INDEX, and REVUE D'HISTOIRE LITTÉRAIRE.

Alternate title:

JAHRBUCH DER SCHOPENHAUER-GESELLSCHAFT

SCHWEITZER, ALBERT (1875-1965)

French humanitarian, physician

1. AMIS D'ALBERT SCHWEITZER. Superseded by ASSOCIATION FRANÇAISE DES AMIS D'ALBERT SCHWEITZER (see entry 2). Sponsor: Association des Amis du Dr. Schweitzer, 65, avenue de La Bourdonnais, Paris. 1954-58.

In French.

2. ASSOCIATION FRANÇAISE DES AMIS D'ALBERT SCHWEITZER. Supersedes AMIS D'ALBERT SCHWEITZER (see entry 1). Editor: R. Minder. Sponsor: Association française des Amis d'Albert Schweitzer, Cercle France-Outre-Mer, 79, Champs Elysées, 75008 Paris. New series, April 1959-(?). 2/yr. [30 p.]

   In French.

   Alternate titles:

   Amis d'Albert Schweitzer. CAHIERS

   CAHIERS DE L'ASSOCIATION FRANÇAISE DES AMIS D'ALBERT SCHWEITZER

SCOTT, SIR WALTER (1771-1832)

Scottish novelist, poet, historian, biographer

1. SIR WALTER SCOTT QUARTERLY. Editor: W. Forbes Gray. Publisher: H. and J. Pillans and Wilson, Edinburgh and Glasgow, Scotland. April 1927-January 1928 (vol. 1, nos. 1-4). Quarterly (April, July, October, January). $2.50. [50-60 p.]

   Brief essays on Scott's life, novels, short stories, religion, early critics, influence in other countries, history of Abbotsford; notes of interest to Scott enthusiasts on meetings, memorials, little-known events in Scott's life; previously unpublished letters; "Random Notes"--on Scott's travels, reading habits, friends.

SEALSFIELD, CHARLES

See Postl, Karl Anton.

SEERS, EUGÈNE [LOUIS DANTIN] (1865-1945)

Canadian poet, critic

1. CAHIERS LOUIS DANTIN. Publisher: Editions du Bien public, Trois-Rivières, Quebec, Canada. 1962-(?). Irregular. [60-160 p.] Last issue examined: no. 4, 1967.

   Previously unpublished letters from Dantin to his son; personal reminiscences; genealogy of the Seers family; announcements of new editions, with notes and descriptions, of Dantin's works.

SHAKESPEARE, WILLIAM (1564-1616)

English poet, dramatist

1. BARD: THE JOURNAL OF THE SHAKESPEAREAN AUTHORSHIP SOCIETY. Supersedes SHAKESPEAREAN AUTHORSHIP REVIEW (see entry 18). Sponsor: Shakespearean Authorship Society, London (formerly, 1922-58, the Shakespeare Fellowship). Chairman: The Reverend Francis Edwards, 114 Mount Street, London W.1. Secretary: D.W. Thomson Vessey, 10 Uphill Grove, Mill Hill, London NW7 4NJ. 1975-- . 2/yr. £5 (London members); £3 (country and overseas); £3 (libraries); £1, back issues. [40-50 p.] Last issue examined: vol. 1, no. 4, 1977.

   Official journal of the Shakespearean Authorship Society established for the purpose of seeking the truth about the authorship of the "Shakespeare" works and for promoting discussion and maintaining a library on the problem. Long (10-20 p.) studies of the autobiographical and political aspects of the works; interpretations of allusions and themes; bibliographical references; lists of books and pamphlets for sale; index every three years.

   Indexed by SHAKESPEARE JAHRBUCH (Weimar).

   Alternate subtitle:

   JOURNAL FOR STUDIES BEARING ON THE IDENTITY, LIFE, AND WORK OF THE AUTHOR OF THE SHAKESPEARE PLAYS AND POEMS

2. BULLETIN OF THE SHAKESPEARE ASSOCIATION OF JAPAN. Sponsor and publisher: Shakespeare Association of Japan, Tsubouchi Memorial Theatre Museum, Waseda University, Tokyo, Japan. October 1930-(?). Irregular (no. 2, December 1931; no. 3, January 1933). [50-60 p.]

   Critical articles on the plays, characters, and soliloquies; annual bibliography of Shakespearean studies in Japan; survey of Shakespeare performances and research in other countries; news of Shakespeare Day in Japan, radio programs, lectures, performances. In Japanese or English.

3. Deutsche Shakespeare-Gesellschaft. JAHRBUCH

   See SHAKESPEARE-JAHRBUCH, Weimar (entry 33).

4. Deutsche Shakespeare-Gesellschaft. SCHRIFTEN.

   See SCHRIFTEN DER DEUTSCHEN SHAKESPEARE-GESELLSCHAFT, Weimar (entry 14).

5. Deutsche Shakespeare-Gesellschaft. SCHRIFTENREIHE.

See SCHRIFTENREIHE DER DEUTSCHEN SHAKESPEARE-GESELLSCHAFT, West (entry 15).

6. Deutsche Shakespeare-Gesellschaft West. JAHRBUCH.

See JAHRBUCH DER DEUTSCHEN SHAKESPEARE-GESELLSCHAFT WEST (Heidelberg) (entry 9).

7. FOLGER LIBRARY NEWSLETTER. Supersedes Folger Shakespeare Library. REPORT FROM THE FOLGER LIBRARY (see entry 8). Editor: Janet Alexander. Sponsor and publisher: Folger Shakespeare Library, 201 East Capitol Street, Washington, D.C. 20003. Director: O.B. Hardison, Jr. Administered by the trustees of Amherst College, Amherst, Mass. 01002. October 1969-- . 5/yr. (October, December, February, April, June). Free or $2.50 donation. [4-6 p.] Last issue examined: vol. 9, 1978.

Comments on recent Folger Library acquisitions and new Folger publications; brief articles on subjects of bibliographical interest, such as watermarks; calendar of events at the Library, including daily poetry readings and frequent seminars; news of awards and grants, conferences, benefits, concert series, films, lectures, gifts of paintings and tapestry; report on performances throughout the United States; news of staff activities.

8. Folger Shakespeare Library. REPORT FROM THE FOLGER LIBRARY. Superseded by FOLGER LIBRARY NEWSLETTER (see entry 7). Editor: Louis B. Wright, Director, Folger Library. Sponsor and publisher: Folger Shakespeare Library, 201 East Capitol Street, Washington, D.C. 20003. 1948-61 (nos. 1-10); new series, December 1962-January 1968. Irregular. [10-14 p.]

Editorials on historical and cultural trends, state of the collection, intellectual milieu; informal accounts of recent Folger acquisitions--their contents, importance, history; comments on important publications; informal news of conferences, seminars, bookbinding problems, institutes, staff and friends, donors, visiting scholars; lists of Folger Library publications. Reprints available from the University Press of Virginia, Charlottesville.

9. JAHRBUCH DER DEUTSCHEN SHAKESPEARE-GESELLSCHAFT WEST (Heidelberg). Editors: Hermann Heuer, Freiburg i/Br., Burgunderstrasse 32, Germany (BRD); Ernst Theodor Sehrt; Rudolf Stamm. Sponsor: Deutsche Shakespeare-Gesellschaft West. Publisher: Verlag Quelle und Meyer. 1965-- . Annual. DM46; $21-23. [300-525 p.] Last issue examined: 1978-79.

Numerous long, documented studies of editions, language, motifs, translations, dramatic conventions, myth, and every aspect of Shakespeare's life, works, and times; survey of dramatic productions during the year, with names of producers and directors, dates, and places; long reviews of bibliographies, new editions, criticism from international sources; annual analytical bibliography of the previous year's scholarship (mainly in German), slightly less comprehensive in scope than that of the SHAKESPEARE-JAHRBUCH, Weimar (see entry 33); news of Gesellschaft events--JAHRESBERICHT; illustrations; index. In German, with occasional material in English.

Volume for 1964 (which carries the variant title SHAKESPEARE-JAHRBUCH, West) was called vol. 100, assuming the volume numbering of the original SHAKESPEARE-JAHRBUCH, which itself was published 1864-1963 and which continued with the volume for 1964 as an East German publication in Weimar (see SHAKESPEARE-JAHRBUCH, Weimar, entry 33). Numbering of the West German (Heidelberg) publication was dropped with 1965 and was henceforth titled only JAHRBUCH 1965, JAHRBUCH 1966, etc.

Indexed by ABSTRACTS OF ENGLISH STUDIES, ANNUAL BIBLIOGRAPHY OF ENGLISH LANGUAGE AND LITERATURE, Klapp, Köttelwesch, MLA INTERNATIONAL BIBLIOGRAPHY, and YEAR'S WORK IN ENGLISH STUDIES.

Alternate titles:

Deutsche Shakespeare-Gesellschaft West. JAHRBUCH

JAHRBUCH DER SHAKESPEARE-GESELLSCHAFT (West)

SHAKESPEARE-JAHRBUCH, Heidelberg/West

10. JAHRBUCH DER SHAKESPEARE-GESELLSCHAFT (East).

See SHAKESPEARE-JAHRBUCH, Weimar (entry 33).

11. JAHRBUCH DER SHAKESPEARE-GESELLSCHAFT (West).

See JAHRBUCH DER DEUTSCHEN SHAKESPEARE-GESELLSCHAFT WEST (Heidelberg) (entry 9).

12. NEW-SHAKESPEAREANA: AN INTERNATIONAL REVIEW OF SHAKESPEAREAN AND DRAMATIC STUDY. Supersedes SHAKESPEARIANA (see entry 63). Sponsor: Shakespeare Society of New York, 36 East Hampton Place, Brooklyn, New York, N.Y. Publisher: Shakespeare Press, Westfield, N.J., and Unionist-Gazette Association, Somerville, N.J. September 1901-December 1911 (vols. 1-10, no. 4). Quarterly. $2.50. [30-75 p.]

Long textual and critical studies; long scholary book reviews; "Marginalia"--news on auctions, Society activities all over the world, performances; list of books received; illustrations and facsimiles; advertisements; indexes to each volume.

Reprints available from AMS Press, and Walter J. Johnson; second-hand copies from Kraus Periodicals ($250). Microfilm available from Walter J. Johnson ($45).

Alternate subtitles:

A CRITICAL, CONTEMPORARY, AND CURRENT REVIEW OF SHAKESPEAREAN AND ELIZABETHAN STUDIES

A TWENTIETH CENTURY REVIEW OF SHAKESPEAREAN AND DRAMATIC STUDY

13. New Shakespere Society, London. PUBLICATIONS. Published for the Society by Kegan Paul, Trench, Trübner, in London. 1874-92 (series 1-8, except for series 5, which was never published).

Several series on different projects: numerous reprints, but also authorship problems, interpretive works, old-spelling Shakespeare, parallel texts, allusion books, English mysteries, transactions of the Society, SHAKESPERE'S ENGLAND (series 6), criticism of editions of plays, previously unpublished works, revised and corrected editions. Reprints available from Kraus Reprint ($643) and from Walter J. Johnson ($479). Microfiche available from Walter J. Johnson ($99).

14. SCHRIFTEN DER DEUTSCHEN SHAKESPEARE-GESELLSCHAFT, Weimar. Superseded by SCHRIFTENREIHE (see entry 15). Publisher: Georg Reimer, Berlin, Germany (BDR). 1904-12 (nos. 1-4). Irregular (a series).

A series of scholarly monographs devoted to a single aspect of Shakespeare's works; portraits; index. In German or English.

Alternate title:

Deutsche Shakespeare-Gesellschaft. SCHRIFTEN

15. SCHRIFTENREIHE DER DEUTSCHEN SHAKESPEARE-GESELLSCHAFT, West (Bochum). Supersedes SCHRIFTEN (see entry 14). Sponsor: 1904-63, Deutsche Shakespeare-Gesellschaft; since 1964, Deutsche Shakespeare-Gesellschaft West. Publisher: various publishers, most recently, Verlag Quelle und Meyer. New series, 1931-- . Irregular (a series). [200-300 p.] Last issue examined: vol. 12, 1975.

Scholarly monographs devoted to a single aspect of Shakespeare's works; portraits; index. In German or English.

Alternate title:

Deutsche Shakespeare-Gesellschaft. SCHRIFTENREIHE

16. SHAKESPEARAKAN: AN ARMENIAN YEARBOOK OF SHAKESPEARE. Editor: Rouben Zarian. Sponsor: Armenian Centre of Shakespearian

Studies. Publisher: Armenian Academy of Sciences, Yerevan, Armenia, USSR. 1966-- .

Long critical essays on Shakespeare's life, works, influence on the public, translations, performances; notes on research conferences and festivals; bibliographies. Title in Armenian and Russian; text in Armenian.

17. SHAKESPEAREAN. Publisher: Stratford-upon-Avon, England. May 1895-98 (nos. 1-33).

Official organ of the New York Shakespeare Society in Europe.

18. SHAKESPEAREAN AUTHORSHIP REVIEW. Supersedes SHAKESPEARE FELLOWSHIP QUARTERLY (see entry 29); superseded by BARD (entry 1). Editors: G.M. Bowen and R.M.D. Wainewright, 25, Montagu Square, London W1H 1RE. Sponsor: Shakespearean Authorship Society, London (before January 1959, the Shakespeare Fellowship). Spring 1959-75 (nos. 1-29). 2/yr. Free with membership (£1); $1.20 (libraries). [24 p.] Circulation: 200.

Devoted chiefly to the perpetuation of documentary evidence that Edward de Vere, 17th Earl of Oxford (1550-1604), was author of the works credited to Shakespeare. Brief critical articles, such as those on de Vere's poems, to show the resemblance between his style and that in the works generally attributed to Shakespeare; frequent book reviews; reports of lectures, meetings, the annual dinner of the Society, members' activities, books for sale; reprints; no index.

19. SHAKESPEAREAN QUARTERLY: A JOURNAL DEVOTED TO SHAKESPEAREAN STUDY AND A RECORD OF THE PROFESSIONAL AND AMATEUR PERFORMANCES OF THE PLAYS. Editors: Hector Bolitho; Norman Campbell, Country Press Chambers, 178 Castlereagh Street, Sydney, Australia. Publisher: Sydney, Australia. January 1922-October 1924 (vols. 1-3, no. 4). [40-45 p.]

Brief articles and notes from Australian, English, and American sources on current productions of Shakespeare's plays; news from Stratford; illustrations and photographs.

20. SHAKESPEAREAN RESEARCH AND OPPORTUNITIES (SRO). Supersedes SHAKESPEAREAN RESEARCH OPPORTUNITIES (see entry 21). Editor: W.R. Elton, Ph.D. Program in English, Graduate Center, City University of New York, 33 West 42nd Street, New York, N.Y. 10036. Sponsor: Modern Language Association of America. 1968/69 (no. 4)-- . Irregular. $10 (individuals); $20 (institutions). [200-260 p.] Circulation: 1,000. Last issues examined: nos. 7-8, 1972-74, published in 1975.

Aims to be a guide to opportunities for Shakespeare research--includes scholarly papers on textual, editorial, interpretive, historical, and philosophical problems in Shakespeare's works; book reviews and bibliographies in every issue; annual annotated bibliography of work in progress in thirty countries around the world--arranged by title of play, subject, and author; list of books received; annotated selective list of books, articles, and dissertations pertaining to Shakespeare's Renaissance intellectual milieu (80-120 p., edited by W.R. Elton); other special bibliographies, including one by T.H. Howard-Hill, "Textual Criticism and Bibliography: A Selective Bibliography for Students of English" (nos. 7-8, 1972-74); indexes. No. 9 not yet published (1978).

Indexed by ABSTRACTS OF ENGLISH STUDIES, ANNUAL BIBLIOGRAPHY OF ENGLISH LANGUAGE AND LITERATURE, MLA INTERNATIONAL BIBLIOGRAPHY, and YEAR'S WORK IN ENGLISH STUDIES.

Alternate title (incorrect);

SHAKESPEAREAN RESEARCH OPPORTUNITIES

21. SHAKESPEAREAN RESEARCH OPPORTUNITIES (SRO). Superseded by SHAKESPEAREAN RESEARCH AND OPPORTUNITIES (see entry 20). Editor: W.R. Elton. Sponsor: Department of English, University of California, 4045 Canyon Crest Drive, Riverside, Calif. 92502. 1965-67 (nos. 1-3). Irregular. [200-260 p.]

Aims to be "of maximum help to the working Shakespearean." Includes the annual report of the Modern Language Association conference, "Opportunities for Research in Shakespearean Studies"--scholarly papers on problem areas and surveys of opportunities for research in Shakespearean and Renaissance studies; annual international annotated bibliography of Shakespearean work in progress; special bibliographies, including several on library holdings; summaries of progress on any Shakespeare topic and of problems in any area requiring investigation; notes and queries; comments on Shakespeare scholars, past and present; list of books received; subject and name index.

Title occasionally, and erroneously, appears as SHAKESPEARE RESEARCH OPPORTUNITIES.

22. Shakespeare Association (London). PAPERS. Published for the Shakespeare Association by Oxford University Press. 1917-(?). Irregular. [25-40 p.]

23. Shakespeare Association (London). SHAKESPEARE SURVEY. Editor: Sir I. Gollancz. Sponsor: Shakespeare Association (London). 1923-28 (vols. 1-3).

Each volume is concerned with a specific subject, such as SHAKESPEARE IN SERBIA (vol. 3).

24. SHAKESPEARE ASSOCIATION BULLETIN (SAB). Superseded by the SHAKESPEARE QUARTERLY (see entry 43). Editor: Robert M. Smith, Department of English, Lehigh University, Bethlehem, Pa. 08015. Sponsor: Shakespeare Association of America, National Arts Club, 15 Gramercy Park, New York, N.Y.; later, Lehigh University. June 1924-October 1949 (vols. 1-24, no. 4). Irregular, 1924-27; quarterly, 1928-49 (January, April, July, October). $3. [20-60 p.]

Scholarly studies on all aspects of Shakespeare's life and work --textual, explicative, historical, source, characters; an extremely valuable, annual classified bibliography, by subject and title, with subject and name index; "Quarterly Reviews" which surveys and criticizes selected new books; notes and comments on Society activities, Shakespeare performances, festivals, collections; reports of meetings, and lists of members; portraits. Second-hand copies available from Kraus Periodicals (1924-49, $480); reprints from Walter J. Johnson ($480). Available on microfilm from Walter J. Johnson ($70).

Indexed by ANNUAL BIBLIOGRAPHY OF ENGLISH LANGUAGE AND LITERATURE and MLA INTERNATIONAL BIBLIOGRAPHY.

Alternate title:

Shakespeare Association of America. BULLETIN

25. Shakespeare Association of Japan. BULLETIN. Sponsor and publisher: Shakespeare Association of Japan, Tsubouchi Memorial Theatre Museum, Waseda University, Tokyo, Japan. October 1930-April 1936 (nos. 1-6). 5 yen. [50-60 p.]

Articles concerning stage productions, character interpretations, annual festivals, Japanese interest in Shakespeare, impressions abroad; Shakespeare bibliography in Japan; notes and news; occasional illustrations. In English or Japanese.

26. Shakespeare Association Papers. Published for the Shakespeare Association by H. Milford, Oxford University Press. 1917-(?). Irregular (a series).

Lectures, papers, catalogs, and studies prepared for the Shakespeare Association by various scholars.

27. Shakespeare Club, Cincinnati. JOURNAL OF THE CINCINNATI SHAKESPEARE CLUB. 1860-72 (vols. 1-5).

News of interest to members.

28. SHAKESPEARE FELLOWSHIP NEWS-LETTER. Superseded by SHAKESPEARE FELLOWSHIP QUARTERLY (see entry 29). Editor: Charles W. Barrell. Sponsor during the years of World War II: Shakespeare Fellowship, American Branch, New York. December 1939-October 1943 (vols. 1-4, no. 6). 6/yr. Free with membership ($2.50). [12-16 p.]

Devoted to the question of the authorship of the Shakespeare plays and to promotion of the claim they were written by Edward de Vere, 17th Earl of Oxford. Brief articles, comments, and news items--all with biographical, textual, or historical arguments to enforce the stated beliefs of the editors; brief book reviews; occasional illustrations; annual index.

Alternate spelling: SHAKESPEARE FELLOWSHIP NEWS LETTER.

29. SHAKESPEARE FELLOWSHIP QUARTERLY. Supersedes SHAKESPEARE FELLOWSHIP NEWS-LETTER (see entry 28); superseded by SHAKESPEAREAN AUTHORSHIP REVIEW (see entry 18). Sponsor: Shakespeare Fellowship, American Branch, New York. January 1944-1948 (vols. 5-9, no. 2). Quarterly (January, April, July, October).

Devoted chiefly to the perpetuation of documentary evidence that Edward de Vere, 17th Earl of Oxford (1550-1604), was the author of the works credited to Shakespeare. Brief notes, news items, and comments; illustrations; annual index.

30. SHAKESPEARE-IANA. Editors: Arthur Brickman and Douglas Bonnier. Sponsor: Arthur Brickman Associates, 1133 Broadway, New York, N.Y. 10010. Publisher: Renee Memorial Press. 1965-(?). Annual.

An elementary subject-indexed checklist of critical works and study guides; facsimiles.

31. Shakespeare Institute. University of Birmingham. REPORT OF THE INTERNATIONAL SHAKESPEARE CONFERENCE. Sponsor and publisher: University of Birmingham, Stratford-upon-Avon, in association with the Shakespeare Birthplace Trust, the Royal Shakespeare Theatre, and the British Council. 194(?)-- . Every two yrs. Free. [20-30 p.] Last issue examined: no. 16, 1974.

Report of the International Shakespeare Conference, which is held every second summer at the Shakespeare Institute. Each session concentrates on a specific area, such as SHAKESPEARE AND THE IDEAS OF HIS TIME (1974). Abstracts of papers read at the conference; list of officers and members attending; schedule of social events; announcement of subject and dates of the forthcoming conference; occasional photographs. No index.

32. SHAKESPEARE-JAHRBUCH. Heidelberg/West.

A variant title for JAHRBUCH DER DEUTSCHEN SHAKESPEARE-GESELLSCHAFT WEST (Heidelberg) (see entry 9).

33. SHAKESPEARE-JAHRBUCH, Weimar (SJ, before 1964; since 1964, SJW). Editors: Anselm Schlösser, Humboldt-Universität zu Berlin, 108 Berlin 8,

Unter den Linden 11, Germany (BRD); Armin-Gerd Kuckhoff, 701 Leipzig Theaterhochschule, Germany (DDR). Sponsor: Deutsche Shakespeare-Gesellschaft, Weimar, Berlin. Publisher: Verlag Hermann Böhlaus. 1864-- . Annual. Price varies--DM30. [300-450 p.] Last issue examined: vol. 114, 1978.

Long scholarly essays on every aspect of Shakespeare's life and works, his times, his influences, and his contemporaries; comprehensive (80 p.) international, analytical bibliography in every volume--covers about eighty periodicals; annual survey of dramatic performances; numerous long book reviews in every volume; news of Society events and of Shakespeare scholarship all over the world; international contributors; illustrations and facsimiles; index. Index for 1865-1963 (vols. 1-99). Text in German or English. Reprints available from Kraus Reprint (1865-1935, $1,623; 1950-63, $285); and from Walter J. Johnson (1865-1967, $1,395), microfiche (1865-1914, $175).

Additional information:

Vols. 1-59/60 (1865-1924) titled the Society's JAHRBUCH. Vols. 59/60-82/83 (1924-50) called also "neue Folge." Vols. for 1950-63 published in Heidelberg by Quelle und Meyer; early volumes published by Reimer in Berlin.

In 1964, another Shakespeare annual (a West German publication sponsored by Deutsche Shakespeare-Gesellschaft West) began publication in Heidelberg under the title SHAKESPEARE-JAHRBUCH, Heidelberg/West (for further information see the title which it assumed in 1965: JAHRBUCH DER DEUTSCHEN SHAKESPEARE-GESELLSCHAFT WEST, entry 9).

Indexed by ABSTRACTS OF ENGLISH STUDIES, ANNUAL BIBLIOGRAPHY OF ENGLISH LANGUAGE AND LITERATURE, ENGLISH LANGUAGE NOTES, Köttelwesch, MLA INTERNATIONAL BIBLIOGRAPHY, and YEAR'S WORK IN ENGLISH STUDIES.

Alternate titles:

Deutsche Shakespeare-Gesellschaft. JAHRBUCH

JAHRBUCH DER DEUTSCHEN SHAKESPEARE-GESELLSCHAFT (EAST)

JAHRBUCH DER SHAKESPEARE-GESELLSCHAFT (East)

34. Shakespeare Memorial Theatre. A PHOTOGRAPHIC RECORD. 1948-(?).

35. SHAKESPEARE MONTHLY AND LITERARY COMPANION. Editor: John Phin, 16 Thomas Street, New York, N.Y. March-April 1906 (nos. 1-2). $.50. [20-30 p.]

Informal brief articles explaining difficult passages or references;

book notices; news of relevant publications; brief book reviews; queries and answers; announcements of meetings.

36. SHAKESPEARE MUSEUM. Publisher: Leipzig, Germany (DDR). April 1870-February 1874 (nos. 1-20).

37. SHAKESPEARE NEWS. Editor: Jiro Ozu. Sponsor and publisher: Shakespeare Society of Japan, 18 Naka-machi, Shinjuku-ku, Tokyo, Japan. Summer 1961-- . 3/yr. Free with membership (3,000 yen, Japan; $5; $20, institutions).

Brief articles; reports of performances, seminars, conferences, and foreign visitors; book reviews. In Japanese. Subscription also includes SHAKESPEARE STUDIES (Tokyo) (see entry 58).

38. SHAKESPEARE NEWSLETTER (ShN). Editor and publisher: Louis Marder, Department of English, Box 4348, University of Illinois at Chicago Circle, Chicago, Ill. 60680. March 1951-- . 6/yr. (September-May). Two-year subscriptions only: $8, U.S.; $9 elsewhere. [8-12 p.] Circulation: 2,800. Last issue examined: vol. 28, no. 155, 1978.

Interested in factual rather than interpretive material. News of grants, awards, the World Shakespearean Congress, the International Shakespeare Association, American conferences, auctions and sales, films, television programs, performances, new international publications, and Shakespeare festivals; occasional bibliographies; reviews of books and periodical articles, with several contributing editors; editorial comments on current critical works and projects; abstracts of recently completed works, including dissertations and papers delivered at scholarly meetings; special issues, such as "Film and Shakespeare," "Marxist Criticism of Shakespeare," and "Teaching Shakespeare"; notes of current interest, such as the fact that membership in the Shakespeare Association of America, which is now $30, includes the benefits of reduced rates for the SHAKESPEARE NEWSLETTER, SHAKESPEARE QUARTERLY (entry 43), SHAKESPEARE STUDIES (entry 59), and SHAKESPEARE SURVEY (entry 60); also such specialized information as a continuing glossary of textual and bibliographical terms used in Shakespeare scholarship; advertisements. Annual cumulated index by name, subject, and title. Reprints available from Johnson Reprint and from Walter J. Johnson (1951-64, vols. 1-14, $60).

Indexed by ABSTRACTS OF ENGLISH STUDIES, ANNUAL BIBLIOGRAPHY OF ENGLISH LANGUAGE AND LITERATURE, MLA INTERNATIONAL BIBLIOGRAPHY, and YEAR'S WORK IN ENGLISH STUDIES.

39. SHAKESPEARE ON FILM NEWSLETTER. Editors: Bernice W. Kliman

DINING WITH William Shakespeare

MADGE LORWIN

A highly original and totally functional cookbook, a charming social commentary, a feast for the eyes and the intellect as well as the palate, Madge Lorwin's *DINING WITH WILLIAM SHAKESPEARE* is truly a book for all seasons.

Mrs. Lorwin has gathered together thirteen complete Elizabethan feast menus based upon quotations from Shakespeare's plays and included the original recipe for each dish along with her own meticulously researched and completely workable modern equivalent. Each menu is followed by a fascinating and informative essay on some aspect of the cuisine or social customs of the period.

Profusely illustrated, *DINING WITH WILLIAM SHAKESPEARE* is a book to delight not only those interested in food and cooking, but also Shakespeare buffs and enthusiasts for English social history.

448 Pages, Illustrated, $14.95

"The research is superb, the recipes authentic and workable, the text fascinating. Give it to your local Shakespeare buff for Christmas, and to yourself just for the fun of it."

--*Publishers Weekly*

Quantity $ Amount

DINING WITH WILLIAM SHAKESPEARE.......

by Madge Lorwin

shipping & handling ____ .75

Total $____

Please ship to:

NAME ____

ADDRESS ____

CITY & STATE ____

Mail with Chec.. to
ATHENEUM PUBLISHERS
122 E. 42nd St.
Dept. AC New York, N.Y. 10017

MISSISSIPPI
Folklore
REGISTER

The Editors of *The Mississippi Folklore Register* announce a special issue (Vol. 10, No. 2) devoted to Shakespeare and folklore edited by Philip C. Kolin.

Single copies may be purchased for $3.00. Orders should be sent to the Editors, *Mississippi Folklore Register*, University of Southern Mississippi, Southern Station Box 418, Hattiesburg, Mississippi, 39401.

Introduction: Shakespeare, Folklore, and Literary Criticism
—*Philip C. Kolin*

Folklore Stress in Shakespeare
—*Louis Marder*

Folklore Ritual as Comic Catharsis and *The Merry Wives of Windsor*
—*C. J. Gianakaris*

"Let's talk of graves": *Othello*, V.ii.5
—*David M. Bergeron*

"Despised in Nativity": Unnatural Birth in Shakespeare
—*Linwood E. Orange*

What Did Caliban Look Like?
—*Barry Gaines* and *Michael Lofaro*

Riddles and the Tragic Structure of *Macbeth*
—*Phyllis Gorfain*

A Bibliography of Scholarship on Shakespeare and Folklore
—*Philip C. Kolin*

(Baruch College), 70 Glen Cove Drive, Glen Head, N.Y. 11545; and Kenneth S. Rothwell, Department of English, University of Vermont, Burlington, Vt. 05401. Sponsor and publisher: University of Vermont. December 1976-- . 2/yr. (Fall, Spring). $2 (U.S.); $2.50 (elsewhere). Circulation: 140. Last issue examined: vol. 3, 1979.

Information useful to teachers, scholars, and others interested in the Shakespearean plays as they appear on film and television; abstracts of books, articles, and papers; detailed bibliographies on specific directors, plays (such as Orson Welles's FALSTAFF), the film collection at the Folger Library, and guides to rental sources for films and explanatory narratives for use as teaching aids; information on work in progress, meetings, and subject content of Shakespeare-on-film courses being conducted throughout the country; notes and queries; rebuttals; reviews of books and articles.

40. SHAKESPEARE PICTORIAL: A MONTHLY ILLUSTRATED CHRONICLE OF EVENTS IN SHAKESPEARELAND. Superseded by SHAKESPEARE PICTORIAL: AN INTIMATE CHRONICLE OF EVENTS IN SHAKESPEARELAND (see entry 41). Publisher: E.P. Ray, Stratford-upon-Avon, England. May (July/October?) 1928-September 1939 (nos. 1-139). Monthly. [15 p.]

Brief notes on performances, social events, tourist problems, need for money to build adequate facilities. Picture portfolio, 1930--(?). Supplement, AVON NEWS, 26 March 1930-21 April 1931.

Alternate title, 23 May-13 June 1928: SHAKESPEARE PICTORIAL AND VISITORS' WEEKLY GUIDE.

41. SHAKESPEARE PICTÓRIAL: AN INTIMATE CHRONICLE OF EVENTS IN SHAKESPEARELAND. Supersedes SHAKESPEARE PICTORIAL: A MONTHLY ILLUSTRATED CHRONICLE (see entry 40); incorporated with STRATFORD-UPON-AVON SCENE, September 1946. Publisher: E.P. Ray, Stratford-upon-Avon. June 1940-September 1946. Monthly (irregular).

News of Shakespeare performances, celebrations, and town events.

Alternate title:

SHAKESPEARE PICTORIAL OCCASIONAL PAPERS

42. SHAKESPEARE PROBLEMS. Editors: A.W. Pollard and J. Dover Wilson. Sponsor: new series, New York University, Washington Square, Graduate School of Fine Arts, New York, N.Y. 10003. Publisher: Cambridge, England. 1920-41 (vols. 1-6); new series, April 1952-(?) (vols. 7-8).

43. SHAKESPEARE QUARTERLY (SQ). Supersedes SHAKESPEARE ASSOCIA-

TION BULLETIN (see entry 24). Editor: John F. Andrews, Folger Shakespeare Library, 201 East Capitol Street, S.E., Washington, D.C. 20003. Sponsor: Shakespeare Association of America, 1950-72; publisher, since July 1972: Folger Shakespeare Library. January 1950-- . Quarterly (Winter, Spring, Summer, Autumn). $12.50, $24/two yrs., $35/three yrs. (American); $15, $28/two yrs., $41/three yrs. (foreign). [100-120 p.] Circulation: 3,000. Last issue examined: vol. 29, 1978.

Editorial policy since 1976 has been to stress ways in which Shakespeare "contributes to our own cultural milieu . . . Shakespeare in His Time and Ours."

Long (20 p.) articles and short notes on every aspect of Shakespeare's life, works, and influence; annual, analytical, annotated world bibliography--the best in the field--of bibliographies, general studies, biographies, new editions, critical books and articles, reviews, abstracts of dissertations, all theatrical productions, and conferences, with index of titles, subjects, and names, edited by Harrison T. Meserole since 1976; news, notes, and queries from international sources; annual review of Shakespeare festivals, usually in the autumn issue; long scholarly book reviews of the most important publications of the year; occasional special issues, including one on the production of Shakespeare's plays in our current theatre (Winter 1976); occasional photographs and reproductions; international contributors; cover illustrations; annual index in the autumn by title, names of characters and historical persons, authors, and reviewers (discontinued with vol. 26, 1975). Cumulated index for 1950-64 (vols. 1-15). Second-hand copies available from Kraus Periodicals (1950-68, $633); reprints from AMS Press; reprints from Walter J. Johnson (1950-66, $595), and microfiche ($175).

Indexed by ABSTRACTS OF ENGLISH LITERATURE, AMERICAN LITERATURE, ANNUAL BIBLIOGRAPHY OF ENGLISH LANGUAGE AND LITERATURE, BIOGRAPHY INDEX, FRENCH VII, HUMANITIES INDEX, INDEX TO BOOK REVIEWS IN THE HUMANITIES, Köttelwesch, Leary, MLA ABSTRACTS, MLA INTERNATIONAL BIBLIOGRAPHY, SOCIAL SCIENCES AND HUMANITIES INDEX, VICTORIAN STUDIES, and YEAR'S WORK IN ENGLISH STUDIES.

44. SHAKESPEARE QUARTERLY (Austria). Editor: Richard Flatter, 3, Bramham Gardens, London S.W.5. Sponsor: Austrian Shakespeare Society. Publisher: Austrian State Printing Office. Summer 1948-(?). £1.1. [120 p.]

Long essays on the plays, characters, famous actresses and actors, interpretive problems, and musical adaptations; long book reviews; numerous illustrations and photographs. In English.

45. SHAKESPEARE RENAISSANCE. Publisher: Tokyo, Japan. October 1933-May 1935.

In Japanese.

46. SHAKESPEARE REPOSITORY. Editor: James H. Fennell, London. Publisher: T. Scott, 1, Warwick Court, High Holburn, Middlesex, England. 1853 (nos. 1-4).

Brief articles on problem areas in Shakespeare's life and works --spelling of his name, his will, his ancestry, manuscripts, theatres of his day, early translations; reprints of early reviews, lectures, and proclamations.

Running title: FENNELL'S SHAKESPEARE REPOSITORY.

Subtitle:

INFORMATION RESPECTING SHAKESPEARE AND HIS FAMILY, HIS WORKS, &., COLLECTED FROM OLD MANUSCRIPTS, SCARCE BOOKS, OLD NEWSPAPERS, MAGAZINES, &.

47. SHAKESPEARE REVIEW: A MONTHLY MAGAZINE DEVOTED TO LITERATURE AND THE DRAMA. Editor: A.K. Chesterton. Publisher: Avon Press, 9 Union Street, Stratford-upon-Avon, England. May-October 1928 (nos. 1-6). [70-90 p.]

Brief, informal critical articles; comments on performances; short book reviews; news notes; letters to the editor.

48. SHAKESPEARE-SCHRIFTEN. Editor: Richard Flatter. Several series published under this title by several different publishers: Walter Krieg Verlag, Vienna; Zurich; Schurmann und Klagges, Bochum, Germany (DDR). 1954-(?). [50 p.]

Each small volume is concerned with a specific subject, such as GOETHE UND SHAKESPEARE (vol. 4). In German.

49. Shakespeare Seminar, Stratford, Ontario.

See STRATFORD PAPERS ON SHAKESPEARE (entry 66).

50. Shakespeare Society, London. PUBLICATIONS. Sponsor: Shakespeare Society, London. Publisher: W. Skeffington. 1841-53 (nos. 1-48).

Title page: "Papers of the Shakespeare Society, being contributions too short in themselves for separate publication." Concerned with Renaissance drama, especially Shakespeare's contemporaries and influences; commentaries on works by Shakespeare, Jonson, and others; studies of memoirs, characters, staging, and plots. Reprints available from Kraus Reprint ($562) and from Walter J. Johnson ($395). See also New Shakespere Society, London (entry 13).

51. Shakespeare Society of New South Wales. ANNUAL REPORT OF THE COUNCIL. Publisher: Sydney, Australia. 1924-- .

52. Shakespeare Society of New York. PUBLICATIONS. 1885-1926 (nos. 1-14). Irregular. [40-50 p.]

Long scholarly papers read before the Society, such as those on ecclesiastical law in HAMLET, or on linguistics; facsimiles. Reprints available from Walter J. Johnson ($75).

53. Shakespeare Society of Philadelphia. PUBLICATIONS. Sponsor: Shakespeare Society of Philadelphia, 206 South 4th Street, Philadelphia, Pa. 1860-1903 (nos. 1-5).

Account of banquet proceedings, with relevant quotations, toasts, and menus from Shakespeare's works. Occasionally spelled "Shakespere" Society of Philadelphia.

54. SHAKESPEARE'S PROCLAMATION. Editor: R. Thad Taylor. Sponsor: Shakespeare Society of America at the Globe, 1107 North Kings Road, Los Angeles, Calif. 90069. October 1968-- . Quarterly. $5 (out-of-state and students); $15 (active); $100 (patrons). [12 p.]

Informal news and notes of past and future Shakespeare performances; information about clubs, lectures, workshops; illustrations.

55. SHAKESPEARE STAGE: THE QUARTERLY BULLETIN OF THE SHAKESPEARE STAGE SOCIETY. Editor: C.B. Purdom. Sponsor: Shakespeare Stage Society, 96 Charlotte Street, London W.1. June 1953-September/December 1954 (nos. 1-6/7). Quarterly. [8-10 p.]

Comments on open-stage productions of Shakespeare--their history and essentials, their news of performances, lectures, relevant publications; international coverage.

56. SHAKESPEARE STUDIES. Monograph Series. Studies in the Bibliography of Renaissance Dramatic Texts. Editor: J. Leeds Barroll III, Department of English, University of Tennessee, Knoxville, Tenn. 37916. Sponsor: Center for Shakespeare Studies, Vanderbilt University, Nashville, Tenn. 37203. Publisher: vols. 1-2, William C. Brown; thereafter, Burt Franklin, New York. December 1969-(inactive but not officially ceased). Annual. Price varies. Last issue examined: vol. 2, 1970.

Detailed studies of Renaissance texts, especially Shakespeare's, to determine the extent of their accuracy and corruption--the aim being to arrive at a version which is as close as possible to the author's final intent.

57. SHAKESPEARE STUDIES (Cincinnati) (ShakS).

See SHAKESPEARE STUDIES: AN ANNUAL GATHERING OF RESEARCH, CRITICISM, AND REVIEWS (entry 59), which was inaugurated under the sponsorship of the University of Cincinnati in 1965.

58. SHAKESPEARE STUDIES (Tokyo) (ShStud). Editor: Jiro Ozu. Sponsor and publisher: Shakespeare Society of Japan, 18 Nakamachi, Shinjuku-ku, Tokyo, Japan. 1962-- . Annual. Free with membership (3,000 yen, Japan); elsewhere $5 (individuals), $20 (institutions). [50-170 p.] Last issue examined: vol. 12, 1973-74.

Long scholarly studies on structure, textual and printing problems, relationship with other authors, characters, themes, philosophy; occasional bibliographical surveys; no index. Subscription also includes SHAKESPEARE NEWS (Tokyo) (see entry 37). Vol. 13 not yet published (1978).

Indexed by ANNUAL BIBLIOGRAPHY OF ENGLISH LANGUAGE AND LITERATURE, MLA INTERNATIONAL BIBLIOGRAPHY, and YEAR'S WORK IN ENGLISH STUDIES.

59. SHAKESPEARE STUDIES: AN ANNUAL GATHERING OF RESEARCH, CRITICISM, AND REVIEWS (ShakS). Editor: J. Leeds Barroll, III, Department of English, University of Tennessee, Knoxville, Tenn. 37916. Sponsor: 1965-67, University of Cincinnati, Cincinnati, Ohio 45221; 1968-70, Center for Shakespeare Studies, Vanderbilt University, Nashville, Tenn. 37203; 1971-74, University of South Carolina, Columbia, S.C. 29208. Publisher: since 1975, Burt Franklin, New York. 1965-- . Annual. $25. [400-500 p.] Last issue examined: vol. 11, 1978.

Numerous long scholarly essays on characters, plots, motifs, historical background, structure, language, and every aspect of Shakespeare's life and work; numerous long book reviews on Shakespeare-related scholarship; list of books received; occasional facsimiles; no index.

Indexed by ABSTRACTS OF ENGLISH STUDIES, ANNUAL BIBLIOGRAPHY OF ENGLISH LANGUAGE AND LITERATURE, ESSAY AND GENERAL LITERATURE INDEX, MLA INTERNATIONAL BIBLIOGRAPHY, and YEAR'S WORK IN ENGLISH STUDIES.

60. SHAKESPEARE SURVEY: AN ANNUAL SURVEY OF SHAKESPEARIAN STUDY AND PRODUCTION (ShS). Editors: Vols. 1-20, Allardyce Nicoll; vol. 21-- , Kenneth Muir, University of Liverpool, Box 147, Liverpool L69 3BX, England. Sponsor: vols. 1-18, University of Birmingham, University of Manchester, Royal Shakespeare Theatre, Shakespeare Birthplace Trust. Publisher: Cambridge University Press, London and New York. 1948-- . Annual. Price varies ($6-17). [200 p.] Last issue examined: vol. 31, 1978.

Each volume is concerned with a specific subject, such as

Shakespeare's problem plays (vol. 25, 1972). Numerous scholarly essays in each volume; survey of scholarship entitled "The Year's Contributions to Shakespearian Study"; occasional illustrations; author and title index. Cumulative index for vols. 1-10 in vol. 11, for vols. 11-20 in vol. 21. Secondhand copies available from Kraus Periodicals (1948-64, $189); reprints from Walter J. Johnson (1948-71, $295). Another publication with the same title was published in London from 1923 to 1928--see entry 23: Shakespeare Association (London). SHAKESPEARE SURVEY.

Indexed by ABSTRACTS OF ENGLISH STUDIES, ANNUAL BIBLIOGRAPHY OF ENGLISH LANGUAGE AND LITERATURE, ENGLISH LANGUAGE NOTES, ESSAY AND GENERAL LITERATURE INDEX, HUMANITIES INDEX, MLA INTERNATIONAL BIBLIOGRAPHY, and YEAR'S WORK IN ENGLISH STUDIES.

61. SHAKESPEARE-TAGE WEIMAR. Sponsor: Deutsche Shakespeare-Gesellschaft. 1971.

In German.

62. SHAKESPEARE TRANSLATION. Chairman: Toshikazu Oyama, Department of English, Seijo University, 6-1-20 Seijo, Setagaya-ku, Tokyo. Sponsor: Investigative Committee on Shakespeare Translation of the World Shakespeare Congress. Publisher: Yushodo Shoten, 29 San-ei-cho, Shinjuku-ku, Tokyo. 1974-- . Annual. $22. [100-125 p.] Last issue examined: vol. 4, 1977.

Annual publication on Shakespeare translation. Collections of long studies on the theory and principle, practice and methodology; historical surveys; research in problem areas; specific studies of passages in Shakespeare's works; examinations of translations of specific titles; surveys of the state of Shakespeare translations in various countries; international contributors; annual index. Cumulated index to vols. 1-3 in vol. 3. In English, with passages in numerous other languages. Distributed in the United States by AMS Press.

63. SHAKESPEARIANA: A CRITICAL AND CONTEMPORARY REVIEW OF SHAKESPEARIAN LITERATURE. Superseded by NEW-SHAKESPEAREANA (see entry 12). Sponsor: Shakespeare Society of New York, vols. 7-10. Publisher: Leonard Scott, Philadelphia, Pa. November 1883-93 (vols. 1-10, no. 90). Monthly, 1883-89; quarterly, 1890-93. [50-60 p.]

Long studies of stage performances, problems in stage presentations, characters, old and new editions, editorial and textual problems; book reviews; notes and queries; "Miscellany"--current events, plays, lectures, libraries; reports of meetings; illustrations, portraits, and charts; cumulative name, title, and subject index for each annual volume. Reprints available from AMS Press, Walter J. Johnson, or Kraus Periodicals ($225).

Title varies, 1883-89:

SHAKESPEARIANA

64. SHAKESPERE NEWSPAPER. 1847 (nos. 1-2).

65. Shakspere Society of Philadelphia.

See Shakespeare Society of Philadelphia (entry 53).

66. STRATFORD PAPERS ON SHAKESPEARE. Editor: B.A.W. Jackson, Department of English, McMaster University. Sponsor: Prepared for the Shakespeare Seminar, which is sponsored by the Universities of Canada in cooperation with the Stratford Festival Theatre and McMaster University. Publisher: McMaster University Library Press, Mills Memorial Library, McMaster University, Hamilton, Ontario L8S 4L6, Canada. 1960-69. Irregular. $2.50-6. [110-240 p.] Last issue examined: vol. 5, 1968-69.

Collections of papers delivered at the annual sessions of the Shakespeare seminars in Stratford, Ontario--studies on structure, characters, fashions in production, reception in other countries and centuries, and other aspects of the plays; well-known contributors, such as Frye, Coghill; no index. Available in microform from Irish University Microforms, Shannon, Ireland.

Alternate title:

Shakespeare Seminar, Stratford, Ontario

67. STRATFORD-UPON-AVON SCENE.

See SHAKESPEARE PICTORIAL: AN INTIMATE CHRONICLE OF EVENTS IN SHAKESPEARELAND (entry 41).

68. SWAN OF AVON: A QUARTERLY DEALING WITH NEW SHAKESPEAREAN RESEARCH. Publisher: Melander Shakespeare Society, Santa Barbara, Calif. March-September 1948 (vol. 1, nos. 1-3). [20-45 p.]

SHAW, GEORGE BERNARD (1856-1950)

Irish dramatist, critic, social reformer

1. CALIFORNIA SHAVIAN. Editor: E.S. Feldman, 1933 South Broadway, Los Angeles, Calif. 90007. Sponsor: Shaw Society of California. 1958-(?). 6/yr. Free to members. Circulation: 250.

No reply to query.

2. INDEPENDENT SHAVIAN: JOURNAL OF THE NEW YORK SHAVIANS.

Editor: Mrs. Vera Scriabine, 14 Washington Place, New York, N.Y. 10003. Sponsor: New York Shavians. October 1962-- . 3/yr. (Fall, Winter, Spring). Membership dues: $10 (individuals within 50 miles of Manhattan); $5 (U.S.); $3.50 (elsewhere). Subscriptions: $3 (U.S.); $3.50 (elsewhere). [16 p.] Circulation: 200. Last issue examined: vol. 15, 1977.

Brief informal biographical and critical studies of Shaw and his circle; occasional reprints of Shaw letters and other inaccessible material; book, film, and play reviews in every issue; collectors' news; announcements of festivals, programs, films, Society meetings, members' activities; sketches, photographs, and illustrations; annual index, usually in the fall. Indexes for 1962-67 (vols. 1-5), 1968-69 (vols. 6-7); thereafter annually. Available in microfilm from University Microfilms International and in reprint from Kraus Reprint.

Indexed by ABSTRACTS OF ENGLISH STUDIES, ANNUAL BIBLIOGRAPHY OF ENGLISH LANGUAGE AND LITERATURE, ENGLISH LITERATURE IN TRANSITION, VICTORIAN STUDIES, and YEAR'S WORK IN ENGLISH STUDIES.

3. SHAVIAN: THE JOURNAL OF THE SHAW SOCIETY. Supersedes the Shaw Society, London. BULLETIN (see entry 12). Editor: 1953-65, Eric J. Batson; since 1965, T.F. Evans, High Orchard, 125 Markyate Road, Dagenham, Essex RM8 2LB, England. Managing editor: Eric F.J. Ford. Sponsor: Shaw Society, 45, Steeplestone Close, London N.18; later, 3 Chestnut Court, Middle Lane, London N.8. New series, December 1953 (no. 1/no. 51; no. 2/no. 52, etc.)-- . 2-3/yr. $5. [35-40 p.] Circulation: 600. Last issue examined: vol. 5, no. 2, 1975.

"Seeks to promote a wider interest in and deeper understanding of the work of Bernard Shaw." Brief notes and long articles on Shaw's interests, technique, ideas, influence, plots, characters, and relationship with other writers; book reviews in every issue; bibliographies; news of performances, films; photographs. Cumulative indexes for vol. 1 (December 1953-October 1959) and vol. 2 (1960-63). Reprints available from Walter J. Johnson (1953/59-69, vols. 1-4, no. 1, $36); microform available from University Microfilms. The Shaw Society also publishes and distributes SHAVIAN TRACT (see entry 4) and OCCASIONAL PAPERS (see entry 11). Vol. 6 not yet published (1978).

Indexed by INDEX TO BOOK REVIEWS IN THE HUMANITIES, MLA INTERNATIONAL BIBLIOGRAPHY, TWENTIETH CENTURY LITERATURE, and VICTORIAN STUDIES.

4. SHAVIAN TRACT. Sponsor: Shaw Society, London. 1950-58 (nos. 1-6); resumed publication (?).

Available from Walter J. Johnson ($6). See SHAVIAN (entry 3).

THE SHAW REVIEW
VOL. XIX, No. 1
JANUARY, 1976
PUBLISHED BY THE PENNSYLVANIA STATE UNIVERSITY PRESS

Alternate title:

Shaw Society (London). TRACT

5. SHAW BULLETIN. Supersedes Shaw Society of America. BULLETIN (see entry 14); superseded by SHAW REVIEW (see entry 8). Editors: William D. Chase, Dan H. Laurence, and Stanley Weintraub. Sponsors: 1952-56, Shaw Society of America; 1957-58, Pennsylvania State University Press. May 1952-September 1958 (vol. 1, no. 3-vol. 2, no. 6). Irregular, 1951-55; 3/yr. (January, May, September), 1956-58. Free with membership ($5); $3 (libraries). [15-30 p.]

   Long studies and brief notes on new editions, influences, interviews, films, theatre, collections of Shaviana; "Continuing Checklist of Shaviana," including primary and secondary works; report on Shaw plays in performances, with casts and evaluations; letters from England on publications and performances; news of meetings.

   Indexed by FRENCH VII and MLA INTERNATIONAL BIBLIOGRAPHY.

6. SHAW BULLETIN (London).

   See alternate title (entry 12): Shaw Society (London). BULLETIN.

7. SHAW CHILDREN IN AMERICA. Publisher: Jacksonville, Fla. October 1959-(?). Quarterly.

8. SHAW REVIEW (ShawR). Supersedes SHAW BULLETIN (see entry 5). Editor: Stanley Weintraub, S234 Burrowes Building South, University Park, Pa. 16802. Sponsor: Pennsylvania State University Press, 215 Wagner Building, University Park, Pa. 16802. January 1959 (vol. 2, no. 7)-- . 3/yr. (January, May, September). $6.75. [45-65 p.] Circulation: 700. Last issue examined: vol. 22, 1979.

   Welcomes scholarship that "either explicitly or implicitly adds to or alters our understanding of Shaw and his milieu . . . its personalities, works, relevance to his age and ours." Long (5-20 p.) critical articles on sources, individual titles, influences; "Continuing Checklist of Shaviana" in every issue, edited and annotated by John R. Pfeiffer--new editions, books, articles, pamphlets, dissertations, recordings; long book reviews; reprints of lectures; special issues, such as "Shaw and Woman," and the twenty-fifth anniversary issue, 1950-75; occasional illustrations; index in the last issue of each year. Cumulated index for 1950-75. Available in microform from University Microfilms International. Reprints available from Kraus Reprint (1951-65, $75; 1966-70, $35) and from Walter J. Johnson (1951-70, $95).

Indexed by ABSTRACTS OF ENGLISH STUDIES, AMERICAN HUMANITIES INDEX, ANNUAL BIBLIOGRAPHY OF ENGLISH LANGUAGE AND LITERATURE, ENGLISH LANGUAGE NOTES, INDEX TO BOOK REVIEWS IN THE HUMANITIES, MLA INTERNATIONAL BIBLIOGRAPHY, MODERN DRAMA (Toronto), TWENTIETH CENTURY LITERATURE, VICTORIAN STUDIES, and YEAR'S WORK IN ENGLISH STUDIES.

9. SHAW'S CORNER. Sponsor: Shaw Society of America, New York (?). November 1954-(?). Irregular (no. 2, July 1956; no. 3, October 1956).

10. SHAW-SCRIPT: A QUARTERLY IN THE SHAVIAN ALPHABET. Editor: Kingsley Read, Abbots Morton, Worcester, England. Publisher: Abbots Morton, England. 1963-65 (nos. 1-8). Quarterly. $2. [16 p.]

    Explanation of the Shaw alphabet, with the purpose of informing, entertaining, and practicing its use. Brief notes; letters to the editor; news; extracts; occasional illustrations. Text is in Shaw-script. "Ever-circulators" pass the issues around. Title also in Shavian alphabet.

11. Shaw Society (England). OCCASIONAL PAPERS. Sponsor: Shaw Society. (?)-(?).

    See SHAVIAN (entry 3).

12. Shaw Society (London). BULLETIN. Superseded by SHAVIAN (see entry 3). Editor: Eric J. Batson. Sponsor and publisher: Shaw Society (London), 45, Steeplechase Close, London N.18. September 1946-September 1953 (nos. 1-50). Free with membership ($2). [15 p.]

    Reminiscences; previously unpublished letters; programs of the Society, Society publications, members' activities, news of forthcoming meetings; comments on new publications; book reviews.

    Indexed by FRENCH VII.

    Alternate title:

    SHAW BULLETIN (London)

13. SHAW SOCIETY NEWSLETTER. Sponsor: Shaw Society of Chicago. October 1956-(?).

    Alternate spelling: SHAW NEWS LETTER.

14. Shaw Society of America. BULLETIN. Superseded by SHAW BULLETIN (see entry 5). Sponsor and publisher: Shaw Society of America, P.O. Box 871, Flint, Mich. 48500. February-Autumn, 1951 (vol. 1, nos. 1-2). Irregular. $5. [10-15 p.]

Purpose: "to study and interpret G.B. Shaw's writings, work, and personality; to make him more widely understood and appreciated; and to provide a meeting ground for those who admire and respect the man." Brief articles on Shaw's life, influence, and friendships; reminiscences; continuing checklist of current Shaviana; report of Shaw's plays in current performance; news of Society meetings and of members' publications.

Alternate title:

BULLETIN OF THE SHAW SOCIETY OF AMERICA

SHELLEY, PERCY BYSSHE (1792-1822)

English poet

See Keats, John.

SJÖBERG, BIRGER (1885-1929)

Swedish poet, critic, journalist

1. Birger Sjöberg Sällskapet (BSS). SKRIFTER. Publisher: Albert Bonniers Vorlag, Sveavägen 56, S-111 34 Stockholm, Sweden. 1962-- . Annual. S kr 40-50. [200 p.] Last issue examined: 1977.

    Long scholarly biographical and critical articles on Sjöberg's youth and influences, his relationship with other authors, the prevailing motifs in his works; examinations of specific titles; textual studies; previously unpublished letters, works, and other pertinent documents; primary bibliographies; bibliographies of Sjöberg scholarship in Sweden and other countries. In Swedish.

    Indexed by MLA INTERNATIONAL BIBLIOGRAPHY.

SPENSER, EDMUND (1522-99)

English poet

1. SPENSER NEWSLETTER. Editor: Foster Provost, Department of English, Duquesne University, Pittsburgh, Pa. 15219. Sponsor: Department of English, University of Massachusetts at Amherst, and Holyoke Community College. 1968-- . 3/yr. (Winter, Spring, Summer). $2 (individuals); $3 (institutions). [20 p.] Circulation: 600. Last issue examined: vol. 9, 1978.

    Specializes in news of Spenser-related research and events; complete coverage of Spenser-related publications, including abstracts of books, dissertations, and articles in journals;

report of work published, forthcoming, and in progress; numerous brief book reviews; report of Spenser at MLA, including summaries of the papers; announcement of future seminars and conferences; queries; annual index in winter issue. Available in microform.

The Spenser Society (inaugurated 1976) plans to publish a membership and work-in-progress booklet and to adopt as its official organ the SPENSER NEWSLETTER, which will be expanded to include brief articles and notes (contact Thomas P. Roche, Department of English, Princeton University, Princeton, N.J. 08540).

Indexed by AMERICAN HUMANITIES INDEX and MLA INTERNATIONAL BIBLIOGRAPHY.

SPINOZA, BARUCH (1632-77)

Dutch philosopher

1. MEDEDELINGEN VANWEGE HET SPINOZAHUIS. Editor and publisher: E.J. Brill, Leiden, the Netherlands. Sponsor: Spinozahuis, Rijnsburg, the Netherlands. 1934-- . Irregular. F2-5.50. [10-35 p.] Last issue examined: no. 27, 1971.

   Each issue concerns a specific subject, such as HEGEL EN SPINOZA (1971); brief studies of Spinoza's life or works. In Dutch.

2. SPINOZA IN AMERICA. Superseded by SPINOZA QUARTERLY (see entry 3). 1931-32 (vol. 1).

3. SPINOZA QUARTERLY. Supersedes SPINOZA IN AMERICA (see entry 2); superseded by BIOSOPHICAL REVIEW. 1932-33 (vol. 2).

4. SPINOZISTISCH BULLETIN. Editor: J.H. Carp, Spinozahuis, Paviljoensgracht 72/74, 's-Gravenhage, the Netherlands. Sponsor: Societas Spinozana, Afdeeling, the Netherlands. Publisher: Uitgave van J. Ploegsma-Zeist. September 1938-August 1940 (nos. 1-4). Irregular. [15-30 p.]

   Long essays on Spinoza's philosophy and his relationship to other authors. Index for 1938-40 in no. 4, 1940. In Dutch.

SPIRE, ANDRÉ (1868-1966)

French poet

1. CAHIERS ANDRÉ SPIRE. Editor: Rougerie, 11, rue des Sapeurs, 87000 Limoges, France. 1972-- .

Long critical essays on Spire's life and writing; previously unpublished works. In French.

Indexed by BIBLIOGRAPHIE DE LA LITTÉRATURE FRANÇAISE.

STAËL, MADAME DE, ANNE LOUISE, BARONNE DE (1766-1817)

French author

1. CAHIERS STAËLIENS (CahiersS). Supersedes OCCIDENT ET CAHIERS STAËLIENS (see entry 2). Editor: S. Balayé. Sponsor: Société des Études staëliens, 148, rue de Longchamp, 75016 Paris. Publisher: Éditions Victor Attinger, Paris. New series, March 1962-- . Irregular. 10-30 Fr. [40-90 p.] Last issue examined: vol. 23, 1978.

   Official organ of the Society. Long studies of Madame de Staël's importance and her contribution to her era; essays on her relationship with other writers, as Benjamin Constant (q.v.), her writing style, the problems of publication and government, and the state of the theatre during her lifetime; annotated bibliographies of new editions, critical works, and reviews; previously unpublished letters and extracts from contemporary correspondence that give insight into Madame de Staël's personality and intelligence; long book reviews for important scholarship; brief annotations for other new publications; news of conferences, colloquia, and Society activities; list of members. In French.

   Indexed by BIBLIOGRAPHIE DE LA LITTÉRATURE FRANÇAISE, Klapp, MLA INTERNATIONAL BIBLIOGRAPHY, and REVUE D'HISTOIRE LITTÉRAIRE.

2. OCCIDENT ET CAHIERS STAËLIENS. Superseded by CAHIERS STAËLIENS (see entry 1). Old series, 1929-39.

   In French.

3. PUBLICATIONS DE LA SOCIÉTÉ D'ÉTUDES STAËLIENNES. Publisher: Éditions Victor Attinger, Paris. 1938-(?). Irregular. [40 p.]

   Every volume is devoted to a different subject, such as bibliographies or portraits; no index. In French.

STEIN, GERTRUDE (1874-1946)

American poet, novelist, critic

1. LOST GENERATION JOURNAL (LGJ). Editor and publisher: Tom Wood, American University, Cairo, Egypt. Executive editor and business manager: J. Catherine O'Bryant, School of Journalism, Southern Illinois University, Carbondale, Ill. 62901. Sponsor: Literary Enterprises, c/o

Michael Zacharias, P.O. Box 99, Claremore, Okla. 74017. May 1973-- . 3/yr. $5 (U.S.); $6 (Canada, Mexico); $7 (elsewhere). [30-40 p.] Last issue examined: vol. 5, 1977.

The JOURNAL's "mission is to trace the steps of Lost Generation people, to stimulate the survivors into further expression, and to strive for the creation of an archival holding worthy of a great era." Interested in scholarship not only on Stein, who is credited with originating the expression "Lost Generation," but also on Pound, Hemingway, and other Americans who went to Europe and lived there between World Wars I and II. Contains numerous informal articles centering mainly on the life of the authors, their interrelationships, and their contribution to the literature of the times; reminiscences; informal notes on library holdings; "Between the Bookends"--brief book reviews; numerous photographs and other art work; annual index in last issue of each year.

Indexed by AMERICAN HUMANITIES INDEX, ANNUAL BIBLIOGRAPHY OF ENGLISH LANGUAGE AND LITERATURE, MLA INTERNATIONAL BIBLIOGRAPHY, and TWENTIETH CENTURY LITERATURE.

STEINBECK, JOHN (1902-68)

American novelist, short-story writer

1. REPORT OF THE JOHN STEINBECK BIBLIOGRAPHICAL SOCIETY. Editor and publisher: Tetsumaro Hayashi, Department of English, Ball State University, Muncie, Ind. 47306. March 1968-- .

   News of collections, new publications, members' activities.

2. Steinbeck Monograph Series. Editor: Tetsumaro Hayashi. Sponsor: John Steinbeck Society of America and English Department, Ball State University, Muncie, Ind. 47306. 1971-- . Annual. $1.50. [30-50 p.] Last issue examined: vol. 8, 1978.

   Publications on one specific aspect of Steinbeck scholarship, such as JOHN STEINBECK: A GUIDE TO THE DOCTORAL DISSERTATION--A COLLECTION OF DISSERTATION ABSTRACTS, 1946-1969 (vol. 1), and STEINBECK CRITICISM: A REVIEW OF BOOK-LENGTH STUDIES, 1939-1973 (vol. 4). Indexes.

3. STEINBECK NEWSLETTER. Superseded by STEINBECK QUARTERLY (see entry 4). Editors: Tetsumaro Hayashi, English Department, Ball State University, Muncie, Ind. 47306; and Robert DeMott, English Department, Kent State University, Kent, Ohio 44240. Sponsor: John Steinbeck Bibliographical Society and English Department, Ball State University. March 1968-Summer 1969 (vols. 1-2, no. 2). Free. Irregular.

Brief biographical and critical articles; bibliographies of critical works; notes on new editions, translations, acquisitions, members' activities; book reviews.

4. STEINBECK QUARTERLY. Supersedes STEINBECK NEWSLETTER (see entry 3). Editors: Tetsumaro Hayashi, English Department, Ball State University, Muncie, Ind. 47306; and Robert DeMott, English Department, Kent State University, Kent, Ohio 44240. Sponsor: until 1977, the John Steinbeck Society of America and Ball State University; since 1978, the Steinbeck Society International. Fall 1969 (vol. 2, no. 3)-- . Quarterly through 1975; since 1976, 3/yr. (Winter, Spring, Summer). $10 (includes the Steinbeck Monograph Series [see entry 2], and the annual membership directory). [32 p.] Circulation: 350. Last issue examined: vol. 11, 1978.

   Articles on Steinbeck's early publications, travels, criticism in other countries, new biographical material, and every aspect of his life and work; reminiscences; annual bibliographic issue on Steinbeck and related fields; occasional bibliographies on special subjects; occasional book reviews; occasional abstracts of dissertations and articles; reports of work in progress; news of auctions, publications, films, and members' activities; annual index. Reprints available from Kraus Reprint (1968-70, $19); microfilm from University Microfilms International.

   Indexed by ABSTRACTS OF ENGLISH STUDIES, AMERICAN HUMANITIES INDEX, ANNUAL BIBLIOGRAPHY OF ENGLISH LANGUAGE AND LITERATURE, FRENCH XX, and TWENTIETH CENTURY LITERATURE.

STEINER, RUDOLF (1861-1925)

Austrian philosopher

1. BEITRÄGE ZUR RUDOLF STEINER GESAMTAUSGABE. Supersedes NACHRICHTEN DER RUDOLF STEINER-NACHLASSVERWALTUNG (see entry 3). Editor: Wolfram Groddeck. Sponsor: Rudolf Steiner-Nachlassverwaltung, Rudolf-Steiner Halde, CH 4143 Dornach, Switzerland. Publisher: Rudolf Steiner Verlag, Haus Duldeck, CH 4143 Dornach, Switzerland. Easter 1970 (no. 29)-- . 3-4/yr. (irregular). DM22.50; 18 Fr. [30-70 p.] Last issue examined: nos. 49-50, 1975.

   Long bibliographical and textual studies of the holdings of the Steiner Archivs; numerous reprints of inaccessible Steiner works; previously unpublished material; news of activities; occasional photographs, numerous facsimiles; no index. In German. No. 51 not yet published (1978).

   Alternate subtitle:

   VERÖFFENTLICHUNGEN AUS DEM ARCHIV DER RUDOLF STEINER-NACHLASSVERWALTUNG, Dornach

2. BULLETIN DES AMIS DE L'ÉCOLE RUDOLF STEINER. Publisher: 22 bis, rue d'Alesia, Paris. 1958-- .

3. NACHRICHTEN DER RUDOLF STEINER-NACHLASSVERWALTUNG. Superseded by BEITRÄGE ZUR RUDOLF STEINER GESAMTAUSGABE (see entry 1). Editor: Wolfram Groddeck. Sponsor and publisher: Rudolf Steiner-Nachlassverwaltung, Haus Duldeck, CH 4143 Dornach, Switzerland. March 1949-69 (nos. 1-27/28). Irregular. DM4; 4 Fr. [30-40 p.]

   Essays describing the holdings of the Steiner Archivs; numerous reprints of Steiner works; previously unpublished material; news notes of interest to Steiner scholars; facsimiles; no index. Includes VERÖFFENTLICHUNGEN AUS DEM ARCHIV. In German.

   Alternate titles:

   NACHRICHTEN MIT VERÖFFENTLICHUNGEN AUS DEM ARCHIV

   Rudolf Steiner-Nachlassverwaltung. NACHRICHTEN

4. RUDOLF-STEINER SCHOOL: A QUARTERLY EXPONENT OF ANTHROPOSOPHY IN EDUCATION. Publisher: New York: October 1928-April 1930 (vols. 1-3, no. 2).

STENDHAL

See Beyle, Marie Henri.

STERNE, LAURENCE (1713-68)

English novelist, clergyman

1. SHANDEAN. Editors: Kenneth Monkman and J.C.T. Oates. Sponsor: Laurence Sterne Trust in association with the Scolar Press. Publisher: Scolar Press, London. Fall 1978-- . Annual. £4. [100-150 p.]

   Devoted to original work by and about Laurence Sterne and his circle. Facsimiles and transcripts of hitherto unpublished manuscripts and letters; anonymous newspaper articles ascribed to Sterne; bibliographical studies of Sterne's sources; biographical, textual, and interpretive essays.

STEVENS, WALLACE (1879-1955)

American poet

1. WALLACE STEVENS JOURNAL: A PUBLICATION OF THE WALLACE STEVENS SOCIETY. Editor: R.H. Deutsch, Department of English, California State University, 18111 Nordhoff Street, Northridge, Calif.

91324. Associate editor: W.T. Ford. Sponsor: Wallace Stevens Society. Spring 1977-- . Quarterly. $10. [45-50 p.] Last issue examined: vol. 2, 1978.

Scholarly articles on Stevens' life, personality, and poetic themes; reminiscences; catalogs of library collections; annotated current bibliography of articles; book reviews; news of exhibitions, book sales, work in progress, dissertations, and MLA conventions; abstracts of dissertations.

Indexed by AMERICAN LITERATURE.

2. WALLACE STEVENS NEWSLETTER (WSN). Editor: W.T. Ford, Northwestern University Library, Evanston, Ill. 60201. October 1969-April 1971 (vols. 1-2, no. 2). 2/yr. (October, April). $4/two yrs. [8-15 p.] Circulation: 250.

Brief informal essays of a critical, historical, or biographical nature; bibliographical notes; current annotated bibliography; abstracts of dissertations; book reviews; news on work in progress, recent publications of interest to Stevens scholars, book prices, and recordings; letters to the editor; occasional photographs.

Indexed by ABSTRACTS OF ENGLISH STUDIES and ANNUAL BIBLIOGRAPHY OF ENGLISH LANGUAGE AND LITERATURE.

STIFTER, ADALBERT (1805-68)

Austrian novelist, painter, poet

1. ADALBERT STIFTER-ALMANACH. Sponsor: Adalbert-Stifter-Gesellschaft, Vienna, Austria. Publisher: early issues, Paul Zsolnay, Vienna; later issues, Österreichische Verlagsanstalt, Innsbruck, Austria. 1937-42; suspended publication, 1942-47; 1947-53(?). [100-125 p.]

Scholarly essays on Stifter, his ideas, art, and interaction with other authors and artists; comments on previously unpublished works; illustrations, portraits, facsimiles; no index. In German.

Alternate title:

STIFTER-ALMANACH

2. Adalbert Stifter-Gesellschaft. MITTEILUNGSBLATT. Sponsor: Adalbert Stifter-Gesellschaft, Munich, Germany (BRD). October 1949-- . Irregular.

News; bibliographies. In German.

3. Adalbert Stifter-Gesellschaft. SCHRIFTENREIHE. Sponsor: Adalbert Stifter-Gesellschaft, Munich. 1949-- . [400 p.]

Each volume concerns a different subject. In German.

Alternate title:

SCHRIFTENREIHE DER ALDALBERT STIFTER-GESELLSCHAFT

4. Adalbert Stifter-Institut des Landes Oberösterreich. SCHRIFTENREIHE. Editors: early volumes, Aldemar Schiffkorn; later volumes, Alois Grossschopf. Sponsor: Adalbert Stifter-Institut, Graz, Austria. Publishers: early issues, H. Carl, Nürnberg, Germany (BRD); later issues, Oberösterreichischer Landesverlag, Linz, Austria. 1950(?)-- . Irregular. AS 70-250. [40-70 p.] Last issue examined: vol. 30, 1977.

Monographs on Stifter and such related subjects as ADALBERT STIFTER UND PRAG (no. 24) or ZU DEN QUELLEN DES RECHTSDENKEN BEI ADALBERT STIFTER (no. 25); bibliographies; illustrations and portraits; no index. In German.

Alternate title:

SCHRIFTENREIHE DES ADALBERT STIFTER-INSTITUTS DES LANDES OBERÖSTERREICH

5. Adalbert Stifter-Institut des Landes Oberösterreich. VIERTELJAHRESSCHRIFT (ASILO). Editor: Herlinde Rigby. Sponsor and publisher: Adalbert Stifter-Institut, Untere Donaulände 6/II, 4020 Linz/Donau, Austria. 1952-- . Quarterly. DM8; $4.65. [25-75 p.] Last issue examined: vol. 26, 1977.

Biographical and critical studies of Stifter's life and works; textual studies in preparation for a critical edition; brief book reviews; close studies of individual titles; notes on new books, articles, dissertations, reviews in newspapers, lectures, films, auctions, activities at the Stifter-Gesellschaft in Vienna and the Stifter-Institut in Linz; news on members' publications and activities; bibliographical references; illustrations; excellent facsimiles; portraits. In German, with occasional English contributions.

Indexed by Köttelwesch and MLA INTERNATIONAL BIBLIOGRAPHY.

Alternate title:

VIERTELJAHRESSCHRIFT DES ADALBERT STIFTER-INSTITUT DES LANDES OBERÖSTERREICH

6. LITERARISCHE ADALBERT-STIFTER-GESELLSCHAFT. Sponsor: Literarische Adalbert-Stifter-Gesellschaft. Publisher: J. Standa, Augsburg, Germany (BRD). 1925-31 (nos. 1-2, 4-10, 12, 14, 16, 18, 21-25, 26, 31-32; gaps were not published). [30-70 p.]

Each issue is a study of a specific subject concerning either Stifter or others related to him. In German.

Alternate subtitle:

SUDETENDEUTSCHE SAMMLUNG

7. STIFTER-JAHRBUCH (StJb). Editor: Helmut G. Preidel. Sponsor: Adalbert Stifter-Verein, Munich, Germany (BRD). Publisher: Delp'sche Verlagsbuchhandlung, Munich. 1949-64 (vols. 1-8); new series, 1971 (vol. 9)-- . Irregular. [160-290 p.]

Not confined to Stifter, although some essays do explain his contributions and influence; coverage extends to many areas of art and history--museum holdings, archaeological finds, manuscripts, architecture, linguistic problems; facsimiles, illustrations, and portraits. In German.

Indexed by Köttelwesch and MLA INTERNATIONAL BIBLIOGRAPHY.

Subtitle:

JAHRBUCH DER WISSENSCHAFTLICHEN ABTEILUNG

STORM, THEODOR (1817-88)

German poet, author of novellas

1. SCHRIFTEN DER THEODOR-STORM-GESELLSCHAFT (SSG). Editor: Karl Ernst Laage and Volkmar Hand. Sponsor: Theodor-Storm-Gesellschaft, im Storm-Haus, Wasserreihe 31, 225 Husum, Germany (BRD). Publisher: Westholsteinische Verlagsanstalt Boyens, Heide in Holstein, Germany (BRD). 1952-- . Annual. Free with membership (DM20). [60-175 p.] Last issue examined: vol. 26, 1977.

Scholarly studies and collections of essays on Storm--his life, works, friends, and influence, with most volumes specializing on a specific subject, such as THEODOR STORM UND IWAN TURGENJEW (1967); occasional comprehensive bibliographies covering several years' research, such as "Storm-Bibliographie, 1967-73" (1974); occasional bibliographies of primary works, library holdings, new editions, and critical works; bibliographical references; previously unpublished works; reports of research ("Storm-Forschung"); news of Gesellschaft events and of activities in the Storm-Haus; lists of members; occasional illustrations and portraits. In German.

Indexed by Köttelwesch and MLA INTERNATIONAL BIBLIOGRAPHY.

Alternate title:

Theodor-Storm-Gesellschaft. SCHRIFTEN

STREHLENAU, NIKOLAUS NIEMBSCH VON [NIKOLAUS LENAU] (1802-50)

Hungarian poet

1. LENAU-ALMANACH. Editor: Nikolaus Britz. Sponsor: Internationale Lenau-Gesellschaft, Vienna, Austria. Publisher: Kulturamt der Stadt Stockerau, Vienna, Austria. 1959-68. Annual. [70-150 p.]

   Long articles on Lenau's life and works--his language, themes, symbolism, style, and love of music and nature; textual studies toward a new edition of his works; close studies of the poems; book reviews; notes on the annual meeting, programs, and members; photographs; no index. In German or Hungarian.

   Indexed by Köttelwesch.

   Alternate title:

   L'ALMANACH

2. LENAU-FORUM: VIERTELJAHRESSCHRIFT FÜR VERGLEICHENDE LITERATURFORSCHUNG (LenauF). Editor: Nikolaus Britz, Lercenfelderstrasse 14, Alle A-1080 Vienna, Austria. Sponsor and publisher: Internationale Lenau-Gesellschaft, Vienna. 1969-- . Quarterly (published in one volume). AS 125; DM34; $6.50. [70-140 p.] Last issue examined: vol. 6, 1974.

   Long articles on Lenau's work, his friendships, the influence of his travels and reading, his FAUST, DON JUAN, and other titles; coverage extends to other authors and literatures, particularly of East European countries; reprints of papers read at the Gesellschaft's annual meetings; bibliographical references; contributors from East European countries; no index. In German. Vol. 7 not yet published (1978).

   Indexed by Köttelwesch and MLA INTERNATIONAL BIBLIOGRAPHY.

STRINDBERG, AUGUST (1849-1912)

Swedish dramatist, novelist, poet

1. MEDDELANDEN FRÅN STRINDBERGSSÅLLSKAPET (MfS). Sponsor: Strindberg Society, Stockholm, Sweden. 1945-- . 2/yr. (May, December). Last issue examined: vol. 48, 1971.

   Long critical studies of Strindberg's poems, characters, plots, and style; brief interpretive notes; articles on his influence and reception in his own and other countries and on his place in literary history; annual bibliography of Strindberg scholarship. Cumulative index for 1945-64 (nos. 1-36). In Swedish.

   Indexed by MLA INTERNATIONAL BIBLIOGRAPHY.

Alternate title:

Strindbergssällskapet. SKRIFTER

STUART, JESSE (1907-)

American poet, novelist, short-story writer

1. Jesse Stuart Creative Writing Workshop. Editor: Jesse Stuart, W-Hollow, Greenup, Ky. 42244. Coordinator: L.J. Hortin. Sponsor: Murray State University, Murray, Ky. 42071. April 1970-- . Annual. $3.25. Circulation: 700-1,000.

   Title of issues: "1st Summer," "2nd Summer," etc. See also JACK LONDON NEWSLETTER, entry 1 under London, Jack.

SUARÈS, ANDRÉ

See Scantrel, Félix-André-Yves.

SWEDENBORG, EMANUEL (1688-1772)

Swedish theologian, scientist, philosopher

1. NEW PHILOSOPHY: A QUARTERLY MAGAZINE DEVOTED TO THE INTEREST OF THE SWEDENBORG SCIENTIFIC ASSOCIATION. Publisher: Lennart Alfelt, Bryn Athyn, Pa. 19009. 1898-- . Quarterly. Free with membership ($4).

2. STUDIA SWEDENBORGIANA. Editor: William R. Woofenden. Sponsor: Swedenborg School of Religion, 48 Sargent Street, Newton, Mass. 02158. January 1974-- . 2/yr. $.75; free to libraries. [50 p.] Circulation: 500.

   Interested in exchanging and disseminating contemporary views on Swedenborg's science, philosophy, and theology. Contains long articles; translations from Swedenborg's Latin; bibliographies; occasional book reviews; occasional illustrations.

3. SWEDENBORG-BÜCHEREI. Publisher: Swedenborg Verlag, Zurich. 1956-- . Irregular. $4. Last issue examined: vol. 6, 1975.

4. Swedenborg Society, London. REPORT. No. 58 (1968). [40 p.]

5. Swedenborg Society, London. TRANSACTIONS. Sponsor: Swedenborg Society, London. 1934-- . Irregular. [60-65 p.] Last issue examined: no. 3, 1936.

   Lectures delivered at the international Swedenborg congresses.

SWIFT, JONATHAN (1667-1745)

English satirist

See Pope, Alexander.

TAGORE, RABINDRANATH (1861-1941)

Indian poet, novelist, story writer, essayist, dramatist, painter

1. Rabindranath Tagore Memorial Lectures. Publisher: University of California Press, 2223 Fulton Street, Berkeley, Calif. 94720. 1962-(?). Irregular. [100-200 p.]

   Includes bibliographical lectures.

2. TAGORE CENTENARY BULLETIN. Sponsor: Rabindranath Tagore Centenary Committee, c/o Ministry of Scientific Research and Cultural Affairs, New Delhi, India. August 1960-September 1961 (nos. 1-4). Quarterly (irregular).

   Brief accounts of international celebrations--symposia, special editions, films, radio programs, exhibitions of Tagore's works, recordings, receptions, opening of museums and theatres, and performances of plays.

3. Tagore Lectures. Sponsor: Tagore Centenary Lectureship, London, in cooperation with the Indian Council for Cultural Relations, New Delhi, and the University of London, School of Oriental and African Studies. Publisher: School of Oriental and African Studies, University of London, London. 1961-(?). [70 p.]

   Reprints of lectures, such as on "Tagore--the Humanist."

4. TAGORE STUDIES. Editor: Somendra Nath Bose. Sponsor: Miss Pronoti Mukherji, Tagore Research Institute, 4 Elgin Road, Calcutta-20, India. 1969-- . Annual. Rs5.00; $2.

   Essays; illustrations.

TARDIVEAU, RENÉ M.A. [RENÉ BOYLESVE] (1867-1926)

French novelist

1. AMIS DE RENÉ BOYLESVE. Sponsor: Amis de René Boylesve, Tours, France. March 1953-55 (nos. 1-2). Quarterly.

   In French.

2. HEURES BOYLESVIENNES. Sponsor and publisher: Groupe Loches-

Descartes des Amis de René Boylesve, Loches, France. June 1969-- . Irregular. $8. [15-70 p.] Last issue examined: no. 10, 1974.

Reprints of lectures delivered at conferences in honor of René Boylesve, his life, and his works. Several issues by Abbé Georges Marchais with bibliographies and indexes. In French. No. 11 not yet published (1978).

TASSO, TORQUATO (1544-95)

Italian poet

1. STUDI TASSIANI (ST). Sponsor: Centro di Studi Tassiani, Bergamo, Italy. Publisher: Tipografia Editrice Secomandi, Bergamo. 1951-- . Annual. L.3.000. Last issue examined: vol. 22, 1972.

   Long scholarly articles on the life, works, style, and influence of Tasso--his lyrics, friendships, epic theory, and criticism; occasional comprehensive enumerative bibliographies of Tasso scholarship; annual bibliographical surveys of recent studies; previously unpublished works; translations. Cumulative indexes for vols. 1-10 and vols. 11-20. Scattered volumes at present available in reprint from Walter J. Johnson ($12.50 per volume).

   Indexed by MLA INTERNATIONAL BIBLIOGRAPHY.

2. STUDI TASSIANI/QUADERNI. Sponsor: Centro Tassiano, Bergamo, Italy. 1963-- . Irregular. [200 p.] Last issue examined: vol. 2, 1974.

   Monographs on aspects of Tassiani's works.

   Alternate title:

   QUADERNI DEGLI "STUDI TASSIANI"

TEILHARD DE CHARDIN, PIERRE (1881-1955)

French priest, anthropologist, geologist, paleontologist, philosopher, author

1. ACTA TEILHARDIANA. Editor: Gerhard-H. Sitzmann, Postfach 102371, D-8900 Augsburg, Germany (BRD). Sponsor and publisher: Gesellschaft Teilhard de Chardin für den deutschen Sprachraum, D-8900 Augsburg, Germany (BRD). 1963-- . Irregular. Price varies. [120-40 p.] Last issue examined: vol. 12, 1975.

   An international, interdisciplinary publication devoted to Teilhard de Chardin, his times, sources, and influence--includes essays and information of the Gesellschaft for the German language area. Each issue is concerned with a specific subject such as MENSCH UND NATUR (reprints of papers prepared for the International Congress in 1973); bibliographies; international contributors. In German. Vol. 13 not yet published (1978).

Alternate subtitle:

STUDIEN UND MITTEILUNGEN DER GESELLSCHAFT TEILHARD DE CHARDIN FÜR DEN DEUTSCHEN SPRACHRAUM

2. Bibliothek Teilhard de Chardin. Sponsor: Bibliothek Teilhard de Chardin. Publisher: Het Spectrum, Utrecht-Antwerpen, Belgium. No. 10, 1963-- . Irregular (a series). [75-200 p.] Last issue examined: no. 19, 1967.

3. CAHIERS DE LA FONDATION TEILHARD DE CHARDIN. Supersedes CAHIERS PIERRE TEILHARD DE CHARDIN (see entry 4). Sponsor: Fondation Pierre Teilhard de Chardin, 38, rue Geoffroy-St-Hilaire, 75005 Paris. President: Jean Piveteau. Publisher: Éditions du Seuil, Paris. 1968 (no. 6)-- . Irregular. 15-30 Fr. [160-240 p.] Last issue examined: no. 8, 1974.

The Fondation Teilhard de Chardin collects and preserves manuscripts and works related to Father Teilhard, publishes previously unpublished works, upholds his beliefs, and promotes studies of his ideas by means of conferences, seminars, scholarship, and publications. It also publishes an annual bulletin of the organization's accomplishments. The CAHIERS are collections of long scholarly studies examining changing religious theories, Teilhard's travels, influence, and conflict with science; occasional bibliographies of dissertations, completed and in progress, and of scholarship in France and all over the world; previously unpublished correspondence or extracts from his works; abstracts of dissertations; activities of the Fondation; international scope. In French. No. 9 not yet published (1978).

Indexed by FRENCH XX.

Alternate titles:

CAHIERS DE LA FONDATION ET ASSOCIATION TEILHARD DE CHARDIN

CAHIERS PIERRE TEILHARD DE CHARDIN

Fondation . . . Teilhard de Chardin. CAHIERS

4. CAHIERS PIERRE TEILHARD DE CHARDIN. Superseded by CAHIERS DE LA FONDATION TEILHARD DE CHARDIN (see entry 3). Sponsor: Association des Amis de Pierre Teilhard de Chardin, Paris. Publisher: Éditions du Seuil, Paris. 1958-65 (nos. 1-5). Irregular.

Each volume is centered on a different subject--some are collections of brief reminiscences, interpretations, memorials, and personal reactions; others contain extracts from Teilhard's works with introductions and notes; others feature scholarly essays interpreting his philosophy and influences. In French.

Indexed by FRENCH XX.

Alternate titles:

CAHIERS DE L'ASSOCIATION DES AMIS DE PIERRE TEILHARD DE CHARDIN

Association des Amis de Pierre Teilhard de Chardin. CAHIERS

5. Cahiers teilhardiens. Publisher: G.H. Baudry, 60, boulevard Vauban, 59000 Lille, France. 1972-- . Last issue published: no. 4, 1976.

6. Carnets Teilhard. Sponsor: Société Pierre Teilhard de Chardin, Paris. Publisher: Éditions Universitaires, Paris. 1962-(?). Irregular (a series). [60-100 p.] Last issue examined: Carnet 20, 1964.

   Each volume focuses on a different subject--for example, TEILHARD, CLAUDEL, AND MAURIAC. In French.

   Indexed by FRENCH XX.

7. Études et recherches sur Teilhard de Chardin. Publisher: Éditions du Seuil, Paris. 1965(?)-- . Irregular (a series). [220-300 p.]

   Each volume of this series concentrates on a different subject --for example, TEILHARD DE CHARDIN ET LA PENSÉE CATHOLIQUE. In French.

8. ÉTUDES TEILHARDIENNES/TEILHARDIAN STUDIES. Publisher: Édition du Seuil, Paris. 1958-- . Irregular. 17.50 Fr. [120 p.] Last issue examined: vol. 3, 1971.

9. REVUE TEILHARD DE CHARDIN. Supersedes TEILHARD DE CHARDIN (see entry 10). Editor: Dominique de Wespin, rue des Champs-Elysées 42, 1050 Brussels, Belgium. Sponsor: Société Pierre Teilhard de Chardin, 99, rue Souveraine, Brussels 5, Belgium. Published with the approval of the Minister of National Education and of Culture, Belgium. Subscriptions: Kredietbank, rue d'Arenberg 7, Brussels; in France: Mlle. Audrain Madeleine, 32, rue Kervegan, F-44000 Nantes, France. June 1961 (no. 6)-- . Quarterly. $5; $4 (institutions); 500 FB (Europe); 600 FB (others). [40-60 p.] Last issue examined: no. 73, 1978.

   Aims to promote cooperation and good will among all people through an exchange of ideas that will lead to understanding and sympathy. Long scholarly essays on philosophy, language, ethics, responsibility of authors, relationship of science and religion, evolution--all as they are reflected in Teilhard's teaching; long reviews or annotations for important new publications; reminiscences; excerpts from letters and lectures; news of the annual international symposium. In French.

Indexed by FRENCH XX and PHILOSOPHER'S INDEX.

Alternate title:

REVUE INTERNATIONALE PIERRE TEILHARD DE CHARDIN

10. TEILHARD DE CHARDIN: REVUE ÉDITÉE PAR LA SOCIÉTÉ PIERRE TEILHARD DE CHARDIN. Superseded by REVUE TEILHARD DE CHARDIN (see entry 9). Sponsor: Société Pierre Teilhard de Chardin, 99, rue Souveraine, Brussels 5, Belgium. Secretary: Dominique de Wespin, rue des Champs-Elysées 42, 1050 Brussels, Belgium. June 1960-April 1961 (nos. 1-5). 160 Fr (Belgium); 16 NF (France).

Long critical articles on Teilhard's theology, his influence and convictions, his travels in the Far East; previously unpublished material, such as letters from the front in World War I, with annotations; book reviews; reminiscences; information on conferences, expeditions, prizes; bulletin of the activities of the Society; photographs and facsimiles. In French.

Indexed by FRENCH XX.

11. TEILHARD REVIEW. Editor: The Reverend John D. Newson, Christ Church College, Canterbury, Kent CT1 1QU, England. Sponsor and publisher since 1970 (vol. 5, no. 2): Teilhard Centre for the Future of Man, 81, Cromwell Road, London SW7 5BW. Summer 1966-- . 2/yr., 1966-71; 3/yr., since 1972. £3 or $6 (individuals); £4.50 or $9 (institutions); free with membership (£5; $10, U.S. and Canada); students ($6, U.S. and Canada; £3, Great Britain and other countries); institutions ($50, U.S. and Canada; £25, Great Britain and other countries). [30-40 p.] Last issue examined: vol. 12, 1977.

The Teilhard Center is dedicated to "the critical study, development, and dissemination of Teilhard's view of reality, and its application to the art and science of human evaluation." Long critical articles on Teilhard's ethics and influence, his relationship with such contemporaries as Gide and Bergson, and with such classical authors as Empedocles; interdisciplinary studies, including one entitled "The future of humanity increasingly responsible for its own evolution," especially as this idea was espoused by Teilhard de Chardin; brief notes on his friendships, vision , travels; extensive international news report of past and future Society conferences and branch activities; comments on translations, symposia, films, radio and

The Teilhard Review

Volume XII, Number 1 *February 1977*

television programs, and new publications; reprints of important international lectures; bibliographical references; long scholarly book reviews.

Indexed by CATHOLIC PERIODICAL AND LITERATURE INDEX, FRENCH XX, and PHILOSOPHER'S INDEX.

Alternate name for sponsor and publisher, 1966-Summer 1970 (vols. 1-5, no. 1): Pierre Teilhard de Chardin Association of Great Britain and Ireland.

12. Teilhard Study Library. Editors: Anthony Dyson and Bernard Towers. Sponsor: 1966-70, Pierre Teilhard de Chardin Association of Great Britain and Ireland, 3, Cromwell Place, London S.W.7; since 1970, Teilhard Centre for the Future of Man, 81, Cromwell Road, London SW7 5BW. Publisher: Garnstone Press, London. 1966(?)-- . Irregular (a series). £1.20-2.40. [115-40 p.] Last issue examined: vol. 7, 1974.

    Collections of studies that explore and explain ways in which man can find significance to his life and live in helpful harmony with others. All are based on or emanate from Teilhard's teaching--for example, CHINA AND THE WEST (1970).

TENNYSON, ALFRED (1809-92)

English poet

1. TENNYSON RESEARCH BULLETIN. Editorial board and publisher: Tennyson Research Centre, City Library, Free School Lane, Lincoln LN2 1FZ, England. Chairman: Christopher Ricks. Secretary: Miss E.M. Jahn. October 1967-- . Annual. Free with membership (£1.50 or $4.50, individuals; £2 or $6, institutions). [20-60 p.] Circulation: 557. Last issue examined: vol. 3, 1978.

    Scholarly articles and explications; studies of biography, themes, motifs, biblical echoes, political aspects, textual changes; selective bibliographies; descriptive reports of international research in progress; brief book reviews; announcements of publications; reprints of letters and lectures; previously unpublished material; notes and queries; news notes on the Research Centre's acquisitions, library holdings, conferences, courses, lectures, and excursions; illustrations and facsimiles; select subject index. An index with binder's title page is available for all parts of vol. 1 (1967-71); similar cumulations will be published at five-year intervals.

    Membership also includes Tennyson Society MONOGRAPHS (see entry 3), ANNUAL REPORTS (see entry 2), and special rates on publications and recordings. Early publications of the Society were offprints (including some from VICTORIAN STUDIES), but since 1967 all have been new titles.

Indexed by ABSTRACTS OF ENGLISH STUDIES, ANNUAL BIBLIOGRAPHY OF ENGLISH LANGUAGE AND LITERATURE, and VICTORIAN STUDIES.

Alternate title:

TENNYSON SOCIETY BULLETIN

2. Tennyson Society. ANNUAL REPORT. Editorial board and publisher: Tennyson Research Centre, City Library, Free School Lane, Lincoln LN2 1FZ, England. 1961-- . Annual. Free with membership (£1.50 or $4.50, individuals; £2 or $6, institutions). [4-20 p.] Circulation: 500. Last issue examined: 17th report, 1977.

   Summary of Society activities--lectures, tours, meetings, church services, dinners, readings, competitions, recordings; lists of acquisitions by the Tennyson Research Centre; lists of officers and members; lists of publications; financial report.

3. Tennyson Society. MONOGRAPHS. Sponsor and publisher: Tennyson Society, Tennyson Research Centre, City Library, Free School Lane, Lincoln LN2 1FZ, England. 1969-- . Irregular. Free with membership (£1.50 or $4.50, individuals; £2 or $6, institutions). [30-60 p.] Last issue examined: vol. 8, 1977.

   Long studies on one aspect of Tennyson's life or work, such as TENNYSON IN PARODY AND JEST (1975); occasional bibliographies, like that of Sir Charles Tennyson's works; reprints of inaccessible works, including poems by Tennyson and other authors appearing in periodicals during Tennyson's lifetime; bibliographical references; reviews of film versions of the works; illustrations and portraits.

   Indexed by ABSTRACTS OF ENGLISH STUDIES.

   Alternate title:

   Tennyson Society Monograph Series

4. Tennyson Society. OCCASIONAL PAPERS. Sponsor and publisher: Tennyson Society, Tennyson Research Centre, City Library, Free School Lane, Lincoln LN2 1FZ, England. 1974-- . Irregular. Price varies. [20-50 p.] Last issue examined: no. 3, 1974.

   Each issue focuses on a specific subject, such as TENNYSON AND DR. GULLY (no. 2), and is written by a different author. No. 4 not yet published (1979).

5. Tennyson Society. PUBLICATIONS. Sponsor: Publications Board of the Tennyson Society, Lincoln LN2 1FZ. England. Secretary: H.W. Wood, 138, Wragby Road, Lincoln LN2 1FZ. Publisher: Bloomington, Indiana. 1963-- . Price varies.

Each volume is concerned with a specific subject, such as THE SOMERSBY TENNYSONS (1963). Bibliographies of library holdings; photographs and facsimiles.

6. Tennyson Society. TENNYSON MEMORIAL SERMON. Sponsor and publisher: Tennyson Society, Tennyson Research Centre, City Library, Free School Lane, Lincoln LN2 1FZ, England. 1968-- . Irregular (1968, 1971, 1972). Free with membership (£1.50 or $4.50, individuals; £2 or $6, institutions). [8 p.]

   Reprints of lectures delivered at various churches in England in memory of Tennyson; biographical and interpretive studies. No sermons have been printed since 1972.

THACKERAY, WILLIAM MAKEPEACE (1811-63)

English novelist

1. THACKERAY NEWSLETTER. Editor and publisher: Peter L. Shillingsburg, Department of English, Mississippi State University, Jackson, Miss. 39762. May 1975-- . 2/yr. (May, November). $1.50. [4-8 p.] Circulation: 30. Last issue examined: May 1978.

   Designed to help active Thackerayans keep each other informed on the state of Thackeray studies. Brief notes; news announcements; lists of recent and forthcoming publications; occasional book reviews; updates on manuscript locations; queries; announcements of work in progress, including dissertations and theses; book exchange offers.

   Indexed by AMERICAN HUMANITIES INDEX.

THIBAULT, JACQUES ANATOLE FRANÇOIS [ANATOLE FRANCE] (1844-1924)

French novelist, critic

1. CAHIERS FRANCIENS. Sponsor: Société Anatole France, 133, rue de la Pompe, 75016 Paris. 1971-- . Irregular. Price varies. [40-60 p.] Circulation: 600. Last issue examined: no. 2, 1975.

   Previously unpublished works with accompanying biographical studies and critical notes; facsimiles. In French.

   Indexed by FRENCH XX.

2. LE LYS ROUGE. Editor: Mme. Jacques Lion. Sponsor: Société Anatole France, 133, rue de la Pompe, 75016 Paris. Publisher: Delayance, La Charité, France. January 1933-68 (vols. 1-36, nos. 1-104); new series, 1969 (vol. 37, no. 1)-- . Irregular. Last issue examined: n.s. no. 4, 1976.

Brief bibliographical and critical articles; previously unpublished letters. Originally a quarterly published by a "Groupe d'admirateurs d'Anatole France" at the Sorbonne. In French.

Indexed by BIBLIOGRAPHIE DE LA LITTÉRATURE FRANÇAISE, FRENCH VII, FRENCH XX, and Klapp.

THOMPSON, FRANCIS (1859-1907)

English poet

1. Francis Thompson Society. JOURNAL. Editor: G. Krishnamurti. Sponsor: Francis Thompson Society, 3 Kemplay Road, Hampstead, London NW3 17A. 1964/65-74/75 (nos. 1-7). £1.50. Circulation: 300.

   Critical articles; book reviews. Now incorporated in the Eighteen Nineties Society, same address.

   Indexed by ABSTRACTS OF ENGLISH STUDIES.

THOREAU, HENRY (1817-62)

American essayist, naturalist, poet

1. CONCORD SAUNTERER. Editor: Malcolm M. Ferguson, Thoreau Lyceum, 156 Belknap Street, Concord, Mass. 01742. Sponsor: Thoreau Foundation. November 1966-- . Quarterly. $3. [15 p.] Circulation: 450.

   Brief biographical or critical articles; information on material available at the Thoreau Lyceum; occasional book reviews; Society events; notes on forthcoming Thoreau scholarship.

2. Thoreau Fellowship. NEWSLETTER. Sponsor and publisher: Thoreau Fellowship, Box 551, Old Town, Maine 04468. April 1971-- . Irregular. [2 p.] Last issue examined: no. 22, July 1976.

   News of the Thoreau Museum exhibits, college courses, expeditions, members' activities, paperback editions of Thoreau works.

3. THOREAU JOURNAL QUARTERLY (TJQ). Editor: Richard F. Fleck, English Department, University of Wyoming, Laramie, Wyo. 82071. Managing editor: Mary P. Sherwood, P.O. Box 551, Old Town, Maine 04468. Sponsor: Thoreau Fellowship, National and International. January 1969-- . 4/yr. (January, April, July, October). $6. [30-35 p.]. Circulation: 500. Last issue examined: vol. 10, 1978.

   Brief critical articles on Thoreau, his home, his interest in natural history, his followers, his integrity, and any subject concerning Thoreau interests; occasional related material on

Hawthorne, Emerson, Alcott, and others of the era; occasional book reviews, such as that of William White's ALL NATURE IS MY BRIDE (1975), in which White takes passages from Thoreau's JOURNAL and arranges them in the shape of poems; quotations from Thoreau; letters to the editor; contemporary poems in Thoreau's style; occasional photographs and illustrations. Newsletter material included in the JOURNAL until Spring 1971, then published separately (see entry 2: Thoreau Fellowship. NEWSLETTER).

Indexed by ABSTRACTS OF ENGLISH STUDIES, AMERICAN HUMANITIES INDEX, AMERICAN LITERATURE, ANNUAL BIBLIOGRAPHY OF ENGLISH LANGUAGE AND LITERATURE, and MLA INTERNATIONAL BIBLIOGRAPHY.

Alternate title:

THOREAU JOURNAL

4. THOREAU SOCIETY BOOKLET (TSBooklet). Editor: Walter Harding, State University College, Geneseo, N.Y. 14454. Sponsor: Thoreau Society, State University. 1942-- . Irregular (approximately 1/yr.). Price varies. [2-400 p.] Circulation: 1,200. Last issue examined: no. 29, 1978.

Publications of various shapes and sizes containing material valuable to Thoreau scholars--collections of critical essays; announcement and production of newly acquired material; facsimiles of and notes on previously unpublished work; reminiscences; notes on Thoreau's friends; occasional bibliographies and illustrations; guide to current book prices; descriptions of various library holdings; no index.

Indexed by ABSTRACTS OF ENGLISH STUDIES, AMERICAN LITERATURE, ANNUAL BIBLIOGRAPHY OF ENGLISH LANGUAGE AND LITERATURE, Leary, and MLA INTERNATIONAL BIBLIOGRAPHY.

Alternate title:

Thoreau Society. BOOKLET

5. THOREAU SOCIETY BULLETIN (TSB). Editor: Walter Harding, State University College, Geneseo, N.Y. 14454. Sponsor: Thoreau Society, State University. October 1941-- . Quarterly. $3; life membership, $100. [8 p.] Circulation: 1,200. Last issue examined: no. 146, 1979.

Brief critical articles and notes on Thoreau, his writings and influence; checklist in every issue of current books, pamphlets, periodical and newspaper articles; occasional surveys of current Thoreau literature; abstracts of dissertations; previously unpublished material; reprints of work by Thoreau, his contemporaries, and his admirers that illustrate his wit and wisdom; queries; occasional hand-drawn illustrations; charts and maps; reports of meetings; news of recent publications that include anecdotes related to Thoreau--as, for example, the one about the touring motorcyclist and his son who carried WALDEN with them to discuss during evenings by the wayside, or the one about the doctor who retired after only twenty years' practice because, like Thoreau, "Perhaps it seemed to me that I had several more lives to live, and could not spare any more time for that one. . . ." Available in microform. Reprints available from Walter J. Johnson (1941-67, $15).

A cumulation of the BULLETIN's checklists arranged alphabetically by author with their original annotations has been published under the title BIBLIOGRAPHY OF THE THOREAU SOCIETY BULLETINS, 1941-1969; A CUMULATION AND INDEX (Troy, N.Y.: Whitston, 1971; $12.50).

Indexed by ABSTRACTS OF ENGLISH STUDIES, AMERICAN HUMANITIES INDEX, AMERICAN LITERATURE, AMERICAN LITERATURE ABSTRACTS, ANNUAL BIBLIOGRAPHY OF ENGLISH LANGUAGE AND LITERATURE, Leary, MLA ABSTRACTS, and MLA INTERNATIONAL BIBLIOGRAPHY.

Alternate title:

Thoreau Society of America. BULLETIN

TOLKIEN, JOHN R.R. (1892-1973)

English author, professor of medieval literature

1. AMON HEN: BULLETIN OF THE TOLKIEN SOCIETY. Editor: J. Kemball-Cook, 110 Breakspears Road, London SE4 1UD, England. Sponsor: Tolkien Society. £ 2.50; $6.

2. ANDURIL: MAGAZINE OF FANTASY. Sponsor and editor: John Martin, 27, Highland Drive, Bushey, Hertfordshire, England. 1972-- . Irregular. 30 p; $1 per issue. [30-50 p.] Last issue examined: no. 3, 1972.

   Informal articles and notes on fantasy, especially that of Tolkien but also that of Charles Williams, C.S. Lewis, and others; brief annotations on newly published fantasy; news and notes of Tolkien Society publications; "Mail from Middle Earth"--letters from readers; book exchange; poetry; numerous drawings. No. 4 not yet published (1978).

   Subtitle for nos. 1-2:

   BULLETIN OF THE TOLKIEN SOCIETY AND MAGAZINE OF FANTASY

3. CARANDAITH: JOURNAL OF THE AUSTRALIAN TOLKIEN SOCIETY. Editors: Alpajpuri, 1690 East 26th Avenue, Eugene, Oreg. 97403; and Michael O'Brien, 158 Liverpool Street, Hobart, Tasmania 7000, Australia. Sponsor: Australian Tolkien Society. 1968-69 (nos. 1-3). Quarterly. $2. [13-19 p.]

   Analyses of the works and their appeal to contemporary readers; interviews; reviews.

4. ENTMOOT. Editor: Greg Shaw, 2707B McAllister, San Francisco, Calif. 1965-66 (nos. 1-4). Irregular. [8-28 p.]

   Devoted entirely to Tolkien, with emphasis on the lighter side; articles on his descriptions, costuming, terms, sources; articles on textual problems. No reply to query.

5. GREEN DRAGON. Editor: Edmund R. Meskys, Box 233, Center Harbor, N.H. 03226. Sponsor: Tolkien Society of America. 1965-(?). Irregular. Free with membership. Circulation: 2,000. Last issue examined: no. 5, December 1968.

   Brief notes; occasional bibliographies; book reviews; news items. Issue no. 1 published separately; no. 2 combined with no. 7 of the TOLKIEN JOURNAL (see entry 12) to function henceforth as a newsletter for members of the Society.

6. I PALANTIR. Editor: Bruce Pelz, Box 100, 308 Westwood Plaza, Los Angeles, Calif. 90024. Sponsor: Fellowship of the Ring. August 1960-64; 1966 (nos. 1-4). Irregular. Free with membership ($1).

   Features reprints of outstanding Tolkien articles from the early years of Tolkien fandom; brief articles on Tolkien fandom; parodies; sketches and cartoons.

7. MALLORN: OFFICIAL JOURNAL OF THE TOLKIEN SOCIETY (England). Sponsor: Tolkien Society, The Carrock, 31, Great Dell, Welwyn Garden City, Hertfordshire, England. Treasurer: Archie Mercer, 21, Trenethick Parc, Helston, Cornwall, England. November 1970-- . Quarterly. $3; £1. [30 p.] Circulation: 130.

   Articles on Tolkien and his critics, Middle-Earth heraldry, genealogy, language, with occasional material on other writers of fantasy and related fields; book reviews; report on new publications. Cumulated index for 1970-75.

8. MYTHLORE. Editor: Glen H. Goodknight, Box 7641, Whittier, Calif. 90607. Sponsor: Mythopoeic Society, P.O. Box 24150, Los Angeles, Calif. 90024. (Absorbed the Tolkien Society of America and the TOLKIEN JOURNAL beginning with no. 16, 1972.) January 1969-- . Quarterly (irregular). Free with membership in the Mythopoeic Society ($3.50); $1 per issue. Circulation: 1,000.

The literary journal of the Mythopoeic Society--concerned with works of Tolkien, C.S. Lewis, Charles Williams, and others. Articles interpreting myths, characters, descriptions, landscape, popularity with readers, religious meaning, imagination; book notes or long review articles in every issue; examinations of translations; occasional bibliographies; letters to the editor; excellent art work.

Indexed by ABSTRACTS OF ENGLISH STUDIES, AMERICAN HUMANITIES INDEX, and MLA INTERNATIONAL BIBLIOGRAPHY.

9. MYTHPRINT. Editor: Glen H. Goodknight, Box 7641, Whittier, Calif. 90607. Sponsor: Mythopoeic Society, Box 24150, Los Angeles, Calif. 90024. October 1967-- . Monthly. Free with membership ($8). [16 p.] Circulation: 1,400.

Monthly bulletin and newsletter of the Mythopoeic Society, which absorbed the Tolkien Society of America in 1972. Concerned with works of Tolkien, C.S. Lewis, Charles Williams, and others. Brief informal articles and notes; occasional book reviews; report of current activities in the numerous Society branches; letters to the editor.

10. NIEKAS. Editors: Edmund R. Meskys, Belknap College, Center Harbor, N.H. 03226; and Felice Rolfe, 1360 Emerson, Palo Alto, Calif. 94300. Sponsor: Tolkien Society of America. 1962-78. 1-2/yr. $3. [45-65 p.] Last issue examined: 1973.

Interested in all contemporary epic fantasy but especially in Tolkien and children's literature. Brief articles interpreting characters, allusions, myths; analyses of editorial problems; satire and creative material encouraged; interviews; some criticism of Gilbert and Sullivan works, and some of science fiction; letters to the editor.

11. ORCRIST: A JOURNAL OF FANTASY IN THE ARTS. Editor: Richard C. West, 1922 Madison Street, Madison, Wis. 53711. Publisher: Originally University of Wisconsin J.R.R. Tolkien Society; nos. 3-5 published in conjunction with the Tolkien Society of America and issued with the TOLKIEN JOURNAL, nos. 11, 13-14 (see entry 12); no. 6 and succeeding issues published by Modern Language Association seminar on "Medieval Tradition in the Modern Arts." March 1966/67-- . Irregular (no. 7, 1973). $1. per issue. [25-90 p.] Circulation: 200. Last issue examined: no. 8, 1977.

Interpretations and analyses of Tolkien's and C.S. Lewis's works; reprints or excerpts from Tolkien-Lewis letters; reminiscences; reprints of lectures at Society meetings; parodies; annotated bibliographies of works by and about Tolkien, including reviews; book reviews in every issue beginning with no. 5; facsimiles; index.

Indexed by ABSTRACTS OF ENGLISH STUDIES and MLA INTERNATIONAL BIBLIOGRAPHY.

Alternate title:

BULLETIN OF THE UNIVERSITY OF WISCONSIN J.R.R. TOLKIEN SOCIETY

12. TOLKIEN JOURNAL. Editor: Edmund R. Meskys, Box 233, Center Harbor, N.H. 03226. Sponsors: Nos. 1-2 (1965), New York Tolkien Society (Chairman Dick Plotz); nos. 3-10 (vols. 2-3, 1966-69), Tolkien Society of America (merged with the Mythopoeic Society, 1972); nos. 11-15 (1970-72), University of Wisconsin J.R.R. Tolkien Society, or Mythopoeic Society, Box 24150, Los Angeles, Calif. 90024. Spring 1965-Summer 1972 (nos. 1-15, beginning with no. 16, absorbed by MYTHLORE, entry 8). Quarterly (irregular). $3. [20-35 p.]. Circulation: 2,000.

Coverage extends beyond Tolkien to C.S. Lewis, Charles Williams, and fantasy in general. Informal articles on Tolkien's life and works, such as interpretations of the rings, Middle-Earth, the Inklings, and sources; essays investigating specific myths; occasional annotated bibliographies or general surveys of Tolkien scholarship; long reviews of books and/or articles in every issue; occasional film reviews; chronicle of events related to Tolkien and his works, radio programs, meetings, new publications; report of annual conferences; letters to the editor; poems; numerous sketches, maps, and imaginative illustrations.

Indexed by ABSTRACTS OF ENGLISH STUDIES.

Nos. 1-14 also called vols. 1-4.

No. 7 absorbed the GREEN DRAGON, no. 2 (see entry 5).

Nos. 11, 13-14 issued with ORCRIST, nos. 3-5 (see entry 11).

No. 12 issued with MYTHLORE, no. 5 (see entry 8).

TORSVAN, BERICK TRAVEN [B. TRAVEN] (1890-)

American novelist

1. B. TRAVEN NEWSLETTER. Editor: T.L. Ponick, P.O. Box 900, Purcellville, Va. 22132. 1975-- . 2/yr., 1975-76; quarterly since 1977. Free, 1975-76; since 1977, $2.

Brief articles; bibliographical data; notes; queries; correspondence.

TOUSSEUL, JEAN

See Degée, Olivier.

TRAKL, GEORG (1887-1914)

German poet

1. TRAKL-STUDIEN. Editor: Ignaz Zangerle. Publisher: Otto Müller Verlag, Salzburg. 1954-- . Irregular. [180-250 p.] Last issue examined: vol. 8, 1971.

   Promotes every aspect of Trakl scholarship--long studies of Trakl's poetry and style; comparisons with his contemporaries; Trakl bibliography, vol. 3, and concordance, vol. 7; bibliographical references. In German.

   Indexed by Köttelwesch.

TRAVEN, B.

See Torsvan, Berick Traven.

TROLLOPE, ANTHONY (1815-82)

English novelist

1. TROLLOPIAN; A JOURNAL OF VICTORIAN FICTION. Superseded by NINETEENTH-CENTURY FICTION. Editor: Bradford A. Booth. Sponsor: University of California Press, Berkeley, Calif. 94720. Summer 1945-March 1949 (vols. 1-3). 2/yr., then quarterly. $3. [50-80 p.]

   Long textual, historical, biographical, and interpretive essays; survey of current books; occasional bibliographies, such as that of the Brontë manuscripts; book reviews; notes and queries; report of work in progress; news of meetings, radio plays, lectures.

   Alternate subtitle:

   A JOURNAL DEVOTED TO STUDIES IN ANTHONY TROLLOPE AND HIS CONTEMPORARIES IN VICTORIAN FICTION

TWAIN, MARK

See Clemens, Samuel L.

UNAMUNO, MIGUEL DE (1864-1936)

Spanish philosopher, poet, novelist

1. CUADERNOS DE LA CÁTEDRA DE UNAMUNO (CCU). Director: Eugenio de Bustos Tovar. Sponsor and publisher: Facultad de Filosofía y Letras de la Universidad de Salamanca, Apartado 20, Salamanca, Spain. 1948-- . Annual (irregular). 150-800 pesetas. [100-200 p.] Last issue examined: vol. 24, 1976.

   Collections of essays on the life, works, and philosophy of Unamuno; surveys of his influence in other countries, with pertinent bibliographies; in almost every issue a "Cronica unamuniana"--an account of international events including lectures, seminars, special publications, courses at universities, expositions; frequent extensive bibliographical surveys of current scholarship arranged by subject and country; previously unpublished material; reminiscences. In Spanish and French.

   Indexed by AMERICA: HISTORY AND LIFE and MLA INTERNATIONAL BIBLIOGRAPHY.

   Alternate title:

   Cátedra Miguel de Unamuno. CUADERNOS

UPDIKE, JOHN (1932-)

American novelist, poet

1. JOHN UPDIKE NEWSLETTER. Editor: Herb Yellin, 19073 Los Alimos Street, Northridge, Calif. 91326. Winter 1977-- . Quarterly (Winter, Spring, Summer, Fall). $5; $6 (overseas); $1.50 per issue. [4 p.] Last issue examined: no. 6, 1978.

   Aims to "provide continuing coverage and information on the past, present, and future writings of John Updike." News of Updike work appearing in unusual or obscure publications; news of performances based on his works; reproductions of rare or little-known material, including Updike poems and letters; current checklist of Updike's published works; listings of bibliographies, critical studies, anthologies, introductions, interviews, British editions, foreign translations, magazine articles; listings of rare book trade; book exchange; letters to the editor; queries and answers; occasional facsimiles.

   Alternate title:

   UPDIKE NEWSLETTER

VALÉRY, PAUL (1871-1945)

French poet, critic

1. Archives Paul Valéry. Subseries of Archives des Lettres Modernes. 1964-- . Irregular. Equivalent numbers are provided below for both the parent series (Archives des Lettres Modernes) and the individual author series on Valéry.

Valéry subseries	Archives series	Date
No. 1	No. 55	1964
No. 2	No. 170	1977

In French. See Camus, Albert, entry 2, for a full description of Archives des Lettres Modernes.

Indexed by BULLETIN CRITIQUE, FRENCH VII, FRENCH XX, Klapp, and MLA INTERNATIONAL BIBLIOGRAPHY.

2. Bibliothèque Paul Valéry. Publisher: Minard, Paris. 1955-- . Irregular (a series). Last issue examined: no. 3, 1975.

   Each volume is concerned with a specific subject--a regrouping of criticism originally published in Lettres Modernes. In French.

3. BULLETIN DES ÉTUDES VALÉRYENNES. Editor: Daniel Moutote. Sponsor: Le Centre d'Études valéryennes, Bibliothèque Universitaire-Section Lettres, Université Paul-Valéry, 1, place de la Voie Domitienne, B.P. 5043, 34032 Montpellier Cedex, France. April 1974-- . Quarterly. 20 Fr; 28 Fr (foreign). [50 p.] Last issue examined: no. 12, 1977.

   News of interest to Valéry scholars; reprints of lectures; transactions of conferences; book reviews. In French.

   Indexed by BIBLIOGRAPHIE DE LA LITTÉRATURE FRANÇAISE, Klapp, and REVUE D'HISTOIRE LITTÉRAIRE.

4. Cahiers Paul Valéry. Editor: Jean Levaillant. Sponsor: Société Paul Valéry, 17, rue de l'Université, 75007 Paris, France. Publisher: Gallimard, Paris. 1975-- . Irregular (vol. 2, 1977). 36 Fr. [250 p.]

   Scholarly studies of Valéry's works; analyses of language, problems, and style; previously unpublished material; bibliographies of scholarship, including translations, book reviews, and papers delivered at colloquia; list of members of the Société. In French.

   Indexed by FRENCH XX.

5. Paul Valéry. Subseries of La Revue des Lettres Modernes. Editor:

Huguette Laurenti. 1974-- . Irregular. Equivalent numbers are provided below for both the parent series (La Revue des Lettres Modernes) and the individual author series on Valéry.

Valéry subseries	La Revue series	Date
No. 1	Nos. 413-18	1974
No. 2	Nos. 498-503	1977

In French. See Camus, Albert, entry 1, for a full description of La Revue des Lettres Modernes.

Indexed by BULLETIN CRITIQUE, FRENCH XX, Klapp, and MLA INTERNATIONAL BIBLIOGRAPHY.

VELDE, HENRY VAN DE (1863-1957)

Belgian architect, craftsman

1. CAHIERS HENRY VAN DE VELDE. Sponsor: Association Henry van de Velde, C.C.P. 515.11, A.S.B.L., Brussels, Belgium. New series, 1965-- .

    Text in French or Dutch.

VENDEL, HENRI [HENRI NADEL] (1892-)

French novelist, poet

1. BULLETIN DE LA SOCIÉTÉ DES AMIS D'HENRI VENDEL. Publisher: Baudena, Grasse, France. November 1954-62 (nos. 1-6).

    In French.

VERGIL [PUBLIUS VERGILIUS MARO] (70-19 B.C.)

Latin poet

1. PROCEEDINGS OF THE VIRGIL SOCIETY. Sponsor: Virgil Society of London. Publisher: H.W. Walden, London. 1961-- . Annual. [100 p.] Last issue examined: no. 15, 1975-76.

    Long scholarly essays and reprints of lectures; book reviews; no index. The Virgil Society also publishes an annual address, 1944-- .

    Alternate title:

    Virgil Society. PROCEEDINGS

2. VERGILIAN DIGEST. Superseded by VERGILIUS (see entry 4). Editor: Rogers V. Scudder, Brooks School, Andover, Mass. 01810. Sponsor:

Vergil Society of America. 1956-Fall 1958 (nos. 1-4). Irregular. $1.

Formed for the purpose of promoting and diffusing Vergilian and classical studies. News of summer sessions, tours, filmstrips, meetings; brief articles on excavations at Cumae, on ancient script, and on Vergil's works; occasional bibliographies, such as that on the AENEID (no. 1).

3. VERGILIAN SOCIETY NEWSLETTER. Editor: Adele I. Knight, 37946 Barber Avenue, Willoughby, Ohio 44094. Sponsor: Vergilian Society of America, Choate School, Charles P. Twichell, Wallingford, Conn. 06492. February 1961-(?). Annual. Free with membership ($3.50).

Notes on activities and publications of interest to members.

4. VERGILIUS. Supersedes VERGILIAN DIGEST (see entry 2). Editor: Janice M. Benario, Department of Foreign Languages, Georgia State University, University Plaza, Atlanta, Ga. 30303. Sponsor: Vergilian Society of America, Choate School, Charles P. Twichell, Box 385, Wallingford, Conn. 06492. Fall 1959 (no. 5)-- . Annual. Free with membership ($4.50). [50-65 p.] Circulation: 1,700. Last issue examined: vol. 24, 1978.

Interested in scholarship concerned with the life, works, and times of Vergil and in other Latin literature and Roman archaeology. Long critical and biographical articles as well as archaeological and historical surveys; bibliographies, including information on work in progress; occasional brief book reviews; annual list and survey of all newly published scholarship, with occasional annotations; occasional special issues; annual report of the secretary, including information on the Villa in Cumae, Italy, which is maintained by the Society for its members; report of the annual Classical Summer School; list of officers; announcement of tours, classical study programs in Greece and Italy; notes on new translations and other relevant publications; numerous maps and illustrations of archaeological finds; no index.

Indexed by L'ANNÉE PHILOLOGIQUE.

5. VERGILIVS: THE BULLETIN OF THE VERGILIAN SOCIETY. Editor: E.L. Highbarger, Northwestern University, Evanston, Ill. 60200. Sponsor: Vergilian Society. June 1938-December 1940 (nos. 1-6). 3/yr. Free with membership ($35); $2 (U.S. and Canada); $2.25 (elsewhere).

Articles on Vergil's life and works, including background, friendships, use of myth, and influence throughout the ages; selected bibliography of recent work on Vergil; book reviews; numerous quotations; notes on important new publications; international contributors; illustrations of Vergil's home and countryside.

VERLAINE, PAUL (1844-96)

French poet, essayist

1. CAHIERS PAUL VERLAINE. Supersedes NUANCES (see entry 3). Editor: André Guibert-Lassalle. Publisher: Revue littéraire des Verlainiens, 39, rue Descartes, 75005 Paris. New series, 1953-February 1960 (nos. 1-74); (?)-(?). Monthly, then irregular.

   Brief articles; news and notes. In French. Reprints available from Walter J. Johnson (1953-69/70, $275).

   Subtitle in REPERTOIRE DE LA PRESSE:

   REVUE LITTÉRAIRE DES VERLAINIENS

2. ÉTUDES VERLAINIENNES. Editor: Jacques-Henry Bornecque. Publisher: A.-G. Nizet, Paris. 1952 (vol. 1); 1959 (vol. 2)-(?). Irregular. [200 p.]

   Critical texts of Verlaine's work with extensive commentary and bibliographies; plates; portraits; index. In French.

   Indexed by FRENCH VII.

3. NUANCES. Superseded by CAHIERS PAUL VERLAINE (see entry 1). 1934-39 (nos. 1-11).

   Devoted to the defense of Verlaine's concept of symbolism. In French.

   Alternate titles:

   BULLETIN OFFICIEL DES VERLAINIENS

   JOURNAL DES VERLAINIENS

VERNE, JULES (1828-1905)

French novelist

1. Archives Jules Verne. Subseries of Archives des Lettres Modernes. Editors: François Raymond and Daniel Compère. 1976-- . Irregular. Equivalent numbers are provided below for both the parent series (Archives des Lettres Modernes) and the individual author series on Verne.

Verne subseries	Archives series	Date
No. 1	No. 161	1976
No. 2	No. 174	1977

   In French. See Camus, Albert, entry 2, for a full description of Archives des Lettres Modernes.

Indexed by BULLETIN CRITIQUE, FRENCH XX, Klapp, and MLA INTERNATIONAL BIBLIOGRAPHY.

2. BULLETIN DE LA SOCIÉTÉ JULES VERNE. Sponsor: Société Jules Verne, Librairie des Alpes, 6, rue de Seine, 75006 Paris. Publisher: 93, rue du Dessous-des-Berges, 75005 Paris. November 1935-December 1938 (vols. 1-3); new series, 1967-- . Quarterly. Last issues examined: nos. 41-44, 1977.

   Brief articles and notes on Verne's imagination in science and language; studies of his canon and his influence on other authors and literatures; source and character studies; news of the inauguration of the Centre du documentation Verne in Amiens. In French.

   Indexed by BIBLIOGRAPHIE DE LA LITTÉRATURE FRANÇAISE, FRENCH XX, Klapp, and REVUE D'HISTOIRE LITTÉRAIRE.

3. Jules Verne. Subseries of La Revue des Lettres Modernes. Editor: François Raymond. 1976-- . Irregular. Equivalent numbers are provided below for both the parent series (La Revue des Lettres Modernes) and the individual author series on Verne.

Verne subseries	La Revue series	Date
No. 1	Nos. 456-61	1976

   In French. See Camus, Albert, entry 1, for a full description of La Revue des Lettres Modernes.

   Indexed by BULLETIN CRITIQUE, FRENCH XX, Klapp, and MLA INTERNATIONAL BIBLIOGRAPHY.

VIAUD, JULIEN [PIERRE LOTI] (1850-1923)

French novelist

1. ASSOCIATION INTERNATIONALE DES AMIS DE PIERRE LOTI. Superseded by CAHIERS PIERRE LOTI (see entry 2). March 1933-35 (nos. 1-11); 1950-51.

   Articles; news. In French.

   Indexed by FRENCH VII.

2. CAHIERS PIERRE LOTI. Supersedes ASSOCIATION INTERNATIONALE DES AMIS DE PIERRE LOTI (see entry 1). Editor: André Moulis, 66, rue Pargaminières, 31000 Toulouse, France. Sponsor: Association internationale des Amis de Pierre Loti, Paris. President: Claude Farrère. May(?) 1952-- . 2/yr. Last issue examined: no. 70, December 1977.

   Brief articles on the technique in Loti's novels; notes on his friendships with contemporaries such as Van Gogh; previously unpublished journals, letters, and other documents. In French.

Indexed by BIBLIOGRAPHIE DE LA LITTÉRATURE FRANÇAISE, FRENCH VII, FRENCH XX, and Klapp.

Alternate information in LIBRAIRIE FRANÇAISE: Director of the publication: Henri Borgeaud, Académie de marine, 3, avenue Octave-Gréard, Paris.

VIGNY, ALFRED VICTOR, COMTE DE (1797-1863)

French poet, dramatist, novelist

1. Archives des Lettres Modernes. 1967-- . Irregular. Series numbers for the issues on Vigny are provided below.

Vigny series	Archives series	Date
Unnumbered	No. 83	1967
Unnumbered	No. 115	1970
Unnumbered	No. 149	1974

In French. See Camus, Albert, entry 2, for a full description of Archives des Lettres Modernes.

Indexed by BULLETIN CRITIQUE, Klapp, and MLA INTERNATIONAL BIBLIOGRAPHY.

2. Association des Amis d'Alfred de Vigny. BULLETIN. Editor: Mme. Christiane Lefranc, 6, avenue Constant-Coquelin, 75007 Paris. Sponsor: Association des Amis d'Alfred de Vigny. 1964(?)-- . Irregular. 25 Fr; 15 Fr (students). [75-80 p.] Last issue examined: vol. 6, 1974-75.

Long biographical and critical studies on Vigny's background, patriotism, political ideas, poetic theory, themes; brief analyses; textual notes; brief bibliography of dissertations, books, and articles concerning Vigny; previously unpublished letters and extracts from letters; abstracts of dissertations; report of Association activities throughout the year--General Assembly, lectures, dinners, performances, commemorations; lists of officers and members; facsimiles, photographs, and reproductions. In French.

Indexed by BIBLIOGRAPHIE DE LA LITTÉRATURE FRANÇAISE and Klapp.

Alternate titles:

Amis d'Alfred de Vigny. BULLETIN

BULLETIN DE L'ASSOCIATION DES AMIS D'ALFRED DE VIGNY

VINCENT OF BEAUVAIS (c. 1190-c. 1264)

French encyclopedist

1. VINCENT OF BEAUVAIS NEWSLETTER. Editor and publisher: Gregory G. Guzman, Department of History, Bradley University, Peoria, Ill. 61625. Sponsor: Department of History, Bradley University. October 1976-- . Annual. First issue, free; succeeding issues, at cost. [10-15 p.] Circulation: 50. Last issue examined: vol. 3, 1978.

   Report on scholars currently interested in Vincent of Beauvais, with names and addresses; report on the international project concerned with the manuscripts for Vincent's encyclopedia; news of acquisitions, conferences and papers, recent publications, forthcoming Vincent activities; queries.

VOLTAIRE

See Arouet, François Marie.

WALLACE, EDGAR (1875-1932)

English author of mystery and adventure stories

1. EDGAR WALLACE NEWSLETTER. Editor: Penelope Wallace, 4, Bradmore Road, Oxford OX2 6QW, England. January 1969-- . Quarterly. $2.50. [6 p.] Circulation: 400.

   Informal brief comments on books and events of interest to Wallace fans.

WARD, ARTHUR S. [SAX ROHMER] (1883-1959)

English author of mystery stories

1. ROHMER REVIEW. Editor and publisher: Douglas A. Rossman, Baton Rouge, La., July 1968-March 1970; since August 1970 (no. 5), Robert E. Briney, 4 Forest Avenue, Salem, Mass. 01970. Sponsor: Sax Rohmer Society. July 1968-- . Irregular (2-3/yr.). $2.25/three issues; $3/overseas; $1 per issue. [25-35 p.] Circulation: 225. Last issue examined: no. 15, September 1976.

   Concerned with the life and works of Sax Rohmer, creator of Dr. Fu Manchu and popular author of mystery thrillers. Biographical notes; bibliographic information, opinion, and commentary; critical interpretations; news and reviews of current publications; reprints of inaccessible material written by Rohmer, his widow, and his biographer, Cay Van Ash; occasional material on other popular-literature subjects if related to Rohmer or his work; letters; photographs and sketches. Author index to nos. 1-10 in no. 10.

Abstracted by ABSTRACTS OF POPULAR CULTURE.

WAUGH, EVELYN (1903-66)

English novelist

1. EVELYN WAUGH NEWSLETTER (EWN). Editor and sponsor: Paul A. Doyle, Department of English, Nassau Community College, State University of New York, Stewart Avenue, Garden City, N.Y. 11530. Spring 1967-- . 3/yr. (Spring, Autumn, Winter). $2.50; £1.10 (England); $1.25 per issue. [6-10 p.] Circulation: 200. Last issue examined: vol. 12, 1978.

   "Designed to stimulate interest and continue interest in the life and writings of Evelyn Waugh." Brief articles and notes on Waugh's sources, characters, images, themes, technique, influence, textual problems, and relationship with other authors; previously unpublished letters; annual critical survey in the Spring issue of the previous year's scholarship; occasional supplementary checklists, including criticism in other countries such as Ireland, Germany, and France; news of MLA seminars, paperbacks, library acquisitions and holdings, work in progress; reviews of new publications concerning Waugh and other authors related to him; letters to the editor. No cover.

   Indexed by ABSTRACTS OF ENGLISH STUDIES, AMERICAN HUMANITIES INDEX, ANNUAL BIBLIOGRAPHY OF ENGLISH LANGUAGE AND LITERATURE, MLA ABSTRACTS, MLA INTERNATIONAL BIBLIOGRAPHY, and YEAR'S WORK IN ENGLISH STUDIES.

   Alternate title:

   WAUGH NEWSLETTER

WEIL, SIMONE (1909-43)

French philosopher, writer

1. Archives des Lettres Modernes. 1959-- . Irregular. Series numbers for the issues on Weil are provided below.

Weil subseries	Archives series	Date
Unnumbered	Nos. 25-26	1959

   In French. See Camus, Albert, entry 2, for a full description of Archives des Lettres Modernes.

   Indexed by FRENCH XX, Klapp, and MLA INTERNATIONAL BIBLIOGRAPHY.

2. Association pour l'étude de la pensée de Simone Weil. BULLETIN. Publisher: Chambéry, France. 1974-- . Irregular. [25-30 p.] Last issue examined: no. 2, 1975.

   Critical notes; bibliographies; news of seminars.

   Indexed by FRENCH XX.

3. Cahiers Simone Weil. Publisher: Plön, Paris. 1970-- .

   A new, revised, enlarged edition of Weil's works, with introductions and copious notes. In French.

WEINHEBER, JOSEF (1892-1945)

Austrian poet

1. JAHRESGABE. Sponsor and publisher: Josef Weinheber-Gesellschaft, Bierhäuselberggasse 39, 1140 Vienna, Austria. President: Karl Rohm, Kraelitzgasse 36, 1130 Vienna. 1956-- . Annual. AS 53; $23.50. [15-50 p.] Last issue examined: 1974-75.

   Brief articles on Weinheber's life, work, and influence on Austrian and world literature; surveys of current studies of his work; studies of his relationship with other authors, his sources, language, and themes; reprints of lectures, conferences; previously unpublished letters; primary bibliographies; numerous quotations from his poetry; notes on new publications; calendar of Gesellschaft activities; no index. In German.

   Indexed by Köttelwesch.

   Alternate title:

   Josef Weinheber-Gesellschaft. JAHRESGABE

WELLS, HERBERT GEORGE (1866-1946)

English novelist, journalist

1. BULLETIN. Superseded by the JOURNAL OF THE H.G. WELLS SOCIETY (see entry 5). Sponsor: H.G. Wells Society International, 24, Wellin Lane, Edwalton, Nottingham, England. April-August 1963 (nos. 1-2); new series, February 1964-Autumn 1971 (nos. 1-20). Irregular. Free to members. [2-16 p.]

   News and notes of interest to members--cultural events, activities of Wells scholars, publications. In 1968, the BULLETIN absorbed the Society's WELLSIAN (see entry 7).

Alternate titles:

H.G. WELLS SOCIETY BULLETIN

BULLETIN OF THE H.G. WELLS SOCIETY

2. COSMOPOLIS MONTHLY BULLETIN. Superseded by COSMOPOLIS WEEKLY BULLETIN (see entry 3). Sponsor: H.G. Wells Society, London. June 1934-February 1936 (nos. 1-20).

Alternate titles:

MONTHLY BULLETIN, nos. 1-4

OPEN CONSPIRACY, nos. 5-18

3. COSMOPOLIS WEEKLY BULLETIN. Supersedes COSMOPOLIS MONTHLY BULLETIN (see entry 2). Sponsor: H.G. Wells Society, London. March 1936-May 1937 (nos. 1-3).

4. H.G. Wells Society. OCCASIONAL PAPERS. Publisher: H.G. Wells Society, 125 Markyate Road, Dagenham, Essex RM8 2LB, England. 1973-- . Irregular. £2. Last issue examined: vol. 2, 1976.

   Issued as a supplement to the Society's WELLSIAN: THE JOURNAL OF THE H.G. WELLS SOCIETY, new series (see entry 8). Vol. 3 not yet published (1978).

5. JOURNAL OF THE H.G. WELLS SOCIETY. Supersedes the BULLETIN (see entry 1); superseded by WELLSIAN: THE JOURNAL OF THE H.G. WELLS SOCIETY, new series (see entry 8). Editor: Eric F.J. Ford, 125 Markyate Road, Dagenham, Essex RM8 2LB, England. Sponsor: H.G. Wells Society International. Spring 1972-Winter 1973 (nos. 1-5). Irregular. Free with membership ($3.50, individuals; $7, institutions). [4-24 p.] Circulation: 300.

   Articles on Wells's life and works, his contemporaries, his influence on and relevance to modern culture; bibliographies; book reviews; report of new publications; information on works in progress; cumulated index. Available on microfilm. Supplement (see entry 4).

Alternate subtitle:

WORLD OF H.G. WELLS

Alternate title:

H.G. Wells Society. JOURNAL

6. NEWSLETTER. Sponsor: H.G. Wells Society, 24, Wellin Lane, Edwalton, Nottingham, England. April 1975-- . Quarterly (irregular). Free with membership (£2); £4 (institutions). [2-4 p.]

News of interest to members--cultural events, publications, activities of Wells scholars.

7. WELLSIAN. Superseded by WELLSIAN: THE JOURNAL OF THE H.G. WELLS SOCIETY, new series (see entry 8). Editor: John Ovenden, 125 Markyate Road, Dagenham, Essex RM8 2LB, England. Sponsor: H.G. Wells Society International, 21 Fawe Park Road, Putney, London S.W. 15. October 1960-68 (vol. 1, nos. 1-10-vol. 2, no. 3). Irregular. Free with membership ($3.50, individuals; $7, institutions--two copies). [20-35 p.] Circulation: 300.

Studies of Wells's style, satirical intent, relationship with Shaw and other authors; reprints of lectures by Wells; book reviews; editorial comments on works in progress, new reports, critical works, anthologies. Incorporated in 1968 with the Society's BULLETIN (see entry 1). Out-of-print issues available from Michael Katanka (Books), 103 Stanmore Hill, Stanmore, Middlesex, England.

Alternate subtitle:

JOURNAL OF THE H.G. WELLS SOCIETY, NOTTINGHAM

8. WELLSIAN: THE JOURNAL OF THE H.G. WELLS SOCIETY (new series). Supersedes the WELLSIAN (see entry 7). Editor: J.P. Vernier. Secretary: J.R. Hammond. Sponsor: H.G. Wells Society, 24, Wellin Lane, Edwalton, Nottingham, England; and 17, Anson Road, Tufnell Park, London N7 0RB. Subscriptions: Michael Katanka (Books), 103 Stanmore Hill, Stanmore, Middlesex, England. New series, 1976 (no. 1)-- . Annual. Free with membership (£2); £4 (institutions). [35-45 p.]

The Society "aims to promote a widespread interest in the life, work, and thought of Herbert George Wells, and generally to stimulate a Wellsian outlook on the many old and new problems facing Man in the latter part of the twentieth century." Brief articles examining sources, themes, autobiographical background in Wells's novels, influences; reprints of lectures delivered to the Society; bibliographies of critical books and articles; brief book reviews; notes on forthcoming books and work in progress; news of cultural events and members' activities. The Society also publishes a quarterly NEWSLETTER (see entry 6), reprints of inaccessible titles by Wells, and supplements to the Wells bibliography, the first comprehensive edition of which it produced in 1966. Additional duties of the Society include arranging meetings in London, sponsoring exhibitions in Britain and abroad, and scheduling lectures and school study groups.

THE WELLSIAN

The journal of The H.G.Wells Society

WELTY, EUDORA (1909-   )

American author of short stories and novels

1. EUDORA WELTY NEWSLETTER. Editor and publisher: W.U. McDonald, Jr., University of Toledo, 2801 West Bancroft Street, Toledo, Ohio 43606. January 1977-- . 2/yr. (Winter, Summer). $1. [10-12 p.] Circulation: 100. Last issue examined: vol. 3, 1979.

    An informal newsletter designed to increase communication among students and collectors. Checklists in every issue of works published by Welty since the preceding issue; annual checklist of Welty scholarship; brief bibliographic notes about unpublished works and location of rare copies or editions; queries and answers concerning location of material, with bibliographic details; notes of interest to book collectors, as, for instance, library acquisitions; information on collections, scholarly works in progress, conferences, papers; exchange column of items for sale or loan.

    Indexed by AMERICAN HUMANITIES INDEX.

WHITEHEAD, ALFRED NORTH (1861-1947)

English philosopher, mathematician

1. PROCESS STUDIES. Editors: Lewis S. Ford, 3157 Trumpet Road, Chesapeake, Va. 23321. Director of the Center for Process Studies: John B. Cobb, Jr., School of Theology at Claremont, 1325 North College Avenue, Claremont, Calif. 91711. Managing editor: Robert W. Hutton, School of Theology at Claremont. Sponsor: School of Theology at Claremont. Spring 1971-- . Quarterly. Individuals: $8, $14/two yrs., $20/three yrs.; institutions: $10, $17/two yrs., $24/three yrs. [70-95 p.] Circulation: 800. Last issue examined: vol. 8, 1978.

    Long scholarly studies concerned with Process Philosophy, especially that of Whitehead, as it is related to theology, literary criticism, history of religions, and other disciplines; numerous abstracts of dissertations; occasional bibliographies, such as that of dissertations and theses on Charles Hartshorne; book reviews; announcements of conferences, relevant publications, work in progress, seminars; annual index.

    Alternate address for Lewis S. Ford: Old Dominion University, P.O. Box 6173, Norfolk, Va. 23508.

    Indexed by INDEX TO RELIGIOUS PERIODICAL LITERATURE and PHILOSOPHER'S INDEX.

WHITMAN, WALT (1819-92)

American poet, journalist, essayist

1. CALAMUS: WALT WHITMAN QUARTERLY: INTERNATIONAL. Editor: William L. Moore, Toho Gakuen University of Music, Sengawa, Chofu, Tokyo, Japan. Sponsor and publisher: Taizo Shinozaki, president, Taibundo Ltd., 1-13, Kanda-Nishikicho, Chiyoda-ku, Tokyo, Japan. September 1969-- . 3/yr. $3.50. [35-50 p.] Circulation: 600. Last issue examined: no. 16, July 1978.

   Encourages "writings from nations where Whitman ideas are leavening our times" because Whitman believed literature should serve not as "a plaything, a display, but as a furthering of the cause of the masses--a means whereby men may be revealed to each other as brothers." Brief articles on individual works, on Whitman's humor and philosophy, his Americanism and influence on other literatures; notes on scholars and teachers of Whitman, on methods of teaching his works; reports of research; reprints; excerpts from dissertations; international contributors and committee of advisors. Title in English and Japanese, but text in English only.

   Indexed by ANNUAL BIBLIOGRAPHY OF ENGLISH LANGUAGE AND LITERATURE and ÉTUDES ANGLAISES.

2. WALT WHITMAN BIRTHPLACE ASSOCIATION NEWSLETTER. Supersedes WALT WHITMAN BIRTHPLACE BULLETIN (see entry 3). Editor: Helen H. Andrew, 246 Walt Whitman Road, Huntington Station, Long Island, N.Y. 11746. Sponsor: Walt Whitman Birthplace Association, 246 Walt Whitman Road, Huntington Station, Long Island, N.Y. 11746. 1961(?)-- . Annual. Free to membership. [1-2 p.] Circulation: 150. Last issue examined: 1975.

   Brief articles and notes about acquisitions and activities.

   Indexed by Leary.

3. WALT WHITMAN BIRTHPLACE BULLETIN. Superseded by WALT WHITMAN BIRTHPLACE ASSOCIATION NEWSLETTER (see entry 2). Editor: Verne Dyson, 1 Commercial Boulevard, Brentwood, Long Island, N.Y. 11717. Publisher: Walt Whitman Birthplace Association, 246 Walt Whitman Road, Huntington Station, Long Island, N.Y. 11746. October 1957-July 1961 (vols. 1-4). Quarterly (October, January, April, July). $1; free with membership. [25 p.]

   Brief critical and biographical articles; reminiscences; occasional bibliographies; book reviews; news of ceremonies, members' activities, musical programs, gifts, library collections; photographs. Index for 1957-61 (vols. 1-4) in vol. 4, no. 4.

   Indexed by Leary.

4. Walt Whitman Fellowship, International. PAPERS. Publisher: Philadelphia, Pa. May 1894-May 1918. Annual. Free with membership. [4-30 p.]

    Reprints of papers read at organizational meetings of the fellowship; program of activities.

    Alternate title:

    WALT WHITMAN FELLOWSHIP PAPERS

5. WALT WHITMAN FOUNDATION BULLETIN. Sponsor and publisher: Walt Whitman Foundation, 330 Mickle Street, Camden, N.J. 08103. January 1948-April 1955 (vols. 1-8, no. 2). Annual. $1; free to members of the Walt Whitman Foundation. [10-20 p.]

    Scholarly essays; bibliography of the previous year's scholarship on Whitman; occasional book reviews; news notes from the Foundation; illustrations. New publication is planned to supersede this title--information from the Walt Whitman Foundation.

    Alternate title:

    Walt Whitman Foundation. BULLETIN

6. WALT WHITMAN NEWSLETTER (WWN). Superseded by WALT WHITMAN REVIEW (see entry 7). Editor: 1955, Gay Wilson Allen; 1956-58, William White, Wayne State University, Detroit, Mich. 48202. Publisher: January-December 1955, New York University Press; March 1956-December 1958, Wayne State University Press. January 1955-December 1958 (vols. 1-4). Quarterly. $2. [15-25 p.]

    Brief articles on Whitman's life, friendships, language, manuscripts; brief notes explicating specific sections or ideas in Whitman's works; bibliographies of Whitman criticism; reviews; letters to the editor.

    Indexed by MLA INTERNATIONAL BIBLIOGRAPHY.

7. WALT WHITMAN REVIEW (WWR). Supersedes WALT WHITMAN NEWSLETTER (see entry 6). Editors: William White, Director, Journalism Program, Oakland University, Rochester, Mich. 48063; and Charles E. Feinberg, Detroit, Mich. Publisher: Wayne State University Press, Detroit, Mich. 48202. March 1959 (vol. 5, no. 1)-- . Quarterly (March, June, September, December). $8/yr.; $14/two yrs.; $20/three yrs. [30-40 p.] Circulation: 800. Last issue examined: vol. 24, 1978.

    Scholarly biographical and interpretive articles that refer to Whitman's allusions, sources, background, influence on other authors, philosophy, style, and travels; notes on textual problems, revisions of manuscripts, language, library acquisitions, and Whitman publications; in every issue--"Whitman: A Current

WALT WHITMAN REVIEW

Volume 22 • Number 4

December 1976

Bibliography" of books, dissertations, articles, with brief notes, edited by William White; previously unpublished material; book reviews; facsimiles and photographs. Cumulative index every five years, the latest covering March 1970-December 1974 (vols. 16-20), arranged by author, title, books reviewed. Available in microfiche ($4.95). Reprints, including NEWSLETTER, available from Kraus Reprint (1955-64, $52); and from Walter J. Johnson (1955-71, $105).

Indexed by ABSTRACTS OF ENGLISH STUDIES, AMERICAN HUMANITIES INDEX, AMERICAN LITERATURE, AMERICAN LITERATURE ABSTRACTS, ANNUAL BIBLIOGRAPHY OF ENGLISH LANGUAGE AND LITERATURE, FRENCH XX, INDEX TO BOOK REVIEWS IN THE HUMANITIES, Leary, MLA INTERNATIONAL BIBLIOGRAPHY, VICTORIAN STUDIES, and YEAR'S WORK IN ENGLISH STUDIES.

WHITTIER, JOHN GREENLEAF (1807-92)

American poet, editor

1. WHITTIER NEWSLETTER. Editor: John B. Pickard, Department of English, University of Florida, Gainesville, Fla. 32611. Sponsor: Whittier Clubs and Homes of Haverhill, Mass. 01830, and Amesbury, Mass. 01913. Fall 1966-- . Annual. Free. [4 p.] Circulation: 700. Last issue examined: vol. 17, 1978.

   In each Fall issue a survey and appraisal of the previous year's scholarship; report of research in progress and work recently completed; news on library collections, new acquisitions; report of Whittier Club activities--meetings, lectures, appointment of officers; notes and queries; illustrations; no index. Occasional special Spring issues (four between 1966 and 1976).

WILLIAMS, WILLIAM CARLOS (1883-1963)

American poet

1. WILLIAM CARLOS WILLIAMS NEWSLETTER (WCWN). Editor: Norman Holmes Pearson, deceased 1975. Managing editor: Theodora R. Graham, Capitol Campus, Pennsylvania State University, Middletown, Pa. 17057. Sponsor: with the cooperation of the Humanities Program, Capitol Campus, Pennsylvania State University. Fall 1975-- . 2/yr. (Spring, Fall). $5 (U.S.); $5.50 (foreign). [20 p.] Last issue examined: vol. 3, 1977.

   Brief biographical and historical articles; notes on comparative analysis and influence; explication of individual works or their parts; reports of translations, library collections, seminars, broadcasts; primary and secondary bibliographies; reprints of letters; report on work in progress and forthcoming works; lists of dissertations completed and in progress; announcements of conferences and seminars; book reviews; queries and answers; reproductions.

Indexed by AMERICAN HUMANITIES INDEX and MLA INTERNATIONAL BIBLIOGRAPHY.

WINCKELMANN, JOHANN JOACHIM (1717-68)

German classical scholar

1. SCHRIFTEN DER WINCKELMANN-GESELLSCHAFT. Editor: Johannes Irmscher and Berthold Häsler. Sponsor: Winckelmann-Gesellschaft, Stendal, Germany (DDR). Publisher: Akademie-Verlag, Berlin. 1973-- . Irregular. $6. [120 p.] Last issue examined: vol. 4, 1977.

   A collection of scholarly essays on Winckelmann's contributions to history and his influence in our times--for example, BEITRÄGE ZU EINEM NEUEN WINCKELMANNBILD (vol. 1). In German.

   Alternate title:

   Winckelmann-Gesellschaft. SCHRIFTEN

2. Winckelmann-Gesellschaft, Stendal. JAHRESGABE. Sponsor: Winckelmann-Gesellschaft, Stendal, Germany (DDR). Publisher: Akademie-Verlag, Berlin. 1941-68(?). Annual. [20-380 p.]

   Each volume is concerned with a specific subject, such as WINCKELMANN UND SEINE WELT (1962). Long studies of Winckelmann's life, his contributions to his era, his aesthetics, his world view; occasional comprehensive Winckelmann bibliographies, including one for the years 1955-66 (1967), edited by Hans Henning; previously unpublished letters and other documents; list of members; numerous facsimiles and illustrations; indexes. Includes "Beiträge zur Gestalt Winckelmanns." Volume for 1942 includes a comprehensive bibliography of publications by and about Winckelmann. In German.

   Indexed by Köttelwesch.

WOLFE, THOMAS (1900-1938)

American novelist

1. THOMAS WOLFE NEWSLETTER. Editors: John S. Phillipson, Department of English, University of Akron, Akron, Ohio 44325; and Aldo P. Magi, 415 Meigs Street, Sandusky, Ohio 44870. Sponsor and publisher: Department of English, Buchtel College, University of Akron. April 1977-- . 2/yr. (Spring, Fall). Free in 1977; $2 thereafter. [30-35 p.] Last issue examined: vol. 2, 1978.

Brief critical articles and notes; reminiscences; book reviews; "The Wolfe Pack"--bibliography with abstracts; "Wolfe Calls" --queries and answers; "Wolfe Trails"--news of general interest to Wolfe scholars, including an account of events and publications at the Wolfe Memorial in Asheville; biographical contributions, such as a description of Wolfe's travels through Vermont; news of forthcoming publications; news of work in progress; photographs and line drawings; no index.

Indexed by AMERICAN HUMANITIES INDEX.

WOLFRAM VON ESCHENBACH (12th century)

German medieval poet

1. WOLFRAM-JAHRBUCH (WJ). Editor: Wolfgang Stammler. Sponsor: Wolfram-von-Eschenbach-Bund, Miltenberg, Germany (BRD); Wiesbaden, Germany (BRD). Publisher: Volkhardt, Miltenberg, Germany (BRD). 1952-56 (?). Annual. [50-300 p.]

   Long scholarly essays on Wolfram's works, including specific titles, such as PARSIFAL, and themes, such as humanity; close studies of fragments of manuscripts; examinations of Wolfram's cultural milieu; occasional bibliographies of scholarship. In German.

   Indexed by Köttelwesch and MLA INTERNATIONAL BIBLIOGRAPHY.

2. WOLFRAM-STUDIEN (WOLFRAM STUDIES). Editor: Werner Schröder. Sponsor: Wolfram-von-Eschenbach-Gesellschaft. Publisher: Erich Schmidt, Berlin. 1970-- . Irregular. DM45-75. [250-300 p.] Last issue examined: vol. 4, 1977.

   Collections of long scholarly essays on various aspects of Wolfram's life, works, influence, and themes, especially those of Parsifal, Gawain, and the Holy Grail; surveys of the current state of Wolfram research; reports on colloquia. In English or German. Published as part of the VERÖFFENTLICHUNGEN of the Wolfram-von-Eschenbach-Gesellschaft (see entry 4).

   Indexed by Köttelwesch.

3. Wolfram von Eschenbach-Bund, Würzburg. MITTEILUNGEN. Sponsor: Wolfram von Eschenbach-Bund, Würzburg, Germany (BRD). Publisher: Amorbach, Germany (BRD). 1936-(?).

   In German.

4. Wolfram-von-Eschenbach-Gesellschaft. VERÖFFENTLICHUNGEN. Editors: Kurt Ruh, Werner Schröder, Ludwig Wolff, and Walter Haug.

Sponsor: Wolfram-von-Eschenbach-Gesellschaft. Publisher: Erich Schmidt, Berlin.

Each volume is on a different subject--includes WOLFRAM-STUDIEN (see entry 2). In English or German.

Alternate title:

VERÖFFENTLICHUNGEN DER WOLFRAM-VON-ESCHENBACH-GESELLSCHAFT

WOLLSTONECRAFT, MARY (1759-97)

English author

1. MARY WOLLSTONECRAFT NEWSLETTER: A JOURNAL OF LITERATURE BY AND ABOUT WOMEN OF THE EIGHTEENTH AND NINETEENTH CENTURIES (MWJ). Superseded by WOMEN AND LITERATURE. Editor: Janet M. Todd, Department of English, Douglass College, Rutgers University, New Brunswick, N.J. 08903. July 1972-Fall 1974 (vols. 1-2). 2/yr. $4.

   Concerned with (1) women writers of the late eighteenth and early nineteenth century, especially Mary Wollstonecraft, Harriet Martineau, and Maria Edgeworth, and (2) the treatment of women in the literature of the period. Short historical, critical, or biographical articles; biographical and bibliographical notes; report of work in progress; occasional book reviews; announcements and checklists of new editions; news notes.

   Indexed by ABSTRACTS OF ENGLISH STUDIES, ANNUAL BIBLIOGRAPHY OF ENGLISH LANGUAGE AND LITERATURE, and ENGLISH LANGUAGE NOTES.

   Alternate title:

   MARY WOLLSTONECRAFT JOURNAL

WOOLF, VIRGINIA (1882-1941)

English novelist, critic

1. VIRGINIA WOOLF MISCELLANY. Editors (editorship rotates): Lucio Ruotolo, Department of English, Stanford University, Stanford, Calif. 94305; J.J. Wilson, Department of English, California State College, Sonoma, 1801 East Cotati Avenue, Rohnert Park, Calif. 94928; Ellen Hawkes, Boston University, Boston, Mass. 02215; Margaret Comstock, New York University, Washington Square, New York, N.Y. 10003. 1973-- . 2/yr. (irregular). Free (donations welcome). [4-10 p.] Last issue examined: no. 9, 1977.

Brief articles on sources, allusions, biographical facts, and textual problems; short critical essays on Woolf's works; reminiscences on her life; reviews of new editions and critical works; reports on library holdings and acquisitions; queries and answers; reports of work in progress; announcements of colloquia, sales, formation of the Virginia Woolf Society, MLA seminars, and social functions; letters to the editor.

Indexed by ANNUAL BIBLIOGRAPHY OF ENGLISH LANGUAGE AND LITERATURE.

2. VIRGINIA WOOLF NEWSLETTER. Editor: Carolyn G. Heilbrun, Department of English, 602 Philosophy Hall, Columbia University, New York, N.Y. 10023. 1971-- . $5.

Product of the Modern Language Association seminar on Virginia Woolf. Brief critical and biographical articles; news and notes.

Indexed by ABSTRACTS OF ENGLISH STUDIES and ANNUAL BIBLIOGRAPHY OF ENGLISH LANGUAGE AND LITERATURE.

3. VIRGINIA WOOLF QUARTERLY (VWQ). Editor: Suzanne Henig (San Diego State University), 6762 Cibola Road, San Diego, Calif. 92120. Publisher: Aeolian Press, San Diego, Calif. Subscriptions: Linda Pluth, 24 Colmar Road, Cherry Hill, N.J. 08002. November 1972-- . Irregular (temporarily suspended, 1973-75; resumed publication with vol. 2, nos. 1-2, 1975; in 1976, one double issue, vol. 2, nos. 3-4; in 1977, one double issue, vol. 3, nos. 1-2). $12 (individuals); $24 (libraries); add $4 for all overseas mail. [150-200 p.] Circulation: 2,500. Last issue examined: vol. 3, 1977.

"Published for the purpose of studying, elucidating, documenting, appreciating, and perpetuating the memory of Virginia Woolf . . . the Bloomsbury Group, their . . . acquaintances and the times in which they lived." Long essays on sources, individual titles, and influences, including philosophy, economics, and science; creative writing and art section; bibliographies and book reviews in every issue; numerous illustrations, photographs, and sketches. Vol. 2, nos. 1-2, contains abstracts of earlier articles and reviews, and a name, title, and subject index to previous issues.

Indexed by AMERICAN HUMANITIES INDEX, ANNUAL BIBLIOGRAPHY OF ENGLISH LANGUAGE AND LITERATURE, MLA INTERNATIONAL BIBLIOGRAPHY, TWENTIETH CENTURY LITERATURE, VICTORIAN STUDIES, and YEAR'S WORK IN ENGLISH STUDIES.

Alternate subtitle:

A SCHOLARLY, CRITICAL, AND LITERARY JOURNAL

WORDSWORTH, WILLIAM (1770-1850)

English poet

1. WORDSWORTH CIRCLE (WC; TWC). Editor: Marilyn Gaull, Department of English, Temple University, Philadelphia, Pa. 19122. Review editor: Paul A. Magnuson. Subscriptions in the United Kingdom: Basil Savage, 46, Brookfield, Highgate West Hill, London N6 6AT. Winter 1970-- . Quarterly. Free with membership in the Wordsworth-Coleridge Association ($7/one yr., $13/two yrs., $19/three yrs.--individuals); $7 (libraries). [60-90 p.] Circulation: 900. Last issue examined: vol. 9, 1978.

   "Founded to improve communication among colleagues interested in the first generation English Romantic writers: Wordsworth, Coleridge, Hazlitt, De Quincey, Lamb, Southey, Landor, Jane Austen, Sir Walter Scott" and their times. Long biographical, critical, and textual studies; special issues, such as those on Landor, Lamb, or Austen, with guest editors who are specialists in their fields; summer issue devoted to long book reviews and notices, often with long critical comments, of all new publications including books, articles, and dissertations "relevant to both English and continental Romanticism"; "An Annual Register" which summarizes but does not evaluate publications of the previous year on Coleridge and Wordsworth; news notes --MLA and regional programs, lecture tours, European conferences, exhibitions, foreign publications; news of the Wordsworth-Coleridge Association and the Wordsworth-Coleridge Summer Conference in the Lake District; information on work in progress and library collections; queries; lists of books received, most of which are reviewed in later issues; occasional illustrations; index for the year in the autumn issue, no. 4, arranged by Romantic author and by reviewer or critic. Available in microform from University Microfilms International.

   Indexed by ABSTRACTS OF ENGLISH STUDIES, AMERICAN HUMANITIES INDEX, ANNUAL BIBLIOGRAPHY OF ENGLISH LANGUAGE AND LITERATURE, ENGLISH LANGUAGE NOTES, MLA ABSTRACTS, MLA INTERNATIONAL BIBLIOGRAPHY, and YEAR'S WORK IN ENGLISH STUDIES.

2. WORDSWORTH SOCIETY: TRANSACTIONS. Publisher: Edinburgh, Scotland, and Grasmere, England. 1882-87 (nos. 1-8).

   Valuable contributions by some of the most famous literary figures of the period. Facsimile reprint in two volumes, with illustrations and portraits, available from Dawson's or Walter J. Johnson ($38).

Alternate information in BRITISH UNION CATALOGUE OF PERIODICALS: 1880-88.

WYCLIF, JOHN (1320?-84)

English religious reformer, theologian

1. Wyclif Society, London. REPORT OF THE EXECUTIVE COMMITTEE. Sponsor and publisher: Wyclif Society, London (founded by Frederick J. Furnivall in 1882). 1882/83-1925. Irregular (no. 14, 1915; no. 15, 1925). One guinea. [4-8 p.]

   "Founded to remove from England the disgrace of having till now left buried in manuscript the most important works of her great early reformer, John Wyclif." Brief notes on progress made in publishing Wyclif's works; list of members; financial statement. Alternate spellings: Wycliffe, Wiclif.

YEATS, WILLIAM BUTLER (1865-1939)

Irish poet, dramatist

1. New Yeats Papers. Editor: Liam Miller. Publisher: Dolmen Press, Dublin, Ireland. Distributor in the United States and Canada: Humanities Press, 171 First Avenue, Atlantic Highlands, N.J. 07716. 1971-- . Irregular (a series). $5-15. [40-130 p.] Circulation: 2,000. Last issue examined: vol. 15, 1978.

   Authoritative monographs devoted to one aspect of Yeats's life, Irish background, and works, such as his symbolism, his use of Cuchulain, his exile, the Irish Renaissance, and the Dun Emer Press; bibliographies and footnotes; portraits and illustrations; no index.

2. YEATS CENTENARY PAPERS. Editor: Liam Miller. Publisher: Dolmen Press, Dublin, Ireland. Distributor in the United States and Canada: Dufour Editions, Chester Springs, Pa. 19425. March 1965-April 1968. Irregular. [20-30 p.]

   Each publication is a critical study of one particular aspect of Yeats's life or works, such as YEATS AND JOYCE (1967); reprints of lectures delivered at the Yeats International Summer School in Sligo, Ireland; bibliographies; illustrations, portraits, and facsimiles.

3. YEATS-ELIOT REVIEW: A JOURNAL OF CRITICISM AND SCHOLARSHIP (YER). Supersedes T.S. ELIOT REVIEW (see Eliot, T.S., entry 3). Editor: Shyamal Bagchee, Department of English, University of Alberta, Edmonton T6G 2E5, Canada. Summer 1978 (vol. 5, no. 1)-- . 2/yr. (Spring, Fall). Two-year subscriptions only: Individuals, U.S., $8;

institutions, U.S., $10; $4 per issue and $6 per double issue. Circulation: 400.

Long articles and brief notes relating to all aspects of Yeats and Eliot studies, individual and comparative; book reviews; occasional news notes and information on work in progress; regular "Bibliographical Update"; no index.

Indexed by ABSTRACTS OF ENGLISH STUDIES, AMERICAN LITERATURE, and MLA INTERNATIONAL BIBLIOGRAPHY.

4. Yeats Society of Japan. BULLETIN. Sponsor and publisher: Yeats Society of Japan, Tokyo, Japan. April 1966-- .

5. Yeats Society of Japan. REPORT. Sponsor and publisher: Yeats Society of Japan, Tokyo, Japan. 1966-- . Annual.

6. YEATS STUDIES: AN INTERNATIONAL JOURNAL. Superseded by Yeats Studies Series (see entry 7). Editors: Robert O'Driscoll and Lorna Reynolds, Irish University Press, Dublin, Ireland. Sponsor: University College, Galway, Ireland, and St. Michael's College, University of Toronto, Toronto M5S 1A6, Canada. Publisher: Irish University Press, Shannon, Ireland. Autumn 1971-72 (vols. 1-2). Annual. $10.60; £2.10. [140-200 p.]

Each volume is concerned with one subject--for example, THEATRE AND THE VISUAL ARTS: A CENTENARY CELEBRATION OF JACK YEATS AND JOHN SYNGE. Collections of critical essays on Yeats, Synge, their families and friends, works, style, language, and ideas; interviews; previously unpublished material; international contributors; numerous portraits and illustrations; facsimiles.

7. Yeats Studies Series. Supersedes YEATS STUDIES (see entry 6). Editors: Robert O'Driscoll and Lorna Reynolds, 2647 Main Street, Niagara Falls, N.Y. 14305. Publisher: Macmillan, Toronto, Canada; Maclean-Hunter Press, Niagara Falls, N.Y. 14300. 1975-- . Irregular (a series). $20-25. [300 p.] Last issue examined: vol. 2, 1976.

Collections of critical and textual studies of Yeats's unpublished writings (and occasionally other authors, such as Shaw) which aim at helping to establish definitive texts to understand the creative process. Each volume is concerned with a specific subject--for example, YEATS AND THE OCCULT (1975), edited by George Mills Harper. Illustrations and facsimiles; no indexes.

ZOLA, ÉMILE (1840-1902)

French novelist

1. Archives des Lettres Modernes. 1970-- . Irregular. The series number for the issue on Zola is provided below.

Zola subseries	Archives series	Date
Unnumbered	No. 114	1970

In French. See Camus, Albert, entry 2, for a full description of Archives des Lettres Modernes.

Indexed by BULLETIN CRITIQUE, FRENCH XX, Klapp, and MLA INTERNATIONAL BIBLIOGRAPHY.

2. BULLETIN DE LA SOCIÉTÉ LITTÉRAIRE DES AMIS D'ÉMILE ZOLA. Sponsor and publisher: Société des Amis de Zola, Paris. 1910-13 (nos. 1-9); new series, 1922-37 (nos. 1-23). Irregular. [30 p.]

Reprints of lectures, letters, and selected works by Zola; news of performances and readings of Zola's works; notes on radio programs, Zola's friendships, pictures. In French.

Alternate titles:

ASSOCIATION ÉMILE ZOLA BULLETIN

BULLETIN DE L'ASSOCIATION ÉMILE ZOLA

Société littéraire des Amis d'Émile Zola. BULLETIN

3. CAHIERS NATURALISTES. Editor: Henri Mitterand, 4, rue du Cuif, 94410 Saint-Maurice, France. Sponsor: Société littéraire des Amis d'Émile Zola, 61, rue des Saints-Pères, 75006 Paris. Publisher: Éditions Fasquelle, Paris. 1955-- . Annual since 1976; formerly 2/yr. (irregular). 60 Fr; 65 Fr (foreign). [100-120 p.] Last issue examined: no. 52, 1978.

Official bulletin of the Société littéraire des Amis d'Émile Zola, which does not confine itself solely to the life and works of Zola but extends to the entire naturalist movement, its influence on Zola's contemporaries, and the study of the sociohistorical novel in French literature. Long articles and brief notes on Zola's political and social theories, his life and family, his interaction with other celebrities; literary analyses of the characters and plots of his works, his naturalism, themes, and treatment of myth; occasional bibliographies of library holdings; comprehensive bibliographies covering recent international Zola scholarship--new editions, books, articles, book reviews, and dissertations; previously unpublished works and letters; report of work in progress; book reviews of important international publications; international contributors. Index to 1955-74 (nos. 1-48) in no. 49 (1975), arranged by subject and name of critic. In French.

Indexed by BIBLIOGRAPHIE DE LA LITTÉRATURE FRANÇAISE, ENGLISH LANGUAGE NOTES, FRENCH XX, Klapp, MLA INTERNATIONAL BIBLIOGRAPHY, and REVUE D' HISTOIRE LITTÉRAIRE.

ZWEIG, STEFAN (1881-1942)

Austrian poet, novelist

1. ARCHIV DER INTERNATIONALEN STEFAN ZWEIG-GESELLSCHAFT. Editor: Arthur Werner. Sponsor and publisher: International Stefan-Zweig-Gesellschaft, Sandwirtgasse 21, 1060 Vienna, Austria. 1966-68 (nos. 1-2). AS 28; DM4; $1.50. [20-25 p.]

   Brief essays on Zweig's contribution to literature, his influence on the younger generation, and his reception and popularity in his own times; information on lectures and programs; quotations from reviews; previously unpublished letters; facsimiles. In German.

2. BLÄTTER DER INTERNATIONALEN STEFAN-ZWEIG-GESELLSCHAFT. Editor: Erich Fitzbauer, Piaristengasse 46/17, Vienna VIII, Austria. Sponsor and publisher: Stefan-Zweig-Gesellschaft, Postfach 90, Vienna 64, Austria. April 1958-January 1963 (nos. 1-15). AS 5; DM1 per issue. [10-25 p.]

   Brief articles on Zweig's life and works; brief excerpts from Zweig's works; discussion of new editions and other important publications; notes on members' activities and gatherings. In German.

   Alternate titles:

   BLÄTTER DER STEFAN-ZWEIG-GESELLSCHAFT (nos. 1-10)

   Internationale Stefan-Zweig-Gesellschaft. BLÄTTER

ZWINGLI, ULRICH (1484-1531)

Swiss religious reformer

1. ZWINGLIANA: MITTEILUNGEN ZUR GESCHICHTE ZWINGLIS UND DER REFORMATION. Sponsor: Zwingliverein, Zentralbibliothek, 6, Zäringerplatz, 8025 Zurich, Switzerland. 1897/1904-- . Irregular. $3. [250 p.] Last issue examined: vol. 14, 1977.

   Articles; brief notes; news. In German. Second-hand copies

available from Kraus Periodicals (1897/1904–1964/1968, vols. 1-12, $222).

Indexed by Köttelwesch.

Alternate subtitles:

BEITRÄGE ZUR GESCHICHTE ZWINGLIS, DER REFORMATION, UND DES PROTESTANTISMUS IN DER SCHWEIZ

MITTEILUNGEN ZUR GESCHICHTE ZWINGLIS, DER REFORMATION, UND DES PROTESTANTISMUS IN DER SCHWEIZ

VEREINIGUNG FÜR DAS ZWINGLIMUSEUM

ADDENDA

Information on the following periodicals was located after the remainder of the book had been prepared for the binder. For statistical purposes, these periodicals are included in the 1,129 referred to on p. ix, and the additional authors make a grand total of 435, but the titles themselves are not listed in the Index, and statistics concerning their contents are not included in the surveys enumerated in the appendixes.

ASIMOV, ISAAC (1920-)

Russian-born American science fiction writer

1. ISAAC ASIMOV'S SCIENCE FICTION. Publisher: Davis Publications, P.O. Box 1855 GPO, N.Y. 10001. Spring 1977-- . 2/month. $5.95.

BAECK, LEO (1873-1956)

Rabbi, leader of German Jewry

1. BULLETIN OF THE LEO BAECK INSTITUTE. Sponsor: Leo Baeck Institute. Publisher: Tel Aviv, Jerusalem. August 1957-- . Irregular (vol. 12, 1969; N.F. 13, 1974).

    A bulletin for the sponsoring and contributing members of the Leo Baeck Institute, Inc. Text in German.

    Indexed by Köttelwesch.

    Alternate titles:

    BULLETIN DES LEO BAECK INSTITUTS

    Leo Baeck Institute of Jews from Germany. BULLETIN

2. LEO BAECK INSTITUTE LIBRARY AND ARCHIVES NEWS. Sponsor and publisher: Leo Baeck Institute, 129 East 73rd Street, New York, N.Y. 10021. February 1975-- .

An excellent source for all information on German, Austrian, Yiddish, and Exile literature.

3. Leo Baeck Institute of Jews from Germany. PUBLICATIONS. Publisher: London, England. 1958-- .

4. Leo Baeck Institute of Jews from Germany. SCHRIFTENREIHE WISSENSCHAFTLICHER ABHANDLUNGEN. Publisher: J.C.B. Mohr, Tübingen, Germany (BRD). 1959-- . Irregular (13 vols. from 1959-65). [70-600 p.]

   Every volume concerns some aspect of the Jewish culture--not confined solely to Leo Baeck, but inspired by him.

5. Leo Baeck Memorial Lecture. Sponsor: Leo Baeck Institute, 129 East 73rd Street, New York, N.Y. 10021. 1958-- .

6. Publications of the Leo Baeck Institute of Jews from Germany. YEARBOOK. Sponsor: Issued for the Institute by the East and West Library, London, England. Publisher: London, Jerusalem, New York. 1956-- . Annual. Last issue examined: vol. 22, 1977.

   Report of activities.

   Indexed by Köttelwesch.

   Alternate title:

   Leo Baeck Institute of Jews from Germany. YEARBOOK.

BALZAC, HONORÉ (see main entry)

1. Archives balzaciennes. Subseries of Archives des Lettres Modernes. 1978-- . Irregular. Equivalent numbers are provided below for both the parent series (Archives des Lettres Modernes) and the individual author series on Balzac.

Balzac subseries	Archives series	Date
No. 1	No. 182	1978

   In French. See Camus, Albert, entry 2, for a full description of Archives des Lettres Modernes.

   Indexed by BULLETIN CRITIQUE, FRENCH VII, FRENCH XX, Klapp, and MLA INTERNATIONAL BIBLIOGRAPHY.

BECKETT, SAMUEL (1906-)

Irish-born French novelist, dramatist, poet

1. JOURNAL OF BECKETT STUDIES. Editor: James Knowlson. Sponsor: University of Reading, Reading, Berkshire RG6 2AH, England. Publisher: John Calder, London, and Beckett Archives, University of Reading. Winter 1976-- . 2/yr. $7.50.

2. Samuel Beckett. Subseries of La Revue des Lettres Modernes. 1964-- . Irregular (a series). Series numbers for the issues on Beckett are provided below.

Beckett subseries	La Revue series	Date
Unnumbered	No. 100	1964

In French. See Camus, Albert, entry 1, for a full description of La Revue des Lettres Modernes.

Indexed by FRENCH VII, Klapp, and MLA INTERNATIONAL BIBLIOGRAPHY.

BURROUGHS, EDGAR RICE (see main entry)

1. FANTASTIC WORLDS OF EDGAR RICE BURROUGHS. Sponsor: British Edgar Rice Burroughs Society, 113 Chertsey Rise, Stevenage, Hertfordshire, SGZ 9JQ, England. 1976-- . Quarterly. $2.50.

BYRON, GEORGE GORDON, LORD (see main entry)

1. Byron Society. NEWSLETTER. Editor: Marsha M. Manns. Sponsor: Byron Society, New York. Publisher: Byron Society, The American Committee, 259 New Jersey Avenue, Collingswood, N.J. 08108. 1973-- . Annual. Free to members. [20 p.] Last issue examined: vol. 5, 1977.

   Brief critical and biographical articles; news of annual Byron seminars and annual international councils; report of Byron Society activities around the world; announcement of members' publications.

CARLYLE, THOMAS (1795-1881)

Scottish historian, philosopher, essayist

1. CARLYLE NEWSLETTER. Edinburgh editors: K.J. Fielding and Ian Campbell, English Department, University of Edinburgh, David Hume Tower, George Square, Edinburgh EH8 9JK, Scotland. American editor: Anne Skabarnicki, English Department, Lafayette College, Easton, Penn. 18042.

Publisher: University of Edinburgh in collaboration with Lafayette College. March 1979-- . Annual. £2 ; $5 (three issues).

Short articles, news, and notes.

CRAWFORD, FRANCIS MARION (1854-1909)

American novelist

1. ROMANTIST. Editors: John C. Moran and Don Herron. Sponsor: Francis Marion Crawford Memorial Society, Saracinesca House, 3610 Meadowbrook Avenue, Nashville, Tenn. 37205. 1977-- . Annual. $5. Circulation: 500.

   Concerned with the Romantic tradition from the late nineteenth century to the present day in both literature and the arts, with special attention to the life and works of Crawford.

DERLETH, AUGUST (1909-71)

American poet, novelist

1. August Derleth Society. NEWSLETTER. Editor: Richard H. Fawcett. Sponsor: August Derleth Society, 61 Teecomwas Drive, Uncasville, Conn. 06382. 1977-- . Irregular.

DESTOUCHES, LOUIS-FERDINAND [LOUIS-FERDINAND CÉLINE]

(see main entry)

1. Cahiers Céline. Publisher: Gallimard, Paris. 1976-- . [250-300 p.] Last issue examined: no. 3, 1977.

   Previously unpublished works; critical notes; interviews. In French.

   Indexed by Klapp.

DICKINSON, EMILY (see main entry)

1. DICKINSON STUDIES. Supersedes EMILY DICKINSON BULLETIN (see Dickinson, Emily, entry 3). Editor and publisher: Frederick L. Morey, Higginson Press, 4508 38th Street, Brentwood, Md. 20722. Sponsor: Emily Dickinson Society. 1978 (no. 34)-- . 2/yr. (June, December). $5; $10 (institutions); renewals for three years only: $14; $30 (institutions). [50-75 p.]

   Explications of the poetry; bibliographies of critical books and articles, dissertations, poems, drama, films, and recordings; notes on new publications.

DIDEROT, DENIS (see main entry)

1. Cahiers diderotiens. Sponsor: 4, rue de l'Université, 75007 Paris. 1978-- .

   Each volume is on a different subject. In French.

FARIGOULE, LOUIS H.J. [JULES ROMAINS] (see main entry)

1. Cahiers Jules Romains. Publisher: Flammarion, Paris. 1976-- . 50 Fr. [250 p.] Last issue examined: no. 2, 1978.

   Previously unpublished letters; notes and explanations. In French.

FREEMAN, R. AUSTIN (1862-1943)

English author of detective stories

1. THORNDYKE FILE. Editor: Philip T. Asdell, R.R. no. 5, Box 355, Frederick, Md. 21701. Spring 1976-- . 2/yr. $5. Last issue published: vol. 3, no. 3, July-September 1977.

IRVING, WASHINGTON (1783-1859)

American essayist, biographer, historian

1. SKETCH BOOK. Sponsor: Irving Association of Starkey Seminary, Elmira, N.Y. 14901. September 22-November 3, 1954 (vol. 1, nos. 1-4).

KIERKEGAARD, SØREN (see main entry)

1. Cahiers du Centre Soeren-Kierkegaard. Superseded by EXISTER. Editor: Xavier Lacroix. Sponsor: Centry Soeren Kierkegaard, 1, rue de l'Ancienne-Préfecture, 69002 Lyon, France. 1974(?)-75 (nos. 1-4). 3/yr. 15 Fr.

LAMENNAIS, HUGUES-FÉLICITÉ-ROBERT DE (1782-1854)

French priest, philosopher, editor

1. CAHIERS LAMENNAIS. 1975-- .

2. CAHIERS MENNAISIENS. Sponsor: Société des amis de Lamennais,

Brest, France. 1963-- . Irregular (nos. 7-8, 1977). [150 p.]

Long critical studies; previously unpublished documents; bibliographies. In French.

Indexed by Klapp.

LÉGER, ALEXIS [SAINT-JOHN PERSE] (1887-1975)

French poet, diplomat

1. Cahiers Saint-John Perse. Editor: Jean-Louis Lalanne. Publisher: Gallimard, Paris. 1978-- .

   In French.

LEROUX, GASTON (1868-1927)

French journalist, author of mystery stories

1. Cahiers semestriels du Cercle Gaston Leroux. Editor: Pierre Lépine. Sponsor: Cercle Gaston Leroux, 86, avenue Félix-Faure, 75015 Paris. 1977-- . Free.

   In French.

LOUIS, PIERRE [PIERRE LOUŸS] (1870-1925)

French novelist, poet

1. BULLETIN DES AMIS DE PIERRE LOUŸS. Editor: William Théry. Sponsor: Les Amis de Pierre Louÿs, 79, rue du Barbâtre, 51100 Reims, France. 1977-- . Quarterly. Last issue examined: no. 4, 1977. [35-40 p.]

   Brief articles; news and notes; bibliographies; previously unpublished documents; reviews. In French.

   Indexed by Klapp.

2. CAHIERS LOUŸS. Sponsor: Les Amis de Pierre Louÿs, 79, rue du Barbâtre, 51100 Reims, France. 1977-- . Annual. [150 p.]

   Previously unpublished letters, works, and other documents; interpretive and biographical articles; studies of the manuscripts; bibliographies. In French.

   Indexed by Klapp.

LOUŸS, PIERRE

See LOUIS, PIERRE.

MAISTRE, JOSEPH MARIA (see main entry)

1. Études maistriennes. Sponsor: Association des Amis de Joseph et de Xavier de Maistre, Centre universitaire de Savoie, Chambéry, France. 1975-- . Irregular. [100 p.]

   Special issues, including a catalogue of Maistre's library (1975). In French.

   Indexed by Klapp.

MAURIAC, FRANÇOIS (see main entry)

1. Travaux du Centre d'études et de recherches sur François Mauriac. Sponsor: Université de Bordeaux III, U.E.R. Esplanade de Michel-Montaigne, domaine universitaire, 33400 Talence, France. 1977-- . 15 Fr; 23 Fr (foreign). [30-40 p.]

   Articles on the manuscripts; bibliographies of theses in progress or completed; news notes. In French.

   Indexed by Klapp.

MORLEY, CHRISTOPHER (1890-1957)

American novelist, journalist, essayist

1. Christopher Morley Knothole Association. ANNUAL LETTER TO MEMBERS. 1961-- . Annual. President: Helen Oakley. Sponsor: Christopher Morley Knothole Association, Bryant Library, Paper Mill Road, Roslyn, N.Y. 11576.

   Report of activities in Christopher Morley Park and in Morley's log-cabin writing studio; news on programs, publications, and acquisitions by the Morley Alcove in Bryant Library.

NABOKOV, VLADIMIR (1899-1977)

Russian-born novelist, poet

1. VLADIMIR NABOKOV RESEARCH NEWSLETTER. Sponsor and Publisher: Vladimir Nabokov Society, Department of Slavic Languages and Literatures, Univ. of Kansas, Lawrence, Kans. 66045. 1978-- . 2/yr. (Spring, Fall). Free with membership ($2).

Abstracts of theses, dissertations, articles, and books; bibliographical materials; book reviews; announcements of work in progress; annotations of Nabokov's works; notes and queries pertinent to Nabokov research interests.

PÉGUY, CHARLES (see main entry)

1. BULLETIN D'INFORMATIONS ET DE RECHERCHES: L'AMITIÉ CHARLES PÉGUY. Supersedes L'AMITIÉ CHARLES PÉGUY (see Péguy, Charles, entry 1). Editor: André-A. Devaux. Sponsor: L'Amitié Charles Péguy, 4 rue Auguste-Bartholdi, 75015 Paris. 1978-- .

   A description of the contents may be found under the periodical's previous title.

PERSE, SAINT-JOHN

See LÉGER, ALEXIS.

POUND, EZRA (see main entry)

1. AMAGOGIC AND PAIDEUMIC REVIEW. Editor: 15 Lynch Street, San Francisco, Calif. 94109.

READ, SIR HERBERT (1893-1968)

English poet, art and literary critic

1. Herbert Read Series. Editor: Philip Ward, 210 Fifth Avenue, New York, N.Y. 10010. Publisher: Oleander Press, 17 Stansgate Avenue, Cambridge CB2 2QZ, England. 1961-- . Irregular. $1.25. [52 p.]

SAPIR, EDWARD (1884-1939)

American linguist, anthropologist

1. Edward Sapir Monograph Series in Language, Culture, and Cognition. 1977-- . Irregular (vol. 4, 1979).

SPINOZA, BARUCH (see main entry)

1. Cahiers Spinoza. Sponsor and publisher: Réplique, 9, rue Dupont-des-Loges, 75007 Paris. 1977-- . Irregular. 40 Fr.

TURGENEV, IVAN (1818-83)

Russian novelist

1. Cahiers Ivan Tourgueniev, Pauline Viardot, Maria Malibran. Editor: Alexander Ziguilsky. Sponsor: Association des Amis de Ivan Tourgueniev, Pauline Viardot, Maria Malibran, 20 bis, avenue Mac-Mahon, 75017 Paris. October 1977-- . 30 Fr.

VERNE, JULES (see main entry)

1. Bibliothèque Jules Verne. Publisher: Minard, Paris. 1974-- . Irregular. Last issue examined: no. 2, 1977.

   Each volume focuses on a specific subject--a regrouping of criticism originally published in Lettres Modernes. In French.

WILLIAMS, TENNESSEE (1911-)

American dramatist and author of fiction

1. TENNESSEE WILLIAMS NEWSLETTER. Editor: Stephen S. Stanton, Department of Humanities, 1079 East Engineering Building, University of Michigan, Ann Arbor, Mich. 48109. January 1979-- . 2/yr.

   Short academic and theatrical notes of interest to drama scholars and teachers; reviews or abstracts of books and articles; reports of dissertations in progress; news and reviews of performances; interpretive notes on plays and fiction; letters of inquiry.

Appendix 1
COUNTRIES AND THEIR AUTHORS

The 28 countries represented in this international bibliography have produced 1,129 newsletters, journals, annuals, and other serials dedicated to research on the life and works of individual authors. France leads all other countries in the number of different individuals who have inspired these publications: 134, ranging from Rabelais and Racine to Gide and Giono. England is second with 83, counting the Browning, Brontë, and Powys families as one unit each because the pertinent titles are invariably concerned with the family as a whole, their interrelationship and influence, as well as with the writing style of the individual members. The United States is third, with 70 authors; then Germany, 52; Italy, 20; Austria, 13; and Switzerland, 9.

English and French authors have inspired most of these highly specialized publications: 326 and 302 titles respectively. German authors are the subject of 160 serials; United States authors, 130; Italian authors, 68; Austrian, 29; and Swiss, 10. Interest in these authors, however, crosses all international boundaries, as the following table illustrates.

SHAKESPEARE (57 titles)

Country	Titles
United States	21
England	16
Germany	7
Japan	6
Australia	2
Armenia	1
Austria	1
Canada	1

DOYLE (52 titles)

Country	Titles
United States	41
Denmark	3
Canada	2
Sweden	2
England	1

GOETHE (24 titles)

Country	Titles
Germany	14
Argentina	2
Austria	2
Japan	2
Australia	1
England	1
France	1
Switzerland	1

Countries and Their Authors

DANTE (23 titles)

Country	Titles
Italy	9
United States	4
Germany	3
England	2
Argentina	1
Canada	1
France	1
Russia	1

SHAW (13 titles)

Country	Titles
United States	8
England	5

BROWNING (12 titles)

Country	Titles
United States	7
England	5

TEILHARD DE CHARDIN (12 titles)

Country	Titles
France	6
Belgium	3
England	2
Germany	1

TOLKIEN (12 titles)

Country	Titles
United States	8
England	2
Australia	1

BALZAC (11 titles)

Country	Titles
France	9
United States	2

CLAUDEL (10 titles)

Country	Titles
France	5
United States	2
Belgium	1
Canada	1
Japan	1

SAINT AUGUSTINE (10 titles)

Country	Titles
France	3
Italy	2
Spain	2
United States	2
Belgium	1

JOYCE (9 titles)

Country	Titles
United States	4
England	2
France	2

NIETZSCHE (9 titles)

Country	Titles
Germany	5
France	4

RIMBAUD (9 titles)

Country	Titles
France	9

BURROUGHS (8 titles)

Country	Titles
United States	7
Canada	1

WELLS, H.G. (8 titles)

Country	Titles
England	8

CLEMENS [Mark Twain] (7 titles)

Country	Titles
United States	7

LUTHER (7 titles)

Country	Titles
Germany	5

LUTHER (cont.)

Country	Titles
Austria	1
United States	1

RENAN (7 titles)

Country	Titles
France	7

STIFTER (7 titles)

Country	Titles
Germany	4
Austria	3

WHITMAN (7 titles)

Country	Titles
United States	6
Japan	1

YEATS (7 titles)

Country	Titles
Ireland	3
Japan	2
United States	2

Not all countries of the world are covered in this Guide, of course--only those for which we have readily accessible literature in our scholarly libraries. But, even though a number of the serials described herein are edited by hobbyists and enthusiasts more from personal taste than academic interest, we hope that almost all of the most durable and worthy scholarship devoted to the genre of the author newsletter or journal has found its way into these pages.

The count by country and author which follows aims at demonstrating national interests in relation to these serial publications. Such a survey can not only give us some idea of literary interest and scholarship concerning specific authors, it can also establish the contributions and value of individual author newsletters, journals, and serials at this particular time in literary history.

ARGENTINA (1 author; 2 titles)

Author	Titles
San Martín, José de	2

AUSTRIA (13 authors; 29 titles)

Author	Titles
Freud, Sigmund	2
Grillparzer, Franz	2
Herzl, Theodor	1
Hofmannsthal, Hugo von	3
Musil, Robert	3
Raimund, Ferdinand	1
Rank, Otto	1
Reinhardt, Max	1
Schnitzler, Arthur	1
Steiner, Rudolf	4
Stifter, Adalbert	7
Weinheber, Josef	1
Zweig, Stefan	2

BELGIUM (6 authors; 8 titles)

Author	Titles
Baillon, André	1
Bolland, Jean de	1
Degée, Olivier [Jean Tousseul]	1
Maeterlinck, Maurice	1
Plisnier, Charles	3
Velde, Henry van de	1

BRAZIL (1 author; 1 title)

Author	Titles
Machado de Assis	1

CANADA (3 authors; 3 titles)

Author	Titles
Choquette, Robert	1
Leacock, Stephen	1
Seers, Eugène [Louis Dantin]	1

CUBA (1 author; 3 titles)

Author	Titles
Martí, José	3

DENMARK (2 authors; 5 titles)

Author	Titles
Andersen, Hans Christian	1
Kierkegaard, Søren	4

ENGLAND, SCOTLAND, IRELAND, WALES (83 authors, counting as one unit each the families of Brontë, Powys, and Browning; 326 titles)

Author	Titles
Arnold, Matthew	2
Austen, Jane	1
Bacon, Francis	5
Bennett, Arnold	1
Blackmore, Richard D.	1
Blake, William	3
Brontë	1
Browning	12
Bulwer-Lytton, Edward	1
Burke, Edmund	2
Burns, Robert	3
Butler, Samuel	1
Byron, Lord	4
Carleton, William	1
Carlyle, Thomas	3
Chaucer, Geoffrey	4
Chesterton, G.K.	1
Conrad, Joseph	6
Coward, Noel	1
Dickens, Charles	5
Disraeli, Benjamin	1
Dodgson, Charles L. [Lewis Carroll]	3
Doyle, Sir Arthur Conan	52
Durrell, Lawrence	1
Esdaile, Arundell	1
Evans, Mary Ann [George Eliot]	1
Forester, C.S.	1
Forster, John	1
Gissing, George	1
Graves, Robert	1
Greenaway, Kate	1
Hardy, Thomas	3
Herbert, George	1
Hopkins, Gerard Manley	4
Housman, A.E.	1
Hume, David	1
Johnson, Samuel	4
Joyce, James	9
Keats, John	3
Kipling, Rudyard	3
Knox, John	1
Lamb, Charles	6
Lawrence, D.H.	6
Lawrence, T.E.	1
Lessing, Doris	1
Lewis, C.S.	3
Lewis, Wyndham	1
Locke, John	2
Lydgate, John	1
Machen, Arthur	2
Mill, John Stuart	1
Milton, John	5
More, Saint Thomas	3
Morris, William	3
Newman, John Henry	1
O'Casey, Sean	1
Paine, Thomas	2
Peake, Mervyn	2
Pope, Alexander	2
Powys	1
Russell, Bertrand	2
Scott, Sir Walter	1
Shakespeare, William	57
Shaw, George Bernard	13
Shelley, Percy Bysshe. See Keats	
Spenser, Edmund	1
Sterne, Laurence	1
Swift, Jonathan. See Pope	
Tennyson, Alfred, 1st baron	6

ENGLAND, SCOTLAND, IRELAND, WALES (cont.)

Author	Titles
Thackeray, William Makepeace	1
Thompson, Francis	1
Tolkien, J.R.R.	12
Trollope, Anthony	1
Wallace, Edgar	1
Ward, Arthur S. [Sax Rohmer]	1
Waugh, Evelyn	1
Wells, H.G.	8
Whitehead, Alfred North	1
Wollstonecraft, Mary	1
Woolf, Virginia	3
Wordsworth, William	2
Wyclif, John	1
Yeats, William Butler	7

FRANCE (134 authors; 302 titles)

Author	Titles
Ampère, André-Marie	1
Arouet, François Marie [Voltaire]	3
Audoux, Marguèrite. See Philippe	
Balzac, Honoré	11
Barbey d'Aurevilly, Jules	3
Barrault, Jean-Louis. See Renaud	
Baty, Gaston	1
Baudelaire, Charles	5
Bergson, Henri Louis	1
Bernanos, Georges	6
Beyle, Marie Henri [Stendhal]	6
Bloch, Jean-Richard	1
Blondel, Maurice	3
Bloy, Léon	3
Blum, Léon	3
Bodin, Jean	1
Bonaparte, Napoleon	1
Bosco, Henri	2
Bossuet, Jacques-Bénigne	2
Bourdaloue, Louis	1
Boutelleau, Jacques [Chardonne]	1
Brasillach, Robert	2
Bremond, Henri	1
Budé, Guillaume	3
Camus, Albert	4
Cathlin, Léon	1
Chartier, Émile [Alain]	3
Chateaubriand, François-René	4
Chatrian, Alexandre. See Erckmann	
Claudel, Paul	10
Cocteau, Jean	2
Constant de Rebecque, Henri	1
Corneille, Pierre	1
Courier, Paul-Louis	2
Couté, Gaston	1
Daniélou, Cardinal	1
de Gaulle, Charles	2
Delisle, Léopold	1
Descartes, René	1
Destouches, Louis-Ferdinand [Céline]	2
Deubel, Léon	1
Diderot, Denis	2
Dieudonné, Lucien [Lucien Jean]. See Philippe	
Doucet, Jacques	1
Du Bellay, Joachim	1
du Bos, Charles	2
Dudevant, Mme. [George Sand]	4
Dullin, Charles	1
Dumas, Alexandre, père	2
Erckmann, Émile [Erckmann-Chatrian]	1
Farigoule, Louis [Jules Romains]	2
Fénelon, François	1
Flaubert, Gustave	3
Fleg, Edmond	1
Foucauld, Charles	2
Fournier, Henri-Alban [Alain-Fournier]	2
Fustel de Coulanges	1
Ghil, Raimond	1
Gide, André	6
Giono, Jean	2
Giraudoux, Jean	2

FRANCE (cont.)

Author	Titles
Gobineau, Joseph-Arthur	2
Gourmont, Rémy de	1
Grindel, Eugène [Paul Éluard]	1
Guérin, Eugénie and Maurice de	2
Guillaumin, Émile. See Philippe	
Hugo, Victor	4
Huysmans, Joris-Karl	1
Jacob, Max [Morven le Gaëlique]	2
Jaurès, Jean	1
Jouvenal, Sidonie-Gabrielle de [Colette]	1
Kostrowitzky, Wilhelm [Apollinaire]	5
Labrunie, Gérard [Gérard de Nerval]	3
Lacordaire, Jean-Baptiste-Henri	1
La Fontaine, Jean de	2
Larbaud, Valéry	1
La Varende, Jean	1
Lazare, Bernard	1
Maistre, Joseph	1
Mallarmé, Stéphane	1
Malraux, André	4
Massignon, Louis	1
Maupassant, Guy de	1
Mauriac, François	3
Maurras, Charles	3
Maynard, François de	1
Mercier, Louis	1
Milosz, Oscar Venceslas	2
Montaigne, Michel	4
Montesquieu, Charles Louis	1
Mounier, Emmanuel	1
Musset, Alfred de	3
Ner, Henri [Han Ryner]	1
Nouveau, Germain	1
Péguy, Charles	3
Pergaud, Louis	1
Philippe, Charles-Louis	2
Poquelin, Jean-Baptiste [Molière]	1
Proudhon, Pierre-Joseph	1

Author	Titles
Proust, Marcel	6
Rabelais, François	4
Racine, Jean Baptiste	4
Randon de Saint-Amand, Gabriel [Jehan Rictus]	1
Renan, Joseph Ernest	7
Renaud, Madeleine	1
Retté, Adolphe	1
Richter, Jean Paul [Jean Paul]	4
Rimbaud, Arthur	9
Rivière, Jacques	2
Rohner, Lucien	1
Rolland, Romain	4
Rollinat, Maurice	1
Ronsard, Pierre de	1
Rouget, Marie Mélanie [Marie Noël]	1
Rousseau, Jean-Jacques	4
Sainte-Beuve, Charles-Augustin	1
Saint-Simon, Claude-Henri	1
Sartre, Jean Paul	1
Scantrel, Félix-André-Yves [André Suarès]	3
Schweitzer, Albert	2
Spire, André	1
Staël, Madame de	3
Tardiveau, René [René Boylesve]	2
Teilhard de Chardin, Pierre	12
Thibault, Anatole François [Anatole France]	2
Valéry, Paul	5
Vendel, Henri [Henri Nadel]	1
Verlaine, Paul	3
Verne, Jules	3
Viaud, Julien [Pierre Loti]	2
Vigny, Alfred Victor	2
Vincent of Beauvais	1
Weil, Simone	3
Zola, Émile	3

GERMANY (52 authors; 160 titles)

Author	Titles
Barlach, Ernst	3

GERMANY (cont.)

Author	Titles
Blunck, Hans Friedrich	1
Boehme, Jacob	1
Brecht, Bertolt	3
Busch, Wilhelm	3
Cusanus, Nicolaus	3
Droste-Hülshoff, Annette von	3
Eichendorff, Baron Joseph	4
Ernst, Paul	4
Erwin von Steinbach	2
Fontane, Theodor	1
Freytag, Gustav	1
Görres, Joseph von	3
Goethe, Johann Wolfgang von	24
Grimm, Jacob and Wilhelm	2
Groth, Klaus	1
Gutenberg, Johannes	3
Hansjakob, Heinrich	2
Hauptmann, Gerhart	3
Hebbel, Friedrich	4
Hegel, Georg	6
Heidegger, Martin	1
Heine, Heinrich	5
Hesse, Hermann	2
Hölderlin, Friedrich	5
Hoffmann, August Heinrich	2
Hoffmann, Ernst T.A.	1
Hohenheim, Theophrastus [Paracelsus]	1
Kant, Immanuel	3
Kircher, Athanasius	1
Kleist, Heinrich von	4
Kolbenheyer, Erwin	1
Leibniz, Gottfried	2
Lessing, Gotthold	1
Ludwig, Otto	2
Luther, Martin	7
Mann, Heinrich	1
Mann, Thomas	2
May, Karl	3
Nietzsche, Friedrich	9
Pirckheimer, Willibald	1
Raabe, Wilhelm	5
Richter, Jean Paul [Jean Paul]	4
Rilke, Rainer Maria	2
Rückert, Friedrich and Heinrich	2
Schiller, Friedrich von	3
Schneider, Reinhold	2
Schopenhauer, Arthur	3
Storm, Theodor	1
Trakl, Georg	1
Winckelmann, Johann	2
Wolfram von Eschenbach	4

GREECE (1 author; 1 title)

Author	Titles
Aristotle	1

HUNGARY (1 author; 2 titles)

Author	Titles
Strehlenau, Nikolaus [Nikolaus Lenau]	2

INDIA (3 authors; 10 titles)

Author	Titles
Gandhi, Mohandas	5
Krishnamurti, Jiddu	1
Tagore, Rabindranath	4

ITALY (20 authors; 68 titles)

Author	Titles
Annunzio, Gabriele d'	1
Aquinas, Saint Thomas	4
Augustine, Saint	10
Barbieri, Cesare	1
Bernardino da Siena, Saint	1
Boccaccio, Giovanni	3
Buzzati, Dino	1
Casanova de Seingalt, Jacques	1
Cicero, Marcus Tullius	2
Croce, Benedetto	1
Dante Alighieri	23
Garibaldi, Guiseppe	1
Goldoni, Carlo	1
Gregory VII, Saint	1
Mazzini, Guiseppe	1
Muratori, Ludovico	1
Petrarch, Francesco	6
Pirandello, Luigi	2
Tasso, Torquato	2
Vergil	5

MARTINIQUE (1 author; 1 title)

Author	Titles
Césaire, Aimé	1

NETHERLANDS (2 authors; 6 titles)

Author	Titles
Cramer, Samuel. See Baudelaire	
Erasmus, Desiderius	2
Spinoza, Baruch	4

NORWAY (1 author; 1 title)

Author	Titles
Ibsen, Henrik	1

POLAND (1 author; 1 title)

Author	Titles
Mickiewicz, Adam	1

PORTUGAL (1 author; 1 title)

Author	Titles
Carvalho, Joaquim de	1

RUSSIA (2 authors; 3 titles)

Author	Titles
Dostoevsky, Feodor	2
Lenin, Nikolai	1

SPAIN (5 authors; 6 titles)

Author	Titles
Cervantes Saavedra, Miguel de	1
García Lorca, Federico	1
Menéndez (y) Pelayo, Marcelino	2
Pérez Galdós, Benito	1
Unamuno, Miguel de	1

SWEDEN (6 authors; 10 titles)

Author	Titles
Bergman, Hjalmar	1
Fröding, Gustaf	1
Lagerlöf, Selma	1
Sjöberg, Birger	1
Strindberg, August	1
Swedenborg, Emanuel	5

SWITZERLAND (9 authors; 10 titles)

Author	Titles
Burckhardt, Jacob	1
Calvin, John	1
Häberlin, Paul	2
Keller, Gottfried	1
Pareto, Vilfredo	1
Postl, Karl Anton [Charles Sealsfield]	1
Ramuz, Charles-Ferdinand	1
Saussure, Ferdinand de	1
Zwingli, Ulrich	1

UNITED STATES (70 authors; 130 titles)

Author	Titles
Alger, Horatio	2
Anderson, Sherwood	2
Baum, L. Frank	1
Berryman, John	1
Burroughs, Edgar Rice	8
Cabell, James Branch	2
Cather, Willa	3
Chaney, William H.	1
Chopin, Kate	1
Clemens, Samuel L. [Mark Twain]	7
Collier, John	1
Crane, Hart	1
Crane, Stephen	1
Curwood, James Oliver	1
Dannay, Frederic [Ellery Queen]	2
Dewey, John	2
Dickinson, Emily	3
Dreiser, Theodore	1
Eliot, T.S.	3
Emerson, Ralph Waldo	3
Faulkner, William	4
Faust, Frederick [Max Brand]	1
Fitzgerald, F. Scott	2
Frederic, Harold	1
George, Henry	1

UNITED STATES (cont.)

Author	Titles
Glasgow, Ellen	1
Grey, Zane	1
Hartmann, Sadakichi	1
Hawthorne, Nathaniel	2
Hemingway, Ernest	2
Higginson, Thomas Wentworth	1
Howard, Robert E.	2
Howells, William Dean	1
Jeffers, Robinson	1
Lee, Edward Edson [Leo Edwards]	1
Lee, Manfred B. See Dannay	
Lewis, Sinclair	1
Lindsay, Vachel	1
London, Jack	3
MacDonald, John D.	1
Markham, Edwin	1
Melville, Herman	4
Mencken, H.L.	1
Miller, Henry	2
Moore, Marianne	1
Nin, Anaïs	2
Nock, Albert Jay	1
O'Connor, Flannery	1
O'Hara, John	1

Authors	Titles
Olson, Charles J.	1
O'Neill, Eugene	1
Peirce, Charles Sanders	2
Poe, Edgar Allan	6
Pound, Ezra	3
Rand, Ayn	1
Riley, James Whitcomb	1
Roosevelt, Theodore	1
Sandoz, Mari [Suzette]	1
Stein, Gertrude	1
Steinbeck, John	4
Stevens, Wallace	2
Stuart, Jesse	1
Thoreau, Henry	5
Torsvan, Berick Traven [B. Traven]	1
Updike, John	1
Welty, Eudora	1
Whitman, Walt	7
Whittier, John Greenleaf	1
Williams, William Carlos	1
Wolfe, Thomas	1

VENEZUELA (1 author; 4 titles)

Author	Titles
Bolívar, Simón	4

Appendix 2

CENTURIES AND THEIR AUTHORS

B.C. (3 authors)

Aristotle
Cicero
Vergil

FIFTH CENTURY (1 author)

Augustine, Saint

ELEVENTH CENTURY (1 author)

Gregory VII, Saint

TWELFTH CENTURY (1 author)

Wolfram von Eschenbach

THIRTEENTH CENTURY (3 authors)

Aquinas, Saint Thomas
Erwin von Steinbach
Vincent of Beauvais

FOURTEENTH CENTURY (5 authors)

Boccaccio, Giovanni
Chaucer, Geoffrey
Dante Alighieri
Petrarch, Francesco
Wyclif, John

FIFTEENTH CENTURY (4 authors)

Bernardino da Siena, Saint
Cusanus, Nicolaus
Gutenberg, Johannes
Lydgate, John

SIXTEENTH CENTURY (17 authors)

Bodin, Jean
Budé, Guillaume
Calvin, John
Du Bellay, Joachim
Erasmus, Desiderius
Hohenheim, Theophrastus (Paracelsus)
Knox, John
Luther, Martin
Montaigne, Michel
More, Saint Thomas
Pirckheimer, Willibald
Rabelais, François
Ronsard, Pierre de
Shakespeare, William
Spenser, Edmund
Tasso, Torquato
Zwingli, Ulrich

SEVENTEENTH CENTURY (18 authors)

Bacon, Francis
Boehme, Jacob
Bolland, Jean de
Bossuet, Jacques-Bénigne
Bourdaloue, Louis
Cervantes Saavedra, Miguel de
Corneille, Pierre
Descartes, René
Fénelon, François
Herbert, George

SEVENTEENTH CENTURY (cont.)

Kircher, Athanasius
La Fontaine, Jean de
Locke, John
Maynard, François de
Milton, John
Poquelin, Jean-Baptiste [Molière]
Racine, Jean Baptiste
Spinoza, Baruch

EIGHTEENTH CENTURY (24 authors)

Arouet, François Marie [Voltaire]
Burke, Edmund
Burns, Robert
Casanova de Seingalt, Jacques
Diderot, Denis
Goldoni, Carlo
Hume, David
Johnson, Samuel
Kant, Immanuel
Leibniz, Gottfried Wilhelm
Lessing, Gotthold Ephraim
Mercier, Louis
Montesquieu, Charles Louis
Muratori, Ludovico
Paine, Thomas
Pope, Alexander
Rousseau, Jean-Jacques
Schiller, Friedrich von
Staël, Madame de
Sterne, Laurence
Swedenborg, Emanuel
Swift, Jonathan
Winckelmann, Johann
Wollstonecraft, Mary

NINETEENTH CENTURY (132 authors)

Alger, Horatio
Ampère, André-Marie
Andersen, Hans Christian
Arnold, Matthew
Austen, Jane
Balzac, Honoré
Barbey d'Aurevilly, Jules
Baudelaire, Charles
Beyle, Marie Henri [Stendhal]
Blackmore, Richard
Blake, William
Bolívar, Simón
Bonaparte, Napoleon
Brontë, Charlotte, Emily, Anne, and Branwell
Browning, Robert and Elizabeth
Bulwer-Lytton, Edward George
Burckhardt, Jacob
Busch, Wilhelm
Butler, Samuel
Byron, George Gordon, Lord
Carleton, William
Carlyle, Thomas
Chaney, William H.
Chateaubriand, François-René
Chatrian, Alexandre
Chopin, Kate
Clemens, Samuel L. [Mark Twain]
Constant de Rebecque, Henri
Courier, Paul-Louis
Crane, Stephen
Delisle, Léopold
Dickens, Charles
Dickinson, Emily
Disraeli, Benjamin
Dodgson, Charles Lutwidge [Lewis Carroll]
Dostoevsky, Feodor
Droste-Hülshoff, Annette von
Dudevant, Lucile-Aurore Dupin [George Sand]
Dumas, Alexandre, père
Eichendorff, Baron Joseph
Emerson, Ralph Waldo
Erckmann, Émile [Erckmann-Chatrian]
Evans, Mary Ann [George Eliot]
Flaubert, Gustave
Fontane, Theodor
Forster, John
Frederic, Harold
Freytag, Gustav
Fustel de Coulanges, Numa-Denis
Garibaldi, Guiseppe
George, Henry
Gissing, George
Gobineau, Joseph-Arthur
Görres, Joseph von
Goethe, Johann Wolfgang von
Greenaway, Kate
Grillparzer, Franz
Grimm, Jacob and Wilhelm

NINETEENTH CENTURY (cont.)

Groth, Klaus
Guérin, Eugénie and Maurice de
Hansjakob, Heinrich
Hardy, Thomas
Hawthorne, Nathaniel
Hebbel, Friedrich
Hegel, Georg
Heine, Heinrich
Herzl, Theodor
Higginson, Thomas Wentworth
Hölderlin, Friedrich
Hoffmann, August Heinrich
Hoffmann, Ernst T.A.
Hopkins, Gerard Manley
Howells, William Dean
Hugo, Victor
Huysmans, Joris-Karl
Ibsen, Henrik
Keats, John
Keller, Gottfried
Kierkegaard, Søren
Kleist, Heinrich von
Labrunie, Gérard [Gérard de Nerval]
Lacordaire, Jean-Baptiste-Henri
Lamb, Charles
Lazare, Bernard
Ludwig, Otto
Machado de Assis, Joaquim
Maistre, Joseph
Mallarmé, Stéphane
Martí, José
Maupassant, Guy de
May, Karl
Mazzini, Guiseppe
Melville, Herman
Mickiewicz, Adam
Mill, John Stuart
Morris, William
Musset, Alfred de
Newman, John Henry
Nietzsche, Friedrich
Peirce, Charles S.
Poe, Edgar Allan
Postl, Karl [Charles Sealsfield]
Proudhon, Pierre-Joseph
Raabe, Wilhelm
Raimund, Ferdinand
Renan, Joseph Ernest
Richter, Jean Paul [Jean Paul]
Riley, James Whitcomb
Rimbaud, Arthur
Rollinat, Maurice
Rückert, Friedrich and Heinrich
Sainte-Beuve, Charles-Augustin
Saint-Simon, Claude-Henri
San Martín, José de
Schopenhauer, Arthur
Scott, Sir Walter
Shelley, Percy Bysshe
Stifter, Adalbert
Storm, Theodor
Strehlenau, Nikolaus [Nikolaus Lenau]
Strindberg, August
Tennyson, Alfred, 1st baron
Thackeray, William Makepeace
Thompson, Francis
Thoreau, Henry
Trollope, Anthony
Verlaine, Paul
Verne, Jules
Vigny, Alfred Victor
Whitman, Walt
Whittier, John Greenleaf
Wordsworth, William
Zola, Émile

TWENTIETH CENTURY (206 authors)

Anderson, Sherwood
Annunzio, Gabriele d'
Baillon, André
Barbieri, Cesare
Barlach, Ernst
Barrault, Jean-Louis
Baty, Gaston
Baum, L. Frank
Bennett, Arnold
Bergman, Hjalmar
Bergson, Henri Louis
Bernanos, Georges
Berryman, John
Bloch, Jean-Richard
Blondel, Maurice
Bloy, Léon
Blum, Léon
Blunck, Hans Friedrich
Bosco, Henri
Boutelleau, Jacques [Chardonne]

TWENTIETH CENTURY (cont.)

Brasillach, Robert
Brecht, Bertolt
Bremond, Henri
Burroughs, Edgar Rice
Buzzati, Dino
Cabell, James Branch
Camus, Albert
Carvalho, Joaquim de
Cather, Willa
Cathlin, Léon
Césaire, Aimé
Chartier, Émile Auguste [Alain]
Chesterton, G.K.
Choquette, Robert
Claudel, Paul
Cocteau, Jean
Collier, John
Conrad, Joseph
Couté, Gaston
Coward, Noel
Crane, Hart
Croce, Benedetto
Curwood, James Oliver
Daniélou, Cardinal
Dannay, Frederic [Ellery Queen]
de Gaulle, Charles
Degée, Olivier [Jean Tousseul]
Destouches, Louis-Ferdinand [Céline]
Deubel, Léon
Dewey, John
Doucet, Jacques
Doyle, Sir Arthur Conan
Dreiser, Theodore
du Bos, Charles
Dullin, Charles
Durrell, Lawrence
Eliot, T.S.
Ernst, Paul
Esdaile, Arundell
Farigoule, Louis [Jules Romains]
Faulkner, William
Faust, Frederick [Max Brand]
Fitzgerald, F. Scott
Fleg, Edmond
Forester, C.S.
Foucauld, Charles, vicomte de
Fournier, Henri-Alban [Alain-Fournier]
Freud, Sigmund
Fröding, Gustaf
Gandhi, Mohandas
García Lorca, Federico
Ghil, Raimond
Gide, André
Giono, Jean
Giraudoux, Jean
Glasgow, Ellen
Gourmont, Rémy de
Graves, Robert
Grey, Zane
Grindel, Eugène [Paul Éluard]
Häberlin, Paul
Hartmann, Sadakichi
Hauptmann, Gerhart
Heidegger, Martin
Hemingway, Ernest
Hesse, Hermann
Hofmannsthal, Hugo von
Housman, A.E.
Howard, Robert E.
Jacob, Max [Morven le Gaëlique]
Jaurès, Jean
Jeffers, Robinson
Jouvenal, Sidonie-Gabrielle de [Colette]
Joyce, James
Kipling, Rudyard
Kolbenheyer, Erwin
Kostrowitzky, Wilhelm [Apollinaire]
Krishnamurti, Jiddu
Lagerlöf, Selma
Larbaud, Valéry
La Varende, Jean Mallard
Lawrence, D.H.
Lawrence, T.E.
Leacock, Stephen
Lee, Edward Edson [Leo Edwards]
Lee, Manfred B.
Lenin, Nikolai
Lessing, Doris
Lewis, C.S.
Lewis, Sinclair
Lewis, Wyndham
Lindsay, Vachel
London, Jack
MacDonald, John D.
Machen, Arthur
Maeterlinck, Maurice

TWENTIETH CENTURY (cont.)

Malraux, André
Mann, Heinrich
Mann, Thomas
Markham, Edwin
Massignon, Louis
Mauriac, François
Maurras, Charles
Mencken, H.L.
Menéndez (y) Pelayo, Marcelino
Miller, Henry
Milosz, Oscar Venceslas
Moore, Marianne
Mounier, Emmanuel
Musil, Robert
Ner, Henri [Han Ryner]
Nin, Anaïs
Nock, Albert Jay
Nouveau, Germain
O'Casey, Sean
O'Connor, Flannery
O'Hara, John
Olson, Charles J.
O'Neill, Eugene
Pareto, Vilfredo
Peake, Mervyn
Péguy, Charles
Pérez Galdós, Benito
Pergaud, Louis
Philippe, Charles-Louis
Pirandello, Luigi
Plisnier, Charles
Pound, Ezra
Powys, Llewelyn, John Cowper, and Theodore
Proust, Marcel
Ramuz, Charles-Ferdinand
Rand, Ayn
Randon de Saint-Armand, Gabriel [Jehan Rictus]
Rank, Otto
Reinhardt, Max
Renaud, Madeleine
Retté, Adolphe
Rilke, Rainer Maria
Rivière, Jacques
Rohner, Lucien
Rolland, Romain
Roosevelt, Theodore
Rouget, Marie Mélanie [Marie Noël]
Russell, Bertrand
Sandoz, Mari [Suzette]
Sartre, Jean Paul
Saussure, Ferdinand de
Scantrel, Félix-André-Yves [André Suarès]
Schneider, Reinhold
Schnitzler, Arthur
Schweitzer, Albert
Seers, Eugène [Louis Dantin]
Shaw, George Bernard
Sjöberg, Birger
Spire, André
Stein, Gertrude
Steinbeck, John
Steiner, Rudolf
Stevens, Wallace
Stuart, Jesse
Tagore, Rabindranath
Tardiveau, René [René Boylesve]
Teilhard de Chardin, Pierre
Thibault, Anatole François [Anatole France]
Tolkien, J.R.R.
Torsvan, Berick Traven [B. Traven]
Trakl, Georg
Unamuno, Miguel de
Updike, John
Valéry, Paul
Velde, Henry van de
Vendel, Henri [Henri Nadel]
Viaud, Julien [Pierre Loti]
Wallace, Edgar
Ward, Arthur S. [Sax Rohmer]
Waugh, Evelyn
Weil, Simone
Weinheber, Josef
Wells, H.G.
Welty, Eudora
Whitehead, Alfred North
Williams, William Carlos
Wolfe, Thomas
Woolf, Virginia
Yeats, William Butler
Zweig, Stefan

Appendix 3
SPONSORING INSTITUTIONS

All institutions that sponsor publications devoted to the life and works of individual authors are here listed in letter-by-letter alphabetical order, with the following exceptions: (1) all societies are listed under the subject heading "Societies" and all Gesellschaften under "Gesellschaften"; (2) only the parent institution is identified, not, for instance, the English Department within the specified university, because all such information is provided in the annotation itself; (3) to conserve space, the numerous small, defunct Sherlock Holmes sponsoring groups are excluded; and (4) no publishing houses or individual persons are cited as sponsors.

A

Academie raciniennes
Accademia Petrarca di Lettere, Arti e Scienze
Adalbert Stifter-Institut
Adalbert Stifter-Verein
Akademiia nauka U.S.S.R. (Dante)
Amici Thomae Mori (More)
Amigos de Menéndez y Pelayo
Amis d'Adolphe Retté
Amis d'Alain
Amis d'Alexandre Dumas
Amis de Charles-Louis Philippe
Amis de Flaubert
Amis de Guérin
Amis de Guillaume Apollinaire
Amis de Jacques Chardonne
Amis de La Fontaine
Amis de La Varende
Amis de Louis Pergaud
Amis de Max Jacob
Amis de Milosz
Amis d'Emmanuel Mounier
Amis de Paul Claudel en Belgique
Amis de Raimond Ghil
Amis de René Boylesve
Amis de Rimbaud
Amis de Samuel Cramer
Amis de Valéry Larbaud
L'Amitié Charles Péguy
Amt für Kultur, Lübeck (H. Mann)
Andrew W. Mellon Foundation (Erasmus)
Armenian Academy of Sciences (Shakespeare)
Armstrong Browning Library
Arthur Brickman Associates (Shakespeare)
Associación Dante Alighieri
Association Charles de Foucald
Association Charles Dullin
Association des Amis d'Alain
Association des Amis d'Alfred de Vigny
Association des Amis d'André Gide
Association des Amis de Benjamin Constant
Association des Amis Dino Buzzati
Association des Amis de Flaubert

Sponsoring Institutions

Association des Amis de François Mauriac
Association des Amis de Gaston Baty
Association des Amis de Guy de Maupassant
Association des Amis de Jacques Rivière
Association des Amis de Jean Giono
Association des Amis de Jean Tousseul
Association des Amis de Jean-Jacques Rousseau
Association des Amis de Marie Noël
Association des Amis de Maynard
Association des Amis de Pierre Teilhard de Chardin
Association des Amis de Rabelais
Association des Amis de Robert Brasillach
Association des Amis de Ronsard
Association des Amis d'Henri Bergson
Association des Amis du Dr. Schweitzer
Association des Amis du Fonds Romain Rolland
Association et Musée Joachim Du Bellay
Association française des Amis d'Albert Schweitzer
Association Guillaume Budé
Association hégelienne internationale
Association Henry van de Velde
Association internationale des Amis de Guillaume Apollinaire
Association internationale des Amis de Pierre Loti
Association "Jeunesse de Racine"
Association "Les Amis de George Sand"
Association pour l'étude de la pensée de Simone Weil
Association Saint-Vincent-Ferrier (Lacordaire)
Augustinian Institute
Ayn Rand Letter

B

Baker Street Irregulars (Doyle)
Ball State University (Steinbeck)
Biblioteca-Museu Joaquim de Carvalho
Bibliothek Teilhard de Chardin
Bibliothèque André Gide
Bootmakers of Toronto (Doyle)
Bradley University (Vincent of Beauvais)
Brigham Young University Press (Pirandello)
Browning Institute
Buchtel College (Wolfe)
Bulwer-Lytton Circle
Burns Federation
Burroughs Bibliophiles
Byron House
BYRON SOCIETY JOURNAL

C

Canada Council (Erasmus)
Carlyle House
Casa di Dante
Casa di Goldoni
Cavendish Squares (Doyle)
Center for Baudelaire Studies
Center for Dewey Studies
Centre Charles Maurras
Centre Charles Péguy
Centre d'Études Proustiennes
Centre d'Études Valéryennes
Centre National des Lettres (Rivière)
Centro di studi ciceroniani
Centro di Studi Tassiani
Centro Tassiano
Cercle Bernard Lazare
Cercle Ernest-Renan
Cercles Universitaires . . . Gaulliennes
Cesare Barbieri Center of Italian Studies
Chaucer Group, MLA
Colgate University (Powys)
Collège de Saint-Laurent (Choquette)
Comité pour le monument de Bossuet
Consejo corporativo . . . (Martí)
Consejo Nacional . . . (Martí)
Cultural Services . . . French Embassy (Claudel)
Cusanus-Institut

D

D.H. Lawrence Association

Dickens Fellowship, London
DICKENS STUDIES ANNUAL
Dickinson College (Hemingway)
Domus Mazziniana
Düsseldorf, City of (Heine)
Dumas Association

E

Eastern Michigan University (Arnold)
Edgar Allan Poe Museum
Emerson College (Dickens)
English Association (Esdaile)
Enoch Pratt Free Library (Mencken)
Ente nazionale Francesco Petrarca
Ente nazionale Giovanni Boccaccio
Erwin von Steinbach-Stiftung
Estudio Teológico Agustiniano
Études Augustiniennes
Evangelischer Bund (Luther)

F

Faulkner Concordance Project
Fellowship of the Ring (Tolkien)
Fifth Northumberland Fusiliers (Doyle)
Folger Shakespeare Library
Fondation Charles-Ferdinand Ramuz
Fondation Charles Plisnier
Fondation Maurice Maeterlinck
Fondation Pierre Teilhard de Chardin
Fondation Sand
Fonds de documentation Henri Bosco
Fonds Rimbaud
Fonds Romain Rolland
Ford Humanities Fund (Powys)
Frankfurter Goethe-Museum
French Embassy, Cultural Services of (Claudel)

G

Gandhi Peace Foundation
George Eliot Fellowship
Georgia College (O'Connor)
Gesellschaften
- Adalbert-Stifter-Gesellschaft
- Charles Sealsfield-Gesellschaft
- Cusanus-Gesellschaft
- Deutsche Dante-Gesellschaft
- Deutsche Gustav-Freytag-Gesellschaft
- Deutsche Schillergesellschaft
- Deutsche Shakespeare-Gesellschaft, Weimar
- Deutsche Shakespeare-Gesellschaft West
- Droste-Gesellschaft
- Eichendorff-Gesellschaft
- Ernst Barlach-Gesellschaft
- E.T.A. Hoffmann-Gesellschaft
- Friedrich Hölderlin-Gesellschaft
- Gesellschaft der Freunde Wilhelm Raabes
- Gesellschaft Teilhard de Chardin
- Görres-Gesellschaft
- Goethe-Gesellschaft, Japan
- Goethe-Gesellschaft (Weimar)
- Gottfried Keller-Gesellschaft
- Gottfried-Wilhelm-Leibniz-Gesellschaft
- Grillparzer-Gesellschaft
- Gutenberg-Gesellschaft
- Hans Friedrich Blunck-Gesellschaft
- Hebbel-Gesellschaft
- Hegel-Gesellschaft
- Heinrich-Hansjakob-Gesellschaft
- Heinrich-Heine-Gesellschaft
- Heinrich-von-Kleist-Gesellschaft
- Hölderlin-Gesellschaft
- Hoffmann von Fallersleben-Gesellschaft
- Hugo von Hofmannsthal-Gesellschaft
- Internationale Athanasius Kircher Forschungs Gesellschaft
- Internationale Brecht-Gesellschaft
- Internationale Lenau-Gesellschaft
- Internationale Paracelsus-Gesellschaft
- Internationale Robert-Musil-Gesellschaft
- Internationale Stefan-Zweig-Gesellschaft
- Jean-Paul-Gesellschaft
- Josef Weinheber-Gesellschaft
- Kant-Gesellschaft (Hamburg, Berlin)
- Kantgesellschaft (Rheinland)
- Karl-May-Gesellschaft
- Klaus-Groth-Gesellschaft
- Kleist Gesellschaft
- Kolbenheyer-Gesellschaft

Gesellschaften (cont.)
- Literarische Adalbert-Stifter-Gesellschaft
- Luther-Gesellschaft (Gütersloh)
- Luthergesellschaft (Hamburg)
- Nietzsche-Gesellschaft
- Österreichischer Freundeskreis der Luther-Gesellschaft
- Paul-Ernst-Gesellschaft
- Paul Häberlin-Gesellschaft
- Pirckheimer-Gesellschaft
- Raabe-Gesellschaft
- Raimundgesellschaft
- Rilke-Gesellschaft
- Rückert-Gesellschaft
- Schopenhauer-Gesellschaft
- Stefan-Zweig-Gesellschaft
- Theodor-Storm-Gesellschaft
- Thomas-Mann-Gesellschaft
- Wilhelm-Busch-Gesellschaft
- Winckelmann-Gesellschaft
- Wolfram-von-Eschenbach-Gesellschaft

Great Alkali Plainsmen (Doyle)
Grillparzer-Forum Forchtenstein
Gustaf-Fröding-sällskapet

H

H.C. Andersens Haus
Hegel-Archiv
Hegel-Kommission
Heinrich-Heine-Institut
Henry George School of Social Science
Hölderlin-Archiv
Hofstra University (George Sand)
Holyoke Community College (Spenser)
House of Greystoke (Burroughs)
Hugo's Companions (Doyle)
Humanities Research Council of Canada (Erasmus)

I

Indiana State University (Dreiser)
Indian Council for Cultural Relations (Tagore)
Institut Charles de Gaulle
Institut français de Damas (Massignon)
Institut Historique Augustinien
Instituto Miguel de Cervantes
Instituto Nacional Sanmartiniano
Institutum Historicum . . . Augustini
Institutum Patristicum "Augustinianum"
Institut Voltaire en Belgique
International Arthur Schnitzler Research Association
Internationale Cardinal Newman Kuratorium
International Hopkins Association
International Wizard of Oz Club (Baum)
Investigative Committee on Shakespeare Translation
Istituto "Civitas garibaldini"
Istituto di studi pirandelliani
Istituto Francesedi Studi Storici (Casanova)

J

James Whitcomb Riley Memorial Association
Johannes Gutenberg-Universität (Cusanus)
John Knox House Association

K

Karl-May-Verlag
Keats-Shelley Association of America
Keats-Shelley Memorial Association
Kent State University Press (Melville)

L

Laurence Sterne Trust
Leo Edwards' . . . Detectives (Lee, E.E.)
Lesley College (Dickens)
Library Association, Chaucer House, (Esdaile)
Literary Enterprises (Stein)
Luther College

M

McMaster University Library Press (Russell, Shakespeare)

Société des Amis de Balzac
Société des Amis de Bossuet
Société des Amis de Charles du Bos
Société des Amis de Colette
Société des Amis d'Edmond Fleg
Société des Amis de Georges Bernanos
Société des Amis de Germain Nouveau
Société des Amis de Han Ryner
Société des Amis de Jean Cocteau
Société des Amis de Jean Giraudoux
Société des Amis de Jules Romains
Société des Amis de Léon Blum
Société des Amis de Marcel Proust
Société des Amis de Montaigne
Société des Amis de Paul-Louis Courier
Société des Amis de Rimbaud
Société des Amis de Zola
Société des Amis du Cardinal Daniélou
Société des Amis du Musée de Stendhal
Société des Bollandistes
Société des études rabelaisiennes
Société des Études renaniennes
Société des Études staëliennes
Société d'études Dantesque . . . Méditerranéen
Société d'Études jaurésiennes
Société Ernest-Renan
Société française d'études nietzschéennes
Société genevoise de linguistique (Saussure)
Société Honoré de Balzac de Touraine
Société Jean Bodin
Société Jean-Jacques Rousseau
Société J.-K. Huysmans
Société Jules Verne
Société "Les Amis de M. Rollinat"
Société littéraire des Amis d'Émile Zola
Société litteraire des Mussettistes
Société nationale des Amis de Balzac
Société Parisienne d'Histoire (Delisle)
Société Paul Claudel
Société Paul Valéry
Société Pierre Corneille
Société Pierre Teilhard de Chardin
Société racinienne
Société vauclusienne des Amis de Pétrarque

Societies

American Dante Society
American Lessing Society
Aquinas Society of London
Aristotelian Society (Aquinas)
Arthur Machen Society
Australian Goethe Society
Australian Tolkien Society
Austrian Shakespeare Society
Bacon Society, London
Bacon Society of America
Balzac Society of America
Balzac Society of Brooklyn
Bertrand Russell Society
Blackmore Society
Boston Browning Society
Brontë Society
Browning Society, London
Burns Society
Byron Society
Cabell Society
Carlyle Society
Charles Lamb Society
Charles S. Peirce Society
Chaucer Society, London
Chesterton Society
Dante Society, Cambridge, Mass.
Dante Society, London
Dante Society of Toronto
D.H. Lawrence Society, Nottingham
D.H. Lawrence Society, U.S.
D.H. Lawrence Society of Japan
Dickens Society
Edgar Allan Poe Society
Ellen Glasgow Society
Emerson Society
English Goethe Society
Francis Bacon Society, London
Francis Thompson Society
Hegel Society of America
Henry Miller Literary Society
Hermann Hesse Society
H.G. Wells Society, Essex, England
H.G. Wells Society, London
H.G. Wells Society, Nottingham
H.G. Wells Society International
Hjalmar Bergman Society
Hopkins Society
Horatio Alger Society
Housman Society

Societies (cont.)
- International Brecht Society
- International Mark Twain Society
- Jacob Boehme Society
- James Branch Cabell Society
- James Joyce Society
- Jane Austen Society
- John Dewey Society
- Johnson Society of Lichfield
- Johnson Society of London
- John Steinbeck Bibliographical Society
- John Steinbeck Society of America
- Joseph Conrad Society, U.K.
- Joseph Conrad Society of America
- Kate Greenaway Society
- Kierkegaard Society
- Kipling Society
- Lewis Carroll Society, England
- Lewis Carroll Society of North America
- Lydgate Society of America
- Malraux Society
- Mark Twain Society of Chicago
- Melville Society of America
- Mervyn Peake Society, England
- Mervyn Peake Society, Wales
- Milton Society of America
- Mythopoeic Society (Tolkien)
- Nathaniel Hawthorne Society
- New York Browning Society
- New York C.S. Lewis Society
- New York Tolkien Society
- Nietzsche Society
- Paul Claudel Society of Canada
- Portland C.S. Lewis Society
- Rook Society (Berryman)
- Samuel Butler Society
- Samuel Johnson Society of the Northwest
- Sax Rohmer Society
- Shakespearean Authorship Society
- Shakespeare Society, London
- Shakespeare Society of America at the Globe
- Shakespeare Society of Japan
- Shakespeare Society of New South Wales
- Shakespeare Society of New York
- Shakespeare Society of Philadelphia
- Shakespeare Stage Society
- Shaw Society, London
- Shaw Society of America
- Shaw Society of California
- Shaw Society of Chicago
- Sherlock Holmes Klubben i Danmark (Doyle)
- Sherlock Holmes Society of London (Doyle)
- Sherlock Holmes Society of North Carolina (Doyle)
- Sherwood Anderson Society
- Sigmund Freud Society
- Søren Kierkegaard Selskabet
- Southern California C.S. Lewis Society
- Steinbeck Society, International
- Strindberg Society
- Swedenborg Society
- Tennyson Society
- Thomas Hardy Society
- Thomas More Society of London
- Thomas Paine Society
- Thoreau Society
- Tolkien Society, England
- Tolkien Society of America
- University of Wisconsin J.R.R. Tolkien Society
- Vergilian Society of America
- Vergil Society of America
- Virgil Society of London
- Wallace Stevens Society
- William Morris Society
- William Morris Society and Kelmscott Fellowship
- Wyclif Society
- Wyndham Lewis Society
- Yeats Society of Japan

Solitary Cyclists of Sweden (Doyle)
Søren Kierkegaard Selskabet
Southern Illinois University (Dewey)
Southern Illinois University Press (Dickens)
Spinozahuis
Stephen Leacock Associates
Suffolk University (O'Neill)
Swedenborg School of Religion
Syracuse University Press (Diderot)

Appendix 4

INDEXING AND ABSTRACTING SERVICES ANNUAL AND QUARTERLY BIBLIOGRAPHIES

About fifty of the indexes and bibliographies most often used by literary scholars to locate articles and essays within periodicals and other serials are here analyzed for coverage so that librarians and researchers can see at a glance which of these reference sources are most useful for their purposes. For instance, students of literature know that ABSTRACTS OF ENGLISH STUDIES is an excellent source to consult for a quick overview of research that has appeared in the JAMES JOYCE QUARTERLY because its regular duty is to abstract and summarize that quarterly's more important articles.

In this appendix, every newsletter, journal, or other serial devoted to the life and works of one author is listed under every source that has ever indexed or analyzed its contents. This does not necessarily mean that the indexing source is currently analyzing the contents, or even that its coverage has been consistent or comprehensive over the years. In some cases, the periodical may have ceased publication long ago, but the information that it was indexed during a part or all of its lifetime may be of great assistance to some researchers. In other cases, the indexing source indicates at the front of its contents that a certain periodical is analyzed, but no citations to that periodical appear in the text. The reader can only assume that there may have been nothing worthy of analysis or that perhaps the abstractors and editors did not have time--or space--to cover the periodical adequately. In still other cases, the index or bibliography does not list the periodical as being covered, but examination of the text proves that it does include citations to the contents of that periodical. Only the editors themselves can explain this anomaly. For the purposes of this guide, however, every serial is included in the lists below if its contents were ever analyzed by any of the indexing sources. Researchers who use the sources will discover the vagaries and inconsistencies of each one.

The titles below are worded and spelled exactly as they appear in the indexing source; thus, these lists will show that ABSTRACTS OF ENGLISH STUDIES has abstracted both EMERSON SOCIETY QUARTERLY and the same publication by its later name, ESQ. Because editors, fashions, and thus titles, change, and because this guide has selected the latest, or current, title as its main entry, students may have to consult the Title Index at the back of this book to ascertain precisely where a specific title is described in the author, or main, section of this guide. For example, if a student is looking for a title he knows as PUBLICATIONS OF THE ENGLISH GOETHE SOCIETY, he will see in the Title Index that it is located in the author section under Goethe, entry 4. There it is entered under the title ENGLISH GOETHE SOCIETY: PUBLICATIONS because that is the form used most recently by its editors.

Titles in a series (which are generally published irregularly) are not capitalized to distinguish them from titles of newsletters, journals, and annuals, which are capitalized. Notice the difference, for instance, between YEATS STUDIES: AN INTERNATIONAL JOURNAL (an annual) and New Yeats Papers (a series), or between PROUST RESEARCH ASSOCIATION NEWSLETTER (two issues a year) and Cahiers Marcel Proust (a series which has published seven issues in five years).

A. INDEXING AND ABSTRACTING SOURCES

ABSTRACTS OF ENGLISH STUDIES
ABSTRACTS OF POPULAR CULTURE
AMERICA: HISTORY AND LIFE
AMERICAN HUMANITIES INDEX
AMERICAN LITERATURE
AMERICAN LITERATURE ABSTRACTS
L'ANNÉE PHILOLOGIQUE
ANNUAL BIBLIOGRAPHY OF ENGLISH LANGUAGE AND LITERATURE
BIBLIOGRAPHIE DE LA LITTÉRATURE FRANÇAISE DU MOYEN AGE À NOS JOURS
BIOGRAPHY INDEX
BRITISH HUMANITIES INDEX
BROWNING INSTITUTE STUDIES
BULLETIN CRITIQUE
CATHOLIC PERIODICAL AND LITERATURE INDEX
ENGLISH LANGUAGE NOTES (ROMANTIC MOVEMENT BIBLIOGRAPHY, 1937-70)
ENGLISH LITERATURE IN TRANSITION
ESSAY AND GENERAL LITERATURE INDEX
ÉTUDES ANGLAISES
FRENCH VI BIBLIOGRAPHY
FRENCH VII BIBLIOGRAPHY
FRENCH XX BIBLIOGRAPHY
HISTORICAL ABSTRACTS
HUMANITIES INDEX
INDEX TO BOOK REVIEWS IN THE HUMANITIES
JOURNAL OF MODERN LITERATURE
KLAPP (BIBLIOGRAPHIE DER FRANZÖSISCHEN LITERATURWISSENSCHAFTEN/ BIBLIOGRAPHIE D'HISTOIRE LITTÉRAIRE FRANÇAISE)
KÖTTELWESCH (BIBLIOGRAPHIE DER DEUTSCHEN LITERATURWISSENSCHAFT and its successor, BIBLIOGRAPHIE DER DEUTSCHEN SPRACH- UND LITERATURWISSENSCHAFT)

Leary (ARTICLES ON AMERICAN LITERATURE)
MANUAL DE BIBLIOGRAFÍA DE LA LITERATURA ESPAÑOLA
MISSISSIPPI QUARTERLY
MLA ABSTRACTS (ceased publication)
MLA INTERNATIONAL BIBLIOGRAPHY
MODERN DRAMA (Toronto)
NEO-LATIN NEWS
PHILOSOPHER'S INDEX
PSYCHOLOGICAL ABSTRACTS
REVUE D'HISTOIRE LITTÉRAIRE DE LA FRANCE
SOCIAL SCIENCES AND HUMANITIES INDEX
STUDIES IN BROWNING AND HIS CIRCLE
TWENTIETH CENTURY LITERATURE
VICTORIAN STUDIES
YEAR'S WORK IN ENGLISH STUDIES

B. ANALYSIS OF COVERAGE BY INDEXING AND ABSTRACTING SOURCES

ABSTRACTS OF ENGLISH STUDIES

Arnold, Matthew
  ARNOLD NEWSLETTER

Berryman, John
  JOHN BERRYMAN STUDIES

Blake, William
  BLAKE STUDIES

Brontë, Charlotte, Emily, Anne, and Branwell
  Brontë Society. TRANSACTIONS

Browning, Robert and Elizabeth
  BROWNING NEWSLETTER
  STUDIES IN BROWNING AND HIS CIRCLE

Bulwer-Lytton, Edward
  BULWER-LYTTON CHRONICLE

Burke, Edmund
  STUDIES IN BURKE AND HIS TIME

Cabell, James Branch
  CABELLIAN

Chaucer, Geoffrey
  CHAUCER REVIEW

Clemens, Samuel L. [Mark Twain]
  MARK TWAIN JOURNAL
  TWAINIAN

Conrad, Joseph
  CONRADIANA

ABSTRACTS OF ENGLISH STUDIES (cont.)

Crane, Stephen
STEPHEN CRANE NEWSLETTER

Dickens, Charles
DICKENSIAN
DICKENS STUDIES ANNUAL
DICKENS STUDIES NEWSLETTER

Doyle, Sir Arthur Conan
BAKER STREET JOURNAL

Dreiser, Theodore
DREISER NEWSLETTER

Eliot, T.S.
T.S. ELIOT REVIEW

Emerson, Ralph Waldo
EMERSON SOCIETY QUARTERLY
ESQ

Hemingway, Ernest
HEMINGWAY NOTES

Hopkins, Gerard Manley
HOPKINS QUARTERLY

Johnson, Samuel
Johnson Society. TRANSACTIONS
NEW RAMBLER

Joyce, James
JAMES JOYCE QUARTERLY
A WAKE NEWSLITTER

Keats, John
KEATS-SHELLEY JOURNAL

Kipling, Rudyard
KIPLING JOURNAL

Lawrence, D.H.
D.H. LAWRENCE NEWS
D.H. LAWRENCE REVIEW

Lewis, Sinclair
SINCLAIR LEWIS NEWSLETTER

London, Jack
JACK LONDON NEWSLETTER

Markham, Edwin
MARKHAM REVIEW

Melville, Herman
EXTRACTS (Melville Society)

ABSTRACTS OF ENGLISH STUDIES (cont.)

Mencken, H.L.
MENCKENIANA

Mill, John Stuart
MILL NEWS LETTER

Milton, John

MILTON QUARTERLY
MILTON STUDIES

More, Saint Thomas
MOREANA

O'Connor, Flannery
FLANNERY O'CONNOR BULLETIN

Paine, Thomas
THOMAS PAINE SOCIETY BULLETIN

Poe, Edgar Allan
POE STUDIES

Pope, Alexander
SCRIBLERIAN: A NEWSJOURNAL
SCRIBLERIAN AND THE KIT-CATS

Pound, Ezra
PAIDEUMA

Shakespeare, William
SHAKESPEAREAN RESEARCH AND OPPORTUNITIES
SHAKESPEARE-JAHRBUCH (Heidelberg)
SHAKESPEARE-JAHRBUCH (Weimar)
SHAKESPEARE NEWSLETTER
SHAKESPEARE QUARTERLY
SHAKESPEARE STUDIES
SHAKESPEARE SURVEY

Shaw, George Bernard
INDEPENDENT SHAVIAN
SHAW REVIEW

Shelley, Percy Bysshe
KEATS-SHELLEY JOURNAL

Steinbeck, John
STEINBECK QUARTERLY

Stevens, Wallace
WALLACE STEVENS NEWSLETTER

Swift, Jonathan
SCRIBLERIAN AND THE KIT-CATS

Tennyson, Alfred, 1st baron
TENNYSON RESEARCH BULLETIN
Tennyson Society. MONOGRAPHS

ABSTRACTS OF ENGLISH STUDIES (cont.)

Thompson, Francis
Francis Thompson Society. JOURNAL

Thoreau, Henry
THOREAU JOURNAL QUARTERLY
THOREAU SOCIETY BOOKLET
THOREAU SOCIETY BULLETIN

Tolkien, J.R.R.
MYTHLORE
ORCRIST
TOLKIEN JOURNAL

Waugh, Evelyn
EVELYN WAUGH NEWSLETTER

Whitman, Walt
WALT WHITMAN REVIEW

Wollstonecraft, Mary
MARY WOLLSTONECRAFT NEWSLETTER

Woolf, Virginia
VIRGINIA WOOLF MISCELLANY

Wordsworth, William
WORDSWORTH CIRCLE

ABSTRACTS OF POPULAR CULTURE

Ward, Arthur S. (Sax Rohmer)
ROHMER REVIEW

AMERICA: HISTORY AND LIFE

Bolívar, Simón
REVISTA BOLIVARIANA

Burke, Edmund
STUDIES IN BURKE AND HIS TIME

Chesterton, G.K.
CHESTERTON REVIEW

Clemens, Samuel L. [Mark Twain]
TWAINIAN

Gandhi, Mohandas
GANDHI MARG

Hume, David
HUME STUDIES

Menéndez Pelayo, Marcelino
BOLETÍN DE LA BIBLIOTECA MENÉNDEZ PELAYO

AMERICA: HISTORY AND LIFE (cont.)

More, Saint Thomas
MOREANA

Unamuno, Miguel de
CUADERNOS DE LA CÁTEDRA DE UNAMUNO

AMERICAN HUMANITIES INDEX

Blake, William
BLAKE: AN ILLUSTRATED QUARTERLY
BLAKE NEWSLETTER
BLAKE STUDIES

Browning, Robert and Elizabeth
BROWNING INSTITUTE STUDIES
STUDIES IN BROWNING AND HIS CIRCLE

Burke, Edmund
STUDIES IN BURKE AND HIS TIME

Burns, Robert
BURNS CHRONICLE

Cabell, James Branch
KALKI

Cather, Willa
WILLA CATHER PIONEER MEMORIAL NEWSLETTER

Chopin, Kate
KATE CHOPIN NEWSLETTER

Clemens, Samuel L. [Mark Twain]
MARK TWAIN JOURNAL
TWAINIAN

Conrad, Joseph
CONRADIANA

Crane, Stephen
STEPHEN CRANE NEWSLETTER

Dickens, Charles
DICKENS STUDIES ANNUAL
DICKENS STUDIES NEWSLETTER

Dickinson, Emily
EMILY DICKINSON BULLETIN

Doyle, Sir Arthur Conan
BAKER STREET JOURNAL

Dreiser, Theodore
DREISER NEWSLETTER

AMERICAN HUMANITIES INDEX (cont.)

Eliot, T.S.
T.S. ELIOT REVIEW

Emerson, Ralph Waldo
ESQ

Fitzgerald, F. Scott
FITZGERALD/HEMINGWAY ANNUAL

Hawthorne, Nathaniel
NATHANIEL HAWTHORNE JOURNAL

Hemingway, Ernst
FITZGERALD/HEMINGWAY ANNUAL
HEMINGWAY NOTES

Joyce, James
JAMES JOYCE QUARTERLY

Lawrence, D.H.
D.H. LAWRENCE REVIEW

London, Jack
JACK LONDON NEWSLETTER

Markham, Edwin
MARKHAM REVIEW

Mencken, H.L.
MENCKENIANA

Mill, John Stuart
MILL NEWS LETTER

Milton, John
MILTON AND THE ROMANTICS
MILTON QUARTERLY
MILTON STUDIES

Moore, Marianne
MARIANNE MOORE NEWSLETTER

Nin, Anaïs
UNDER THE SIGN OF PISCES

O'Connor, Flannery
FLANNERY O'CONNOR BULLETIN

Olson, Charles J.
OLSON

Pirandello, Luigi
PIRANDELLO STUDIES

Poe, Edgar Allan
POE STUDIES

AMERICAN HUMANITIES INDEX (cont.)

Pope, Alexander
SCRIBLERIAN AND THE KIT-CATS

Pound, Ezra
PAIDEUMA

Rank, Otto
JOURNAL OF THE OTTO RANK FOUNDATION

Shaw, George Bernard
SHAW REVIEW

Spenser, Edmund
SPENSER NEWSLETTER

Stein, Gertrude
LOST GENERATION JOURNAL

Steinbeck, John
STEINBECK QUARTERLY

Thackeray, William Makepeace
THACKERAY NEWSLETTER

Thoreau, Henry
THOREAU JOURNAL QUARTERLY
THOREAU SOCIETY BULLETIN

Tolkien, J.R.R.
MYTHLORE

Waugh, Evelyn
EVELYN WAUGH NEWSLETTER

Welty, Eudora
EUDORA WELTY NEWSLETTER

Whitman, Walt
WALT WHITMAN REVIEW

Williams, William Carlos
WILLIAM CARLOS WILLIAMS NEWSLETTER

Wolfe, Thomas
THOMAS WOLFE NEWSLETTER

Woolf, Virginia
VIRGINIA WOOLF QUARTERLY

Wordsworth, William
WORDSWORTH CIRCLE

AMERICAN LITERATURE

Baum, Frank
BAUM BUGLE

AMERICAN LITERATURE (cont.)

Cabell, James Branch
CABELLIAN

Clemens, Samuel L. [Mark Twain]
MARK TWAIN JOURNAL
TWAINIAN

Crane, Stephen
STEPHEN CRANE NEWSLETTER

Eliot, T.S.
T.S. ELIOT REVIEW

Emerson, Ralph Waldo
EMERSON SOCIETY QUARTERLY
ESQ

Fitzgerald, F. Scott
FITZGERALD/HEMINGWAY ANNUAL
FITZGERALD NEWSLETTER

Hawthorne, Nathaniel
NATHANIEL HAWTHORNE JOURNAL

Hemingway, Ernest
FITZGERALD/HEMINGWAY ANNUAL

Mencken, H.L.
MENCKENIANA

Pound, Ezra
PAIDEUMA

Shakespeare, William
SHAKESPEARE QUARTERLY

Stevens, Wallace
WALLACE STEVENS JOURNAL

Thoreau, Henry
THOREAU JOURNAL QUARTERLY
THOREAU SOCIETY BOOKLET
THOREAU SOCIETY BULLETIN

Whitman, Walt
WALT WHITMAN REVIEW

Williams, William Carlos
WILLIAM CARLOS WILLIAMS NEWSLETTER

AMERICAN LITERATURE ABSTRACTS

Clemens, Samuel L. [Mark Twain]
MARK TWAIN JOURNAL

Emerson, Ralph Waldo
ESQ

AMERICAN LITERATURE ABSTRACTS (cont.)

Fitzgerald, F. Scott
FITZGERALD NEWSLETTER

London, Jack
JACK LONDON NEWSLETTER

Thoreau, Henry
THOREAU SOCIETY BULLETIN

Whitman, Walt
WALT WHITMAN REVIEW

L'ANNÉE PHILOLOGIQUE

Augustine, Saint
AUGUSTINIANA
AUGUSTINIAN STUDIES
AUGUSTINIANUM
AUGUSTINUS
REVUE DES ÉTUDES AUGUSTINIENNES

Bolland, Jean de
ANALECTA BOLLANDIA

Budé, Guillaume
BULLETIN DE L'ASSOCIATION GUILLAUME BUDÉ

Kant, Immanuel
KANT-STUDIEN

Vergil
VERGILIUS

ANNUAL BIBLIOGRAPHY OF ENGLISH LANGUAGE AND LITERATURE

Archives des Lettres Modernes
Minard, Paris

Arnold, Matthew
ARNOLD NEWSLETTER

Blake, William
BLAKE: AN ILLUSTRATED QUARTERLY
BLAKE NEWSLETTER
BLAKE STUDIES

Brontë, Charlotte, Emily, Anne, and Branwell
Brontë Society. TRANSACTIONS

Browning, Robert and Elizabeth
BROWNING INSTITUTE STUDIES
BROWNING NEWSLETTER
BROWNING SOCIETY NOTES
STUDIES IN BROWNING AND HIS CIRCLE

ANNUAL BIBLIOGRAPHY OF ENGLISH LANGUAGE AND LITERATURE (cont.)

Burke, Edmund
STUDIES IN BURKE AND HIS TIME

Burns, Robert
BURNS CHRONICLE AND CLUB DIRECTORY

Cabell, James Branch
KALKI

Carleton, William
CARLETON NEWSLETTER

Chaucer, Geoffrey
CHAUCER REVIEW

Clemens, Samuel L. [Mark Twain]
MARK TWAIN JOURNAL
TWAINIAN

Collier, John
PRESENTING MOONSHINE

Conrad, Joseph
CONRADIANA

Crane, Stephen
STEPHEN CRANE NEWSLETTER

Dickens, Charles
DICKENSIAN
DICKENS STUDIES
DICKENS STUDIES ANNUAL
DICKENS STUDIES NEWSLETTER

Dickinson, Emily
EMILY DICKINSON BULLETIN

Doyle, Sir Arthur Conan
BAKER STREET JOURNAL

Dreiser, Theodore
DREISER NEWSLETTER

Emerson, Ralph Waldo
EMERSON SOCIETY QUARTERLY
ESQ

Fitzgerald, F. Scott
FITZGERALD/HEMINGWAY ANNUAL
FITZGERALD NEWSLETTER

Graves, Robert
FOCUS ON ROBERT GRAVES

Hawthorne, Nathaniel
NATHANIEL HAWTHORNE JOURNAL

ANNUAL BIBLIOGRAPHY OF ENGLISH LANGUAGE AND LITERATURE (cont.)

Hemingway, Ernest
FITZGERALD/HEMINGWAY ANNUAL

Higginson, Thomas Wentworth
HIGGINSON JOURNAL OF POETRY

Hopkins, Gerard Manley
HOPKINS RESEARCH BULLETIN

Housman, A.E.
HOUSMAN SOCIETY JOURNAL

Johnson, Samuel
JOHNSONIAN NEWS LETTER
NEW RAMBLER

Joyce, James
JAMES JOYCE QUARTERLY

Keats, John
KEATS-SHELLEY JOURNAL
KEATS-SHELLEY MEMORIAL BULLETIN

Kipling, Rudyard
KIPLING JOURNAL

Lawrence, D.H.
D.H. LAWRENCE REVIEW

Lewis, Sinclair
SINCLAIR LEWIS NEWSLETTER

London, Jack
JACK LONDON NEWSLETTER

Lydgate, John
LYDGATE NEWSLETTER

Markham, Edwin
MARKHAM REVIEW

Mencken, H.L.
MENCKENIANA

Mill, John Stuart
MILL NEWS LETTER

Milton, John
MILTON QUARTERLY
MILTON STUDIES

More, Saint Thomas
MOREANA

Morris, William
JOURNAL OF THE WILLIAM MORRIS SOCIETY

ANNUAL BIBLIOGRAPHY OF ENGLISH LANGUAGE AND LITERATURE (cont.)

O'Connor, Flannery
FLANNERY O'CONNOR BULLETIN

Poe, Edgar Allan
POE STUDIES

Pope, Alexander
SCRIBLERIAN AND THE KIT-CATS

Pound, Ezra
PAIDEUMA

Shakespeare, William
SHAKESPEAREAN RESEARCH AND OPPORTUNITIES
SHAKESPEARE ASSOCIATION BULLETIN
SHAKESPEARE-JAHRBUCH (Heidelberg)
SHAKESPEARE-JAHRBUCH (Weimar)
SHAKESPEARE NEWSLETTER
SHAKESPEARE QUARTERLY
SHAKESPEARE STUDIES (Tokyo)
SHAKESPEARE STUDIES: AN ANNUAL GATHERING
SHAKESPEARE SURVEY

Shaw, George Bernard
INDEPENDENT SHAVIAN
SHAW REVIEW

Shelley, Percy Bysshe
KEATS-SHELLEY JOURNAL

Stein, Gertrude
LOST GENERATION JOURNAL

Steinbeck, John
STEINBECK QUARTERLY

Stevens, Wallace
WALLACE STEVENS NEWSLETTER

Tennyson, Alfred, 1st baron
TENNYSON RESEARCH BULLETIN

Thoreau, Henry
THOREAU JOURNAL QUARTERLY
THOREAU SOCIETY BOOKLET
THOREAU SOCIETY BULLETIN

Waugh, Evelyn
EVELYN WAUGH NEWSLETTER

Whitman, Walt
CALAMUS
WALT WHITMAN REVIEW

ANNUAL BIBLIOGRAPHY OF ENGLISH LANGUAGE AND LITERATURE (cont.)

Wollstonecraft, Mary
MARY WOLLSTONECRAFT JOURNAL

Woolf, Virginia
VIRGINIA WOOLF MISCELLANY
VIRGINIA WOOLF NEWSLETTER
VIRGINIA WOOLF QUARTERLY

Wordsworth, William
WORDSWORTH CIRCLE

BIBLIOGRAPHIE DE LA LITTÉRATURE FRANÇAISE DU MOYEN AGE À NOS JOURS

Annunzio, Gabriele d'
QUADERNI DANNUNZIANI

Aquinas, Saint Thomas
AQUINAS

Arouet, François [Voltaire]
STUDIES ON VOLTAIRE AND THE EIGHTEENTH CENTURY

Augustine, Saint
REVUE DES ÉTUDES AUGUSTINIENNES

Balzac, Honoré
L'ANNÉE BALZACIENNE
BALZAC A SACHÉ
COURRIER BALZACIEN

Barrault, Jean-Louis
CAHIERS DE LA COMPAGNIE MADELEINE RENAUD--JEAN-LOUIS BARRAULT

Baty, Gaston
CAHIERS GASTON BATY

Baudelaire, Charles
BULLETIN BAUDELAIRIEN
CRAMÉRIEN

Bernanos, Georges
COURRIER GEORGES BERNANOS

Beyle, Marie Henri [Stendhal]
STENDHAL CLUB

Bloch, Jean-Richard
EUROPE

Bosco, Henri
CAHIERS DE L'AMITIÉ HENRI BOSCO

Bossuet, Jacques-Bénigne
AMIS DE BOSSUET

BIBLIOGRAPHIE DE LA LITTÉRATURE FRANÇAISE DU MOYEN AGE À NOS JOURS (cont.)

Boutelleau, Jacques [Jacques Chardonne]
CAHIERS JACQUES CHARDONNE

Brasillach, Robert
CAHIERS DES AMIS DE ROBERT BRASILLACH

Budé, Guillaume
BULLETIN DE L'ASSOCIATION GUILLAUME BUDÉ
BULLETIN DES JEUNES DE L'ASSOCIATION GUILLAUME BUDÉ

Casanova de Seingalt, Giovanni
CASANOVA GLEANINGS

Chartier, Émile Auguste [Alain]
Association des Amis d'Alain. BULLETIN

Chateaubriand, François-René
BULLETIN DE LA SOCIÉTÉ CHATEAUBRIAND

Claudel, Paul
BULLETIN DE LA SOCIÉTÉ PAUL CLAUDEL
BULLETIN DE LA SOCIÉTÉ PAUL CLAUDEL DU JAPON
CLAUDEL NEWSLETTER
CLAUDEL STUDIES
Société Claudel en Belgique. BULLETIN RÉGIONAL

Cocteau, Jean
Cahiers Jean Cocteau

Courier, Paul-Louis
CAHIERS PAUL-LOUIS COURIER

Cramer, Samuel. See Baudelaire

Croce, Benedetto
RIVISTA DI STUDI CROCIANI

Degée, Olivier [Jean Tousseul]
CAHIERS JEAN TOUSSEUL

Deubel, Léon
Société des Amis de Léon Deubel. BULLETIN

du Bos, Charles
CAHIERS CHARLES DU BOS

Dumas, Alexandre (père)
Association des Amis d'Alexandre Dumas. BULLETIN

Farigoule, Louis [Jules Romains]
Société des Amis de Jules Romains. BULLETIN

Flaubert, Gustave
AMIS DE FLAUBERT

Fleg, Edmond
BULLETIN DE LA SOCIÉTÉ DES AMIS D'EDMOND FLEG

BIBLIOGRAPHIE DE LA LITTÉRATURE FRANÇAISE DU MOYEN AGE À NOS JOURS (cont.)

Freud, Sigmund
ÉTUDES FREUDIENNES

Gide, André
BULLETIN DES AMIS D'ANDRÉ GIDE
Cahiers André Gide

Giono, Jean
Association des Amis de Jean Giono. BULLETIN

Giraudoux, Jean
CAHIERS JEAN GIRAUDOUX

Gobineau, Joseph-Arthur
ÉTUDES GOBINIENNES

Grindel, Eugène [Paul Éluard]
CAHIERS PAUL ÉLUARD

Guérin, Eugénie and Maurice de
L'AMITIÉ GUÉRINIENNE

Gutenberg, Johannes
GUTENBERG-JAHRBUCH

Huysmans, Joris-Karl
BULLETIN DE LA SOCIÉTÉ J.-K. HUYSMANS

Jaurès, Jean
BULLETIN DE LA SOCIÉTÉ D'ÉTUDES JAURÉSIENNES

Jouvenal, Sidonie-Gabrielle [Colette]
BULLETIN DE LA SOCIÉTÉ DES AMIS DE COLETTE

Joyce, James
JAMES JOYCE QUARTERLY

Kant, Immanuel
KANT-STUDIEN

Kostrowitzky, Wilhelm [Apollinaire]
QUE VLO-VE?

Larbaud, Valéry
CAHIERS DES AMIS DE VALÉRY LARBAUD

La Varende, Jean
AMIS DE LA VARENDE

Leibniz, Gottfried
STUDIA LEIBNITIANA: ZEITSCHRIFT

Maeterlinck, Maurice
Fondation Maurice Maeterlinck. ANNALES

Malraux, André
MÉLANGES MALRAUX MISCELLANY

Mauriac, François
CAHIERS FRANÇOIS MAURIAC

BIBLIOGRAPHIE DE LA LITTÉRATURE FRANÇAISE DU MOYEN AGE À NOS JOURS (cont.)

Maurras, Charles
CAHIERS CHARLES MAURRAS
ÉTUDES MAURRASSIENNES

Maynard, François de
Association des Amis de Maynard. BULLETIN

Menéndez Pelayo, Marcelino
BOLETÍN DE LA BIBLIOTECA MENÉNDEZ PELAYO

Milosz, Oscar Venceslas de Lubicz
Amis de Milosz. CAHIERS DE L'ASSOCIATION

Montaigne, Michel
BULLETIN DE LA SOCIÉTÉ DES AMIS DE MONTAIGNE

More, Saint Thomas
MOREANA

Ner, Henri [Han Ryner]
CAHIERS DES AMIS DE HAN RYNER

Nouveau, Germain
CAHIERS GERMAIN NOUVEAU

Péguy, Charles
L'AMITIÉ CHARLES PÉGUY
COURRIER D'ORLÉANS

Pergaud, Louis
Amis de Louis Pergaud. BULLETIN

Philippe, Charles-Louis
Amis de Charles-Louis Philippe. BULLETIN

Proust, Marcel
BULLETIN DE LA SOCIÉTÉ DES AMIS DE MARCEL PROUST
BULLETIN D'INFORMATIONS PROUSTIENNES
ÉTUDES PROUSTIENNES
PROUST RESEARCH ASSOCIATION NEWSLETTER

Rabelais, François
AMIS DE RABELAIS ET DE LA DEVINIÈRE
ÉTUDES RABELAISIENNES

Racine, Jean
CAHIERS RACINIENS
JEUNESSE DE RACINE

Ramuz, Charles-Ferdinand
Fondation Charles-Ferdinand Ramuz. BULLETIN

Renan, Joseph Ernest
Cahiers renaniens
ÉTUDES RENANIENNES: BULLETIN

BIBLIOGRAPHIE DE LA LITTÉRATURE FRANÇAISE DU MOYEN AGE À NOS JOURS (cont.)

Renaud, Madeleine
CAHIERS DE LA COMPAGNIE MADELEINE RENAUD--JEAN-LOUIS BARRAULT

Retté, Adolphe
BULLETIN DES AMIS D'ADOLPHE RETTÉ

Rimbaud, Arthur
RIMBAUD VIVANT

Rolland, Romain
BULLETIN DE L'ASSOCIATION DES AMIS DU FONDS ROMAIN ROLLAND

Rollinat, Maurice
BULLETIN DE LA SOCIÉTÉ "LES AMIS DE MAURICE ROLLINAT"

Rouget, Marie Mélanie [Marie Noël]
CAHIERS MARIE NOËL

Rousseau, Jean-Jacques
ANNALES DE LA SOCIÉTÉ JEAN-JACQUES ROUSSEAU
Association des Amis de Jean-Jacques Rousseau. BULLETIN D'INFORMATION

Saint-Simon, Claude-Henri
CAHIERS SAINT-SIMON

Schopenhauer, Arthur
SCHOPENHAUER-JAHRBUCH

Spire, André
CAHIERS ANDRÉ SPIRE

Staël, Madame de
CAHIERS STAËLIENS

Thibault, Anatole [Anatole France]
LE LYS ROUGE

Valéry, Paul
BULLETIN DES ÉTUDES VALÉRYENNES

Verne, Jules
BULLETIN DE LA SOCIÉTÉ JULES VERNE

Viaud, Julien [Pierre Loti]
CAHIERS PIERRE LOTI

Vigny, Alfred Victor de
Association des Amis d'Alfred de Vigny. BULLETIN

Zola, Émile
CAHIERS NATURALISTES

BIBLIOGRAPHY OF FRENCH SEVENTEENTH CENTURY STUDIES

Arouet, François Marie [Voltaire]
STUDIES ON VOLTAIRE AND THE EIGHTEENTH CENTURY

Budé, Guillaume
BULLETIN DE L'ASSOCIATION GUILLAUME BUDÉ

Racine, Jean Baptiste
CAHIERS RACINIENS

Revue des Lettres Modernes
Minard, Paris

BIOGRAPHY INDEX

Shakespeare, William
SHAKESPEARE QUARTERLY

BRITISH HUMANITIES INDEX

Brontë, Charlotte, Emily, Anne, and Branwell
Brontë Society. TRANSACTIONS

Dickens, Charles
DICKENSIAN

Hardy, Thomas
THOMAS HARDY YEAR BOOK

Kipling, Rudyard
KIPLING JOURNAL

BROWNING INSTITUTE STUDIES

Browning, Robert and Elizabeth
BROWNING SOCIETY NOTES

BULLETIN CRITIQUE

Archives des Lettres Modernes
Minard, Paris

Balzac, Honoré
COURRIER BALZACIEN
ÉTUDES BALZACIENNES

Baudelaire, Charles
Études baudelairiens

Beyle, Marie Henri [Stendhal]
STENDHAL CLUB

Blondel, Maurice
ÉTUDES BLONDÉLIENNES

BULLETIN CRITIQUE (cont.)

Budé, Guillaume
BULLETIN DE L'ASSOCIATION GUILLAUME BUDÉ

Chateaubriand, François-René
Société Chateaubriand. BULLETIN

Claudel, Paul
Cahiers Paul Claudel

Cocteau, Jean
Cahiers Jean Cocteau

Foucauld, Charles
CAHIERS CHARLES DE FOUCAULD

Giraudoux, Jean
CAHIERS JEAN GIRAUDOUX

Gobineau, Joseph-Arthur
ÉTUDES GOBINIENNES

Huysmans, Joris-Karl
BULLETIN DE LA SOCIÉTÉ J.-K. HUYSMANS

Larbaud, Valéry
CAHIERS DES AMIS DE VALÉRY LARBAUD

Ner, Henri [Han Ryner]
CAHIERS DES AMIS DE HAN RYNER

Proust, Marcel
Cahiers Marcel Proust

Racine, Jean Baptiste
CAHIERS RACINIENS

Renan, Ernest
CAHIERS RENAN

Renaud, Madeleine
CAHIERS RENAUD-BARRAULT

Revue des Lettres Modernes
Minard, Paris

CATHOLIC PERIODICAL AND LITERATURE INDEX

Augustine, Saint
AUGUSTINIAN STUDIES

Teilhard de Chardin, Pierre
TEILHARD REVIEW

ENGLISH LANGUAGE NOTES, ANNUAL SUPPLEMENTS, and ROMANTIC MOVEMENT BIBLIOGRAPHY, 1937-70

Arouet, François Marie [Voltaire]
STUDIES ON VOLTAIRE AND THE EIGHTEENTH CENTURY

Beyle, Marie Henri [Stendhal]
STENDHAL CLUB

Blake, William
BLAKE: AN ILLUSTRATED QUARTERLY
BLAKE NEWSLETTER
BLAKE STUDIES

Browning, Robert and Elizabeth
STUDIES IN BROWNING AND HIS CIRCLES

Budé, Guillaume
BULLETIN DE L'ASSOCIATION GUILLAUME BUDÉ

Burke, Edmund
STUDIES IN BURKE AND HIS TIME

Chateaubriand, François-René
Société Chateaubriand. BULLETIN

Dickens, Charles
DICKENS STUDIES NEWSLETTER

Eichendorff, Joseph Freiherr von
AURORA: EICHENDORFF-ALMANACH
AURORA: JAHRBUCH DER EICHENDORFF-GESELLSCHAFT

Emerson, Ralph Waldo
EMERSON SOCIETY QUARTERLY
ESQ

Görres, Joseph von
LITERATURWISSENSCHAFTLICHES JAHRBUCH

Goethe, Johann Wolfgang
ENGLISH GOETHE SOCIETY: PUBLICATIONS
GOETHE-JAHRBUCH (Tokyo)
JAHRBUCH DES FREIEN DEUTSCHEN HOCHSTIFTS
JAHRBUCH DES WIENER GOETHE-VEREINS

Guérin, Eugénie and Maurice de
L'AMITIÉ GUÉRINIENNE

Heine, Heinrich
HEINE-JAHRBUCH

Hölderlin, Friedrich
HÖLDERLIN-JAHRBUCH

Hoffmann, Ernst T.A.
MITTEILUNGEN DER E.T.A. HOFFMANN-GESELLSCHAFT

ENGLISH LANGUAGE NOTES, ANNUAL SUPPLEMENTS, and ROMANTIC MOVEMENT BIBLIOGRAPHY, 1937-70 (cont.)

Johnson, Samuel
JOHNSONIAN NEWS LETTER

Kant, Immanuel
KANT-STUDIEN

Keats, John
KEATS-SHELLEY JOURNAL
KEATS-SHELLEY MEMORIAL BULLETIN

Lamb, Charles
CHARLES LAMB BULLETIN

Lessing, Gotthold
LESSING YEARBOOK

Menéndez (y) Pelayo, Marcelino
BOLETÍN DE LA BIBLIOTECA MENÉNDEZ PELAYO

Milton, John
MILTON AND THE ROMANTICS

Raabe, Wilhelm
JAHRBUCH DER RAABE-GESELLSCHAFT

Richter, Jean Paul [Jean Paul]
JAHRBUCH DER JEAN-PAUL-GESELLSCHAFT

Schiller, Friedrich von
JAHRBUCH DER DEUTSCHEN SCHILLERGESELLSCHAFT

Shakespeare, William
SHAKESPEARE-JAHRBUCH (Weimar)
SHAKESPEARE SURVEY

Shaw, George Bernard
SHAW REVIEW

Wollstonecraft, Mary
MARY WOLLSTONECRAFT NEWSLETTER

Wordsworth, William
WORDSWORTH CIRCLE

Zola, Émile
CAHIERS NATURALISTES

ENGLISH LITERATURE IN TRANSITION

Shaw, George Bernard
INDEPENDENT SHAVIAN

ESSAY AND GENERAL LITERATURE INDEX

Dickens, Charles
DICKENS STUDIES ANNUAL

ESSAY AND GENERAL LITERATURE INDEX (cont.)

Joyce, James
JAMES JOYCE MISCELLANY

Shakespeare, William
SHAKESPEARE STUDIES: AN ANNUAL GATHERING
SHAKESPEARE SURVEY

ÉTUDES ANGLAISES

Browning, Robert and Elizabeth
STUDIES IN BROWNING AND HIS CIRCLE

Conrad, Joseph
CONRADIANA

Dickens, Charles
DICKENSIAN

Eliot, T.S.
T.S. ELIOT NEWSLETTER
T.S. ELIOT REVIEW

Joyce, James
JAMES JOYCE QUARTERLY

Keats, John
KEATS-SHELLEY MEMORIAL BULLETIN

Milton, John
MILTON QUARTERLY

More, Saint Thomas
MOREANA

Shakespeare, William
SHAKESPEARE QUARTERLY
SHAKESPEARE STUDIES (Tokyo)

Whitman, Walt
CALAMUS

FRENCH VI BIBLIOGRAPHY: FOR THE STUDY OF NINETEENTH-CENTURY FRENCH LITERATURE

Baudelaire, Charles
BULLETIN BAUDELAIRIEN

Beyle, Marie Henri [Stendhal]
STENDHAL CLUB

Dumas, Alexandre, père
DUMASIAN

Flaubert, Gustave
AMIS DE FLAUBERT

FRENCH VI BIBLIOGRAPHY: FOR THE STUDY OF NINETEENTH-CENTURY FRENCH LITERATURE (cont.)

Labrunie, Gérard [Gérard de Nerval]
Nouvelle bibliothèque nervalienne

Montaigne, Michel
BULLETIN DE LA SOCIÉTÉ DES AMIS DE MONTAIGNE

Proust, Marcel
BULLETIN MARCEL PROUST

FRENCH VII BIBLIOGRAPHY: CRITICAL AND BIOGRAPHICAL REFERENCES FOR THE STUDY OF CONTEMPORARY FRENCH LITERATURE

Annunzio, Gabriele d'
QUADERNI DANNUNZIANI

Archives des Lettres Modernes
Minard, Paris

Barbieri, Cesare
CESARE BARBIERI COURIER

Barrault, Jean-Louis
CAHIERS RENAUD-BARRAULT

Baty, Gaston
Cahiers Gaston Baty

Bergson, Henri
ÉTUDES BERGSONIENNES

Bernanos, Georges
BULLETIN DE LA SOCIÉTÉ DES AMIS DE GEORGES BERNANOS
Société des Amis de Georges Bernanos. BULLETIN

Bloch, Jean-Richard
EUROPE

Bloy, Léon
BLOYANA

Brasillach, Robert
CAHIERS DES AMIS DE ROBERT BRASILLACH

Chartier, Émile Auguste [Alain]
Association des Amis d'Alain. BULLETIN

Claudel, Paul
BULLETIN DE LA SOCIÉTÉ PAUL CLAUDEL
Cahier Canadien Claudel
Cahiers Paul Claudel
Société Claudel en Belgique. BULLETIN RÉGIONAL

Croce, Benedetto
RIVISTA DI STUDI CROCIANI

FRENCH VII BIBLIOGRAPHY: CRITICAL AND BIOGRAPHICAL REFERENCES FOR THE STUDY OF CONTEMPORARY FRENCH LITERATURE (cont.)

Deubel, Léon
Société des Amis de Léon Deubel. BULLETIN

du Bos, Charles
CAHIERS CHARLES DU BOS

Dullin, Charles
Association Charles Dullin. BULLETIN

Gandhi, Mohandas
GANDHI MARG

Görres, Joseph von
LITERATURWISSENSCHAFTLICHES JAHRBUCH

Goethe, Johann
ENGLISH GOETHE SOCIETY: PUBLICATIONS

Huysmans, Joris-Karl
BULLETIN DE LA SOCIÉTÉ J.-K. HUYSMANS

Jaurès, Jean
BULLETIN DE LA SOCIÉTÉ D'ÉTUDES JAURÉSIENNES

Kant, Immanuel
KANT-STUDIEN

La Varende, Jean
AMIS DE LA VARENDE

Maeterlinck, Maurice
Fondation M. Maeterlinck. ANNALES

Maurras, Charles
CAHIERS CHARLES MAURRAS

Montaigne, Michel
BULLETIN DE LA SOCIÉTÉ DES AMIS DE MONTAIGNE

Ner, Henri (Han Ryner)
CAHIERS DES AMIS DE HAN RYNER

Péguy, Charles
L'AMITIÉ CHARLES PÉGUY
CAHIERS DE L'AMITIÉ CHARLES PÉGUY

Pergaud, Louis
Amis de Louis Pergaud. BULLETIN
Amis de Louis Pergaud. CAHIERS

Philippe, Charles-Louis
Amis de Charles-Louis Philippe. BULLETIN

Proust, Marcel
BULLETIN DE LA SOCIÉTÉ DES AMIS DE MARCEL PROUST

Ramuz, Charles-Ferdinand
Fondation Charles-Ferdinand Ramuz. BULLETIN

FRENCH VII BIBLIOGRAPHY: CRITICAL AND BIOGRAPHICAL REFERENCES FOR THE STUDY OF CONTEMPORARY FRENCH LITERATURE (cont.)

Renaud, Madeleine
CAHIERS RENAUD-BARRAULT

Retté, Adolphe
BULLETIN DES AMIS D'ADOLPHE RETTÉ

Revue des Lettres Modernes
Minard, Paris

Rimbaud, Arthur
BATEAU IVRE
BULLETIN DES AMIS DE RIMBAUD
RIMBALDIEN

Rolland, Romain
Association des Amis de Romain Rolland. BULLETIN
Cahiers Romain Rolland
ÉTUDES SUR ROMAIN ROLLAND

Rollinat, Maurice
BULLETIN DE LA SOCIÉTÉ "LES AMIS DE MAURICE ROLLINAT"

Shakespeare, William
SHAKESPEARE QUARTERLY

Shaw, George Bernard
SHAW BULLETIN
Shaw Society (London). BULLETIN

Thibault, Anatole [Anatole France]
LE LYS ROUGE

Verlaine, Paul
ÉTUDES VERLAINIENNES

Viaud, Julien [Pierre Loti]
ASSOCIATION INTERNATIONALE DES AMIS DE PIERRE LOTI
CAHIERS PIERRE LOTI

FRENCH XX BIBLIOGRAPHY: CRITICAL AND BIOGRAPHICAL REFERENCES FOR THE STUDY OF FRENCH LITERATURE SINCE 1885

Archives des Lettres Modernes
Minard, Paris

Augustine, Saint
RECHERCHES AUGUSTINIENNES

Barrault, Jean-Louis
CAHIERS RENAUD-BARRAULT

Baty, Gaston
CAHIERS GASTON BATY

FRENCH XX BIBLIOGRAPHY: CRITICAL AND BIOGRAPHICAL REFERENCES FOR THE STUDY OF FRENCH LITERATURE SINCE 1885 (cont.)

Baudelaire, Charles
  BULLETIN BAUDELAIRIEN

Bergson, Henri-Louis
  ÉTUDES BERGSONIENNES

Bernanos, Georges
  COURRIER GEORGES BERNANOS

Beyle, Marie Henri [Stendhal]
  STENDHAL CLUB

Bloch, Henri
  EUROPE

Bloy, Léon
  BLOYANA

Bosco, Henri
  CAHIERS DE L'AMITIÉ HENRI BOSCO

Brasillach, Robert
  CAHIERS DES AMIS DE ROBERT BRASILLACH

Budé, Guillaume
  BULLETIN DE L'ASSOCIATION GUILLAUME BUDÉ

Camus, Albert
  Cahiers Albert Camus

Césaire, Aimé
  CAHIERS CÉSAIRIENS

Chartier, Émile Auguste [Alain]
  Association des Amis d'Alain. BULLETIN

Chateaubriand, François-René
  Société Chateaubriand. BULLETIN

Claudel, Paul
  BULLETIN DE LA SOCIÉTÉ PAUL CLAUDEL
  Cahier Canadien Claudel
  Cahiers Paul Claudel
  CLAUDEL NEWSLETTER
  CLAUDEL STUDIES
  Société Claudel en Belgique. BULLETIN RÉGIONAL

Cocteau, Jean
  Cahiers Jean Cocteau

Croce, Benedetto
  RIVISTA DI STUDI CROCIANI

de Gaulle, Charles
  ESPOIR

FRENCH XX BIBLIOGRAPHY: CRITICAL AND BIOGRAPHICAL REFERENCES FOR THE STUDY OF FRENCH LITERATURE SINCE 1885 (cont.)

Destouches, Louis-Ferdinand [Louis-Ferdinand Céline]
    Archives Céline
    L.-F. Céline

du Bos, Charles
    CAHIERS CHARLES DU BOS

Flaubert, Gustave
    AMIS DE FLAUBERT

Fournier, Henri-Alban [Alain-Fournier]. See Rivière, Jacques

Gandhi, Mohandas
    GANDHI MARG

Gide, André
    BULLETIN DES AMIS D'ANDRÉ GIDE
    Cahiers André Gide

Giono, Jean
    Association des Amis de Jean Giono. BULLETIN

Giraudoux, Jean
    CAHIERS JEAN GIRAUDOUX

Huysmans, Joris-Karl
    BULLETIN DE LA SOCIÉTÉ J.-K. HUYSMANS

Jaurés, Jean
    BULLETIN DE LA SOCIÉTÉ D'ÉTUDES JAURÉSIENNES

Joyce, James
    JAMES JOYCE QUARTERLY

Kostrowitzky, Wilhelm [Apollinaire]
    Bibliothèque Guillaume Apollinaire
    BULLETIN DE L'ASSOCIATION INTERNATIONALE DES AMIS DE GUILLAUME APOLLINAIRE
    QUE VLO-VE?

Larbaud, Valéry
    Amis de Valéry Larbaud. CAHIERS

Maeterlinck, Maurice
    ANNALES DE LA FONDATION M. MAETERLINCK

Malraux, André
    MÉLANGES MALRAUX MISCELLANY

Mauriac, François
    CAHIERS FRANÇOIS MAURIAC

Maurras, Charles
    CAHIERS CHARLES MAURRAS

Milosz, Oscar Venceslas
    Amis de Milosz. CAHIERS DE L'ASSOCIATION

FRENCH XX BIBLIOGRAPHY: CRITICAL AND BIOGRAPHICAL REFERENCES FOR THE STUDY OF FRENCH LITERATURE SINCE 1885 (cont.)

Montaigne, Michel
BULLETIN DE LA SOCIÉTÉ DES AMIS DE MONTAIGNE

Ner, Henri [Han Ryner]
CAHIERS DES AMIS DE HAN RYNER

Pareto, Vilfredo
CAHIERS VILFREDO PARETO

Péguy, Charles
L'AMITIÉ CHARLES PÉGUY: FEUILLETS MENSUELS
CAHIERS DE L'AMITIÉ CHARLES PÉGUY

Pergaud, Louis
Amis de Louis Pergaud. BULLETIN

Philippe, Charles-Louis
Amis de Charles-Louis Philippe. BULLETIN
Amis de Charles-Louis Philippe. CAHIERS

Proust, Marcel
BULLETIN DE LA SOCIÉTÉ DES AMIS DE MARCEL PROUST
ÉTUDES PROUSTIENNES
PROUST RESEARCH ASSOCIATION NEWSLETTER

Racine, Jean Baptiste
CAHIERS RACINIENS

Ramuz, Charles-Ferdinand
Fondation Charles-Ferdinand Ramuz. BULLETIN

Renaud, Madeleine
CAHIERS RENAUD-BARRAULT

Revue des Lettres Modernes
Minard, Paris

Rimbaud, Arthur
ÉTUDES RIMBALDIENNES
RIMBAUD VIVANT

Rivière, Jacques
Association des Amis de Jacques Rivière et Alain-Fournier. BULLETIN

Rolland, Romain
Association des Amis de Romain Rolland. BULLETIN
Cahiers Romain Rolland

Rollinat, Maurice
BULLETIN DE LA SOCIÉTÉ "LES AMIS DE MAURICE ROLLINAT"

Rouget, Marie Mélanie [Marie Noël]
CAHIERS MARIE NOËL

Rousseau, Jean-Jacques
ANNALES DE LA SOCIÉTÉ JEAN-JACQUES ROUSSEAU

FRENCH XX BIBLIOGRAPHY: CRITICAL AND BIOGRAPHICAL REFERENCES FOR THE STUDY OF FRENCH LITERATURE SINCE 1885 (cont.)

Steinbeck, John
STEINBECK QUARTERLY

Teilhard de Chardin, Pierre
CAHIERS DE LA FONDATION TEILHARD DE CHARDIN
CAHIERS PIERRE TEILHARD DE CHARDIN
Carnets Teilhard
REVUE TEILHARD DE CHARDIN
TEILHARD DE CHARDIN
TEILHARD REVIEW

Thibault, Anatole [Anatole France]
CAHIERS FRANCIENS
LE LYS ROUGE

Valéry, Paul
Cahiers Paul Valéry

Verne, Jules
BULLETIN DE LA SOCIÉTÉ JULES VERNE

Viaud, Julien [Pierre Loti]
CAHIERS PIERRE LOTI

Weil, Simone
Association pour l'étude de la pensée de Simone Weil. BULLETIN

Whitman, Walt
WALT WHITMAN REVIEW

Zola, Émile
CAHIERS NATURALISTES

HISTORICAL ABSTRACTS

Bolívar, Simón
REVISTA BOLIVARIANA

Burke, Edmund
STUDIES IN BURKE AND HIS TIME

Chesterton, G.K.
CHESTERTON REVIEW

Clemens, Samuel L. [Mark Twain]
TWAINIAN

Gandhi, Mohandas
GANDHI MARG

Hume, David
HUME STUDIES

Menéndez Pelayo, Marcelino
BOLETÍN DE LA BIBLIOTECA MENÉNDEZ PELAYO

HISTORICAL ABSTRACTS (cont.)

More, Saint Thomas
MOREANA

Unamuno, Miguel de
CUADERNOS DE LA CÁTEDRA DE UNAMUNO

HUMANITIES INDEX

Chaucer, Geoffrey
CHAUCER REVIEW

Keats, John
KEATS-SHELLEY JOURNAL

Shakespeare, William
SHAKESPEARE QUARTERLY
SHAKESPEARE SURVEY

Shelley, Percy Bysshe
KEATS-SHELLEY JOURNAL

INDEX TO BOOK REVIEWS IN THE HUMANITIES

Browning, Robert and Elizabeth
BROWNING NEWSLETTER
STUDIES IN BROWNING AND HIS CIRCLE

Conrad, Joseph
CONRADIANA

Dickens, Charles
DICKENSIAN

Joyce, James
JAMES JOYCE QUARTERLY

Kant, Immanuel
KANT-STUDIEN

Pope, Alexander
SCRIBLERIAN: A NEWSJOURNAL
SCRIBLERIAN AND THE KIT-CATS

Shakespeare, William
SHAKESPEARE QUARTERLY

Shaw, George Bernard
SHAVIAN
SHAW REVIEW

Swift, Jonathan
SCRIBLERIAN: A NEWSJOURNAL
SCRIBLERIAN AND THE KIT-CATS

Whitman, Walt
WALT WHITMAN REVIEW

JOURNAL OF MODERN LITERATURE

Eliot, T.S.
T.S. ELIOT REVIEW

Klapp (BIBLIOGRAPHIE DER FRANZÖSISCHEN LITERATURWISSENSCHAFT/ BIBLIOGRAPHIE D'HISTOIRE LITTÉRAIRE FRANÇAISE)

Archives des Lettres Modernes
Minard, Paris

Arouet, François Marie [Voltaire]
STUDIES ON VOLTAIRE AND THE EIGHTEENTH CENTURY

Balzac, Honoré
L'ANNÉE BALZACIENNE
ÉTUDES BALZACIENNES

Barrault, Jean-Louis
CAHIERS RENAUD-BARRAULT

Baudelaire, Charles
BULLETIN BAUDELAIRIEN
Études baudelairiennes

Bergson, Henri Louis
ÉTUDES BERGSONIENNES

Bernanos, Georges
COURRIER GEORGES BERNANOS

Beyle, Marie Henri [Stendhal]
DIVAN
STENDHAL CLUB

Bloch, Jean-Richard
EUROPE

Bosco, Henri
BULLETIN HENRI BOSCO

Brasillach, Robert
CAHIERS DES AMIS DE ROBERT BRASILLACH

Budé, Guillaume
BULLETIN DE L'ASSOCIATION GUILLAUME BUDÉ

Burke, Edmund
STUDIES IN BURKE AND HIS TIME

Casanova de Seingalt, Jacques
CASANOVA GLEANINGS

Chateaubriand, François-René
BULLETIN DE LA SOCIÉTÉ CHATEAUBRIAND

Klapp (BIBLIOGRAPHIE DER FRANZÖSISCHEN LITERATURWISSENSCHAFT/ BIBLIOGRAPHIE D'HISTOIRE LITTÉRAIRE FRANÇAISE) (cont.)

Claudel, Paul
BULLETIN DE LA SOCIÉTÉ PAUL CLAUDEL
Cahier Canadien Claudel
Cahiers Paul Claudel
CLAUDEL STUDIES

Cocteau, Jean
Cahiers Jean Cocteau

Constant, Benjamin
CAHIERS BENJAMIN CONSTANT

Corneille, Pierre
CAHIERS PIERRE CORNEILLE

Dante Alighieri
DEUTSCHE DANTE-JAHRBUCH

Degée, Olivier [Jean Tousseul]
CAHIERS JEAN TOUSSEUL

Delisle, Léopold
CAHIERS LÉOPOLD DELISLE

Deubel, Léon
Société des Amis de Léon Deubel. BULLETIN

Diderot, Denis
Diderot Studies

du Bos, Charles
CAHIERS CHARLES DU BOS

Flaubert, Gustave
AMIS DE FLAUBERT

Freud, Sigmund
ÉTUDES FREUDIENNES

Gide, André
BULLETIN DES AMIS D'ANDRÉ GIDE
Cahiers André Gide

Giono, Jean
BULLETIN. Association des Amis de Jean Giono.

Giraudoux, Jean
CAHIERS JEAN GIRAUDOUX

Gobineau, Joseph-Arthur de
ÉTUDES GOBINIENNES

Goethe, Johannes Wolfgang
GOETHE JAHRBUCH (Weimar)

Grindel, Eugène [Paul Éluard]
CAHIERS PAUL ÉLUARD

Klapp (BIBLIOGRAPHIE DER FRANZÖSISCHEN LITERATURWISSENSCHAFT/ BIBLIOGRAPHIE D'HISTOIRE LITTÉRAIRE FRANÇAISE) (cont.)

Guérin, Eugénie and Maurice de
L'AMITIÉ GUÉRINIENNE

Gutenberg, Johannes
GUTENBERG-JAHRBUCH

Huysmans, Joris-Karl
BULLETIN DE LA SOCIÉTÉ J.-K. HUYSMANS

Joyce, James
JAMES JOYCE QUARTERLY

Kostrowitzky, Wilhelm [Apollinaire]
QUE VLO-VE?

Larbaud, Valéry
CAHIERS DES AMIS DE VALÉRY LARBAUD

La Varende, Jean
AMIS DE LA VARENDE

Maeterlinck, Maurice
Fondation Maurice Maeterlinck. ANNALES

Maupassant, Guy de
BEL AMI

Mauriac, François
CAHIERS FRANÇOIS MAURIAC

Maurras, Charles
CAHIERS CHARLES MAURRAS

Milosz, Oscar Venceslas
Amis de Milosz. CAHIERS DE L'ASSOCIATION

Montaigne, Michel
BULLETIN DE LA SOCIÉTÉ DES AMIS DE MONTAIGNE

Ner, Henri [Han Ryner]
CAHIERS DES AMIS DE HAN RYNER

Péguy, Charles
L'AMITIÉ CHARLES PÉGUY

Pergaud, Louis
Amis de Louis Pergaud. BULLETIN

Philippe, Charles-Louis
Amis de Charles-Louis Philippe. BULLETIN

Proust, Marcel
BULLETIN DE LA SOCIÉTÉ DES AMIS DE MARCEL PROUST
Cahiers Marcel Proust
ÉTUDES PROUSTIENNES

Rabelais, François
BULLETIN DE LA SOCIÉTÉ DES AMIS DE RABELAIS
ÉTUDES RABELAISIENNES

Klapp (BIBLIOGRAPHIE DER FRANZÖSISCHEN LITERATURWISSENSCHAFT/ BIBLIOGRAPHIE D'HISTOIRE LITTÉRAIRE FRANÇAISE) (cont.)

Racine, Jean Baptiste
CAHIERS RACINIENS
JEUNESSE DE RACINE

Renan, Joseph Ernest
Cahiers renaniens
ÉTUDES RENANIENNES: BULLETIN

Renaud, Madeleine
CAHIERS RENAUD-BARRAULT

Revue des Lettres Modernes
Minard, Paris

Rimbaud, Arthur
Amis de Rimbaud. ÉTUDES RIMBALDIENNES
CAHIERS DU CENTRE CULTUREL ARTHUR RIMBAUD
RIMBAUD VIVANT

Rivière, Jacques
BULLETIN DES AMIS DE JACQUES RIVIÈRE ET ALAIN-FOURNIER

Rolland, Romain
Association des Amis de Romain Rolland. BULLETIN

Rollinat, Maurice
BULLETIN DE LA SOCIÉTÉ "LES AMIS DE MAURICE ROLLINAT"

Rouget, Marie Mélanie [Marie Noël]
CAHIERS MARIE NOËL

Rousseau, Jean-Jacques
ANNALES DE LA SOCIÉTÉ JEAN-JACQUES ROUSSEAU

Saint-Simon, Claude-Henri
CAHIERS SAINT-SIMON

Saussure, Ferdinand de
CAHIERS FERDINAND DE SAUSSURE

Schiller, Friedrich von
Deutsche Schiller-Gesellschaft. JAHRBUCH

Shakespeare, William
SHAKESPEARE JAHRBUCH (Heidelberg)

Staël, Madame de
CAHIERS STAËLIENS

Thibault, Anatole [Anatole France]
LE LYS ROUGE

Valéry, Paul
BULLETIN DES ÉTUDES VALÉRYENNES

Verne, Jules
BULLETIN DE LA SOCIÉTÉ JULES VERNE

Klapp (BIBLIOGRAPHIE DER FRANZÖSISCHEN LITERATURWISSENSCHAFT/ BIBLIOGRAPHIE D'HISTOIRE LITTÉRAIRE FRANÇAISE) (cont.)

Viaud, Julien [Pierre Loti]
CAHIERS PIERRE LOTI

Vigny, Alfred Victor de
Amis d'Alfred de Vigny. BULLETIN

Zola, Émile
CAHIERS NATURALISTES

Köttelwesch (BIBLIOGRAPHIE DER DEUTSCHEN LITERATURWISSENSCHAFT and its successor, BIBLIOGRAPHIE DER DEUTSCHEN SPRACH- UND LITERATURWISSENSCHAFT)

Barlach, Ernst
DEN MITGLIEDERN UND FREUNDEN ZUR JAHRESWENDE

Blunck, Hans
HANS FRIEDRICH BLUNCK-JAHRBUCH

Bolland, Jean de
ANALECTA BOLLANDIA

Brecht, Bertolt
BRECHT HEUTE
BRECHT-JAHRBUCH

Budé, Guillaume
BULLETIN DE L'ASSOCIATION GUILLAUME BUDÉ

Busch, Wilhelm
JAHRBUCH DER WILHELM-BUSCH-GESELLSCHAFT
Wilhelm-Busch-Gesellschaft. MITTEILUNGEN
WILHELM-BUSCH-JAHRBUCH

Cusanus, Nicolaus
MITTEILUNGEN UND FORSCHUNGSBEITRÄGE DER CUSANUS-GESELLSCHAFT

Dante Alighieri
DEUTSCHE DANTE-JAHRBUCH
MITTEILUNGSBLATT DER DEUTSCHEN DANTE-GESELLSCHAFT

Droste-Hülshoff, Annette von
JAHRBUCH DER DROSTE-GESELLSCHAFT
KLEINE BEITRÄGE ZUR DROSTE-FORSCHUNG

Eichendorff, Joseph Freiherr von
AURORA: JAHRBUCH DER DEUTSCHEN EICHENDORFF-STIFTUNG

Ernst, Paul
Paul-Ernst-Gesellschaft. JAHRESGABE
WILLE ZUR FORM

Erwin von Steinbach
STUDIEN DER ERWIN VON STEINBACH-STIFTUNG

Köttelwesch (BIBLIOGRAPHIE DER DEUTSCHEN LITERATURWISSENSCHAFT and its successor, BIBLIOGRAPHIE DER DEUTSCHEN SPRACH- UND LITERATURWISSENSCHAFT) (cont.)

Fontane, Theodor
FONTANE-BLÄTTER

Freytag, Gustav
GUSTAV-FREYTAG-BLÄTTER

Görres, Joseph von
HISTORISCHES JAHRBUCH DER GÖRRES-GESELLSCHAFT
PHILOSOPHISCHES JAHRBUCH DER GÖRRES-GESELLSCHAFT

Goethe, Johann Wolfgang
AUSTRALIAN GOETHE SOCIETY PROCEEDINGS
CHRONIK DES WIENER GOETHE-VEREINS
ENGLISH GOETHE SOCIETY: PUBLICATIONS
GOETHE-ALMANACH AUF DAS JAHR
GOETHE-JAHRBUCH (Tokyo)
GOETHE-JAHRBUCH (Weimar)
JAHRBUCH DES FREIEN DEUTSCHEN HOCHSTIFTS
JAHRBUCH DES WIENER GOETHE-VEREINS

Grillparzer, Franz
GRILLPARZER-FORUM FORCHTENSTEIN
JAHRBUCH DER GRILLPARZER-GESELLSCHAFT

Groth, Klaus
JAHRESGABE DER KLAUS-GROTH-GESELLSCHAFT

Gutenberg, Johannes
GUTENBERG-JAHRBUCH

Hansjakob, Heinrich
HANSJAKOB-JAHRBUCH

Hauptmann, Gerhart
GERHART-HAUPTMANN-JAHRBUCH

Hebbel, Friedrich
HEBBEL-JAHRBUCH

Hegel, Georg
HEGEL-STUDIEN

Heine, Heinrich
HEINE-JAHRBUCH

Hölderlin, Friedrich
HÖLDERLIN-JAHRBUCH

Hoffmann, Ernst T.A.
MITTEILUNGEN DER E.T.A. HOFFMANN-GESELLSCHAFT

Hofmannsthal, Hugo von
HOFMANNSTHAL-BLÄTTER

Köttelwesch (BIBLIOGRAPHIE DER DEUTSCHEN LITERATURWISSENSCHAFT and its successor BIBLIOGRAPHIE DER DEUTSCHEN SPRACH- UND LITERATURWISSENSCHAFT) (cont.)

Ibsen, Henrik
IBSENÅRBOK

Kant, Immanuel
KANT-STUDIEN

Keller, Gottfried
Gottfried Keller-Gesellschaft. JAHRESBERICHT

Kleist, Heinrich von
JAHRESGABE DER HEINRICH-VON-KLEIST-GESELLSCHAFT

Lessing, Gotthold
LESSING YEARBOOK

Luther, Martin
LUTHER-JAHRBUCH

Mann, Heinrich
Arbeitkreis Heinrich Mann. MITTEILUNGSBLATT

Mann, Thomas
BLÄTTER DER THOMAS-MANN-GESELLSCHAFT

May, Karl
JAHRBUCH DER KARL-MAY-GESELLSCHAFT

Mickiewicz, Adam
MICKIEWICZ-BLÄTTER

Nietzsche, Friedrich
NIETZSCHE-STUDIEN

Pirckheimer, Willibald
MARGINALIEN

Raabe, Wilhelm
JAHRBUCH DER RAABE-GESELLSCHAFT
MITTEILUNGEN DER RAABE-GESELLSCHAFT
RAABE-JAHRBUCH
WILHELM RAABE-KALENDER

Raimund, Ferdinand
RAIMUND-ALMANACH

Renaud, Madeleine
CAHIERS RENAUD-BARRAULT

Richter, Jean Paul [Jean Paul]
HESPERUS
JAHRBUCH DER JEAN-PAUL-GESELLSCHAFT

Rilke, Rainer Maria
BLÄTTER DER RILKE-GESELLSCHAFT

Köttelwesch (BIBLIOGRAPHIE DER DEUTSCHEN LITERATURWISSENSCHAFT and its successor BIBLIOGRAPHIE DER DEUTSCHEN SPRACH- UND LITERATURWISSENSCHAFT) (cont.)

Rousseau, Jean-Jacques
ANNALES DE LA SOCIÉTÉ JEAN-JACQUES ROUSSEAU

Saussure, Ferdinand de
CAHIERS FERDINAND SAUSSURE

Schiller, Friedrich von
JAHRBUCH DER DEUTSCHEN SCHILLERGESELLSCHAFT

Schneider, Reinhold
Reinhold-Schneider-Gesellschaft. MITTEILUNGEN

Schopenhauer, Arthur
SCHOPENHAUER-JAHRBUCH

Shakespeare, William
JAHRBUCH DER DEUTSCHEN SHAKESPEARE-GESELLSCHAFT WEST (Heidelberg)
SHAKESPEARE-JAHRBUCH (Weimar)
SHAKESPEARE QUARTERLY

Stifter, Adalbert
Adalbert Stifter-Institut des Landes Oberösterreich. VIERTELJAHRESSCHRIFT
STIFTER-JAHRBUCH

Storm, Theodor
SCHRIFTEN DER THEODOR-STORM-GESELLSCHAFT

Strehlenau, Nikolaus [Nikolaus Lenau]
LENAU-ALMANACH
LENAU-FORUM

Trakl, Georg
TRAKL-STUDIEN

Weinheber, Josef
JAHRESGABE

Winckelmann, Johann
Winckelmann-Gesellschaft, Stendal. JAHRESGABE

Wolfram von Eschenbach
WOLFRAM-JAHRBUCH
WOLFRAM-STUDIEN

Zwingli, Ulrich
ZWINGLIANA

Leary (ARTICLES ON AMERICAN LITERATURE)

Clemens, Samuel L. [Mark Twain]
MARK TWAIN JOURNAL

Leary (ARTICLES ON AMERICAN LITERATURE) (cont.)

Crane, Stephen
STEPHEN CRANE NEWSLETTER

Emerson, Ralph Waldo
EMERSON SOCIETY QUARTERLY
ESQ

Fitzgerald, F. Scott
FITZGERALD NEWSLETTER

Gutenberg, Johannes
GUTENBERG-JAHRBUCH

Melville, Herman
EXTRACTS (Melville Society)

Shakespeare, William
SHAKESPEARE QUARTERLY

Thoreau, Henry
THOREAU SOCIETY BOOKLET
THOREAU SOCIETY BULLETIN

Whitman, Walt
WALT WHITMAN BIRTHPLACE ASSOCIATION NEWSLETTER
WALT WHITMAN BIRTHPLACE BULLETIN
WALT WHITMAN REVIEW

MANUAL DE BIBLIOGRAFÍA DE LA LITERATURA ESPAÑOLA

Cervantes
ANALES CERVANTINOS

More, Saint Thomas
MOREANA

MISSISSIPPI QUARTERLY

Cabell, James Branch
CABELLIAN

Clemens, Samuel L. [Mark Twain]
MARK TWAIN JOURNAL

Faulkner, William
FAULKNER CONCORDANCE NEWSLETTER

Glasgow, Ellen
ELLEN GLASGOW NEWSLETTER

Mencken, H.L.
MENCKENIANA

MISSISSIPPI QUARTERLY (cont.)

O'Connor, Flannery
FLANNERY O'CONNOR BULLETIN

Poe, Edgar Allan
POE STUDIES

MODERN DRAMA (Toronto)

Claudel, Paul
CLAUDEL STUDIES

O'Casey, Sean
SEAN O'CASEY REVIEW

Shaw, George Bernard
SHAW REVIEW

MODERN LANGUAGE ASSOCIATION ABSTRACTS

Blake, William
BLAKE NEWSLETTER

Burke, Edmund
STUDIES IN BURKE AND HIS TIME

Chaucer, Geoffrey
CHAUCER REVIEW

Claudel, Paul
CLAUDEL STUDIES

Clemens, Samuel L. [Mark Twain]
MARK TWAIN JOURNAL

Conrad, Joseph
CONRADIANA

Eliot, T.S.
T.S. ELIOT REVIEW

Emerson, Ralph Waldo
ESQ

Fitzgerald, F. Scott
FITZGERALD/HEMINGWAY ANNUAL

Hemingway, Ernest
FITZGERALD/HEMINGWAY ANNUAL

Keats, John
KEATS-SHELLEY JOURNAL

Malraux, André
MÉLANGES MALRAUX MISCELLANY

Markham, Edwin
MARKHAM REVIEW

MODERN LANGUAGE ASSOCIATION ABSTRACTS (cont.)

Milton, John
MILTON QUARTERLY
MILTON STUDIES

More, Saint Thomas
MOREANA

O'Casey, Sean
SEAN O'CASEY REVIEW

Poe, Edgar Allan
POE STUDIES

Shakespeare, William
SHAKESPEARE QUARTERLY

Shelley, Percy Bysshe
KEATS-SHELLEY JOURNAL

Thoreau, Henry
THOREAU SOCIETY BULLETIN

Waugh, Evelyn
EVELYN WAUGH NEWSLETTER

Wordsworth, William
WORDSWORTH CIRCLE

MODERN LANGUAGE ASSOCIATION INTERNATIONAL BIBLIOGRAPHY

Andersen, Hans Christian
ANDERSENIANA

Anderson, Sherwood
WINESBURG EAGLE

Annunzio, Gabriele d'
QUADERNI DANNUNZIANI

Aquinas, Saint Thomas
AQUINAS

Archives des Lettres Modernes
Minard, Paris

Arouet, François Marie [Voltaire]
STUDIES ON VOLTAIRE AND THE EIGHTEENTH CENTURY

Augustine, Saint
AUGUSTINIANA
AUGUSTINIANUM
AUGUSTINUS
RECHERCHES AUGUSTINIENNES
REVUE DES ÉTUDES AUGUSTINIENNES

MODERN LANGUAGE ASSOCIATION INTERNATIONAL BIBLIOGRAPHY (cont.)

Balzac, Honoré
L'ANNÉE BALZACIENNE
ÉTUDES BALZACIENNES

Barbieri, Cesare
CESARE BARBIERI COURIER

Barlach, Ernst
JAHRBUCH DER BARLACH-GESELLSCHAFT

Barrault, Jean-Louis
CAHIERS RENAUD-BARRAULT

Baudelaire, Charles
BULLETIN BAUDELAIRIEN

Baum, Frank
BAUM BUGLE

Bergman, Hjalmar
HJALMAR BERGMAN SAMFUNDET ÅRSBOK

Berryman, John
JOHN BERRYMAN STUDIES

Beyle, Marie Henri [Stendhal]
DIVAN
STENDHAL CLUB

Blake, William
BLAKE: AN ILLUSTRATED QUARTERLY
BLAKE NEWSLETTER

Boccaccio, Giovanni
STUDI SUL BOCCACCIO

Bolland, Jean de
ANALECTA BOLLANDIA

Brecht, Bertolt
BRECHT HEUTE
BRECHT JAHRBUCH

Brontë, Charlotte, Emily, Anne, and Branwell
Brontë Society. TRANSACTIONS

Browning, Robert and Elizabeth
BROWNING INSTITUTE STUDIES
BROWNING NEWSLETTER
BROWNING SOCIETY NOTES
STUDIES IN BROWNING AND HIS CIRCLE

Budé, Guillaume
BULLETIN DE L'ASSOCIATION GUILLAUME BUDÉ

Burke, Edmund
STUDIES IN BURKE AND HIS TIME

MODERN LANGUAGE ASSOCIATION INTERNATIONAL BIBLIOGRAPHY (cont.)

Cabell, James Branch
CABELLIAN
KALKI

Carvalho, Joaquim de
MISCELÂNEA DE ESTUDOS A JOAQUIM DE CARVALHO

Cervantes, Miguel
ANALES CERVANTINOS

Césaire, Aimé
CAHIERS CÉSAIRIENS

Chateaubriand, François-René
Société Chateaubriand. BULLETIN
Société Chateaubriand. GRAND BULLETIN

Chaucer, Geoffrey
CHAUCER REVIEW

Claudel, Paul
Cahier Canadien Claudel
CLAUDEL STUDIES

Clemens, Samuel L. [Mark Twain]
MARK TWAIN JOURNAL
TWAINIAN

Cocteau, Jean
Cahiers Jean Cocteau

Conrad, Joseph
CONRADIANA

Crane, Stephen
STEPHEN CRANE NEWSLETTER

Croce, Benedetto
RIVISTA DI STUDI CROCIANI

Cusanus
MITTEILUNGEN UND FORSCHUNGSBEITRÄGE DER CUSANUS-GESELLSCHAFT

Dante
L'ALIGHIERI
ANNALI DELL'ISTITUTO DI STUDI DANTESCHI
BULLETIN DE LA SOCIÉTÉ D'ÉTUDES DANTESQUE DU CENTRE UNIVERSITAIRE MÉDITERRANÉEN
DANTE STUDIES
DEUTSCHE DANTE-JAHRBUCH
STUDI DANTESCHI

MODERN LANGUAGE ASSOCIATION INTERNATIONAL BIBLIOGRAPHY (cont.)

Dickens, Charles
DICKENSIAN
DICKENS STUDIES
DICKENS STUDIES ANNUAL
DICKENS STUDIES NEWSLETTER

Diderot, Denis
Diderot Studies

Doyle, Sir Arthur Conan
BAKER STREET JOURNAL

Dreiser, Theodore
DREISER NEWSLETTER

Droste-Hülshoff, Annette von
KLEINE BEITRÄGE ZUR DROSTE-FORSCHUNG
SCHRIFTEN DER DROSTE-GESELLSCHAFT

Eichendorff, Joseph Freiherr von
AURORA: EICHENDORFF-ALMANACH
AURORA: JAHRBUCH DER DEUTSCHEN EICHENDORFF-STIFTUNG

Eliot, T.S.
T.S. ELIOT REVIEW

Emerson, Ralph Waldo
EMERSON SOCIETY QUARTERLY
ESQ

Erasmus, Desiderius
ERASMUS IN ENGLISH

Fitzgerald, F. Scott
FITZGERALD/HEMINGWAY ANNUAL
FITZGERALD NEWSLETTER

Flaubert, Gustave
AMIS DE FLAUBERT

Fontane, Theodor
FONTANE-BLÄTTER

Frederic, Harold
FREDERIC HERALD

Freytag, Gustav
GUSTAV-FREYTAG-BLÄTTER

Gandhi, Mohandas
GANDHI MARG

García Lorca, Federico
GARCÍA LORCA REVIEW

Giraudoux, Jean
CAHIERS JEAN GIRAUDOUX

MODERN LANGUAGE ASSOCIATION INTERNATIONAL BIBLIOGRAPHY (cont.)

Glasgow, Ellen
ELLEN GLASGOW NEWSLETTER

Görres, Joseph
LITERATURWISSENSCHAFTLICHES JAHRBUCH
PHILOSOPHISCHES JAHRBUCH DER GÖRRES-GESELLSCHAFT

Goethe, Johann
CHRONIK DES WIENER GOETHE-VEREINS
ENGLISH GOETHE SOCIETY: PUBLICATIONS
GOETHE-ALMANACH AUF DAS JAHR
GOETHE JAHRBUCH (Weimar)
Goethezeit
JAHRBUCH DER GOETHE-GESELLSCHAFT (Weimar)
JAHRBUCH DES FREIEN DEUTSCHEN HOCHSTIFTS
Wiener Goethe-Verein. JAHRBUCH

Goldoni, Carlo
STUDI GOLDONIANI

Graves, Robert
FOCUS ON ROBERT GRAVES

Grillparzer, Franz
GRILLPARZER-FORUM FORCHTENSTEIN
JAHRBUCH DER GRILLPARZER-GESELLSCHAFT

Groth, Klaus
JAHRESGABE DER KLAUS-GROTH-GESELLSCHAFT

Gutenberg, Johannes
GUTENBERG-JAHRBUCH

Hardy, Thomas
THOMAS HARDY YEAR BOOK

Hawthorne, Nathaniel
NATHANIEL HAWTHORNE JOURNAL

Hebbel, Friedrich
HEBBEL-JAHRBUCH

Heine, Heinrich
HEINE-JAHRBUCH

Hemingway, Ernest
FITZGERALD/HEMINGWAY ANNUAL

Hölderlin, Friedrich
HÖLDERLIN-JAHRBUCH

Hoffmann, Ernst T.A.
MITTEILUNGEN DER E.T.A. HOFFMANN-GESELLSCHAFT

Hofmannsthal, Hugo von
HOFMANNSTHAL-BLÄTTER

MODERN LANGUAGE ASSOCIATION INTERNATIONAL BIBLIOGRAPHY (cont.)

Hopkins, Gerard Manley
HOPKINS QUARTERLY

Ibsen, Henrik
IBSENÅRBOK

Jeffers, Robinson
ROBINSON JEFFERS NEWSLETTER

Johnson, Samuel
NEW RAMBLER

Joyce, James
JAMES JOYCE MISCELLANY
JAMES JOYCE QUARTERLY
JAMES JOYCE REVIEW
A WAKE NEWSLITTER

Kant, Immanuel
KANT-STUDIEN

Keats, John
KEATS-SHELLEY JOURNAL
KEATS-SHELLEY MEMORIAL BULLETIN

Kipling, Rudyard
KIPLING JOURNAL

Lamb, Charles
CHARLES LAMB BULLETIN

Lawrence, D.H.
D.H. LAWRENCE REVIEW

Lessing, Gotthold
LESSING YEARBOOK

Lewis, C.S.
BULLETIN OF THE NEW YORK C.S. LEWIS SOCIETY

London, Jack
JACK LONDON NEWSLETTER

Luther, Martin
LUTHER-JAHRBUCH

Maeterlinck, Maurice
Fondation Maurice Maeterlinck. ANNALES

Malraux, André
MÉLANGES MALRAUX MISCELLANY

Mann, Thomas
BLÄTTER DER THOMAS-MANN-GESELLSCHAFT
Thomas Mann-Studien

MODERN LANGUAGE ASSOCIATION INTERNATIONAL BIBLIOGRAPHY (cont.)

Markham, Edwin
MARKHAM REVIEW

Martí, José
ARCHIVO JOSÉ MARTÍ

May, Karl
JAHRBUCH DER KARL-MAY-GESELLSCHAFT

Mazzini, Guiseppe
BOLLETTINO DEL DOMUS MAZZINIANA

Melville, Herman
EXTRACTS (Melville Society)

Mencken, H.L.
MENCKENIANA

Menéndez (y) Pelayo, Marcelino
BOLETÍN DE LA BIBLIOTECA MENÉNDEZ PELAYO

Milton, John
MILTON QUARTERLY
MILTON STUDIES

Montaigne, Michel
BULLETIN DE LA SOCIÉTÉ DES AMIS DE MONTAIGNE

More, Saint Thomas
MOREANA

Muratori, Ludovico
ARCHIVIO MURATORIANO

Musil, Robert
Musil-Studien

Nietzsche, Friedrich
NIETZSCHE-STUDIEN

O'Casey, Sean
SEAN O'CASEY REVIEW

Péguy, Charles
L'AMITIÉ CHARLES PÉGUY
CAHIERS DE L'AMITIÉ CHARLES PÉGUY

Pérez Galdós, Benito
ANALES GALDOSIANOS

Petrarch, Francesco
STUDI PETRARCHESCHI

Pirckheimer, Willibald
MARGINALIEN

Poe, Edgar Allan
POE NEWSLETTER
POE STUDIES

MODERN LANGUAGE ASSOCIATION INTERNATIONAL BIBLIOGRAPHY (cont.)

Pope, Alexander
SCRIBLERIAN: A NEWSJOURNAL
SCRIBLERIAN AND THE KIT-CATS

Pound, Ezra
PAIDEUMA

Proust, Marcel
PROUST RESEARCH ASSOCIATION NEWSLETTER

Raabe, Wilhelm
JAHRBUCH DER RAABE-GESELLSCHAFT
MITTEILUNGEN DER RAABE-GESELLSCHAFT
SCHRIFTEN DER RAABE-GESELLSCHAFT

Rabelais, François
AMIS DE RABELAIS ET DE LA DEVINIÈRE
BULLETIN DE L'ASSOCIATION DES AMIS DE RABELAIS
ÉTUDES RABELAISIENNES

Racine, Jean Baptiste
CAHIERS RACINIENS

Renan, Ernest
Cahiers renaniens

Renaud, Madeleine
CAHIERS RENAUD-BARRAULT

Revue des Lettres Modernes
Minard, Paris

Richter, Jean Paul [Jean Paul]
HESPERUS
JAHRBUCH DER JEAN-PAUL-GESELLSCHAFT

Rilke, Rainer Maria
BLÄTTER DER RILKE-GESELLSCHAFT

Rimbaud, Arthur
ÉTUDES RIMBALDIENNES

Saussure, Ferdinand de
CAHIERS FERDINAND DE SAUSSURE

Schiller, Friedrich von
Deutsche Schillergesellschaft. JAHRBUCH
Deutsche Schillergesellschaft. VERÖFFENTLICHUNGEN

Shakespeare, William
SHAKESPEAREAN RESEARCH AND OPPORTUNITIES
SHAKESPEARE ASSOCIATION BULLETIN
SHAKESPEARE-JAHRBUCH (Heidelberg)
SHAKESPEARE-JAHRBUCH (Weimar)
SHAKESPEARE NEWSLETTER
SHAKESPEARE QUARTERLY

MODERN LANGUAGE ASSOCIATION INTERNATIONAL BIBLIOGRAPHY (cont.)

SHAKESPEARE STUDIES (Tokyo)
SHAKESPEARE STUDIES: AN ANNUAL GATHERING
SHAKESPEARE SURVEY

Shaw, George Bernard
SHAVIAN
SHAW BULLETIN
SHAW REVIEW

Shelley, Percy Bysshe
KEATS-SHELLEY JOURNAL
KEATS-SHELLEY MEMORIAL BULLETIN

Sjöberg, Birger
Birger Sjöberg Sällskapet. SKRIFTER

Spenser, Edmund
SPENSER NEWSLETTER

Staël, Madame de
CAHIERS STAËLIENS

Stifter, Adalbert
Adalbert Stifter-Institut. VIERTELJAHRESSCHRIFT
STIFTER-JAHRBUCH

Storm, Theodor
SCHRIFTEN DER THEODOR-STORM-GESELLSCHAFT

Strehlenau, Nikolaus [Nikolaus Lenau]
LENAU-FORUM

Strindberg, August
MEDDELANDEN FRÅN STRINDBERGSSÅLLSKAPET

Swift, Jonathan
SCRIBLERIAN AND THE KIT-CATS

Tasso, Torquato
STUDI TASSIANI

Thoreau, Henry
THOREAU JOURNAL QUARTERLY
THOREAU SOCIETY BOOKLET
THOREAU SOCIETY BULLETIN

Tolkien, J.R.R.
MYTHLORE
ORCRIST

Unamuno, Miguel de
CUADERNOS DE LA CÁTEDRA DE UNAMUNO

Waugh, Evelyn
EVELYN WAUGH NEWSLETTER

MODERN LANGUAGE ASSOCIATION INTERNATIONAL BIBLIOGRAPHY (cont.)

Whitman, Walt
WALT WHITMAN NEWSLETTER
WALT WHITMAN REVIEW

Wolfram von Eschenbach
WOLFRAM-JAHRBUCH

Woolf, Virginia
VIRGINIA WOOLF QUARTERLY

Wordsworth, William
WORDSWORTH CIRCLE

Zola, Émile
CAHIERS NATURALISTES

NEO-LATIN NEWS

More, Saint Thomas
MOREANA

PHILOLOGICAL QUARTERLY

Arouet, François Marie [Voltaire]
STUDIES ON VOLTAIRE AND THE EIGHTEENTH CENTURY

Blake, William
BLAKE NEWSLETTER
BLAKE STUDIES

Burke, Edmund
STUDIES IN BURKE AND HIS TIME

Emerson, Ralph Waldo
ESQ

Goethe, Johann Wolfgang von
GOETHE-JAHRBUCH (Weimar)

Kant, Immanuel
KANT-STUDIEN

Leibniz, Gottfried
STUDIA LEIBNITIANA

Lessing, Gotthold
LESSING YEARBOOK

Pope, Alexander
SCRIBLERIANA

Schiller, Friedrich von
JAHRBUCH DER DEUTSCHEN SCHILLERGESELLSCHAFT

Swift, Jonathan
SCRIBLERIANA

PHILOSOPHER'S INDEX

Aquinas, Saint Thomas
AQUINAS: RIVISTA INTERNAZIONALE

Augustine, Saint
AUGUSTINIAN STUDIES
AUGUSTINUS
REVUE DES ÉTUDES AUGUSTINIENNES

Croce, Benedetto
RIVISTA DI STUDI CROCIANI

Hegel, Georg
HEGEL-JAHRBUCH
OWL OF MINERVA

Hume, David
HUME STUDIES

Kant, Immanuel
KANT-STUDIEN

Leibniz, Gottfried
STUDIA LEIBNITIANA

Locke, John
LOCKE NEWSLETTER

Mill, John Stuart
MILL NEWS LETTER

Peirce, Charles S.
TRANSACTIONS OF THE CHARLES S. PEIRCE SOCIETY

Russell, Bertrand
RUSSELL

Schopenhauer, Arthur
SCHOPENHAUER-JAHRBUCH

Teilhard de Chardin, Pierre
REVUE TEILHARD DE CHARDIN
TEILHARD REVIEW

Whitehead, Alfred North
PROCESS STUDIES

PSYCHOLOGICAL ABSTRACTS

Rank, Otto
JOURNAL OF THE OTTO RANK ASSOCIATION

REVUE D'HISTOIRE LITTÉRAIRE DE LA FRANCE

Arouet, François Marie [Voltaire]
STUDIES ON VOLTAIRE AND THE EIGHTEENTH CENTURY

REVUE D'HISTOIRE LITTÉRAIRE DE LA FRANCE (cont.)

Balzac, Honoré
L'ANNÉE BALZACIENNE

Baudelaire, Charles
BULLETIN BAUDELAIRIEN
ÉTUDES BAUDELAIRIENNES

Beyle, Marie Henri [Stendhal]
STENDHAL CLUB

Bosco, Henri
CAHIERS DE L'AMITIÉ HENRI BOSCO

Budé, Guillaume
BULLETIN DE L'ASSOCIATION GUILLAUME BUDÉ

Chateaubriand, François-René
Société Chateaubriand. BULLETIN

Claudel, Paul
BULLETIN DE LA SOCIÉTÉ PAUL CLAUDEL
Cahiers Paul Claudel

Courier, Paul-Louis
Société des Amis de Paul-Louis Courier. PUBLICATIONS

du Bos, Charles
CAHIERS CHARLES DU BOS

Dudevant, Mme. [George Sand]
Association "Les Amis de George Sand." BULLETIN DE LIAISON

Dumas, Alexandre, père
BULLETIN DE L'ASSOCIATION DES AMIS D'ALEXANDRE DUMAS

Flaubert, Gustave
AMIS DE FLAUBERT

Fournier, Henri-Alban [Alain-Fournier]
DOSSIERS DE LA SOCIÉTÉ DES AMIS DE JACQUES RIVIÈRE ET ALAIN-FOURNIER

Gide, André
BULLETIN DES AMIS D'ANDRÉ GIDE

Giraudoux, Jean
CAHIERS JEAN GIRAUDOUX

Guérin, Eugénie and Maurice de
L'AMITIÉ GUÉRINIENNE

Huysmans, Joris-Karl
BULLETIN DE LA SOCIÉTÉ J.-K. HUYSMANS

Kostrowitzky, Wilhelm [Apollinaire]
QUE VLO-VE?

REVUE D'HISTOIRE LITTÉRAIRE DE LA FRANCE (cont.)

Larbaud, Valéry
CAHIERS DES AMIS DE VALÉRY LARBAUD

Maeterlinck, Maurice
Fondation Maurice Maeterlinck. ANNALES

Mauriac, François
CAHIERS FRANÇOIS MAURIAC

Maurras, Charles
CAHIERS CHARLES MAURRAS
ÉTUDES MAURRASSIENNES

Milosz, Oscar Venceslas
CAHIERS DE L'ASSOCIATION LES AMIS DE MILOSZ

Montaigne, Michel
BULLETIN DE LA SOCIÉTÉ DES AMIS DE MONTAIGNE

More, Saint Thomas
MOREANA

Péguy, Charles
L'AMITIÉ CHARLES PÉGUY

Pergaud, Louis
Amis de Louis Pergaud. BULLETIN

Proust, Marcel
BULLETIN DE LA SOCIÉTÉ DES AMIS DE MARCEL PROUST

Rabelais, François
AMIS DE RABELAIS ET DE LA DEVINIÈRE
ÉTUDES RABELAISIENNES

Renan, Joseph Ernest
Cahiers renaniens
ÉTUDES RENANIENNES: BULLETIN
Société des études renaniennes. BULLETIN

Rimbaud, Arthur
RIMBAUD VIVANT

Rivière, Jacques
DOSSIERS DE LA SOCIÉTÉ DES AMIS DE JACQUES RIVIÈRE ET ALAIN-FOURNIER

Rollinat, Maurice
BULLETIN DE LA SOCIÉTÉ "LES AMIS DE MAURICE ROLLINAT"

Rousseau, Jean-Jacques
ANNALES DE LA SOCIÉTÉ DE JEAN-JACQUES ROUSSEAU
Association des Amis de Jean-Jacques Rousseau. BULLETIN D'INFORMATION

Schopenhauer, Arthur
SCHOPENHAUER-JAHRBUCH

REVUE D'HISTOIRE LITTÉRAIRE DE LA FRANCE (cont.)

Staël, Madame de
CAHIERS STAËLIENS

Valéry, Paul
BULLETIN DES ÉTUDES VALÉRYENNES

Verne, Jules
BULLETIN DE LA SOCIÉTÉ JULES VERNE

Zola, Émile
CAHIERS NATURALISTES

SOCIAL SCIENCES AND HUMANITIES INDEX

Shakespeare, William
SHAKESPEARE QUARTERLY

STUDIES IN BROWNING AND HIS CIRCLE

Browning, Robert and Elizabeth
BROWNING SOCIETY NOTES

TWENTIETH CENTURY LITERATURE

Clemens, Samuel L. [Mark Twain]
MARK TWAIN JOURNAL

Conrad, Joseph
CONRADIANA

Eliot, T.S.
T.S. ELIOT REVIEW

Fitzgerald, F. Scott
FITZGERALD/HEMINGWAY ANNUAL

Hemingway, Ernest
FITZGERALD/HEMINGWAY ANNUAL

Joyce, James
JAMES JOYCE QUARTERLY
JAMES JOYCE REVIEW

Kipling, Rudyard
KIPLING JOURNAL

Lawrence, D.H.
D.H. LAWRENCE REVIEW

Mencken, H.L.
MENCKENIANA

Nin, Anaïs
UNDER THE SIGN OF PISCES

TWENTIETH CENTURY LITERATURE (cont.)

Shaw, George Bernard
SHAVIAN
SHAW REVIEW

Stein, Gertrude
LOST GENERATION JOURNAL

Steinbeck, John
STEINBECK QUARTERLY

Woolf, Virginia
VIRGINIA WOOLF QUARTERLY

VICTORIAN STUDIES

Brontë, Charlotte, Emily, Anne, and Branwell
BRONTË SOCIETY TRANSACTIONS

Browning, Robert and Elizabeth
BROWNING INSTITUTE STUDIES
BROWNING SOCIETY NOTES
STUDIES IN BROWNING AND HIS CIRCLE

Clemens, Samuel L. [Mark Twain]
MARK TWAIN JOURNAL

Conrad, Joseph
CONRADIANA

Dickens, Charles
DICKENSIAN
DICKENS STUDIES ANNUAL
DICKENS STUDIES NEWSLETTER

Disraeli, Benjamin
DISRAELI NEWSLETTER

Dodgson, Charles Lutwidge [Lewis Carroll]
JABBERWOCKY

Doyle, Sir Arthur Conan
BAKER STREET JOURNAL

Emerson, Ralph Waldo
EMERSON SOCIETY QUARTERLY

Hopkins, Gerard Manley
HOPKINS RESEARCH BULLETIN
HOPKINS QUARTERLY

Housman, A.E.
HOUSMAN SOCIETY JOURNAL

Kant, Immanuel
KANT-STUDIEN

VICTORIAN STUDIES (cont.)

Keats, John
KEATS-SHELLEY JOURNAL

Kipling, Rudyard
KIPLING JOURNAL

Mill, John Stuart
MILL NEWS LETTER

Morris, William
JOURNAL OF THE WILLIAM MORRIS SOCIETY

Pound, Ezra
PAIDEUMA

Shakespeare, William
SHAKESPEARE QUARTERLY

Shaw, George Bernard
INDEPENDENT SHAVIAN
SHAVIAN
SHAW REVIEW

Shelley, Percy Bysshe
KEATS-SHELLEY JOURNAL

Tennyson, Alfred, 1st baron
TENNYSON RESEARCH BULLETIN
Tennyson Society. PUBLICATIONS

Whitman, Walt
WALT WHITMAN REVIEW

Woolf, Virginia
VIRGINIA WOOLF QUARTERLY

YEAR'S WORK IN ENGLISH STUDIES

Blake, William
BLAKE NEWSLETTER
BLAKE STUDIES

Brontë, Charlotte, Emily, Anne, and Branwell
Brontë Society. TRANSACTIONS

Browning, Robert and Elizabeth
STUDIES IN BROWNING AND HIS CIRCLE

Burke, Edmund
STUDIES IN BURKE AND HIS TIME

Chaucer, Geoffrey
CHAUCER REVIEW

YEAR'S WORK IN ENGLISH STUDIES (cont.)

Dickens, Charles
DICKENS STUDIES
DICKENS STUDIES ANNUAL
DICKENS STUDIES NEWSLETTER

Emerson, Ralph Waldo
ESQ

Hardy, Thomas
THOMAS HARDY YEAR BOOK

Joyce, James
JAMES JOYCE QUARTERLY

Keats, John
KEATS-SHELLEY JOURNAL
KEATS-SHELLEY MEMORIAL BULLETIN

Lawrence, D.H.
D.H. LAWRENCE REVIEW

Markham, Edwin
MARKHAM REVIEW

Milton, John
MILTON NEWSLETTER
MILTON QUARTERLY
MILTON STUDIES

More, Saint Thomas
MOREANA

Poe, Edgar Allan
POE NEWSLETTER
POE STUDIES

Shakespeare, William
SHAKESPEAREAN RESEARCH AND OPPORTUNITIES
SHAKESPEARE-JAHRBUCH (Heidelberg)
SHAKESPEARE-JAHRBUCH (Weimar)
SHAKESPEARE NEWSLETTER
SHAKESPEARE QUARTERLY
SHAKESPEARE STUDIES: AN ANNUAL GATHERING
SHAKESPEARE STUDIES (Tokyo)
SHAKESPEARE SURVEY

Shaw, George Bernard
INDEPENDENT SHAVIAN
SHAW REVIEW

Shelley, Percy Bysshe
KEATS-SHELLEY JOURNAL

Waugh, Evelyn
EVELYN WAUGH NEWSLETTER

YEAR'S WORK IN ENGLISH STUDIES (cont.)

Whitman, Walt
WALT WHITMAN REVIEW

Woolf, Virginia
VIRGINIA WOOLF QUARTERLY

Wordsworth, William
WORDSWORTH CIRCLE

Appendix 5
PUBLISHERS

Publishers are arranged alphabetically by their last name except for a few cases where the commonly accepted trade name, such as "Éditions" and "Verlag," is given preference. Addresses for defunct publishers and publications are included as identification aids for acquisition and interlibrary loan librarians. University and university press addresses are generally provided in the entries themselves because with few exceptions they are identical with the address of the editor.

Aeolian Press
6762 Cibola Road
San Diego, Calif. 92120

Akademie-Verlag
Leipziger Strasse 3-4
108 Berlin 8, Germany

AMS Press
56 East 13th Street
New York, N.Y. 10003

E. Appelhans
Braunschweig, Germany (BRD)

Aquin Press
Woodchester Lodge
Woodchester
Gloucestershire, England

Artemis Verlag
Limmatquai 18
Zurich 1, Switzerland
or
Alexanderstrasse 63
Postfach 3173
7000 Stuttgart 1, Germany

Athenaeum Press
Bream's Building
Chancery Lane
London, England

Athenäum Verlag
Falkensteinerstrasse 7577
6000 Frankfurt/am/Main, Germany (BRD)

Amable Audin
3, rue Marius Audin
69 Lyon 3, France

Aufbau Verlag
Postfach 1217
Französischestrasse 32
108 Berlin, Germany

Badenia Verlag
Rudolph-Freytag-strasse 6
D-7500 Karlsruhe, Germany (BRD)

Baker and Taylor
50 Kirby Avenue
Somerville, N.J. 08876

Publishers

C.H. Beck'sche Verlagsbuchhandlung
Wilhelmstrasse 9
8 Munich 40, Germany (BRD)

John Benjamins
Amsteldijk 44
Amsterdam, Netherlands

Bergland Verlag
Kärntnerring 17
1010 Vienna, Austria

Rolf Bernhart
Darmstadt, Germany (BRD)

Blackwell and Mott
49, Broad Street
Oxford OX1 3BP, England

Auguste Blaizot et fils
164, faubourg Saint-Honoré
75008 Paris, France

Hermann Böhlaus Nachfolger
Meyerstrasse 50a
53 Weimar, Germany (DDR)
or
8043 Graz-Kroisbach, Austria
or
Schmalzhofgasse 4
A-1061 Vienna, Austria
or
Schwerinstrasse 40
5 Köln 60, Germany (BRD)

Bouvier Verlag Herbert Grundmann
am Hof 32
D-5300 Bonn 1, Germany (BRD)

Brigham Young University Press
Marketing 205 UPB
Provo, Utah 84602

William C. Brown
135 Locust Street
Dubuque, Iowa 52001

Cambridge University Press
Syndics, Bentley House
200 Euston Road
London NW1 2DB, England
or
32 East 57th Street
New York, N.Y. 10022

Honoré Champion
7 Quai Malaquais
75006 Paris, France

Colgate University Press
304 Lawrence Hall
Hamilton, N.Y. 13346

William Dawson and Sons
Cannon House, Park Farm Road
Folkstone
Kent CT19 5EE, England

Delp'sche Verlagsbuchhandlung
St. Blasienstrasse 5
D-8 Munich 13, Germany (BRD)

Denoël
14, rue Amélie
75007 Paris, France

Deutsche Volksbücherei
Goslar, Germany (BRD)

La Direzione
via Gino Capponi, 46
Florence, Italy

Dolmen Press
North Richmond Industrial Estate
North Richmond Street
Dublin 1, Ireland

Librairie Droz
11, rue Massot
1206 Geneva, Switzerland

Duncker und Humblot
Dietrich-Schäfer-Weg 9
D-1 Berlin 41, Germany

A. Durel
Libraire de la Société de Amis de Montaigne
18, rue de l'Ancienne-Comédie
Paris, France

Éditions André Silvaire
20 rue Domat
75007 Paris, France

Éditions Arthaud
6, rue de Fontenay
Clamart, Seine, France

Éditions Bernard Grasset
61, rue des Saints-Pères
75006 Paris, France

Éditions de la Baconnière
2017 Boudry
Neuchâtel, Switzerland
or
106, boulevard St.-Germain
75006 Paris, France

Éditions des Sept-Couleurs
27, rue de l'Abbé-Grégoire
75006 Paris, France

Éditions du Bien public
Trois-Rivières
Quebec, Canada

Éditions du Divan
37, rue Bonaparte
75006 Paris, France

Éditions du Grand Chêne
1603 Aran
Lausanne, Switzerland

Éditions du Seuil
27, rue Jacob
75006 Paris, France

Éditions Fasquelle
61, rue des Saints-Pères
75006 Paris, France

Éditions Grasset et Fasquelle
61, rue des Saints-Pères
75006 Paris, France

Éditions Robert Laffont
6 place St. Sulpice
70006 Paris, France

Éditions Universitaires
115, rue du Cherche-Midi
75006 Paris, France

Éditions Victor Attinger
4, rue le Goff
75005 Paris, France

Editrice Antenore
via G. Rusca 15
Padua (Padova), Italy

Editrice Felice le Monnier
via Scipione Ammirato 100
I-50136 Florence, Italy

Edizioni del mondo
Postfach 2640
6200 Wiesbaden, Germany (BRD)

N.G. Elwert Verlag
Reitgasse 7-9, Postfach 1118
D-355 Marburg an der Lahn, Germany (BRD)

Ely House
37, Dover Street
London WIX 4AH, England

Falcon Press
1617 Wood Street
Philadelphia, Pa. 19100

Feffer and Simons
100 Park Avenue
New York, N.Y. 10017

Wilhelm Fink Verlag
Nikolaistrasse 2
8000 Munich 19, Germany (BRD)

Flammarion
26, rue Racine
75006 Paris, France

A. Francke Verlag
Hochfeldstrasse 113
CH-3000 Bern 26, Switzerland
or
Dachauer Strasse 42
D-8000 Munich 2, Germany (BRD)

Publishers

Burt Franklin
235 East 44th Street
New York, N.Y. 10017

Gale Research
Book Tower
Detroit, Mich. 48226

Gallimard
5, rue Sébastien-Bottin
75007 Paris, France

Garnier-Arnoul
39, rue de Seine
75006 Paris, France

Garnier Frères
19, rue des Plantes
75014 Paris, France

Garnstone Press
59, Brompton Road
London S.W.3, England

Gregg Associates
Brussels, Belgium

Matthias-Grünewald-Verlag
Bischofsplatz 6
D-6500 Mainz, Germany (BRD)

Walter de Gruyter
Genthinerstrasse 13
1000 Berlin 30, Germany

Gütersloher Verlagshaus Gerd Mohn
Königstrasse 23
Postfach 2368
4830 Gütersloh 1, Germany (BRD)

Hansa-Verlag
Erdkampsweg 33
2000 Hamburg 63, Germany (BRD)

Harvester Press
2 Standford Terrace
Hassocks, West Sussex, England

Het Spectrum
Marsstraat 66
2600-Berchem
Utrecht-Antwerpen
Vitgeverij, Belgium

Hoffmann und Campe Verlag
Harvestehuder Weg 45
2 Hamburg 13, Germany (BRD)

Max Hueber Verlag
Krausstrasse 30
8045 Ismaning, Germany (BRD)

Irish University Press
81 Merrion Square
Dublin 2, Ireland

Walter J. Johnson
355 Chestnut Street
Norwood, N.J. 07648
or
Geschaftsstelle in Deutschland
Goldberweg 4
6 Frankfurt/am/Main 70 (Oberrad), Germany

Johnson Associates
P.O. Box 1017
Greenwich, Conn. 06830

Johnson Reprint Corp.
111 Fifth Avenue
New York, N.Y. 10003

A. Jullien
Au Bourg-de-Four 32
1204 Geneva, Switzerland

Michael Katanka (Books)
103 Stanmore Hill
Stanmore, Middlesex, England

Kelmscott House
26, Upper Mall
London W.6, England

Ernst Klett
Rotebühlstrasse 77
7000 Stuttgart-W, Germany (BRD)

Librairie Klincksieck
11, rue de Lille
75007 Paris, France

Kraus Periodicals
16 East 46th Street
New York, N.Y. 10017

Kraus Reprint Corp.
Route 100
Millwood, N.Y. 10546
or
FI-9491 Nendeln, Liechtenstein

Alfred Kröner Verlag
Reuchlinstrasse 4B
D-7000 Stuttgart W, Germany (BRD)

Libreria Editrice Minerva
via Castiglione 13-15
Bologna, Italy

Macmillan
70 Bond Street
Toronto M5B 1X3, Canada

Marquette University Press
1131 West Wisconsin Avenue
Milwaukee, Wis. 53233

Maruschke und Berendt Verlag
Breslau, Germany (now Poland)

Albin Michel
22, rue Huyghens
75014 Paris, France

Microcard Editions
Denver Technological Center
5500 South Valentia Way
Englewood, Colo. 80110

Michel J. Minard
73, rue du Cardinal-Lemoine
75005 Paris, France

J.C.B. Mohr
Wilhelmstrasse 18
74 Tübingen, Germany (BRD)

Otto Müller Verlag
Ernest-Thun Strasse 11
5021 Salzburg, Austria

Ejnar Munksgaard
Prags Boulevard 47
Copenhagen, Denmark

NCR/Microcard Editions
901 26th Street, N.W.
Washington, D.C.

Max Niemayer Verlag
Pfrondorfer Strasse 4
D-74 Tübingen, Germany (BRD)

A.-G. Nizet
3 bis, place de la Sorbonne
75005 Paris, France

Notring-Verlag
Judenplatz 6
A-1010 Vienna, Austria

NWT:s Förlag
Värmlandstryck, 1
Karlstad AB, Sweden

Oberkirchenrat Jakob Wolfer
Martinstrasse 25
A-1180 Vienna, Austria

Leo S. Olschki
Viuzzo del Pozzetto
Viale Europa
I-50126 Florence, Italy
or
Piazza S. Marco, 71
Venice, Italy

Ophrys
avenue d'Embrun
05 Gap; or 10, rue de Nesle
75006 Paris, France

Oxford University Press
200 Madison Avenue
New York, N.Y. 10016

Publishers

Pahl-Rugenstein Verlag
Vorgebirgstrasse 115
D-5000 Köln 51, Germany

Paulinus-Verlag
Fleischstrasse 61/54
5500 Trier, Germany (BRD)

H. and J. Pillans and Wilson
20 Bernard Terrace
Edinburgh, Scotland
or
58 Renfield Street
Glasgow, Scotland

Pontificio Ateneo Salesiano
Piazza dell'Ateneo Salesiano 1
00139 Rome, Italy

Presses Universitaires de France
108, boulevard St-Germain
75006 Paris, France

Publicações Europa-América
Rua das Flores, 45
Lisbon, Portugal

Quelle und Meyer
Schloss-Wolfsbrunnes-Veg 29
Postfach 1340
6900 Heidelberg, Germany (BRD)

Rombach
Lörracher Strasse 3
7800 Freiburg im Breisgau, Germany (BRD)

Rosenkilde og Bagger
Kron-Prinsens-Gade 3
1114 Copenhagen, Denmark

Rötzer-Verlag
Haydngasse 41
7000 Eisenstadt, Austria

G.C. Sansoni Editore
via Lamarmore, 45
50121 Florence, Itahly
or
Viale Mazzine, 46
50132 Florence, Italy

Richard Scherpe Verlag
Glockenspitz 140
4150 Krefeld, Germany (BRD)

Erich Schmidt
Genthinerstrasse 30 G
D-1000 Berlin 30, Germany

Schweizer Spiegel Verlag
Hirschengraben 20
CH-8023 Zurich, Switzerland

Scolar Press
39, Great Russell Street
London WCIB 3PH, England

Angelo Signorelli
via Paola Falconieri 84
00152 Rome, Italy

Slatkine Reprints
5, rue des Chaudronniers
1211 Geneva 3, Switzerland

Società Editrice Vita e Pensiero
Largo Gemelli 1
20123 Milan, Italy

Société d'édition les Belles Lettres
95, boulevard Raspail
75006 Paris, France

Souchon
10, avenue de Paris
Roanne, France

René Soulié
Hotel de Ville, 32, rue de Meaux
La Ferté-Milon (Aisne), France

State University of New York Press
99 Washington Street
Albany, N.Y. 12210

Franz Steiner Verlag
Bahnhofstrasse 39
6200 Wiesbaden, Germany (BRD)

Lothar Stiehm Verlag
Hausackerweg 16
6900 Heidelberg, Germany (BRD)

Subervie
21, rue de l'Embergue
1200 Rodez, France

Suhrkamp
Lindenstrasse 29-35
Postfach 2446
D-6000 Frankfurt/am/Main, Germany (BRD)

Swets and Zeitlinger
Heereweg 347B
Lisse, Netherlands
or
P.O. Box 517
Berwyn, Pa. 19312

Tipografia Editrice Secomandi
via Pignolo 103
24100 Bergamo, Italy

University Microfilms International
or
University Microfilm Library Services
P.O. Box 1346
Ann Arbor, Mich. 48106

University of Toronto Press
St. George Street Campus
Toronto M5S 1A6, Ontario

University Press of Virginia
Box 3608, University Station
Charlottesville, Va. 22903

Vandenhoeck und Ruprecht
Postfach 77
34 Göttingen, Germany (BRD)

Van Gorcum
Postbus 43
Assen, Netherlands

Verlag Anton Hain KG
Postfach 180
6554 Meisenheim am Glan, Germany (BRD)

Verlag Aschendorff
Gallitzinstrasse 13
Münster, Germany (BRD)

Verlag Der Oberschlesier
Oppeln (Opole), Poland

Verlag Friedrich Wittig
Bebelallee 11
2 Hamburg 39, Germany (BRD)

Verlag für Angewandte Wissenschaften
Hardstrasse 1
7570 Baden-Baden, Germany (BRD)

Verlag Regensberg
(Regensbergsche Verlagsbuchhandlung)
Schaumbergstrasse
4400 Münster/Westphalia, Germany (BRD)

Verlag Waldemar Kramer
Bornheimer Landwehr 57a
6000 Frankfurt/am/Main, Germany (BRD)

Waisenhaus-Buchdruckerei und Verlag
Waisenhausdamm 13
3300 Braunschweig, Germany (BRD)

H.W. Walden and Co.
18 Station Approach
Clapham Junction
London S.W. 11, England

Westholsteinische Verlagsanstalt Boyens and Co.
Postfach 1880, Am Wulf-Isebrand-Platz
224 Heide in Holstein, Germany (BRD)

L.C. Wittich
Wittichstrasse 6
6100 Darmstadt, Germany (BRD)

Yale University Press
302 Temple Street
New Haven, Conn. 06511

Appendix 6

GLOSSARY OF FOREIGN TERMS

Abhandlung - critical article
Abstammung - source
Abteilung - division
AS, S - Austrian shilling
Beiheft - supplement
Beitrag - contribution to a journal
Bericht - report
Bestandsverzeichnis - current index
BF - Belgian franc
BRD - Bundesrepublik Deutschland (West Germany)
Buchbesprechung - book review
Cahiers - notebook or collection, sometimes of critical essays, sometimes of the author's works, and sometimes a combination of both
d.(der, das) - the
DDR - Deutsche Demokratische Republik (East Germany)
Ergänzungsheft - supplemental issue
ersch. - published
FB - Belgian franc
fl - florin
Förderung - patron
Forschung - research
Fr, F - franc
gegenwärtig - current
Gesamtausgabe - complete edition
Geschäftsstelle - office address
Geschichte - history
Gesellschaft - society
H., Heft - issue
Jahresgabe - annual publication for members
Jahreswende - new year, turn of the year
KR - Danish kroner
L. - Italian lira
libraire - bookseller-publisher
librairie - bookstore
Mitglied - member

Glossary of Foreign Terms

Mitgliedergabe - publication for members
Mitteilungsblatt - newsletter
NF - new francs
N.F., n.F. - neue Folge, new series
Nachlassverwaltung - executor of the author's manuscripts
Nachricht - report, news, information
p - English pence
Rs - rupees
S, AS - Austrian shilling
Sållskapet - society
Sammlung - collection
sämtliche - complete
Schriftenreihe - publications series
Schrr., Schriften - writings
S Fr - Swiss franc
S Kr - Swedish kronor
Sonderheft - special issue, supplement
Stifter - sponsor
Tätigkeitsbericht - activity report of a society
Überblick - survey
Vereinigung - corporation
Verlag - publishing house
Verleger - publisher
Veröffentlichung - publication
Verzeichnis - index
vierteljahresschrift - quarterly
wissenschaft - learned
z., zu - to, in, at, by, for
zeitgenössisch - contemporary

Appendix 7

SOURCES CONSULTED AND THEIR ABBREVIATIONS

The following reference sources proved to be of great value in compiling this international bibliography. Titles which were of little or no value are not included. The abbreviations are those which appear most frequently in general reference books.

ABSTRACTS OF ENGLISH STUDIES	AES
ALLGEMEINE DEUTSCHE BIOGRAPHIE	
AMERICA: HISTORY AND LIFE	AMERICA
AMERICAN HUMANITIES INDEX	AM.HUM.IND., AHI
AMERICAN LITERATURE	AM.LIT., AL
AMERICAN LITERATURE ABSTRACTS	AM.LIT.ABST., ALA
L'ANNÉE PHILOLOGIQUE	L'ANNÉE
ANNUAL BIBLIOGRAPHY OF ENGLISH LANGUAGE AND LITERATURE	ABELL, MHRA
Archives des Lettres Modernes	Archives
ARTICLES ON AMERICAN LITERATURE	Leary
BIBLIOGRAPHIE DE LA FRANCE/ BIBLIO: REVUES ET PÉRIODIQUES	FRANCE/BIBLIO
BIBLIOGRAPHIE DE LA LITTÉRATURE FRANÇAISE DU MOYEN AGE À NOS JOURS	BIBL.LITT.FR., Rancoeur
BIBLIOGRAPHIE DER DEUTSCHEN LITERATURWISSENSCHAFT (continued by BIBLIOGRAPHIE DER DEUTSCHEN SPRACH- UND LITERATURWISSEN-SCHAFT)	Köttelwesch
BIBLIOGRAPHIE DER FRANZÖSISCHEN LITERATURWISSENSCHAFT (title in French: BIBLIOGRAPHIE D'HISTOIRE LITTÉRAIRE FRANÇAISE	Klapp

Sources and Abbreviations

Source	Abbreviation
BIBLIOGRAPHISCHES HANDBUCH DER DEUTSCHEN LITERATURWISSEN-SCHAFT	HANDBUCH
BIBLIOGRAPHISCHES HANDBUCH DES DEUTSCHEN SCHRIFTTUMS	Körner
BIOGRAPHISCHES WÖRTERBUCH ZUR DEUTSCHEN GESCHICHTE	
BIOGRAPHY INDEX	BIOG.IND., BI
BOOK REVIEW DIGEST	BK.REV.DIG., BRD
BOOK REVIEW INDEX	BK.REV.IND., BRI
BRITISH HUMANITIES INDEX	BR.HUM.IND., BHI
BRITISH UNION-CATALOGUE OF PERIODICALS	BRIT.U-C OF PER.
BULLETIN CRITIQUE DU LIVRE FRANÇAIS	BULL.CRIT.
BULLETIN OF BIBLIOGRAPHY	BULL. OF BIBL., B OF B
CATHOLIC PERIODICAL AND LITERATURE INDEX	
DEUTSCHE BUCH	
DIRECTORY OF PUBLISHING OPPORTUNITIES	
EBSCO BULLETIN OF SERIALS CHANGES	
ENGLISH LANGUAGE NOTES: THE ROMANTIC MOVEMENT, A SELECTIVE AND CRITICAL BIBLIOG-RAPHY	ELN
ENGLISH LITERATURE IN TRANSITION	ELT
EPPELSHEIMER UND KÖTTELWESCH See BIBLIOGRAPHIE DER DEUTSCHEN LITERATURWISSENSCHAFT	
ESSAY AND GENERAL LITERATURE INDEX	EGLI
FOURTH DIRECTORY OF PERIODICALS PUBLISHING ARTICLES ON ENGLISH AND AMERICAN LITERATURE AND LANGUAGE	Gerstenberger and Hendrick
FRENCH VI BIBLIOGRAPHY: FOR THE STUDY OF NINETEENTH-CENTURY FRENCH LITERATURE	FRENCH VI

FRENCH VII BIBLIOGRAPHY: CRITICAL AND BIOGRAPHICAL REFERENCES FOR THE STUDY OF CONTEMPORARY FRENCH LITERATURE	FRENCH VII
FRENCH XX BIBLIOGRAPHY: CRITICAL AND BIOGRAPHICAL REFERENCES FOR THE STUDY OF FRENCH LITERATURE SINCE 1885	FRENCH XX
GERMAN PERIODICAL PUBLICATIONS. Hoover Institution	
GUIDE TO CURRENT BRITISH JOURNALS	Woodworth
GUIDE TO CURRENT LATIN AMERICAN PERIODICALS: HUMANITIES AND SOCIAL SCIENCES	Zimmerman
HANDBUCH DER DEUTSCHEN LITERATURGESCHICHTE ABTEILUNG BIBLIOGRAPHIEN	
HISTORICAL ABSTRACTS	
HUMANITIES INDEX	HUM.IND., HI
INDEX TO BOOK REVIEWS IN THE HUMANITIES	IND.BK.REV.HUM.
INDEX TO LITTLE MAGAZINES	
INTERNATIONALE BIBLIOGRAPHIE ZUR GESCHICHTE DER DEUTSCHEN LITERATUR	
IRREGULAR SERIALS AND ANNUALS: AN INTERNATIONAL DIRECTORY (Bowker)	
JOHNSON REPRINT	
JOURNAL OF MODERN LITERATURE	JML
KRAUS PERIODICALS	
LIBRAIRIE FRANÇAISE: LES LIVRES DE L'ANNÉE	
LIBRAIRIE FRANÇAISE, 1956-1965	
LISTE DES SOCIÉTÉS SAVANTES ET LITTÉRAIRES	
LITTÉRATURE FRANÇAISE: CRITIQUE LITTÉRAIRE, LINGUISTIE	Slatkine Reprints
LIVRES DE L'ANNÉE-BIBLIO	BIBLIO

Sources and Abbreviations

LIVRES DU MOIS	
MAGAZINES FOR LIBRARIES	Katz
MANUAL DE BIBLIOGRAFÍA DE LA LITERATURA ESPAÑOLA	BIBL.LIT.ESP.
MLA ABSTRACTS	
MLA INTERNATIONAL BIBLIOGRAPHY	MLA INT'L BIBL., MLAIB
Modern Language Association	MLA
NEW SERIAL TITLES	NST
NEW SERIAL TITLES--CLASSED SUBJECT ARRANGEMENT	
NEW SERIAL TITLES--SUBJECT INDEX	
PERIODICALS AND REFERENCE WORKS	Walter J. Johnson
PHILOLOGICAL QUARTERLY	PQ
PHILOSOPHER'S INDEX	PHIL. IND.
PUBLISHERS' INTERNATIONAL DIRECTORY	
PUBLISHERS' INTERNATIONAL YEAR BOOK	
RÉPERTOIRE DE LA PRESSE ET DES PUBLICATIONS PÉRIODIQUES FRANÇAISES	RÉPERTOIRE
REPERTÒRIO BIBLIOGRAFICO DELLA LETTERATURA ITALIANA	
Revue des Lettres Modernes	La Revue
REVUE D'HISTOIRE LITTÉRAIRE DE LA FRANCE	REVUE D'HISTOIRE
RIVISTA DI LETTERATURE MODERNE E COMPARATE	
ROMANTIC MOVEMENT BIBLIOGRAPHY, 1936-1970	
SERIAL BIBLIOGRAPHIES IN THE HUMANITIES AND SOCIAL SCIENCES	Gray
SERIALS UPDATING SERVICE ANNUAL	
SERIALS UPDATING SERVICE QUARTERLY	
SOCIAL SCIENCES AND HUMANITIES INDEX	SSHI
SOURCEBOOK FOR HISPANIC LITERA-TURE AND LANGAUGE	Bleznick

STANDARD PERIODICAL DIRECTORY	
TWENTIETH CENTURY LITERATURE	TCL
ULRICH'S INTERNATIONAL PERIODICALS DIRECTORY	Ulrich's
ULRICH'S QUARTERLY	
UNION LIST OF SERIALS	ULS
VERZEICHNIS LIEFERBARER BÜCHER	
VICTORIAN STUDIES	VS
WEBSTER'S AMERICAN BIOGRAPHIES	
YEAR'S WORK IN ENGLISH STUDIES	YWES

TITLE INDEX

All titles are listed in alphabetical order letter by letter, whether they are current, defunct, superseded, alternate, or variant titles. Each title is followed by an author's name and an entry number which indicates the location of its annotation in the main author-periodical section of this Guide. ACTA TEILHARDIANA, for instance, is entry 1 in the section on Teilhard de Chardin. References are made from alternate and variant titles to the entry for the correct title, which for the purposes of this Guide is generally that title appearing on the title page of the most recent or the current issue of the publication.

A

Title Index

B

C

D

E

F

G

H

I

J

K

L

M

N

O

P

Q

R

S

T

U

V

W

Y

Z

WITHDRAWN
UML LIBRARIES